Artificial Intelligence

Artificial Intelligence

Second Edition

Elaine Rich

*Microelectronics and Computer
Technology Corporation*

Kevin Knight

Carnegie Mellon University

McGraw-Hill, Inc.
New York St. Louis San Francisco Auckland Bogotá Caracas
Hamburg Lisbon London Madrid Mexico Milan Montreal
New Delhi Paris San Juan São Paulo Singapore Sydney
Tokyo Toronto

Artificial Intelligence

2 3 4 5 6 7 8 9 0 DOC DOC 9 5 4 3 2 1

ISBN 0-07-052263-4

The editors were David M. Shapiro and Joseph F. Murphy;
the production supervisor was Louise Karam.
R. R. Donnelley & Sons Company was printer and binder.

Library of Congress Cataloging in Publication Data

Rich, Elaine
     Artificial Intelligence / Elaine Rich, Kevin Knight.—2nd ed.
        p.   cm.
     Includes bibliographical references and index.
     ISBN 0-07-052263-4
        1. Artificial intelligence.   I. Knight, Kevin.   II. Title.
Q335.R53   1991
006.3 — dc20   90-20608

About the Authors

Elaine Rich is Director of the Artificial Intelligence Laboratory at the Microelectronics and Computer Technology Corporation (MCC). Formerly on the faculty in computer sciences at the University of Texas, she received her Ph.D. from Carnegie Mellon University. Her research interests include natural language processing, knowledge representation, and machine translation.

Kevin Knight received his B.A. from Harvard University and is presently completing his Ph.D. in computer science at Carnegie Mellon University. A regular consultant at MCC, his research interests include natural language processing, unification, machine translation, and search.

For our fathers

Robert Rich

and

Gary Knight

Contents

Preface

In the years since the first edition of this book appeared, Artificial Intelligence (AI) has grown from a small-scale laboratory science into a technological and industrial success. We now possess an arsenal of techniques for creating computer programs that control manufacturing processes, diagnose computer faults and human diseases, design computers, do insurance underwriting, play grandmaster-level chess, and so on. Basic research in AI has expanded enormously during this period. For the student, extracting theoretical and practical knowledge from such a large body of scientific knowledge is a daunting task. The goal of the first edition of this book was to provide a readable introduction to the problems and techniques of AI. In this edition, we have tried to achieve the same goal for the expanded field that AI has become. In particular, we have tried to present both the theoretical foundations of AI and an indication of the ways that current techniques can be used in application programs.

As a result of this effort, the book has grown. It is probably no longer possible to cover everything in a single semester. Because of this, we have structured the book so that an instructor can choose from a variety of paths through the chapters. The book is divided into three parts:

Part I.   Problems and Search.
Part II.   Knowledge Representation.
Part III. Advanced Topics.

Part I introduces AI by examining the nature of the difficult problems that AI seeks to solve. It then develops the theory and practice of heuristic search, providing detailed algorithms for standard search methods, including best-first search, hill climbing, simulated annealing, means-ends analysis, and constraint satisfaction.

The last thirty years of AI have demonstrated that intelligence requires more than the ability to reason. It also requires a great deal of knowledge about the world. So Part II explores a variety of methods for encoding knowledge in computer systems. These methods include predicate logic, production rules, semantic networks, frames, and scripts. There are also chapters on both symbolic and numeric techniques for reasoning under uncertainty. In addition, we present some very specific frameworks in which particular commitments to a set of representational primitives are made.

Parts I and II should be covered in any basic course in AI. They provide the foundation for the advanced topics and applications that are presented in Part III. While the chapters in Parts I and II should be covered in order since they build on each other, the chapters in Part III are, for the most part, independent and can be covered in almost any combination, depending on the goals of a particular course. The topics that are covered include: game playing, planning, understanding, natural language processing (which depends on the understanding chapter), parallel and distributed AI (which depends on planning and natural language), learning, connectionist models, common sense, expert systems, and perception and action.

To use this book effectively, students should have some background in both computer science and mathematics. As computer science background, they should have experience programming and they should feel comfortable with the material in an undergraduate data structures course. They should be familiar with the use of recursion as a program control structure. And they should be able to do simple analyses of the time complexity of algorithms. As mathematical background, students should have the equivalent of an undergraduate course in logic, including predicate logic with quantifiers and the basic notion of a decision procedure.

This book contains, spread throughout it, many references to the AI research literature. These references are important for two reasons. First, they make it possible for the student to pursue individual topics in greater depth than is possible within the space restrictions of this book. This is the common reason for including references in a survey text. The second reason that these references have been included is more specific to the content of this book. AI is a relatively new discipline. In many areas of the field there is still not complete agreement on how things should be done. The references to the source literature guarantee that students have access not just to one approach, but to as many as possible of those whose eventual success still needs to be determined by further research, both theoretical and empirical.

Since the ultimate goal of AI is the construction of programs that solve hard problems, no study of AI is complete without some experience writing programs. Most AI programs are written in LISP, PROLOG, or some specialized AI shell. Recently though, as AI has spread out into the mainstream computing world, AI programs are being written in a wide variety of programming languages. The algorithms presented in this book are described in sufficient detail to enable students to exploit them in their programs, but they are not expressed in code. This book should probably be supplemented with a good book on whatever language is being used for programming in the course.

This book would not have happened without the help of many people. The content of the manuscript has been greatly improved by the comments of Srinivas Akella, Jim Blevins, Clay Bridges, R. Martin Chavez, Alan Cline, Adam Farquar, Anwar Ghuloum, Yolanda Gil, R. V. Guha, Lucy Hadden, Ajay Jain, Craig Knoblock, John Laird, Clifford Mercer, Michael Newton, Charles Petrie, Robert Rich, Steve Shafer, Reid Simmons, Herbert Simon, Munindar Singh, Milind Tambe, David Touretzky, Manuela Veloso, David Wroblewski, and Marco Zagha.

Special thanks to Yolanda Gil and Alan Cline for help above and beyond. Yolanda kept the project going under desperate circumstances, and Alan spent innumerable hours designing the cover and bringing it into the world. We thank them for these things and much, much more.

Linda Mitchell helped us put together many draft editions along the way. Some of those drafts were used in actual courses, where students found innumerable bugs for us. We would like to thank them as well as their instructors, Tom Mitchell and Jean Scholtz. Thanks also to Don Speray for his help in producing the cover.

David Shapiro and Joe Murphy deserve credit for superb editing, and for keeping us on schedule.

We would also like to thank Nicole Vecchi for her wisdom and patience in the world of high resolution printing. Thanks to David Long and Lily Mummert for pointing us to the right fonts.

Thanks to the following reviewers for their comments: Yigal Arens, University of Southern California; Jaime Carbonell, Carnegie Mellon University; Charles Dyer, University of Wisconsin, Madison; George Ernst, Case Western Reserve University; Pat Langley, University of California, Irvine; Brian Schunck, University of Michigan; and James Slagle, University of Minnesota.

Carnegie Mellon University and MCC provided us the environment in which we could write and produce this book. We would like to thank our colleagues, particularly Jim Barnett and Masaru Tomita, for putting up with us while we were writing this book instead of doing the other things we were supposed to be doing.

Elaine Rich
Kevin Knight

Part I

Problems and Search

Chapter 1

What Is Artificial Intelligence?

What exactly is artificial intelligence? Although most attempts to define complex and widely used terms precisely are exercises in futility, it is useful to draw at least an approximate boundary around the concept to provide a perspective on the discussion that follows. To do this, we propose the following by no means universally accepted definition. *Artificial intelligence* (AI) is the study of how to make computers do things which, at the moment, people do better. This definition is, of course, somewhat ephemeral because of its reference to the current state of computer science. And it fails to include some areas of potentially very large impact, namely problems that cannot now be solved well by either computers or people. But it provides a good outline of what constitutes artificial intelligence, and it avoids the philosophical issues that dominate attempts to define the meaning of either *artificial* or *intelligence*. Interestingly, though, it suggests a similarity with philosophy at the same time it is avoiding it. Philosophy has always been the study of those branches of knowledge that were so poorly understood that they had not yet become separate disciplines in their own right. As fields such as mathematics or physics became more advanced, they broke off from philosophy. Perhaps if AI succeeds it can reduce itself to the empty set.

1.1   The AI Problems

What then are some of the problems contained within AI? Much of the early work in the field focused on formal tasks, such as game playing and theorem proving. Samuel wrote a checkers-playing program that not only played games with opponents but also used its experience at those games to improve its later performance. Chess also received a good deal of attention. The Logic Theorist was an early attempt to prove mathematical theorems. It was able to prove several theorems from the first chapter of Whitehead and Russell's *Principia Mathematica*. Gelernter's theorem prover explored another area of mathematics: geometry. Game playing and theorem proving share the property that people who do them well are considered to be displaying intelligence. Despite this, it appeared initially that computers could perform well at those tasks simply by being fast at exploring a large number of solution paths and then selecting the best one. It was thought that this process required very little knowledge and could therefore be programmed easily. As we will see later, this assumption turned out to be false since no computer is fast enough to overcome the combinatorial explosion generated by most problems.

Another early foray into AI focused on the sort of problem solving that we do every day when we decide how to get to work in the morning, often called *commonsense reasoning*. It includes reasoning about physical objects and their relationships to each other (e.g., an object can be in only one place at a time), as well as reasoning about actions and their consequences (e.g., if you let go of something, it will fall to the floor and maybe break). To investigate this sort of reasoning, Newell, Shaw, and Simon built the General Problem Solver (GPS), which they applied to several commonsense tasks as well as to the problem of performing symbolic manipulations of logical expressions. Again, no attempt was made to create a program with a large amount of knowledge about a particular problem domain. Only quite simple tasks were selected.

As AI research progressed and techniques for handling larger amounts of world knowledge were developed, some progress was made on the tasks just described and new tasks could reasonably be attempted. These include perception (vision and speech), natural language understanding, and problem solving in specialized domains such as medical diagnosis and chemical analysis.

Perception of the world around us is crucial to our survival. Animals with much less intelligence than people are capable of more sophisticated visual perception than are current machines. Perceptual tasks are difficult because they involve analog (rather than digital) signals; the signals are typically very noisy and usually a large number of things (some of which may be partially obscuring others) must be perceived at once. The problems of perception are discussed in greater detail in Chapter 21.

The ability to use language to communicate a wide variety of ideas is perhaps the most important thing that separates humans from the other animals. The problem of understanding spoken language is a perceptual problem and is hard to solve for the reasons just discussed. But suppose we simplify the problem by restricting it to written language. This problem, usually referred to as *natural language understanding*, is still extremely difficult. In order to understand sentences about a topic, it is necessary to know not only a lot about the language itself (its vocabulary and grammar) but also a good deal about the topic so that unstated assumptions can be recognized. We discuss this problem again later in this chapter and then in more detail in Chapter 15.

In addition to these mundane tasks, many people can also perform one or maybe more specialized tasks in which carefully acquired expertise is necessary. Examples of such tasks include engineering design, scientific discovery, medical diagnosis, and financial planning. Programs that can solve problems in these domains also fall under the aegis of artificial intelligence. Figure 1.1 lists some of the tasks that are the targets of work in AI.

A person who knows how to perform tasks from several of the categories shown in the figure learns the necessary skills in a standard order. First perceptual, linguistic, and commonsense skills are learned. Later (and of course for some people, never) expert skills such as engineering, medicine, or finance are acquired. It might seem to make sense then that the earlier skills are easier and thus more amenable to computerized duplication than are the later, more specialized ones. For this reason, much of the initial AI work was concentrated in those early areas. But it turns out that this naive assumption is not right. Although expert skills require knowledge that many of us do not have, they

Mundane Tasks

- Perception
    - Vision
    - Speech
- Natural language
    - Understanding
    - Generation
    - Translation
- Commonsense reasoning
- Robot control

Formal Tasks

- Games
    - Chess
    - Backgammon
    - Checkers
    - Go
- Mathematics
    - Geometry
    - Logic
    - Integral calculus
    - Proving properties of programs

Expert Tasks

- Engineering
    - Design
    - Fault finding
    - Manufacturing planning
- Scientific analysis
- Medical diagnosis
- Financial analysis

Figure 1.1: Some of the Task Domains of Artificial Intelligence

often require much less knowledge than do the more mundane skills and that knowledge is usually easier to represent and deal with inside programs.

As a result, the problem areas where AI is now flourishing most as a practical discipline (as opposed to a purely research one) are primarily the domains that require only specialized expertise without the assistance of commonsense knowledge. There are now thousands of programs called *expert systems* in day-to-day operation throughout all areas of industry and government. Each of these systems attempts to solve part, or perhaps all, of a practical, significant problem that previously required scarce human expertise. In Chapter 20 we examine several of these systems and explore techniques for constructing them.

Before embarking on a study of specific AI problems and solution techniques, it is important at least to discuss, if not to answer, the following four questions:

1. What are our underlying assumptions about intelligence?

2. What kinds of techniques will be useful for solving AI problems?

3. At what level of detail, if at all, are we trying to model human intelligence?

4. How will we know when we have succeeded in building an intelligent program?

The next four sections of this chapter address these questions. Following that is a survey of some AI books that may be of interest and a summary of the chapter.

1.2   The Underlying Assumption

At the heart of research in artificial intelligence lies what Newell and Simon [1976] call the *physical symbol system hypothesis*. They define a physical symbol system as follows:

> A physical symbol system consists of a set of entities, called symbols, which are physical patterns that can occur as components of another type of entity called an expression (or symbol structure). Thus, a symbol structure is composed of a number of instances (or tokens) of symbols related in some physical way (such as one token being next to another). At any instant of time the system will contain a collection of these symbol structures. Besides these structures, the system also contains a collection of processes that operate on expressions to produce other expressions: processes of creation, modification, reproduction and destruction. A physical symbol system is a machine that produces through time an evolving collection of symbol structures. Such a system exists in a world of objects wider than just these symbolic expressions themselves.

They then state the hypothesis as

> *The Physical Symbol System Hypothesis.* A physical symbol system has the necessary and sufficient means for general intelligent action.

This hypothesis is only a hypothesis. There appears to be no way to prove or disprove it on logical grounds. So it must be subjected to empirical validation. We may find that it is false. We may find that the bulk of the evidence says that it is true. But the only way to determine its truth is by experimentation.

Computers provide the perfect medium for this experimentation since they can be programmed to simulate any physical symbol system we like. This ability of computers to serve as arbitrary symbol manipulators was noticed very early in the history of computing. Lady Lovelace made the following observation about Babbage's proposed Analytical Engine in 1842:

> The operating mechanism can even be thrown into action independently of any object to operate upon (although of course no result could then be developed). Again, it might act upon other things besides numbers, were objects found whose mutual fundamental relations could be expressed by those of the abstract science of operations, and which should be also susceptible of adaptations to the action of the operating notation and mechanism of the engine. Supposing, for instance, that the fundamental relations of pitched sounds in the science of harmony and of musical composition were susceptible of such expression and adaptations, the engine might compose elaborate and scientific pieces of music of any degree of complexity or extent. [Lovelace, 1961]

As it has become increasingly easy to build computing machines, so it has become increasingly possible to conduct empirical investigations of the physical symbol system hypothesis. In each such investigation, a particular task that might be regarded as requiring intelligence is selected. A program to perform the task is proposed and then tested. Although we have not been completely successful at creating programs that perform all the selected tasks, most scientists believe that many of the problems that have been encountered will ultimately prove to be surmountable by more sophisticated programs than we have yet produced.

Evidence in support of the physical symbol system hypothesis has come not only from areas such as game playing, where one might most expect to find it, but also from areas such as visual perception, where it is more tempting to suspect the influence of subsymbolic processes. However, subsymbolic models (for example, neural networks) are beginning to challenge symbolic ones at such low-level tasks. Such models are discussed in Chapter 18. Whether certain subsymbolic models conflict with the physical symbol system hypothesis is a topic still under debate (e.g., Smolensky [1988]). And it is important to note that even the success of subsymbolic systems is not necessarily evidence against the hypothesis. It is often possible to accomplish a task in more than one way.

One interesting attempt to reduce a particularly human activity, the understanding of jokes, to a process of symbol manipulation is provided in the book *Mathematics and Humor* [Paulos, 1980]. It is, of course, possible that the hypothesis will turn out to be only partially true. Perhaps physical symbol systems will prove able to model some aspects of human intelligence and not others. Only time and effort will tell.

The importance of the physical symbol system hypothesis is twofold. It is a significant theory of the nature of human intelligence and so is of great interest to psychologists. It also forms the basis of the belief that it is possible to build programs that can perform intelligent tasks now performed by people. Our major concern here is with the latter of these implications, although as we will soon see, the two issues are not unrelated.

1.3   What Is an AI Technique?

Artificial intelligence problems span a very broad spectrum. They appear to have very little in common except that they are hard. Are there any techniques that are appropriate for the solution of a variety of these problems? The answer to this question is yes, there are. What, then, if anything, can we say about those techniques besides the fact that they manipulate symbols? How could we tell if those techniques might be useful in solving other problems, perhaps ones not traditionally regarded as AI tasks? The rest of this book is an attempt to answer those questions in detail. But before we begin examining closely the individual techniques, it is enlightening to take a broad look at them to see what properties they ought to possess.

One of the few hard and fast results to come out of the first three decades of AI research is that *intelligence requires knowledge*. To compensate for its one overpowering asset, indispensability, knowledge possesses some less desirable properties, including:

- It is voluminous.

- It is hard to characterize accurately.

- It is constantly changing.

- It differs from data by being organized in a way that corresponds to the ways it will be used.

So where does this leave us in our attempt to define AI techniques? We are forced to conclude that an AI technique is a method that exploits knowledge that should be represented in such a way that:

- The knowledge captures generalizations. In other words, it is not necessary to represent separately each individual situation. Instead, situations that share important properties are grouped together. If knowledge does not have this property, inordinate amounts of memory and updating will be required. So we usually call something without this property "data" rather than knowledge.

- It can be understood by people who must provide it. Although for many programs, the bulk of the data can be acquired automatically (for example, by taking readings from a variety of instruments), in many AI domains, most of the knowledge a program has must ultimately be provided by people in terms they understand.

- It can easily be modified to correct errors and to reflect changes in the world and in our world view.

- It can be used in a great many situations even if it is not totally accurate or complete.

- It can be used to help overcome its own sheer bulk by helping to narrow the range of possibilities that must usually be considered.

Although AI techniques must be designed in keeping with these constraints imposed by AI problems, there is some degree of independence between problems and problem-solving techniques. It is possible to solve AI problems without using AI techniques (although, as we suggested above, those solutions are not likely to be very good). And it is possible to apply AI techniques to the solution of non-AI problems. This is likely to be a good thing to do for problems that possess many of the same characteristics as do AI problems. In order to try to characterize AI techniques in as problem-independent a way as possible, let's look at two very different problems and a series of approaches for solving each of them.

1.3.1 Tic-Tac-Toe

In this section, we present a series of three programs to play tic-tac-toe. The programs in this series increase in:

- Their complexity

- Their use of generalizations

- The clarity of their knowledge

- The extensibility of their approach

Thus they move toward being representations of what we call AI techniques.

Program 1

Data Structures

Board

A nine-element vector representing the board, where the elements of the vector correspond to the board positions as follows:

1	2	3
4	5	6
7	8	9

An element contains the value 0 if the corresponding square is blank, 1 if it is filled with an X, or 2 if it is filled with an O.

Movetable

A large vector of 19,683 elements (3^9), each element of which is a nine-element vector. The contents of this vector are chosen specifically to allow the algorithm to work.

The Algorithm

To make a move, do the following:

1. View the vector Board as a ternary (base three) number. Convert it to a decimal number.

2. Use the number computed in step 1 as an index into Movetable and access the vector stored there.

3. The vector selected in step 2 represents the way the board will look after the move that should be made. So set Board equal to that vector.

Comments

This program is very efficient in terms of time. And, in theory, it could play an optimal game of tic-tac-toe. But it has several disadvantages:

- It takes a lot of space to store the table that specifies the correct move to make from each board position.

- Someone will have to do a lot of work specifying all the entries in the movetable.

- It is very unlikely that all the required movetable entries can be determined and entered without any errors.

- If we want to extend the game, say to three dimensions, we would have to start from scratch, and in fact this technique would no longer work at all, since 3^{27} board positions would have to be stored, thus overwhelming present computer memories.

The technique embodied in this program does not appear to meet any of our requirements for a good AI technique. Let's see if we can do better.

Program 2

Data Structures

Board   A nine-element vector representing the board, as described for Program 1. But instead of using the numbers 0, 1, or 2 in each element, we store 2 (indicating blank), 3 (indicating X), or 5 (indicating O).

Turn   An integer indicating which move of the game is about to be played; 1 indicates the first move, 9 the last.

The Algorithm

The main algorithm uses three subprocedures:

Make2   Returns 5 if the center square of the board is blank, that is, if Board[5] = 2. Otherwise, this function returns any blank noncorner square (2, 4, 6, or 8).

Posswin(p)   Returns 0 if player p cannot win on his next move; otherwise, it returns the number of the square that constitutes a winning move. This function will enable the program both to win and to block the opponent's win. Posswin operates by checking, one at a time, each of the rows, columns, and diagonals. Because of the way values are numbered, it can test an entire row (column or diagonal) to see if it is a possible win by multiplying the values of its squares together. If the product is 18 (3 x 3 x 2), then X can win. If the product is 50 (5 x 5 x 2), then O can win. If we find a winning row, we determine which element is blank, and return the number of that square.

Go(*n*)   Makes a move in square *n*. This procedure sets Board[*n*] to 3 if Turn is odd, or 5 if Turn is even. It also increments Turn by one.

The algorithm has a built-in strategy for each move it may have to make. It makes the odd-numbered moves if it is playing X, the even-numbered moves if it is playing O. The strategy for each turn is as follows:

Turn=1   Go(1) (upper left corner).

Turn=2   If Board[5] is blank, Go(5), else Go(1).

Turn=3   If Board[9] is blank, Go(9), else Go(3).

Turn=4   If Posswin(X) is not 0, then Go(Posswin(X)) [i.e., block opponent's win], else Go(Make2).

Turn=5   If Posswin(X) is not 0 then Go(Posswin(X)) [i.e., win] else if Posswin(O) is not 0, then Go(Posswin(O)) [i.e., block win], else if Board[7] is blank, then Go(7), else Go(3). [Here the program is trying to make a fork.]

Turn=6   If Posswin(O) is not 0 then Go(Posswin(O)), else if Posswin(X) is not 0, then Go(Posswin(X)), else Go(Make2).

Turn=7   If Posswin(X) is not 0 then Go(Posswin(X)), else if Posswin(O) is not 0, then Go(Posswin(O)), else go anywhere that is blank.

Turn=8   If Posswin(O) is not 0 then Go(Posswin(O)), else if Posswin(X) is not 0, then Go(Posswin(X)), else go anywhere that is blank.

Turn=9   Same as Turn=7.

Comments

This program is not quite as efficient in terms of time as the first one since it has to check several conditions before making each move. But it is a lot more efficient in terms of space. It is also a lot easier to understand the program's strategy or to change the strategy if desired. But the total strategy has still been figured out in advance by the programmer. Any bugs in the programmer's tic-tac-toe playing skill will show up in the program's play. And we still cannot generalize any of the program's knowledge to a different domain, such as three-dimensional tic-tac-toe.

Program 2′

This program is identical to Program 2 except for one change in the representation of the board. We again represent the board as a nine-element vector, but this time we assign board positions to vector elements as follows:

8	3	4
1	5	9
6	7	2

Notice that this numbering of the board produces a magic square: all the rows, columns, and diagonals sum to 15. This means that we can simplify the process of checking for a possible win. In addition to marking the board as moves are made, we keep a list, for each player, of the squares in which he or she has played. To check for a possible win for one player, we consider each pair of squares owned by that player and compute the difference between 15 and the sum of the two squares. If this difference is not positive or if it is greater than 9, then the original two squares were not collinear and so can be ignored. Otherwise, if the square representing the difference is blank, a move there will produce a win. Since no player can have more than four squares at a time, there will be many fewer squares examined using this scheme than there were using the more straightforward approach of Program 2. This shows how the choice of representation can have a major impact on the efficiency of a problem-solving program.

Comments

This comparison raises an interesting question about the relationship between the way people solve problems and the way computers do. Why do people find the row-scan approach easier while the number-counting approach is more efficient for a computer? We do not know enough about how people work to answer that question completely. One part of the answer is that people are parallel processors and can look at several parts of the board at once, whereas the conventional computer must look at the squares one at a time. Sometimes an investigation of how people solve problems sheds great light on how computers should do so. At other times, the differences in the hardware of the two seem so great that different strategies seem best. As we learn more about problem solving both by people and by machines, we may know better whether the same representations and algorithms are best for both people and machines. We will discuss this question further in Section 1.4.

Program 3

Data Structures

BoardPosition   A structure containing a nine-element vector representing the board, a list of board positions that could result from the next move, and a number representing an estimate of how likely the board position is to lead to an ultimate win for the player to move.

The Algorithm

To decide on the next move, look ahead at the board positions that result from each possible move. Decide which position is best (as described below), make the move that leads to that position, and assign the rating of that best move to the current position.

To decide which of a set of board positions is best, do the following for each of them:

    1. See if it is a win. If so, call it the best by giving it the highest possible rating.

2. Otherwise, consider all the moves the opponent could make next. See which of them is worst for us (by recursively calling this procedure). Assume the opponent will make that move. Whatever rating that move has, assign it to the node we are considering.

3. The best node is then the one with the highest rating.

This algorithm will look ahead at various sequences of moves in order to find a sequence that leads to a win. It attempts to maximize the likelihood of winning, while assuming that the opponent will try to minimize that likelihood. This algorithm is called the *minimax procedure*, and it is discussed in detail in Chapter 12.

Comments

This program will require much more time than either of the others since it must search a tree representing all possible move sequences before making each move. But it is superior to the other programs in one very big way: It could be extended to handle games more complicated than tic-tac-toe, for which the exhaustive enumeration approach of the other programs would completely fall apart. It can also be augmented by a variety of specific kinds of knowledge about games and how to play them. For example, instead of considering all possible next moves, it might consider only a subset of them that are determined, by some simple algorithm, to be reasonable. And, instead of following each series of moves until one player wins, it could search for a limited time and evaluate the merit of each resulting board position using some static function.

Program 3 is an example of the use of an AI technique. For very small problems, it is less efficient than a variety of more direct methods. However, it can be used in situations where those methods would fail.

1.3.2   Question Answering

In this section we look at a series of programs that read in English text and then answer questions, also stated in English, about that text. This task differs from the last one in that it is more difficult now to state formally and precisely what our problem is and what constitutes correct solutions to it. For example, suppose that the input text were just the single sentence

Russia massed troops on the Czech border.

Then either of the following question-answering dialogues might occur (and in fact did occur with the POLITICS program [Carbonell, 1980]):

Dialogue 1

Q: Why did Russia do this?

A: Because Russia thought that it could take political control of Czechoslovakia by sending troops.

Q: What should the United States do?

A: The United States should intervene militarily.

Dialogue 2

Q: Why did Russia do this?

A: Because Russia wanted to increase its political influence over Czechoslovakia.

Q: What should the United States do?

A: The United States should denounce the Russian action in the United Nations.

In the POLITICS program, answers were constructed by considering both the input text and a separate model of the beliefs and actions of various political entities, including Russia. When the model is changed, as it was between these two dialogues, the system's answers also change. In this example, the first dialogue was produced when POLITICS was given a model that was intended to correspond to the beliefs of a typical American conservative (circa 1977). The second dialogue occurred when POLITICS was given a model that was intended to correspond to the beliefs of a typical American liberal (of the same vintage).

The general point here is that defining what it means to produce a *correct* answer to a question may be very hard. Usually, question-answering programs define what it means to be an answer by the procedure that is used to compute the answer. Then their authors appeal to other people to agree that the answers found by the program "make sense" and so to confirm the model of question answering defined in the program. This is not completely satisfactory, but no better way of defining the problem has yet been found. For lack of a better method, we will do the same here and illustrate three definitions of question answering, each with a corresponding program that implements the definition.

In order to be able to compare the three programs, we illustrate all of them using the following text:

> Mary went shopping for a new coat. She found a red one she really liked. When she got it home, she discovered that it went perfectly with her favorite dress.

We will also attempt to answer each of the following questions with each program:

Q1:   What did Mary go shopping for?

Q2:   What did Mary find that she liked?

Q3:   Did Mary buy anything?

Program 1

This program attempts to answer questions using the literal input text. It simply matches text fragments in the questions against the input text.

Data Structures

QuestionPatterns   A set of templates that match common question forms and produce patterns to be used to match against inputs. Templates and patterns (which we call *text patterns*) are paired so that if a template matches successfully against an input question then its associated text patterns are used to try to find appropriate answers in the text. For example, if the template "Who did x y" matches an input question, then the text pattern "x y z" is matched against the input text and the value of z is given as the answer to the question.

Text   The input text stored simply as a long character string.

Question   The current question also stored as a character string.

The Algorithm

To answer a question, do the following:

1. Compare each element of QuestionPatterns against the Question and use all those that match successfully to generate a set of text patterns.

2. Pass each of these patterns through a substitution process that generates alternative forms of verbs so that, for example, "go" in a question might match "went" in the text. This step generates a new, expanded set of text patterns.

3. Apply each of these text patterns to Text, and collect all the resulting answers.

4. Reply with the set of answers just collected.

Examples

Q1: The template "What did x y" matches this question and generates the text pattern "Mary go shopping for z." After the pattern-substitution step, this pattern is expanded to a set of patterns including "Mary goes shopping for z," and "Mary went shopping for z." The latter pattern matches the input text; the program, using a convention that variables match the longest possible string up to a sentence delimiter (such as a period), assigns z the value, "a new coat," which is given as the answer.

Q2: Unless the template set is very large, allowing for the insertion of the object of "find" between it and the modifying phrase "that she liked," the insertion of the word "really" in the text, and the substitution of "she" for "Mary," this question is not answerable. If all of these variations are accounted for and the question can be answered, then the response is "a red one."

Q3: Since no answer to this question is contained in the text, no answer will be found.

Comments

This approach is clearly inadequate to answer the kinds of questions people could answer after reading a simple text. Even its ability to answer the most direct questions is delicately dependent on the exact form in which questions are stated and on the variations that were anticipated in the design of the templates and the pattern substitutions that the system uses. In fact, the sheer inadequacy of this program to perform the task may make you wonder how such an approach could even be proposed. This program is substantially farther away from being useful than was the initial program we looked at for tic-tac-toe. Is this just a strawman designed to make some other technique look good in comparison? In a way, yes, but it is worth mentioning that the approach that this program uses, namely matching patterns, performing simple text substitutions, and then forming answers using straightforward combinations of canned text and sentence fragments located by the matcher, is the same approach that is used in one of the most famous "AI" programs ever written—ELIZA, which we discuss in Section 6.4.3. But, as you read the rest of this sequence of programs, it should become clear that what we mean by the term "artificial intelligence" does not include programs such as this except by a substantial stretching of definitions.

Program 2

This program first converts the input text into a structured internal form that attempts to capture the meaning of the sentences. It also converts questions into that form. It finds answers by matching structured forms against each other.

Data Structures

EnglishKnow   A description of the words, grammar, and appropriate semantic interpretations of a large enough subset of English to account for the input texts that the system will see. This knowledge of English is used both to map input sentences into an internal, meaning-oriented form and to map from such internal forms back into English. The former process is used when English text is being read; the latter is used to generate English answers from the meaning-oriented form that constitutes the program's knowledge base.

InputText   The input text in character form.

StructuredText   A structured representation of the content of the input text. This structure attempts to capture the essential knowledge contained in the text, independently of the exact way that the knowledge was stated in English. Some things that were not explicit in the English text, such as the referents of pronouns, have been made explicit in this form. Representing knowledge such as this is an important issue in the design of almost all AI programs. Existing programs exploit a variety of frameworks for doing this. There are three important families of such *knowledge representation* systems: production rules (of the form "if x then y"), slot-and-filler structures, and statements in mathematical logic. We discuss all of these methods later in substantial detail, and we look at key questions that need to be answered in order to choose a method for a particular program. For now though, we just pick one arbitrarily. The one we've chosen is a slot-and-filler structure. For example, the sentence "She found a red one she really liked," might be represented as shown in Figure 1.2. Actually, this is a simplified description of the contents of the sentence. Notice that it is not very explicit about temporal relationships (for example, events are just marked as past tense) nor have we made any real attempt to represent the meaning of the qualifier "really." It should, however, illustrate the basic form that representations such as this take. One of the key ideas in this sort

Event2
> *instance :*   *Finding*
> *tense :*   *Past*
> *agent :*   *Mary*
> *object :*   *Thing1*

Thing1
> *instance :*   *Coat*
> *color :*   *Red*

Event2
> *instance :*   *Liking*
> *tense :*   *Past*
> *modifier :*   *Much*
> *object :*   *Thing1*

Figure 1.2: A Structured Representation of a Sentence

of representation is that entities in the representation derive their meaning from their connections to other entities. In the figure, only the entities defined by the sentence are shown. But other entities, corresponding to concepts that the program knew about before it read this sentence, also exist in the representation and can be referred to within these new structures. In this example, for instance, we refer to the entities *Mary*, *Coat* (the general concept of a coat of which *Thing1* is a specific instance), *Liking* (the general concept of liking), and *Finding* (the general concept of finding).

InputQuestion   The input question in character form.

StructQuestion   A structured representation of the content of the user's question. The structure is the same as the one used to represent the content of the input text.

The Algorithm

Convert the InputText into structured form using the knowledge contained in English-Know. This may require considering several different potential structures, for a variety of reasons, including the fact that English words can be ambiguous, English grammatical structures can be ambiguous, and pronouns may have several possible antecedents.

Then, to answer a question, do the following:

1. Convert the question to structured form, again using the knowledge contained in EnglishKnow. Use some special marker in the structure to indicate the part of the structure that should be returned as the answer. This marker will often correspond

to the occurrence of a question word (like "who" or "what") in the sentence. The exact way in which this marking gets done depends on the form chosen for representing StructuredText. If a slot-and-filler structure, such as ours, is used, a special marker can be placed in one or more slots. If a logical system is used, however, markers will appear as variables in the logical formulas that represent the question.

2. Match this structured form against StructuredText.

3. Return as the answer those parts of the text that match the requested segment of the question.

Examples

Q1:   This question is answered straightforwardly with, "a new coat."

Q2:   This one also is answered successfully with, "a red coat."

Q3:   This one, though, cannot be answered, since there is no direct response to it in the text.

Comments

This approach is substantially more meaning (knowledge)-based than that of the first program and so is more effective. It can answer most questions to which replies are contained in the text, and it is much less brittle than the first program with respect to the exact forms of the text and the questions. As we expect, based on our experience with the pattern recognition and tic-tac-toe programs, the price we pay for this increased flexibility is time spent searching the various knowledge bases (i.e., EnglishKnow, StructuredText).

One word of warning is appropriate here. The problem of producing a knowledge base for English that is powerful enough to handle a wide range of English inputs is very difficult. It is discussed at greater length in Chapter 15. In addition, it is now recognized that knowledge of English alone is not adequate in general to enable a program to build the kind of structured representation shown here. Additional knowledge about the world with which the text deals is often required to support lexical and syntactic disambiguation and the correct assignment of antecedents to pronouns, among other things. For example, in the text

> Mary walked up to the salesperson. She asked where the toy department was.

it is not possible to determine what the word "she" refers to without knowledge about the roles of customers and salespeople in stores. To see this, contrast the correct antecedent of "she" in that text with the correct antecedent for the first occurrence of "she" in the following example:

> Mary walked up to the salesperson. She asked her if she needed any help.

In the simple case illustrated in our coat-buying example, it is possible to derive correct answers to our first two questions without any additional knowledge about stores or coats, and the fact that some such additional information may be necessary to support question answering has already been illustrated by the failure of this program to find an answer to question 3. Thus we see that although extracting a structured representation of the meaning of the input text is an improvement over the meaning-free approach of Program 1, it is by no means sufficient in general. So we need to look at an even more sophisticated (i.e., knowledge-rich) approach, which is what we do next.

Program 3

This program converts the input text into a structured form that contains the meanings of the sentences in the text, and then it combines that form with other structured forms that describe prior knowledge about the objects and situations involved in the text. It answers questions using this augmented knowledge structure.

Data Structures

WorldModel   A structured representation of background world knowledge. This structure contains knowledge about objects, actions, and situations that are described in the input text. This structure is used to construct IntegratedText from the input text. For example, Figure 1.3 shows an example of a structure that represents the system's knowledge about shopping. This kind of stored knowledge about stereotypical events is called a *script* and is discussed in more detail in Section 10.2. The notation used here differs from the one normally used in the literature for the sake of simplicity. The prime notation describes an object of the same type as the unprimed symbol that may or may not refer to the identical object. In the case of our text, for example, M is a coat and M′ is a red coat. Branches in the figure describe alternative paths through the script.

EnglishKnow   Same as in Program 2.

InputText   The input text in character form.

IntegratedText   A structured representation of the knowledge contained in the input text (similar to the structured description of Program 2) but combined now with other background, related knowledge.

InputQuestion   The input question in character form.

StructQuestion   A structured representation of the question.

The Algorithm

Convert the InputText into structured form using both the knowledge contained in EnglishKnow and that contained in WorldModel. The number of possible structures will usually be greater now than it was in Program 2 because so much more knowledge is being used. Sometimes, though, it may be possible to consider fewer possibilities by using the additional knowledge to filter the alternatives.

Shopping Script:

roles: C (customer), S (salesperson)
props: M (merchandise), D (dollars)
location: L (a store)

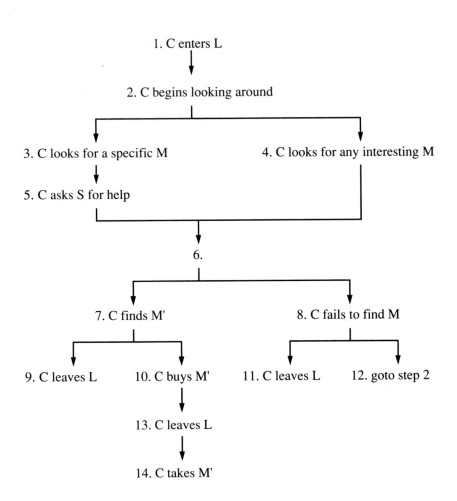

Figure 1.3: A Shopping Script

To answer a question, do the following:

1. Convert the question to structured form as in Program 2 but use WorldModel if necessary to resolve any ambiguities that may arise.

2. Match this structured form against IntegratedText.

3. Return as the answer those parts of the text that match the requested segment of the question.

Examples

Q1:   Same as Program 2.

Q2:   Same as Program 2.

Q3:   Now this question can be answered. The shopping script is instantiated for this text, and because of the last sentence, the path through step 14 of the script is the one that is used in forming the representation of this text. When the script is instantiated M' is bound to the structure representing the red coat (because the script says that M' is what gets taken home and the text says that a red coat is what got taken home). After the script has been instantiated, IntegratedText contains several events that are taken from the script but that are not described in the original text, including the event "Mary buys a red coat" (from step 10 of the script). Thus, using the integrated text as the basis for question answering allows the program to respond "She bought a red coat."

Comments

This program is more powerful than either of the first two because it exploits more knowledge. Thus it, like the final program in each of the other two sequences we have examined, is exploiting what we call AI techniques. But, again, a few caveats are in order. Even the techniques we have exploited in this program are not adequate for complete English question answering. The most important thing that is missing from this program is a general reasoning (inference) mechanism to be used when the requested answer is not contained explicitly even in IntegratedText, but that answer does follow logically from the knowledge that is there. For example, given the text

> Saturday morning Mary went shopping. Her brother tried to call her then, but he couldn't get hold of her.

it should be possible to answer the question

> Why couldn't Mary's brother reach her?

with the reply

> Because she wasn't home.

But to do so requires knowing that one cannot be two places at once and then using that fact to conclude that Mary could not have been home because she was shopping instead. Thus, although we avoided the inference problem temporarily by building IntegratedText, which had some obvious inferences built into it, we cannot avoid it forever. It is simply not practical to anticipate all legitimate inferences. In later chapters, we look at ways of providing a general inference mechanism that could be used to support a program such as the last one in this series.

This limitation does not contradict the main point of this example though. In fact, it is additional evidence for that point, namely, an effective question-answering procedure must be one based soundly on knowledge and the computational use of that knowledge. The purpose of AI techniques is to support this effective use of knowledge.

1.3.3   Conclusion

We have just examined two series of programs to solve two very different problems. In each series, the final program exemplifies what we mean by an AI technique. These two programs are slower to execute than the earlier ones in their respective series, but they illustrate three important AI techniques:

- Search—Provides a way of solving problems for which no more direct approach is available as well as a framework into which any direct techniques that are available can be embedded.

- Use of Knowledge—Provides a way of solving complex problems by exploiting the structures of the objects that are involved.

- Abstraction—Provides a way of separating important features and variations from the many unimportant ones that would otherwise overwhelm any process.

For the solution of hard problems, programs that exploit these techniques have several advantages over those that do not. They are much less fragile; they will not be thrown off completely by a small perturbation in their input. People can easily understand what the program's knowledge is. And these techniques can work for large problems where more direct methods break down.

We have still not given a precise definition of an AI technique. It is probably not possible to do so. But we have given some examples of what one is and what one is not. Throughout the rest of this book, we talk in great detail about what one is. The definition should then become a bit clearer, or less necessary.

1.4   The Level of the Model

Before we set out to do something, it is a good idea to decide exactly what we are trying to do. So we must ask ourselves, "What is our goal in trying to produce programs that do the intelligent things that people do?" Are we trying to produce programs that do the tasks the same way people do? Or, are we attempting to produce programs that simply do the tasks in whatever way appears easiest? There have been AI projects motivated by each of these goals.

Efforts to build programs that perform tasks the way people do can be divided into two classes. Programs in the first class attempt to solve problems that do not really fit our definition of an AI task. They are problems that a computer could easily solve, although that easy solution would exploit mechanisms that do not seem to be available to people. A classical example of this class of program is the Elementary Perceiver and Memorizer (EPAM) [Feigenbaum, 1963], which memorized associated pairs of nonsense syllables. Memorizing pairs of nonsense syllables is easy for a computer. Simply input them. To retrieve a response syllable given its associated stimulus one, the computer just scans for the stimulus syllable and responds with the one stored next to it. But this task is hard for people. EPAM simulated one way people might perform the task. It built a discrimination net through which it could find images of the syllables it had seen. It also stored, with each stimulus image, a cue that it could later pass through the discrimination net to try to find the correct response image. But it stored as a cue only as much information about the response syllable as was necessary to avoid ambiguity at the time the association was stored. This might be just the first letter, for example. But, of course, as the discrimination net grew and more syllables were added, an old cue might no longer be sufficient to identify a response syllable uniquely. Thus EPAM, like people, sometimes "forgot" previously learned responses. Many people regard programs in this first class to be uninteresting, and to some extent they are probably right. These programs can, however, be useful tools for psychologists who want to test theories of human performance.

The second class of programs that attempt to model human performance are those that do things that fall more clearly within our definition of AI tasks; they do things that are not trivial for the computer. There are several reasons one might want to model human performance at these sorts of tasks:

1. To test psychological theories of human performance. One example of a program that was written for this reason is PARRY [Colby, 1975], which exploited a model of human paranoid behavior to simulate the conversational behavior of a paranoid person. The model was good enough that when several psychologists were given the opportunity to converse with the program via a terminal, they diagnosed its behavior as paranoid.

2. To enable computers to understand human reasoning. For example, for a computer to be able to read a newspaper story and then answer a question, such as "Why did the terrorists kill the hostages?" its program must be able to simulate the reasoning processes of people.

3. To enable people to understand computer reasoning. In many circumstances, people are reluctant to rely on the output of a computer unless they can understand how the machine arrived at its result. If the computer's reasoning process is similar to that of people, then producing an acceptable explanation is much easier.

4. To exploit what knowledge we can glean from people. Since people are the best-known performers of most of the tasks with which we are dealing, it makes a lot of sense to look to them for clues as to how to proceed.

This last motivation is probably the most pervasive of the four. It motivated several very early systems that attempted to produce intelligent behavior by imitating people at the level of individual neurons. For examples of this, see the early theoretical work of McCulloch and Pitts [1943], the work on perceptrons, originally developed by Frank Rosenblatt but best described in *Perceptrons* [Minsky and Papert, 1969] and *Design for a Brain* [Ashby, 1952]. It proved impossible, however, to produce even minimally intelligent behavior with such simple devices. One reason was that there were severe theoretical limitations to the particular neural net architecture that was being used. More recently, several new neural net architectures have been proposed. These structures are not subject to the same theoretical limitations as were perceptrons. These new architectures are loosely called *connectionist*, and they have been used as a basis for several learning and problem-solving programs. We have more to say about them in Chapter 18. Also, we must consider that while human brains are highly parallel devices, most current computing systems are essentially serial engines. A highly successful parallel technique may be computationally intractable on a serial computer. But recently, partly because of the existence of the new family of parallel cognitive models, as well as because of the general promise of parallel computing, there is now substantial interest in the design of massively parallel machines to support AI programs.

Human cognitive theories have also influenced AI to look for higher-level (i.e., far above the neuron level) theories that do not require massive parallelism for their implementation. An early example of this approach can be seen in GPS, which are discussed in more detail in Section 3.6. This same approach can also be seen in much current work in natural language understanding. The failure of straightforward syntactic parsing mechanisms to make much of a dent in the problem of interpreting English sentences has led many people who are interested in natural language understanding by machine to look seriously for inspiration at what little we know about how people interpret language. And when people who are trying to build programs to analyze pictures discover that a filter function they have developed is very similar to what we think people use, they take heart that perhaps they are on the right track.

As you can see, this last motivation pervades a great many areas of AI research. In fact, it, in conjunction with the other motivations we mentioned, tends to make the distinction between the goal of simulating human performance and the goal of building an intelligent program any way we can seem much less different than they at first appeared. In either case, what we really need is a good model of the processes involved in intelligent reasoning. The field of *cognitive science*, in which psychologists, linguists, and computer scientists all work together, has as its goal the discovery of such a model. For a good survey of the variety of approaches contained within the field, see Norman [1981], Anderson [1985], and Gardner [1985].

1.5   Criteria for Success

One of the most important questions to answer in any scientific or engineering research project is "How will we know if we have succeeded?" Artificial intelligence is no exception. How will we know if we have constructed a machine that is intelligent? That question is at least as hard as the unanswerable question "What is intelligence?" But can we do anything to measure our progress?

In 1950, Alan Turing proposed the following method for determining whether a machine can think. His method has since become known as the *Turing test*. To conduct this test, we need two people and the machine to be evaluated. One person plays the role of the interrogator, who is in a separate room from the computer and the other person. The interrogator can ask questions of either the person or the computer by typing questions and receiving typed responses. However, the interrogator knows them only as A and B and aims to determine which is the person and which is the machine. The goal of the machine is to fool the interrogator into believing that it is the person. If the machine succeeds at this, then we will conclude that the machine can think. The machine is allowed to do whatever it can to fool the interrogator. So, for example, if asked the question "How much is 12,324 times 73,981?" it could wait several minutes and then respond with the wrong answer [Turing, 1963].

The more serious issue, though, is the amount of knowledge that a machine would need to pass the Turing test. Turing gives the following example of the sort of dialogue a machine would have to be capable of:

Interrogator: In the first line of your sonnet which reads "Shall I compare thee to a summer's day," would not "a spring day" do as well or better?

A: It wouldn't scan.

Interrogator: How about "a winter's day." That would scan all right.

A: Yes, but nobody wants to be compared to a winter's day.

Interrogator: Would you say Mr. Pickwick reminded you of Christmas?

A: In a way.

Interrogator: Yet Christmas is a winter's day, and I do not think Mr. Pickwick would mind the comparison.

A: I don't think you're serious. By a winter's day one means a typical winter's day, rather than a special one like Christmas.

It will be a long time before a computer passes the Turing test. Some people believe none ever will. But suppose we are willing to settle for less than a complete imitation of a person. Can we measure the achievement of AI in more restricted domains?

Often the answer to this question is yes. Sometimes it is possible to get a fairly precise measure of the achievement of a program. For example, a program can acquire a chess rating in the same way as a human player. The rating is based on the ratings of players whom the program can beat. Already programs have acquired chess ratings higher than the vast majority of human players. For other problem domains, a less precise measure of a program's achievement is possible. For example, DENDRAL is a program that analyzes organic compounds to determine their structure. It is hard to get a precise measure of DENDRAL's level of achievement compared to human chemists, but it has produced analyses that have been published as original research results. Thus it is certainly performing competently.

In other technical domains, it is possible to compare the time it takes for a program to complete a task to the time required by a person to do the same thing. For example, there are several programs in use by computer companies to configure particular systems to customers' needs (of which the pioneer was a program called R1). These programs typically require minutes to perform tasks that previously required hours of a skilled engineer's time. Such programs are usually evaluated by looking at the bottom line—whether they save (or make) money.

For many everyday tasks, though, it may be even harder to measure a program's performance. Suppose, for example, we ask a program to paraphrase a newspaper story. For problems such as this, the best test is usually just whether the program responded in a way that a person could have.

If our goal in writing a program is to simulate human performance at a task, then the measure of success is the extent to which the program's behavior corresponds to that performance, as measured by various kinds of experiments and protocol analyses. In this we do not simply want a program that does as well as possible. We want one that fails when people do. Various techniques developed by psychologists for comparing individuals and for testing models can be used to do this analysis.

We are forced to conclude that the question of whether a machine has intelligence or can think is too nebulous to answer precisely. But it is often possible to construct a computer program that meets some performance standard for a particular task. That does not mean that the program does the task in the best possible way. It means only that we understand at least one way of doing at least part of a task. When we set out to design an AI program, we should attempt to specify as well as possible the criteria for success for that particular program functioning in its restricted domain. For the moment, that is the best we can do.

1.6   Some General References

There are a great many sources of information about artificial intelligence. First, some survey books: The broadest are the multi-volume *Handbook of Artificial Intelligence* [Barr *et al.*, 1981] and *Encyclopedia of Artificial Intelligence* [Shapiro and Eckroth, 1987], both of which contain articles on each of the major topics in the field. Four other books that provide good overviews of the field are *Artificial Intelligence* [Winston, 1984], *Introduction to Artificial Intelligence* [Charniak and McDermott, 1985], *Logical Foundations of Artificial Intelligence* [Genesereth and Nilsson, 1987], and *The Elements of Artificial Intelligence* [Tanimoto, 1987]. Of more restricted scope is *Principles of Artificial Intelligence* [Nilsson, 1980], which contains a formal treatment of some general-purpose AI techniques.

The history of research in artificial intelligence is a fascinating story, related by Pamela McCorduck [1979] in her book *Machines Who Think*. Because almost all of what we call AI has been developed over the last 30 years, McCorduck was able to conduct her research for the book by actually interviewing almost all of the people whose work was influential in forming the field.

Most of the work conducted in AI has been originally reported in journal articles, conference proceedings, or technical reports. But some of the most interesting of these papers have later appeared in special collections published as books. *Computers and Thought* [Feigenbaum and Feldman, 1963] is a very early collection of this sort. Later ones include Simon and Siklossy [1972], Schank and Colby [1973], Bobrow and Collins [1975], Waterman and Hayes-Roth [1978], Findler [1979], Webber and Nilsson [1981], Halpern [1986], Shrobe [1988], and several others that are mentioned in later chapters in connection with specific topics.

The major journal of AI research is called simply *Artificial Intelligence*. In addition, *Cognitive Science* is devoted to papers dealing with the overlapping areas of psychology, linguistics, and artificial intelligence. *AI Magazine* is a more ephemeral, less technical magazine that is published by the American Association for Artificial Intelligence (AAAI). *IEEE Expert* and several other journals publish papers about expert systems in a wide variety of application domains.

Since 1969, there has been a major AI conference, the International Joint Conference on Artificial Intelligence (IJCAI), held every two years. The proceedings of these conferences give a good picture of the work that was taking place at the time. The other important AI conference, held three out of every four years starting in 1980, is sponsored by the AAAI, and its proceedings, too, are published.

In addition to these general references, there exists a whole array of papers and books describing individual AI projects. Rather than trying to list them all here, they are referred to as appropriate throughout the rest of this book.

1.7 One Final Word

What conclusions can we draw from this hurried introduction to the major questions of AI? The problems are varied, interesting, and hard. If we solve them, we will have useful programs and perhaps a better understanding of human thought. We should do the best we can to set criteria so that we can tell if we have solved the problems, and then we must try to do so.

How actually to go about solving these problems is the topic for the rest of this book. We need methods to help us solve AI's serious dilemma:

1. An AI system must contain a lot of knowledge if it is to handle anything but trivial toy problems.

2. But as the amount of knowledge grows, it becomes harder to access the appropriate things when needed, so more knowledge must be added to help. But now there is even more knowledge to manage, so more must be added, and so forth.

Our goal in AI is to construct working programs that solve the problems we are interested in. Throughout most of this book we focus on the design of representation mechanisms and algorithms that can be used by programs to solve the problems. We do not spend much time discussing the programming process required to turn these designs into working programs. In theory, it does not matter how this process is carried out, in what language it is done, or on what machine the product is run. In practice, of course, it is often much easier to produce a program using one system rather than another. Specifically, AI programs are easiest to build using languages that have been designed to support symbolic rather than primarily numeric computation.

For a variety of reasons, LISP has historically been the most commonly used language for AI programming. We say little explicitly about LISP in this book, although we occasionally rely on it as a notation. There used to be several competing dialects of LISP, but Common Lisp is now accepted as a standard. If you are unfamiliar with LISP, consult any of the following sources: *LISP* [Winston and Horn, 1989], *Common Lisp* [Hennessey, 1989], *Common LISPcraft* [Wilensky, 1986], and *Common Lisp: A Gentle*

Introduction to Symbolic Computation [Touretzky, 1989a]. For a complete description of Common Lisp, see *Common Lisp: The Reference* [Steele, 1990]. Another language that is often used for AI programming is PROLOG, which is described briefly in Chapter 6. And increasingly, as AI makes its way into the conventional programming world, AI systems are being written in general purpose programming languages such as C. One reason for this is that AI programs are ceasing to be standalone systems; instead, they are becoming components of larger systems, which may include conventional programs and databases of various forms. Real code does not form a big part of this book precisely because it is possible to implement the techniques we discuss in any of several languages and it is important not to confuse the ideas with their specific implementations. But you should keep in mind as you read the rest of this book that both the knowledge structures and the problem-solving strategies we discuss must ultimately be coded and integrated into a working program.

AI is still a young discipline. We have learned many things, some of which are presented in this book. But it is still hard to know exactly the perspective from which those things should be viewed. We cannot resist quoting an observation made by Lady Lovelace more than 100 years ago:

> In considering any new subject, there is frequently a tendency, first, to *overrate* what we find to be already interesting or remarkable; and, secondly, by a sort of natural reaction, to *undervalue* the true state of the case, when we do discover that our notions have surpassed those that were really tenable. [Lovelace, 1961]

She was talking about Babbage's Analytical Engine. But she could have been describing artificial intelligence.

1.8   Exercises

1. Pick a specific topic within the scope of AI and use the sources described in this chapter to do a preliminary literature search to determine what the current state of understanding of that topic is. If you cannot think of a more novel topic, try one of the following: expert systems for some specific domain (e.g., cancer therapy, computer design, financial planning), recognizing motion in images, using natural (i.e., humanlike) methods for proving mathematical theorems, resolving pronominal references in natural language texts, representing sequences of events in time, or designing a memory organization scheme for knowledge in a computer system based on our knowledge of human memory organization.

2. Explore the spectrum from static to AI-based techniques for a problem other than the two discussed in this chapter. Think of your own problem or use one of the following:

   - Translating an English sentence into Japanese
   - Teaching a child to subtract integers
   - Discovering patterns in empirical data taken from scientific experiments, and suggesting further experiments to find more patterns

Chapter 2

Problems, Problem Spaces, and Search

In the last chapter, we gave a brief description of the kinds of problems with which AI is typically concerned, as well as a couple of examples of the techniques it offers to solve those problems. To build a system to solve a particular problem, we need to do four things:

1. Define the problem precisely. This definition must include precise specifications of what the initial situation(s) will be as well as what final situations constitute acceptable solutions to the problem.

2. Analyze the problem. A few very important features can have an immense impact on the appropriateness of various possible techniques for solving the problem.

3. Isolate and represent the task knowledge that is necessary to solve the problem.

4. Choose the best problem-solving technique(s) and apply it (them) to the particular problem.

In this chapter and the next, we discuss the first two and the last of these issues. Then, in the chapters in Part II, we focus on the issue of knowledge representation.

2.1 Defining the Problem as a State Space Search

Suppose we start with the problem statement "Play chess." Although there are a lot of people to whom we could say that and reasonably expect that they will do as we intended, as our request now stands it is a very incomplete statement of the problem we want solved. To build a program that could "Play chess," we would first have to specify the starting position of the chess board, the rules that define the legal moves, and the board positions that represent a win for one side or the other. In addition, we must make explicit the previously implicit goal of not only playing a legal game of chess but also winning the game, if possible.

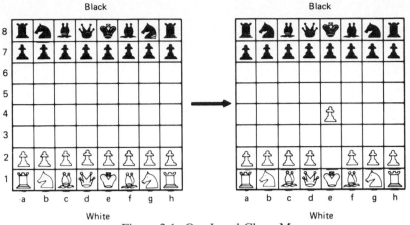

Figure 2.1: One Legal Chess Move

For the problem "Play chess," it is fairly easy to provide a formal and complete problem description. The starting position can be described as an 8-by-8 array where each position contains a symbol standing for the appropriate piece in the official chess opening position. We can define as our goal any board position in which the opponent does not have a legal move and his or her king is under attack. The legal moves provide the way of getting from the initial state to a goal state. They can be described easily as a set of rules consisting of two parts: a left side that serves as a pattern to be matched against the current board position and a right side that describes the change to be made to the board position to reflect the move. There are several ways in which these rules can be written. For example, we could write a rule such as that shown in Figure 2.1.

However, if we write rules like the one above, we have to write a very large number of them since there has to be a separate rule for each of the roughly 10^{120} possible board positions. Using so many rules poses two serious practical difficulties:

- No person could ever supply a complete set of such rules. It would take too long and could certainly not be done without mistakes.

- No program could easily handle all those rules. Although a hashing scheme could be used to find the relevant rules for each move fairly quickly, just storing that many rules poses serious difficulties.

In order to minimize such problems, we should look for a way to write the rules describing the legal moves in as general a way as possible. To do this, it is useful to introduce some convenient notation for describing patterns and substitutions. For example, the rule described in Figure 2.1, as well as many like it, could be written as shown in Figure 2.2.[1] In general, the more succinctly we can describe the rules we need, the less work we will have to do to provide them and the more efficient the program that uses them can be.

We have just defined the problem of playing chess as a problem of moving around in a *state space*, where each state corresponds to a legal position of the board. We can

---

[1] To be completely accurate, this rule should include a check for pinned pieces, which have been ignored here.

White pawn at
   Square(file e, rank 2)
      AND
Square(file e, rank 3)
   is empty
      AND
Square(file e, rank 4)
   is empty

$\rightarrow$

move pawn from
   Square(file e, rank 2)
   to Square(file e, rank 4)

Figure 2.2: Another Way to Describe Chess Moves

then play chess by starting at an initial state, using a set of rules to move from one state to another, and attempting to end up in one of a set of final states. This state space representation seems natural for chess because the set of states, which corresponds to the set of board positions, is artificial and well-organized. This same kind of representation is also useful for naturally occurring, less well-structured problems, although it may be necessary to use more complex structures than a matrix to describe an individual state. The state space representation forms the basis of most of the AI methods we discuss here. Its structure corresponds to the structure of problem solving in two important ways:

- It allows for a formal definition of a problem as the need to convert some given situation into some desired situation using a set of permissible operations.

- It permits us to define the process of solving a particular problem as a combination of known techniques (each represented as a rule defining a single step in the space) and search, the general technique of exploring the space to try to find some path from the current state to a goal state. Search is a very important process in the solution of hard problems for which no more direct techniques are available.

In order to show the generality of the state space representation, we use it to describe a problem very different from that of chess.

A Water Jug Problem: You are given two jugs, a 4-gallon one and a 3-gallon one. Neither has any measuring markers on it. There is a pump that can be used to fill the jugs with water. How can you get exactly 2 gallons of water into the 4-gallon jug?

The state space for this problem can be described as the set of ordered pairs of integers (x, y), such that $x = 0, 1, 2, 3,$ or 4 and $y = 0, 1, 2,$ or 3; x represents the number of gallons of water in the 4-gallon jug, and y represents the quantity of water in the 3-gallon jug. The start state is $(0, 0)$. The goal state is $(2, n)$ for any value of n (since the problem does not specify how many gallons need to be in the 3-gallon jug).

The operators[2] to be used to solve the problem can be described as shown in Figure 2.3. As in the chess problem, they are represented as rules whose left sides are

---

[2] The word "operator" refers to some representation of an action. An operator usually includes information about what must be true in the world before the action can take place, and how the world is changed by the action.

matched against the current state and whose right sides describe the new state that results from applying the rule. Notice that in order to describe the operators completely, it was necessary to make explicit some assumptions not mentioned in the problem statement. We have assumed that we can fill a jug from the pump, that we can pour water out of a jug onto the ground, that we can pour water from one jug to another, and that there are no other measuring devices available. Additional assumptions such as these are almost always required when converting from a typical problem statement given in English to a formal representation of the problem suitable for use by a program.

To solve the water jug problem, all we need, in addition to the problem description given above, is a control structure that loops through a simple cycle in which some rule whose left side matches the current state is chosen, the appropriate change to the state is made as described in the corresponding right side, and the resulting state is checked to see if it corresponds to a goal state. As long as it does not, the cycle continues. Clearly the speed with which the problem gets solved depends on the mechanism that is used to select the next operation to be performed. In Chapter 3, we discuss several ways of making that selection.

For the water jug problem, as with many others, there are several sequences of operators that solve the problem. One such sequence is shown in Figure 2.4. Often, a problem contains the explicit or implied statement that the shortest (or cheapest) such sequence be found. If present, this requirement will have a significant effect on the choice of an appropriate mechanism to guide the search for a solution. We discuss this issue in Section 2.3.4.

Several issues that often arise in converting an informal problem statement into a formal problem description are illustrated by this sample water jug problem. The first of these issues concerns the role of the conditions that occur in the left sides of the rules. All but one of the rules shown in Figure 2.3 contain conditions that must be satisfied before the operator described by the rule can be applied. For example, the first rule says, "If the 4-gallon jug is not already full, fill it." This rule could, however, have been written as, "Fill the 4-gallon jug," since it is physically possible to fill the jug even if it is already full. It is stupid to do so since no change in the problem state results, but it is possible. By encoding in the left sides of the rules constraints that are not strictly necessary but that restrict the application of the rules to states in which the rules are most likely to lead to a solution, we can generally increase the efficiency of the problem-solving program that uses the rules.

The extreme of this approach is shown in the first tic-tac-toe program of Chapter 1. Each entry in the move vector corresponds to a rule that describes an operation. The left side of each rule describes a board configuration and is represented implicitly by the index position. The right side of each rule describes the operation to be performed and is represented by a nine-element vector that corresponds to the resulting board configuration. Each of these rules is maximally specific; it applies only to a single board configuration, and, as a result, no search is required when such rules are used. However, the drawback to this extreme approach is that the problem solver can take no action at all in a novel situation. In fact, essentially no problem *solving* ever really occurs. For a tic-tac-toe playing program, this is not a serious problem, since it is possible to enumerate all the situations (i.e., board configurations) that may occur. But for most problems, this is not the case. In order to solve new problems, more general rules must be available.

1	(x, y)	$\rightarrow (4, y)$	Fill the 4-gallon jug
	if $x < 4$		
2	(x, y)	$\rightarrow (x, 3)$	Fill the 3-gallon jug
	if $y < 3$		
3	(x, y)	$\rightarrow (x - d, y)$	Pour some water out of
	if $x > 0$		the 4-gallon jug
4	(x, y)	$\rightarrow (x, y - d)$	Pour some water out of
	if $y > 0$		the 3-gallon jug
5	(x, y)	$\rightarrow (0, y)$	Empty the 4-gallon jug
	if $x > 0$		on the ground
6	(x, y)	$\rightarrow (x, 0)$	Empty the 3-gallon jug
	if $y > 0$		on the ground
7	(x, y)	$\rightarrow (4, y - (4 - x))$	Pour water from the
	if $x + y \geq 4$ and $y > 0$		3-gallon jug into the
			4-gallon jug until the
			4-gallon jug is full
8	(x, y)	$\rightarrow (x - (3 - y), 3)$	Pour water from the
	if $x + y \geq 3$ and $x > 0$		4-gallon jug into the
			3-gallon jug until the
			3-gallon jug is full
9	(x, y)	$\rightarrow (x + y, 0)$	Pour all the water
	if $x + y \leq 4$ and $y > 0$		from the 3-gallon jug
			into the 4-gallon jug
10	(x, y)	$\rightarrow (0, x + y)$	Pour all the water
	if $x + y \leq 3$ and $x > 0$		from the 4-gallon jug
			into the 3-gallon jug
11	$(0, 2)$	$\rightarrow (2, 0)$	Pour the 2 gallons
			from the 3-gallon jug
			into the 4-gallon jug
12	$(2, y)$	$\rightarrow (0, y)$	Empty the 2 gallons in
			the 4-gallon jug on
			the ground

Figure 2.3: Production Rules for the Water Jug Problem

Gallons in the 4-Gallon Jug	Gallons in the 3-Gallon Jug	Rule Applied
0	0	
		2
0	3	
		9
3	0	
		2
3	3	
		7
4	2	
		5 or 12
0	2	
		9 or 11
2	0	

Figure 2.4: One Solution to the Water Jug Problem

A second issue is exemplified by rules 3 and 4 in Figure 2.3. Should they or should they not be included in the list of available operators? Emptying an unmeasured amount of water onto the ground is certainly allowed by the problem statement. But a superficial preliminary analysis of the problem makes it clear that doing so will never get us any closer to a solution. Again, we see the tradeoff between writing a set of rules that describe just the problem itself, as opposed to a set of rules that describe both the problem and some knowledge about its solution.

Rules 11 and 12 illustrate a third issue. To see the problem-solving knowledge that these rules represent, look at the last two steps of the solution shown in Figure 2.4. Once the state (4, 2) is reached, it is obvious what to do next. The desired 2 gallons have been produced, but they are in the wrong jug. So the thing to do is to move them (rule 11). But before that can be done, the water that is already in the 4-gallon jug must be emptied out (rule 12). The idea behind these special-purpose rules is to capture the special-case knowledge that can be used at this stage in solving the problem. These rules do not actually add power to the system since the operations they describe are already provided by rule 9 (in the case of rule 11) and by rule 5 (in the case of rule 12). In fact, depending on the control strategy that is used for selecting rules to use during problem solving, the use of these rules may degrade performance. But the use of these rules may also improve performance if preference is given to special-case rules (as we discuss in Section 6.4.3).

We have now discussed two quite different problems, chess and the water jug problem. From these discussions, it should be clear that the first step toward the design of a program to solve a problem must be the creation of a formal and manipulable description of the problem itself. Ultimately, we would like to be able to write programs that can themselves produce such formal descriptions from informal ones. This process is called *operationalization*. It is not at all well-understood how to construct such programs, but see Section 17.3 for a description of one program that solves a piece of this problem. Until it becomes possible to automate this process, it must be done by hand, however. For simple problems, such as chess or the water jug, this is not very difficult. The problems are artificial and highly structured. For other problems, particularly naturally occurring ones, this step is much more difficult. Consider, for example, the task of specifying precisely what it means to understand an English sentence. Although such a specification must somehow be provided before we can design a program to solve the problem, producing such a specification is itself a very hard problem. Although our ultimate goal is to be able to solve difficult, unstructured problems, such as natural language understanding, it is useful to explore simpler problems, such as the water jug problem, in order to gain insight into the details of methods that can form the basis for solutions to the harder problems.

Summarizing what we have just said, in order to provide a formal description of a problem, we must do the following:

1. Define a state space that contains all the possible configurations of the relevant objects (and perhaps some impossible ones). It is, of course, possible to define this space without explicitly enumerating all of the states it contains.

2. Specify one or more states within that space that describe possible situations from which the problem-solving process may start. These states are called the *initial states*.

3. Specify one or more states that would be acceptable as solutions to the problem. These states are called *goal states*.

4. Specify a set of rules that describe the actions (operators) available. Doing this will require giving thought to the following issues:

   - What unstated assumptions are present in the informal problem description?
   - How general should the rules be?
   - How much of the work required to solve the problem should be precomputed and represented in the rules?

The problem can then be solved by using the rules, in combination with an appropriate control strategy, to move through the problem space until a path from an initial state to a goal state is found. Thus the process of search is fundamental to the problem-solving process. The fact that search provides the basis for the process of problem solving does not, however, mean that other, more direct approaches cannot also be exploited. Whenever possible, they can be included as steps in the search by encoding them into the rules. For example, in the water jug problem, we use the standard arithmetic operations as single steps in the rules. We do not use search to find a number with the property that it is equal to $y - (4 - x)$. Of course, for complex problems, more sophisticated computations will be needed. Search is a general mechanism that can be used when no more direct method is known. At the same time, it provides the framework into which more direct methods for solving subparts of a problem can be embedded.

2.2   Production Systems

Since search forms the core of many intelligent processes, it is useful to structure AI programs in a way that facilitates describing and performing the search process. Production systems provide such structures. A definition of a production system is given below. Do not be confused by other uses of the word *production*, such as to describe what is done in factories. A *production system* consists of:

- A set of rules, each consisting of a left side (a pattern) that determines the applicability of the rule and a right side that describes the operation to be performed if the rule is applied.[3]

- One or more knowledge/databases that contain whatever information is appropriate for the particular task. Some parts of the database may be permanent, while other parts of it may pertain only to the solution of the current problem. The information in these databases may be structured in any appropriate way.

- A control strategy that specifies the order in which the rules will be compared to the database and a way of resolving the conflicts that arise when several rules match at once.

- A rule applier.

So far, our definition of a production system has been very general. It encompasses a great many systems, including our descriptions of both a chess player and a water jug problem solver. It also encompasses a family of general production system interpreters, including:

- Basic production system languages, such as OPS5 [Brownston *et al.*, 1985] and ACT* [Anderson, 1983].

- More complex, often hybrid systems called *expert system shells*, which provide complete (relatively speaking) environments for the construction of knowledge-based expert systems.

- General problem-solving architectures like SOAR [Laird *et al.*, 1987], a system based on a specific set of cognitively motivated hypotheses about the nature of problem solving.

All of these systems provide the overall architecture of a production system and allow the programmer to write rules that define particular problems to be solved. We discuss production system issues further in Chapter 6.

We have now seen that in order to solve a problem, we must first reduce it to one for which a precise statement can be given. This can be done by defining the problem's state space (including the start and goal states) and a set of operators for moving in that space. The problem can then be solved by searching for a path through the space from an initial state to a goal state. The process of solving the problem can usefully be

---

[3]This convention for the use of left and right sides is natural for forward rules. As we will see later, many backward rule systems reverse the sides.

modeled as a production system. In the rest of this section, we look at the problem of choosing the appropriate control structure for the production system so that the search can be as efficient as possible.

2.2.1   Control Strategies

So far, we have completely ignored the question of how to decide which rule to apply next during the process of searching for a solution to a problem. This question arises since often more than one rule (and sometimes fewer than one rule) will have its left side match the current state. Even without a great deal of thought, it is clear that how such decisions are made will have a crucial impact on how quickly, and even whether, a problem is finally solved.

- *The first requirement of a good control strategy is that it cause motion.* Consider again the water jug problem of the last section. Suppose we implemented the simple control strategy of starting each time at the top of the list of rules and choosing the first applicable one. If we did that, we would never solve the problem. We would continue indefinitely filling the 4-gallon jug with water. Control strategies that do not cause motion will never lead to a solution.

- *The second requirement of a good control strategy is that it be systematic.* Here is another simple control strategy for the water jug problem: On each cycle, choose at random from among the applicable rules. This strategy is better than the first. It causes motion. It will lead to a solution eventually. But we are likely to arrive at the same state several times during the process and to use many more steps than are necessary. Because the control strategy is not systematic, we may explore a particular useless sequence of operators several times before we finally find a solution. The requirement that a control strategy be systematic corresponds to the need for global motion (over the course of several steps) as well as for local motion (over the course of a single step). One systematic control strategy for the water jug problem is the following. Construct a tree with the initial state as its root. Generate all the offspring of the root by applying each of the applicable rules to the initial state. Figure 2.5 shows how the tree looks at this point. Now, for each leaf node, generate all its successors by applying all the rules that are appropriate. The tree at this point is shown in Figure 2.6.[4] Continue this process until some rule produces a goal state. This process, called *breadth-first search*, can be described precisely as follows.

Algorithm: Breadth-First Search

1. Create a variable called *NODE-LIST* and set it to the initial state.

2. Until a goal state is found or *NODE-LIST* is empty do:

    (a) Remove the first element from *NODE-LIST* and call it *E*. If *NODE-LIST* was empty, quit.

---

[4]Rules 3, 4, 11, and 12 have been ignored in constructing the search tree.

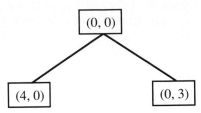

Figure 2.5: One Level of a Breadth-First Search Tree

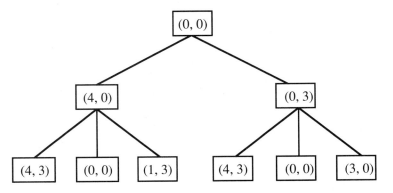

Figure 2.6: Two Levels of a Breadth-First Search Tree

(b) For each way that each rule can match the state described in *E* do:

    i. Apply the rule to generate a new state.

    ii. If the new state is a goal state, quit and return this state.

    iii. Otherwise, add the new state to the end of *NODE-LIST*.

Other systematic control strategies are also available. For example, we could pursue a single branch of the tree until it yields a solution or until a decision to terminate the path is made. It makes sense to terminate a path if it reaches a dead-end, produces a previous state, or becomes longer than some prespecified "futility" limit. In such a case, backtracking occurs. The most recently created state from which alternative moves are available will be revisited and a new state will be created. This form of backtracking is called *chronological backtracking* because the order in which steps are undone depends only on the temporal sequence in which the steps were originally made. Specifically, the most recent step is always the first to be undone. This form of backtracking is what is usually meant by the simple term *backtracking*. But there are other ways of retracting steps of a computation. We discuss one important such way, dependency-directed backtracking, in Chapter 7. Until then, though, when we use the term backtracking, it means chronological backtracking.

The search procedure we have just described is also called *depth-first search*. The following algorithm describes this precisely.

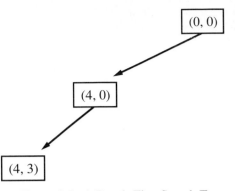

Figure 2.7: A Depth-First Search Tree

Algorithm: Depth-First Search

1. If the initial state is a goal state, quit and return success.

2. Otherwise, do the following until success or failure is signaled:

   (a) Generate a successor, E, of the initial state. If there are no more successors, signal failure.

   (b) Call Depth-First Search with E as the initial state.

   (c) If success is returned, signal success. Otherwise continue in this loop.

Figure 2.7 shows a snapshot of a depth-first search for the water jug problem. A comparison of these two simple methods produces the following observations.

Advantages of Depth-First Search

- Depth-first search requires less memory since only the nodes on the current path are stored. This contrasts with breadth-first search, where all of the tree that has so far been generated must be stored.

- By chance (or if care is taken in ordering the alternative successor states), depth-first search may find a solution without examining much of the search space at all. This contrasts with breadth-first search in which all parts of the tree must be examined to level n before any nodes on level $n + 1$ can be examined. This is particularly significant if many acceptable solutions exist. Depth-first search can stop when one of them is found.

Advantages of Breadth-First Search

- Breadth-first search will not get trapped exploring a blind alley. This contrasts with depth-first searching, which may follow a single, unfruitful path for a very long time, perhaps forever, before the path actually terminates in a state that has no successors. This is a particular problem in depth-first search if there are loops (i.e., a state has a successor that is also one of its ancestors) unless special care is expended to test for such a situation. The example in Figure 2.7, if it continues always choosing the first (in numerical sequence) rule that applies, will have exactly this problem.

- If there is a solution, then breadth-first search is guaranteed to find it. Furthermore, if there are multiple solutions, then a minimal solution (i.e., one that requires the minimum number of steps) will be found. This is guaranteed by the fact that longer paths are never explored until all shorter ones have already been examined. This contrasts with depth-first search, which may find a long path to a solution in one part of the tree, when a shorter path exists in some other, unexplored part of the tree.

Clearly what we would like is a way to combine the advantages of both of these methods. In Section 3.3 we will talk about one way of doing this when we have some additional information. Later, in Section 12.5, we will describe an uninformed way of doing so.

For the water jug problem, most control strategies that cause motion and are systematic will lead to an answer. The problem is simple. But this is not always the case. In order to solve some problems during our lifetime, we must also demand a control structure that is efficient.

Consider the following problem.

> **The Traveling Salesman Problem:** A salesman has a list of cities, each of which he must visit exactly once. There are direct roads between each pair of cities on the list. Find the route the salesman should follow for the shortest possible round trip that both starts and finishes at any one of the cities.

A simple, motion-causing and systematic control structure could, in principle, solve this problem. It would simply explore all possible paths in the tree and return the one with the shortest length. This approach will even work in practice for very short lists of cities. But it breaks down quickly as the number of cities grows. If there are N cities, then the number of different paths among them is $1 \cdot 2 \cdots (N-1)$, or $(N-1)!$. The time to examine a single path is proportional to N. So the total time required to perform this search is proportional to $N!$. Assuming there are only 10 cities, 10! is 3,628,800, which is a very large number. The salesman could easily have 25 cities to visit. To solve this problem would take more time than he would be willing to spend. This phenomenon is called *combinatorial explosion*. To combat it, we need a new control strategy.

We can beat the simple strategy outlined above using a technique called *branch-and-bound*. Begin generating complete paths, keeping track of the shortest path found so far. Give up exploring any path as soon as its partial length becomes greater than the shortest path found so far. Using this technique, we are still guaranteed to find the shortest path. Unfortunately, although this algorithm is more efficient than the first one, it still requires exponential time. The exact amount of time it saves for a particular problem depends on the order in which the paths are explored. But it is still inadequate for solving large problems.

2.2.2 Heuristic Search

In order to solve many hard problems efficiently, it is often necessary to compromise the requirements of mobility and systematicity and to construct a control structure that is no longer guaranteed to find the best answer but that will almost always find a very good answer. Thus we introduce the idea of a heuristic.[5] A *heuristic* is a technique that improves the efficiency of a search process, possibly by sacrificing claims of completeness. Heuristics are like tour guides. They are good to the extent that they point in generally interesting directions; they are bad to the extent that they may miss points of interest to particular individuals. Some heuristics help to guide a search process without sacrificing any claims to completeness that the process might previously have had. Others (in fact, many of the best ones) may occasionally cause an excellent path to be overlooked. But, on the average, they improve the quality of the paths that are explored. Using good heuristics, we can hope to get good (though possibly nonoptimal) solutions to hard problems, such as the traveling salesman, in less than exponential time. There are some good general-purpose heuristics that are useful in a wide variety of problem domains. In addition, it is possible to construct special-purpose heuristics that exploit domain-specific knowledge to solve particular problems.

One example of a good general-purpose heuristic that is useful for a variety of combinatorial problems is the *nearest neighbor heuristic*, which works by selecting the locally superior alternative at each step. Applying it to the traveling salesman problem, we produce the following procedure:

1. Arbitrarily select a starting city.

2. To select the next city, look at all cities not yet visited, and select the one closest to the current city. Go to it next.

3. Repeat step 2 until all cities have been visited.

This procedure executes in time proportional to N^2, a significant improvement over $N!$, and it is possible to prove an upper bound on the error it incurs. For general-purpose heuristics, such as nearest neighbor, it is often possible to prove such error bounds, which provides reassurance that one is not paying too high a price in accuracy for speed.

In many AI problems, however, it is not possible to produce such reassuring bounds. This is true for two reasons:

- For real world problems, it is often hard to measure precisely the value of a particular solution. Although the length of a trip to several cities is a precise notion, the appropriateness of a particular response to such questions as "Why has inflation increased?" is much less so.

- For real world problems, it is often useful to introduce heuristics based on relatively unstructured knowledge. It is often impossible to define this knowledge in such a way that a mathematical analysis of its effect on the search process can be performed.

---

[5]The word *heuristic* comes from the Greek word *heuriskein*, meaning "to discover," which is also the origin of *eureka*, derived from Archimedes' reputed exclamation, *heurika* (for "I have found"), uttered when he had discovered a method for determining the purity of gold.

There are many heuristics that, although they are not as general as the nearest neighbor heuristic, are nevertheless useful in a wide variety of domains. For example, consider the task of discovering interesting ideas in some specified area. The following heuristic [Lenat, 1983b] is often useful:

> If there is an interesting function of two arguments $f(x, y)$, look at what happens if the two arguments are identical.

In the domain of mathematics, this heuristic leads to the discovery of *squaring* if f is the multiplication function, and it leads to the discovery of an *identity* function if f is the function of set union. In less formal domains, this same heuristic leads to the discovery of *introspection* if f is the function contemplate or it leads to the notion of *suicide* if f is the function kill.

Without heuristics, we would become hopelessly ensnarled in a combinatorial explosion. This alone might be a sufficient argument in favor of their use. But there are other arguments as well:

- Rarely do we actually need the optimum solution; a good approximation will usually serve very well. In fact, there is some evidence that people, when they solve problems, are not optimizers but rather are *satisficers* [Simon, 1981]. In other words, they seek any solution that satisfies some set of requirements, and as soon as they find one they quit. A good example of this is the search for a parking space. Most people stop as soon as they find a fairly good space, even if there might be a slightly better space up ahead.

- Although the approximations produced by heuristics may not be very good in the worst case, worst cases rarely arise in the real world. For example, although many graphs are not separable (or even nearly so) and thus cannot be considered as a set of small problems rather than one large one, a lot of graphs describing the real world are.[6]

- Trying to understand why a heuristic works, or why it doesn't work, often leads to a deeper understanding of the problem.

One of the best descriptions of the importance of heuristics in solving interesting problems is *How to Solve It* [Polya, 1957]. Although the focus of the book is the solution of mathematical problems, many of the techniques it describes are more generally applicable. For example, given a problem to solve, look for a similar problem you have solved before. Ask whether you can use either the solution of that problem or the method that was used to obtain the solution to help solve the new problem. Polya's work serves as an excellent guide for people who want to become better problem solvers. Unfortunately, it is not a panacea for AI for a couple of reasons. One is that it relies on human abilities that we must first understand well enough to build into a program. For example, many of the problems Polya discusses are geometric ones in which once an appropriate picture is drawn, the answer can be seen immediately. But to exploit such techniques in programs, we must develop a good way of representing and manipulating descriptions of those figures. Another is that the rules are very general.

---

[6]For arguments in support of this, see Simon [1981].

They have extremely underspecified left sides, so it is hard to use them to guide a search—too many of them are applicable at once. Many of the rules are really only useful for looking back and rationalizing a solution after it has been found. In essence, the problem is that Polya's rules have not been operationalized.

Nevertheless, Polya was several steps ahead of AI. A comment he made in the preface to the first printing (1944) of the book is interesting in this respect:

> The following pages are written somewhat concisely, but as simply as possible, and are based on a long and serious study of methods of solution. This sort of study, called *heuristic* by some writers, is not in fashion nowadays but has a long past and, perhaps, some future.

There are two major ways in which domain-specific, heuristic knowledge can be incorporated into a rule-based search procedure:

- In the rules themselves. For example, the rules for a chess-playing system might describe not simply the set of legal moves but rather a set of "sensible" moves, as determined by the rule writer.

- As a heuristic function that evaluates individual problem states and determines how desirable they are.

A *heuristic function* is a function that maps from problem state descriptions to measures of desirability, usually represented as numbers. Which aspects of the problem state are considered, how those aspects are evaluated, and the weights given to individual aspects are chosen in such a way that the value of the heuristic function at a given node in the search process gives as good an estimate as possible of whether that node is on the desired path to a solution.

Well-designed heuristic functions can play an important part in efficiently guiding a search process toward a solution. Sometimes very simple heuristic functions can provide a fairly good estimate of whether a path is any good or not. In other situations, more complex heuristic functions should be employed. Figure 2.8 shows some simple heuristic functions for a few problems. Notice that sometimes a high value of the heuristic function indicates a relatively good position (as shown for chess and tic-tac-toe), while at other times a low value indicates an advantageous situation (as shown for the traveling salesman). It does not matter, in general, which way the function is stated. The program that uses the values of the function can attempt to minimize it or to maximize it as appropriate.

The purpose of a heuristic function is to guide the search process in the most profitable direction by suggesting which path to follow first when more than one is available. The more accurately the heuristic function estimates the true merits of each node in the search tree (or graph), the more direct the solution process. In the extreme, the heuristic function would be so good that essentially no search would be required. The system would move directly to a solution. But for many problems, the cost of computing the value of such a function would outweigh the effort saved in the search process. After all, it would be possible to compute a perfect heuristic function by doing a complete search from the node in question and determining whether it leads to a good solution. In general, there is a trade-off between the cost of evaluating a heuristic function and the savings in search time that the function provides.

Chess	the material advantage of our side over the opponent
Traveling Salesman	the sum of the distances so far
Tic-Tac-Toe	1 for each row in which we could win and in which we already have one piece plus 2 for each such row in which we have two pieces

Figure 2.8: Some Simple Heuristic Functions

In the previous section, the solutions to AI problems were described as centering on a search process. From the discussion in this section, it should be clear that it can more precisely be described as a process of heuristic search. Some heuristics will be used to define the control structure that guides the application of rules in the search process. Others, as we shall see, will be encoded in the rules themselves. In both cases, they will represent either general or specific world knowledge that makes the solution of hard problems feasible. This leads to another way that one could define artificial intelligence: the study of techniques for solving exponentially hard problems in polynomial time by exploiting knowledge about the problem domain.

2.3   Problem Characteristics

Heuristic search is a very general method applicable to a large class of problems. It encompasses a variety of specific techniques, each of which is particularly effective for a small class of problems. In order to choose the most appropriate method (or combination of methods) for a particular problem, it is necessary to analyze the problem along several key dimensions:

- Is the problem decomposable into a set of (nearly) independent smaller or easier subproblems?

- Can solution steps be ignored or at least undone if they prove unwise?

- Is the problem's universe predictable?

- Is a good solution to the problem obvious without comparison to all other possible solutions?

- Is the desired solution a state of the world or a path to a state?

- Is a large amount of knowledge absolutely required to solve the problem, or is knowledge important only to constrain the search?

- Can a computer that is simply given the problem return the solution, or will the solution of the problem require interaction between the computer and a person?

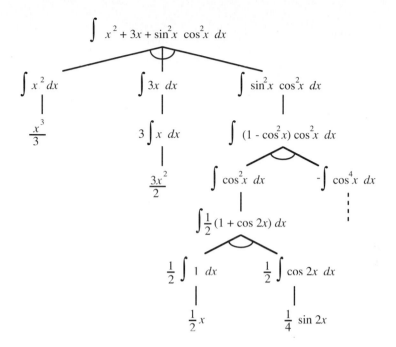

Figure 2.9: A Decomposable Problem

In the rest of this section, we examine each of these questions in greater detail. Notice that some of these questions involve not just the statement of the problem itself but also characteristics of the solution that is desired and the circumstances under which the solution must take place.

2.3.1 Is the Problem Decomposable?

Suppose we want to solve the problem of computing the expression

$$\int (x^2 + 3x + \sin^2 x \cdot \cos^2 x) \, dx$$

We can solve this problem by breaking it down into three smaller problems, each of which we can then solve by using a small collection of specific rules. Figure 2.9 shows the problem tree that will be generated by the process of problem decomposition as it can be exploited by a simple recursive integration program that works as follows: At each step, it checks to see whether the problem it is working on is immediately solvable. If so, then the answer is returned directly. If the problem is not easily solvable, the integrator checks to see whether it can decompose the problem into smaller problems. If it can, it creates those problems and calls itself recursively on them. Using this technique of *problem decomposition*, we can often solve very large problems easily.

Now consider the problem illustrated in Figure 2.10. This problem is drawn from the domain often referred to in AI literature as the *blocks world*. Assume that the following operators are available:

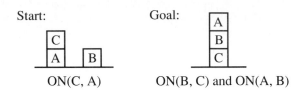

Figure 2.10: A Simple Blocks World Problem

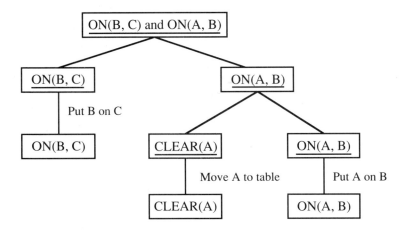

Figure 2.11: A Proposed Solution for the Blocks Problem

1. CLEAR(*x*) [block *x* has nothing on it] → ON(*x*, Table) [pick up *x* and put it on the table]

2. CLEAR(*x*) and CLEAR(*y*) → ON(*x*, *y*) [put *x* on *y*]

Applying the technique of problem decomposition to this simple blocks world example would lead to a solution tree such as that shown in Figure 2.11. In the figure, goals are underlined. States that have been achieved are not underlined. The idea of this solution is to reduce the problem of getting B on C and A on B to two separate problems. The first of these new problems, getting B on C, is simple, given the start state. Simply put B on C. The second subgoal is not quite so simple. Since the only operators we have allow us to pick up single blocks at a time, we have to clear off A by removing C before we can pick up A and put it on B. This can easily be done. However, if we now try to combine the two subsolutions into one solution, we will fail. Regardless of which one we do first, we will not be able to do the second as we had planned. In this problem, the two subproblems are not independent. They interact and those interactions must be considered in order to arrive at a solution for the entire problem.

These two examples, symbolic integration and the blocks world, illustrate the difference between decomposable and nondecomposable problems. In Chapter 3, we present a specific algorithm for problem decomposition, and in Chapter 13, we look at what happens when decomposition is impossible.

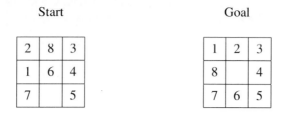

Figure 2.12: An Example of the 8-Puzzle

2.3.2 Can Solution Steps Be Ignored or Undone?

Suppose we are trying to prove a mathematical theorem. We proceed by first proving a lemma that we think will be useful. Eventually, we realize that the lemma is no help at all. Are we in trouble?

No. Everything we need to know to prove the theorem is still true and in memory, if it ever was. Any rules that could have been applied at the outset can still be applied. We can just proceed as we should have in the first place. All we have lost is the effort that was spent exploring the blind alley.

Now consider a different problem.

> **The 8-Puzzle:** The 8-puzzle is a square tray in which are placed eight square tiles. The remaining ninth square is uncovered. Each tile has a number on it. A tile that is adjacent to the blank space can be slid into that space. A game consists of a starting position and a specified goal position. The goal is to transform the starting position into the goal position by sliding the tiles around.

A sample game using the 8-puzzle is shown in Figure 2.12. In attempting to solve the 8-puzzle, we might make a stupid move. For example, in the game shown above, we might start by sliding tile 5 into the empty space. Having done that, we cannot change our mind and immediately slide tile 6 into the empty space since the empty space will essentially have moved. But we can backtrack and undo the first move, sliding tile 5 back to where it was. Then we can move tile 6. Mistakes can still be recovered from but not quite as easily as in the theorem-proving problem. An additional step must be performed to undo each incorrect step, whereas no action was required to "undo" a useless lemma. In addition, the control mechanism for an 8-puzzle solver must keep track of the order in which operations are performed so that the operations can be undone one at a time if necessary. The control structure for a theorem prover does not need to record all that information.

Now consider again the problem of playing chess. Suppose a chess-playing program makes a stupid move and realizes it a couple of moves later. It cannot simply play as though it had never made the stupid move. Nor can it simply back up and start the game over from that point. All it can do is to try to make the best of the current situation and go on from there.

These three problems—theorem proving, the 8-puzzle, and chess—illustrate the differences between three important classes of problems:

- Ignorable (e.g., theorem proving), in which solution steps can be ignored

- Recoverable (e.g., 8-puzzle), in which solution steps can be undone

- Irrecoverable (e.g., chess), in which solution steps cannot be undone

These three definitions make reference to the steps of the solution to a problem and thus may appear to characterize particular production systems for solving a problem rather than the problem itself. Perhaps a different formulation of the same problem would lead to the problem being characterized differently. Strictly speaking, this is true. But for a great many problems, there is only one (or a small number of essentially equivalent) formulations that *naturally* describe the problem. This was true for each of the problems used as examples above. When this is the case, it makes sense to view the recoverability of a problem as equivalent to the recoverability of a natural formulation of it.

The recoverability of a problem plays an important role in determining the complexity of the control structure necessary for the problem's solution. Ignorable problems can be solved using a simple control structure that never backtracks. Such a control structure is easy to implement. Recoverable problems can be solved by a slightly more complicated control strategy that does sometimes make mistakes. Backtracking will be necessary to recover from such mistakes, so the control structure must be implemented using a push-down stack, in which decisions are recorded in case they need to be undone later. Irrecoverable problems, on the other hand, will need to be solved by a system that expends a great deal of effort making each decision since the decision must be final. Some irrecoverable problems can be solved by recoverable style methods used in a *planning* process, in which an entire sequence of steps is analyzed in advance to discover where it will lead before the first step is actually taken. We discuss next the kinds of problems in which this is possible.

2.3.3   Is the Universe Predictable?

Again suppose that we are playing with the 8-puzzle. Every time we make a move, we know exactly what will happen. This means that it is possible to plan an entire sequence of moves and be confident that we know what the resulting state will be. We can use planning to avoid having to undo actual moves, although it will still be necessary to backtrack past those moves one at a time during the planning process. Thus a control structure that allows backtracking will be necessary.

However, in games other than the 8-puzzle, this planning process may not be possible. Suppose we want to play bridge. One of the decisions we will have to make is which card to play on the first trick. What we would like to do is to plan the entire hand before making that first play. But now it is not possible to do such planning with certainty since we cannot know exactly where all the cards are or what the other players will do on their turns. The best we can do is to investigate several plans and use probabilities of the various outcomes to choose a plan that has the highest estimated probability of leading to a good score on the hand.

These two games illustrate the difference between certain-outcome (e.g., 8-puzzle) and uncertain-outcome (e.g., bridge) problems. One way of describing planning is that it is problem solving without feedback from the environment. For solving certain-outcome problems, this open-loop approach will work fine since the result of an action can be predicted perfectly. Thus, planning can be used to generate a sequence of operators that is guaranteed to lead to a solution. For uncertain-outcome problems, however, planning can at best generate a sequence of operators that has a good probability of leading to a solution. To solve such problems, we need to allow for a process of *plan revision* to take place as the plan is carried out and the necessary feedback is provided. In addition to providing no guarantee of an actual solution, planning for uncertain-outcome problems has the drawback that it is often very expensive since the number of solution paths that need to be explored increases exponentially with the number of points at which the outcome cannot be predicted.

The last two problem characteristics we have discussed, ignorable versus recoverable versus irrecoverable and certain-outcome versus uncertain-outcome, interact in an interesting way. As has already been mentioned, one way to solve irrecoverable problems is to plan an entire solution before embarking on an implementation of the plan. But this planning process can only be done effectively for certain-outcome problems. Thus one of the hardest types of problems to solve is the irrecoverable, uncertain-outcome. A few examples of such problems are:

- Playing bridge. But we can do fairly well since we have available accurate estimates of the probabilities of each of the possible outcomes.

- Controlling a robot arm. The outcome is uncertain for a variety of reasons. Someone might move something into the path of the arm. The gears of the arm might stick. A slight error could cause the arm to knock over a whole stack of things.

- Helping a lawyer decide how to defend his client against a murder charge. Here we probably cannot even list all the possible outcomes, much less assess their probabilities.

2.3.4 Is a Good Solution Absolute or Relative?

Consider the problem of answering questions based on a database of simple facts, such as the following:

1. Marcus was a man.
2. Marcus was a Pompeian.
3. Marcus was born in 40 A.D.
4. All men are mortal.
5. All Pompeians died when the volcano erupted in 79 A.D.
6. No mortal lives longer than 150 years.
7. It is now 1991 A.D.

Suppose we ask the question "Is Marcus alive?" By representing each of these facts in a formal language, such as predicate logic, and then using formal inference methods,

		Justification
1.	Marcus was a man.	axiom 1
4.	All men are mortal.	axiom 4
8.	Marcus is mortal.	1, 4
3.	Marcus was born in 40 A.D.	axiom 3
7.	It is now 1991 A.D.	axiom 7
9.	Marcus' age is 1951 years.	3, 7
6.	No mortal lives longer than 150 years.	axiom 6
10.	Marcus is dead.	8, 6, 9

OR

7.	It is now 1991 A.D.	axiom 7
5.	All Pompeians died in 79 A.D.	axiom 5
11.	All Pompeians are dead now.	7, 5
2.	Marcus was a Pompeian.	axiom 2
12.	Marcus is dead.	11, 2

Figure 2.13: Two Ways of Deciding That Marcus Is Dead

	Boston	New York	Miami	Dallas	S.F.
Boston		250	1450	1700	3000
New York	250		1200	1500	2900
Miami	1450	1200		1600	3300
Dallas	1700	1500	1600		1700
S.F.	3000	2900	3300	1700	

Figure 2.14: An Instance of the Traveling Salesman Problem

we can fairly easily derive an answer to the question.[7] In fact, either of two reasoning paths will lead to the answer, as shown in Figure 2.13. Since all we are interested in is the answer to the question, it does not matter which path we follow. If we do follow one path successfully to the answer, there is no reason to go back and see if some other path might also lead to a solution.

But now consider again the traveling salesman problem. Our goal is to find the shortest route that visits each city exactly once. Suppose the cities to be visited and the distances between them are as shown in Figure 2.14.

One place the salesman could start is Boston. In that case, one path that might be followed is the one shown in Figure 2.15, which is 8850 miles long. But is this the solution to the problem? The answer is that we cannot be sure unless we also try all

---

[7]Of course, representing these statements so that a mechanical procedure could exploit them to answer the question also requires the explicit mention of other facts, such as "dead implies not alive." We do this in Chapter 5.

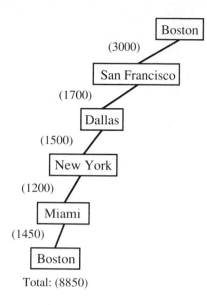

Figure 2.15: One Path among the Cities

other paths to make sure that none of them is shorter. In this case, as can be seen from Figure 2.16, the first path is definitely not the solution to the salesman's problem.

These two examples illustrate the difference between any-path problems and best-path problems. Best-path problems are, in general, computationally harder than any-path problems. Any-path problems can often be solved in a reasonable amount of time by using heuristics that suggest good paths to explore. (See the discussion of best-first search in Chapter 3 for one way of doing this.) If the heuristics are not perfect, the search for a solution may not be as direct as possible, but that does not matter. For true best-path problems, however, no heuristic that could possibly miss the best solution can be used. So a much more exhaustive search will be performed.

2.3.5 Is the Solution a State or a Path?

Consider the problem of finding a consistent interpretation for the sentence

The bank president ate a dish of pasta salad with the fork.

There are several components of this sentence, each of which, in isolation, may have more than one interpretation. But the components must form a coherent whole, and so they constrain each other's interpretations. Some of the sources of ambiguity in this sentence are the following:

The word "bank" may refer either to a financial institution or to a side of a river. But only one of these may have a president.

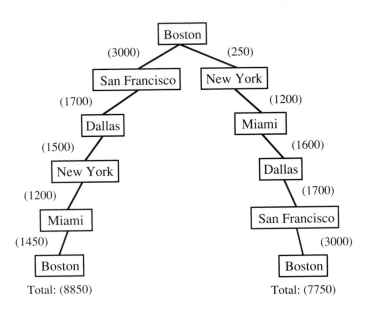

Figure 2.16: Two Paths Among the Cities

- The word "dish" is the object of the verb "eat." It is possible that a dish was eaten. But it is more likely that the pasta salad in the dish was eaten.

- Pasta salad is a salad containing pasta. But there are other ways meanings can be formed from pairs of nouns. For example, dog food does not normally contain dogs.

- The phrase "with the fork" could modify several parts of the sentence. In this case, it modifies the verb "eat." But, if the phrase had been "with vegetables," then the modification structure would be different. And if the phrase had been "with her friends," the structure would be different still.

Because of the interaction among the interpretations of the constituents of this sentence, some search may be required to find a complete interpretation for the sentence. But to solve the problem of finding the interpretation we need to produce only the interpretation itself. No record of the processing by which the interpretation was found is necessary.

Contrast this with the water jug problem. Here it is not sufficient to report that we have solved the problem and that the final state is $(2, 0)$. For this kind of problem, what we really must report is not the final state but the path that we found to that state. Thus a statement of a solution to this problem must be a sequence of operations (sometimes called a *plan*) that produces the final state.

These two examples, natural language understanding and the water jug problem, illustrate the difference between problems whose solution is a state of the world and problems whose solution is a path to a state. At one level, this difference can be ignored and all problems can be formulated as ones in which only a state is required to be reported. If we do this for problems such as the water jug, then we must redescribe our states so that each state represents a partial path to a solution rather than just a single state of the world. So this question is not a formally significant one. But, just as for the question of ignorability versus recoverability, there is often a natural (and economical) formulation of a problem in which problem states correspond to situations in the world, not sequences of operations. In this case, the answer to this question tells us whether it is necessary to record the path of the problem-solving process as it proceeds.

2.3.6 What Is the Role of Knowledge?

Consider again the problem of playing chess. Suppose you had unlimited computing power available. How much knowledge would be required by a perfect program? The answer to this question is very little—just the rules for determining legal moves and some simple control mechanism that implements an appropriate search procedure. Additional knowledge about such things as good strategy and tactics could of course help considerably to constrain the search and speed up the execution of the program.

But now consider the problem of scanning daily newspapers to decide which are supporting the Democrats and which are supporting the Republicans in some upcoming election. Again assuming unlimited computing power, how much knowledge would be required by a computer trying to solve this problem? This time the answer is a great deal. It would have to know such things as:

- The names of the candidates in each party.

- The fact that if the major thing you want to see done is have taxes lowered, you are probably supporting the Republicans.

- The fact that if the major thing you want to see done is improved education for minority students, you are probably supporting the Democrats.

- The fact that if you are opposed to big government, you are probably supporting the Republicans.

- And so on . . .

These two problems, chess and newspaper story understanding, illustrate the difference between problems for which a lot of knowledge is important only to constrain the search for a solution and those for which a lot of knowledge is required even to be able to recognize a solution.

2.3.7 Does the Task Require Interaction with a Person?

Sometimes it is useful to program computers to solve problems in ways that the majority of people would not be able to understand. This is fine if the level of the interaction between the computer and its human users is problem-in solution-out. But increasingly we are building programs that require intermediate interaction with people, both to provide additional input to the program and to provide additional reassurance to the user.

Consider, for example, the problem of proving mathematical theorems. If

1. All we want is to know that there is a proof

2. The program is capable of finding a proof by itself

then it does not matter what strategy the program takes to find the proof. It can use, for example, the *resolution* procedure (see Chapter 5), which can be very efficient but which does not appear natural to people. But if either of those conditions is violated, it may matter very much how a proof is found. Suppose that we are trying to prove some new, very difficult theorem. We might demand a proof that follows traditional patterns so that a mathematician can read the proof and check to make sure it is correct. Alternatively, finding a proof of the theorem might be sufficiently difficult that the program does not know where to start. At the moment, people are still better at doing the high-level strategy required for a proof. So the computer might like to be able to ask for advice. For example, it is often much easier to do a proof in geometry if someone suggests the right line to draw into the figure. To exploit such advice, the computer's reasoning must be analogous to that of its human advisor, at least on a few levels. As computers move into areas of great significance to human lives, such as medical diagnosis, people will be very unwilling to accept the verdict of a program whose reasoning they cannot follow.

Thus we must distinguish between two types of problems:

- Solitary, in which the computer is given a problem description and produces an answer with no intermediate communication and with no demand for an explanation of the reasoning process

- Conversational, in which there is intermediate communication between a person and the computer, either to provide additional assistance to the computer or to provide additional information to the user, or both

Of course, this distinction is not a strict one describing particular problem domains. As we just showed, mathematical theorem proving could be regarded as either. But for a particular application, one or the other of these types of systems will usually be desired and that decision will be important in the choice of a problem-solving method.

2.3.8   Problem Classification

When actual problems are examined from the point of view of all of these questions, it becomes apparent that there are several broad classes into which the problems fall. These classes can each be associated with a generic control strategy that is appropriate for solving the problem. For example, consider the generic problem of *classification*. The task here is to examine an input and then decide which of a set of known classes the input is an instance of. Most diagnostic tasks, including medical diagnosis as well as diagnosis of faults in mechanical devices, are examples of classification. Another example of a generic strategy is *propose and refine*. Many design and planning problems can be attacked with this strategy.

Depending on the granularity at which we attempt to classify problems and control strategies, we may come up with different lists of generic tasks and procedures. See Chandrasekaran [1986] and McDermott [1988] for two approaches to constructing such lists. The important thing to remember here, though, since we are about to embark on a discussion of a variety of problem-solving methods, is that there is no one single way of solving all problems. But neither must each new problem be considered totally *ab initio*. Instead, if we analyze our problems carefully and sort our problem-solving methods by the kinds of problems for which they are suitable, we will be able to bring to each new problem much of what we have learned from solving other, similar problems.

2.4 Production System Characteristics

We have just examined a set of characteristics that distinguish various classes of problems. We have also argued that production systems are a good way to describe the operations that can be performed in a search for a solution to a problem. Two questions we might reasonably ask at this point are:

1. Can production systems, like problems, be described by a set of characteristics that shed some light on how they can easily be implemented?

2. If so, what relationships are there between problem types and the types of production systems best suited to solving the problems?

The answer to the first question is yes. Consider the following definitions of classes of production systems. A *monotonic production system* is a production system in which the application of a rule never prevents the later application of another rule that could also have been applied at the time the first rule was selected. A *nonmonotonic production system* is one in which this is not true. A *partially commutative production system* is a production system with the property that if the application of a particular sequence of rules transforms state *x* into state *y*, then any permutation of those rules that is allowable (i.e., each rule's preconditions are satisfied when it is applied) also transforms state *x* into state *y*. A *commutative production system* is a production system that is both monotonic and partially commutative.[8]

The significance of these categories of production systems lies in the relationship between the categories and appropriate implementation strategies. But before discussing that relationship, it may be helpful to make the meanings of the definitions clearer by showing how they relate to specific problems.

Thus we arrive at the second question above, which asked whether there is an interesting relationship between classes of production systems and classes of problems. For any solvable problem, there exist an infinite number of production systems that describe ways to find solutions. Some will be more natural or efficient than others. Any problem that can be solved by any production system can be solved by a commutative one (our most restricted class), but the commutative one may be so unwieldy as to be practically useless. It may use individual states to represent entire sequences of applications of rules of a simpler, noncommutative system. So in a formal sense, there is no relationship between kinds of problems and kinds of production systems since all problems can be solved by all kinds of systems. But in a practical sense, there definitely is such a relationship between kinds of problems and the kinds of systems that lend themselves naturally to describing those problems. To see this, let us look at a few examples. Figure 2.17 shows the four categories of production systems produced by the two dichotomies, monotonic versus nonmonotonic and partially commutative versus

---

[8]This corresponds to the definition of a commutative production system given in Nilsson [1980].

	Monotonic	Nonmonotonic
Partially commutative	Theorem proving	Robot navigation
Not partially commutative	Chemical synthesis	Bridge

Figure 2.17: The Four Categories of Production Systems

nonpartially commutative, along with some problems that can naturally be solved by each type of system. The upper left corner represents commutative systems.

Partially commutative, monotonic production systems are useful for solving ignorable problems. This is not surprising since the definitions of the two are essentially the same. But recall that ignorable problems are those for which a *natural* formulation leads to solution steps that can be ignored. Such a natural formulation will then be a partially commutative, monotonic system. Problems that involve creating new things rather than changing old ones are generally ignorable. Theorem proving, as we have described it, is one example of such a creative process. Making deductions from some known facts is a similar creative process. Both of those processes can easily be implemented with a partially commutative, monotonic system.

Partially commutative, monotonic production systems are important from an implementation standpoint because they can be implemented without the ability to backtrack to previous states when it is discovered that an incorrect path has been followed. Although it is often useful to implement such systems with backtracking in order to guarantee a systematic search, the actual database representing the problem state need not be restored. This often results in a considerable increase in efficiency, particularly because, since the database will never have to be restored, it is not necessary to keep track of where in the search process every change was made.

We have now discussed partially commutative production systems that are also monotonic. They are good for problems where things do not change; new things get created. Nonmonotonic, partially commutative systems, on the other hand, are useful for problems in which changes occur but can be reversed and in which order of operations is not critical. This is usually the case in physical manipulation problems, such as robot navigation on a flat plane. Suppose that a robot has the following operators: go north (N), go east (E), go south (S), and go west (W). To reach its goal, it does not matter whether the robot executes N-N-E or N-E-N. Depending on how the operators are chosen, the 8-Puzzle and the blocks world problem can also be considered partially commutative.

Both types of partially commutative production systems are significant from an implementation point of view because they tend to lead to many duplications of individual states during the search process. This is discussed further in Section 2.5.

Production systems that are not partially commutative are useful for many problems in which irreversible changes occur. For example, consider the problem of determining a process to produce a desired chemical compound. The operators available include such things as "Add chemical x to the pot" or "Change the temperature to t degrees." These operators may cause irreversible changes to the potion being brewed. The order

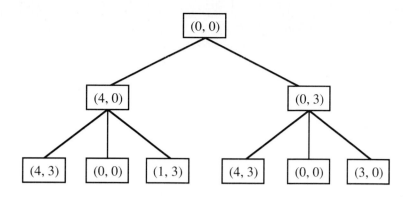

Figure 2.18: A Search Tree for the Water Jug Problem

in which they are performed can be very important in determining the final output. It is possible that if x is added to y, a stable compound will be formed, so later addition of z will have no effect; if z is added to y, however, a different stable compound may be formed, so later addition of x will have no effect. Nonpartially commutative production systems are less likely to produce the same node many times in the search process. When dealing with ones that describe irreversible processes, it is particularly important to make correct decisions the first time, although if the universe is predictable, planning can be used to make that less important.

2.5   Issues in the Design of Search Programs

Every search process can be viewed as a traversal of a tree structure in which each node represents a problem state and each arc represents a relationship between the states represented by the nodes it connects. For example, Figure 2.18 shows part of a search tree for a water jug problem. The arcs have not been labeled in the figure, but they correspond to particular water-pouring operations. The search process must find a path or paths through the tree that connect an initial state with one or more final states. The tree that must be searched could, in principle, be constructed in its entirety from the rules that define allowable moves in the problem space. But, in practice, most of it never is. It is too large and most of it need never be explored. Instead of first building the tree *explicitly* and then searching it, most search programs represent the tree *implicitly* in the rules and generate explicitly only those parts that they decide to explore. Throughout our discussion of search methods, it is important to keep in mind this distinction between implicit search trees and the explicit partial search trees that are actually constructed by the search program.

In the next chapter, we present a family of general-purpose search techniques. But before doing so, we need to mention some important issues that arise in all of them:

- The direction in which to conduct the search (*forward* versus *backward* reasoning). We can search forward through the state space from the start state to a goal state, or we can search backward from the goal.

- How to select applicable rules (*matching*). Production systems typically spend most of their time looking for rules to apply, so it is critical to have efficient procedures for matching rules against states.

- How to represent each node of the search process (the *knowledge representation problem* and the *frame problem*). For problems like chess, a node can be fully represented by a simple array. In more complex problem solving, however, it is inefficient and/or impossible to represent all of the facts in the world and to determine all of the side effects an action may have.

We discuss the knowledge representation and frame problems further in Chapter 4. We investigate matching and forward versus backward reasoning when we return to production systems in Chapter 6.

One other issue we should consider at this point is that of search trees versus search graphs. As mentioned above, we can think of production rules as generating nodes in a search tree. Each node can be expanded in turn, generating a set of successors. This process continues until a node representing a solution is found. Implementing such a procedure requires little bookkeeping. However, this process often results in the same node being generated as part of several paths and so being processed more than once. This happens because the search space may really be an arbitrary directed graph rather than a tree.

For example, in the tree shown in Figure 2.18, the node (4, 3), representing 4 gallons of water in one jug and 3 gallons in the other, can be generated either by first filling the 4-gallon jug and then the 3-gallon one or by filling them in the opposite order. Since the order does not matter, continuing to process both these nodes would be redundant. This example also illustrates another problem that often arises when the search process operates as a tree walk. On the third level, the node (0, 0) appears. (In fact, it appears twice.) But this is the same as the top node of the tree, which has already been expanded. Those two paths have not gotten us anywhere. So we would like to eliminate them and continue only along the other branches.

The waste of effort that arises when the same node is generated more than once can be avoided at the price of additional bookkeeping. Instead of traversing a search tree, we traverse a directed graph. This graph differs from a tree in that several paths may come together at a node. The graph corresponding to the tree of Figure 2.18 is shown in Figure 2.19.

Any tree search procedure that keeps track of all the nodes that have been generated so far can be converted to a graph search procedure by modifying the action performed each time a node is generated. Notice that of the two systematic search procedures we have discussed so far, this requirement that nodes be kept track of is met by breadth-first search but not by depth-first search. But, of course, depth-first search could be modified, at the expense of additional storage, to retain in memory nodes that have been expanded and then backed-up over. Since all nodes are saved in the search graph, we must use the following algorithm instead of simply adding a new node to the graph.

Algorithm: Check Duplicate Nodes

1. Examine the set of nodes that have been created so far to see if the new node already exists.

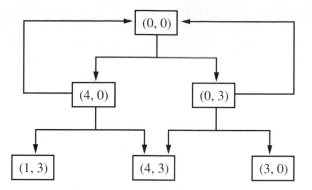

Figure 2.19: A Search Graph for the Water Jug Problem

2. If it does not, simply add it to the graph just as for a tree.

3. If it does already exist, then do the following:

   (a) Set the node that is being expanded to point to the already existing node corresponding to its successor rather than to the new one. The new one can simply be thrown away.

   (b) If you are keeping track of the best (shortest or otherwise least-cost) path to each node, then check to see if the new path is better or worse than the old one. If worse, do nothing. If better, record the new path as the correct path to use to get to the node and propagate the corresponding change in cost down through successor nodes as necessary.

One problem that may arise here is that cycles may be introduced into the search graph. A *cycle* is a path through the graph in which a given node appears more than once. For example, the graph of Figure 2.19 contains two cycles of length two. One includes the nodes (0, 0) and (4, 0); the other includes the nodes (0, 0) and (0, 3). Whenever there is a cycle, there can be paths of arbitrary length. Thus it may become more difficult to show that a graph traversal algorithm is guaranteed to terminate.

Treating the search process as a graph search rather than as a tree search reduces the amount of effort that is spent exploring essentially the same path several times. But it requires additional effort each time a node is generated to see if it has been generated before. Whether this effort is justified depends on the particular problem. If it is very likely that the same node will be generated in several different ways, then it is more worthwhile to use a graph procedure than if such duplication will happen only rarely.

Graph search procedures are especially useful for dealing with partially commutative production systems in which a given set of operations will produce the same result regardless of the order in which the operations are applied. A systematic search procedure will try many of the permutations of these operators and so will generate the same node many times. This is exactly what happened in the water jug example shown above.

2.6   Additional Problems

Several specific problems have been discussed throughout this chapter. Other problems have not yet been mentioned, but are common throughout the AI literature. Some have become such classics that no AI book could be complete without them, so we present them in this section. A useful exercise, at this point, would be to evaluate each of them in light of the seven problem characteristics we have just discussed.

A brief justification is perhaps required before this parade of toy problems is presented. Artificial intelligence is not merely a science of toy problems and microworlds (such as the blocks world). Many of the techniques that have been developed for these problems have become the core of systems that solve very nontoy problems. So think about these problems not as defining the scope of AI but rather as providing a core from which much more has developed.

The Missionaries and Cannibals Problem

Three missionaries and three cannibals find themselves on one side of a river. They have agreed that they would all like to get to the other side. But the missionaries are not sure what else the cannibals have agreed to. So the missionaries want to manage the trip across the river in such a way that the number of missionaries on either side of the river is never less than the number of cannibals who are on the same side. The only boat available holds only two people at a time. How can everyone get across the river without the missionaries risking being eaten?

The Tower of Hanoi

Somewhere near Hanoi there is a monastery whose monks devote their lives to a very important task. In their courtyard are three tall posts. On these posts is a set of sixty-four disks, each with a hole in the center and each of a different radius. When the monastery was established, all of the disks were on one of the posts, each disk resting on the one just larger than it. The monks' task is to move all of the disks to one of the other pegs. Only one disk may be moved at a time, and all the other disks must be on one of the pegs. In addition, at no time during the process may a disk be placed on top of a smaller disk. The third peg can, of course, be used as a temporary resting place for the disks. What is the quickest way for the monks to accomplish their mission?

Even the best solution to this problem will take the monks a very long time. This is fortunate, since legend has it that the world will end when they have finished.

The Monkey and Bananas Problem

A hungry monkey finds himself in a room in which a bunch of bananas is hanging from the ceiling. The monkey, unfortunately, cannot reach the bananas. However, in the room there are also a chair and a stick. The ceiling is just the right height so that a monkey standing on a chair could knock the bananas down with the stick. The monkey knows how to move around, carry other things around, reach for the bananas, and wave a stick in the air. What is the best sequence of actions for the monkey to take to acquire lunch?

```
     SEND              DONALD              CROSS
    +MORE             +GERALD            +ROADS
    -----             -------            ------
    MONEY              ROBERT             DANGER
```

Figure 2.20: Some Cryptarithmetic Problems

Cryptarithmetic

Consider an arithmetic problem represented in letters, as shown in the examples in Figure 2.20. Assign a decimal digit to each of the letters in such a way that the answer to the problem is correct. If the same letter occurs more than once, it must be assigned the same digit each time. No two different letters may be assigned the same digit.

People's strategies for solving cryptarithmetic problems have been studied intensively by Newell and Simon [1972].

2.7   Summary

In this chapter we have discussed the first two steps that must be taken toward the design of a program to solve a particular problem:

1. Define the problem precisely. Specify the problem space, the operators for moving within the space, and the starting and goal state(s).

2. Analyze the problem to determine where it falls with respect to seven important issues.

The last two steps for developing a program to solve that problem are, of course:

3. Identify and represent the knowledge required by the task.

4. Choose one or more techniques for problem solving, and apply those techniques to the problem.

Several general-purpose, problem-solving techniques are presented in the next chapter, and several of them have already been alluded to in the discussion of the problem characteristics in this chapter. The relationships between problem characteristics and specific techniques should become even clearer as we go on. Then, in Part II, we discuss the issue of how domain knowledge is to be represented.

2.8   Exercises

1. In this chapter, the following problems were mentioned:

   • Chess

   • Water jug

- 8-puzzle
- Traveling salesman
- Missionaries and cannibals
- Tower of Hanoi
- Monkey and bananas
- Cryptarithmetic
- Bridge

Analyze each of them with respect to the seven problem characteristics discussed in Section 2.3.

2. Before we can solve a problem using state space search, we must define an appropriate state space. For each of the problems mentioned above for which it was not done in the text, find a good state space representation.

3. Describe how the branch-and-bound technique could be used to find the shortest solution to a water jug problem.

4. For each of the following types of problems, try to describe a good heuristic function:

   (a) Blocks world

   (b) Theorem proving

   (c) Missionaries and cannibals

5. Give an example of a problem for which breadth-first search would work better than depth-first search. Give an example of a problem for which depth-first search would work better than breadth-first search.

6. Write an algorithm to perform breadth-first search of a problem *graph*. Make sure your algorithm works properly when a single node is generated at more than one level in the graph.

7. Try to construct an algorithm for solving blocks world problems, such as the one in Figure 2.10. Do not cheat by looking ahead to Chapter 13.

Chapter 3

Heuristic Search Techniques

In the last chapter, we saw that many of the problems that fall within the purview of artificial intelligence are too complex to be solved by direct techniques; rather they must be attacked by appropriate search methods armed with whatever direct techniques are available to guide the search. In this chapter, a framework for describing search methods is provided and several general-purpose search techniques are discussed. These methods are all varieties of heuristic search. They can be described independently of any particular task or problem domain. But when applied to particular problems, their efficacy is highly dependent on the way they exploit domain-specific knowledge since in and of themselves they are unable to overcome the combinatorial explosion to which search processes are so vulnerable. For this reason, these techniques are often called *weak methods*. Although a realization of the limited effectiveness of these weak methods to solve hard problems by themselves has been an important result that emerged from the last three decades of AI research, these techniques continue to provide the framework into which domain-specific knowledge can be placed, either by hand or as a result of automatic learning. Thus they continue to form the core of most AI systems.

We have already discussed two very basic search strategies:

- Depth-first search

- Breadth-first search

In the rest of this chapter, we present some others:

- Generate and test

- Hill climbing

- Best-first search

- Problem reduction

- Constraint satisfaction

- Means-ends analysis

3.1   Generate-and-Test

The generate-and-test strategy is the simplest of all the approaches we discuss. It consists of the following steps:

Algorithm: Generate-and-Test

1. Generate a possible solution. For some problems, this means generating a particular point in the problem space. For others, it means generating a path from a start state.

2. Test to see if this is actually a solution by comparing the chosen point or the endpoint of the chosen path to the set of acceptable goal states.

3. If a solution has been found, quit. Otherwise, return to step 1.

If the generation of possible solutions is done systematically, then this procedure will find a solution eventually, if one exists. Unfortunately, if the problem space is very large, "eventually" may be a very long time.

The generate-and-test algorithm is a depth-first search procedure since complete solutions must be generated before they can be tested. In its most systematic form, it is simply an exhaustive search of the problem space. Generate-and-test can, of course, also operate by generating solutions randomly, but then there is no guarantee that a solution will ever be found. In this form, it is also known as the British Museum algorithm, a reference to a method for finding an object in the British Museum by wandering randomly.[1] Between these two extremes lies a practical middle ground in which the search process proceeds systematically, but some paths are not considered because they seem unlikely to lead to a solution. This evaluation is performed by a heuristic function, as described in Section 2.2.2.

The most straightforward way to implement systematic generate-and-test is as a depth-first search tree with backtracking. If some intermediate states are likely to appear often in the tree, however, it may be better to modify that procedure, as described above, to traverse a graph rather than a tree.

For simple problems, exhaustive generate-and-test is often a reasonable technique. For example, consider the puzzle that consists of four six-sided cubes, with each side of each cube painted one of four colors. A solution to the puzzle consists of an arrangement of the cubes in a row such that on all four sides of the row one block face of each color is showing. This problem can be solved by a person (who is a much slower processor for this sort of thing than even a very cheap computer) in several minutes by systematically and exhaustively trying all possibilities. It can be solved even more quickly using a heuristic generate-and-test procedure. A quick glance at the four blocks reveals that there are more, say, red faces than there are of other colors. Thus when placing a block with several red faces, it would be a good idea to use as few of them as possible as outside faces. As many of them as possible should be placed to abut the next block. Using this heuristic, many configurations need never be explored and a solution can be found quite quickly.

---

[1] Or, as another story goes, if a sufficient number of monkeys were placed in front of a set of typewriters and left alone long enough, then they would eventually produce all of the works of Shakespeare.

Unfortunately, for problems much harder than this, even heuristic generate-and-test, all by itself, is not a very effective technique. But when combined with other techniques to restrict the space in which to search even further, the technique can be very effective.

For example, one early example of a successful AI program is DENDRAL [Lindsay *et al.*, 1980], which infers the structure of organic compounds using mass spectrogram and nuclear magnetic resonance (NMR) data. It uses a strategy called *plan-generate-test*, in which a planning process that uses constraint-satisfaction techniques (see Section 3.5) creates lists of recommended and contraindicated substructures. The generate-and-test procedure then uses those lists so that it can explore only a fairly limited set of structures. Constrained in this way, the generate-and-test procedure has proved highly effective.

This combination of planning, using one problem-solving method (in this case, constraint satisfaction) with the use of the plan by another problem-solving method, generate-and-test, is an excellent example of the way techniques can be combined to overcome the limitations that each possesses individually. A major weakness of planning is that it often produces somewhat inaccurate solutions since there is no feedback from the world. But by using it only to produce pieces of solutions that will then be exploited in the generate-and-test process, the lack of detailed accuracy becomes unimportant. And, at the same time, the combinatorial problems that arise in simple generate-and-test are avoided by judicious reference to the plans.

3.2 Hill Climbing

Hill climbing is a variant of generate-and-test in which feedback from the test procedure is used to help the generator decide which direction to move in the search space. In a pure generate-and-test procedure, the test function responds with only a yes or no. But if the test function is augmented with a heuristic function[2] that provides an estimate of how close a given state is to a goal state, the generate procedure can exploit it as shown in the procedure below. This is particularly nice because often the computation of the heuristic function can be done at almost no cost at the same time that the test for a solution is being performed. Hill climbing is often used when a good heuristic function is available for evaluating states but when no other useful knowledge is available. For example, suppose you are in an unfamiliar city without a map and you want to get downtown. You simply aim for the tall buildings. The heuristic function is just distance between the current location and the location of the tall buildings and the desirable states are those in which this distance is minimized.

Recall from Section 2.3.4 that one way to characterize problems is according to their answer to the question, "Is a good solution absolute or relative?" Absolute solutions exist whenever it is possible to recognize a goal state just by examining it. Getting downtown is an example of such a problem. For these problems, hill climbing can terminate whenever a goal state is reached. Only relative solutions exist, however, for maximization (or minimization) problems, such as the traveling salesman problem. In these problems, there is no *a priori* goal state. For problems of this sort, it makes sense to terminate hill climbing when there is no reasonable alternative state to move to.

---

[2]What we are calling the heuristic function is sometimes also called the *objective function*, particularly in the literature of mathematical optimization.

3.2.1   Simple Hill Climbing

The simplest way to implement hill climbing is as follows.

Algorithm: Simple Hill Climbing

1. Evaluate the initial state. If it is also a goal state, then return it and quit. Otherwise, continue with the initial state as the current state.

2. Loop until a solution is found or until there are no new operators left to be applied in the current state:

   (a) Select an operator that has not yet been applied to the current state and apply it to produce a new state.

   (b) Evaluate the new state.

      i. If it is a goal state, then return it and quit.
      ii. If it is not a goal state but it is better than the current state, then make it the current state.
      iii. If it is not better than the current state, then continue in the loop.

The key difference between this algorithm and the one we gave for generate-and-test is the use of an evaluation function as a way to inject task-specific knowledge into the control process. It is the use of such knowledge that makes this and the other methods discussed in the rest of this chapter *heuristic* search methods, and it is that same knowledge that gives these methods their power to solve some otherwise intractable problems.

Notice that in this algorithm, we have asked the relatively vague question, "Is one state *better* than another?" For the algorithm to work, a precise definition of *better* must be provided. In some cases, it means a higher value of the heuristic function. In others, it means a lower value. It does not matter which, as long as a particular hill-climbing program is consistent in its interpretation.

To see how hill climbing works, let's return to the puzzle of the four colored blocks. To solve the problem, we first need to define a heuristic function that describes how close a particular configuration is to being a solution. One such function is simply the sum of the number of different colors on each of the four sides. A solution to the puzzle will have a value of 16. Next we need to define a set of rules that describe ways of transforming one configuration into another. Actually, one rule will suffice. It says simply pick a block and rotate it 90 degrees in any direction. Having provided these definitions, the next step is to generate a starting configuration. This can either be done at random or with the aid of the heuristic function described in the last section. Now hill climbing can begin. We generate a new state by selecting a block and rotating it. If the resulting state is better, then we keep it. If not, we return to the previous state and try a different perturbation.

3.2.2   Steepest-Ascent Hill Climbing

A useful variation on simple hill climbing considers all the moves from the current state and selects the best one as the next state. This method is called *steepest-ascent hill climbing* or *gradient search*. Notice that this contrasts with the basic method in which the first state that is better than the current state is selected. The algorithm works as follows.

Algorithm: Steepest-Ascent Hill Climbing

1. Evaluate the initial state. If it is also a goal state, then return it and quit. Otherwise, continue with the initial state as the current state.

2. Loop until a solution is found or until a complete iteration produces no change to current state:

   (a) Let *SUCC* be a state such that any possible successor of the current state will be better than *SUCC*.

   (b) For each operator that applies to the current state do:

      i. Apply the operator and generate a new state.
      ii. Evaluate the new state. If it is a goal state, then return it and quit. If not, compare it to *SUCC*. If it is better, then set *SUCC* to this state. If it is not better, leave *SUCC* alone.

   (c) If the *SUCC* is better than current state, then set current state to *SUCC*.

To apply steepest-ascent hill climbing to the colored blocks problem, we must consider all perturbations of the initial state and choose the best. For this problem, this is difficult since there are so many possible moves. There is a trade-off between the time required to select a move (usually longer for steepest-ascent hill climbing) and the number of moves required to get to a solution (usually longer for basic hill climbing) that must be considered when deciding which method will work better for a particular problem.

Both basic and steepest-ascent hill climbing may fail to find a solution. Either algorithm may terminate not by finding a goal state but by getting to a state from which no better states can be generated. This will happen if the program has reached either a local maximum, a plateau, or a ridge.

A *local maximum* is a state that is better than all its neighbors but is not better than some other states farther away. At a local maximum, all moves appear to make things worse. Local maxima are particularly frustrating because they often occur almost within sight of a solution. In this case, they are called *foothills*.

A *plateau* is a flat area of the search space in which a whole set of neighboring states have the same value. On a plateau, it is not possible to determine the best direction in which to move by making local comparisons.

A *ridge* is a special kind of local maximum. It is an area of the search space that is higher than surrounding areas and that itself has a slope (which one would like to climb). But the orientation of the high region, compared to the set of available moves and the directions in which they move, makes it impossible to traverse a ridge by single moves.

There are some ways of dealing with these problems, although these methods are by no means guaranteed:

- Backtrack to some earlier node and try going in a different direction. This is particularly reasonable if at that node there was another direction that looked as promising or almost as promising as the one that was chosen earlier. To implement this strategy, maintain a list of paths almost taken and go back to one of them if the path that was taken leads to a dead end. This is a fairly good way of dealing with local maxima.

- Make a big jump in some direction to try to get to a new section of the search space. This is a particularly good way of dealing with plateaus. If the only rules available describe single small steps, apply them several times in the same direction.

- Apply two or more rules before doing the test. This corresponds to moving in several directions at once. This is a particularly good strategy for dealing with ridges.

Even with these first-aid measures, hill climbing is not always very effective. It is particularly unsuited to problems where the value of the heuristic function drops off suddenly as you move away from a solution. This is often the case whenever any sort of threshold effect is present. Hill climbing is a local method, by which we mean that it decides what to do next by looking only at the "immediate" consequences of its choice rather than by exhaustively exploring all the consequences. It shares with other local methods, such as the nearest neighbor heuristic described in Section 2.2.2, the advantage of being less combinatorially explosive than comparable global methods. But it also shares with other local methods a lack of a guarantee that it will be effective. Although it is true that the hill-climbing procedure itself looks only one move ahead and not any farther, that examination may in fact exploit an arbitrary amount of global information if that information is encoded in the heuristic function. Consider the blocks world problem shown in Figure 3.1. Assume the same operators (i.e., pick up one block and put it on the table; pick up one block and put it on another one) that were used in Section 2.3.1. Suppose we use the following heuristic function:

Local: Add one point for every block that is resting on the thing it is supposed to be resting on. Subtract one point for every block that is sitting on the wrong thing.

Using this function, the goal state has a score of 8. The initial state has a score of 4 (since it gets one point added for blocks C, D, E, F, G, and H and one point subtracted for blocks A and B). There is only one move from the initial state, namely to move block A to the table. That produces a state with a score of 6 (since now A's position causes a point to be added rather than subtracted). The hill-climbing procedure will accept that move. From the new state, there are three possible moves, leading to the three states shown in Figure 3.2. These states have the scores: (a) 4, (b) 4, and (c) 4. Hill climbing will halt because all these states have lower scores than the current state. The process has reached a local maximum that is not the global maximum. The problem is that by purely local examination of support structures, the current state appears to be better

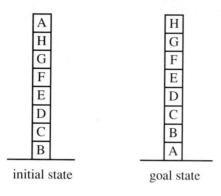

initial state   goal state

Figure 3.1: A Hill-Climbing Problem

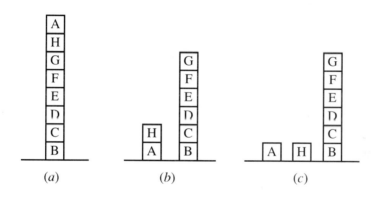

(a)   (b)   (c)

Figure 3.2: Three Possible Moves

than any of its successors because more blocks rest on the correct objects. To solve this problem, it is necessary to disassemble a good local structure (the stack B through H) because it is in the wrong global context.

We could blame hill climbing itself for this failure to look far enough ahead to find a solution. But we could also blame the heuristic function and try to modify it. Suppose we try the following heuristic function in place of the first one:

> **Global:** For each block that has the correct support structure (i.e., the complete structure underneath it is exactly as it should be), add one point for every block in the support structure. For each block that has an incorrect support structure, subtract one point for every block in the existing support structure.

Using this function, the goal state has the score 28 (1 for B, 2 for C, etc.). The initial state has the score −28. Moving A to the table yields a state with a score of −21 since A no longer has seven wrong blocks under it. The three states that can be produced next now have the following scores: (a) -28, (b) -16, and (c) -15. This time, steepest-ascent hill climbing will choose move (c), which is the correct one. This new heuristic function captures the two key aspects of this problem: incorrect structures are bad and should be taken apart; and correct structures are good and should be built up. As a result, the same hill climbing procedure that failed with the earlier heuristic function now works perfectly.

Unfortunately, it is not always possible to construct such a perfect heuristic function. For example, consider again the problem of driving downtown. The perfect heuristic function would need to have knowledge about one-way and dead-end streets, which, in the case of a strange city, is not always available. And even if perfect knowledge is, in principle, available, it may not be computationally tractable to use. As an extreme example, imagine a heuristic function that computes a value for a state by invoking its own problem-solving procedure to look ahead from the state it is given to find a solution. It then knows the exact cost of finding that solution and can return that cost as its value. A heuristic function that does this converts the local hill-climbing procedure into a global method by embedding a global method within it. But now the computational advantages of a local method have been lost. Thus it is still true that hill climbing can be very inefficient in a large, rough problem space. But it is often useful when combined with other methods that get it started in the right general neighborhood.

3.2.3   Simulated Annealing

Simulated annealing is a variation of hill climbing in which, at the beginning of the process, some downhill moves may be made. The idea is to do enough exploration of the whole space early on so that the final solution is relatively insensitive to the starting state. This should lower the chances of getting caught at a local maximum, a plateau, or a ridge.

In order to be compatible with standard usage in discussions of simulated annealing, we make two notational changes for the duration of this section. We use the term *objective function* in place of the term *heuristic function*.

And we attempt to *minimize* rather than maximize the value of the objective function. Thus we actually describe a process of valley descending rather than hill climbing.

Simulated annealing [Kirkpatrick *et al.*, 1983] as a computational process is patterned after the physical process of *annealing*, in which physical substances such as metals are melted (i.e., raised to high energy levels) and then gradually cooled until some solid state is reached. The goal of this process is to produce a minimal-energy final state. Thus this process is one of valley descending in which the objective function is the energy level. Physical substances usually move from higher energy configurations to lower ones, so the valley descending occurs naturally. But there is some probability that a transition to a higher energy state will occur. This probability is given by the function

$$p = e^{-\Delta E/kT}$$

where ΔE is the positive change in the energy level, T is the temperature, and k is Boltzmann's constant. Thus, in the physical valley descending that occurs during annealing, the probability of a large uphill move is lower than the probability of a small one. Also, the probability that an uphill move will be made decreases as the temperature decreases. Thus such moves are more likely during the beginning of the process when the temperature is high, and they become less likely at the end as the temperature becomes lower. One way to characterize this process is that downhill moves are allowed anytime. Large upward moves may occur early on, but as the process progresses, only relatively small upward moves are allowed until finally the process converges to a local minimum configuration.

The rate at which the system is cooled is called the *annealing schedule*. Physical annealing processes are very sensitive to the annealing schedule. If cooling occurs too rapidly, stable regions of high energy will form. In other words, a local but not global minimum is reached. If, however, a slower schedule is used, a uniform crystalline structure, which corresponds to a global minimum, is more likely to develop. But, if the schedule is too slow, time is wasted. At high temperatures, where essentially random motion is allowed, nothing useful happens. At low temperatures a lot of time may be wasted after the final structure has already been formed. The optimal annealing schedule for each particular annealing problem must usually be discovered empirically.

These properties of physical annealing can be used to define an analogous process of simulated annealing, which can be used (although not always effectively) whenever simple hill climbing can be used. In this analogous process, ΔE is generalized so that it represents not specifically the change in energy but more generally, the change in the value of the objective function, whatever it is. The analogy for kT is slightly less straightforward. In the physical process, temperature is a well-defined notion, measured in standard units. The variable k describes the correspondence between the units of temperature and the units of energy. Since, in the analogous process, the units for both E and T are artificial, it makes sense to incorporate k into T, selecting values for T that produce desirable behavior on the part of the algorithm. Thus we use the revised probability formula

$$p' = e^{-\Delta E / T}$$

But we still need to choose a schedule of values for T (which we still call temperature). We discuss this briefly below after we present the simulated annealing algorithm.

The algorithm for simulated annealing is only slightly different from the simple hill-climbing procedure. The three differences are:

- The annealing schedule must be maintained.

- Moves to worse states may be accepted.

- It is a good idea to maintain, in addition to the current state, the best state found so far. Then, if the final state is worse than that earlier state (because of bad luck in accepting moves to worse states), the earlier state is still available.

Algorithm: Simulated Annealing

1. Evaluate the initial state. If it is also a goal state, then return it and quit. Otherwise, continue with the initial state as the current state.

2. Initialize *BEST-SO-FAR* to the current state.

3. Initialize T according to the annealing schedule.

4. Loop until a solution is found or until there are no new operators left to be applied in the current state.

    (a) Select an operator that has not yet been applied to the current state and apply it to produce a new state.

    (b) Evaluate the new state. Compute

$$\Delta E = \text{(value of current)} - \text{(value of new state)}$$

- If the new state is a goal state, then return it and quit.
- If it is not a goal state but is better than the current state, then make it the current state. Also set *BEST-SO-FAR* to this new state.
- If it is not better than the current state, then make it the current state with probability p' as defined above. This step is usually implemented by invoking a random number generator to produce a number in the range [0,1]. If that number is less than p', then the move is accepted. Otherwise, do nothing.

    (c) Revise T as necessary according to the annealing schedule.

5. Return *BEST-SO-FAR* as the answer.

To implement this revised algorithm, it is necessary to select an annealing schedule, which has three components. The first is the initial value to be used for temperature. The second is the criteria that will be used to decide when the temperature of the system should be reduced. The third is the amount by which the temperature will be reduced each time it is changed. There may also be a fourth component of the schedule, namely, when to quit. Simulated annealing is often used to solve problems in which the number of moves from a given state is very large (such as the number of permutations that can be made to a proposed traveling salesman route). For such problems, it may not make sense to try all possible moves. Instead, it may be useful to exploit some criterion involving the number of moves that have been tried since an improvement was found.

Experiments that have been done with simulated annealing on a variety of problems suggest that the best way to select an annealing schedule is by trying several and observing the effect on both the quality of the solution that is found and the rate at which the process converges. To begin to get a feel for how to come up with a schedule, the first thing to notice is that as T approaches zero, the probability of accepting a move to a worse state goes to zero and simulated annealing becomes identical to simple hill climbing. The second thing to notice is that what really matters in computing the probability of accepting a move is the ratio $\Delta E/T$. Thus it is important that values of T be scaled so that this ratio is meaningful. For example, T could be initialized to a value such that, for an average ΔE, p' would be 0.5.

Chapter 18 returns to simulated annealing in the context of neural networks.

3.3 Best-First Search

Until now, we have really only discussed two systematic control strategies, breadth-first search and depth-first search (of several varieties). In this section, we discuss a new method, best-first search, which is a way of combining the advantages of both depth-first and breadth-first search into a single method.

3.3.1 OR Graphs

Depth-first search is good because it allows a solution to be found without all competing branches having to be expanded. Breadth-first search is good because it does not get trapped on dead-end paths. One way of combining the two is to follow a single path at a time, but switch paths whenever some competing path looks more promising than the current one does.

At each step of the best-first search process, we select the most promising of the nodes we have generated so far. This is done by applying an appropriate heuristic function to each of them. We then expand the chosen node by using the rules to generate its successors. If one of them is a solution, we can quit. If not, all those new nodes are added to the set of nodes generated so far. Again the most promising node is selected and the process continues. Usually what happens is that a bit of depth-first searching occurs as the most promising branch is explored. But eventually, if a solution is not found, that branch will start to look less promising than one of the top-level branches that had been ignored. At that point, the now more promising, previously ignored branch will be explored. But the old branch is not forgotten. Its last node remains in the set of generated but unexpanded nodes. The search can return to it whenever all the others get bad enough that it is again the most promising path.

Figure 3.3 shows the beginning of a best-first search procedure. Initially, there is only one node, so it will be expanded. Doing so generates three new nodes. The heuristic function, which, in this example, is an estimate of the cost of getting to a solution from a given node, is applied to each of these new nodes. Since node D is the most promising, it is expanded next, producing two successor nodes, E and F. But then the heuristic function is applied to them. Now another path, that going through node B, looks more promising, so it is pursued, generating nodes G and H. But again when these new nodes are evaluated they look less promising than another path, so attention is returned to the path through D to E. E is then expanded, yielding nodes I and J. At the next step, J will be expanded, since it is the most promising. This process can continue until a solution is found.

Notice that this procedure is very similar to the procedure for steepest ascent hill climbing, with two exceptions. In hill climbing, one move is selected and all the others are rejected, never to be reconsidered. This produces the straightline behavior that is characteristic of hill climbing. In best-first search, one move is selected, but the others are kept around so that they can be revisited later if the selected path becomes less promising.[3] Further, the best available state is selected in best-first search, even if that state has a value that is lower than the value of the state that was just explored. This

---

[3]In a variation of best-first search, called *beam search*, only the n most promising states are kept for future consideration. This procedure is more efficient with respect to memory but introduces the possibility of missing a solution altogether by pruning the search tree too early.

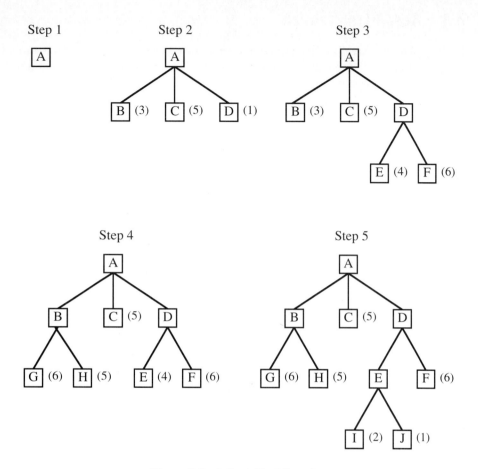

Figure 3.3: A Best-First Search

contrasts with hill climbing, which will stop if there are no successor states with better values than the current state.

Although the example shown above illustrates a best-first search of a tree, it is sometimes important to search a graph instead so that duplicate paths will not be pursued. An algorithm to do this will operate by searching a directed graph in which each node represents a point in the problem space. Each node will contain, in addition to a description of the problem state it represents, an indication of how promising it is, a parent link that points back to the best node from which it came, and a list of the nodes that were generated from it. The parent link will make it possible to recover the path to the goal once the goal is found. The list of successors will make it possible, if a better path is found to an already existing node, to propagate the improvement down to its successors. We will call a graph of this sort an *OR graph*, since each of its branches represents an alternative problem-solving path.

To implement such a graph-search procedure, we will need to use two lists of nodes:

- *OPEN*—nodes that have been generated and have had the heuristic function applied to them but which have not yet been examined (i.e., had their successors generated). *OPEN* is actually a priority queue in which the elements with the highest priority are those with the most promising value of the heuristic function. Standard techniques for manipulating priority queues can be used to manipulate the list.

- *CLOSED*—nodes that have already been examined. We need to keep these nodes in memory if we want to search a graph rather than a tree, since whenever a new node is generated, we need to check whether it has been generated before.

We will also need a heuristic function that estimates the merits of each node we generate. This will enable the algorithm to search more promising paths first. Call this function f' (to indicate that it is an approximation to a function f that gives the true evaluation of the node). For many applications, it is convenient to define this function as the sum of two components that we call g and h'. The function g is a measure of the cost of getting from the initial state to the current node. Note that g is not an estimate of anything; it is known to be the exact sum of the costs of applying each of the rules that were applied along the best path to the node. The function h' is an estimate of the additional cost of getting from the current node to a goal state. This is the place where knowledge about the problem domain is exploited. The combined function f', then, represents an estimate of the cost of getting from the initial state to a goal state along the path that generated the current node. If more than one path generated the node, then the algorithm will record the best one. Note that because g and h' must be added, it is important that h' be a measure of the cost of getting from the node to a solution (i.e., good nodes get low values; bad nodes get high values) rather than a measure of the goodness of a node (i.e., good nodes get high values). But that is easy to arrange with judicious placement of minus signs. It is also important that g be nonnegative. If this is not true, then paths that traverse cycles in the graph will appear to get better as they get longer.

The actual operation of the algorithm is very simple. It proceeds in steps, expanding one node at each step, until it generates a node that corresponds to a goal state. At each step, it picks the most promising of the nodes that have so far been generated but not expanded. It generates the successors of the chosen node, applies the heuristic function to them, and adds them to the list of open nodes, after checking to see if any of them have been generated before. By doing this check, we can guarantee that each node only appears once in the graph, although many nodes may point to it as a successor. Then the next step begins.

This process can be summarized as follows.

Algorithm: Best-First Search

1. Start with *OPEN* containing just the initial state.

2. Until a goal is found or there are no nodes left on *OPEN* do:

    (a) Pick the best node on *OPEN*.

    (b) Generate its successors.

    (c) For each successor do:

    i. If it has not been generated before, evaluate it, add it to *OPEN*, and record its parent.

    ii. If it has been generated before, change the parent if this new path is better than the previous one. In that case, update the cost of getting to this node and to any successors that this node may already have.

The basic idea of this algorithm is simple. Unfortunately, it is rarely the case that graph traversal algorithms are simple to write correctly. And it is even rarer that it is simple to guarantee the correctness of such algorithms. In the section that follows, we describe this algorithm in more detail as an example of the design and analysis of a graph-search program.

3.3.2   The A* Algorithm

The best-first search algorithm that was just presented is a simplification of an algorithm called A*, which was first presented by Hart *et al.* [1968; 1972]. This algorithm uses the same f', g, and h' functions, as well as the lists *OPEN* and *CLOSED*, that we have already described.

Algorithm: A*

1. Start with *OPEN* containing only the initial node. Set that node's g value to 0, its h' value to whatever it is, and its f' value to $h' + 0$, or h'. Set *CLOSED* to the empty list.

2. Until a goal node is found, repeat the following procedure: If there are no nodes on *OPEN*, report failure. Otherwise, pick the node on *OPEN* with the lowest f' value. Call it *BESTNODE*. Remove it from *OPEN*. Place it on *CLOSED*. See if *BESTNODE* is a goal node. If so, exit and report a solution (either *BESTNODE* if all we want is the node or the path that has been created between the initial state and *BESTNODE* if we are interested in the path). Otherwise, generate the successors of *BESTNODE* but do not set *BESTNODE* to point to them yet. (First we need to see if any of them have already been generated.) For each such *SUCCESSOR*, do the following:

    (a) Set *SUCCESSOR* to point back to *BESTNODE*. These backwards links will make it possible to recover the path once a solution is found.

    (b) Compute $g(SUCCESSOR) = g(BESTNODE)$ + the cost of getting from *BESTNODE* to *SUCCESSOR*.

    (c) See if *SUCCESSOR* is the same as any node on *OPEN* (i.e., it has already been generated but not processed). If so, call that node *OLD*. Since this node already exists in the graph, we can throw *SUCCESSOR* away and add *OLD* to the list of *BESTNODE*'s successors. Now we must decide whether *OLD*'s parent link should be reset to point to *BESTNODE*. It should be if the path we have just found to *SUCCESSOR* is cheaper than the current best path to *OLD* (since *SUCCESSOR* and *OLD* are really the same node). So see whether it is cheaper to get to *OLD* via its current parent or to *SUCCESSOR* via *BESTNODE* by comparing their g values. If *OLD* is cheaper (or just as cheap), then we need do nothing. If *SUCCESSOR* is cheaper, then reset *OLD*'s parent link to point to *BESTNODE*, record the new cheaper path in $g(OLD)$, and update $f'(OLD)$.

(d) If *SUCCESSOR* was not on *OPEN*, see if it is on *CLOSED*. If so, call the node on *CLOSED OLD* and add *OLD* to the list of *BESTNODE*'s successors. Check to see if the new path or the old path is better just as in step 2(c), and set the parent link and g and f' values appropriately. If we have just found a better path to *OLD*, we must propagate the improvement to *OLD*'s successors. This is a bit tricky. *OLD* points to its successors. Each successor in turn points to its successors, and so forth, until each branch terminates with a node that either is still on *OPEN* or has no successors. So to propagate the new cost downward, do a depth-first traversal of the tree starting at *OLD*, changing each node's g value (and thus also its f' value), terminating each branch when you reach either a node with no successors or a node to which an equivalent or better path has already been found.[4] This condition is easy to check for. Each node's parent link points back to its best known parent. As we propagate down to a node, see if its parent points to the node we are coming from. If so, continue the propagation. If not, then its g value already reflects the better path of which it is part. So the propagation may stop here. But it is possible that with the new value of g being propagated downward, the path we are following may become better than the path through the current parent. So compare the two. If the path through the current parent is still better, stop the propagation. If the path we are propagating through is now better, reset the parent and continue propagation.

(e) If *SUCCESSOR* was not already on either *OPEN* or *CLOSED*, then put it on *OPEN*, and add it to the list of *BESTNODE*'s successors. Compute $f'(SUCCESSOR) - g(SUCCESSOR) + h'(SUCCESSOR)$.

Several interesting observations can be made about this algorithm. The first concerns the role of the g function. It lets us choose which node to expand next on the basis not only of how good the node itself looks (as measured by h'), but also on the basis of how good the path to the node was. By incorporating g into f', we will not always choose as our next node to expand the node that appears to be closest to the goal. This is useful if we care about the path we find. If, on the other hand, we only care about getting to a solution somehow, we can define g always to be 0, thus always choosing the node that seems closest to a goal. If we want to find a path involving the fewest number of steps, then we set the cost of going from a node to its successor as a constant, usually 1. If, on the other hand, we want to find the cheapest path and some operators cost more than others, then we set the cost of going from one node to another to reflect those costs. Thus the A* algorithm can be used whether we are interested in finding a minimal-cost overall path or simply any path as quickly as possible.

The second observation involves h', the estimator of h, the distance of a node to the goal. If h' is a perfect estimator of h, then A* will converge immediately to the goal

---

[4]This second check guarantees that the algorithm will terminate even if there are cycles in the graph. If there is a cycle, then the second time that a given node is visited, the path will be no better than the first time and so propagation will stop.

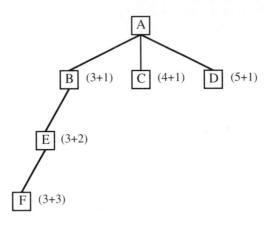

Figure 3.4: h' Underestimates h

with no search. The better h' is, the closer we will get to that direct approach. If, on
the other hand, the value of h' is always 0, the search will be controlled by g. If the
value of g is also 0, the search strategy will be random. If the value of g is always 1, the
search will be breadth first. All nodes on one level will have lower g values, and thus
lower f' values than will all nodes on the next level. What if, on the other hand, h' is
neither perfect nor 0? Can we say anything interesting about the behavior of the search?
The answer is yes if we can guarantee that h' never overestimates h. In that case, the
A* algorithm is guaranteed to find an optimal (as determined by g) path to a goal, if one
exists. This can easily be seen from a few examples.[5]

Consider the situation shown in Figure 3.4. Assume that the cost of all arcs is 1.
Initially, all nodes except A are on *OPEN* (although the figure shows the situation two
steps later, after B and E have been expanded). For each node, f' is indicated as the
sum of h' and g. In this example, node B has the lowest f', 4, so it is expanded first.
Suppose it has only one successor E, which also appears to be three moves away from
a goal. Now $f'(E)$ is 5, the same as $f'(C)$. Suppose we resolve this in favor of the
path we are currently following. Then we will expand E next. Suppose it too has a
single successor F, also judged to be three moves from a goal. We are clearly using up
moves and making no progress. But $f'(F) = 6$, which is greater than $f'(C)$. So we will
expand C next. Thus we see that by underestimating $h(B)$ we have wasted some effort.
But eventually we discover that B was farther away than we thought and we go back
and try another path.

Now consider the situation shown in Figure 3.5. Again we expand B on the first
step. On the second step we again expand E. At the next step we expand F, and finally
we generate G, for a solution path of length 4. But suppose there is a direct path from D
to a solution, giving a path of length 2. We will never find it. By overestimating
$h'(D)$ we make D look so bad that we may find some other, worse solution without
ever expanding D. In general, if h' might overestimate h, we cannot be guaranteed of
finding the cheapest path solution unless we expand the entire graph until all paths are

---

[5]A search algorithm that is guaranteed to find an optimal path to a goal, if one exists, is called *admissible*
[Nilsson, 1980].

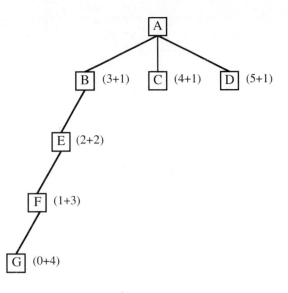

Figure 3.5: h' Overestimates h

longer than the best solution. An interesting question is, "Of what practical significance is the theorem that if h' never overestimates h then A* is admissible?" The answer is, "almost none," because, for most real problems, the only way to guarantee that h' never overestimates h is to set it to zero. But then we are back to breadth-first search, which is admissible but not efficient. But there is a corollary to this theorem that is very useful. We can state it loosely as follows:

> **Graceful Decay of Admissibility:** If h' rarely overestimates h by more than δ, then the A* algorithm will rarely find a solution whose cost is more than δ greater than the cost of the optimal solution.

The formalization and proof of this corollary will be left as an exercise.

The third observation we can make about the A* algorithm has to do with the relationship between trees and graphs. The algorithm was stated in its most general form as it applies to graphs. It can, of course, be simplified to apply to trees by not bothering to check whether a new node is already on *OPEN* or *CLOSED*. This makes it faster to generate nodes but may result in the same search being conducted many times if nodes are often duplicated.

Under certain conditions, the A* algorithm can be shown to be optimal in that it generates the fewest nodes in the process of finding a solution to a problem. Under other conditions it is not optimal. For formal discussions of these conditions, see Gelperin [1977] and Martelli [1977].

3.3.3 Agendas

In our discussion of best-first search in OR graphs, we assumed that we could evaluate multiple paths to the same node independently of each other. For example, in the water jug problem, it makes no difference to the evaluation of the merit of the position (4, 3) that there are at least two separate paths by which it could be reached. This is not true, however, in all situations, e.g., especially when there is no single, simple heuristic function that measures the distance between a given node and a goal.

Consider, for example, the task faced by the mathematics discovery program AM, written by Lenat [1977; 1982]. AM was given a small set of starting facts about number theory and a set of operators it could use to develop new ideas. These operators included such things as "Find examples of a concept you already know." AM's goal was to generate new "interesting" mathematical concepts. It succeeded in discovering such things as prime numbers and Goldbach's conjecture.

Armed solely with its basic operators, AM would have been able to create a great many new concepts, most of which would have been worthless. It needed a way to decide intelligently which rules to apply. For this it was provided with a set of heuristic rules that said such things as "The extreme cases of any concept are likely to be interesting." "Interest" was then used as the measure of merit of individual tasks that the system could perform. The system operated by selecting at each cycle the most interesting task, doing it, and possibly generating new tasks in the process. This corresponds to the selection of the most promising node in the best-first search procedure. But in AM's situation the fact that several paths recommend the same task does matter. Each contributes a reason why the task would lead to an interesting result. The more such reasons there are, the more likely it is that the task really would lead to something good. So we need a way to record proposed tasks along with the reasons they have been proposed. AM used a task agenda. An *agenda* is a list of tasks a system could perform. Associated with each task there are usually two things: a list of reasons why the task is being proposed (often called *justifications*) and a rating representing the overall weight of evidence suggesting that the task would be useful.

An agenda-driven system uses the following procedure.

Algorithm: Agenda-Driven Search

1. Do until a goal state is reached or the agenda is empty:

    (a) Choose the most promising task from the agenda. Notice that this task can be represented in any desired form. It can be thought of as an explicit statement of what to do next or simply as an indication of the next node to be expanded.

    (b) Execute the task by devoting to it the number of resources determined by its importance. The important resources to consider are time and space. Executing the task will probably generate additional tasks (successor nodes). For each of them, do the following:

        i. See if it is already on the agenda. If so, then see if this same reason for doing it is already on its list of justifications. If so, ignore this current evidence. If this justification was not already present, add it to the list. If the task was not on the agenda, insert it.

        ii. Compute the new task's rating, combining the evidence from all its justifications. Not all justifications need have equal weight. It is often useful to associate with each justification a measure of how strong a reason it is. These measures are then combined at this step to produce an overall rating for the task.

One important question that arises in agenda-driven systems is how to find the most promising task on each cycle. One way to do this is simple. Maintain the agenda sorted by rating. When a new task is created, insert it into the agenda in its proper place. When a task has its justifications changed, recompute its rating and move it to the correct place in the list. But this method causes a great deal of time to be spent keeping the agenda in perfect order. Much of this time is wasted since we do not need perfect order. We only need to know the proper first element. The following modified strategy may occasionally cause a task other than the best to be executed, but it is significantly cheaper than the perfect method. When a task is proposed, or a new justification is added to an existing task, compute the new rating and compare it against the top few (e.g., five or ten) elements on the agenda. If it is better, insert the node into its proper position at the top of the list. Otherwise, leave it where it is or simply insert it at the end of the agenda. At the beginning of each cycle, choose the first task on the agenda. In addition, once in a while, go through the agenda and reorder it properly.

An agenda-driven control structure is also useful if some tasks (or nodes) provide negative evidence about the merits of other tasks (or nodes). This can be represented by justifications with negative weightings. If these negative weightings are used, it may be important to check not only for the possibility of moving a task to the head of the agenda but also of moving a top task to the bottom if new, negative justifications appear. But this is easy to do.

As you can see, the agenda mechanism provides a good way of focusing the attention of a complex system in the areas suggested by the greatest number of positive indicators. But the overhead for each task executed may be fairly high. This raises the question of the proper grain size for the division of the entire problem-solving process into individual tasks. Suppose each task is very small. Then we will never do even a very small thing unless it really is the best thing to do. But we will spend a large percentage of our total effort on figuring out what to do next. If, on the other hand, the size of an individual task is very large, then some effort may be spent finishing one task when there are more promising ones that could be done. But a smaller percentage of the total time will be spent on the overhead of figuring out what to do. The exact choice of task size for a particular system depends on the extent to which doing one small thing really means that a set of other small things is likely to be very good to do too. It often requires some experimentation to get right.

There are some problem domains for which an agenda mechanism is inappropriate. The agenda mechanism assumes that if there is good reason to do something now, then there will also be the same good reason to do something later unless something better comes along in the interim. But this is not always the case, particularly for systems that are interacting with people. The following dialogue would not be acceptable to most people:

Person: I don't want to read any more about China. Give me something else.

Computer: OK. What else are you interested in?

Person: How about Italy? I think I'd find Italy fascinating.

Computer: What things about Italy are you interested in reading about?

Person: I think I'd like to start with its history.

Computer: Why don't you want to read any more about China?

It would have been fine to have tried to find out why the person was no longer interested in China right after he or she mentioned it. The computer chose instead to try to find a new area of positive interest, also a very reasonable thing to do. But in conversations, the fact that something is reasonable now does not mean that it will continue to be so after the conversation has proceeded for a while. So it is not a good idea simply to put possible statements on an agenda, wait until a later lull, and then pop out with them. More precisely, agendas are a good way to implement monotonic production systems (in the sense of Section 2.4) and a poor way to implement nonmonotonic ones.

Despite these difficulties, agenda-driven control structures are very useful. They provide an excellent way of integrating information from a variety of sources into one program since each source simply adds tasks and justifications to the agenda. As AI programs become more complex and their knowledge bases grow, this becomes a particularly significant advantage.

3.4   Problem Reduction

So far, we have considered search strategies for OR graphs through which we want to find a single path to a goal. Such structures represent the fact that we will know how to get from a node to a goal state if we can discover how to get from that node to a goal state along any one of the branches leaving it.

3.4.1   AND-OR Graphs

Another kind of structure, the AND-OR graph (or tree), is useful for representing the solution of problems that can be solved by decomposing them into a set of smaller problems, all of which must then be solved. This decomposition, or reduction, generates arcs that we call AND arcs. One AND arc may point to any number of successor nodes, all of which must be solved in order for the arc to point to a solution. Just as in an OR graph, several arcs may emerge from a single node, indicating a variety of ways in which the original problem might be solved. This is why the structure is called not simply an AND graph but rather an AND-OR graph. An example of an AND-OR graph (which also happens to be an AND-OR tree) is given in Figure 3.6. AND arcs are indicated with a line connecting all the components.

In order to find solutions in an AND-OR graph, we need an algorithm similar to best-first search but with the ability to handle the AND arcs appropriately. This algorithm should find a path from the starting node of the graph to a set of nodes representing solution states. Notice that it may be necessary to get to more than one solution state since each arm of an AND arc must lead to its own solution node.

To see why our best-first search algorithm is not adequate for searching AND-OR graphs, consider Figure 3.7(a). The top node, A, has been expanded, producing two arcs, one leading to B and one leading to C and D. The numbers at each node represent the value of f' at that node. We assume, for simplicity, that every operation has a uniform cost, so each arc with a single successor has a cost of 1 and each AND arc with

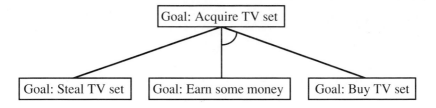

Figure 3.6: A Simple AND-OR Graph

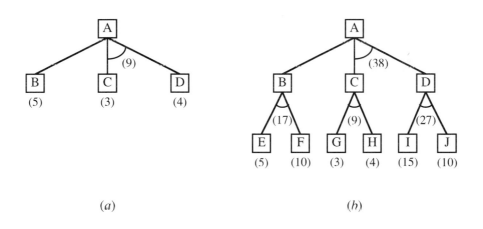

Figure 3.7: AND-OR Graphs

multiple successors has a cost of 1 for each of its components. If we look just at the nodes and choose for expansion the one with the lowest f' value, we must select C. But using the information now available, it would be better to explore the path going through B since to use C we must also use D, for a total cost of 9 (C+D+2) compared to the cost of 6 that we get by going through B. The problem is that the choice of which node to expand next must depend not only on the f' value of that node but also on whether that node is part of the current best path from the initial node. The tree shown in Figure 3.7(b) makes this even clearer. The most promising single node is G with an f' value of 3. It is even part of the most promising arc G-H, with a total cost of 9. But that arc is not part of the current best path since to use it we must also use the arc I-J, with a cost of 27. The path from A, through B, to E and F is better, with a total cost of 18. So we should not expand G next; rather we should examine either E or F.

In order to describe an algorithm for searching an AND-OR graph, we need to exploit a value that we call *FUTILITY*. If the estimated cost of a solution becomes greater than the value of *FUTILITY*, then we abandon the search. *FUTILITY* should be chosen to correspond to a threshold such that any solution with a cost above it is too expensive to be practical, even if it could ever be found. Now we can state the algorithm.

Algorithm: Problem Reduction

1. Initialize the graph to the starting node.

2. Loop until the starting node is labeled *SOLVED* or until its cost goes above *FUTILITY*:

   (a) Traverse the graph, starting at the initial node and following the current best path, and accumulate the set of nodes that are on that path and have not yet been expanded or labeled as solved.

   (b) Pick one of these unexpanded nodes and expand it. If there are no successors, assign *FUTILITY* as the value of this node. Otherwise, add its successors to the graph and for each of them compute f' (use only h' and ignore g, for reasons we discuss below). If f' of any node is 0, mark that node as *SOLVED*.

   (c) Change the f' estimate of the newly expanded node to reflect the new information provided by its successors. Propagate this change backward through the graph. If any node contains a successor arc whose descendants are all solved, label the node itself as *SOLVED*. At each node that is visited while going up the graph, decide which of its successor arcs is the most promising and mark it as part of the current best path. This may cause the current best path to change. This propagation of revised cost estimates back up the tree was not necessary in the best-first search algorithm because only unexpanded nodes were examined. But now expanded nodes must be reexamined so that the best current path can be selected. Thus it is important that their f' values be the best estimates available.

This process is illustrated in Figure 3.8. At step 1, A is the only node, so it is at the end of the current best path. It is expanded, yielding nodes B, C, and D. The arc to D is labeled as the most promising one emerging from A, since it costs 6 compared to B and C, which costs 9. (Marked arcs are indicated in the figures by arrows.) In step 2, node D is chosen for expansion. This process produces one new arc, the AND arc to E and F, with a combined cost estimate of 10. So we update the f' value of D to 10. Going back one more level, we see that this makes the AND arc B-C better than the arc to D, so it is labeled as the current best path. At step 3, we traverse that arc from A and discover the unexpanded nodes B and C. If we are going to find a solution along this path, we will have to expand both B and C eventually, so let's choose to explore B first. This generates two new arcs, the ones to G and to H. Propagating their f' values backward, we update f' of B to 6 (since that is the best we think we can do, which we can achieve by going through G). This requires updating the cost of the AND arc B-C to 12 (6+4+2). After doing that, the arc to D is again the better path from A, so we record that as the current best path and either node E or node F will be chosen for expansion at step 4. This process continues until either a solution is found or all paths have led to dead ends, indicating that there is no solution.

In addition to the difference discussed above, there is a second important way in which an algorithm for searching an AND-OR graph must differ from one for searching an OR graph. This difference, too, arises from the fact that individual paths from node to node cannot be considered independently of the paths through other nodes connected

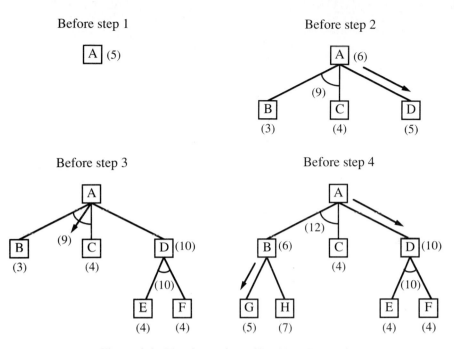

Figure 3.8: The Operation of Problem Reduction

to the original ones by AND arcs. In the best-first search algorithm, the desired path from one node to another was always the one with the lowest cost. But this is not always the case when searching an AND-OR graph.

Consider the example shown in Figure 3.9(a). The nodes were generated in alphabetical order. Now suppose that node J is expanded at the next step and that one of its successors is node E, producing the graph shown in Figure 3.9(b). This new path to E is longer than the previous path to E going through C. But since the path through C will only lead to a solution if there is also a solution to D, which we know there is not, the path through J is better.

There is one important limitation of the algorithm we have just described. It fails to take into account any interaction between subgoals. A simple example of this failure is shown in Figure 3.10. Assuming that both node C and node E ultimately lead to a solution, our algorithm will report a complete solution that includes both of them. The AND-OR graph states that for A to be solved, both C and D must be solved. But then the algorithm considers the solution of D as a completely separate process from the solution of C. Looking just at the alternatives from D, E is the best path. But it turns out that C is necessary anyway, so it would be better also to use it to satisfy D. But since our algorithm does not consider such interactions, it will find a nonoptimal path. In Chapter 13, problem-solving methods that can consider interactions among subgoals are presented.

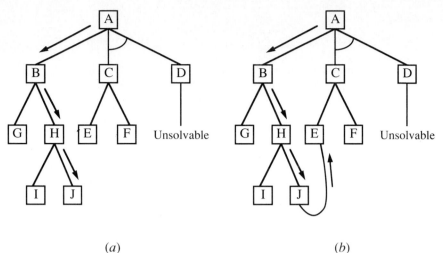

(a)   (b)

Figure 3.9: A Longer Path May Be Better

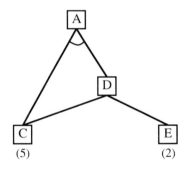

Figure 3.10: Interacting Subgoals

3.4.2   The AO* Algorithm

The problem reduction algorithm we just described is a simplification of an algorithm described in Martelli and Montanari [1973], Martelli and Montanari [1978], and Nilsson [1980]. Nilsson calls it the AO* algorithm, the name we assume.

Rather than the two lists, *OPEN* and *CLOSED*, that were used in the A* algorithm, the AO* algorithm will use a single structure *GRAPH*, representing the part of the search graph that has been explicitly generated so far. Each node in the graph will point both down to its immediate successors and up to its immediate predecessors. Each node in the graph will also have associated with it an h' value, an estimate of the cost of a path from itself to a set of solution nodes. We will not store g (the cost of getting from the start node to the current node) as we did in the A* algorithm. It is not possible to compute a single such value since there may be many paths to the same state. And such a value is not necessary because of the top-down traversing of the best-known path, which guarantees that only nodes that are on the best path will ever be considered for expansion. So h' will serve as the estimate of goodness of a node.

Algorithm: AO*

1. Let *GRAPH* consist only of the node representing the initial state. (Call this node *INIT*.) Compute $h'(INIT)$.

2. Until *INIT* is labeled *SOLVED* or until *INIT*'s h' value becomes greater than *FUTILITY*, repeat the following procedure:

   (a) Trace the labeled arcs from *INIT* and select for expansion one of the as yet unexpanded nodes that occurs on this path. Call the selected node *NODE*.

   (b) Generate the successors of *NODE*. If there are none, then assign *FUTILITY* as the h' value of *NODE*. This is equivalent to saying that *NODE* is not solvable. If there are successors, then for each one (called *SUCCESSOR*) that is not also an ancestor of *NODE* do the following:

      i. Add *SUCCESSOR* to *GRAPH*.

      ii. If *SUCCESSOR* is a terminal node, label it *SOLVED* and assign it an h' value of 0.

      iii. If *SUCCESSOR* is not a terminal node, compute its h' value.

   (c) Propagate the newly discovered information up the graph by doing the following: Let *S* be a set of nodes that have been labeled *SOLVED* or whose h' values have been changed and so need to have values propagated back to their parents. Initialize *S* to *NODE*. Until *S* is empty, repeat the following procedure:

      i. If possible, select from *S* a node none of whose descendants in *GRAPH* occurs in *S*. If there is no such node, select any node from *S*. Call this node *CURRENT*, and remove it from *S*.

      ii. Compute the cost of each of the arcs emerging from *CURRENT*. The cost of each arc is equal to the sum of the h' values of each of the nodes at the end of the arc plus whatever the cost of the arc itself is. Assign as *CURRENT*'s new h' value the minimum of the costs just computed for the arcs emerging from it.

      iii. Mark the best path out of *CURRENT* by marking the arc that had the minimum cost as computed in the previous step.

      iv. Mark *CURRENT SOLVED* if all of the nodes connected to it through the new labeled arc have been labeled *SOLVED*.

      v. If *CURRENT* has been labeled *SOLVED* or if the cost of *CURRENT* was just changed, then its new status must be propagated back up the graph. So add all of the ancestors of *CURRENT* to *S*.

It is worth noticing a couple of points about the operation of this algorithm. In step 2(*c*)*v*, the ancestors of a node whose cost was altered are added to the set of nodes whose costs must also be revised. As stated, the algorithm will insert all the node's ancestors into the set, which may result in the propagation of the cost change back up through a large number of paths that are already known not to be very good. For example, in Figure 3.11, it is clear that the path through C will always be better than the path through B, so work expended on the path through B is wasted. But if the cost of E is

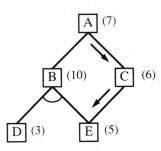

Figure 3.11: An Unnecessary Backward Propagation

revised and that change is not propagated up through B as well as through C, B may appear to be better. For example, if, as a result of expanding node E, we update its cost to 10, then the cost of C will be updated to 11. If this is all that is done, then when A is examined, the path through B will have a cost of only 11 compared to 12 for the path through C, and it will be labeled erroneously as the most promising path. In this example, the mistake might be detected at the next step, during which D will be expanded. If its cost changes and is propagated back to B, B's cost will be recomputed and the new cost of E will be used. Then the new cost of B will propagate back to A. At that point, the path through C will again be better. All that happened was that some time was wasted in expanding D. But if the node whose cost has changed is farther down in the search graph, the error may never be detected. An example of this is shown in Figure 3.12(*a*). If the cost of G is revised as shown in Figure 3.12(*b*) and if it is not immediately propagated back to E, then the change will never be recorded and a nonoptimal solution through B may be discovered.

A second point concerns the termination of the backward cost propagation of step 2(*c*). Because *GRAPH* may contain cycles, there is no guarantee that this process will terminate simply because it reaches the "top" of the graph. It turns out that the process can be guaranteed to terminate for a different reason, though. One of the exercises at the end of this chapter explores why.

3.5   Constraint Satisfaction

Many problems in AI can be viewed as problems of *constraint satisfaction* in which the goal is to discover some problem state that satisfies a given set of constraints. Examples of this sort of problem include cryptarithmetic puzzles (as described in Section 2.6) and many real-world perceptual labeling problems. Design tasks can also be viewed as constraint-satisfaction problems in which a design must be created within fixed limits on time, cost, and materials.

By viewing a problem as one of constraint satisfaction, it is often possible to reduce substantially the amount of search that is required as compared with a method that attempts to form partial solutions directly by choosing specific values for components of the eventual solution. For example, a straightforward search procedure to solve a cryptarithmetic problem might operate in a state space of partial solutions in which letters

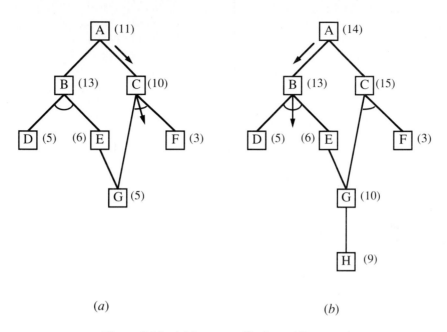

(*a*)   (*b*)

Figure 3.12: A Necessary Backward Propagation

are assigned particular numbers as their values. A depth-first control scheme could then follow a path of assignments until either a solution or an inconsistency is discovered. In contrast to this, a constraint satisfaction approach to solving this problem avoids making guesses on particular assignments of numbers to letters until it has to. Instead, the initial set of constraints, which says that each number may correspond to only one letter and that the sums of the digits must be as they are given in the problem, is first augmented to include restrictions that can be inferred from the rules of arithmetic. Then, although guessing may still be required, the number of allowable guesses is reduced and so the degree of search is curtailed.

Constraint satisfaction is a search procedure that operates in a space of constraint sets. The initial state contains the constraints that are originally given in the problem description. A goal state is any state that has been constrained "enough," where "enough" must be defined for each problem. For example, for cryptarithmetic, enough means that each letter has been assigned a unique numeric value.

Constraint satisfaction is a two-step process. First, constraints are discovered and propagated as far as possible throughout the system. Then, if there is still not a solution, search begins. A guess about something is made and added as a new constraint. Propagation can then occur with this new constraint, and so forth.

The first step, propagation, arises from the fact that there are usually dependencies among the constraints. These dependencies occur because many constraints involve more than one object and many objects participate in more than one constraint. So, for example, assume we start with one constraint, $N = E + 1$. Then, if we added the constraint $N = 3$, we could propagate that to get a stronger constraint on E, namely that $E = 2$. Constraint propagation also arises from the presence of inference rules that allow additional constraints to be inferred from the ones that are given. Constraint propagation terminates for one of two reasons. First, a contradiction may be detected. If this happens, then there is no solution consistent with all the known constraints. If the contradiction involves only those constraints that were given as part of the problem specification (as opposed to ones that were guessed during problem solving), then no solution exists. The second possible reason for termination is that the propagation has run out of steam and there are no further changes that can be made on the basis of current knowledge. If this happens and a solution has not yet been adequately specified, then search is necessary to get the process moving again.

At this point, the second step begins. Some hypothesis about a way to strengthen the constraints must be made. In the case of the cryptarithmetic problem, for example, this usually means guessing a particular value for some letter. Once this has been done, constraint propagation can begin again from this new state. If a solution is found, it can be reported. If still more guesses are required, they can be made. If a contradiction is detected, then backtracking can be used to try a different guess and proceed with it. We can state this procedure more precisely as follows:

Algorithm: Constraint Satisfaction

1. Propagate available constraints. To do this, first set *OPEN* to the set of all objects that must have values assigned to them in a complete solution. Then do until an inconsistency is detected or until *OPEN* is empty:

    (a) Select an object *OB* from *OPEN*. Strengthen as much as possible the set of constraints that apply to *OB*.

    (b) If this set is different from the set that was assigned the last time *OB* was examined or if this is the first time *OB* has been examined, then add to *OPEN* all objects that share any constraints with *OB*.

    (c) Remove *OB* from *OPEN*.

2. If the union of the constraints discovered above defines a solution, then quit and report the solution.

3. If the union of the constraints discovered above defines a contradiction, then return failure.

4. If neither of the above occurs, then it is necessary to make a guess at something in order to proceed. To do this, loop until a solution is found or all possible solutions have been eliminated:

    (a) Select an object whose value is not yet determined and select a way of strengthening the constraints on that object.

    (b) Recursively invoke constraint satisfaction with the current set of constraints augmented by the strengthening constraint just selected.

This algorithm has been stated as generally as possible. To apply it in a particular problem domain requires the use of two kinds of rules: rules that define the way constraints may validly be propagated and rules that suggest guesses when guesses are

Problem:

```
        SEND
       +MORE
       -----
       MONEY
```

Initial State:

No two letters have the same value.

The sums of the digits must be as shown in
the problem.

Figure 3.13: A Cryptarithmetic Problem

necessary. It is worth noting, though, that in some problem domains guessing may
not be required. For example, the Waltz algorithm for propagating line labels in a
picture, which is described in Chapter 14, is a version of this constraint satisfaction
algorithm with the guessing step eliminated. In general, the more powerful the rules for
propagating constraints, the less need there is for guessing.

To see how this algorithm works, consider the cryptarithmetic problem shown in
Figure 3.13. The goal state is a problem state in which all letters have been assigned a
digit in such a way that all the initial constraints are satisfied.

The solution process proceeds in cycles. At each cycle, two significant things are
done (corresponding to steps 1 and 4 of this algorithm):

1. Constraints are propagated by using rules that correspond to the properties of
   arithmetic.

2. A value is guessed for some letter whose value is not yet determined.

In the first step, it does not usually matter a great deal what order the propagation is
done in, since all available propagations will be performed before the step ends. In the
second step, though, the order in which guesses are tried may have a substantial impact
on the degree of search that is necessary. A few useful heuristics can help to select the
best guess to try first. For example, if there is a letter that has only two possible values
and another with six possible values, there is a better chance of guessing right on the first
than on the second. Another useful heuristic is that if there is a letter that participates
in many constraints then it is a good idea to prefer it to a letter that participates in a
few. A guess on such a highly constrained letter will usually lead quickly either to a
contradiction (if it is wrong) or to the generation of many additional constraints (if it is
right). A guess on a less constrained letter, on the other hand, provides less information.

The result of the first few cycles of processing this example is shown in Figure 3.14.
Since constraints never disappear at lower levels, only the ones being added are shown

for each level. It will not be much harder for the problem solver to access the constraints as a set of lists than as one long list, and this approach is efficient both in terms of storage space and the ease of backtracking. Another reasonable approach for this problem would be to store all the constraints in one central database and also to record at each node the changes that must be undone during backtracking. C1, C2, C3, and C4 indicate the carry bits out of the columns, numbering from the right.

Initially, rules for propagating constraints generate the following additional constraints:

- $M = 1$, since two single-digit numbers plus a carry cannot total more than 19.

- $S = 8$ or 9, since $S + M + C3 > 9$ (to generate the carry) and $M = 1$, $S + 1 + C3 > 9$, so $S + C3 > 8$ and C3 is at most 1.

- $O = 0$, since $S + M(1) + C3$ $(<= 1)$ must be at least 10 to generate a carry and it can be at most 11. But M is already 1, so O must be 0.

- $N = E$ or $E + 1$, depending on the value of C2. But N cannot have the same value as E. So $N = E + 1$ and C2 is 1.

- In order for C2 to be 1, the sum of $N + R + C1$ must be greater than 9, so $N + R$ must be greater than 8.

- $N + R$ cannot be greater than 18, even with a carry in, so E cannot be 9.

At this point, let us assume that no more constraints can be generated. Then, to make progress from here, we must guess. Suppose E is assigned the value 2. (We chose to guess a value for E because it occurs three times and thus interacts highly with the other letters.) Now the next cycle begins.

The constraint propagator now observes that:

- $N = 3$, since $N = E + 1$.

- $R = 8$ or 9, since $R + N (3) + C1$ (1 or 0) = 2 or 12. But since N is already 3, the sum of these nonnegative numbers cannot be less than 3. Thus $R + 3 + (0$ or $1) = 12$ and $R = 8$ or 9.

- $2 + D = Y$ or $2 + D = 10 + Y$, from the sum in the rightmost column.

Again, assuming no further constraints can be generated, a guess is required. Suppose C1 is chosen to guess a value for. If we try the value 1, then we eventually reach dead ends, as shown in the figure. When this happens, the process will backtrack and try $C1 = 0$.

A couple of observations are worth making on this process. Notice that all that is required of the constraint propagation rules is that they not infer spurious constraints. They do not have to infer all legal ones. For example, we could have reasoned through to the result that C1 equals 0. We could have done so by observing that for C1 to be 1, the following must hold: $2 + D = 10 + Y$. For this to be the case, D would have to be 8 or 9. But both S and R must be either 8 or 9 and three letters cannot share two values. So C1 cannot be 1. If we had realized this initially, some search could have been avoided. But since the constraint propagation rules we used were not that sophisticated,

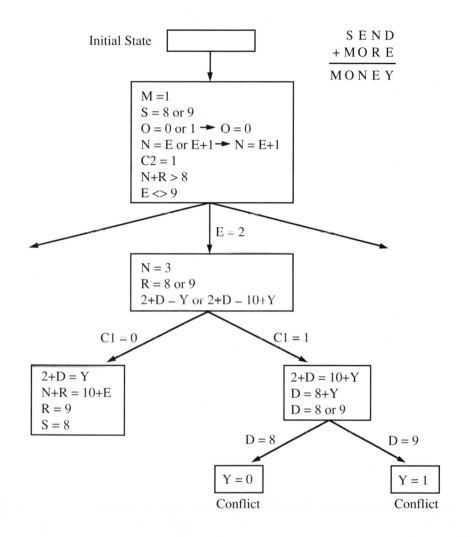

Figure 3.14: Solving a Cryptarithmetic Problem

it took some search. Whether the search route takes more or less actual time than does the constraint propagation route depends on how long it takes to perform the reasoning required for constraint propagation.

A second thing to notice is that there are often two kinds of constraints. The first kind are simple; they just list possible values for a single object. The second kind are more complex; they describe relationships between or among objects. Both kinds of constraints play the same role in the constraint satisfaction process, and in the cryptarithmetic example they were treated identically. For some problems, however, it may be useful to represent the two kinds of constraints differently. The simple, value-listing constraints are always dynamic, and so must always be represented explicitly in each problem state. The more complicated, relationship-expressing constraints are dynamic in the cryptarithmetic domain since they are different for each cryptarithmetic problem. But in many other domains they are static. For example, in the Waltz line labeling algorithm, the only binary constraints arise from the nature of the physical world, in which surfaces can meet in only a fixed number of possible ways. These ways are the same for all pictures that that algorithm may see. Whenever the binary constraints are static, it may be computationally efficient not to represent them explicitly in the state description but rather to encode them in the algorithm directly. When this is done, the only things that get propagated are possible values. But the essential algorithm is the same in both cases.

So far, we have described a fairly simple algorithm for constraint satisfaction in which chronological backtracking is used when guessing leads to an inconsistent set of constraints. An alternative is to use a more sophisticated scheme in which the specific cause of the inconsistency is identified and only constraints that depend on that culprit are undone. Others, even though they may have been generated after the culprit, are left alone if they are independent of the problem and its cause. This approach is called dependency-directed backtracking (DDB). It is described in detail in Section 7.5.1.

3.6   Means-Ends Analysis

So far, we have presented a collection of search strategies that can reason either forward or backward, but for a given problem, one direction or the other must be chosen. Often, however, a mixture of the two directions is appropriate. Such a mixed strategy would make it possible to solve the major parts of a problem first and then go back and solve the small problems that arise in "gluing" the big pieces together. A technique known as *means-ends analysis* allows us to do that.

The means-ends analysis process centers around the detection of differences between the current state and the goal state. Once such a difference is isolated, an operator that can reduce the difference must be found. But perhaps that operator cannot be applied to the current state. So we set up a subproblem of getting to a state in which it can be applied. The kind of backward chaining in which operators are selected and then subgoals are set up to establish the preconditions of the operators is called *operator subgoaling*. But maybe the operator does not produce exactly the goal state we want. Then we have a second subproblem of getting from the state it does produce to the goal. But if the difference was chosen correctly and if the operator is really effective at reducing the difference, then the two subproblems should be easier to solve than the

Operator	Preconditions	Results
PUSH(obj, loc)	at(robot, obj) ∧ large(obj) ∧ clear(obj) ∧ armempty	at(obj, loc) ∧ at(robot, loc)
CARRY(obj, loc)	at(robot, obj) ∧ small(obj)	at(obj, loc) ∧ at(robot, loc)
WALK(loc)	none	at(robot, loc)
PICKUP(obj)	at(robot, obj)	holding(obj)
PUTDOWN(obj)	holding(obj)	¬ holding(obj)
PLACE(obj1, obj2)	at(robot, obj2) ∧ holding(obj1)	on(obj1, obj2)

Figure 3.15: The Robot's Operators

original problem. The means-ends analysis process can then be applied recursively. In order to focus the system's attention on the big problems first, the differences can be assigned priority levels. Differences of higher priority can then be considered before lower priority ones.

The first AI program to exploit means-ends analysis was the General Problem Solver (GPS) [Newell and Simon, 1963; Ernst and Newell, 1969]. Its design was motivated by the observation that people often use this technique when they solve problems. But GPS provides a good example of the fuzziness of the boundary between building programs that simulate what people do and building programs that simply solve a problem any way they can.

Just like the other problem-solving techniques we have discussed, means-ends analysis relies on a set of rules that can transform one problem state into another. These rules are usually not represented with complete state descriptions on each side. Instead, they are represented as a left side that describes the conditions that must be met for the rule to be applicable (these conditions are called the rule's *preconditions*) and a right side that describes those aspects of the problem state that will be changed by the application of the rule. A separate data structure called a *difference table* indexes the rules by the differences that they can be used to reduce.

Consider a simple household robot domain. The available operators are shown in Figure 3.15, along with their preconditions and results. Figure 3.16 shows the difference table that describes when each of the operators is appropriate. Notice that sometimes there may be more than one operator that can reduce a given difference and that a given operator may be able to reduce more than one difference.

Suppose that the robot in this domain were given the problem of moving a desk with two things on it from one room to another. The objects on top must also be moved. The

	Push	Carry	Walk	Pickup	Putdown	Place
Move object	*	*				
Move robot			*			
Clear object				*		
Get object on object						*
Get arm empty					*	*
Be holding object				*		

Figure 3.16: A Difference Table

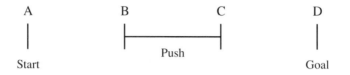

Figure 3.17: The Progress of the Means-Ends Analysis Method

main difference between the start state and the goal state would be the location of the desk. To reduce this difference, either PUSH or CARRY could be chosen. If CARRY is chosen first, its preconditions must be met. This results in two more differences that must be reduced: the location of the robot and the size of the desk. The location of the robot can be handled by applying WALK, but there are no operators than can change the size of an object (since we did not include SAW-APART). So this path leads to a dead-end. Following the other branch, we attempt to apply PUSH. Figure 3.17 shows the problem solver's progress at this point. It has found a way of doing something useful. But it is not yet in a position to do that thing. And the thing does not get it quite to the goal state. So now the differences between A and B and between C and D must be reduced.

PUSH has four preconditions, two of which produce differences between the start and the goal states: the robot must be at the desk, and the desk must be clear. Since the desk is already large, and the robot's arm is empty, those two preconditions can be ignored. The robot can be brought to the correct location by using WALK. And the surface of the desk can be cleared by two uses of PICKUP. But after one PICKUP, an attempt to do the second results in another difference—the arm must be empty. PUTDOWN can be used to reduce that difference.

Once PUSH is performed, the problem state is close to the goal state, but not quite. The objects must be placed back on the desk. PLACE will put them there. But it cannot be applied immediately. Another difference must be eliminated, since the robot must be holding the objects. The progress of the problem solver at this point is shown in Figure 3.18.

The final difference between C and E can be reduced by using WALK to get the robot back to the objects, followed by PICKUP and CARRY.

The process we have just illustrated (which we call MEA for short) can be summarized as follows:

A   B   C   E   D

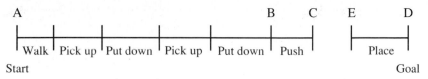

Walk   Pick up   Put down   Pick up   Put down   Push   Place

Start   Goal

Figure 3.18: More Progress of the Means-Ends Method

Algorithm: Means-Ends Analysis (*CURRENT*, *GOAL*)

1. Compare *CURRENT* to *GOAL*. If there are no differences between them then return.

2. Otherwise, select the most important difference and reduce it by doing the following until success or failure is signaled:

   (a) Select an as yet untried operator *O* that is applicable to the current difference. If there are no such operators, then signal failure.

   (b) Attempt to apply *O* to *CURRENT*. Generate descriptions of two states: *O-START*, a state in which *O*'s preconditions are satisfied and *O-RESULT*, the state that would result if *O* were applied in *O-START*.

   (c) If
   (*FIRST-PART* ← MEA(*CURRENT*, *O-START*))
   and
   (*LAST-PART* ← MEA(*O-RESULT*, *GOAL*))
   are successful, then signal success and return the result of concatenating *FIRST-PART*, *O*, and *LAST-PART*.

   Many of the details of this process have been omitted in this discussion. In particular, the order in which differences are considered can be critical. It is important that significant differences be reduced before less critical ones. If this is not done, a great deal of effort may be wasted on situations that take care of themselves once the main parts of the problem are solved.

   The simple process we have described is usually not adequate for solving complex problems. The number of permutations of differences may get too large. Working on one difference may interfere with the plan for reducing another. And in complex worlds, the required difference tables would be immense. In Chapter 13 we look at some ways in which the basic means-ends analysis approach can be extended to tackle some of these problems.

3.7   Summary

In Chapter 2, we listed four steps that must be taken to design a program to solve an AI problem. The first two steps were:

1. Define the problem precisely. Specify the problem space, the operators for moving within the space, and the starting and goal state(s).

2. Analyze the problem to determine where it falls with respect to seven important issues.

The other two steps were to isolate and represent the task knowledge required, and to choose problem solving techniques and apply them to the problem. In this chapter, we began our discussion of the last step of this process by presenting some general-purpose, problem-solving methods. There are several important ways in which these algorithms differ, including:

- What the states in the search space(s) represent. Sometimes the states represent complete potential solutions (as in hill climbing). Sometimes they represent solutions that are partially specified (as in constraint satisfaction).

- How, at each stage of the search process, a state is selected for expansion.

- How operators to be applied to that node are selected.

- Whether an optimal solution can be guaranteed.

- Whether a given state may end up being considered more than once.

- How many state descriptions must be maintained throughout the search process.

- Under what circumstances should a particular search path be abandoned.

In the chapters that follow, we talk about ways that knowledge about task domains can be encoded in problem-solving programs and we discuss techniques for combining problem-solving techniques with knowledge to solve several important classes of problems.

3.8   Exercises

1. When would best-first search be worse than simple breadth-first search?

2. Suppose we have a problem that we intend to solve using a heuristic best-first search procedure. We need to decide whether to implement it as a tree search or as a graph search. Suppose that we know that, on the average, each distinct node will be generated N times during the search process. We also know that if we use a graph, it will take, on the average, the same amount of time to check a node to see if it has already been generated as it takes to process M nodes if no checking is done. How can we decide whether to use a tree or a graph? In addition to the parameters N and M, what other assumptions must be made?

3. Consider trying to solve the 8-puzzle using hill climbing. Can you find a heuristic function that makes this work? Make sure it works on the following example:

Start   Goal

1	2	3
8	5	6
4	7	

1	2	3
4	5	6
7	8	

4. Describe the behavior of a revised version of the steepest ascent hill climbing algorithm in which step 2(c) is replaced by "set current state to best successor."

5. Suppose that the first step of the operation of the best-first search algorithm results in the following situation ($a + b$ means that the value of h' at a node is a and the value of g is b):

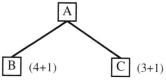

The second and third steps then result in the following sequence of situations:

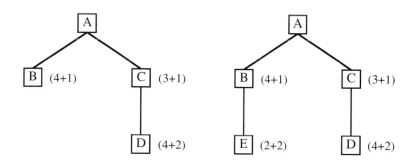

   (a) What node will be expanded at the next step?

   (b) Can we guarantee that the best solution will be found?

6. Why must the A* algorithm work properly on graphs containing cycles? Cycles could be prevented if when a new path is generated to an existing node, that path were simply thrown away if it is no better than the existing recorded one. If g is nonnegative, a cyclic path can never be better than the same path with the cycle omitted. For example, consider the first graph shown below, in which the nodes were generated in alphabetical order. The fact that node D is a successor of node F could simply not be recorded since the path through node F is longer than the one through node B. This same reasoning would also prevent us from recording node E as a successor of node F, if such was the case. But what would happen in the situation shown in the second graph below if the path from node G to node F were not recorded and, at the next step, it were discovered that node G

is a successor of node C?

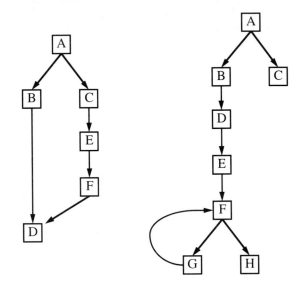

7. Formalize the Graceful Decay of Admissibility Corollary and prove that it is true of the A* algorithm.

8. In step 2(*a*) of the AO* algorithm, a random state at the end of the current best path is chosen for expansion. But there are heuristics that can be used to influence this choice. For example, it may make sense to choose the state whose current cost estimate is the lowest. The argument for this is that for such nodes, only a few steps are required before either a solution is found or a revised cost estimate is produced. With nodes whose current cost estimate is large, on the other hand, many steps may be required before any new information is obtained. How would the algorithm have to be changed to implement this state-selection heuristic?

9. The backward cost propagation step 2(*c*) of the AO* algorithm must be guaranteed to terminate even on graphs containing cycles. How can we guarantee that it does? To help answer this question, consider what happens for the following two graphs, assuming in each case that node F is expanded next and that its only successor is A:

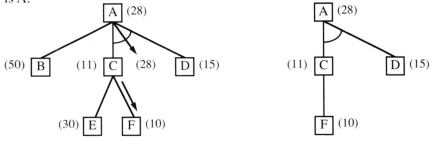

Also consider what happens in the following graph if the cost of node C is changed to 3:

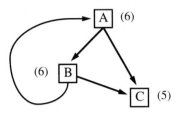

10. The AO* algorithm, in step 2(c)i, requires that a node with no descendants in S be selected from S, if possible. How should the manipulation of S be implemented so that such a node can be chosen efficiently? Make sure that your technique works correctly on the following graph, if the cost of node E is changed:

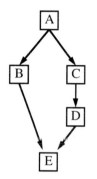

11. Consider again the AO* algorithm. Under what circumstances will it happen that there are nodes in S but there are no nodes in S that have no descendants also in S?

12. Trace the constraint satisfaction procedure solving the following cryptarithmetic problem:

```
  CROSS
 +ROADS
 ------
 DANGER
```

13. The constraint satisfaction procedure we have described performs depth-first search whenever some kind of search is necessary. But depth-first is not the only way to conduct such a search (although it is perhaps the simplest).

    (a) Rewrite the constraint satisfaction procedure to use breadth-first search.

    (b) Rewrite the constraint satisfaction procedure to use best-first search.

14. Show how means-ends analysis could be used to solve the problem of getting from one place to another. Assume that the available operators are walk, drive, take the bus, take a cab, and fly.

Part II

Knowledge Representation

Chapter 4

Knowledge Representation Issues

In Chapter 1, we discussed the role that knowledge plays in AI systems. In succeeding chapters up until now, though, we have paid little attention to knowledge and its importance as we instead focused on basic frameworks for building search based problem-solving programs. These methods are sufficiently general that we have been able to discuss them without reference to how the knowledge they need is to be represented. For example, in discussing the best-first search algorithm, we hid all the references to domain specific knowledge in the generation of successors and the computation of the h' function. Although these methods are useful and form the skeleton of many of the methods we are about to discuss, their problem-solving power is limited precisely because of their generality. As we look in more detail at ways of representing knowledge, it becomes clear that particular knowledge representation models allow for more specific, more powerful problem-solving mechanisms that operate on them. In this part of the book, we return to the topic of knowledge and examine specific techniques that can be used for representing and manipulating knowledge within programs.

4.1 Representations and Mappings

In order to solve the complex problems encountered in artificial intelligence, one needs both a large amount of knowledge and some mechanisms for manipulating that knowledge to create solutions to new problems. A variety of ways of representing knowledge (facts) have been exploited in AI programs. But before we can talk about them individually, we must consider the following point that pertains to all discussions of representation, namely that we are dealing with two different kinds of entities:

- Facts: truths in some relevant world. These are the things we want to represent.

- Representations of facts in some chosen formalism. These are the things we will actually be able to manipulate.

One way to think of structuring these entities is as two levels:

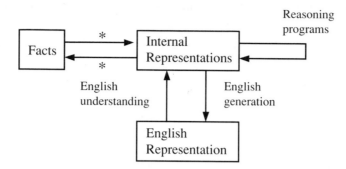

Figure 4.1: Mappings between Facts and Representations

- The *knowledge level*, at which facts (including each agent's behaviors and current goals) are described.

- The *symbol level*, at which representations of objects at the knowledge level are defined in terms of symbols that can be manipulated by programs.

See Newell [1982] for a detailed exposition of this view in the context of agents and their goals and behaviors. In the rest of our discussion here, we will follow a model more like the one shown in Figure 4.1. Rather than thinking of one level on top of another, we will focus on facts, on representations, and on the two-way mappings that must exist between them. We will call these links *representation mappings*. The forward representation mapping maps from facts to representations. The backward representation mapping goes the other way, from representations to facts.

One representation of facts is so common that it deserves special mention: natural language (particularly English) sentences. Regardless of the representation for facts that we use in a program, we may also need to be concerned with an English representation of those facts in order to facilitate getting information into and out of the system. In this case, we must also have mapping functions from English sentences to the representation we are actually going to use and from it back to sentences. Figure 4.1 shows how these three kinds of objects relate to each other.

Let's look at a simple example using mathematical logic as the representational formalism. Consider the English sentence:

Spot is a dog.

The fact represented by that English sentence can also be represented in logic as:

dog(Spot)

Suppose that we also have a logical representation of the fact that all dogs have tails:

$\forall x : dog(x) \rightarrow hastail(x)$

Then, using the deductive mechanisms of logic, we may generate the new representation object:

hastail(*Spot*)

Using an appropriate backward mapping function, we could then generate the English sentence:

Spot has a tail.

Or we could make use of this representation of a new fact to cause us to take some appropriate action or to derive representations of additional facts.

It is important to keep in mind that usually the available mapping functions are not one-to-one. In fact, they are often not even functions but rather many-to-many relations. (In other words, each object in the domain may map to several elements in the range, and several elements in the domain may map to the same element of the range.) This is particularly true of the mappings involving English representations of facts. For example, the two sentences "All dogs have tails" and "Every dog has a tail" could both represent the same fact, namely that every dog has at least one tail. On the other hand, the former could represent either the fact that every dog has at least one tail or the fact that each dog has several tails. The latter may represent either the fact that every dog has at least one tail or the fact that there is a tail that every dog has. As we will see shortly, when we try to convert English sentences into some other representation, such as logical propositions, we must first decide what facts the sentences represent and then convert those facts into the new representation.

The starred links of Figure 4.1 are key components of the design of any knowledge-based program. To see why, we need to understand the role that the internal representation of a fact plays in a program. What an AI program does is to manipulate the internal representations of the facts it is given. This manipulation should result in new structures that can also be interpreted as internal representations of facts. More precisely, these structures should be the internal representations of facts that correspond to the answer to the problem described by the starting set of facts.

Sometimes, a good representation makes the operation of a reasoning program not only correct but trivial. A well-known example of this occurs in the context of the mutilated checkerboard problem, which can be stated as follows:

> **The Mutilated Checkerboard Problem.** Consider a normal checker board from which two squares, in opposite corners, have been removed. The task is to cover all the remaining squares exactly with dominoes, each of which covers two squares. No overlapping, either of dominoes on top of each other or of dominoes over the boundary of the mutilated board are allowed. Can this task be done?

One way to solve this problem is to try to enumerate, exhaustively, all possible tilings to see if one works. But suppose one wants to be more clever. Figure 4.2 shows three ways in which the mutilated checkerboard could be represented (to a person). The first

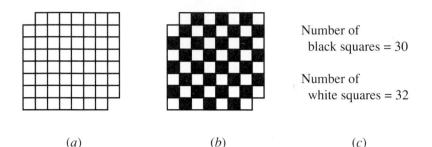

(a)   (b)   (c)

Figure 4.2: Three Representations of a Mutilated Checkerboard

representation does not directly suggest the answer to the problem. The second may; the third does, when combined with the single additional fact that each domino must cover exactly one white square and one black square. Even for human problem solvers a representation shift may make an enormous difference in problem-solving effectiveness. Recall that we saw a slightly less dramatic version of this phenomenon with respect to a problem-solving program in Section 1.3.1, where we considered two different ways of representing a tic-tac-toe board, one of which was as a magic square.

Figure 4.3 shows an expanded view of the starred part of Figure 4.1. The dotted line across the top represents the abstract reasoning process that a program is intended to model. The solid line across the bottom represents the concrete reasoning process that a particular program performs. This program successfully models the abstract process to the extent that, when the backward representation mapping is applied to the program's output, the appropriate final facts are actually generated. If either the program's operation or one of the representation mappings is not faithful to the problem that is being modeled, then the final facts will probably not be the desired ones. The key role that is played by the nature of the representation mapping is apparent from this figure. If no good mapping can be defined for a problem, then no matter how good the program to solve the problem is, it will not be able to produce answers that correspond to real answers to the problem.

It is interesting to note that Figure 4.3 looks very much like the sort of figure that might appear in a general programming book as a description of the relationship between an abstract data type (such as a set) and a concrete implementation of that type (e.g., as a linked list of elements). There are some differences, though, between this figure and the formulation usually used in programming texts (such as Aho *et al.* [1983]). For example, in data type design it is expected that the mapping that we are calling the backward representation mapping is a function (i.e., every representation corresponds to only one fact) and that it is onto (i.e., there is at least one representation for every fact). Unfortunately, in many AI domains, it may not be possible to come up with such a representation mapping, and we may have to live with one that gives less ideal results. But the main idea of what we are doing is the same as what programmers always do, namely to find concrete implementations of abstract concepts.

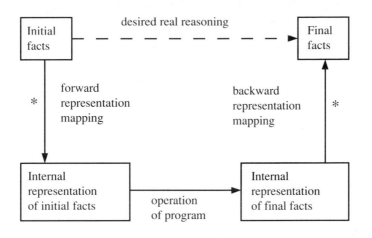

Figure 4.3: Representation of Facts

4.2 Approaches to Knowledge Representation

A good system for the representation of knowledge in a particular domain should possess the following four properties:

Representational Adequacy—the ability to represent all of the kinds of knowledge that are needed in that domain.

Inferential Adequacy—the ability to manipulate the representational structures in such a way as to derive new structures corresponding to new knowledge inferred from old.

Inferential Efficiency—the ability to incorporate into the knowledge structure additional information that can be used to focus the attention of the inference mechanisms in the most promising directions.

Acquisitional Efficiency—the ability to acquire new information easily. The simplest case involves direct insertion, by a person, of new knowledge into the database. Ideally, the program itself would be able to control knowledge acquisition.

Unfortunately, no single system that optimizes all of the capabilities for all kinds of knowledge has yet been found. As a result, multiple techniques for knowledge representation exist. Many programs rely on more than one technique. In the chapters that follow, the most important of these techniques are described in detail. But in this section, we provide a simple, example-based introduction to the important ideas.

Simple Relational Knowledge

The simplest way to represent declarative facts is as a set of relations of the same sort used in database systems. Figure 4.4 shows an example of such a relational system.

Player	Height	Weight	Bats-Throws
Hank Aaron	6-0	180	Right-Right
Willie Mays	5-10	170	Right-Right
Babe Ruth	6-2	215	Left-Left
Ted Williams	6-3	205	Left-Right

Figure 4.4: Simple Relational Knowledge

The reason that this representation is simple is that standing alone it provides very weak inferential capabilities. But knowledge represented in this form may serve as the input to more powerful inference engines. For example, given just the facts of Figure 4.4, it is not possible even to answer the simple question, "Who is the heaviest player?" But if a procedure for finding the heaviest player is provided, then these facts will enable the procedure to compute an answer. If, instead, we are provided with a set of rules for deciding which hitter to put up against a given pitcher (based on right- and left-handedness, say), then this same relation can provide at least some of the information required by those rules.

Providing support for relational knowledge is what database systems are designed to do. Thus we do not need to discuss this kind of knowledge representation structure further here. The practical issues that arise in linking a database system that provides this kind of support to a knowledge representation system that provides some of the other capabilities that we are about to discuss have already been solved in several commercial products.

Inheritable Knowledge

The relational knowledge of Figure 4.4 corresponds to a set of attributes and associated values that together describe the objects of the knowledge base. Knowledge about objects, their attributes, and their values need not be as simple as that shown in our example. In particular, it is possible to augment the basic representation with inference mechanisms that operate on the structure of the representation. For this to be effective, the structure must be designed to correspond to the inference mechanisms that are desired. One of the most useful forms of inference is *property inheritance*, in which elements of specific classes inherit attributes and values from more general classes in which they are included.

In order to support property inheritance, objects must be organized into classes and classes must be arranged in a generalization hierarchy. Figure 4.5 shows some additional baseball knowledge inserted into a structure that is so arranged. Lines represent attributes. Boxed nodes represent objects and values of attributes of objects. These values can also be viewed as objects with attributes and values, and so on. The arrows on the lines point from an object to its value along the corresponding attribute line. The structure shown in the figure is a *slot-and-filler structure*. It may also be called a *semantic network* or a collection of *frames*. In the latter case, each individual frame represents the collection of attributes and values associated with a particular node. Figure 4.6 shows the node for baseball player displayed as a frame.

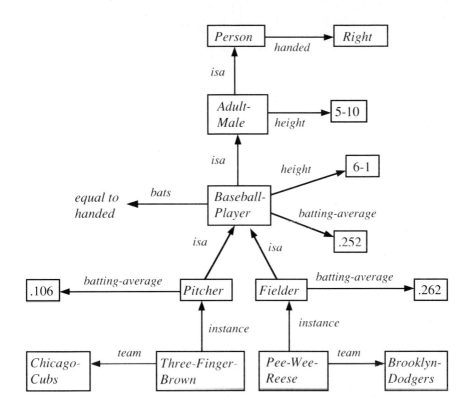

Figure 4.5: Inheritable Knowledge

Do not be put off by the confusion in terminology here. There is so much flexibility in the way that this (and the other structures described in this section) can be used to solve particular representation problems that it is difficult to reserve precise words for particular representations. Usually the use of the term *frame system* implies somewhat more structure on the attributes and the inference mechanisms that are available to apply to them than does the term *semantic network*.

In Chapter 9 we discuss structures such as these in substantial detail. But to get an idea of how these structures support inference using the knowledge they contain, we discuss them briefly here. All of the objects and most of the attributes shown in this example have been chosen to correspond to the baseball domain, and they have no general significance. The two exceptions to this are the attribute *isa*, which is being used to show class inclusion, and the attribute *instance*, which is being used to show class membership. These two specific (and generally useful) attributes provide the basis for property inheritance as an inference technique. Using this technique, the knowledge base can support retrieval both of facts that have been explicitly stored and of facts that can be derived from those that are explicitly stored.

An idealized form of the property inheritance algorithm can be stated as follows.

Baseball-Player
    isa :   *Adult-Male*
    bats :   (EQUAL *handed*)
    height :   6-1
    batting-average :   .252

Figure 4.6: Viewing a Node as a Frame

Algorithm: Property Inheritance

To retrieve a value *V* for attribute *A* of an instance object *O*:

1. Find *O* in the knowledge base.

2. If there is a value there for the attribute *A*, report that value.

3. Otherwise, see if there is a value for the attribute *instance*. If not, then fail.

4. Otherwise, move to the node corresponding to that value and look for a value for the attribute *A*. If one is found, report it.

5. Otherwise, do until there is no value for the *isa* attribute or until an answer is found:

   (a) Get the value of the *isa* attribute and move to that node.

   (b) See if there is a value for the attribute *A*. If there is, report it.

This procedure is simplistic. It does not say what we should do if there is more than one value of the *instance* or *isa* attribute. But it does describe the basic mechanism of inheritance. We can apply this procedure to our example knowledge base to derive answers to the following queries:

- *team(Pee-Wee-Reese)* = *Brooklyn-Dodgers*. This attribute had a value stored explicitly in the knowledge base.

- *batting-average(Three-Finger-Brown)* = .106. Since there is no value for batting average stored explicitly for Three Finger Brown, we follow the *instance* attribute to *Pitcher* and extract the value stored there. Now we observe one of the critical characteristics of property inheritance, namely that it may produce default values that are not guaranteed to be correct but that represent "best guesses" in the face of a lack of more precise information. In fact, in 1906, Brown's batting average was .204.

- *height(Pee-Wee-Reese)* = 6-1. This represents another default inference. Notice here that because we get to it first, the more specific fact about the height of baseball players overrides a more general fact about the height of adult males.

$$\forall x : Ball(x) \land Fly(x) \land Fair(x) \land Infield\text{-}Catchable\,(x) \land$$
$$Occupied\text{-}Base(First) \land Occupied\text{-}Base(Second) \land (Outs < 2) \land$$
$$\neg[Line\text{-}Drive(x) \lor Attempted\text{-}Bunt(x)]$$
$$\rightarrow Infield\text{-}Fly(x)$$

$$\forall x, y : Batter(x) \land batted(x, y) \land Infield\text{-}Fly(y) \rightarrow Out(x)$$

Figure 4.7: Inferential Knowledge

- *bats(Three-Finger-Brown) = Right.* To get a value for the attribute *bats* required going up the *isa* hierarchy to the class *Baseball-Player*. But what we found there was not a value but a rule for computing a value. This rule required another value (that for *handed*) as input. So the entire process must be begun again recursively to find a value for *handed*. This time, it is necessary to go all the way up to *Person* to discover that the default value for handedness for people is *Right*. Now the rule for *bats* can be applied, producing the result *Right*. In this case, that turns out to be wrong, since Brown is a switch hitter (i.e., he can hit both left- and right-handed).

Inferential Knowledge

Property inheritance is a powerful form of inference, but it is not the only useful form. Sometimes all the power of traditional logic (and sometimes even more than that) is necessary to describe the inferences that are needed. Figure 4.7 shows two examples of the use of first-order predicate logic to represent additional knowledge about baseball.

Of course, this knowledge is useless unless there is also an inference procedure that can exploit it (just as the default knowledge in the previous example would have been useless without our algorithm for moving through the knowledge structure). The required inference procedure now is one that implements the standard logical rules of inference. There are many such procedures, some of which reason forward from given facts to conclusions, others of which reason backward from desired conclusions to given facts. One of the most commonly used of these procedures is *resolution*, which exploits a proof by contradiction strategy. Resolution is described in detail in Chapter 5.

Recall that we hinted at the need for something besides stored primitive values with the *bats* attribute of our previous example. Logic provides a powerful structure in which to describe relationships among values. It is often useful to combine this, or some other powerful description language, with an *isa* hierarchy. In general, in fact, all of the techniques we are describing here should not be regarded as complete and incompatible ways of representing knowledge. Instead, they should be viewed as building blocks of a complete representational system.

Procedural Knowledge

So far, our examples of baseball knowledge have concentrated on relatively static, declarative facts. But another, equally useful, kind of knowledge is operational, or procedural knowledge, that specifies what to do when. Procedural knowledge can be

Baseball-Player
   isa :   *Adult-Male*
   bats :   (lambda (x)

```
          (prog ()
       L1
       (cond ((caddr x) (return (caddr x)))
             (t (setq x (eval (cadr x)))
             (cond (x (go L1))
                   (t (return nil)))))))))
```

   height :   6-1
   batting-average :   .252

Figure 4.8: Using LISP Code to Define a Value

represented in programs in many ways. The most common way is simply as code (in some programming language such as LISP) for doing something. The machine uses the knowledge when it executes the code to perform a task. Unfortunately, this way of representing procedural knowledge gets low scores with respect to the properties of inferential adequacy (because it is very difficult to write a program that can reason about another program's behavior) and acquisitional efficiency (because the process of updating and debugging large pieces of code becomes unwieldy).

As an extreme example, compare the representation of the way to compute the value of *bats* shown in Figure 4.6 to one in LISP shown in Figure 4.8. Although the LISP one will work given a particular way of storing attributes and values in a list, it does not lend itself to being reasoned about in the same straightforward way as the representation of Figure 4.6 does. The LISP representation is slightly more powerful since it makes explicit use of the name of the node whose value for *handed* is to be found. But if this matters, the simpler representation can be augmented to do this as well.

Because of this difficulty in reasoning with LISP, attempts have been made to find other ways of representing procedural knowledge so that it can relatively easily be manipulated both by other programs and by people.

The most commonly used technique for representing procedural knowledge in AI programs is the use of production rules. Figure 4.9 shows an example of a production rule that represents a piece of operational knowledge typically possessed by a baseball player.

Production rules, particularly ones that are augmented with information on how they are to be used, are more procedural than are the other representation methods discussed in this chapter. But making a clean distinction between declarative and procedural knowledge is difficult. Although at an intuitive level such a distinction makes some sense, at a formal level it disappears, as discussed in Section 6.1. In fact, as you can see, the structure of the declarative knowledge of Figure 4.7 is not substantially different from that of the operational knowledge of Figure 4.9. The important difference is in how the knowledge is used by the procedures that manipulate it.

If: ninth inning, and
         score is close, and
         less than 2 outs, and
         first base is vacant, and
         batter is better hitter than next batter,
Then: walk the batter.

Figure 4.9: Procedural Knowledge as Rules

4.3   Issues in Knowledge Representation

Before embarking on a discussion of specific mechanisms that have been used to represent various kinds of real-world knowledge, we need briefly to discuss several issues that cut across all of them:

- Are any attributes of objects so basic that they occur in almost every problem domain? If there are, we need to make sure that they are handled appropriately in each of the mechanisms we propose. If such attributes exist, what are they?

- Are there any important relationships that exist among attributes of objects?

- At what level should knowledge be represented? Is there a good set of *primitives* into which all knowledge can be broken down? Is it helpful to use such primitives?

- How should sets of objects be represented?

- Given a large amount of knowledge stored in a database, how can relevant parts be accessed when they are needed?

We will talk about each of these questions briefly in the next five sections.

4.3.1   Important Attributes

There are two attributes that are of very general significance, and we have already seen their use: *instance* and *isa*. These attributes are important because they support property inheritance. They are called a variety of things in AI systems, but the names do not matter. What does matter is that they represent class membership and class inclusion and that class inclusion is transitive. In slot-and-filler systems, such as those described in Chapters 9 and 10, these attributes are usually represented explicitly in a way much like that shown in Figures 4.5 and 4.6. In logic-based systems, these relationships may be represented this way or they may be represented implicitly by a set of predicates describing particular classes. See Section 5.2 for some examples of this.

4.3.2   Relationships among Attributes

The attributes that we use to describe objects are themselves entities that we represent. What properties do they have independent of the specific knowledge they encode? There are four such properties that deserve mention here:

- Inverses

- Existence in an *isa* hierarchy

- Techniques for reasoning about values

- Single-valued attributes

Inverses

Entities in the world are related to each other in many different ways. But as soon as we decide to describe those relationships as attributes, we commit to a perspective in which we focus on one object and look for binary relationships between it and others. Attributes are those relationships. So, for example, in Figure 4.5, we used the attributes *instance*, *isa*, and *team*. Each of these was shown in the figure with a directed arrow, originating at the object that was being described and terminating at the object representing the value of the specified attribute. But we could equally well have focused on the object representing the value. If we do that, then there is still a relationship between the two entities, although it is a different one since the original relationship was not symmetric (although some relationships, such as *sibling*, are). In many cases, it is important to represent this other view of relationships. There are two good ways to do this.

The first is to represent both relationships in a single representation that ignores focus. Logical representations are usually interpreted as doing this. For example, the assertion:

   team(Pee-Wee-Reese, Brooklyn-Dodgers)

can equally easily be interpreted as a statement about Pee Wee Reese or about the Brooklyn Dodgers. How it is actually used depends on the other assertions that a system contains.

The second approach is to use attributes that focus on a single entity but to use them in pairs, one the inverse of the other. In this approach, we would represent the team information with two attributes:

- one associated with Pee Wee Reese:

   team = Brooklyn-Dodgers

- one associated with Brooklyn Dodgers:

   team-members = Pee-Wee-Reese, . . .

This is the approach that is taken in semantic net and frame-based systems. When it is used, it is usually accompanied by a knowledge acquisition tool that guarantees the consistency of inverse slots by forcing them to be declared and then checking each time a value is added to one attribute that the corresponding value is added to the inverse.

An Isa Hierarchy of Attributes

Just as there are classes of objects and specialized subsets of those classes, there are attributes and specializations of attributes. Consider, for example, the attribute *height*. It is actually a specialization of the more general attribute *physical-size* which is, in turn, a specialization of *physical-attribute*. These generalization-specialization relationships are important for attributes for the same reason that they are important for other concepts—they support inheritance. In the case of attributes, they support inheriting information about such things as constraints on the values that the attribute can have and mechanisms for computing those values.

Techniques for Reasoning about Values

Sometimes values of attributes are specified explicitly when a knowledge base is created. We saw several examples of that in the baseball example of Figure 4.5. But often the reasoning system must reason about values it has not been given explicitly. Several kinds of information can play a role in this reasoning, including:

- Information about the type of the value. For example, the value of *height* must be a number measured in a unit of length.

- Constraints on the value, often stated in terms of related entities. For example, the age of a person cannot be greater than the age of either of that person's parents.

- Rules for computing the value when it is needed. We showed an example of such a rule in Figure 4.5 for the *bats* attribute. These rules are called *backward* rules. Such rules have also been called *if-needed rules*.

- Rules that describe actions that should be taken if a value ever becomes known. These rules are called *forward* rules, or sometimes *if-added rules*.

We discuss forward and backward rules again in Chapter 6, in the context of rule-based knowledge representation.

Single-Valued Attributes

A specific but very useful kind of attribute is one that is guaranteed to take a unique value. For example, a baseball player can, at any one time, have only a single height and be a member of only one team. If there is already a value present for one of these attributes and a different value is asserted, then one of two things has happened. Either a change has occurred in the world or there is now a contradiction in the knowledge base that needs to be resolved. Knowledge-representation systems have taken several different approaches to providing support for single-valued attributes, including:

- Introduce an explicit notation for temporal interval. If two different values are ever asserted for the same temporal interval, signal a contradiction automatically.

- Assume that the only temporal interval that is of interest is now. So if a new value is asserted, replace the old value.

- Provide no explicit support. Logic-based systems are in this category. But in these systems, knowledge-base builders can add axioms that state that if an attribute has one value then it is known not to have all other values.

4.3.3   Choosing the Granularity of Representation

Regardless of the particular representation formalism we choose, it is necessary to answer the question "At what level of detail should the world be represented?" Another way this question is often phrased is "What should be our primitives?" Should there be a small number of low-level ones or should there be a larger number covering a range of granularities? A brief example illustrates the problem. Suppose we are interested in the following fact:

John spotted Sue.

We could represent this as[1]

$$spotted(agent(John),$$
$$object(Sue))$$

Such a representation would make it easy to answer questions such as:

Who spotted Sue?

But now suppose we want to know:

Did John see Sue?

The obvious answer is "yes," but given only the one fact we have, we cannot discover that answer. We could, of course, add other facts, such as

$$spotted(x, y) \rightarrow saw(x, y)$$

We could then infer the answer to the question.

An alternative solution to this problem is to represent the fact that spotting is really a special type of seeing explicitly in the representation of the fact. We might write something such as

$$saw(agent(John),$$
$$object(Sue),$$
$$timespan(briefly))$$

---

[1]The arguments *agent* and *object* are usually called *cases*. They represent roles involved in the event. This semantic way of analyzing sentences contrasts with the probably more familiar syntactic approach in which sentences have a surface subject, direct object, indirect object, and so forth. We will discuss case grammar [Fillmore, 1968] and its use in natural language understanding in Section 15.3.2. For the moment, you can safely assume that the cases mean what their names suggest.

In this representation, we have broken the idea of *spotting* apart into more primitive concepts of *seeing* and *timespan*. Using this representation, the fact that John saw Sue is immediately accessible. But the fact that he spotted her is more difficult to get to.

The major advantage of converting all statements into a representation in terms of a small set of primitives is that the rules that are used to derive inferences from that knowledge need be written only in terms of the primitives rather than in terms of the many ways in which the knowledge may originally have appeared. Thus what is really being argued for is simply some sort of canonical form. Several AI programs, including those described by Schank and Abelson [1977] and Wilks [1972], are based on knowledge bases described in terms of a small number of low-level primitives.

There are several arguments against the use of low-level primitives. One is that simple high-level facts may require a lot of storage when broken down into primitives. Much of that storage is really wasted since the low-level rendition of a particular high-level concept will appear many times, once for each time the high-level concept is referenced. For example, suppose that actions are being represented as combinations of a small set of primitive actions. Then the fact that John punched Mary might be represented as shown in Figure 4.10(*a*). The representation says that there was physical contact between John's fist and Mary. The contact was caused by John propelling his fist toward Mary, and in order to do that John first went to where Mary was.[2] But suppose we also know that Mary punched John. Then we must also store the structure shown in Figure 4.10(*b*). If, however, punching were represented simply as punching, then most of the detail of both structures could be omitted from the structures themselves. It could instead be stored just once in a common representation of the concept of punching.

A second but related problem is that if knowledge is initially presented to the system in a relatively high-level form, such as English, then substantial work must be done to reduce the knowledge into primitive form. Yet, for many purposes, this detailed primitive representation may be unnecessary. Both in understanding language and in interpreting the world that we see, many things appear that later turn out to be irrelevant. For the sake of efficiency, it may be desirable to store these things at a very high level and then to analyze in detail only those inputs that appear to be important.

A third problem with the use of low-level primitives is that in many domains, it is not at all clear what the primitives should be. And even in domains in which there may be an obvious set of primitives, there may not be enough information present in each use of the high-level constructs to enable them to be converted into their primitive components. When this is true, there is no way to avoid representing facts at a variety of granularities.

The classical example of this sort of situation is provided by kinship terminology [Lindsay, 1963]. There exists at least one obvious set of primitives: mother, father, son, daughter, and possibly brother and sister. But now suppose we are told that Mary is Sue's cousin. An attempt to describe the cousin relationship in terms of the primitives could produce any of the following interpretations:

- Mary = *daughter*(*brother*(*mother*(Sue)))

- Mary = *daughter*(*sister*(*mother*(Sue)))

---

[2]The representation shown in this example is called *conceptual dependency* and is discussed in detail in Section 10.1.

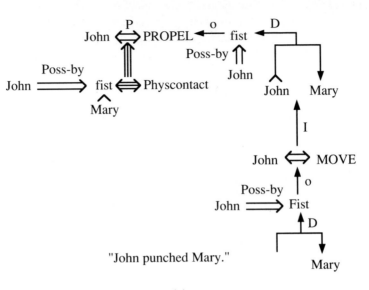

"John punched Mary."

(*a*)

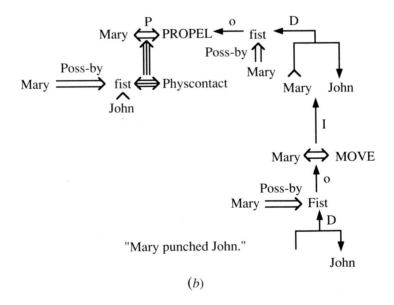

"Mary punched John."

(*b*)

Figure 4.10: Redundant Representations

- Mary = *daughter*(*brother*(*father*(Sue)))

- Mary = *daughter*(*sister*(*father*(Sue)))

If we do not already know that Mary is female, then of course there are four more possibilities as well. Since in general we may have no way of choosing among these representations, we have no choice but to represent the fact using the nonprimitive relation *cousin*.

The other way to solve this problem is to change our primitives. We could use the set: *parent*, *child*, *sibling*, *male*, and *female*. Then the fact that Mary is Sue's cousin could be represented as

- Mary = *child*(*sibling*(*parent*(Sue)))

But now the primitives incorporate some generalizations that may or may not be appropriate. The main point to be learned from this example is that even in very simple domains, the correct set of primitives is not obvious.

In less well-structured domains, even more problems arise. For example, given just the fact

John broke the window.

a program would not be able to decide if John's actions consisted of the primitive sequence:

1. Pick up a hard object.

2. Hurl the object through the window.

or the sequence:

1. Pick up a hard object.

2. Hold onto the object while causing it to crash into the window.

or the single action:

1. Cause hand (or foot) to move fast and crash into the window.

or the single action:

1. Shut the window so hard that the glass breaks.

As these examples have shown, the problem of choosing the correct granularity of representation for a particular body of knowledge is not easy. Clearly, the lower the level we choose, the less inference required to reason with it in some cases, but the more inference required to create the representation from English and the more room it takes to store, since many inferences will be represented many times. The answer for any particular task domain must come to a large extent from the domain itself—to what use is the knowledge to be put?

One way of looking at the question of whether there exists a good set of low-level primitives is that it is a question of the existence of a unique representation. Does there exist a single, canonical way in which large bodies of knowledge can be represented independently of how they were originally stated? Another, closely related, uniqueness question asks whether individual objects can be represented uniquely and independently of how they are described. This issue is raised in the following quotation from Quine [1961] and discussed in Woods [1975]:

> The phrase *Evening Star* names a certain large physical object of spherical form, which is hurtling through space some scores of millions of miles from here. The phrase *Morning Star* names the same thing, as was probably first established by some observant Babylonian. But the two phrases cannot be regarded as having the same meaning; otherwise that Babylonian could have dispensed with his observations and contented himself with reflecting on the meaning of his words. The meanings, then, being different from one another, must be other than the named object, which is one and the same in both cases.

In order for a program to be able to reason as did the Babylonian, it must be able to handle several distinct representations that turn out to stand for the same object.

We discuss the question of the correct granularity of representation, as well as issues involving redundant storage of information, throughout the next several chapters, particularly in the section on conceptual dependency, since that theory explicitly proposes that a small set of low-level primitives should be used for representing actions.

4.3.4   Representing Sets of Objects

It is important to be able to represent sets of objects for several reasons. One is that there are some properties that are true of sets that are not true of the individual members of a set. As examples, consider the assertions that are being made in the sentences "There are more sheep than people in Australia" and "English speakers can be found all over the world." The only way to represent the facts described in these sentences is to attach assertions to the sets representing people, sheep, and English speakers, since, for example, no single English speaker can be found all over the world. The other reason that it is important to be able to represent sets of objects is that if a property is true of all (or even most) elements of a set, then it is more efficient to associate it once with the set rather than to associate it explicitly with every element of the set. We have already looked at ways of doing that, both in logical representations through the use of the universal quantifier and in slot-and-filler structures, where we used nodes to represent sets and inheritance to propagate set-level assertions down to individuals. As we consider ways to represent sets, we will want to consider both of these uses of set-level representations. We will also need to remember that the two uses must be kept distinct. Thus if we assert something like *large(Elephant)*, it must be clear whether we are asserting some property of the set itself (i.e., that the set of elephants is large) or some property that holds for individual elements of the set (i.e., that anything that is an elephant is large).

There are three obvious ways in which sets may be represented. The simplest is just by a name. This is essentially what we did in Section 4.2 when we used the node named *Baseball-Player* in our semantic net and when we used predicates such as *Ball* and

Batter in our logical representation. This simple representation does make it possible to associate predicates with sets. But it does not, by itself, provide any information about the set it represents. It does not, for example, tell how to determine whether a particular object is a member of the set or not.

There are two ways to state a definition of a set and its elements. The first is to list the members. Such a specification is called an *extensional* definition. The second is to provide a rule that, when a particular object is evaluated, returns true or false depending on whether the object is in the set or not. Such a rule is called an *intensional* definition. For example, an extensional description of the set of our sun's planets on which people live is $\{Earth\}$. An intensional description is

$$\{x : sun\text{-}planet(x) \land human\text{-}inhabited(x)\}$$

For simple sets, it may not matter, except possibly with respect to efficiency concerns, which representation is used. But the two kinds of representations can function differently in some cases.

One way in which extensional and intensional representations differ is that they do not necessarily correspond one-to-one with each other. For example, the extensionally defined set $\{Earth\}$ has many intensional definitions in addition to the one we just gave. Others include:

$$\{x : sun\text{-}planet(x) \land nth\text{-}farthest\text{-}from\text{-}sun(x, 3)\}$$
$$\{x : sun\text{-}planet(x) \land nth\text{-}biggest(x, 5)\}$$

Thus, while it is trivial to determine whether two sets are identical if extensional descriptions are used, it may be very difficult to do so using intensional descriptions.

Intensional representations have two important properties that extensional ones lack, however. The first is that they can be used to describe infinite sets and sets not all of whose elements are explicitly known. Thus we can describe intensionally such sets as prime numbers (of which there are infinitely many) or kings of England (even though we do not know who all of them are or even how many of them there have been). The second thing we can do with intensional descriptions is to allow them to depend on parameters that can change, such as time or spatial location. If we do that, then the actual set that is represented by the description will change as a function of the value of those parameters. To see the effect of this, consider the sentence, "The president of the United States used to be a Democrat," uttered when the current president is a Republican. This sentence can mean two things. The first is that the specific person who is now president was once a Democrat. This meaning can be captured straightforwardly with an extensional representation of "the president of the United States." We just specify the individual. But there is a second meaning, namely that there was once someone who was the president and who was a Democrat. To represent the meaning of "the president of the United States" given this interpretation requires an intensional description that depends on time. Thus we might write *president(t)*, where *president* is some function that maps instances of time onto instances of people, namely U.S. presidents.

4.3.5   Finding the Right Structures as Needed

Recall that in Chapter 2, we briefly touched on the problem of matching rules against state descriptions during the problem-solving process. This same issue now rears its head with respect to locating appropriate knowledge structures that have been stored in memory.

For example, suppose we have a script (a description of a class of events in terms of contexts, participants, and subevents) that describes the typical sequence of events in a restaurant.[3] This script would enable us to take a text such as

> John went to Steak and Ale last night. He ordered a large rare steak, paid his bill, and left.

and answer "yes" to the question

> Did John eat dinner last night?

Notice that nowhere in the story was John's eating anything mentioned explicitly. But the fact that when one goes to a restaurant one eats will be contained in the restaurant script. If we know in advance to use the restaurant script, then we can answer the question easily. But in order to be able to reason about a variety of things, a system must have many scripts for everything from going to work to sailing around the world. How will it select the appropriate one each time? For example, nowhere in our story was the word "restaurant" mentioned.

In fact, in order to have access to the right structure for describing a particular situation, it is necessary to solve all of the following problems.[4]

- How to perform an initial selection of the most appropriate structure.

- How to fill in appropriate details from the current situation.

- How to find a better structure if the one chosen initially turns out not to be appropriate.

- What to do if none of the available structures is appropriate.

- When to create and remember a new structure.

There is no good, general purpose method for solving all these problems. Some knowledge-representation techniques solve some of them. In this section we survey some solutions to two of these problems: how to select an initial structure to consider and how to find a better structure if that one turns out not to be a good match.

Selecting an Initial Structure

Selecting candidate knowledge structures to match a particular problem-solving situation is a hard problem; there are several ways in which it can be done. Three important approaches are the following:

---

[3]We discuss such a script in detail in Chapter 10.
[4]This list is taken from Minsky [1975].

- Index the structures directly by the significant English words that can be used to describe them. For example, let each verb have associated with it a structure that describes its meaning. This is the approach taken in conceptual dependency theory, discussed in Chapter 10. Even for selecting simple structures, such as those representing the meanings of individual words, though, this approach may not be adequate, since many words may have several distinct meanings. For example, the word "fly" has a different meaning in each of the following sentences:

  - John flew to New York. (He rode in a plane from one place to another.)
  - John flew a kite. (He held a kite that was up in the air.)
  - John flew down the street. (He moved very rapidly.)
  - John flew into a rage. (An idiom)

Another problem with this approach is that it is only useful when there is an English description of the problem to be solved.

- Consider each major concept as a pointer to all of the structures (such as scripts) in which it might be involved. This may produce several sets of prospective structures. For example, the concept *Steak* might point to two scripts, one for restaurant and one for supermarket. The concept *Bill* might point to a restaurant and a shopping script. Take the intersection of those sets to get the structure(s), preferably precisely one, that involves all the content words. Given the pointers just described and the story about John's trip to Steak and Ale, the restaurant script would be evoked. One important problem with this method is that if the problem description contains any even slightly extraneous concepts, then the intersection of their associated structures will be empty. This might occur if we had said, for example, "John rode his bicycle to Steak and Ale last night." Another problem is that it may require a great deal of computation to compute all of the possibility sets and then to intersect them. However, if computing such sets and intersecting them could be done in parallel, then the time required to produce an answer would be reasonable even if the total number of computations is large. For an exploration of this parallel approach to clue intersection, see Fahlman [1979].

- Locate one major clue in the problem description and use it to select an initial structure. As other clues appear, use them to refine the initial selection or to make a completely new one if necessary. For a discussion of this approach, see Charniak [1978]. The major problem with this method is that in some situations there is not an easily identifiable major clue. A second problem is that it is necessary to anticipate which clues are going to be important and which are not. But the relative importance of clues can change dramatically from one situation to another. For example, in many contexts, the color of the objects involved is not important. But if we are told "The light turned red," then the color of the light is the most important feature to consider.

None of these proposals seems to be the complete answer to the problem. It often turns out, unfortunately, that the more complex the knowledge structures are, the harder it is to tell when a particular one is appropriate.

Revising the Choice When Necessary

Once we find a candidate knowledge structure, we must attempt to do a detailed match of it to the problem at hand. Depending on the representation we are using, the details of the matching process will vary. It may require variables to be bound to objects. It may require attributes to have their values compared. In any case, if values that satisfy the required restrictions as imposed by the knowledge structure can be found, they are put into the appropriate places in the structure. If no appropriate values can be found, then a new structure must be selected. The way in which the attempt to instantiate this first structure failed may provide useful cues as to which one to try next. If, on the other hand, appropriate values can be found, then the current structure can be taken to be appropriate for describing the current situation. But, of course, that situation may change. Then information about what happened (for example, we walked around the room we were looking at) may be useful in selecting a new structure to describe the revised situation.

As was suggested above, the process of instantiating a structure in a particular situation often does not proceed smoothly. When the process runs into a snag, though, it is often not necessary to abandon the effort and start over. Rather, there are a variety of things that can be done:

- Select the fragments of the current structure that do correspond to the situation and match them against candidate alternatives. Choose the best match. If the current structure was at all close to being appropriate, much of the work that has been done to build substructures to fit into it will be preserved.

- Make an excuse for the current structure's failure and continue to use it. For example, a proposed chair with only three legs might simply be broken. Or there might be another object in front of it which occludes one leg. Part of the structure should contain information about the features for which it is acceptable to make excuses. Also, there are general heuristics, such as the fact that a structure is more likely to be appropriate if a desired feature is missing (perhaps because it is hidden from view) than if an inappropriate feature is present. For example, a person with one leg is more plausible than a person with a tail.

- Refer to specific stored links between structures to suggest new directions in which to explore. An example of this sort of linking among a set of frames is shown in the similarity network shown in Figure 4.11.[5]

- If the knowledge structures are stored in an *isa* hierarchy, traverse upward in it until a structure is found that is sufficiently general that it does not conflict with the evidence. Either use this structure if it is specific enough to provide the required knowledge or consider creating a new structure just below the matching one.

4.4   The Frame Problem

So far in this chapter, we have seen several methods for representing knowledge that would allow us to form complex state descriptions for a search program. Another issue

---

[5]This example is taken from Minsky [1975].

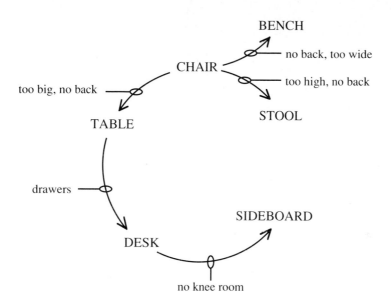

Figure 4.11: A Similarity Net

concerns how to represent efficiently *sequences* of problem states that arise from a search process. For complex ill-structured problems, this can be a serious matter.

Consider the world of a household robot. There are many objects and relationships in the world, and a state description must somehow include facts like *on(Plant12, Table34)*, *under(Table34, Window13)*, and *in(Table34, Room15)*. One strategy is to store each state description as a list of such facts. But what happens during the problem-solving process if each of those descriptions is very long? Most of the facts will not change from one state to another, yet each fact will be represented once at every node, and we will quickly run out of memory. Furthermore, we will spend the majority of our time creating these nodes and copying these facts—most of which do not change often—from one node to another. For example, in the robot world, we could spend a lot of time recording *above(Ceiling, Floor)* at every node. All of this is, of course, in addition to the real problem of figuring out which facts *should* be different at each node.

This whole problem of representing the facts that change as well as those that do not is known as the *frame problem* [McCarthy and Hayes, 1969]. In some domains, the only hard part is representing all the facts. In others, though, figuring out which ones change is nontrivial. For example, in the robot world, there might be a table with a plant on it under the window. Suppose we move the table to the center of the room. We must also infer that the plant is now in the center of the room too but that the window is not.

To support this kind of reasoning, some systems make use of an explicit set of axioms called *frame axioms*, which describe all the things that do not change when a particular operator is applied in state n to produce state $n + 1$. (The things that do change must be mentioned as part of the operator itself.) Thus, in the robot domain, we might write axioms such as

$$color(x, y, s_1) \land move(x, s_1, s_2) \to color(x, y, s_2)$$

which can be read as, "If x has color y in state s_1 and the operation of moving x is applied in state s1 to produce state s_2, then the color of x in s_2 is still y." Unfortunately, in any complex domain, a huge number of these axioms becomes necessary. An alternative approach is to make the assumption that the only things that change are the things that must. By "must" here we mean that the change is either required explicitly by the axioms that describe the operator or that it follows logically from some change that is asserted explicitly. This idea of *circumscribing* the set of unusual things is a very powerful one; it can be used as a partial solution to the frame problem and as a way of reasoning with incomplete knowledge. We return to it in Chapter 7.

But now let's return briefly to the problem of representing a changing problem state. We could do it by simply starting with a description of the initial state and then making changes to that description as indicated by the rules we apply. This solves the problem of the wasted space and time involved in copying the information for each node. And it works fine until the first time the search has to backtrack. Then, unless all the changes that were made can simply be ignored (as they could be if, for example, they were simply additions of new theorems), we are faced with the problem of backing up to some earlier node. But how do we know what changes in the problem state description need to be undone? For example, what do we have to change to undo the effect of moving the table to the center of the room? There are two ways this problem can be solved:

- Do not modify the initial state description at all. At each node, store an indication of the specific changes that should be made at this node. Whenever it is necessary to refer to the description of the current problem state, look at the initial state description and also look back through all the nodes on the path from the start state to the current state. This is what we did in our solution to the cryptarithmetic problem in Section 3.5. This approach makes backtracking very easy, but it makes referring to the state description fairly complex.

- Modify the initial state description as appropriate, but also record at each node an indication of what to do to undo the move should it ever be necessary to backtrack through the node. Then, whenever it is necessary to backtrack, check each node along the way and perform the indicated operations on the state description.

Sometimes, even these solutions are not enough. We might want to remember, for example, in the robot world, that before the table was moved, it was under the window and after being moved, it was in the center of the room. This can be handled by adding to the representation of each fact a specific indication of the time at which that fact was true. This indication is called a *state variable*. But to apply the same technique to a real-world problem, we need, for example, separate facts to indicate all the times at which the Statue of Liberty is in New York.

There is no simple answer either to the question of knowledge representation or to the frame problem. Each of them is discussed in greater depth later in the context of specific problems. But it is important to keep these questions in mind when considering search strategies, since the representation of knowledge and the search process depend heavily on each other.

4.5 Summary

The purpose of this chapter has been to outline the need for knowledge in reasoning programs and to survey issues that must be addressed in the design of a good knowledge-representation structure. Of course, we have not covered everything. In the chapters that follow, we describe some specific representations and look at their relative strengths and weaknesses.

The following collections all contain further discussions of the fundamental issues in knowledge representation, along with specific techniques to address these issues: Bobrow [1975], Winograd [1978], Brachman and Levesque [1985], and Halpern [1986]. For especially clear discussions of specific issues on the topic of knowledge representation and use see Woods [1975] and Brachman [1985].

Chapter 5

Using Predicate Logic

In this chapter, we begin exploring one particular way of representing facts—the language of logic. Other representational formalisms are discussed in later chapters. The logical formalism is appealing because it immediately suggests a powerful way of deriving new knowledge from old   mathematical deduction. In this formalism, we can conclude that a new statement is true by proving that it follows from the statements that are already known. Thus the idea of a proof, as developed in mathematics as a rigorous way of demonstrating the truth of an already believed proposition, can be extended to include deduction as a way of deriving answers to questions and solutions to problems.

One of the early domains in which AI techniques were explored was mechanical theorem proving, by which was meant proving statements in various areas of mathematics. For example, the Logic Theorist [Newell *et al.*, 1963] proved theorems from the first chapter of Whitehead and Russell's *Principia Mathematica* [1950]. Another theorem prover [Gelernter *et al.*, 1963] proved theorems in geometry. Mathematical theorem proving is still an active area of AI research. (See, for example, Wos *et al.* [1984].) But, as we show in this chapter, the usefulness of some mathematical techniques extends well beyond the traditional scope of mathematics. It turns out that mathematics is no different from any other complex intellectual endeavor in requiring both reliable deductive mechanisms and a mass of heuristic knowledge to control what would otherwise be a completely intractable search problem.

At this point, readers who are unfamiliar with propositional and predicate logic may want to consult a good introductory logic text before reading the rest of this chapter. Readers who want a more complete and formal presentation of the material in this chapter should consult Chang and Lee [1973]. Throughout the chapter, we use the following standard logic symbols: "→" (*material implication*), "¬" (*not*), "∨" (*or*), "∧" (*and*), "∀" (*for all*), and "∃" (*there exists*).

5.1   Representing Simple Facts in Logic

Let's first explore the use of propositional logic as a way of representing the sort of world knowledge that an AI system might need. Propositional logic is appealing because it is simple to deal with and a decision procedure for it exists. We can easily

It is raining.
RAINING

It is sunny.
SUNNY

It is windy.
WINDY

If it is raining, then it is not sunny.
RAINING $\rightarrow \neg$ *SUNNY*

Figure 5.1: Some Simple Facts in Propositional Logic

represent real-world facts as logical *propositions* written as *well-formed formulas (wff's)* in propositional logic, as shown in Figure 5.1. Using these propositions, we could, for example, conclude from the fact that it is raining the fact that it is not sunny. But very quickly we run up against the limitations of propositional logic. Suppose we want to represent the obvious fact stated by the classical sentence

Socrates is a man.

We could write:

SOCRATESMAN

But if we also wanted to represent

Plato is a man.

we would have to write something such as:

PLATOMAN

which would be a totally separate assertion, and we would not be able to draw any conclusions about similarities between Socrates and Plato. It would be much better to represent these facts as:

MAN(SOCRATES)
MAN(PLATO)

since now the structure of the representation reflects the structure of the knowledge itself. But to do that, we need to be able to use predicates applied to arguments. We are in even more difficulty if we try to represent the equally classic sentence

All men are mortal.

We could represent this as:

MORTALMAN

But that fails to capture the relationship between any individual being a man and that individual being a mortal. To do that, we really need variables and quantification unless we are willing to write separate statements about the mortality of every known man.

So we appear to be forced to move to first-order predicate logic (or just predicate logic, since we do not discuss higher order theories in this chapter) as a way of representing knowledge because it permits representations of things that cannot reasonably be represented in propositional logic. In predicate logic, we can represent real-world facts as *statements* written as wff's.

But a major motivation for choosing to use logic at all is that if we use logical statements as a way of representing knowledge, then we have available a good way of reasoning with that knowledge. Determining the validity of a proposition in propositional logic is straightforward, although it may be computationally hard. So before we adopt predicate logic as a good medium for representing knowledge, we need to ask whether it also provides a good way of reasoning with the knowledge. At first glance, the answer is yes. It provides a way of deducing new statements from old ones. Unfortunately, however, unlike propositional logic, it does not possess a decision procedure, even an exponential one. There do exist procedures that will find a proof of a proposed theorem if indeed it is a theorem. But these procedures are not guaranteed to halt if the proposed statement is not a theorem. In other words, although first-order predicate logic is not decidable, it is semidecidable. A simple such procedure is to use the rules of inference to generate theorems from the axioms in some orderly fashion, testing each to see if it is the one for which a proof is sought. This method is not particularly efficient, however, and we will want to try to find a better one.

Although negative results, such as the fact that there can exist no decision procedure for predicate logic, generally have little direct effect on a science such as AI, which seeks positive methods for doing things, this particular negative result is helpful since it tells us that in our search for an efficient proof procedure, we should be content if we find one that will prove theorems, even if it is not guaranteed to halt if given a nontheorem. And the fact that there cannot exist a decision procedure that halts on all possible inputs does not mean that there cannot exist one that will halt on almost all the inputs it would see in the process of trying to solve real problems. So despite the theoretical undecidability of predicate logic, it can still serve as a useful way of representing and manipulating some of the kinds of knowledge that an AI system might need.

Let's now explore the use of predicate logic as a way of representing knowledge by looking at a specific example. Consider the following set of sentences:

1. Marcus was a man.
2. Marcus was a Pompeian.
3. All Pompeians were Romans.
4. Caesar was a ruler.
5. All Romans were either loyal to Caesar or hated him.
6. Everyone is loyal to someone.
7. People only try to assassinate rulers they are not loyal to.
8. Marcus tried to assassinate Caesar.

The facts described by these sentences can be represented as a set of wff's in predicate logic as follows:

1. Marcus was a man.

   man(Marcus)

   This representation captures the critical fact of Marcus being a man. It fails to capture some of the information in the English sentence, namely the notion of past tense. Whether this omission is acceptable or not depends on the use to which we intend to put the knowledge. For this simple example, it will be all right.

2. Marcus was a Pompeian.

   Pompeian(Marcus)

3. All Pompeians were Romans.

   $\forall x : Pompeian(x) \rightarrow Roman(x)$

4. Caesar was a ruler.

   ruler(Caesar)

   Here we ignore the fact that proper names are often not references to unique individuals, since many people share the same name. Sometimes deciding which of several people of the same name is being referred to in a particular statement may require a fair amount of knowledge and reasoning.

5. All Romans were either loyal to Caesar or hated him.

   $\forall x : Roman(x) \rightarrow loyalto(x, Caesar) \lor hate(x, Caesar)$

   In English, the word "or" sometimes means the logical *inclusive-or* and sometimes means the logical *exclusive-or* (XOR). Here we have used the inclusive interpretation. Some people will argue, however, that this English sentence is really stating an exclusive-or. To express that, we would have to write:

   $\forall x : Roman(x) \rightarrow [(loyalto(x, Caesar) \lor hate(x, Caesar)) \land$
   $\qquad \neg(loyalto(x, Caesar) \land hate(x, Caesar))]$

6. Everyone is loyal to someone.

   $\forall x : \exists y : loyalto(x, y)$

   A major problem that arises when trying to convert English sentences into logical statements is the scope of quantifiers. Does this sentence say, as we have assumed in writing the logical formula above, that for each person there exists someone to whom he or she is loyal, possibly a different someone for everyone? Or does it say that there exists someone to whom everyone is loyal (which would be written as $\exists y : \forall x : loyalto(x, y)$)? Often only one of the two interpretations seems likely, so people tend to favor it.

7. People only try to assassinate rulers they are not loyal to.

$\forall x : \forall y : person(x) \wedge ruler(y) \wedge tryassassinate(x, y) \rightarrow \neg loyalto(x, y)$

This sentence, too, is ambiguous. Does it mean that the only rulers that people try to assassinate are those to whom they are not loyal (the interpretation used here), or does it mean that the only thing people try to do is to assassinate rulers to whom they are not loyal?

In representing this sentence the way we did, we have chosen to write "try to assassinate" as a single predicate. This gives a fairly simple representation with which we can reason about trying to assassinate. But using this representation, the connections between trying to assassinate and trying to do other things and between trying to assassinate and actually assassinating could not be made easily. If such connections were necessary, we would need to choose a different representation.

8. Marcus tried to assassinate Caesar.

$tryassassinate(Marcus, Caesar)$

From this brief attempt to convert English sentences into logical statements, it should be clear how difficult the task is. For a good description of many issues involved in this process, see Reichenbach [1947].

Now suppose that we want to use these statements to answer the question

Was Marcus loyal to Caesar?

It seems that using 7 and 8, we should be able to prove that Marcus was not loyal to Caesar (again ignoring the distinction between past and present tense). Now let's try to produce a formal proof, reasoning backward from the desired goal:

$\neg loyalto(Marcus, Caesar)$

In order to prove the goal, we need to use the rules of inference to transform it into another goal (or possibly a set of goals) that can in turn be transformed, and so on, until there are no unsatisfied goals remaining. This process may require the search of an AND-OR graph (as described in Section 3.4) when there are alternative ways of satisfying individual goals. Here, for simplicity, we show only a single path. Figure 5.2 shows an attempt to produce a proof of the goal by reducing the set of necessary but as yet unattained goals to the empty set. The attempt fails, however, since there is no way to satisfy the goal $person(Marcus)$ with the statements we have available.

The problem is that, although we know that Marcus was a man, we do not have any way to conclude from that that Marcus was a person. We need to add the representation of another fact to our system, namely:

$\neg loyalto(Marcus, Caesar)$

$\uparrow$ (7, substitution)

$person(Marcus) \land$
$ruler(Caesar) \land$
$tryassassinate(Marcus, Caesar)$

$\uparrow$ (4)

$person(Marcus)$
$tryassassinate(Marcus, Caesar)$

$\uparrow$ (8)

$person(Marcus)$

Figure 5.2: An Attempt to Prove $\neg loyalto(Marcus, Caesar)$

9. All men are people.

$\forall x : man(x) \rightarrow person(x)$

Now we can satisfy the last goal and produce a proof that Marcus was not loyal to Caesar.

From this simple example, we see that three important issues must be addressed in the process of converting English sentences into logical statements and then using those statements to deduce new ones:

- Many English sentences are ambiguous (for example, 5, 6, and 7 above). Choosing the correct interpretation may be difficult.

- There is often a choice of how to represent the knowledge (as discussed in connection with 1 and 7 above). Simple representations are desirable, but they may preclude certain kinds of reasoning. The expedient representation for a particular set of sentences depends on the use to which the knowledge contained in the sentences will be put.

- Even in very simple situations, a set of sentences is unlikely to contain all the information necessary to reason about the topic at hand. In order to be able to use a set of statements effectively, it is usually necessary to have access to another set of statements that represent facts that people consider too obvious to mention. We discuss this issue further in Section 10.3.

An additional problem arises in situations where we do not know in advance which statements to deduce. In the example just presented, the object was to answer the question "Was Marcus loyal to Caesar?" How would a program decide whether it should try to prove

$loyalto(Marcus, Caesar)$

or

$\neg loyalto(Marcus, Caesar)$

There are several things it could do. It could abandon the strategy we have outlined of reasoning backward from a proposed truth to the axioms and instead try to reason forward and see which answer it gets to. The problem with this approach is that, in general, the branching factor going forward from the axioms is so great that it would probably not get to either answer in any reasonable amount of time. A second thing it could do is use some sort of heuristic rules for deciding which answer is more likely and then try to prove that one first. If it fails to find a proof after some reasonable amount of effort, it can try the other answer. This notion of limited effort is important, since any proof procedure we use may not halt if given a nontheorem. Another thing it could do is simply try to prove both answers simultaneously and stop when one effort is successful. Even here, however, if there is not enough information available to answer the question with certainty, the program may never halt. Yet a fourth strategy is to try both to prove one answer and to disprove it, and to use information gained in one of the processes to guide the other.

5.2 Representing Instance and Isa Relationships

In Chapter 4, we discussed the specific attributes *instance* and *isa* and described the important role they play in a particularly useful form of reasoning, property inheritance. But if we look back at the way we just represented our knowledge about Marcus and Caesar, we do not appear to have used these attributes at all. We certainly have not used predicates with those names. Why not? The answer is that although we have not used the predicates *instance* and *isa* explicitly, we have captured the relationships they are used to express, namely class membership and class inclusion.

Figure 5.3 shows the first five sentences of the last section represented in logic in three different ways. The first part of the figure contains the representations we have already discussed. In these representations, class membership is represented with unary predicates (such as *Roman*), each of which corresponds to a class. Asserting that $P(x)$ is true is equivalent to asserting that x is an instance (or element) of P. The second part of the figure contains representations that use the *instance* predicate explicitly. The predicate *instance* is a binary one, whose first argument is an object and whose second argument is a class to which the object belongs. But these representations do not use an explicit *isa* predicate. Instead, subclass relationships, such as that between Pompeians and Romans, are described as shown in sentence 3. The implication rule there states that if an object is an instance of the subclass *Pompeian* then it is an instance of the superclass *Roman*. Note that this rule is equivalent to the standard set-theoretic definition of the subclass-superclass relationship. The third part contains representations that use both the *instance* and *isa* predicates explicitly. The use of the *isa* predicate simplifies the representation of sentence 3, but it requires that one additional axiom (shown here as number 6) be provided. This additional axiom describes how an *instance* relation and an *isa* relation can be combined to derive a new *instance* relation. This one additional axiom is general, though, and does not need to be provided separately for additional *isa* relations.

1.   *man(Marcus)*
2.   *Pompeian(Marcus)*
3. $\forall x : Pompeian(x) \rightarrow Roman(x)$
4.   *ruler(Caesar)*
5. $\forall x : Roman(x) \rightarrow loyalto(x, Caesar) \lor hate(x, Caesar)$

1.   *instance(Marcus, man)*
2.   *instance(Marcus, Pompeian)*
3. $\forall x : instance(x, Pompeian) \rightarrow instance(x, Roman)$
4.   *instance(Caesar, ruler)*
5. $\forall x : instance(x, Roman) \rightarrow loyalto(x, Caesar) \lor hate(x, Caesar)$

1.   *instance(Marcus, man)*
2.   *instance(Marcus, Pompeian)*
3.   *isa(Pompeian, Roman)*
4.   *instance(Caesar, ruler)*
5. $\forall x : instance(x, Roman) \rightarrow loyalto(x, Caesar) \lor hate(x, Caesar)$
6. $\forall x : \forall y : \forall z : instance(x, y) \land isa(y, z) \rightarrow instance(x, z)$

Figure 5.3: Three Ways of Representing Class Membership

These examples illustrate two points. The first is fairly specific. It is that, although class and superclass memberships are important facts that need to be represented, those memberships need not be represented with predicates labeled *instance* and *isa*. In fact, in a logical framework it is usually unwieldy to do that, and instead unary predicates corresponding to the classes are often used. The second point is more general. There are usually several different ways of representing a given fact within a particular representational framework, be it logic or anything else. The choice depends partly on which deductions need to be supported most efficiently and partly on taste. The only important thing is that within a particular knowledge base consistency of representation is critical. Since any particular inference rule is designed to work on one particular form of representation, it is necessary that all the knowledge to which that rule is intended to apply be in the form that the rule demands. Many errors in the reasoning performed by knowledge-based programs are the result of inconsistent representation decisions. The moral is simply to be careful.

There is one additional point that needs to be made here on the subject of the use of *isa* hierarchies in logic-based systems. The reason that these hierarchies are so important is not that they permit the inference of superclass membership. It is that by permitting the inference of superclass membership, they permit the inference of other properties associated with membership in that superclass. So, for example, in our sample knowledge base it is important to be able to conclude that Marcus is a Roman because we have some relevant knowledge about Romans, namely that they either hate

Caesar or are loyal to him. But recall that in the baseball example of Chapter 4, we were able to associate knowledge with superclasses that could then be overridden by more specific knowledge associated either with individual instances or with subclasses. In other words, we recorded default values that could be accessed whenever necessary. For example, there was a height associated with adult males and a different height associated with baseball players. Our procedure for manipulating the *isa* hierarchy guaranteed that we always found the correct (i.e., most specific) value for any attribute. Unfortunately, reproducing this result in logic is difficult.

Suppose, for example, that, in addition to the facts we already have, we add the following.[1]

> *Pompeian(Paulus)*
> ¬[*loyalto(Paulus, Caesar)* ∨ *hate(Paulus, Caesar)*]

In other words, suppose we want to make Paulus an exception to the general rule about Romans and their feelings toward Caesar. Unfortunately, we cannot simply add these facts to our existing knowledge base the way we could just add new nodes into a semantic net. The difficulty is that if the old assertions are left unchanged, then the addition of the new assertions makes the knowledge base inconsistent. In order to restore consistency, it is necessary to modify the original assertion to which an exception is being made. So our original sentence 5 must become:

$$\forall x : Roman(x) \wedge \neg eq(x, Paulus) \rightarrow loyalto(x, Caesar) \vee hate(x, Caesar)$$

In this framework, every exception to a general rule must be stated twice, once in a particular statement and once in an exception list that forms part of the general rule. This makes the use of general rules in this framework less convenient and less efficient when there are exceptions than is the use of general rules in a semantic net.

A further problem arises when information is incomplete and it is not possible to prove that no exceptions apply in a particular instance. But we defer consideration of this problem until Chapter 7.

5.3 Computable Functions and Predicates

In the example we explored in the last section, all the simple facts were expressed as combinations of individual predicates, such as:

> *tryassassinate(Marcus, Caesar)*

This is fine if the number of facts is not very large or if the facts themselves are sufficiently unstructured that there is little alternative. But suppose we want to express simple facts, such as the following greater-than and less-than relationships:

---

[1] For convenience, we now return to our original notation using unary predicates to denote class relations.

$$gt(1, 0) \quad lt(0, 1)$$
$$gt(2, 1) \quad lt(1, 2)$$
$$gt(3, 2) \quad lt(2, 3)$$
$$\vdots \qquad \vdots$$

Clearly we do not want to have to write out the representation of each of these facts individually. For one thing, there are infinitely many of them. But even if we only consider the finite number of them that can be represented, say, using a single machine word per number, it would be extremely inefficient to store explicitly a large set of statements when we could, instead, so easily compute each one as we need it. Thus it becomes useful to augment our representation by these *computable predicates*. Whatever proof procedure we use, when it comes upon one of these predicates, instead of searching for it explicitly in the database or attempting to deduce it by further reasoning, we can simply invoke a procedure, which we will specify in addition to our regular rules, that will evaluate it and return true or false.

It is often also useful to have computable functions as well as computable predicates. Thus we might want to be able to evaluate the truth of

$$gt(2 + 3, 1)$$

To do so requires that we first compute the value of the plus function given the arguments 2 and 3, and then send the arguments 5 and 1 to *gt*.

The next example shows how these ideas of computable functions and predicates can be useful. It also makes use of the notion of equality and allows equal objects to be substituted for each other whenever it appears helpful to do so during a proof.

Consider the following set of facts, again involving Marcus:

1. Marcus was a man.

   man(Marcus)

   Again we ignore the issue of tense.

2. Marcus was a Pompeian.

   Pompeian(Marcus)

3. Marcus was born in 40 A.D.

   born(Marcus, 40)

   For simplicity, we will not represent A.D. explicitly, just as we normally omit it in everyday discussions. If we ever need to represent dates B.C., then we will have to decide on a way to do that, such as by using negative numbers. Notice that the representation of a sentence does not have to look like the sentence itself as long as there is a way to convert back and forth between them. This allows us to choose a representation, such as positive and negative numbers, that is easy for a program to work with.

4. All men are mortal.

   $\forall x : man(x) \rightarrow mortal(x)$

5. All Pompeians died when the volcano erupted in 79 A.D.

   $erupted(volcano, 79) \wedge \forall x : [Pompeian(x) \rightarrow died(x, 79)]$

   This sentence clearly asserts the two facts represented above. It may also assert another that we have not shown, namely that the eruption of the volcano caused the death of the Pompeians. People often assume causality between concurrent events if such causality seems plausible.

   Another problem that arises in interpreting this sentence is that of determining the referent of the phrase "the volcano." There is more than one volcano in the world. Clearly the one referred to here is Vesuvius, which is near Pompeii and erupted in 79 A.D. In general, resolving references such as these can require both a lot of reasoning and a lot of additional knowledge.

6. No mortal lives longer than 150 years.

   $\forall x : \forall t_1 : \forall t_2 : mortal(x) \wedge born(x, t_1) \wedge gt(t_2 - t_1, 150) \rightarrow dead(x, t_2)$

   There are several ways that the content of this sentence could be expressed. For example, we could introduce a function *age* and assert that its value is never greater than 150. The representation shown above is simpler, though, and it will suffice for this example.

7. It is now 1991.

   $now = 1991$

   Here we will exploit the idea of equal quantities that can be substituted for each other.

   Now suppose we want to answer the question "Is Marcus alive?" A quick glance through the statements we have suggests that there may be two ways of deducing an answer. Either we can show that Marcus is dead because he was killed by the volcano or we can show that he must be dead because he would otherwise be more than 150 years old, which we know is not possible. As soon as we attempt to follow either of those paths rigorously, however, we discover, just as we did in the last example, that we need some additional knowledge. For example, our statements talk about dying, but they say nothing that relates to being alive, which is what the question is asking. So we add the following facts:

8. Alive means not dead.

   $\forall x : \forall t : [alive(x, t) \rightarrow \neg dead(x, t)] \wedge [\neg dead(x, t) \rightarrow alive(x, t)]$

   This is not strictly correct, since $\neg dead$ implies alive only for animate objects. (Chairs can be neither dead nor alive.) Again, we will ignore this for now. This is an example of the fact that rarely do two expressions have truly identical meanings in all circumstances.

9. If someone dies, then he is dead at all later times.

   $\forall x : \forall t_1 : \forall t_2 : died(x, t_1) \wedge gt(t_2, t_1) \rightarrow dead(x, t_2)$

   This representation says that one is dead in all years after the one in which one died. It ignores the question of whether one is dead in the year in which one died.

1. *man(Marcus)*
2. *Pompeian(Marcus)*
3. *born(Marcus, 40)*
4. $\forall x : man(x) \rightarrow mortal(x)$
5. $\forall x : Pompeian(x) \rightarrow died(x, 79)$
6. *erupted(volcano, 79)*
7. $\forall x : \forall t_1 : \forall t_2 : mortal(x) \land born(x, t_1) \land gt(t_2 - t_1, 150) \rightarrow dead(x, t_2)$
8. *now* = 1991
9. $\forall x : \forall t : [alive(x, t) \rightarrow \neg dead(x, t)] \land [\neg dead(x, t) \rightarrow alive(x, t)]$
10. $\forall x : \forall t_1 : \forall t_2 : died(x, t_1) \land gt(t_2, t_1) \rightarrow dead(x, t_2)$

Figure 5.4: A Set of Facts about Marcus

To answer that requires breaking time up into smaller units than years. If we do that, we can then add rules that say such things as "One is dead at *time(year1, month1)* if one died during *(year1, month2)* and *month2* precedes *month1*." We can extend this to days, hours, etc., as necessary. But we do not want to reduce all time statements to that level of detail, which is unnecessary and often not available.

A summary of all the facts we have now represented is given in Figure 5.4. (The numbering is changed slightly because sentence 5 has been split into two parts.) Now let's attempt to answer the question "Is Marcus alive?" by proving:

$\neg alive(Marcus, now)$

Two such proofs are shown in Figures 5.5 and 5.6. The term *nil* at the end of each proof indicates that the list of conditions remaining to be proved is empty and so the proof has succeeded. Notice in those proofs that whenever a statement of the form:

$a \land b \rightarrow c$

was used, *a* and *b* were set up as independent subgoals. In one sense they are, but in another sense they are not if they share the same bound variables, since, in that case, consistent substitutions must be made in each of them. For example, in Figure 5.6 look at the step justified by statement 3. We can satisfy the goal

$born(Marcus, t_1)$

using statement 3 by binding t_1 to 40, but then we must also bind t_1 to 40 in

$gt(now - t_1, 150)$

since the two t_1's were the same variable in statement 4, from which the two goals came. A good computational proof procedure has to include both a way of determining

$$\neg alive(Marcus, now)$$

$$\uparrow \quad \text{(9, substitution)}$$

$$dead(Marcus, now)$$

$$\uparrow \quad \text{(10, substitution)}$$

$$died(Marcus, t_1) \wedge gt(now, t_1)$$

$$\uparrow \quad \text{(5, substitution)}$$

$$Pompeian(Marcus) \wedge gt(now, 79)$$

$$\uparrow \quad (2)$$

$$gt(now, 79)$$

$$\uparrow \quad \text{(8, substitute equals)}$$

$$gt(1991, 79)$$

$$\uparrow \quad \text{(compute gt)}$$

$$nil$$

Figure 5.5: One Way of Proving That Marcus Is Dead

that a match exists and a way of guaranteeing uniform substitutions throughout a proof. Mechanisms for doing both those things are discussed below.

From looking at the proofs we have just shown, two things should be clear:

- Even very simple conclusions can require many steps to prove.

- A variety of processes, such as matching, substitution, and application of *modus ponens* are involved in the production of a proof. This is true even for the simple statements we are using. It would be worse if we had implications with more than a single term on the right or with complicated expressions involving *ands* and *ors* on the left.

The first of these observations suggests that if we want to be able to do nontrivial reasoning, we are going to need some statements that allow us to take bigger steps along the way. These should represent the facts that people gradually acquire as they become experts. How to get computers to acquire them is a hard problem for which no very good answer is known.

The second observation suggests that actually building a program to do what people do in producing proofs such as these may not be easy. In the next section, we introduce a proof procedure called *resolution* that reduces some of the complexity because it operates on statements that have first been converted to a single canonical form.

5.4 Resolution

As we suggest above, it would be useful from a computational point of view if we had a proof procedure that carried out in a single operation the variety of processes involved

$\neg alive(Marcus, now)$

$\uparrow$ (9, substitution)

$dead(Marcus, now)$

$\uparrow$ (7, substitution)

$mortal(Marcus) \wedge$
$born(Marcus, t_1) \wedge$
$gt(now - t_1, 150)$

$\uparrow$ (4, substitution)

$man(Marcus) \wedge$
$born(Marcus, t_1) \wedge$
$gt(now - t_1, 150)$

$\uparrow$ (1)

$born(Marcus, t_1) \wedge$
$gt(now - t_1, 150)$

$\uparrow$ (3)

$gt(now - 40, 150)$

$\uparrow$ (8)

$gt(1991 - 40, 150)$

$\uparrow$ (compute minus)

$gt(1951, 150)$

$\uparrow$ (compute gt)

nil

Figure 5.6: Another Way of Proving That Marcus Is Dead

in reasoning with statements in predicate logic. Resolution is such a procedure, which gains its efficiency from the fact that it operates on statements that have been converted to a very convenient standard form, which is described below.

Resolution produces proofs by *refutation*. In other words, to prove a statement (i.e., show that it is valid), resolution attempts to show that the negation of the statement produces a contradiction with the known statements (i.e., that it is unsatisfiable). This approach contrasts with the technique that we have been using to generate proofs by chaining backward from the theorem to be proved to the axioms. Further discussion of how resolution operates will be much more straightforward after we have discussed the standard form in which statements will be represented, so we defer it until then.

5.4.1 Conversion to Clause Form

Suppose we know that all Romans who know Marcus either hate Caesar or think that anyone who hates anyone is crazy. We could represent that in the following wff:

$\forall x : [Roman(x) \wedge know(x, Marcus)] \rightarrow$
$\quad [hate(x, Caesar) \vee (\forall y : \exists z : hate(y, z) \rightarrow thinkcrazy(x, y))]$

To use this formula in a proof requires a complex matching process. Then, having matched one piece of it, such as *thinkcrazy*(x, y), it is necessary to do the right thing with the rest of the formula including the pieces in which the matched part is embedded and those in which it is not. If the formula were in a simpler form, this process would be much easier. The formula would be easier to work with if

- It were flatter, i.e., there was less embedding of components.

- The quantifiers were separated from the rest of the formula so that they did not need to be considered.

Conjunctive normal form [Davis and Putnam, 1960] has both of these properties. For example, the formula given above for the feelings of Romans who know Marcus would be represented in conjunctive normal form as

$\neg Roman(x) \vee \neg know(x, Marcus) \vee$
$\quad hate(x, Caesar) \vee \neg hate(y, z) \vee thinkcrazy(x, z)$

Since there exists an algorithm for converting any wff into conjunctive normal form, we lose no generality if we employ a proof procedure (such as resolution) that operates only on wff's in this form. In fact, for resolution to work, we need to go one step further. We need to reduce a set of wff's to a set of *clauses*, where a clause is defined to be a wff in conjunctive normal form but with no instances of the connector $\wedge$. We can do this by first converting each wff into conjunctive normal form and then breaking apart each such expression into clauses, one for each conjunct. All the conjuncts will be considered to be conjoined together as the proof procedure operates. To convert a wff into clause form, perform the following sequence of steps.

Algorithm: Convert to Clause Form

1. Eliminate $\rightarrow$, using the fact that $a \rightarrow b$ is equivalent to $\neg a \vee b$. Performing this transformation on the wff given above yields

    $\forall x : \neg[Roman(x) \wedge know(x, Marcus)] \vee$
    $\quad [hate(x, Caesar) \vee (\forall y : \neg(\exists z : hate(y, z)) \vee thinkcrazy(x, y))]$

2. Reduce the scope of each $\neg$ to a single term, using the fact that $\neg(\neg p) = p$, deMorgan's laws [which say that $\neg(a \wedge b) = \neg a \vee \neg b$ and $\neg(a \vee b) = \neg a \wedge \neg b$], and the standard correspondences between quantifiers [$\neg \forall x : P(x) = \exists x : \neg P(x)$ and $\neg \exists x : P(x) = \forall x : \neg P(x)$]. Performing this transformation on the wff from step 1 yields

    $\forall x : [\neg Roman(x) \vee \neg know(x, Marcus)] \vee$
    $\quad [hate(x, Caesar) \vee (\forall y : \forall z : \neg hate(y, z) \vee thinkcrazy(x, y))]$

3. Standardize variables so that each quantifier binds a unique variable. Since variables are just dummy names, this process cannot affect the truth value of the wff. For example, the formula

$\forall x : P(x) \lor \forall x : Q(x)$

would be converted to

$\forall x : P(x) \lor \forall y : Q(y)$

This step is in preparation for the next.

4. Move all quantifiers to the left of the formula without changing their relative order. This is possible since there is no conflict among variable names. Performing this operation on the formula of step 2, we get

$\forall x : \forall y : \forall z : [\neg Roman(x) \lor \neg know(x, Marcus)] \lor$
   $[hate(x, Caesar) \lor (\neg hate(y, z) \lor thinkcrazy(x, y))]$

At this point, the formula is in what is known as *prenex normal form*. It consists of a *prefix* of quantifiers followed by a *matrix*, which is quantifier-free.

5. Eliminate existential quantifiers. A formula that contains an existentially quantified variable asserts that there is a value that can be substituted for the variable that makes the formula true. We can eliminate the quantifier by substituting for the variable a reference to a function that produces the desired value. Since we do not necessarily know how to produce the value, we must create a new function name for every such replacement. We make no assertions about these functions except that they must exist. So, for example, the formula

$\exists y : President(y)$

can be transformed into the formula

$President(S1)$

where $S1$ is a function with no arguments that somehow produces a value that satisfies President.

If existential quantifiers occur within the scope of universal quantifiers, then the value that satisfies the predicate may depend on the values of the universally quantified variables. For example, in the formula

$\forall x : \exists y : father\text{-}of(y, x)$

the value of y that satisfies *father-of* depends on the particular value of x. Thus we must generate functions with the same number of arguments as the number of universal quantifiers in whose scope the expression occurs. So this example would be transformed into

$\forall x : father\text{-}of(S2(x), x))$

These generated functions are called *Skolem functions*. Sometimes ones with no arguments are called *Skolem constants*.

6. Drop the prefix. At this point, all remaining variables are universally quantified, so the prefix can just be dropped and any proof procedure we use can simply assume

that any variable it sees is universally quantified. Now the formula produced in step 4 appears as

$[\neg Roman(x) \lor \neg know(x, Marcus)] \lor$
$\quad [hate(x, Caesar) \lor (\neg hate(y, z) \lor thinkcrazy(x, y))]$

7. Convert the matrix into a conjunction of disjuncts. In the case of our example, since there are no *and*'s, it is only necessary to exploit the associative property of *or* [i.e., $a \lor (b \lor c) = (a \lor b) \lor c$] and simply remove the parentheses, giving

$\neg Roman(x) \lor \neg know(x, Marcus) \lor$
$\quad hate(x, Caesar) \lor \neg hate(y, z) \lor thinkcrazy(x, y)$

However, it is also frequently necessary to exploit the distributive property [i.e., $(a \land b) \lor c = (a \lor c) \land (b \lor c)$]. For example, the formula

$(winter \land wearingboots) \lor (summer \land wearingsandals)$

becomes, after one application of the rule

$[winter \lor (summer \land wearingsandals)]$
$\quad \land [wearingboots \lor (summer \land wearingsandals)]$

and then, after a second application, required since there are still conjuncts joined by OR's,

$(winter \lor summer) \land$
$(winter \lor wearingsandals) \land$
$(wearingboots \lor summer) \land$
$(wearingboots \lor wearingsandals)$

8. Create a separate clause corresponding to each conjunct. In order for a wff to be true, all the clauses that are generated from it must be true. If we are going to be working with several wff's, all the clauses generated by each of them can now be combined to represent the same set of facts as were represented by the original wff's.

9. Standardize apart the variables in the set of clauses generated in step 8. By this we mean rename the variables so that no two clauses make reference to the same variable. In making this transformation, we rely on the fact that

$(\forall x : P(x) \land Q(x)) = \forall x : P(x) \land \forall x : Q(x)$

Thus since each clause is a separate conjunct and since all the variables are universally quantified, there need be no relationship between the variables of two clauses, even if they were generated from the same wff.

Performing this final step of standardization is important because during the resolution procedure it is sometimes necessary to instantiate a universally quantified variable (i.e., substitute for it a particular value). But, in general, we want to keep clauses in their most general form as long as possible. So when a variable is instantiated, we want to know the minimum number of substitutions that must be made to preserve the truth value of the system.

After applying this entire procedure to a set of wff's, we will have a set of clauses, each of which is a disjunction of *literals*. These clauses can now be exploited by the resolution procedure to generate proofs.

5.4.2   The Basis of Resolution

The resolution procedure is a simple iterative process: at each step, two clauses, called the *parent clauses*, are compared (*resolved*), yielding a new clause that has been inferred from them. The new clause represents ways that the two parent clauses interact with each other. Suppose that there are two clauses in the system:

> *winter* ∨ *summer*
> ¬*winter* ∨ *cold*

Recall that this means that both clauses must be true (i.e., the clauses, although they look independent, are really conjoined).

Now we observe that precisely one of *winter* and ¬*winter* will be true at any point. If *winter* is true, then *cold* must be true to guarantee the truth of the second clause. If ¬*winter* is true, then *summer* must be true to guarantee the truth of the first clause. Thus we see that from these two clauses we can deduce

> *summer* ∨ *cold*

This is the deduction that the resolution procedure will make. Resolution operates by taking two clauses that each contain the same literal, in this example, *winter*. The literal must occur in positive form in one clause and in negative form in the other. The *resolvent* is obtained by combining all of the literals of the two parent clauses except the ones that cancel.

If the clause that is produced is the empty clause, then a contradiction has been found. For example, the two clauses

> *winter*
> ¬*winter*

will produce the empty clause. If a contradiction exists, then eventually it will be found. Of course, if no contradiction exists, it is possible that the procedure will never terminate, although as we will see, there are often ways of detecting that no contradiction exists.

So far, we have discussed only resolution in propositional logic. In predicate logic, the situation is more complicated since we must consider all possible ways of substituting values for the variables. The theoretical basis of the resolution procedure in predicate logic is Herbrand's theorem [Chang and Lee, 1973], which tells us the following:

- To show that a set of clauses S is unsatisfiable, it is necessary to consider only interpretations over a particular set, called the *Herbrand universe* of S.

- A set of clauses S is unsatisfiable if and only if a finite subset of ground instances (in which all bound variables have had a value substituted for them) of S is unsatisfiable.

The second part of the theorem is important if there is to exist any computational procedure for proving unsatisfiability, since in a finite amount of time no procedure will be able to examine an infinite set. The first part suggests that one way to go about finding a contradiction is to try systematically the possible substitutions and see if each produces a contradiction. But that is highly inefficient. The resolution principle, first introduced by Robinson [1965], provides a way of finding contradictions by trying a minimum number of substitutions. The idea is to keep clauses in their general form as long as possible and only introduce specific substitutions when they are required. For more details on different kinds of resolution, see Stickel [1988].

5.4.3   Resolution in Propositional Logic

In order to make it clear how resolution works, we first present the resolution procedure for propositional logic. We then expand it to include predicate logic.

In propositional logic, the procedure for producing a proof by resolution of proposition P with respect to a set of axioms F is the following.

Algorithm: Propositional Resolution

1. Convert all the propositions of F to clause form.

2. Negate P and convert the result to clause form. Add it to the set of clauses obtained in step 1.

3. Repeat until either a contradiction is found or no progress can be made:

   (a) Select two clauses. Call these the parent clauses.

   (b) Resolve them together. The resulting clause, called the *resolvent*, will be the disjunction of all of the literals of both of the parent clauses with the following exception: If there are any pairs of literals L and $\neg L$ such that one of the parent clauses contains L and the other contains $\neg L$, then select one such pair and eliminate both L and $\neg L$ from the resolvent.

   (c) If the resolvent is the empty clause, then a contradiction has been found. If it is not, then add it to the set of clauses available to the procedure.

Let's look at a simple example. Suppose we are given the axioms shown in the first column of Figure 5.7 and we want to prove R. First we convert the axioms to clause form, as shown in the second column of the figure. Then we negate R, producing $\neg R$, which is already in clause form. Then we begin selecting pairs of clauses to resolve together. Although any pair of clauses can be resolved, only those pairs that contain complementary literals will produce a resolvent that is likely to lead to the goal of producing the empty clause (shown as a box). We might, for example, generate the sequence of resolvents shown in Figure 5.8. We begin by resolving with the clause $\neg R$ since that is one of the clauses that must be involved in the contradiction we are trying to find.

One way of viewing the resolution process is that it takes a set of clauses that are all assumed to be true and, based on information provided by the others, it generates new clauses that represent restrictions on the way each of those original clauses can be made true. A contradiction occurs when a clause becomes so restricted that there is no way it can be true. This is indicated by the generation of the empty clause. To see how this works, let's look again at the example. In order for proposition 2 to be true, one of three things must be true: $\neg P$, $\neg Q$, or R. But we are assuming that $\neg R$ is true. Given

Given Axioms	Converted to Clause Form	
P	P	(1)
$(P \wedge Q) \rightarrow R$	$\neg P \vee \neg Q \vee R$	(2)
$(S \vee T) \rightarrow Q$	$\neg S \vee Q$	(3)
	$\neg T \vee Q$	(4)
T	T	(5)

Figure 5.7: A Few Facts in Propositional Logic

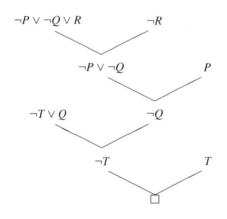

Figure 5.8: Resolution in Propositional Logic

that, the only way for proposition 2 to be true is for one of two things to be true: $\neg P$ or $\neg Q$. That is what the first resolvent clause says. But proposition 1 says that P is true, which means that $\neg P$ cannot be true, which leaves only one way for proposition 2 to be true, namely for $\neg Q$ to be true (as shown in the second resolvent clause). Proposition 4 can be true if either $\neg T$ or Q is true. But since we now know that $\neg Q$ must be true, the only way for proposition 4 to be true is for $\neg T$ to be true (the third resolvent). But proposition 5 says that T is true. Thus there is no way for all of these clauses to be true in a single interpretation. This is indicated by the empty clause (the last resolvent).

5.4.4   The Unification Algorithm

In propositional logic, it is easy to determine that two literals cannot both be true at the same time. Simply look for L and $\neg L$. In predicate logic, this matching process is more complicated since the arguments of the predicates must be considered. For example, *man(John)* and $\neg$*man(John)* is a contradiction, while *man(John)* and $\neg$*man(Spot)* is not. Thus, in order to determine contradictions, we need a matching procedure that compares two literals and discovers whether there exists a set of substitutions that makes them identical. There is a straightforward recursive procedure, called the *unification algorithm*, that does just this.

The basic idea of unification is very simple. To attempt to unify two literals, we first check if their initial predicate symbols are the same. If so, we can proceed. Otherwise, there is no way they can be unified, regardless of their arguments. For example, the two literals

tryassassinate(Marcus, Caesar)
hate(Marcus, Caesar)

cannot be unified. If the predicate symbols match, then we must check the arguments, one pair at a time. If the first matches, we can continue with the second, and so on. To test each argument pair, we can simply call the unification procedure recursively. The matching rules are simple. Different constants or predicates cannot match; identical ones can. A variable can match another variable, any constant, or a predicate expression, with the restriction that the predicate expression must not contain any instances of the variable being matched.

The only complication in this procedure is that we must find a single, consistent substitution for the entire literal, not separate ones for each piece of it. To do this, we must take each substitution that we find and apply it to the remainder of the literals before we continue trying to unify them. For example, suppose we want to unify the expressions

$P(x, x)$
$P(y, z)$

The two instances of P match fine. Next we compare x and y, and decide that if we substitute y for x, they could match. We will write that substitution as

y/x

(We could, of course, have decided instead to substitute x for y, since they are both just dummy variable names. The algorithm will simply pick one of these two substitutions.) But now, if we simply continue and match x and z, we produce the substitution z/x. But we cannot substitute both y and z for x, so we have not produced a consistent substitution.

What we need to do after finding the first substitution y/x is to make that substitution throughout the literals, giving

$P(y, y)$
$P(y, z)$

Now we can attempt to unify arguments y and z, which succeeds with the substitution z/y. The entire unification process has now succeeded with a substitution that is the composition of the two substitutions we found. We write the composition as

$(z/y)(y/x)$

following standard notation for function composition. In general, the substitution $(a_1/a_2, a_3/a_4, \ldots)(b_1/b_2, b_3/b_4, \ldots) \ldots$ means to apply all the substitutions of the right-most list, then take the result and apply all the ones of the next list, and so forth, until all substitutions have been applied.

The object of the unification procedure is to discover at least one substitution that causes two literals to match. Usually, if there is one such substitution there are many. For example, the literals

> $hate(x, y)$
> $hate(Marcus, z)$

could be unified with any of the following substitutions:

> $(Marcus/x, z/y)$
> $(Marcus/x, y/z)$
> $(Marcus/x, Caesar/y, Caesar/z)$
> $(Marcus/x, Polonius/y, Polonius/z)$

The first two of these are equivalent except for lexical variation. But the second two, although they produce a match, also produce a substitution that is more restrictive than absolutely necessary for the match. Because the final substitution produced by the unification process will be used by the resolution procedure, it is useful to generate the most general unifier possible. The algorithm shown below will do that.

Having explained the operation of the unification algorithm, we can now state it concisely. We describe a procedure Unify($L1$, $L2$), which returns as its value a list representing the composition of the substitutions that were performed during the match. The empty list, NIL, indicates that a match was found without any substitutions. The value FAIL indicates that the unification procedure failed.

Algorithm: Unify(L1, L2)

1. If $L1$ or $L2$ is a variable or constant, then:

    (a) If $L1$ and $L2$ are identical, then return NIL.

    (b) Else if $L1$ is a variable, then if $L1$ occurs in $L2$ then return FAIL, else return $\{(L2/L1)\}$.

    (c) Else if $L2$ is a variable then if $L2$ occurs in $L1$ then return FAIL, else return $\{(L1/L2)\}$.

    (d) Else return FAIL.

2. If the initial predicate symbols in $L1$ and $L2$ are not identical, then return FAIL.

3. If $L1$ and $L2$ have a different number of arguments, then return FAIL.

4. Set *SUBST* to NIL. (At the end of this procedure, *SUBST* will contain all the substitutions used to unify $L1$ and $L2$.)

5. For $i \leftarrow 1$ to number of arguments in $L1$:

(a) Call Unify with the *i*th argument of *L*1 and the *i*th argument of *L*2, putting result in *S*.

(b) If *S* = FAIL then return FAIL.

(c) If *S* is not equal to NIL then:

    i. Apply *S* to the remainder of both *L*1 and *L*2.

    ii. *SUBST* := APPEND(*S*, *SUBST*).

6. Return *SUBST*.

The only part of this algorithm that we have not yet discussed is the check in steps 1(*b*) and 1(*c*) to make sure that an expression involving a given variable is not unified with that variable. Suppose we were attempting to unify the expressions

$$f(x, x)$$
$$f(g(x), g(x))$$

If we accepted $g(x)$ as a substitution for x, then we would have to substitute it for x in the remainder of the expressions. But this leads to infinite recursion since it will never be possible to eliminate x.

Unification has deep mathematical roots and is a useful operation in many AI programs, for example, theorem provers and natural language parsers. As a result, efficient data structures and algorithms for unification have been developed. For an introduction to these techniques and applications, see Knight [1989].

5.4.5 Resolution in Predicate Logic

We now have an easy way of determining that two literals are contradictory—they are if one of them can be unified with the negation of the other. So, for example, $man(x)$ and $\neg man(Spot)$ are contradictory, since $man(x)$ and $man(Spot)$ can be unified. This corresponds to the intuition that says that $man(x)$ cannot be true for all x if there is known to be some x, say Spot, for which $man(x)$ is false. Thus in order to use resolution for expressions in the predicate logic, we use the unification algorithm to locate pairs of literals that cancel out.

We also need to use the unifier produced by the unification algorithm to generate the resolvent clause. For example, suppose we want to resolve two clauses:

1. *man(Marcus)*
2. $\neg man(x_1) \lor mortal(x_1)$

The literal *man(Marcus)* can be unified with the literal $man(x_1)$ with the substitution $Marcus/x_1$, telling us that for $x_1 = Marcus$, $\neg man(Marcus)$ is false. But we cannot simply cancel out the two *man* literals as we did in propositional logic and generate the resolvent $mortal(x_1)$. Clause 2 says that for a given x_1, either $\neg man(x_1)$ or $mortal(x_1)$. So for it to be true, we can now conclude only that $mortal(Marcus)$ must be true. It is not necessary that $mortal(x_1)$ be true for all x_1, since for some values of x_1, $\neg man(x_1)$ might be true, making $mortal(x_1)$ irrelevant to the truth of the complete clause. So the resolvent generated by clauses 1 and 2 must be $mortal(Marcus)$, which we get by applying the result of the unification process to the resolvent. The resolution process can then proceed from there to discover whether *mortal(Marcus)* leads to a contradiction with other available clauses.

This example illustrates the importance of standardizing variables apart during the process of converting expressions to clause form. Given that that standardization has been done, it is easy to determine how the unifier must be used to perform substitutions to create the resolvent. If two instances of the same variable occur, then they must be given identical substitutions.

We can now state the resolution algorithm for predicate logic as follows, assuming a set of given statements F and a statement to be proved P:

Algorithm: Resolution

1. Convert all the statements of F to clause form.

2. Negate P and convert the result to clause form. Add it to the set of clauses obtained in 1.

3. Repeat until either a contradiction is found, no progress can be made, or a prede-termined amount of effort has been expended.

   (a) Select two clauses. Call these the parent clauses.

   (b) Resolve them together. The resolvent will be the disjunction of all the literals of both parent clauses with appropriate substitutions performed and with the following exception: If there is one pair of literals $T1$ and $\neg T2$ such that one of the parent clauses contains $T1$ and the other contains $T2$ and if $T1$ and $T2$ are unifiable, then neither $T1$ nor $T2$ should appear in the resolvent. We call $T1$ and $T2$ *complementary literals*. Use the substitution produced by the unification to create the resolvent. If there is more than one pair of complementary literals, only one pair should be omitted from the resolvent.

   (c) If the resolvent is the empty clause, then a contradiction has been found. If it is not, then add it to the set of clauses available to the procedure.

If the choice of clauses to resolve together at each step is made in certain systematic ways, then the resolution procedure will find a contradiction if one exists. However, it may take a very long time. There exist strategies for making the choice that can speed up the process considerably:

- Only resolve pairs of clauses that contain complementary literals, since only such resolutions produce new clauses that are harder to satisfy than their parents. To facilitate this, index clauses by the predicates they contain, combined with an indication of whether the predicate is negated. Then, given a particular clause, possible resolvents that contain a complementary occurrence of one of its predi-cates can be located directly.

- Eliminate certain clauses as soon as they are generated so that they cannot partic-ipate in later resolutions. Two kinds of clauses should be eliminated: tautologies (which can never be unsatisfied) and clauses that are subsumed by other clauses (i.e., they are easier to satisfy). For example, $P \vee Q$ is subsumed by P.)

- Whenever possible, resolve either with one of the clauses that is part of the statement we are trying to refute or with a clause generated by a resolution with such a clause. This is called the *set-of-support strategy* and corresponds to the intuition that the contradiction we are looking for must involve the statement we are trying to prove. Any other contradiction would say that the previously believed statements were inconsistent.

- Whenever possible, resolve with clauses that have a single literal. Such resolutions generate new clauses with fewer literals than the larger of their parent clauses and thus are probably closer to the goal of a resolvent with zero terms. This method is called the *unit-preference strategy*.

Let's now return to our discussion of Marcus and show how resolution can be used to prove new things about him. Let's first consider the set of statements introduced in Section 5.1. To use them in resolution proofs, we must convert them to clause form as described in Section 5.4.1. Figure 5.9(a) shows the results of that conversion. Figure 5.9(b) shows a resolution proof of the statement

$$hate(Marcus, Caesar)$$

Of course, many more resolvents could have been generated than we have shown, but we used the heuristics described above to guide the search. Notice that what we have done here essentially is to reason backward from the statement we want to show is a contradiction through a set of intermediate conclusions to the final conclusion of inconsistency.

Suppose our actual goal in proving the assertion

$$hate(Marcus, Caesar)$$

was to answer the question "Did Marcus hate Caesar?" In that case, we might just as easily have attempted to prove the statement

$$\neg hate(Marcus, Caesar)$$

To do so, we would have added

$$hate(Marcus, Caesar)$$

to the set of available clauses and begun the resolution process. But immediately we notice that there are no clauses that contain a literal involving $\neg hate$. Since the resolution process can only generate new clauses that are composed of combinations of literals from already existing clauses, we know that no such clause can be generated and thus we conclude that $hate(Marcus, Caesar)$ will not produce a contradiction with the known statements. This is an example of the kind of situation in which the resolution procedure can detect that no contradiction exists. Sometimes this situation is detected not at the beginning of a proof, but part way through, as shown in the example in Figure 5.10(a), based on the axioms given in Figure 5.9.

But suppose our knowledge base contained the two additional statements

Axioms in clause form:
1. *man(Marcus)*
2. *Pompeian(Marcus)*
3. ¬*Pompeian(x₁)* ∨ *Roman(x₁)*
4. *ruler(Caesar)*
5. ¬*Roman(x₂)* ∨ *loyalto(x₂, Caesar)* ∨ *hate(x₂, Caesar)*
6. *loyalto(x₃, fl(x₃))*
7. ¬*man(x₄)* ∨ ¬*ruler(y₁)* ∨ ¬*tryassassinate(x₄, y₁)* ∨ *loyalto(x₄, y₁)*
8. *tryassassinate(Marcus, Caesar)*

(a)

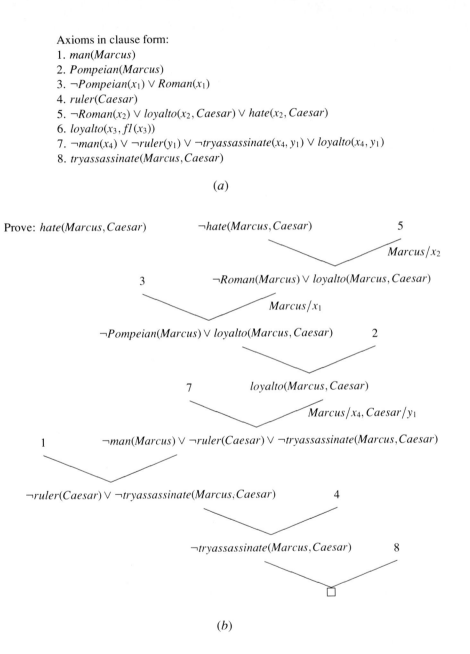

(b)

Figure 5.9: A Resolution Proof

Prove: *loyalto(Marcus, Caesar)*

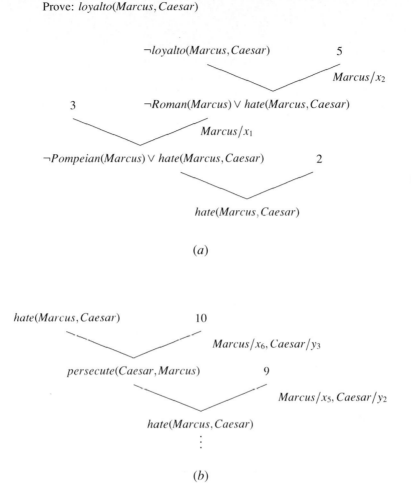

(a)

(b)

Figure 5.10: An Unsuccessful Attempt at Resolution

9. *persecute(x, y) → hate(y, x)*

10. *hate(x, y) → persecute(y, x)*

Converting to clause form, we get

9. $\neg persecute(x_5, y_2) \lor hate(y_2, x_5)$

10. $\neg hate(x_6, y_3) \lor persecute(y_3, x_6)$

These statements enable the proof of Figure 5.10(*a*) to continue as shown in Figure 5.10(*b*). Now to detect that there is no contradiction we must discover that the only resolvents that can be generated have been generated before. In other words, although we can generate resolvents, we can generate no new ones.

Given:

1. ¬*father*(*x*, *y*) ∨ ¬*woman*(*x*)
    (i.e., *father*(*x*, *y*) → ¬*woman*(*x*))
2. ¬*mother*(*x*, *y*) ∨ *woman*(*x*)
    (i.e., *mother*(*x*, *y*) → *woman*(*x*))
3. *mother*(*Chris*, *Mary*)
4. *father*(*Chris*, *Bill*)

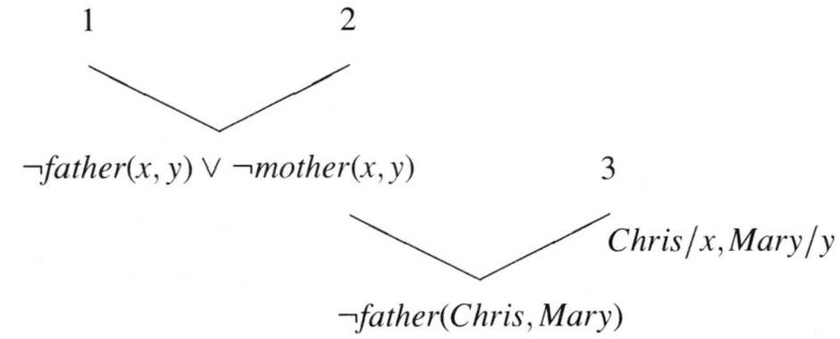

1   2

¬*father*(*x*, *y*) ∨ ¬*mother*(*x*, *y*)   3

                                        Chris/*x*, *Mary*/*y*

¬*father*(*Chris*, *Mary*)

Figure 5.11: The Need to Standardize Variables

Recall that the final step of the process of converting a set of formulas to clause form was to standardize apart the variables that appear in the final clauses. Now that we have discussed the resolution procedure, we can see clearly why this step is so important. Figure 5.11 shows an example of the difficulty that may arise if standardization is not done. Because the variable *y* occurs in both clause 1 and clause 2, the substitution at the second resolution step produces a clause that is too restricted and so does not lead to the contradiction that is present in the database. If, instead, the clause

    ¬*father*(*Chris*, *y*)

had been produced, the contradiction with clause 4 would have emerged. This would have happened if clause 2 had been rewritten as

    ¬*mother*(*a*, *b*) ∨ *woman*(*a*)

In its pure form, resolution requires all the knowledge it uses to be represented in the form of clauses. But as we pointed out in Section 5.3, it is often more efficient to represent certain kinds of information in the form of computable functions, computable predicates, and equality relationships. It is not hard to augment resolution to handle this sort of knowledge. Figure 5.12 shows a resolution proof of the statement

    ¬*alive*(*Marcus*, *now*)

Axioms in clause form:

1. $man(Marcus)$
2. $Pompeian(Marcus)$
3. $born(Marcus, 40)$
4. $\neg man(x_1) \vee mortal(x_1)$
5. $\neg Pompeian(x_2) \vee died(x_2, 79)$
6. $erupted(volcano, 79)$
7. $\neg mortal(x_3) \vee \neg born(x_3, t_1) \vee \neg gt(t_2 - t_1, 150) \vee dead(x_3, t_2)$
8. $now = 1991$
9a. $\neg alive(x_4, t_3) \vee \neg dead(x_4, t_3)$
9b. $dead(x_5, t_4) \vee alive(x_5, t_4)$
10. $\neg died(x_6, t_5) \vee \neg gt(t_6, t_5) \vee dead(x_6, t_6)$

Prove: $\neg alive(Marcus, now)$

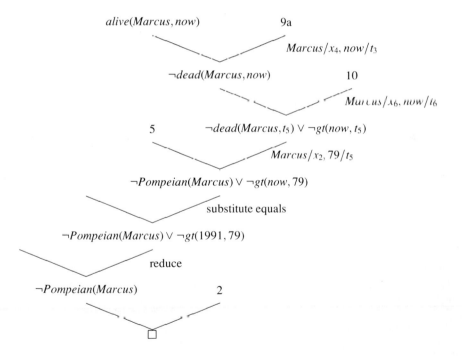

Figure 5.12: Using Resolution with Equality and Reduce

based on the statements given in Section 5.3. We have added two ways of generating new clauses, in addition to the resolution rule:

- Substitution of one value for another to which it is equal.

- Reduction of computable predicates. If the predicate evaluates to FALSE, it can simply be dropped, since adding $\lor$ FALSE to a disjunction cannot change its truth value. If the predicate evaluates to TRUE, then the generated clause is a tautology and cannot lead to a contradiction.

5.4.6 The Need to Try Several Substitutions

Resolution provides a very good way of finding a refutation proof without actually trying all the substitutions that Herbrand's theorem suggests might be necessary. But it does not always eliminate the necessity of trying more than one substitution. For example, suppose we know, in addition to the statements in Section 5.1, that

    hate(Marcus, Paulus)
    hate(Marcus, Julian)

Now if we want to prove that Marcus hates some ruler, we would be likely to try each substitution shown in Figure 5.13(*a*) and (*b*) before finding the contradiction shown in (*c*). Sometimes there is no way short of very good luck to avoid trying several substitutions.

5.4.7 Question Answering

Very early in the history of AI it was realized that theorem-proving techniques could be applied to the problem of answering questions. As we have already suggested, this seems natural since both deriving theorems from axioms and deriving new facts (answers) from old facts employ the process of deduction. We have already shown how resolution can be used to answer yes-no questions, such as "Is Marcus alive?" In this section, we show how resolution can be used to answer fill-in-the-blank questions, such as "When did Marcus die?" or "Who tried to assassinate a ruler?" Answering these questions involves finding a known statement that matches the terms given in the question and then responding with another piece of that same statement that fills the slot demanded by the question. For example, to answer the question "When did Marcus die?" we need a statement of the form

    died(Marcus, ??)

with ?? actually filled in by some particular year. So, since we can prove the statement

    died(Marcus, 79)

we can respond with the answer 79.

It turns out that the resolution procedure provides an easy way of locating just the statement we need and finding a proof for it. Let's continue with the example question

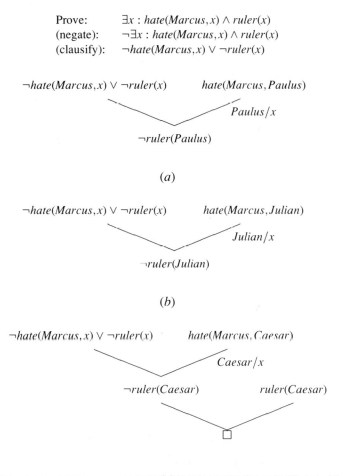

Prove: ∃x : hate(Marcus,x) ∧ ruler(x)
(negate):   ¬∃x : hate(Marcus,x) ∧ ruler(x)
(clausify): ¬hate(Marcus,x) ∨ ¬ruler(x)

¬hate(Marcus,x) ∨ ¬ruler(x)   hate(Marcus,Paulus)

                                    Paulus/x

              ¬ruler(Paulus)

                    (a)

¬hate(Marcus,x) ∨ ¬ruler(x)   hate(Marcus,Julian)

                                    Julian/x

              ¬ruler(Julian)

                    (b)

¬hate(Marcus,x) ∨ ¬ruler(x)   hate(Marcus,Caesar)

                                    Caesar/x

       ¬ruler(Caesar)   ruler(Caesar)

                    □

                    (c)

Figure 5.13: Trying Several Substitutions

"When did Marcus die?" In order to be able to answer this question, it must first be true that Marcus died. Thus it must be the case that

$$\exists t : died(Marcus, t)$$

A reasonable first step then might be to try to prove this. To do so using resolution, we attempt to show that

$$\neg \exists t : died(Marcus, t)$$

produces a contradiction. What does it mean for that statement to produce a contradiction? Either it conflicts with a statement of the form

$$\forall t : died(Marcus, t)$$

where t is a variable, in which case we can either answer the question by reporting that there are many times at which Marcus died, or we can simply pick one such time and respond with it. The other possibility is that we produce a contradiction with one or more specific statements of the form

$$died(Marcus, date)$$

for some specific value of *date*. Whatever value of date we use in producing that contradiction is the answer we want. The value that proves that there is a value (and thus the inconsistency of the statement that there is no such value) is exactly the value we want.

Figure 5.14(*a*) shows how the resolution process finds the statement for which we are looking. The answer to the question can then be derived from the chain of unifications that lead back to the starting clause. We can eliminate the necessity for this final step by adding an additional expression to the one we are going to use to try to find a contradiction. This new expression will simply be the one we are trying to prove true (i.e., it will be the negation of the expression that is actually used in the resolution). We can tag it with a special marker so that it will not interfere with the resolution process. (In the figure, it is underlined.) It will just get carried along, but each time unification is done, the variables in this dummy expression will be bound just as are the ones in the clauses that are actively being used. Instead of terminating on reaching the nil clause, the resolution procedure will terminate when all that is left is the dummy expression. The bindings of its variables at that point provide the answer to the question. Figure 5.14(*b*) shows how this process produces an answer to our question.

Unfortunately, given a particular representation of the facts in a system, there will usually be some questions that cannot be answered using this mechanism. For example, suppose that we want to answer the question "What happened in 79 A.D.?" using the statements in Section 5.3. In order to answer the question, we need to prove that something happened in 79. We need to prove

$$\exists x : event(x, 79)$$

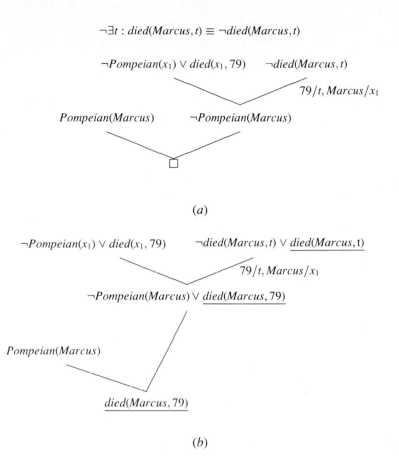

Figure 5.14: Answer Extraction Using Resolution

and to discover a value for *x*. But we do not have any statements of the form *event(x, y)*.

We can, however, answer the question if we change our representation. Instead of saying

erupted(volcano, 79)

we can say

event(erupted(volcano), 79)

Then the simple proof shown in Figure 5.15 enables us to answer the question.

This new representation has the drawback that it is more complex than the old one. And it still does not make it possible to answer all conceivable questions. In general, it is necessary to decide on the kinds of questions that will be asked and to design a representation appropriate for those questions.

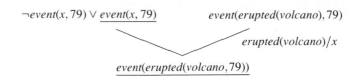

Figure 5.15: Using the New Representation

Of course, yes-no and fill-in-the-blank questions are not the only kinds one could ask. For example, we might ask how to do something. So we have not yet completely solved the problem of question answering. In later chapters, we discuss some other methods for answering a variety of questions. Some of them exploit resolution; others do not.

5.5   Natural Deduction

In the last section, we introduced resolution as an easily implementable proof procedure that relies for its simplicity on a uniform representation of the statements it uses. Unfortunately, uniformity has its price—everything looks the same. Since everything looks the same, there is no easy way to select those statements that are the most likely to be useful in solving a particular problem. In converting everything to clause form, we often lose valuable heuristic information that is contained in the original representation of the facts. For example, suppose we believe that all judges who are not crooked are well-educated, which can be represented as

$\forall x : judge(x) \land \neg crooked(x) \rightarrow educated(x)$

In this form, the statement suggests a way of deducing that someone is educated. But when the same statement is converted to clause form,

$\neg judge(x) \lor crooked(x) \lor educated(x)$

it appears also to be a way of deducing that someone is not a judge by showing that he is not crooked and not educated. Of course, in a logical sense, it is. But it is almost certainly not the best way, or even a very good way, to go about showing that someone is not a judge. The heuristic information contained in the original statement has been lost in the transformation.

Another problem with the use of resolution as the basis of a theorem-proving system is that people do not think in resolution. Thus it is very difficult for a person to interact with a resolution theorem prover, either to give it advice or to be given advice by it. Since proving very hard things is something that computers still do poorly, it is important from a practical standpoint that such interaction be possible. To facilitate it, we are forced to look for a way of doing machine theorem proving that corresponds more closely to the processes used in human theorem proving. We are thus led to what we call, mostly by definition, *natural deduction*.

Natural deduction is not a precise term. Rather it describes a melange of techniques, used in combination to solve problems that are not tractable by any one method alone. One common technique is to arrange knowledge, not by predicates, as we have been doing, but rather by the objects involved in the predicates. Some techniques for doing this are described in Chapter 9. Another technique is to use a set of rewrite rules that not only describe logical implications but also suggest the way that those implications can be exploited in proofs.

For a good survey of the variety of techniques that can be exploited in a natural deduction system, see Bledsoe [1977]. Although the emphasis in that paper is on proving mathematical theorems, many of the ideas in it can be applied to a variety of domains in which it is necessary to deduce new statements from known ones. For another discussion of theorem proving using natural mechanisms, see Boyer and Moore [1988], which describes a system for reasoning about programs. It places particular emphasis on the use of mathematical induction as a proof technique.

5.6 Summary

In this chapter we showed how predicate logic can be used as the basis of a technique for knowledge representation. We also discussed a problem-solving technique, resolution, that can be applied when knowledge is represented in this way. The resolution procedure is not guaranteed to halt if given a nontheorem to prove. But is it guaranteed to halt and find a contradiction if one exists? This is called the *completeness* question. In the form in which we have presented the algorithm, the answer to this question is no. Some small changes, usually not implemented in theorem-proving systems, must be made to guarantee completeness. But, from a computational point of view, completeness is not the only important question. Instead, we must ask whether a proof can be found in the limited amount of time that is available. There are two ways to approach achieving this computational goal. The first is to search for good heuristics that can inform a theorem-proving program. Current theorem-proving research attempts to do this. The other approach is to change not the program but the data given to the program. In this approach, we recognize that a knowledge base that is just a list of logical assertions possesses no structure. Suppose an information-bearing structure could be imposed on such a knowledge base. Then that additional information could be used to guide the program that uses the knowledge. Such a program may not look a lot like a theorem prover, although it will still be a knowledge-based problem solver. We discuss this idea further in Chapter 9.

A second difficulty with the use of theorem proving in AI systems is that there are some kinds of information that are not easily represented in predicate logic. Consider the following examples:

- "It is very hot today." How can relative degrees of heat be represented?

- "Blond-haired people often have blue eyes." How can the amount of certainty be represented?

- "If there is no evidence to the contrary, assume that any adult you meet knows how to read." How can we represent that one fact should be inferred from the absence of another?

- "It's better to have more pieces on the board than the opponent has." How can we represent this kind of heuristic information?

- "I know Bill thinks the Giants will win, but I think they are going to lose." How can several different belief systems be represented at once?

These examples suggest issues in knowledge representation that we have not yet satisfactorily addressed. They deal primarily with the need to make do with a knowledge base that is incomplete, although other problems also exist, such as the difficulty of representing continuous phenomena in a discrete system. Some solutions to these problems are presented in the remaining chapters in this part of the book.

5.7   Exercises

1. Using facts 1-9 of Section 5.1, answer the question, "Did Marcus hate Caesar?"

2. In Section 5.3, we showed that given our facts, there were two ways to prove the statement ¬*alive*(*Marcus*, *now*). In Figure 5.12 a resolution proof corresponding to one of those methods is shown. Use resolution to derive another proof of the statement using the other chain of reasoning.

3. Trace the operation of the unification algorithm on each of the following pairs of literals:

   (a) *f*(*Marcus*) and *f*(*Caesar*)

   (b) *f*(*x*) and *f*(*g*(*y*))

   (c) *f*(*Marcus*, *g*(*x*, *y*)) and *f*(*x*, *g*(*Caesar*, *Marcus*))

4. Consider the following sentences:

   - John likes all kinds of food.
   - Apples are food.
   - Chicken is food.
   - Anything anyone eats and isn't killed by is food.
   - Bill eats peanuts and is still alive.
   - Sue eats everything Bill eats.

   (a) Translate these sentences into formulas in predicate logic.

   (b) Prove that John likes peanuts using backward chaining.

   (c) Convert the formulas of part a into clause form.

   (d) Prove that John likes peanuts using resolution.

    (e) Use resolution to answer the question, "What food does Sue eat?"

5. Consider the following facts:

- The members of the Elm St. Bridge Club are Joe, Sally, Bill, and Ellen.
- Joe is married to Sally.
- Bill is Ellen's brother.
- The spouse of every married person in the club is also in the club.
- The last meeting of the club was at Joe's house.

    (a) Represent these facts in predicate logic.

    (b) From the facts given above, most people would be able to decide on the truth of the following additional statements:

- The last meeting of the club was at Sally's house.
- Ellen is not married.

Can you construct resolution proofs to demonstrate the truth of each of these statements given the five facts listed above? Do so if possible. Otherwise, add the facts you need and then construct the proofs.

6. Assume the following facts:

- Steve only likes easy courses.
- Science courses are hard.
- All the courses in the basketweaving department are easy.
- BK301 is a basketweaving course.

Use resolution to answer the question, "What course would Steve like?"

7. In Section 5.4.7, we answered the question, "When did Marcus die?" by using resolution to show that there was a time when Marcus died. Using the facts given in Figure 5.4, and the additional fact

$$\forall x : \forall t_1 : dead(x, t_1) \rightarrow \exists t_2 : gt(t_1, t_2) \land died(x, t_2)$$

there is another way to show that there was a time when Marcus died.

    (a) Do a resolution proof of this other chain of reasoning.

    (b) What answer will this proof give to the question, "When did Marcus die?"

8. Suppose that we are attempting to resolve the following clauses:

$loves(father(a), a)$
$\lnot loves(y, x) \lor loves(x, y)$

    (a) What will be the result of the unification algorithm when applied to clause 1 and the first term of clause 2?

    (b) What must be generated as a result of resolving these two clauses?

(c) What does this example show about the order in which the substitutions determined by the unification procedure must be performed?

9. Suppose you are given the following facts:

$$\forall x, y, z : gt(x, y) \land gt(y, z) \rightarrow gt(x, z)$$
$$\forall a, b : succ(a, b) \rightarrow gt(a, b)$$
$$\forall x : \neg gt(x, x)$$

You want to prove that

$$gt(5, 2)$$

Consider the following attempt at a resolution proof:

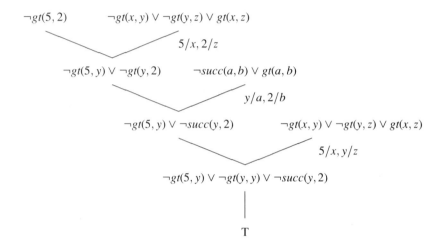

(a) What went wrong?

(b) What needs to be added to the resolution procedure to make sure that this does not happen?

10. The answer to the last problem suggests that the unification procedure could be simplified by omitting the check that prevents x and $f(x)$ from being unified together (the *occur check*). This should be possible since no two clauses will ever share variables. If x occurs in one, $f(x)$ cannot occur in another. But suppose the unification procedure is given the following two clauses (in the notation of Section 5.4.4):

$$p(x, f(x))$$
$$p(f(a), a)$$

Trace the execution of the procedure. What does this example show about the need for the occur check?

11. What is wrong with the following argument [Henle, 1965]?

- Men are widely distributed over the earth.
- Socrates is a man.

- Therefore, Socrates is widely distributed over the earth.

How should the facts represented by these sentences be represented in logic so that this problem does not arise?

12. Consider all the facts about baseball that are represented in the slot-and-filler structure of Figure 4.5. Represent those same facts as a set of assertions in predicate logic. Show how the inferences that were derived from that knowledge in Section 4.2 can be derived using logical deduction.

13. What problems would be encountered in attempting to represent the following statements in predicate logic? It should be possible to deduce the final statement from the others.

- John only likes to see French movies.
- It's safe to assume a movie is American unless explicitly told otherwise.
- The Playhouse rarely shows foreign films.
- People don't do things that will cause them to be in situations that they don't like.
- John doesn't go to the Playhouse very often.

Chapter 6

Representing Knowledge Using Rules

In this chapter, we discuss the use of rules to encode knowledge. This is a particularly important issue since rule-based reasoning systems have played a very important role in the evolution of AI from a purely laboratory science into a commercially significant one, as we see later in Chapter 20.

We have already talked about rules as the basis for a search program. But we gave little consideration to the way knowledge about the world was represented in the rules (although we can see a simple example of this in Section 4.2). In particular, we have been assuming that search control knowledge was maintained completely separately from the rules themselves. We will now relax that assumption and consider a set of rules to represent both knowledge about relationships in the world, as well as knowledge about how to solve problems using the content of the rules.

6.1 Procedural versus Declarative Knowledge

Since our discussion of knowledge representation has concentrated so far on the use of logical assertions, we use logic as a starting point in our discussion of rule-based systems.

In the previous chapter, we viewed logical assertions as declarative representations of knowledge. A *declarative representation* is one in which knowledge is specified, but the use to which that knowledge is to be put is not given. To use a declarative representation, we must augment it with a program that specifies what is to be done to the knowledge and how. For example, a set of logical assertions can be combined with a resolution theorem prover to give a complete program for solving problems. There is a different way, though, in which logical assertions can be viewed, namely as a *program*, rather than as *data* to a program. In this view, the implication statements define the legitimate reasoning paths and the atomic assertions provide the starting points (or, if we reason backward, the ending points) of those paths. These reasoning paths define the possible execution paths of the program in much the same way that traditional control constructs, such as *if-then-else*, define the execution paths through traditional programs. In other words, we could view logical assertions as procedural representations of knowledge. A *procedural representation* is one in which the control information that is necessary to use the knowledge is considered to be embedded in the knowledge itself. To use a procedural representation, we need to augment it with an interpreter that follows the instructions given in the knowledge.

Actually, viewing logical assertions as code is not a very radical idea, given that all programs are really data to other programs that interpret (or compile) and execute them. The real difference between the declarative and the procedural views of knowledge lies in where control information resides. For example, consider the knowledge base:

> *man(Marcus)*
> *man(Caesar)*
> *person(Cleopatra)*
> $\forall x : man(x) \rightarrow person(x)$

Now consider trying to extract from this knowledge base the answer to the question

> $\exists y : person(y)$

We want to bind y to a particular value for which *person* is true. Our knowledge base justifies any of the following answers:

> $y = Marcus$
> $y = Caesar$
> $y = Cleopatra$

Because there is more than one value that satisfies the predicate, but only one value is needed, the answer to the question will depend on the order in which the assertions are examined during the search for a response. If we view the assertions as declarative, then they do not themselves say anything about how they will be examined. If we view them as procedural, then they do. Of course, nondeterministic programs are possible— for example, the concurrent and parallel programming constructs described in Dijkstra [1976], Hoare [1985], and Chandy and Misra [1989]. So, we could view these assertions as a nondeterministic program whose output is simply not defined. If we do this, then we have a "procedural" representation that actually contains no more information than does the "declarative" form. But most systems that view knowledge as procedural do not do this. The reason for this is that, at least if the procedure is to execute on any sequential or on most existing parallel machines, some decision must be made about the order in which the assertions will be examined. There is no hardware support for randomness. So if the interpreter must have a way of deciding, there is no real reason not to specify it as part of the definition of the language and thus to define the meaning of any particular program in the language. For example, we might specify that assertions will be examined in the order in which they appear in the program and that search will proceed depth-first, by which we mean that if a new subgoal is established then it will be pursued immediately and other paths will only be examined if the new one fails. If we do that, then the assertions we gave above describe a program that will answer our question with

$y = Cleopatra$

To see clearly the difference between declarative and procedural representations, consider the following assertions:

man(*Marcus*)
man(*Caesar*)
$\forall x : man(x) \rightarrow person(x)$
person(*Cleopatra*)

Viewed declaratively, this is the same knowledge base that we had before. All the same answers are supported by the system and no one of them is explicitly selected. But viewed procedurally, and using the control model we used to get *Cleopatra* as our answer before, this is a different knowledge base since now the answer to our question is *Marcus*. This happens because the first statement that can achieve the *person* goal is the inference rule $\forall x : man(x) \rightarrow person(x)$. This rule sets up a subgoal to find a man. Again the statements are examined from the beginning, and now *Marcus* is found to satisfy the subgoal and thus also the goal. So *Marcus* is reported as the answer.

It is important to keep in mind that although we have said that a procedural representation encodes control information in the knowledge base, it does so only to the extent that the interpreter for the knowledge base recognizes that control information. So we could have gotten a different answer to the *person* question by leaving our original knowledge base intact and changing the interpreter so that it examines statements from last to first (but still pursuing depth-first search). Following this control regime, we report *Caesar* as our answer.

There has been a great deal of controversy in AI over whether declarative or procedural knowledge representation frameworks are better. There is no clearcut answer to the question. As you can see from this discussion, the distinction between the two forms is often very fuzzy. Rather than try to answer the question of which approach is better, what we do in the rest of this chapter is to describe ways in which rule formalisms and interpreters can be combined to solve problems. We begin with a mechanism called *logic programming*, and then we consider more flexible structures for rule-based systems.

6.2 Logic Programming

Logic programming is a programming language paradigm in which logical assertions are viewed as programs, as described in the previous section. There are several logic programming systems in use today, the most popular of which is PROLOG [Clocksin and Mellish, 1984; Bratko, 1986]. A PROLOG program is described as a series of logical assertions, each of which is a *Horn clause*.[1] A Horn clause is a clause (as defined in Section 5.4.1) that has at most one positive literal. Thus p, $\neg p \lor q$, and $p \rightarrow q$ are all Horn clauses. The last of these does not look like a clause and it appears to have two positive literals. But recall from Section 5.4.1 that any logical expression can be converted to clause form. If we do that for this example, the resulting clause is $\neg p \lor q$,

---

[1] Programs written in pure PROLOG are composed only of Horn clauses. PROLOG, as an actual programming language, however, allows departures from Horn clauses. In the rest of this section, we limit our discussion to pure PROLOG.

$$\forall x : pet(x) \wedge small(x) \rightarrow apartmentpet(x)$$
$$\forall x : cat(x) \vee dog(x) \rightarrow pet(x)$$
$$\forall x : poodle(x) \rightarrow dog(x) \wedge small(x)$$
$$poodle(fluffy)$$

A Representation in Logic

```
apartmentpet(X)  :- pet(X),  small(X).
pet(X)  :- cat(X).
pet(X)  :- dog(X).
dog(X)  :- poodle(X).
small(X)  :- poodle(X).
poodle(fluffy).
```

A Representation in PROLOG

Figure 6.1: A Declarative and a Procedural Representation

which is a well-formed Horn clause. As we will see below, when Horn clauses are written in PROLOG programs, they actually look more like the form we started with (an implication with at most one literal on the right of the implication sign) than the clause form we just produced. Some examples of PROLOG Horn clauses appear below.

The fact that PROLOG programs are composed only of Horn clauses and not of arbitrary logical expressions has two important consequences. The first is that because of the uniform representation a simple and efficient interpreter can be written. The second consequence is even more important. The logic of Horn clause systems is decidable (unlike that of full first-order predicate logic).

The control structure that is imposed on a PROLOG program by the PROLOG interpreter is the same one we used at the beginning of this chapter to find the answers *Cleopatra* and *Marcus*. The input to a program is a goal to be proved. Backward reasoning is applied to try to prove the goal given the assertions in the program. The program is read top to bottom, left to right and search is performed depth-first with backtracking.

Figure 6.1 shows an example of a simple knowledge base represented in standard logical notation and then in PROLOG. Both of these representations contain two types of statements, *facts*, which contain only constants (i.e., no variables) and *rules*, which do contain variables. Facts represent statements about specific objects. Rules represent statements about classes of objects.

Notice that there are several superficial, syntactic differences between the logic and the PROLOG representations, including:

1. In logic, variables are explicitly quantified. In PROLOG, quantification is provided implicitly by the way the variables are interpreted (see below). The distinction between variables and constants is made in PROLOG by having all variables

begin with upper case letters and all constants begin with lower case letters or numbers.

2. In logic, there are explicit symbols for *and* ($\wedge$) and *or* ($\vee$). In PROLOG, there is an explicit symbol for *and* (,), but there is none for *or*. Instead, disjunction must be represented as a list of alternative statements, any one of which may provide the basis for a conclusion.

3. In logic, implications of the form "*p* implies *q*" are written as $p \rightarrow q$. In PROLOG, the same implication is written "backward," as q :- p. This form is natural in PROLOG because the interpreter always works backwards from a goal, and this form causes every rule to begin with the component that must therefore be matched first. This first component is called the *head* of the rule.

The first two of these differences arise naturally from the fact that PROLOG programs are actually sets of Horn clauses that have been transformed as follows:

1. If the Horn clause contains no negative literals (i.e., it contains a single literal which is positive), then leave it as it is.

2. Otherwise, rewrite the Horn clause as an implication, combining all of the negative literals into the antecedent of the implication and leaving the single positive literal (if there is one) as the consequent.

This procedure causes a clause, which originally consisted of a disjunction of literals (all but one of which were negative), to be transformed into a single implication whose antecedent is a conjunction of (what are now positive) literals. Further, recall that in a clause, all variables are implicitly universally quantified. But, when we apply this transformation (which essentially inverts several steps of the procedure we gave in Section 5.4.1 for converting to clause form), any variables that occurred in negative literals and so now occur in the antecedent become existentially quantified, while the variables in the consequent (the head) are still universally quantified. For example, the PROLOG clause

```
P(x)  :- Q(x, y)
```

is equivalent to the logical expression

$$\forall x : \exists y : Q(x, y) \rightarrow P(x)$$

A key difference between logic and the PROLOG representation is that the PROLOG interpreter has a fixed control strategy, and so the assertions in the PROLOG program define a particular search path to an answer to any question. In contrast, the logical assertions define only the set of answers that they justify; they themselves say nothing about how to choose among those answers if there are more than one.

The basic PROLOG control strategy outlined above is simple. Begin with a problem statement, which is viewed as a goal to be proved. Look for assertions that can prove the goal. Consider facts, which prove the goal directly, and also consider any rule whose head matches the goal. To decide whether a fact or a rule can be applied to the current problem, invoke a standard unification procedure (recall Section 5.4.4). Reason backward from that goal until a path is found that terminates with assertions in the program. Consider paths using a depth-first search strategy and using backtracking. At each choice point, consider options in the order in which they appear in the program. If a goal has more than one conjunctive part, prove the parts in the order in which they appear, propagating variable bindings as they are determined during unification. We can illustrate this strategy with a simple example.

Suppose the problem we are given is to find a value of X that satisfies the predicate `apartmentpet(X)`. We state this goal to PROLOG as

```
?- apartmentpet(X).
```

Think of this as the input to the program. The PROLOG interpreter begins looking for a fact with the predicate `apartmentpet` or a rule with that predicate as its head. Usually PROLOG programs are written with the facts containing a given predicate coming before the rules for that predicate so that the facts can be used immediately if they are appropriate and the rules will only be used when the desired fact is not immediately available. In this example, there are no facts with this predicate, though, so the one rule there is must be used. Since the rule will succeed if both of the clauses on its right-hand side can be satisfied, the next thing the interpreter does is to try to prove each of them. They will be tried in the order in which they appear. There are no facts with the predicate `pet` but again there are rules with it on the right-hand side. But this time there are two such rules, rather than one. All that is necessary for a proof though is that one of them succeed. They will be tried in the order in which they occur. The first will fail because there are no assertions about the predicate `cat` in the program. The second will eventually lead to success, using the rule about dogs and poodles and using the fact `poodle(fluffy)`. This results in the variable X being bound to `fluffy`. Now the second clause `small(X)` of the initial rule must be checked. Since X is now bound to fluffy, the more specific goal, `small(fluffy)`, must be proved. This too can be done by reasoning backward to the assertion `poodle(fluffy)`. The program then halts with the result `apartmentpet(fluffy)`.

Logical negation ($\neg$) cannot be represented explicitly in pure PROLOG. So, for example, it is not possible to encode directly the logical assertion

$$\forall x : dog(x) \rightarrow \neg cat(x)$$

Instead, negation is represented implicitly by the lack of an assertion. This leads to the problem-solving strategy called *negation as failure* [Clark, 1978]. If the PROLOG program of Figure 6.1 were given the goal

```
?- cat(fluffy).
```

it would return FALSE because it is unable to prove that Fluffy is a cat. Unfortunately, this program returns the same answer when given the goal

```
?- cat(mittens).
```

even though the program knows nothing about Mittens and specifically knows nothing that might prevent Mittens from being a cat. Negation by failure requires that we make what is called the *closed world assumption*, which states that all relevant, true assertions are contained in our knowledge base or are derivable from assertions that are so contained. Any assertion that is not present can therefore be assumed to be false. This assumption, while often justified, can cause serious problems when knowledge bases are incomplete. We discuss this issue further in Chapter 7.

There is much to say on the topic of PROLOG-style versus LISP-style programming. A great advantage of logic programming is that the programmer need only specify rules and facts since a search engine is built directly into the language. The disadvantage is that the search control is fixed. Although it is possible to write PROLOG code that uses search strategies other than depth-first with backtracking, it is difficult to do so. It is even more difficult to apply domain knowledge to constrain a search. PROLOG does allow for rudimentary control of search through a non-logical operator called *cut*. A cut can be inserted into a rule to specify a point that may not be backtracked over.

More generally, the fact that PROLOG programs must be composed of a restricted set of logical operators can be viewed as a limitation of the expressiveness of the language. But the other side of the coin is that it is possible to build PROLOG compilers that produce very efficient code.

In the rest of this chapter, we retain the rule-based nature of PROLOG, but we relax a number of PROLOG's design constraints, leading to more flexible rule-based architectures.

6.3 Forward versus Backward Reasoning

The object of a search procedure is to discover a path through a problem space from an initial configuration to a goal state. While PROLOG only searches from a goal state, there are actually two directions in which such a search could proceed:

- Forward, from the start states

- Backward, from the goal states

The production system model of the search process provides an easy way of viewing forward and backward reasoning as symmetric processes. Consider the problem of solving a particular instance of the 8-puzzle. The rules to be used for solving the puzzle can be written as shown in Figure 6.2. Using those rules we could attempt to solve the puzzle shown back in Figure 2.12 in one of two ways:

- *Reason forward from the initial states.* Begin building a tree of move sequences that might be solutions by starting with the initial configuration(s) at the root of the tree. Generate the next level of the tree by finding all the rules whose *left* sides match the root node and using their right sides to create the new configurations. Generate the next level by taking each node generated at the previous level and applying to it all of the rules whose left sides match it. Continue until a configuration that matches the goal state is generated.

Assume the areas of the tray are numbered:

1	2	3
4	5	6
7	8	9

Square 1 empty and Square 2 contains tile n $\rightarrow$
Square 2 empty and Square 1 contains tile n
Square 1 empty and Square 4 contains tile n $\rightarrow$
Square 4 empty and Square 1 contains tile n
Square 2 empty and Square 1 contains tile n $\rightarrow$
Square 1 empty and Square 2 contains tile n

$$\vdots$$

Figure 6.2: A Sample of the Rules for Solving the 8-Puzzle

- *Reason backward from the goal states.* Begin building a tree of move sequences that might be solutions by starting with the goal configuration(s) at the root of the tree. Generate the next level of the tree by finding all the rules whose *right* sides match the root node. These are all the rules that, if only we could apply them, would generate the state we want. Use the left sides of the rules to generate the nodes at this second level of the tree. Generate the next level of the tree by taking each node at the previous level and finding all the rules whose right sides match it. Then use the corresponding left sides to generate the new nodes. Continue until a node that matches the initial state is generated. This method of reasoning backward from the desired final state is often called *goal-directed reasoning*.

Notice that the same rules can be used both to reason forward from the initial state and to reason backward from the goal state. To reason forward, the left sides (the preconditions) are matched against the current state and the right sides (the results) are used to generate new nodes until the goal is reached. To reason backward, the right sides are matched against the current node and the left sides are used to generate new nodes representing new goal states to be achieved. This continues until one of these goal states is matched by an initial state.

In the case of the 8-puzzle, it does not make much difference whether we reason forward or backward; about the same number of paths will be explored in either case. But this is not always true. Depending on the topology of the problem space, it may be significantly more efficient to search in one direction rather than the other.

Four factors influence the question of whether it is better to reason forward or backward:

- Are there more possible start states or goal states? We would like to move from the smaller set of states to the larger (and thus easier to find) set of states.

- In which direction is the branching factor (i.e., the average number of nodes that can be reached directly from a single node) greater? We would like to proceed in the direction with the lower branching factor.

- Will the program be asked to justify its reasoning process to a user? If so, it is important to proceed in the direction that corresponds more closely with the way the user will think.

- What kind of event is going to trigger a problem-solving episode? If it is the arrival of a new fact, forward reasoning makes sense. If it is a query to which a response is desired, backward reasoning is more natural.

A few examples make these issues clearer. It seems easier to drive from an unfamiliar place home than from home to an unfamiliar place. Why is this? The branching factor is roughly the same in both directions (unless one-way streets are laid out very strangely). But for the purpose of finding our way around, there are many more locations that count as being home than there are locations that count as the unfamiliar target place. Any place from which we know how to get home can be considered as equivalent to home. If we can get to any such place, we can get home easily. But in order to find a route from where we are to an unfamiliar place, we pretty much have to be already at the unfamiliar place. So in going toward the unfamiliar place, we are aiming at a much smaller target than in going home. This suggests that if our starting position is home and our goal position is the unfamiliar place, we should plan our route by reasoning backward from the unfamiliar place.

On the other hand, consider the problem of symbolic integration. The problem space is the set of formulas, some of which contain integral expressions. The start state is a particular formula containing some integral expression. The desired goal state is a formula that is equivalent to the initial one and that does not contain any integral expressions. So we begin with a single easily identified start state and a huge number of possible goal states. Thus to solve this problem, it is better to reason forward using the rules for integration to try to generate an integral-free expression than to start with arbitrary integral-free expressions, use the rules for differentiation, and try to generate the particular integral we are trying to solve. Again we want to head toward the largest target; this time that means chaining forward.

These two examples have illustrated the importance of the relative number of start states to goal states in determining the optimal direction in which to search when the branching factor is approximately the same in both directions. When the branching factor is not the same, however, it must also be taken into account.

Consider again the problem of proving theorems in some particular domain of mathematics. Our goal state is the particular theorem to be proved. Our initial states are normally a small set of axioms. Neither of these sets is significantly bigger than the other. But consider the branching factor in each of the two directions. From a small set of axioms we can derive a very large number of theorems. On the other hand, this large number of theorems must go back to the small set of axioms. So the branching factor is significantly greater going forward from the axioms to the theorems than it is going backward from theorems to axioms. This suggests that it would be much better to reason backward when trying to prove theorems. Mathematicians have long realized this [Polya, 1957], as have the designers of theorem-proving programs.

The third factor that determines the direction in which search should proceed is the need to generate coherent justifications of the reasoning process as it proceeds. This is often crucial for the acceptance of programs for the performance of very important tasks. For example, doctors are unwilling to accept the advice of a diagnostic program that cannot explain its reasoning to the doctors' satisfaction. This issue was of concern to the designers of MYCIN [Shortliffe, 1976], a program that diagnoses infectious diseases. It reasons backward from its goal of determining the cause of a patient's illness. To do that, it uses rules that tell it such things as "If the organism has the following set of characteristics as determined by the lab results, then it is likely that it is organism x." By reasoning backward using such rules, the program can answer questions like "Why should I perform that test you just asked for?" with such answers as "Because it would help to determine whether organism x is present." (For a discussion of the explanation capabilities of MYCIN, see Chapter 20.)

Most of the search techniques described in Chapter 3 can be used to search either forward or backward. By describing the search process as the application of a set of production rules, it is easy to describe the specific search algorithms without reference to the direction of the search.[2]

We can also search both forward from the start state and backward from the goal simultaneously until two paths meet somewhere in between. This strategy is called *bidirectional search*. It seems appealing if the number of nodes at each step grows exponentially with the number of steps that have been taken. Empirical results [Pohl, 1971] suggest that for blind search, this divide-and-conquer strategy is indeed effective. Unfortunately, other results [Pohl, 1971; de Champeaux and Sint, 1977] suggest that for informed, heuristic search it is much less likely to be so. Figure 6.3 shows why bidirectional search may be ineffective. The two searches may pass each other, resulting in more work than it would have taken for one of them, on its own, to have finished. However, if individual forward and backward steps are performed as specified by a program that has been carefully constructed to exploit each in exactly those situations where it can be the most profitable, the results can be more encouraging. In fact, many successful AI applications have been written using a combination of forward and backward reasoning, and most AI programming environments provide explicit support for such hybrid reasoning.

Although in principle the same set of rules can be used for both forward and backward reasoning, in practice it has proved useful to define two classes of rules, each of which encodes a particular kind of knowledge.

- Forward rules, which encode knowledge about how to respond to certain input configurations.

- Backward rules, which encode knowledge about how to achieve particular goals.

By separating rules into these two classes, we essentially add to each rule an additional piece of information, namely how it should be used in problem solving. In the next three sections, we describe in more detail the two kinds of rule systems and how they can be combined.

---

[2]One exception to this is the means-ends analysis technique, described in Section 3.6, which proceeds not by making successive steps in a single direction but by reducing differences between the current and the goal states, and, as a result, sometimes reasoning backward and sometimes forward.

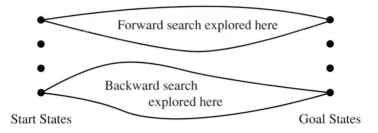

Figure 6.3: A Bad Use of Heuristic Bidirectional Search

6.3.1 Backward-Chaining Rule Systems

Backward-chaining rule systems, of which PROLOG is an example, are good for goal-directed problem solving. For example, a query system would probably use backward chaining to reason about and answer user questions.

In PROLOG, rules are restricted to Horn clauses. This allows for rapid indexing because all of the rules for deducing a given fact share the same rule head. Rules are matched with the unification procedure. Unification tries to find a set of bindings for variables to equate a (sub)goal with the head of some rule. Rules in a PROLOG program are matched in the order in which they appear.

Other backward-chaining systems allow for more complex rules. In MYCIN, for example, rules can be augmented with probabilistic certainty factors to reflect the fact that some rules are more reliable than others. We discuss this in more detail in Chapter 8.

6.3.2 Forward-Chaining Rule Systems

Instead of being directed by goals, we sometimes want to be directed by incoming data. For example, suppose you sense searing heat near your hand. You are likely to jerk your hand away. While this could be construed as goal-directed behavior, it is modeled more naturally by the recognize-act cycle characteristic of forward-chaining rule systems. In forward-chaining systems, left sides of rules are matched against the state description. Rules that match dump their right-hand side assertions into the state, and the process repeats.

Matching is typically more complex for forward-chaining systems than backward ones. For example, consider a rule that checks for some condition in the state description and then adds an assertion. After the rule fires, its conditions are probably still valid, so it could fire again immediately. However, we will need some mechanism to prevent repeated firings, especially if the state remains unchanged.

While simple matching and control strategies are possible, most forward-chaining systems (e.g., OPS5 [Brownston *et al.*, 1985]) implement highly efficient matchers and supply several mechanisms for preferring one rule over another. We discuss matching in more detail in the next section.

6.3.3   Combining Forward and Backward Reasoning

Sometimes certain aspects of a problem are best handled via forward chaining and other aspects by backward chaining. Consider a forward-chaining medical diagnosis program. It might accept twenty or so facts about a patient's condition, then forward chain on those facts to try to deduce the nature and/or cause of the disease. Now suppose that at some point, the left side of a rule was *nearly* satisfied—say, nine out of ten of its preconditions were met. It might be efficient to apply backward reasoning to satisfy the tenth precondition in a directed manner, rather than wait for forward chaining to supply the fact by accident. Or perhaps the tenth condition requires further medical tests. In that case, backward chaining can be used to query the user.

Whether it is possible to use the same rules for both forward and backward reasoning also depends on the form of the rules themselves. If both left sides and right sides contain pure assertions, then forward chaining can match assertions on the left side of a rule and add to the state description the assertions on the right side. But if arbitrary procedures are allowed as the right sides of rules, then the rules will not be reversible. Some production languages allow only reversible rules; others do not. When irreversible rules are used, then a commitment to the direction of the search must be made at the time the rules are written. But, as we suggested above, this is often a useful thing to do anyway because it allows the rule writer to add control knowledge to the rules themselves.

6.4   Matching

So far, we have described the process of using search to solve problems as the application of appropriate rules to individual problem states to generate new states to which the rules can then be applied, and so forth, until a solution is found. We have suggested that clever search involves choosing from among the rules that can be applied at a particular point, the ones that are most likely to lead to a solution. But we have said little about how we extract from the entire collection of rules those that can be applied at a given point. To do so requires some kind of *matching* between the current state and the preconditions of the rules. How should this be done? The answer to this question can be critical to the success of a rule-based system. We discuss a few proposals below.

6.4.1   Indexing

One way to select applicable rules is to do a simple search through all the rules, comparing each one's preconditions to the current state and extracting all the ones that match. But there are two problems with this simple solution:

- In order to solve very interesting problems, it will be necessary to use a large number of rules. Scanning through all of them at every step of the search would be hopelessly inefficient.

- It is not always immediately obvious whether a rule's preconditions are satisfied by a particular state.

Sometimes there are easy ways to deal with the first of these problems. Instead of scarching through the rules, use the current state as an index into the rules and select the

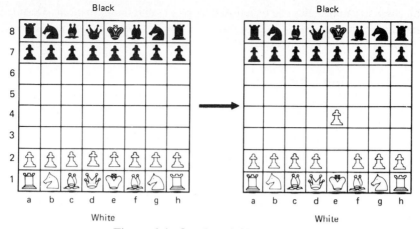

Figure 6.4: One Legal Chess Move

White pawn at
    Square(file e, rank 2)
        AND
Square(file e, rank 3)
    is empty
        AND
Square(file e, rank 4)
    is empty

$\rightarrow$

move pawn from
Square(file e, rank 2)
to Square(file e, rank 4)

Figure 6.5: Another Way to Describe Chess Moves

matching ones immediately. For example, consider the legal-move generation rule for chess shown in in Figure 6.4. To be able to access the appropriate rules immediately, all we need do is assign an index to each board position. This can be done simply by treating the board description as a large number. Any reasonable hashing function can then be used to treat that number as an index into the rules. All the rules that describe a given board position will be stored under the same key and so will be found together. Unfortunately, this simple indexing scheme only works because preconditions of rules match exact board configurations. Thus the matching process is easy but at the price of complete lack of generality in the statement of the rules. As discussed in Section 2.1, it is often better to write rules in a more general form, such as that shown in Figure 6.5. When this is done, such simple indexing is not possible. In fact, there is often a trade-off between the ease of writing rules (which is increased by the use of high-level descriptions) and the simplicity of the matching process (which is decreased by such descriptions).

    All of this does not mean that indexing cannot be helpful even when the preconditions of rules are stated as fairly high-level predicates. In PROLOG and many theorem-proving systems, for example, rules are indexed by the predicates they contain, so all the rules that could be applicable to proving a particular fact can be accessed fairly quickly.

In the chess example, rules can be indexed by pieces and their positions. Despite some limitations of this approach, indexing in some form is very important in the efficient operation of rule-based systems.

6.4.2   Matching with Variables

The problem of selecting applicable rules is made more difficult when preconditions are not stated as exact descriptions of particular situations but rather describe properties (of varying complexity) that the situations must have. It often turns out that discovering whether there is a match between a particular situation and the preconditions of a given rule must itself involve a significant search process.

If we want to match a single condition against a single element in a state description, then the unification procedure of Section 5.4.4 will suffice. However, in many rule-based systems, we need to compute the whole set of rules that match the current state description. Backward-chaining systems usually use depth-first backtracking to select individual rules, but forward-chaining systems generally employ sophisticated *conflict resolution strategies* to choose among the applicable rules.[3] While it is possible to apply unification repeatedly over the cross product of preconditions and state description elements, it is more efficient to consider the *many-many* match problem, in which many rules are matched against many elements in the state description simultaneously.

One efficient many-many match algorithm is RETE, which gains efficiency from three major sources:

- The temporal nature of data. Rules usually do not alter the state description radically. Instead, a rule will typically add one or two elements, or perhaps delete one or two, but most of the state description remains the same. (Recall our discussion of this as part of our treatment of the frame problem in Section 4.4.) If a rule did not match in the previous cycle, it will most likely fail to apply in the current cycle. RETE maintains a network of rule conditions, and it uses changes in the state description to determine which new rules might apply (and which rules might no longer apply). Full matching is only pursued for candidates that could be affected by incoming or outgoing data.

- Structural similarity in rules. Different rules may share a large number of pre-conditions. For example, consider rules for identifying wild animals. One rule concludes *jaguar(x)* if *mammal(x)*, *feline(x)*, *carnivorous(x)*, and *has-spots(x)*. Another rule concludes *tiger(x)* and is identical to the first rule except that it replaces *has-spots* with *has-stripes*. If we match the two rules independently, we will repeat a lot of work unnecessarily. RETE stores the rules so that they share structures in memory; sets of conditions that appear in several rules are matched (at most) once per cycle.

- Persistence of variable binding consistency. While all the individual preconditions of a rule might be met, there may be variable binding conflicts that prevent the rule from firing. For example, suppose we know the facts *son(Mary,Joe)* and *son(Bill,Bob)*. The individual preconditions of the rule

---

[3] Conflict resolution is discussed in the next section.

$$son(x, y) \land son(y, z) \rightarrow grandparent(x, z)$$

can be matched, but not in a manner that satisfies the constraint imposed by the variable y. Fortunately, it is not necessary to compute binding consistency from scratch every time a new condition is satisfied. RETE remembers its previous calculations and is able to merge new binding information efficiently.

For more details about the RETE match algorithm, see Forgy [1982]. Other matching algorithms (e.g., Miranker [1987] and Oflazer [1987]) take different stands on how much time to spend on saving state information between cycles. They can be more or less efficient than RETE, depending on the types of rules written for the domain and on the degree of hardware parallelism available.

6.4.3   Complex and Approximate Matching

A more complex matching process is required when the preconditions of a rule specify required properties that are not stated explicitly in the description of the current state. In this case, a separate set of rules must be used to describe how some properties can be inferred from others.

An even more complex matching process is required if rules should be applied if their preconditions *approximately* match the current situation. This is often the case in situations involving physical descriptions of the world. For example, a speech-understanding program must contain rules that map from a description of a physical waveform to phones (instances of English phonemes, such as p or d). There is so much variability in the physical signal, as a result of background noise, differences in the way individuals speak, and so forth, that one can hope to find only an approximate match between the rule that describes an ideal sound and the input that describes an unideal world. Approximate matching is particularly difficult to deal with because as we increase the tolerance allowed in the match, we also increase the number of rules that will match, thus increasing the size of the main search process. But approximate matching is nevertheless superior to exact matching in situations such as speech understanding, where exact matching may often result in no rules being matched and the search process coming to a grinding halt. Although symbolic techniques for approximate matching exist, there is another, very different approach that can be used to solve this problem. We discuss it in detail in Chapter 18 where we describe connectionist systems (also called neural nets).

For some problems, almost all the action is in the matching of the rules to the problem state. Once that is done, so few rules apply that the remaining search is trivial. This was the case, for example, in ELIZA [Weizenbaum, 1966], an early AI program that simulated the behavior of a Rogerian therapist. A fragment of a dialogue between ELIZA and a user is shown in Figure 6.6. ELIZA's knowledge about both English and psychology was coded in a set of simple rules. Figure 6.7 shows some ELIZA-like rules.

ELIZA operated by matching the left sides of the rules against the user's last sentence and using the appropriate right side to generate a response. For example, if the user typed "My brother is mean to me," ELIZA might respond, "Who else in your family is mean to you?" or "Tell me more about your family." The rules were indexed by keywords so only a few had actually to be matched against a particular sentence. Some

Person: Men are all alike.

ELIZA: In what way?

Person: They're always bugging us about something or other.

ELIZA: Can you think of a specific example?

Person: Well, my boyfriend made me come here.

ELIZA: Your boyfriend made you come here.

Person: He says I'm depressed much of the time.

ELIZA: I am sorry to hear you are depressed.

Person: It's true. I am unhappy.

ELIZA: Do you think coming here will help you not to be unhappy?

Person: I need some help, that much seems certain.

ELIZA: What would it mean to you if you got some help?

Person: Perhaps I could learn to get along with my mother.

ELIZA: Tell me more about your family.

Figure 6.6: A Bit of a Dialogue with ELIZA

(X me Y)   → (X you Y)
(I remember X)   → (Why do remember X just now?)
(My {family-member} is Y)   → (Who else in your family is Y?)
(X {family-member} Y)   → (Tell me more about your family)

Figure 6.7: Some ELIZA-like rules

of the rules had no left side, so the rule could apply anywhere. These rules were used if no other rules matched and they generated replies such as "Tell me more about that." Notice that the rules themselves cause a form of approximate matching to occur. The patterns ask about specific words in the user's sentence. They do not need to match entire sentences. Thus a great variety of sentences can be matched by a single rule, and the grammatical complexity of English is pretty much ignored. This accounts both for ELIZA's major strength, its ability to say something fairly reasonable almost all of the time, and its major weakness, the superficiality of its understanding and its ability to be led completely astray. Approximate matching can easily lead to both these results.

As if the matching process were not already complicated enough, recall the frame problem mentioned in Chapter 4. One way of dealing with the frame problem is to avoid storing entire state descriptions at each node but instead to store only the changes from the previous node. If this is done, the matching process will have to be modified to scan backward from a node through its predecessors, looking for the required objects.

6.4.4   Conflict Resolution

The result of the matching process is a list of rules whose antecedents have matched the current state description along with whatever variable bindings were generated by the matching process. It is the job of the search method to decide on the order in which rules will be applied. But sometimes it is useful to incorporate some of that decision making into the matching process. This phase of the matching process is then called *conflict resolution*.

There are three basic approaches to the problem of conflict resolution in a production system:

- Assign a preference based on the rule that matched.

- Assign a preference based on the objects that matched.

- Assign a preference based on the action that the matched rule would perform.

Preferences Based on Rules

There are two common ways of assigning a preference based on the rules themselves. The first, and simplest, is to consider the rules to have been specified in a particular order, such as the physical order in which they are presented to the system. Then priority is given to the rules in the order in which they appear. This is the scheme used in PROLOG.

The other common rule-directed preference scheme is to give priority to special case rules over rules that are more general. We ran across this in Chapter 2, in the case of the water jug problem of Figure 2.3. Recall that rules 11 and 12 were special cases of rules 9 and 5, respectively. The purpose of such specific rules is to allow for the kind of knowledge that expert problem solvers use when they solve problems directly, without search. If we consider all rules that match, then the addition of such special-purpose rules will increase the size of the search rather than decrease it. In order to prevent that, we build the matcher so that it rejects rules that are more general than other rules that also match. How can the matcher decide that one rule is more general than another? There are a few easy ways:

- If the set of preconditions of one rule contains all the preconditions of another (plus some others), then the second rule is more general than the first.

- If the preconditions of one rule are the same as those of another except that in the first case variables are specified where in the second there are constants, then the first rule is more general than the second.

Preferences Based on Objects

Another way in which the matching process can ease the burden on the search mechanism is to order the matches it finds based on the importance of the objects that are matched. There are a variety of ways this can happen. Consider again ELIZA, which matched patterns against a user's sentence in order to find a rule to generate a reply. The patterns looked for specific combinations of important keywords. Often an input sentence contained several of the keywords that ELIZA knew. If that happened, then ELIZA made use of the fact that some keywords had been marked as being more significant than others. The pattern matcher returned the match involving the highest priority keyword. For example, ELIZA knew the word "I" as a keyword. Matching the input sentence "I know everybody laughed at me" by the keyword "I" would have enabled it to respond, "You say you know everybody laughed at you." But ELIZA also knew the word "everybody" as a keyword. Because "everybody" occurs more rarely than "I," ELIZA knows it to be more semantically significant and thus to be the clue to which it should respond. So it will produce a response such as "Who in particular are you thinking of?" Notice that priority matching such as this is particularly important if only one of the choices will ever be tried. This was true for ELIZA and would also be true, say, for a person who, when leaving a fast-burning room, must choose between turning off the lights (normally a good thing to do) and grabbing the baby (a more important thing to do).

Another form of priority matching can occur as a function of the position of the matchable objects in the current state description. For example, suppose we want to model the behavior of human short-term memory (STM). Rules can be matched against the current contents of STM and then used to generate actions, such as producing output to the environment or storing something in long-term memory. In this situation, we might like to have the matcher first try to match against the objects that have most recently entered STM and only compare against older elements if the newer elements do not trigger a match. For a discussion of this method as a conflict resolution strategy in a production system, see Newell [1973].

Preferences Based on States

Suppose that there are several rules waiting to fire. One way of selecting among them is to fire all of them temporarily and to examine the results of each. Then, using a heuristic function that can evaluate each of the resulting states, compare the merits of the results, and select the preferred one. Throw away (or maybe keep for later if necessary) the remaining ones.

This approach should look familiar—it is identical to the best-first search procedure we saw in Chapter 3. Although conceptually this approach can be thought of as a conflict resolution strategy, it is usually implemented as a search control technique that operates on top of the states generated by rule applications. The drawback to this design is that LISP-coded search control knowledge is procedural and therefore difficult to modify. Many AI search programs, especially ones that learn from their experience, represent their control strategies declaratively. The next section describes some methods for capturing knowledge about control using rules.

6.5   Control Knowledge

A major theme of this book is that while intelligent programs require search, search is computationally intractable unless it is constrained by knowledge about the world. In large knowledge bases that contain thousands of rules, the intractability of search is an overriding concern. When there are many possible paths of reasoning, it is critical that

Under conditions A and B,
Rules that do {not} mention X
    {at all,
    in their left-hand side,
    in their right-hand side}
will
    {definitely be useless,
    probably be useless

      . . .

    probably be especially useful
    definitely be especially useful}

Figure 6.8: Syntax for a Control Rule [Davis, 1980]

fruitless ones not be pursued. Knowledge about which paths are most likely to lead quickly to a goal state is often called *search control knowledge*. It can take many forms:

1. Knowledge about which states are more preferable to others.

2. Knowledge about which rule to apply in a given situation.

3. Knowledge about the order in which to pursue subgoals.

4. Knowledge about useful sequences of rules to apply.

In Chapter 3, we saw how the first type of knowledge could be represented with heuristic evaluation functions. There are many ways of representing the other types of control knowledge. For example, rules can be labeled and partitioned. A medical diagnosis system might have one set of rules for reasoning about bacteriological diseases and another set for immunological diseases. If the system is trying to prove a particular fact by backward chaining, it can probably eliminate one of the two rule sets, depending on what the fact is. Another method [Etzioni, 1989] is to assign cost and probability-of-success measures to rules. The problem solver can then use probabilistic decision analysis to choose a cost-effective alternative at each point in the search.

By now it should be clear that we are discussing how to represent knowledge about knowledge. For this reason, search control knowledge is sometimes called *meta-knowledge*. Davis [1980] first pointed out the need for meta-knowledge, and suggested that it be represented declaratively using rules. The syntax for one type of control rule is shown in Figure 6.8.

A number of AI systems represent their control knowledge with rules. We look briefly at two such systems, SOAR and PRODIGY.

SOAR [Laird *et al.*, 1987] is a general architecture for building intelligent systems. SOAR is based on a set of specific, cognitively motivated hypotheses about the structure of human problem solving. These hypotheses are derived from what we know about short-term memory, practice effects, etc. In SOAR:

1. Long-term memory is stored as a set of productions (or, rules).

2. Short-term memory (also called *working memory*) is a buffer that is affected by perceptions and serves as a storage area for facts deduced by rules in long-term memory. Working memory is analogous to the state description in problem solving.

3. All problem-solving activity takes place as state space traversal. There are several classes of problem-solving activities, including reasoning about which states to explore, which rules to apply in a given situation, and what effects those rules will have.

4. All intermediate and final results of problem solving are remembered (or, *chunked*) for future reference.[4]

The third feature is of most interest to us here. When SOAR is given a start state and a goal state, it sets up an initial problem space. In order to take the first step in that space, it must choose a rule from the set of applicable ones. Instead of employing a fixed conflict resolution strategy, SOAR considers that choice of rules to be a substantial problem in its own right, and it actually sets up another, auxiliary problem space. The rules that apply in this space look something like the rule shown in Figure 6.8. Operator preference rules may be very general, such as the ones described in the previous section on conflict resolution, or they may contain domain-specific knowledge.

SOAR also has rules for expressing a preference for applying a whole sequence of rules in a given situation. In learning mode, SOAR can take useful sequences and build from them more complex productions that it can apply in the future.

We can also write rules based on preferences for some states over others. Such rules can be used to implement the basic search strategies we studied in Chapters 2 and 3. For example, if we always prefer to work from the state we generated last, we will get depth-first behavior. On the other hand, if we prefer states that were generated earlier in time, we will get breadth-first behavior. If we prefer any state that looks better than the current state (according to some heuristic function), we will get hill climbing. Best-first search results when state preference rules prefer the state with the highest heuristic score. Thus we see that all of the weak methods are subsumed by an architecture that reasons with explicit search control knowledge. Different methods may be employed for different problems, and specific domain knowledge can override the more general strategies.

PRODIGY [Minton *et al.*, 1989] is a general-purpose problem-solving system that incorporates several different learning mechanisms. A good deal of the learning in PRODIGY is directed at automatically constructing a set of control rules to improve search in a particular domain. We return to PRODIGY's learning methods in Chapter 17, but we mention here a few facts that bear on the issue of search control rules. PRODIGY can acquire control rules in a number of ways:

- Through hand coding by programmers.

- Through a static analysis of the domain's operators.

- Through looking at traces of its own problem-solving behavior.

---

[4] We return to chunking in Chapter 17.

PRODIGY learns control rules from its experience, but unlike SOAR it also learns from its failures. If PRODIGY pursues an unfruitful path, it will try to come up with an explanation of why that path failed. It will then use that explanation to build control knowledge that will help it avoid fruitless search paths in the future.

One reason why a path may lead to difficulties is that subgoals can interact with one another. In the process of solving one subgoal, we may undo our solution of a previous subgoal. Search control knowledge can tell us something about the order in which we should pursue our subgoals. Suppose we are faced with the problem of building a piece of wooden furniture. The problem specifies that the wood must be sanded, sealed, and painted. Which of the three goals do we pursue first? To humans who have knowledge about this sort of thing, the answer is clear. An AI program, however, might decide to try painting first, since any physical object can be painted, regardless of whether it has been sanded. However, as the program plans further, it will realize that one of the effects of the sanding process is to remove the paint. The program will then be forced to plan a repainting step or else backtrack and try working on another subgoal first. Proper search control knowledge can prevent this wasted computational effort. Rules we might consider include:

- If a problem's subgoals include sanding and painting, then we should solve the sanding subgoal first.

- If subgoals include sealing and painting, then consider what the object is made of. If the object is made of wood, then we should seal it before painting it.

Before closing this section, we should touch on a couple of seemingly paradoxical issues concerning control rules. The first issue is called the *utility problem* [Minton, 1988]. As we add more and more control knowledge to a system, the system is able to search more judiciously. This cuts down on the number of nodes it expands. However, in deliberating about which step to take next in the search space, the system must consider all the control rules. If there are many control rules, simply matching them all can be very time-consuming. It is easy to reach a situation (especially in systems that generate control knowledge automatically) in which the system's problem-solving efficiency, as measured in CPU cycles, is worse with the control rules than without them. Different systems handle this problem in different ways, as demonstrated in Section 17.4.4.

The second issue concerns the complexity of the production system interpreter. As this chapter has progressed, we have seen a trend toward explicitly representing more and more knowledge about how search should proceed. We have found it useful to create meta-rules that talk about when to apply other rules. Now, a production system interpreter must know how to apply various rules and meta-rules, so we should expect that our interpreters will have to become more complex as we progress away from simple backward-chaining systems like PROLOG. And yet, moving to a declarative representation for control knowledge means that previously hand coded LISP functions can be eliminated from the interpreter. In this sense, the interpreter becomes more streamlined.

6.6   Summary

In this chapter, we have seen how to represent knowledge declaratively in rule-based systems and how to reason with that knowledge. We began with a simple mechanism, logic programming, and progressed to more complex production system models that can reason both forward and backward, apply sophisticated and efficient matching techniques, and represent their search control knowledge in rules.

In later chapters, we expand further on rule-based systems. In Chapter 7, we describe the use of rules that allow default reasoning to occur in the absence of specific counter evidence. In Chapter 8, we introduce the idea of attaching probabilistic measures to rules. And, in Chapter 20, we look at how rule-based systems are being used to solve complex, real-world problems.

The book *Pattern-Directed Inference Systems* [Waterman and Hayes-Roth, 1978] is a collection of papers describing the wide variety of uses to which production systems have been put in AI. Its introduction provides a good overview of the subject. Brownston *et al.* [1985] is an introduction to programming in production rules, with an emphasis on the OPS5 programming language.

6.7   Exercises

1. Consider the following knowledge base:

   $\forall x : \forall y : cat(x) \wedge fish(y) \rightarrow likes\text{-}to\text{-}eat(x, y)$
   $\forall x : calico(x) \rightarrow cat(x)$
   $\forall x : tuna(x) \rightarrow fish(x)$
   tuna(Charlie)
   tuna(Herb)
   calico(Puss)

   (a) Convert these wff's into Horn clauses.

   (b) Convert the Horn clauses into a PROLOG program.

   (c) Write a PROLOG query corresponding to the question, "What does Puss like to eat?" and show how it will be answered by your program.

   (d) Write another PROLOG program that corresponds to the same set of wff's but returns a different answer to the same query.

2. A problem-solving search can proceed either forward (from a known start state to a desired goal state) or backward (from a goal state to a start state). What factors determine the choice of direction for a particular problem?

3. If a problem-solving search program were to be written to solve each of the following types of problems, determine whether the search should proceed forward or backward:

   (a) water jug problem

   (b) blocks world

   (c) natural language understanding

4. Program the interpreter for a production system. You will need to build a table that holds the rules and a matcher that compares the current state to the left sides of the rules. You will also need to provide an appropriate control strategy to select among competing rules. Use your interpreter as the basis of a program that solves water jug problems.

Chapter 7

Symbolic Reasoning under Uncertainty

So far, we have described techniques for reasoning with a complete, consistent, and unchanging model of the world. Unfortunately, in many problem domains it is not possible to create such models. In this chapter and the next, we explore techniques for solving problems with incomplete and uncertain models.

7.1 Introduction to Nonmonotonic Reasoning

In their book, *The Web of Belief*, Quine and Ullian [1978] provide an excellent discussion of techniques that can be used to reason effectively even when a complete, consistent, and constant model of the world is not available. One of their examples, which we call the ABC Murder story, clearly illustrates many of the main issues that such techniques must deal with. Quoting Quine and Ullian [1978]:

> Let Abbott, Babbitt, and Cabot be suspects in a murder case. Abbott has an alibi, in the register of a respectable hotel in Albany. Babbitt also has an alibi, for his brother-in-law testified that Babbitt was visiting him in Brooklyn at the time. Cabot pleads alibi too, claiming to have been watching a ski meet in the Catskills, but we have only his word for that. So we believe
>
> (1) That Abbott did not commit the crime,
>
> (2) That Babbitt did not,
>
> (3) That Abbott or Babbitt or Cabot did.
>
>   But presently Cabot documents his alibi—he had the good luck to have been caught by television in the sidelines at the ski meet. A new belief is thus thrust upon us:
>
> (4) That Cabot did not.

Our beliefs (1) through (4) are inconsistent, so we must choose one for rejection. Which has the weakest evidence? The basis for (1) in the hotel register is good, since it is a fine old hotel. The basis for (2) is weaker, since Babbitt's brother-in-law might be lying. The basis for (3) is perhaps twofold: that there is no sign of burglary and that only Abbott, Babbitt, and Cabot seem to have stood to gain from the murder apart from burglary. This exclusion of burglary seems conclusive, but the other consideration does not; there could be some fourth beneficiary. For (4), finally, the basis is conclusive: the evidence from television. Thus (2) and (3) are the weak points. To resolve the inconsistency of (1) through (4) we should reject (2) or (3), thus either incriminating Babbitt or widening our net for some new suspect.

See also how the revision progresses downward. If we reject (2), we also revise our previous underlying belief, however tentative, that the brother-in-law was telling the truth and Babbitt was in Brooklyn. If instead we reject (3), we also revise our previous underlying belief that none but Abbott, Babbitt, and Cabot stood to gain from the murder apart from burglary.

Finally a certain arbitrariness should be noted in the organization of this analysis. The inconsistent beliefs (1) through (4) were singled out, and then various further beliefs were accorded a subordinate status as underlying evidence: a belief about a hotel register, a belief about the prestige of the hotel, a belief about the television, a perhaps unwarranted belief about the veracity of the brother-in-law, and so on. We could instead have listed this full dozen of beliefs on an equal footing, appreciated that they were in contradiction, and proceeded to restore consistency by weeding them out in various ways. But the organization lightened our task. It focused our attention on four prominent beliefs among which to drop one, and then it ranged the other beliefs under these four as mere aids to choosing which of the four to drop.

The strategy illustrated would seem in general to be a good one: divide and conquer. When a set of beliefs has accumulated to the point of contradiction, find the smallest selection of them you can that still involves contradiction; for instance, (1) through (4). For we can be sure that we are going to have to drop some of the beliefs in that subset, whatever else we do. In reviewing and comparing the evidence for the beliefs in the subset, then, we will find ourselves led down in a rather systematic way to other beliefs of the set. Eventually we find ourselves dropping some of them too.

In probing the evidence, where do we stop? In probing the evidence for (1) through (4) we dredged up various underlying beliefs, but we could have probed further, seeking evidence in turn for them. In practice, the probing stops when we are satisfied how best to restore consistency: which ones to discard among the beliefs we have canvassed.

This story illustrates some of the problems posed by uncertain, fuzzy, and often changing knowledge. A variety of logical frameworks and computational methods have been proposed for handling such problems. In this chapter and the next, we discuss two approaches:

- Nonmonotonic reasoning, in which the axioms and/or the rules of inference are extended to make it possible to reason with incomplete information. These systems preserve, however, the property that, at any given moment, a statement is either believed to be true, believed to be false, or not believed to be either.

- Statistical reasoning, in which the representation is extended to allow some kind of numeric measure of certainty (rather than simply TRUE or FALSE) to be associated with each statement.

Other approaches to these issues have also been proposed and used in systems. For example, it is sometimes the case that there is not a single knowledge base that captures the beliefs of all the agents involved in solving a problem. This would happen in our murder scenario if we were to attempt to model the reasoning of Abbott, Babbitt, and Cabot, as well as that of the police investigator. To be able to do this reasoning, we would require a technique for maintaining several parallel *belief spaces*, each of which would correspond to the beliefs of one agent. Such techniques are complicated by the fact that the belief spaces of the various agents, although not identical, are sufficiently similar that it is unacceptably inefficient to represent them as completely separate knowledge bases. In Section 15.4.2 we return briefly to this issue. Meanwhile, in the rest of this chapter, we describe techniques for nonmonotonic reasoning.

Conventional reasoning systems, such first-order predicate logic, are designed to work with information that has three important properties:

- It is complete with respect to the domain of interest. In other words, all the facts that are necessary to solve a problem are present in the system or can be derived from those that are by the conventional rules of first-order logic.

- It is consistent.

- The only way it can change is that new facts can be added as they become available. If these new facts are consistent with all the other facts that have already been asserted, then nothing will ever be retracted from the set of facts that are known to be true. This property is called *monotonicity*.

Unfortunately, if any of these properties is not satisfied, conventional logic-based reasoning systems become inadequate. Nonmonotonic reasoning systems, on the other hand, are designed to be able to solve problems in which all of these properties may be missing.

In order to do this, we must address several key issues, including the following

1. *How can the knowledge base be extended to allow inferences to be made on the basis of lack of knowledge as well as on the presence of it?* For example, we would like to be able to say things like, "If you have no reason to suspect that a particular person committed a crime, then assume he didn't," or "If you have no reason to believe that someone is not getting along with her relatives, then assume that the relatives will try to protect her." Specifically, we need to make clear the distinction between:

   - It is known that $\neg P$.

- It is not known whether P.

First-order predicate logic allows reasoning to be based on the first of these. We need an extended system that allows reasoning to be based on the second as well. In our new system, we call any inference that depends on the lack of some piece of knowledge a *nonmonotonic inference*.[1]

Allowing such reasoning has a significant impact on a knowledge base. Nonmonotonic reasoning systems derive their name from the fact that because of inferences that depend on lack of knowledge, knowledge bases may not grow monotonically as new assertions are made. Adding a new assertion may invalidate an inference that depended on the absence of that assertion. First-order predicate logic systems, on the other hand, are monotonic in this respect. As new axioms are asserted, new wff's may become provable, but no old proofs ever become invalid.

In other words, if some set of axioms T entails the truth of some statement w, then T combined with another set of axioms N also entails w. Because nonmonotonic reasoning does not share this property, it is also called *defeasible*: a nonmonotonic inference may be defeated (rendered invalid) by the addition of new information that violates assumptions that were made during the original reasoning process. It turns out, as we show below, that making this one change has a dramatic impact on the structure of the logical system itself. In particular, most of our ideas of what it means to find a proof will have to be reevaluated.

2. *How can the knowledge base be updated properly when a new fact is added to the system (or when an old one is removed)?* In particular, in nonmonotonic systems, since the addition of a fact can cause previously discovered proofs to be become invalid, how can those proofs, and all the conclusions that depend on them be found? The usual solution to this problem is to keep track of proofs, which are often called *justifications*. This makes it possible to find all the justifications that depended on the absence of the new fact, and those proofs can be marked as invalid. Interestingly, such a recording mechanism also makes it possible to support conventional, monotonic reasoning in the case where axioms must occasionally be retracted to reflect changes in the world that is being modeled. For example, it may be the case that Abbott is in town this week and so is available to testify, but if we wait until next week, he may be out of town. As a result, when we discuss techniques for maintaining valid sets of justifications, we talk both about nonmonotonic reasoning and about monotonic reasoning in a changing world.

3. *How can knowledge be used to help resolve conflicts when there are several inconsistent nonmonotonic inferences that could be drawn?* It turns out that when inferences can be based on the lack of knowledge as well as on its presence, contradictions are much more likely to occur than they were in conventional logical systems in which the only possible contradictions were those that depended

---

[1] Recall that in Section 2.4, we also made a monotonic/nonmonotonic distinction. There the issue was classes of production systems. Although we are applying the distinction to different entities here, it is essentially the same distinction in both cases, since it distinguishes between systems that never shrink as a result of an action (monotonic ones) and ones that can (nonmonotonic ones).

on facts that were explicitly asserted to be true. In particular, in nonmonotonic systems, there are often portions of the knowledge base that are locally consistent but mutually (globally) inconsistent. As we show below, many techniques for reasoning nonmonotonically are able to define the alternatives that could be believed, but most of them provide no way to choose among the options when not all of them can be believed at once.

To do this, we require additional methods for resolving such conflicts in ways that are most appropriate for the particular problem that is being solved. For example, as soon as we conclude that Abbott, Babbitt, and Cabot all claim that they didn't commit a crime, yet we conclude that one of them must have since there's no one else who is believed to have had a motive, we have a contradiction, which we want to resolve in some particular way based on other knowledge that we have. In this case, for example, we choose to resolve the conflict by finding the person with the weakest alibi and believing that he committed the crime (which involves believing other things, such as that the chosen suspect lied).

The rest of this chapter is divided into five parts. In the first, we present several logical formalisms that provide mechanisms for performing nonmonotonic reasoning. In the last four, we discuss approaches to the implementation of such reasoning in problem-solving programs. For more detailed descriptions of many of these systems, see the papers in Ginsberg [1987].

7.2 Logics for Nonmonotonic Reasoning

Because monotonicity is fundamental to the definition of first-order predicate logic, we are forced to find some alternative to support nonmonotonic reasoning. In this section, we look at several formal approaches to doing this. We examine several because no single formalism with all the desired properties has yet emerged (although there are some attempts, e.g., Shoham [1987] and Konolige [1987], to present a unifying framework for these several theories). In particular, we would like to find a formalism that does all of the following things:

- Defines the set of possible worlds that could exist given the facts that we do have. More precisely, we will define an *interpretation* of a set of wff's to be a domain (a set of objects) D, together with a function that assigns: to each predicate, a relation (of corresponding arity); to each n-ary function, an operator that maps from D^n into D; and to each constant, an element of D. A *model* of a set of wff's is an interpretation that satisfies them. Now we can be more precise about this requirement. We require a mechanism for defining the set of models of any set of wff's we are given.

- Provides a way to say that we prefer to believe in some models rather than others.

- Provides the basis for a practical implementation of this kind of reasoning.

- Corresponds to our intuitions about how this kind of reasoning works. In other words, we do not want vagaries of syntax to have a significant impact on the conclusions that can be drawn within our system.

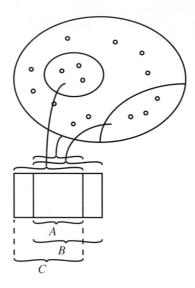

Figure 7.1: Models, Wff's, and Nonmonotonic Reasoning

As we examine each of the theories below, we need to evaluate how well they perform each of these tasks. For a more detailed discussion of these theories and some comparisons among them, see Reiter [1987a], Etherington [1988], and Genesereth and Nilsson [1987].

Before we go into specific theories in detail, let's consider Figure 7.1, which shows one way of visualizing how nonmonotonic reasoning works in all of them. The box labeled A corresponds to an original set of wff's. The large circle contains all the models of A. When we add some nonmonotonic reasoning capabilities to A, we get a new set of wff's, which we've labeled B.[2] B (usually) contains more information than A does. As a result, fewer models satisfy B than A. The set of models corresponding to B is shown at the lower right of the large circle. Now suppose we add some new wff's (representing new information) to A. We represent A with these additions as the box C. A difficulty may arise, however, if the set of models corresponding to C is as shown in the smaller, interior circle, since it is disjoint with the models for B. In order to find a new set of models that satisfy C, we need to accept models that had previously been rejected. To do that, we need to eliminate the wff's that were responsible for those models being thrown away. This is the essence of nonmonotonic reasoning.

7.2.1   Default Reasoning

We want to use nonmonotonic reasoning to perform what is commonly called *default reasoning*. We want to draw conclusions based on what is most likely to be true. In this section, we discuss two approaches to doing this.

---

[2]As we will see below, some techniques add inference rules, which then generate wff's, while others add wff's directly. We'll ignore that difference for the moment.

- Nonmonotonic Logic[3]

- Default Logic

We then describe two common kinds of nonmonotonic reasoning that can be defined in those logics:

- Abduction

- Inheritance

Nonmonotonic Logic

One system that provides a basis for default reasoning is *Nonmonotonic Logic* (NML) [McDermott and Doyle, 1980], in which the language of first-order predicate logic is augmented with a modal operator M, which can be read as "is consistent." For example, the formula

$$\forall x, y: \ Related(x, y) \wedge M \ GetAlong(x, y) \rightarrow WillDefend(x, y)$$

should be read as, "For all x and y, if x and y are related and if the fact that x gets along with y is consistent with everything else that is believed, then conclude that x will defend y."

Once we augment our theory to allow statements of this form, one important issue must be resolved if we want our theory to be even semidecidable. (Recall that even in a standard first-order theory, the question of theoremhood is undecidable, so semidecidability is the best we can hope for.) We must define what "is consistent" means. Because consistency in this system, as in first-order predicate logic, is undecidable, we need some approximation. The one that is usually used is the PROLOG notion of negation as failure, or some variant of it. In other words, to show that P is consistent, we attempt to prove $\neg P$. If we fail, then we assume $\neg P$ to be false and we call P consistent. Unfortunately, this definition does not completely solve our problem. Negation as failure works in pure PROLOG because, if we restrict the rest of our language to Horn clauses, we have a decidable theory. So failure to prove something means that it is not entailed by our theory. If, on the other hand, we start with full first-order predicate logic as our base language, we have no such guarantee. So, as a practical matter, it may be necessary to define consistency on some heuristic basis, such as failure to prove inconsistency within some fixed level of effort.

A second problem that arises in this approach (and others, as we explain below) is what to do when multiple nonmonotonic statements, taken alone, suggest ways of augmenting our knowledge that if taken together would be inconsistent. For example, consider the following set of assertions:

$\forall x: \ Republican(x) \ \wedge M \ \neg Pacifist(x) \rightarrow \neg Pacifist(x)$
$\forall x: \ Quaker(x) \ \wedge M \ Pacifist(x) \rightarrow Pacifist(x)$
$Republican(Dick)$
$Quaker(Dick)$

---

[3]Try not to get confused about names here. We are using the terms "nonmonotonic reasoning" and "default reasoning" generically to describe a kind of reasoning. The terms "Nonmonotonic Logic" and "Default Logic" are, on the other hand, being used to refer to specific formal theories.

The definition of NML that we have given supports two distinct ways of augmenting this knowledge base. In one, we first apply the first assertion, which allows us to conclude ¬*Pacifist(Dick)*. Having done that, the second assertion cannot apply, since it is not consistent to assume *Pacifist(Dick)*. The other thing we could do, however, is apply the second assertion first. This results in the conclusion *Pacifist(Dick)*, which prevents the first one from applying. So what conclusion does the theory actually support?

The answer is that NML defines the set of theorems that can be derived from a set of wff's A to be the intersection of the sets of theorems that result from the various ways in which the wff's of A might be combined. So, in our example, no conclusion about Dick's pacifism can be derived. This theory thus takes a very conservative approach to theoremhood.

It is worth pointing out here that although assertions such as the ones we used to reason about Dick's pacifism look like rules, they are, in this theory, just ordinary wff's which can be manipulated by the standard rules for combining logical expressions. So, for example, given

$$A \wedge M\,B \rightarrow B$$
$$\neg A \wedge M\,B \rightarrow B$$

we can derive the expression

$$M\,B \rightarrow B$$

In the original formulation of NML, the semantics of the modal operator M, which is self-referential, were unclear. A more recent system, *Autoepistemic Logic* [Moore, 1985] is very similar, but solves some of these problems.

Default Logic

An alternative logic for performing default-based reasoning is Reiter's *Default Logic* (DL) [Reiter, 1980], in which a new class of inference rules is introduced. In this approach, we allow inference rules of the form[4]

$$\frac{A\,:\,B}{C}$$

Such a rule should be read as, "If A is provable and it is consistent to assume B then conclude C." As you can see, this is very similar in intent to the nonmonotonic expressions that we used in NML. There are some important differences between the two theories, however. The first is that in DL the new inference rules are used as a basis for computing a set of plausible *extensions* to the knowledge base. Each extension corresponds to one maximal consistent augmentation of the knowledge base.[5] The logic

---

[4] Reiter's original notation had ":M" in place of ":", but since it conveys no additional information, the M is usually omitted.

[5] What we mean by the expression "maximal consistent augmentation" is that no additional default rules can be applied without violating consistency. But it is important to note that only expressions generated by the application of the stated inference rules to the original knowledge are allowed in an extension. Gratuitous additions are not permitted.

then admits as a theorem any expression that is valid in any extension. If a decision among the extensions is necessary to support problem solving, some other mechanism must be provided. So, for example, if we return to the case of Dick the Republican, we can compute two extensions, one corresponding to his being a pacifist and one corresponding to his not being a pacifist. The theory of DL does not say anything about how to choose between the two. But see Reiter and Criscuolo [1981], Touretzky [1986], and Rich [1983] for discussions of this issue.

A second important difference between these two theories is that, in DL, the non-monotonic expressions are rules of inference rather than expressions in the language. Thus they cannot be manipulated by the other rules of inference. This leads to some unexpected results. For example, given the two rules

$$\frac{A : B}{B} \qquad \frac{\neg A : B}{B}$$

and no assertion about A, no conclusion about B will be drawn, since neither inference rule applies.

Abduction

Standard logic performs deduction. Given two axioms:

$$\forall x : A(x) \rightarrow B(x)$$
$$A(C)$$

we can conclude $B(C)$ using deduction. But what about applying the implication in reverse? For example, suppose the axiom we have is

$$\forall x : Measles(x) \rightarrow Spots(x)$$

The axiom says that having measles implies having spots. But suppose we notice spots. We might like to conclude measles. Such a conclusion is not licensed by the rules of standard logic and it may be wrong, but it may be the best guess we can make about what is going on. Deriving conclusions in this way is thus another form of default reasoning. We call this specific form *abductive reasoning*. More precisely, the process of abductive reasoning can be described as, "Given two wff's $(A \rightarrow B)$ and (B), for any expressions A and B, if it is consistent to assume A, do so."

In many domains, abductive reasoning is particularly useful if some measure of certainty is attached to the resulting expressions. These certainty measures quantify the risk that the abductive reasoning process is wrong, which it will be whenever there were other antecedents besides A that could have produced B. We discuss ways of doing this in Chapter 8.

Abductive reasoning is not a kind of logic in the sense that DL and NML are. In fact, it can be described in either of them. But it is a very useful kind of nonmonotonic reasoning, and so we mentioned it explicitly here.

Inheritance

One very common use of nonmonotonic reasoning is as a basis for inheriting attribute values from a prototype description of a class to the individual entities that belong to the class. We considered one example of this kind of reasoning in Chapter 4, when we discussed the baseball knowledge base. Recall that we presented there an algorithm for implementing inheritance. We can describe informally what that algorithm does by saying, "An object inherits attribute values from all the classes of which it is a member unless doing so leads to a contradiction, in which case a value from a more restricted class has precedence over a value from a broader class." Can the logical ideas we have just been discussing provide a basis for describing this idea more formally? The answer is yes. To see how, let's return to the baseball example (as shown in Figure 4.5) and try to write its inheritable knowledge as rules in DL.

We can write a rule to account for the inheritance of a default value for the height of a baseball player as:

$$\frac{Baseball\text{-}Player(x) : height(x, 6\text{-}1)}{height(x, 6\text{-}1)}$$

Now suppose we assert *Pitcher(Three-Finger-Brown)*. Since this enables us to conclude that *Three-Finger-Brown* is a baseball player, our rule allows us to conclude that his height is 6-1. If, on the other hand, we had asserted a conflicting value for Three Finger's height, and if we had an axiom like

$$\forall x, y, z : height(x, y) \wedge height(x, z) \rightarrow y = z,$$

which prohibits someone from having more than one height, then we would not be able to apply the default rule. Thus an explicitly stated value will block the inheritance of a default value, which is exactly what we want. (We'll ignore here the order in which the assertions and the rules occur. As a logical framework, default logic does not care. We'll just assume that somehow it settles out to a consistent state in which no defaults that conflict with explicit assertions have been asserted. In Section 7.5.1 we look at issues that arise in creating an implementation that assures that.)

But now, let's encode the default rule for the height of adult males in general. If we pattern it after the one for baseball players, we get

$$\frac{Adult\text{-}Male(x) : height(x, 5\text{-}10)}{height(x, 5\text{-}10)}$$

Unfortunately, this rule does not work as we would like. In particular, if we again assert *Pitcher(Three-Finger-Brown)*, then the resulting theory contains two extensions: one in which our first rule fires and Brown's height is 6-1 and one in which this new rule applies and Brown's height is 5-10. Neither of these extensions is preferred. In order to state that we prefer to get a value from the more specific category, baseball player, we could rewrite the default rule for adult males in general as:

$$\frac{Adult\text{-}Male(x) : \neg Baseball\text{-}Player(x) \wedge height(x, 5\text{-}10)}{height(x, 5\text{-}10)}$$

This effectively blocks the application of the default knowledge about adult males in the case that more specific information from the class of baseball players is available.

Unfortunately, this approach can become unwieldy as the set of exceptions to the general rule increases. For example, we could end up with a rule like:

$$\frac{Adult\text{-}Male(x) : \neg Baseball\text{-}Player(x) \wedge \neg Midget(x) \wedge \neg Jockey(x) \wedge height(x, 5\text{-}10)}{height(x, 5\text{-}10)}$$

What we have done here is to clutter our knowledge about the general class of adult males with a list of all the known exceptions with respect to height. A clearer approach is to say something like, "Adult males typically have a height of 5-10 unless they are abnormal in some way." We can then associate with other classes the information that they are abnormal in one or another way. So we could write, for example:

$\forall x : Adult\text{-}Male(x) \wedge \neg AB(x, aspect1) \rightarrow height(x, 5\text{-}10)$
$\forall x : Baseball\text{-}Player(x) \rightarrow AB(x, aspect1)$
$\forall x : Midget(x) \rightarrow AB(x, aspect1)$
$\forall x : Jockey(x) \rightarrow AB(x, aspect1)$

Then, if we add the single default rule:

$$\frac{: \neg AB(x, y)}{\neg AB(x, y)}$$

we get the desired result.

7.2.2 Minimalist Reasoning

So far, we have talked about general methods that provide ways of describing things that are generally true. In this section we describe methods for saying a very specific and highly useful class of things that are generally true. These methods are based on some variant of the idea of a *minimal model*. Recall from the beginning of this section that a model of a set of formulas is an interpretation that satisfies them. Although there are several distinct definitions of what constitutes a minimal model, for our purposes, we will define a model to be minimal if there are no other models in which fewer things are true. (As you can probably imagine, there are technical difficulties in making this precise, many of which involve the treatment of sentences with negation.) The idea behind using minimal models as a basis for nonmonotonic reasoning about the world is the following: "There are many fewer true statements than false ones. If something is true and relevant it makes sense to assume that it has been entered into our knowledge base. Therefore, assume that the only true statements are those that necessarily must be true in order to maintain the consistency of the knowledge base." We have already mentioned (in Section 6.2) one kind of reasoning based on this idea, the PROLOG concept of negation as failure, which provides an implementation of the idea for Horn clause-based systems. In the rest of this section we look at some logical issues that arise when we remove the Horn clause limitation.

The Closed World Assumption

A simple kind of minimalist reasoning is suggested by the *Closed World Assumption* or CWA [Reiter, 1978]. The CWA says that the only objects that satisfy any predicate P are those that must. The CWA is particularly powerful as a basis for reasoning with databases, which are assumed to be complete with respect to the properties they describe. For example, a personnel database can safely be assumed to list all of the company's employees. If someone asks whether Smith works for the company, we should reply "no" unless he is explicitly listed as an employee. Similarly, an airline database can be assumed to contain a complete list of all the routes flown by that airline. So if I ask if there is a direct flight from Oshkosh to El Paso, the answer should be "no" if none can be found in the database. The CWA is also useful as a way to deal with *AB* predicates, of the sort we introduced in Section 7.2.1, since we want to take as abnormal only those things that are asserted to be so.

Although the CWA is both simple and powerful, it can fail to produce an appropriate answer for either of two reasons. The first is that its assumptions are not always true in the world; some parts of the world are not realistically "closable." We saw this problem in the murder story example. There were facts that were relevant to the investigation that had not yet been uncovered and so were not present in the knowledge base. The CWA will yield appropriate results exactly to the extent that the assumption that all the relevant positive facts are present in the knowledge base is true.

The second kind of problem that plagues the CWA arises from the fact that it is a purely syntactic reasoning process. Thus, as you would expect, its results depend on the form of the assertions that are provided. Let's look at two specific examples of this problem.

Consider a knowledge base that consists of just a single statement:

$$A(Joe) \lor B(Joe)$$

The CWA allows us to conclude both $\neg A(Joe)$ and $\neg B(Joe)$, since neither A nor B must necessarily be true of Joe. Unfortunately, the resulting extended knowledge base

$$A(Joe) \lor B(Joe)$$
$$\neg A(Joe)$$
$$\neg B(Joe)$$

is inconsistent.

The problem is that we have assigned a special status to positive instances of predicates, as opposed to negative ones. Specifically, the CWA forces completion of a knowledge base by adding the negative assertion $\neg P$ whenever it is consistent to do so. But the assignment of a real world property to some predicate P and its complement to the negation of P may be arbitrary. For example, suppose we define a predicate *Single* and create the following knowledge base:

$$Single(John)$$
$$Single(Mary)$$

Then, if we ask about Jane, the CWA will yield the answer $\neg Single(Jane)$. But now suppose we had chosen instead to use the predicate *Married* rather than *Single*. Then the corresponding knowledge base would be

$$\neg Married(John)$$
$$\neg Married(Mary)$$

If we now ask about Jane, the CWA will yield the result ¬*Married*(*Jane*).

Circumscription

Although the CWA captures part of the idea that anything that must not necessarily be true should be assumed to be false, it does not capture all of it. It has two essential limitations:

- It operates on individual predicates without considering the interactions among predicates that are defined in the knowledge base. We saw an example of this above when we considered the statement $A(Joe) \vee B(Joe)$.

- It assumes that all predicates have all of their instances listed. Although in many database applications this is true, in many knowledge-based systems it is not. Some predicates can reasonably be assumed to be completely defined (i.e., the part of the world they describe is closed), but others cannot (i.e., the part of the world they describe is open). For example, the predicate *has-a-green-shirt* should probably be considered open since in most situations it would not be safe to assume that one has been told all the details of everyone else's wardrobe.

Several theories of *circumscription* (e.g., McCarthy [1980], McCarthy [1986], and Lifschitz [1985]) have been proposed to deal with these problems. In all of these theories, new axioms are added to the existing knowledge base. The effect of these axioms is to force a minimal interpretation on a selected portion of the knowledge base. In particular, each specific axiom describes a way that the set of values for which a particular axiom of the original theory is true is to be delimited (i.e., circumscribed).

As an example, suppose we have the simple assertion

$$\forall x : Adult(x) \wedge \neg AB(x, aspect1) \rightarrow Literate(x)$$

We would like to circumscribe *AB*, since we would like it to apply only to those individuals to which it applies. In essence, what we want to do is to say something about what the predicate *AB* must be (since at this point we have no idea what it is; all we know is its name). To know what it is, we need to know for what values it is true. Even though we may know a few values for which it is true (if any individuals have been asserted to be abnormal in this way), there are many different predicates that would be consistent with what we know so far. Imagine this universe of possible binary predicates. We might ask, which of these predicates could be *AB*? We want to say that *AB* can only be one of the predicates that is true only for those objects that we know it must be true for. We can do this by adding a (second order) axiom that says that *AB* is the smallest predicate that is consistent with our existing knowledge base.

In this simple example, circumscription yields the same result as does the CWA since there are no other assertions in the knowledge base with which a minimization of *AB* must be consistent. In both cases, the only models that are admitted are ones in which there are no individuals who are abnormal in *aspect1*. In other words, *AB* must be the predicate FALSE.

But, now let's return to the example knowledge base

$A(Joe) \lor B(Joe)$

If we circumscribe only A, then this assertion describes exactly those models in which A is true of no one and B is true of at least *Joe*. Similarly, if we circumscribe only B, then we will accept exactly those models in which B is true of no one and A is true of at least *Joe*. If we circumscribe A and B together, then we will admit only those models in which A is true of only *Joe* and B is true of no one or those in which B is true of only *Joe* and A is true of no one. Thus, unlike the CWA, circumscription allows us to describe the logical relationship between A and B.

7.3   Implementation Issues

Although the logical frameworks that we have just discussed take us part of the way toward a basis for implementing nonmonotonic reasoning in problem-solving programs, they are not enough. As we have seen, they all have some weaknesses as logical systems. In addition, they fail to deal with four important problems that arise in real systems.

The first is how to derive exactly those nonmonotonic conclusions that are relevant to solving the problem at hand while not wasting time on those that, while they may be licensed by the logic, are not necessary and are not worth spending time on.

The second problem is how to update our knowledge incrementally as problem-solving progresses. The definitions of the logical systems tell us how to decide on the truth status of a proposition with respect to a given truth status of the rest of the knowledge base. Since the procedure for doing this is a global one (relying on some form of consistency or minimality), any change to the knowledge base may have far-reaching consequences. It would be computationally intractable to handle this problem by starting over with just the facts that are explicitly stated and reapplying the various nonmonotonic reasoning steps that were used before, this time deriving possibly different results.

The third problem is that in nonmonotonic reasoning systems, it often happens that more than one interpretation of the known facts is licensed by the available inference rules. In Reiter's terminology, a given nonmonotonic system may (and often does) have several extensions at the moment, even though many of them will eventually be eliminated as new knowledge becomes available. Thus some kind of search process is necessary. How should it be managed?

The final problem is that, in general, these theories are not computationally effective. None of them is decidable. Some are semidecidable, but only in their propositional forms. And none is efficient.

In the rest of this chapter, we discuss several computational solutions to these problems. In all of these systems, the reasoning process is separated into two parts: a problem solver that uses whatever mechanism it happens to have to draw conclusions as necessary and a truth maintenance system whose job is just to do the bookkeeping required to provide a solution to our second problem. The various logical issues we have been discussing, as well as the heuristic ones we have raised here are issues in the design of the problem solver. We discuss these issues in Section 7.4. Then in the following sections, we describe techniques for tracking nonmonotonic inferences so that changes to the knowledge base are handled properly. Techniques for doing this can be divided into two classes, determined by their approach to the search control problem:

- Depth-first, in which we follow a single, most likely path until some new piece of information comes in that forces us to give up this path and find another.

- Breadth-first, in which we consider all the possibilities as equally likely. We consider them as a group, eliminating some of them as new facts become available. Eventually, it may happen that only one (or a small number) turn out to be consistent with everything we come to know.

It is important to keep in mind throughout the rest of this discussion that there is no exact correspondence between any of the logics that we have described and any of the implementations that we will present. Unfortunately, the details of how the two can be brought together are still unknown.

7.4 Augmenting a Problem Solver

So far, we have described a variety of logical formalisms, all of which describe the theorems that can be derived from a set of axioms. We have said nothing about how we might write a program that solves problems using those axioms. In this section, we do that.

As we have already discussed several times, problem solving can be done using either forward or backward reasoning. Problem solving using uncertain knowledge is no exception. As a result, there are two basic approaches to this kind of problem solving (as well as a variety of hybrids):

- Reason forward from what is known. Treat nonmonotonically derivable conclusions the same way monotonically derivable ones are handled. Nonmonotonic reasoning systems that support this kind of reasoning allow standard forward-chaining rules to be augmented with *unless* clauses, which introduce a basis for reasoning by default. Control (including deciding which default interpretation to choose) is handled in the same way that all other control decisions in the system are made (whatever that may be, for example, via rule ordering or the use of metarules).

- Reason backward to determine whether some expression P is true (or perhaps to find a set of bindings for its variables that make it true). Nonmonotonic reasoning systems that support this kind of reasoning may do either or both of the following two things:

  - Allow default (unless) clauses in backward rules. Resolve conflicts among defaults using the same control strategy that is used for other kinds of reasoning (usually rule ordering).

  - Support a kind of debate in which an attempt is made to construct arguments both in favor of P and opposed to it. Then some additional knowledge is applied to the arguments to determine which side has the stronger case.

Let's look at backward reasoning first. We will begin with the simple case of backward reasoning in which we attempt to prove (and possibly to find bindings for)

Suspect(*x*) ← *Beneficiary*(*x*)
                UNLESS *Alibi*(*x*)

Alibi(*x*) ← *SomewhereElse*(*x*)

SomewhereElse(*x*) ← *RegisteredHotel*(*x*, *y*) and *FarAway*(*y*)
                UNLESS *ForgedRegister*(*y*)

Alibi(*x*) ← *Defends*(*x*, *y*)
                UNLESS *Lies*(*y*)

SomewhereElse(*x*) ← *PictureOf*(*x*, *y*) and *FarAway*(*y*)

Contradiction() ← TRUE
                UNLESS ∃*x*: *Suspect*(*x*)

Beneficiary(*Abbott*)
Beneficiary(*Babbitt*)
Beneficiary(*Cabot*)

Figure 7.2: Backward Rules Using UNLESS

an expression *P*. Suppose that we have a knowledge base that consists of the backward
rules shown in Figure 7.2.

Assume that the problem solver that is using this knowledge base uses the usual
PROLOG-style control structure in which rules are matched top to bottom, left to right.
Then if we ask the question ?*Suspect*(*x*), the program will first try Abbott, who is a fine
suspect given what we know now, so it will return Abbott as its answer. If we had also
included the facts

   RegisteredHotel(*Abbott*, *Albany*)
   FarAway(*Albany*)

then, the program would have failed to conclude that Abbott was a suspect and it would
instead have located Babbitt.

As an alternative to this approach, consider the idea of a debate. In debating systems,
an attempt is made to find multiple answers. In the ABC Murder story case, for example,
all three possible suspects would be considered. Then some attempt to choose among
the arguments would be made. In this case, for example, we might want to have a
choice rule that says that it is more likely that people will lie to defend themselves than
to defend others. We might have a second rule that says that we prefer to believe hotel
registers rather than people. Using these two rules, a problem solver would conclude
that the most likely suspect is Cabot.

Backward rules work exactly as we have described if all of the required facts are
present when the rules are invoked. But what if we begin with the situation shown
in Figure 7.2 and conclude that Abbott is our suspect. Later, we are told that he was

If: *Beneficiary*(*x*),
  UNLESS *Alibi*(*x*),
then *Suspect*(*x*)

If: *SomewhereElse*(*x*),
then *Alibi*(*x*)

If: *RegisteredHotel*(*x*, *y*), and
  FarAway(*y*),
    UNLESS *ForgedRegister*(*y*),
then *SomewhereElse*(*x*)

If *Defends*(*x*, *y*),
  UNLESS *Lies*(*y*),
then *Alibi*(*x*)

If *PictureOf*(*x*, *y*), and
  FarAway(*y*),
then *SomewhereElse*(*x*)

If TRUE,
  UNLESS $\exists x$: *Suspect*(*x*)
then *Contradiction*()

Beneficiary(*Abbott*)
Beneficiary(*Babbitt*)
Beneficiary(*Cabot*)

Figure 7.3: Forward Rules Using UNLESS

registered at a hotel in Albany. Backward rules will never notice that anything has changed. To make our system data-driven, we need to use forward rules. Figure 7.3 shows how the same knowledge could be represented as forward rules. Of course, what we probably want is a system that can exploit both. In such a system, we could use a backward rule whose goal is to find a suspect, coupled with forward rules that fire as new facts that are relevant to finding a suspect appear.

7.5 Implementation: Depth-First Search

7.5.1 Dependency-Directed Backtracking

If we take a depth-first approach to nonmonotonic reasoning, then the following scenario is likely to occur often: We need to know a fact, F, which cannot be derived monotonically from what we already know, but which can be derived by making some assumption A which seems plausible. So we make assumption A, derive F, and then derive some additional facts G and H from F. We later derive some other facts M and N, but they are completely independent of A and F. A little while later, a new fact comes in that invalidates A. We need to rescind our proof of F, and also our proofs of G and H since they depended on F. But what about M and N? They didn't depend on F, so there is no logical need to invalidate them. But if we use a conventional backtracking scheme, we have to back up past conclusions in the order in which we derived them. So we have to backup past M and N, thus undoing them, in order to get back to F, G, H and A. To get around this problem, we need a slightly different notion of backtracking, one that is based on logical dependencies rather than the chronological order in which decisions were made. We call this new method *dependency-directed backtracking* [Stallman and Sussman, 1977], in contrast to *chronological backtracking*, which we have been using up until now.

Before we go into detail on how dependency-directed backtracking works, it is worth pointing out that although one of the big motivations for it is in handling nonmonotonic reasoning, it turns out to be useful for conventional search programs as well. This is not too surprising when you consider that what any depth-first search program does is to "make a guess" at something, thus creating a branch in the search space. If that branch eventually dies out, then we know that at least one guess that led to it must be wrong. It could be any guess along the branch. In chronological backtracking we have to assume it was the most recent guess and back up there to try an alternative. Sometimes, though, we have additional information that tells us which guess caused the problem. We'd like to retract only that guess and the work that explicitly depended on it, leaving everything else that has happened in the meantime intact. This is exactly what dependency-directed backtracking does.

As an example, suppose we want to build a program that generates a solution to a fairly simple problem, such as finding a time at which three busy people can all attend a meeting. One way to solve such a problem is first to make an assumption that the meeting will be held on some particular day, say Wednesday, add to the database an assertion to that effect, suitably tagged as an assumption, and then proceed to find a time, checking along the way for any inconsistencies in people's schedules. If a conflict arises, the statement representing the assumption must be discarded and replaced by another, hopefully noncontradictory, one. But, of course, any statements that have been generated along the way that depend on the now-discarded assumption must also be discarded.

Of course, this kind of situation can be handled by a straightforward tree search with chronological backtracking. All assumptions, as well as the inferences drawn from them, are recorded at the search node that created them. When a node is determined to represent a contradiction, simply backtrack to the next node from which there remain unexplored paths. The assumptions and their inferences will disappear automatically. The drawback to this approach is illustrated in Figure 7.4, which shows part of the search tree of a program that is trying to schedule a meeting. To do so, the program must solve a constraint satisfaction problem to find a day and time at which none of the participants is busy and at which there is a sufficiently large room available.

In order to solve the problem, the system must try to satisfy one constraint at a time. Initially, there is little reason to choose one alternative over another, so it decides to schedule the meeting on Wednesday. That creates a new constraint that must be met by the rest of the solution. The assumption that the meeting will be held on Wednesday

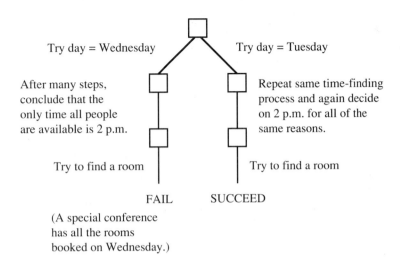

Try day = Wednesday   Try day = Tuesday

After many steps,   Repeat same time-finding
conclude that the   process and again decide
only time all people   on 2 p.m. for all of the
are available is 2 p.m.   same reasons.

Try to find a room   Try to find a room

FAIL   SUCCEED

(A special conference
has all the rooms
booked on Wednesday.)

Figure 7.4: Nondependency-Directed Backtracking

is stored at the node it generated. Next the program tries to select a time at which all participants are available. Among them, they have regularly scheduled daily meetings at all times except 2:00. So 2:00 is chosen as the meeting time. But it would not have mattered which day was chosen. Then the program discovers that on Wednesday there are no rooms available. So it backtracks past the assumption that the day would be Wednesday and tries another day, Tuesday. Now it must duplicate the chain of reasoning that led it to choose 2:00 as the time because that reasoning was lost when it backtracked to redo the choice of day. This occurred even though that reasoning did not depend in any way on the assumption that the day would be Wednesday. By withdrawing statements based on the order in which they were generated by the search process rather than on the basis of responsibility for inconsistency, we may waste a great deal of effort.

If we want to use dependency-directed backtracking instead, so that we do not waste this effort, then we need to do the following things:

- Associate with each node one or more justifications. Each justification corresponds to a derivation process that led to the node. (Since it is possible to derive the same node in several different ways, we want to allow for the possibility of multiple justifications.) Each justification must contain a list of all the nodes (facts, rules, assumptions) on which its derivation depended.

- Provide a mechanism that, when given a contradiction node and its justification, computes the "no-good" set of assumptions that underlie the justification. The no-good set is defined to be the minimal set of assumptions such that if you remove any element from the set, the justification will no longer be valid and the inconsistent node will no longer be believed.

- Provide a mechanism for considering a no-good set and choosing an assumption to retract.

- Provide a mechanism for propagating the result of retracting an assumption. This mechanism must cause all of the justifications that depended, however indirectly, on the retracted assumption to become invalid.

In the next two sections, we will describe two approaches to providing such a system.

7.5.2   Justification-Based Truth Maintenance Systems

The idea of a truth maintenance system or TMS [Doyle, 1979] arose as a way of providing the ability to do dependency-directed backtracking and so to support nonmonotonic reasoning. There was a later attempt to rename it to Reason Maintenance System (a bit less pretentious), but since the old name has stuck, we use it here.

A TMS allows assertions to be connected via a spreadsheet-like network of dependencies. In this section, we describe a simple form of truth maintenance system, a justification-based truth maintenance system (or JTMS). In a JTMS (or just TMS for the rest of this section), the TMS itself does not know anything about the structure of the assertions themselves. (As a result, in our examples, we use an English-like shorthand for representing the contents of nodes.) The TMS's only role is to serve as a bookkeeper for a separate problem-solving system, which in turn provides it with both assertions and dependencies among assertions.

To see how a TMS works, let's return to the ABC Murder story. Initially, we might believe that Abbott is the primary suspect because he was a beneficiary of the deceased and he had no alibi. There are three assertions here, a specific combination of which we now believe, although we may change our beliefs later. We can represent these assertions in shorthand as follows:

- *Suspect Abbott* (Abbott is the primary murder suspect.)

- *Beneficiary Abbott* (Abbott is a beneficiary of the victim.)

- *Alibi Abbott* (Abbott was at an Albany hotel at the time.)

Our reason for possible belief that Abbott is the murderer is nonmonotonic. In the notation of Default Logic, we can state the rule that produced it as

$$\frac{Beneficiary(x) \, : \, \neg Alibi(x)}{Suspect(x)}$$

or we can write it as a backward rule as we did in Section 7.4.

If we currently believe that he is a beneficiary and we have no reason to believe he has a valid alibi, then we will believe that he is our suspect. But if later we come to believe that he does have a valid alibi, we will no longer believe Abbott is a suspect.

But how should belief be represented and how should this change in belief be enforced? There are various *ad hoc* ways we might do this in a rule-based system. But they would all require a developer to construct rules carefully for each possible change in belief. For instance, we would have to have a rule that said that if Abbott ever gets

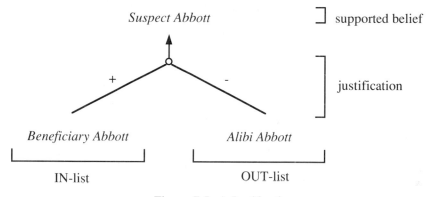

Figure 7.5: A Justification

an alibi, then we should erase from the database the belief that Abbott is a suspect. But suppose that we later fire a rule that erases belief in Abbott's alibi. Then we need another rule that would reconclude that Abbott is a suspect. The task of creating a rule set that consistently maintains beliefs when new assertions are added to the database quickly becomes unmanageable. In contrast, a TMS dependency network offers a purely syntactic, domain independent way to represent belief and change it consistently.

Figure 7.5 shows how these three facts would be represented in a dependency network, which can be created as a result of applying the first rule of either Figure 7.2 or Figure 7.3. The assertion *Suspect Abbott* has an associated TMS *justification*. Each justification consists of two parts: an *IN-list* and an *OUT-list*. In the figure, the assertions on the IN-list are connected to the justification by "+" links, those on the OUT-list by "−" links. The justification is connected by an arrow to the assertion that it supports. In the justification shown, there is exactly one assertion in each list. *Beneficiary Abbott* is in the IN-list and *Alibi Abbott* is in the OUT-list. Such a justification says that Abbott should be a suspect just when it is believed that he is a beneficiary and it is not believed that he has an alibi.

More generally, assertions (usually called nodes) in a TMS dependency network are believed when they have a valid justification. A justification is *valid* if every assertion in the IN-list is believed and none of those in the OUT-list is. A justification is nonmonotonic if its OUT-list is not empty, or, recursively, if any assertion in its IN-list has a nonmonotonic justification. Otherwise, it is monotonic. In a TMS network, nodes are labeled with a *belief status*. If the assertion corresponding to the node should be believed, then in the TMS it is labeled IN. If there is no good reason to believe the assertion, then it is labeled OUT. What does it mean that an assertion "should be believed" or has no "good" reason for belief?

A TMS answers these questions for a dependency network in a way that is independent of any interpretation of the assertions associated with the nodes. The *labeling* task of a TMS is to label each node so that two criteria about the dependency network

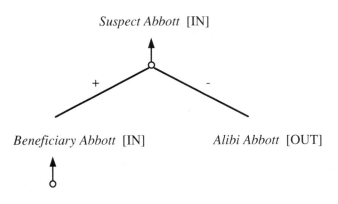

Figure 7.6: Labeled Nodes with Premise Justification

structure are met. The first criterion is *consistency*: every node labeled IN is supported by at least one valid justification and all other nodes are labeled OUT. More specifically than before, a justification is valid if every node in its IN-list is labeled IN and every node in its OUT-list is labeled OUT. Notice that in Figure 7.5, all of the assertions would have to be labeled OUT to be consistent. *Alibi Abbott* has no justification at all, much less a valid one, and so must be labeled OUT. But the same is true for *Beneficiary Abbott*, so it must be OUT as well. Then the justification for *Suspect Abbott* is invalid because an element of its IN-list is labeled OUT. *Suspect Abbott* would then be labeled OUT as well. Thus status labels correspond to our belief or lack of it in assertions, and justifications correspond to our reasons for such belief, with valid justifications being our "good" reasons. Notice that the label OUT may indicate that we have specific reason to believe that a node represents an assertion that is not true, or it may mean simply that we have no information one way or the other.

But the state of affairs in Figure 7.5 is incomplete. We are told that Abbott is a beneficiary. We have no further justification for this fact; we must simply accept it. For such facts, we give a *premise* justification: a justification with empty IN- and OUT-lists. Premise justifications are always valid. Figure 7.6 shows such a justification added to the network and a consistent labeling for that network, which shows *Suspect Abbott* labeled IN.

That Abbot is the primary suspect represents an initial state of the murder investigation. Subsequently, the detective establishes that Abbott is listed on the register of a good Albany hotel on the day of the murder. This provides a valid reason to believe Abbott's alibi. Figure 7.7 shows the effect of adding such a justification to the network, assuming that we have used forward (data-driven) rules as shown in Figure 7.3 for all of our reasoning except possibly establishing the top-level goal. That Abbott was registered at the hotel, *Registered Abbott*, was told to us and has a premise justification and so is labeled IN. That the hotel is far away is also asserted as a premise. The register might have been forged, but we have no good reason to believe it was. Thus

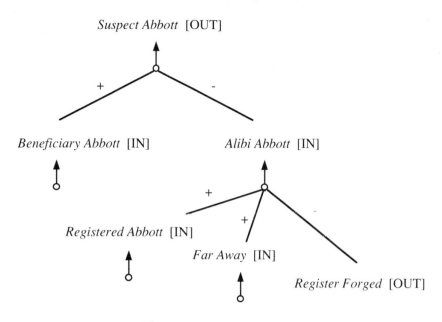

Figure 7.7: Changed Labeling

Register Forged lacks any justification and is labeled OUT. That Abbott was on the register of a far away hotel and the lack of belief that the register was forged will cause the appropriate forward rule to fire and create a justification for *Alibi Abbott*, which is thus labeled IN. This means that *Suspect Abbott* no longer has a valid justification and must be labeled OUT. Abbott is no longer a suspect.

Notice that such a TMS labeling carefully avoids saying that the register definitely was *not* forged. It only says that there is currently no good reason to believe that it was. Just like our original reason for believing that Abbott was a suspect, this is a nonmonotonic justification. Later, if we find that Abbott was secretly married to the desk clerk, we might add to this network a justification that would reverse some of the labeling. Babbitt will have a similar justification based upon lack of belief that his brother-in-law lied as shown in Figure 7.8 (where *B-I-L* stands for "Brother-In-Law").

Abbott's changing state showed how consistency was maintained. There is another criterion that the TMS must meet in labeling a dependency network: *well-foundedness* (i.e., the proper grounding of a chain of justifications on a set of nodes that do not themselves depend on the nodes they support). To illustrate this, consider poor Cabot. Not only does he have fewer *b*s and *t*s in his name, he also lacks a valid justification for his alibi that he was at a ski show. We have only his word that he was. Ignoring the more complicated representation of lying, the simple dependency network in Figure 7.9 illustrates the fact that the only support for the alibi of attending the ski show is that Cabot is telling the truth about being there. The only support for his telling the truth would be if we knew he was at the ski show. But this is a circular argument. Part of the task of a TMS is to disallow such arguments. In particular, if the support for a node only depends on an unbroken chain of positive links (IN-list links) leading back to itself,

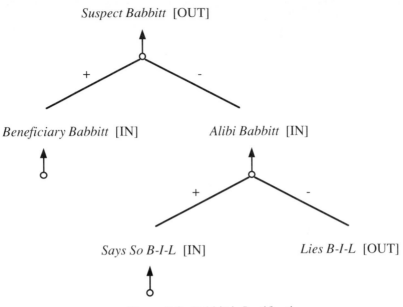

Figure 7.8: Babbitt's Justification

then that node must be labeled OUT if the labeling is to be well-founded.

The TMS task of ensuring a consistent, well-founded labeling has now been outlined. The other major task of a TMS is resolving contradictions. In a TMS, a contradiction node does not represent a logical contradiction but rather a state of the database explicitly declared to be undesirable. (In the next section, we describe a slightly different kind of TMS in which this is not the case.) In our example, we have a contradiction if we do not have at least one murder suspect. Thus a contradiction might have the justification shown in Figure 7.10, where the node *Other Suspects* means that there are suspects other than Abbott, Babbitt, and Cabot. This is one way of explicitly representing an instance of the closed world assumption. Later, if we discover a long-lost relative, this will provide a valid justification for *Other Suspects*. But for now, it has none and must be labeled OUT. Fortunately, even though Abbott and Babbitt are not suspects, *Suspect Cabot* is labeled IN, invalidating the justification for the contradiction. While the contradiction is labeled OUT, there is no contradiction to resolve.

Now we learn that Cabot was seen on television attending the ski tournament. Adding this to the dependency network first illustrates the fact that nodes can have more than one justification as shown in Figure 7.11. Not only does Cabot say he was at the ski slopes, but he was seen there on television, and we have no reason to believe that this was an elaborate forgery. This new valid justification of *Alibi Cabot* causes it to be labeled IN (which also causes *Tells Truth Cabot* to come IN). This change in state propagates to *Suspect Cabot*, which goes OUT. Now we have a problem.

The justification for the contradiction is now valid and the contradiction is IN. The job of the TMS at this point is to determine how the contradiction can be made OUT again. In a TMS network, a node can be made OUT by causing all of its justifications

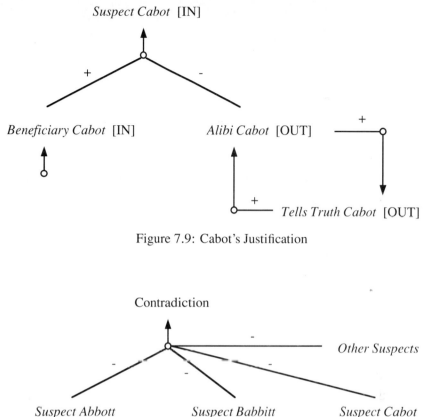

Figure 7.9: Cabot's Justification

Figure 7.10: A Contradiction

to become invalid. Monotonic justifications cannot be made invalid without retracting explicit assertions that have been made to the network. Nonmonotonic justifications can, however, be invalidated by asserting some fact whose absence is required by the justification. We call assertions with nonmonotonic justifications *assumptions*. An assumption can be retracted by making IN some element of its justification's OUT-list (or recursively in some element of the OUT-list of the justification of some element in its IN-list). Unfortunately, there may be many such assumptions in a large dependency network. Fortunately, the network gives us a way to identify those that are relevant to the contradiction at hand. Dependency-directed backtracking algorithms, of the sort we described in Section 7.5.1, can use the dependency links to determine an AND/OR tree of assumptions that might be retracted and ways to retract them by justifying other beliefs.

In Figure 7.10, we see that the contradiction itself is an assumption whenever its justification is valid. We might retract it by believing there were other suspects or by finding a way to believe again that either Abbott, Babbitt, or Cabot was a suspect. Each of the last three could be believed if we disbelieved their alibis, which in turn

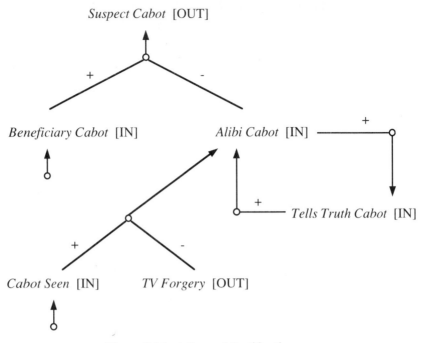

Figure 7.11: A Second Justification

are assumptions. So if we believed that the hotel register was a forgery, that Babbitt's brother-in-law lied, or that the television pictures were faked, we would have a suspect again and the contradiction would go back OUT. So there are four things we might believe to resolve the contradiction. That is as far as DDB will take us. It reports there is an OR tree with four nodes. What should we do?

A TMS has no answer for this question. Early TMSs picked an answer at random. More recent architectures take the more reasonable position that this choice was a problem for the same problem-solving agent that created the dependencies in the first place. But suppose we do pick one. Suppose, in particular, that we choose to believe that Babbitt's brother-in-law lied. What should be the justification for that belief? If we believe it just because not believing it leads to a contradiction, then we should install a justification that should be valid only as long as it needs to be. If later we find another way that the contradiction can be labeled OUT, we will not want to continue in our abductive belief.

For instance, suppose that we believe that the brother-in-law lied, but later we discover that a long-lost relative, jilted by the family, was in town the day of the murder. We would no longer have to believe the brother-in-law lied just to avoid a contradiction. A TMS may also have algorithms to create such justifications, which we call abductive since they are created using abductive reasoning. If they have the property that they are not unnecessarily valid, they are said to be *complete*. Figure 7.12 shows a complete abductive justification for the belief that Babbitt's brother-in-law lied. If we come to

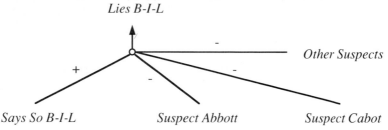

Figure 7.12: A Complete Abductive Justification

believe that Abbott or Cabot is a suspect, or we find a long-lost relative, or we somehow come to believe that Babbitt's brother-in-law didn't really say Babbitt was at his house, then this justification for lying will become invalid.

At this point, we have described the key reasoning operations that are performed by a JTMS:

- consistent labeling

- contradiction resolution

We have also described a set of important reasoning operations that a JTMS does not perform, including:

- applying rules to derive conclusions

- creating justifications for the results of applying rules (although justifications are created as part of contradiction resolution)

- choosing among alternative ways of resolving a contradiction

- detecting contradictions

All of these operations must be performed by the problem-solving program that is using the JTMS. In the next section, we describe a slightly different kind of TMS, in which, although the first three of these operations must still be performed by the problem-solving system, the last can be performed by the TMS.

7.5.3   Logic-Based Truth Maintenance Systems

A *logic-based truth maintenance system* (LTMS) [McAllester, 1980] is very similar to a JTMS. It differs in one important way. In a JTMS, the nodes in the network are treated as atoms by the TMS, which assumes no relationships among them except the ones that are explicitly stated in the justifications. In particular, a JTMS has no problem simultaneously labeling both P and $\neg P$ IN. For example, we could have represented explicitly both *Lies B-I-L* and *Not Lies B-I-L* and labeled both of them IN. No contradiction will be detected automatically. In an LTMS, on the other hand, a contradiction would be asserted automatically in such a case. If we had constructed the ABC example in an

LTMS system, we would not have created an explicit contradiction corresponding to the assertion that there was no suspect. Instead we would replace the contradiction node by one that asserted something like *No Suspect*. Then we would assert *Suspect*. When *No Suspect* came IN, it would cause a contradiction to be asserted automatically.

7.6   Implementation: Breadth-First Search

The *assumption-based truth maintenance system* (ATMS) [de Kleer, 1986] is an alternative way of implementing nonmonotonic reasoning. In both JTMS and LTMS systems, a single line of reasoning is pursued at a time, and dependency-directed backtracking occurs whenever it is necessary to change the system's assumptions. In an ATMS, alternative paths are maintained in parallel. Backtracking is avoided at the expense of maintaining multiple contexts, each of which corresponds to a set of consistent assumptions. As reasoning proceeds in an ATMS-based system, the universe of consistent contexts is pruned as contradictions are discovered. The remaining consistent contexts are used to label assertions, thus indicating the contexts in which each assertion has a valid justification. Assertions that do not have a valid justification in any consistent context can be pruned from consideration by the problem solver. As the set of consistent contexts gets smaller, so too does the set of assertions that can consistently be believed by the problem solver. Essentially, an ATMS system works breadth-first, considering all possible contexts at once, while both JTMS and LTMS systems operate depth-first.

The ATMS, like the JTMS, is designed to be used in conjunction with a separate problem solver. The problem solver's job is to:

- Create nodes that correspond to assertions (both those that are given as axioms and those that are derived by the problem solver).

- Associate with each such node one or more justifications, each of which describes a reasoning chain that led to the node.

- Inform the ATMS of inconsistent contexts.

Notice that this is identical to the role of the problem solver that uses a JTMS, except that no explicit choices among paths to follow need be made as reasoning proceeds. Some decision may be necessary at the end, though, if more than one possible solution still has a consistent context.

The role of the ATMS system is then to:

- Propagate inconsistencies, thus ruling out contexts that include subcontexts (sets of assertions) that are known to be inconsistent.

- Label each problem solver node with the contexts in which it has a valid justification. This is done by combining contexts that correspond to the components of a justification. In particular, given a justification of the form

$$A1 \wedge A2 \wedge \cdots \wedge An \rightarrow C$$

assign as a context for the node corresponding to C the intersection of the contexts corresponding to the nodes $A1$ through An.

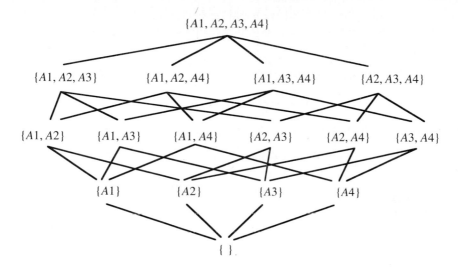

Figure 7.13: A Context Lattice

Contexts get eliminated as a result of the problem solver asserting inconsistencies and the ATMS propagating them. Nodes get created by the problem solver to represent possible components of a problem solution. They may then get pruned from consideration if all their context labels get pruned. Thus a choice among possible solution components gradually evolves in a process very much like the constraint satisfaction procedure that we examined in Section 3.5.

One problem with this approach is that given a set of n assumptions, the number of possible contexts that may have to be considered is 2^n. Fortunately, in many problem-solving scenarios, most of them can be pruned without ever looking at them. Further, the ATMS exploits an efficient labeling system that makes it possible to encode a set of contexts as a single context that delimits the set. To see how both of these things work, it is necessary to think of the set of contexts that are defined by a set of assumptions as forming a lattice, as shown for a simple example with four assumptions in Figure 7.13. Lines going upward indicate a subset relationship.

The first thing this lattice does for us is to illustrate a simple mechanism by which contradictions (inconsistent contexts) can be propagated so that large parts of the space of 2^n contexts can be eliminated. Suppose that the context labeled $\{A2, A3\}$ is asserted to be inconsistent. Then all contexts that include it (i.e., those that are above it) must also be inconsistent.

Now consider how a node can be labeled with all the contexts in which it has a valid justification. Suppose its justification depends on assumption $A1$. Then the context labeled $\{A1\}$ and all the contexts that include it are acceptable. But this can be indicated just by saying $\{A1\}$. It is not necessary to enumerate its supersets. In general, each node will be labeled with the greatest lower bounds of the contexts in which it should be believed.

Clearly, it is important that this lattice not be built explicitly but only used as an implicit structure as the ATMS proceeds.

As an example of how an ATMS-based problem solver works, let's return to the ABC Murder story. Again, our goal is to find a primary suspect. We need (at least) the following assumptions:

- A1. Hotel register was forged.

- A2. Hotel register was not forged.

- A3. Babbitt's brother-in-law lied.

- A4. Babbitt's brother-in-law did not lie.

- A5. Cabot lied.

- A6. Cabot did not lie.

- A7. Abbott, Babbitt, and Cabot are the only possible suspects.

- A8. Abbott, Babbitt, and Cabot are not the only suspects.

The problem solver could then generate the nodes and associated justifications shown in the first two columns of Figure 7.14. In the figure, the justification for a node that corresponds to a decision to make assumption N is shown as $\{N\}$. Justifications for nodes that correspond to the result of applying reasoning rules are shown as the rule involved. Then the ATMS can assign labels to the nodes as shown in the second two columns. The first shows the label that would be generated for each justification taken by itself. The second shows the label (possibly containing multiple contexts) that is actually assigned to the node given all its current justifications. These columns are identical in simple cases, but they may differ in more complex situations as we see for nodes 12, 13, and 14 of our example.

There are several things to notice about this example:

- Nodes may have several justifications if there are several possible reasons for believing them. This is the case for nodes 12, 13, and 14.

- Recall that when we were using a JTMS, a node was labeled IN if it had at least one valid justification. Using an ATMS, a node will end up being labeled with a consistent context if it has at least one justification that can occur in a consistent context.

- The label assignment process is sometimes complicated. We describe it in more detail below.

Suppose that a problem-solving program first created nodes 1 through 14, representing the various dependencies among them without committing to which of them it currently believes. It can indicate known contradictions by marking as no good the context:

- A, B, C are the only suspects; A, B, C are not the only suspects: $\{A7, A8\}$

	Nodes	Justifications		Node Labels
[1]	Register was not forged	$\{A2\}$	$\{A2\}$	$\{A2\}$
[2]	Abbott at hotel	$[1] \rightarrow [2]$	$\{A2\}$	$\{A2\}$
[3]	B-I-L didn't lie	$\{4\}$	$\{A4\}$	$\{A4\}$
[4]	Babbitt at B-I-L	$[3] \rightarrow [4]$	$\{A4\}$	$\{A4\}$
[5]	Cabot didn't lie	$\{6\}$	$\{A6\}$	$\{A6\}$
[6]	Cabot at ski show	$[5] \rightarrow [6]$	$\{A6\}$	$\{A6\}$
[7]	A, B, C only suspects	$\{A7\}$	$\{A7\}$	$\{A7\}$
[8]	Prime Suspect Abbott	$[7] \wedge [13] \wedge [14] \rightarrow [8]$	$\{A7, A4, A6\}$	$\{A7, A4, A6\}$
[9]	Prime Suspect Babbitt	$[7] \wedge [12] \wedge [14] \rightarrow [9]$	$\{A7, A2, A6\}$	$\{A7, A2, A6\}$
[10]	Prime Suspect Cabot	$[7] \wedge [12] \wedge [13] \rightarrow [10]$	$\{A7, A2, A4\}$	$\{A7, A2, A4\}$
[11]	A, B, C not only suspects	$\{A8\}$	$\{A8\}$	$\{A8\}$
[12]	Not prime suspect Abbott	$[2] \rightarrow [12]$	$\{A2\}$	$\{A2\}, \{A8\}$
		$[11] \rightarrow [12]$	$\{A8\}$	
		$[9] \rightarrow [12]$	$\{A7, A2, A6\}$	
		$[10] \rightarrow [12]$	$\{A7, A2, A4\}$	
[13]	Not prime suspect Babbitt	$[4] \rightarrow [13]$	$\{A4\}$	$\{A4\}, \{A8\}$
		$[11] \rightarrow [13]$	$\{A8\}$	
		$[8] \rightarrow [13]$	$\{A7, A4, A6\}$	
		$[10] \rightarrow [13]$	$\{A7, A4, A2\}$	
[14]	Not prime suspect Cabot	$[6] \rightarrow [14]$	$\{A6\}$	$\{A6\}, \{A8\}$
		$[11] \rightarrow [14]$	$\{A8\}$	
		$[8] \rightarrow [14]$	$\{A7, A4, A6\}$	
		$[9] \rightarrow [14]$	$\{A7, A2, A6\}$	

Figure 7.14: Nodes and Their Justifications and Labels

The ATMS would then assign the labels shown in the figure. Let's consider the case of node 12. We generate four possible labels, one for each justification. But we want to assign to the node a label that contains just the greatest lower bounds of all the contexts in which it can occur, since they implicitly encode the superset contexts. The label $\{A2\}$ is the greatest lower bound of the first, third, and fourth label, and $\{A8\}$ is the same for the second label. Thus those two contexts are all that are required as the label for the node. Now let's consider labeling node 8. Its label must be the union of the labels of nodes 7, 13, and 14. But nodes 13 and 14 have complex labels representing alternative justifications. So we must consider all ways of combining the labels of all three nodes. Fortunately, some of these combinations, namely those that contain both $A7$ and $A8$, can be eliminated because they are already known to be contradictory. Thus we are left with a single label as shown.

Now suppose the problem solving program labels the context $\{A2\}$ as no good, meaning that the assumption it contains (namely that the hotel register was not forged) conflicts with what it knows. Then many of the labels that we had disappear since they are now inconsistent. In particular, the labels for nodes 1, 2, 9, 10, and 12 disappear. At this point, the only suspect node that has a label is node 8. But node 12 (Not prime suspect Abbott) also still has a label that corresponds to the assumption that Abbott, Babbitt, and Cabot are not the only suspects. If this assumption is made, then Abbott would not be a clear suspect even if the hotel register were forged. Further information or some choice process is still necessary to choose between these remaining nodes.

7.7   Summary

In this chapter we have discussed several logical systems that provide a basis for nonmonotonic reasoning, including nonmonotonic logic, default logic, abduction, inheritance, the closed world assumption, and circumscription. We have also described a way in which the kind of rules that we discussed in Chapter 6 could be augmented to support nonmonotonic reasoning.

We then presented three kinds of TMS systems, all of which provide a basis for implementing nonmonotonic reasoning. We have considered two dimensions along which TMS systems can vary: whether they automatically detect logical contradictions and whether they maintain single or multiple contexts. The following table summarizes this discussion:

TMS Kinds	single context	multiple context
nonlogical	JTMS	ATMS
logical	LTMS	?

As can be seen in this table, there is currently no TMS with logical contradictions and multiple contexts.

These various TMS systems each have advantages and disadvantages with respect to each other. The major issues that distinguish JTMS and ATMS systems are:

- The JTMS is often better when only a single solution is desired since it does not need to consider alternatives; the ATMS is usually more efficient if all solutions are eventually going to be needed.

- To create the context lattice, the ATMS performs a global operation in which it considers all possible combinations of assumptions. As a result, either all assumptions must be known at the outset of problem solving or an expensive, recompilation process must occur whenever an assumption is added. In the JTMS, on the other hand, the gradual addition of new assumptions poses no problem.

- The JTMS may spend a lot of time switching contexts when backtracking is necessary. Context switching does not happen in the ATMS.

- In an ATMS, inconsistent contexts disappear from consideration. If the initial problem description was overconstrained, then all nodes will end up with empty labels and there will be no problem-solving trace that can serve as a basis for relaxing one or more of the constraints. In a JTMS, on the other hand, the justification that is attached to a contradiction node provides exactly such a trace.

- The ATMS provides a natural way to answer questions of the form, "In what contexts is A true?" The only way to answer such questions using a JTMS is to try all the alternatives and record the ones in which A is labeled IN.

One way to get the best of both of these worlds is to combine an ATMS and a JTMS (or LTMS), letting each handle the part of the problem-solving process to which it is best suited.

The various nonmonotonic systems that we have described in this chapter have served as a basis for a variety of applications. One area of particular significance is diagnosis (for example, of faults in a physical device) [Reiter, 1987b; de Kleer and Williams, 1987]. Diagnosis is a natural application area for minimalist reasoning in particular, since one way to describe the diagnostic task is, "Find the smallest set of abnormally behaving components that would account for the observed behavior." A second application area is reasoning about action, with a particular emphasis on addressing the frame problem [Hanks and McDermott, 1986]. The frame problem is also natural for this kind of reasoning since it can be described as, "Assume that everything stays the same after an action except the things that necessarily change." A third application area is design [Steele *et al.*, 1989]. Here, nonmonotonic reasoning provides a basis for using common design principles to find a promising path quickly even in a huge design space while preserving the option to consider alternatives later if necessary. And yet another application area is in extracting intent from English expressions (see Chapter 15.)

In all the systems that we have discussed, we have assumed that belief status is a binary function. An assertion must eventually be either believed or not. Sometimes, this is too strong an assumption. In the next chapter, we present techniques for dealing with uncertainty without making that assumption. Instead, we allow for varying degrees of belief.

7.8 Exercises

1. Try to formulate the ABC Murder story in predicate logic and see how far you can get.

2. The classic example of nonmonotonic reasoning involves birds and flying. In particular, consider the following facts:

   - Most things do not fly.
   - Most birds do fly, unless they are too young or dead or have a broken wing.
   - Penguins and ostriches do not fly.
   - Magical ostriches fly.
   - Tweety is a bird.
   - Chirpy is either a penguin or an ostrich.
   - Feathers is a magical ostrich.

   Use one or more of the nonmonotonic reasoning systems we have discussed to answer the following questions:

   - Does Tweety fly?
   - Does Chirpy fly?
   - Does Feathers fly?
   - Does Paul fly?

3. Consider the missionaries and cannibals problem of Section 2.6. When you solved that problem, you used the CWA several times (probably without thinking about it). List some of the ways in which you used it.

4. A big technical problem that arises in defining circumscription precisely is the definition of a minimal model. Consider again the problem of Dick, the Quaker and Republican, which we can rewrite using a slightly different kind of *AB* predicate as:

$\forall x : Republican(x) \land \neg AB1(x) \rightarrow \neg Pacifist(x)$
$\forall x : Quaker(x) \land \neg AB2(x) \rightarrow Pacifist(x)$
$Republican(x)$
$Quaker(x)$

   (a) Write down the smallest models you can that describe the two extensions that we computed for that knowledge base.

   (b) Does it make sense to say that either is smaller than the other?

   (c) Prioritized circumscription [McCarthy, 1986] attempts to solve this problem by ranking predicates by the order in which they should be minimized. How could you use this idea to indicate a preference as to which extension to prefer?

5. Consider the problem of finding clothes to wear in the morning. To solve this problem, it is necessary to use knowledge such as:

   • Wear jeans unless either they are dirty or you have a job interview today.

   • Wear a sweater if it's cold.

   • It's usually cold in the winter.

   • Wear sandals if it's warm.

   • It's usually warm in the summer.

   (a) Build a JTMS-style database of the necessary facts to solve this problem.

   (b) Show how the problem can be solved and how the solution changes as the relevant facts (such as time of year and dirtiness of jeans) change.

6. Show how a JTMS could be used in medical diagnosis. Consider rules such as, "If you have a runny nose, assume you have a cold unless it is allergy season."

7. Solve the same medical reasoning problem with an ATMS.

8. Show how a JTMS could be used to select a TV program to watch. Consider rules such as, "If it is 6:00, then watch the news on channel 2 unless there is a football game still going on."

9. TMSs are useful tools in solving constraint satisfaction problems since they facilitate the nonmonotonic reasoning that occurs during the search for a complete solution.

    (a) Show how a JTMS could be used to solve the cryptarithmetic problems of Chapter 2.

    (b) Show how an ATMS would solve the same problem.

10. We described informally the JTMS labeling process. Write a formal description of that algorithm.

11. Work through the details of the ATMS node labeling process whose results are shown in Figure 7.14.

Chapter 8

Statistical Reasoning

So far, we have described several representation techniques that can be used to model belief systems in which, at any given point, a particular fact is believed to be true, believed to be false, or not considered one way or the other. For some kinds of problem solving, though, it is useful to be able to describe beliefs that are not certain but for which there is some supporting evidence. Let's consider two classes of such problems.

The first class contains problems in which there is genuine randomness in the world. Playing card games such as bridge and blackjack is a good example of this class. Although in these problems it is not possible to predict the world with certainty, some knowledge about the likelihood of various outcomes is available, and we would like to be able to exploit it.

The second class contains problems that could, in principle, be modeled using the techniques we described in the last chapter. In these problems, the relevant world is not random; it behaves "normally" unless there is some kind of exception. The difficulty is that there are many more possible exceptions than we care to enumerate explicitly (using techniques such as AB and UNLESS). Many common sense tasks fall into this category, as do many expert reasoning tasks such as medical diagnosis. For problems like this, statistical measures may serve a very useful function as summaries of the world; rather than enumerating all the possible exceptions, we can use a numerical summary that tells us how often an exception of some sort can be expected to occur.

In this chapter we explore several techniques that can be used to augment knowledge representation techniques with statistical measures that describe levels of evidence and belief.

8.1 Probability and Bayes' Theorem

An important goal for many problem-solving systems is to collect evidence as the system goes along and to modify its behavior on the basis of the evidence. To model this behavior, we need a statistical theory of evidence. Bayesian statistics is such a theory. The fundamental notion of Bayesian statistics is that of conditional probability:

$$P(H|E)$$

Read this expression as the probability of hypothesis H given that we have observed evidence E. To compute this, we need to take into account the prior probability of H (the probability that we would assign to H if we had no evidence) and the extent to which E provides evidence of H. To do this, we need to define a universe that contains an exhaustive, mutually exclusive set of H_i's, among which we are trying to discriminate. Then, let

$P(H_i|E)$ =the probability that hypothesis H_i is true given evidence E

$P(E|H_i)$ =the probability that we will observe evidence E given that hypothesis i is true

$P(H_i)$ =the *a priori* probability that hypothesis i is true in the absence of any specific evidence. These probabilities are called prior probabilities or *priors*.

k =the number of possible hypotheses

Bayes' theorem then states that

$$P(H_i|E) = \frac{P(E|H_i) \cdot P(H_i)}{\sum_{n=1}^{k} P(E|H_n) \cdot P(H_n)}$$

Suppose, for example, that we are interested in examining the geological evidence at a particular location to determine whether that would be a good place to dig to find a desired mineral. If we know the prior probabilities of finding each of the various minerals and we know the probabilities that if a mineral is present then certain physical characteristics will be observed, then we can use Bayes' formula to compute, from the evidence we collect, how likely it is that the various minerals are present. This is, in fact, what is done by the PROSPECTOR program [Duda *et al.*, 1979], which has been used successfully to help locate deposits of several minerals, including copper and uranium.

The key to using Bayes' theorem as a basis for uncertain reasoning is to recognize exactly what it says. Specifically, when we say $P(A|B)$, we are describing the conditional probability of A given that the only evidence we have is B. If there is also other relevant evidence, then it too must be considered. Suppose, for example, that we are solving a medical diagnosis problem. Consider the following assertions:

S: patient has spots
M: patient has measles
F: patient has high fever

Without any additional evidence, the presence of spots serves as evidence in favor of measles. It also serves as evidence of fever since measles would cause fever. But suppose we already know that the patient has measles. Then the additional evidence that he has spots actually tells us nothing about the likelihood of fever. Alternatively, either spots alone or fever alone would constitute evidence in favor of measles. If both are present, we need to take both into account in determining the total weight of evidence. But, since spots and fever are not independent events, we cannot just sum their effects. Instead, we need to represent explicitly the conditional probability that arises from their conjunction. In general, given a prior body of evidence e and some new observation E, we need to compute

$$P(H|E, e) = P(H|E) \cdot \frac{P(e|E, H)}{P(e|E)}$$

Unfortunately, in an arbitrarily complex world, the size of the set of joint probabilities that we require in order to compute this function grows as 2^n if there are n different propositions being considered. This makes using Bayes' theorem intractable for several reasons:

- The knowledge acquisition problem is insurmountable; too many probabilities have to be provided. In addition, there is substantial empirical evidence (e.g., Tversky and Kahneman [1974] and Kahneman *et al.* [1982]) that people are very poor probability estimators.

- The space that would be required to store all the probabilities is too large.

- The time required to compute the probabilities is too large.

Despite these problems, though, Bayesian statistics provide an attractive basis for an uncertain reasoning system. As a result, several mechanisms for exploiting its power while at the same time making it tractable have been developed. In the rest of this chapter, we explore three of these:

- Attaching certainty factors to rules

- Bayesian networks

- Dempster-Shafer theory

We also mention one very different numerical approach to uncertainty, fuzzy logic.

There has been an active, strident debate for many years on the question of whether pure Bayesian statistics are adequate as a basis for the development of reasoning pro- grams. (See, for example, Cheeseman [1985] for arguments that it is and Buchanan and Shortliffe [1984] for arguments that it is not.) On the one hand, non-Bayesian approaches have been shown to work well for some kinds of applications (as we see below). On the other hand, there are clear limitations to all known techniques. In essence, the jury is still out. So we sidestep the issue as much as possible and simply describe a set of methods and their characteristics.

8.2 Certainty Factors and Rule-Based Systems

In this section we describe one practical way of compromising on a pure Bayesian system. The approach we discuss was pioneered in the MYCIN system [Shortliffe, 1976; Buchanan and Shortliffe, 1984; Shortliffe and Buchanan, 1975], which attempts to recommend appropriate therapies for patients with bacterial infections. It interacts with the physician to acquire the clinical data it needs. MYCIN is an example of an *expert system*, since it performs a task normally done by a human expert. Here we concentrate on the use of probabilistic reasoning; Chapter 20 provides a broader view of expert systems.

MYCIN represents most of its diagnostic knowledge as a set of rules. Each rule has associated with it a *certainty factor*, which is a measure of the extent to which the evidence that is described by the antecedent of the rule supports the conclusion that is given in the rule's consequent. A typical MYCIN rule looks like:

```
If: (1) the stain of the organism is gram-positive, and
    (2) the morphology of the organism is coccus, and
    (3) the growth conformation of the organism is clumps,
then there is suggestive evidence (0.7) that
  the identity of the organism is staphylococcus.
```

This is the form in which the rules are stated to the user. They are actually represented internally in an easy-to-manipulate LISP list structure. The rule we just saw would be represented internally as

```
PREMISE: ($AND (SAME CNTXT GRAM GRAMPOS)
               (SAME CNTXT MORPH COCCUS)
               (SAME CNTXT CONFORM CLUMPS))
ACTION:  (CONCLUDE CNTXT IDENT STAPHYLOCOCCUS TALLY 0.7)
```

MYCIN uses these rules to reason backward to the clinical data available from its goal of finding significant disease-causing organisms. Once it finds the identities of such organisms, it then attempts to select a therapy by which the disease(s) may be treated. In order to understand how MYCIN exploits uncertain information, we need answers to two questions: "What do certainty factors mean?" and "How does MYCIN combine the estimates of certainty in each of its rules to produce a final estimate of the certainty of its conclusions?" A further question that we need to answer, given our observations about the intractability of pure Bayesian reasoning, is, "What compromises does the MYCIN technique make and what risks are associated with those compromises?" In the rest of this section we answer all these questions.

Let's start first with a simple answer to the first question (to which we return with a more detailed answer later). A certainty factor ($CF[h, e]$) is defined in terms of two components:

- $MB[h, e]$—a measure (between 0 and 1) of belief in hypothesis h given the evidence e. MB measures the extent to which the evidence supports the hypothesis. It is zero if the evidence fails to support the hypothesis.

- $MD[h, e]$—a measure (between 0 and 1) of disbelief in hypothesis h given the evidence e. MD measures the extent to which the evidence supports the negation of the hypothesis. It is zero if the evidence supports the hypothesis.

From these two measures, we can define the certainty factor as

$$CF[h, e] = MB[h, e] - MD[h, e]$$

Since any particular piece of evidence either supports or denies a hypothesis (but not both), and since each MYCIN rule corresponds to one piece of evidence (although it may be a compound piece of evidence), a single number suffices for each rule to define both the MB and MD and thus the CF.

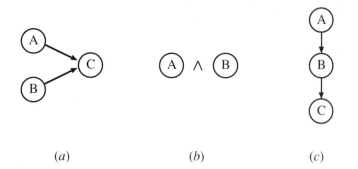

(a) (b) (c)

Figure 8.1: Combining Uncertain Rules

The CF's of MYCIN's rules are provided by the experts who write the rules. They reflect the experts' assessments of the strength of the evidence in support of the hypothesis. As MYCIN reasons, however, these CF's need to be combined to reflect the operation of multiple pieces of evidence and multiple rules applied to a problem. Figure 8.1 illustrates three combination scenarios that we need to consider. In Figure 8.1(a), several rules all provide evidence that relates to a single hypothesis. In Figure 8.1(b), we need to consider our belief in a collection of several propositions taken together. In Figure 8.1(c), the output of one rule provides the input to another.

What formulas should be used to perform these combinations? Before we answer that question, we need first to describe some properties that we would like the combining functions to satisfy:

- Since the order in which evidence is collected is arbitrary, the combining functions should be commutative and associative.

- Until certainty is reached, additional confirming evidence should increase MB (and similarly for disconfirming evidence and MD).

- If uncertain inferences are chained together, then the result should be less certain than either of the inferences alone.

Having accepted the desirability of these properties, let's first consider the scenario in Figure 8.1(a), in which several pieces of evidence are combined to determine the CF of one hypothesis. The measures of belief and disbelief of a hypothesis given two observations s_1 and s_2 are computed from:

$$MB[h, s_1 \wedge s_2] = \begin{cases} 0 & \text{if } MD[h, s_1 \wedge s_2] = 1 \\ MB[h, s_1] + MB[h, s_2] \cdot (1 - MB[h, s_1]) & \text{otherwise} \end{cases}$$

$$MD[h, s_1 \wedge s_2] = \begin{cases} 0 & \text{if } MB[h, s_1 \wedge s_2] = 1 \\ MD[h, s_1] + MD[h, s_2] \cdot (1 - MD[h, s_1]) & \text{otherwise} \end{cases}$$

One way to state these formulas in English is that the measure of belief in h is 0 if h is disbelieved with certainty. Otherwise, the measure of belief in h given two observations is the measure of belief given only one observation plus some increment for the second observation. This increment is computed by first taking the difference between 1 (certainty) and the belief given only the first observation. This difference is the most that can be added by the second observation. The difference is then scaled by the belief in h given only the second observation. A corresponding explanation can be given, then, for the formula for computing disbelief. From MB and MD, CF can be computed. Notice that if several sources of corroborating evidence are pooled, the absolute value of CF will increase. If conflicting evidence is introduced, the absolute value of CF will decrease.

A simple example shows how these functions operate. Suppose we make an initial observation that confirms our belief in h with $MB = 0.3$. Then $MD[h, s_1] = 0$ and $CF[h, s_1] = 0.3$. Now we make a second observation, which also confirms h, with $MB[h, s_2] = 0.2$. Now:

$$
\begin{aligned}
MB[h, s_1 \wedge s_2] &= 0.3 + 0.2 \cdot 0.7 \\
&= 0.44 \\
MD[h, s_1 \wedge s_2] &= 0.0 \\
CF[h, s_1 \wedge s_2] &= 0.44
\end{aligned}
$$

You can see from this example how slight confirmatory evidence can accumulate to produce increasingly larger certainty factors.

Next let's consider the scenario of Figure 8.1(b), in which we need to compute the certainty factor of a combination of hypotheses. In particular, this is necessary when we need to know the certainty factor of a rule antecedent that contains several clauses (as, for example, in the staphylococcus rule given above). The combination certainty factor can be computed from its MB and MD. The formulas MYCIN uses for the MB of the conjunction and the disjunction of two hypotheses are:

$$
MB[h_1 \wedge h_2, e] = \min(MB[h_1, e], MB[h_2, e])
$$

$$
MB[h_1 \vee h_2, e] = \max(MB[h_1, e], MB[h_2, e])
$$

MD can be computed analogously.

Finally, we need to consider the scenario in Figure 8.1(c), in which rules are chained together with the result that the uncertain outcome of one rule must provide the input to another. Our solution to this problem will also handle the case in which we must assign a measure of uncertainty to initial inputs. This could easily happen in situations where the evidence is the outcome of an experiment or a laboratory test whose results are not completely accurate. In such a case, the certainty factor of the hypothesis must take into account both the strength with which the evidence suggests the hypothesis and the level of confidence in the evidence. MYCIN provides a chaining rule that is defined as follows. Let $MB'[h, s]$ be the measure of belief in h given that we are absolutely sure of the validity of s. Let e be the evidence that led us to believe in s (for example, the actual readings of the laboratory instruments or the results of applying other rules). Then:

$$MB[h, s] = MB'[h, s] \cdot \max(0, CF[s, e])$$

Since initial CF's in MYCIN are estimates that are given by experts who write the rules, it is not really necessary to state a more precise definition of what a CF means than the one we have already given. The original work did, however, provide one by defining MB (which can be thought of as a proportionate decrease in disbelief in h as a result of e) as:

$$MB[h, e] = \begin{cases} 1 & \text{if } P(h) = 1 \\ \frac{\max[P(h|e), P(h)] - P(h)}{1 - P(h)} & \text{otherwise} \end{cases}$$

Similarly, the MD is the proportionate decrease in belief in h as a result of e:

$$MD[h, e] = \begin{cases} 1 & \text{if } P(h) = 0 \\ \frac{\min[P(h|e), P(h)] - P(h)}{-P(h)} & \text{otherwise} \end{cases}$$

It turns out that these definitions are incompatible with a Bayesian view of conditional probability. Small changes to them, however, make them compatible [Heckerman, 1986]. In particular, we can redefine MB as

$$MB[h, e] = \begin{cases} 1 & \text{if } P(h) = 1 \\ \frac{\max[P(h|e), P(h)] - P(h)}{(1 - P(h)) \cdot P(h|e)} & \text{otherwise} \end{cases}$$

The definition of MD must also be changed similarly.

With these reinterpretations, there ceases to be any fundamental conflict between MYCIN's techniques and those suggested by Bayesian statistics. We argued at the end of the last section that pure Bayesian statistics usually leads to intractable systems. But MYCIN works [Buchanan and Shortliffe, 1984]. Why?

Each CF in a MYCIN rule represents the contribution of an individual rule to MYCIN's belief in a hypothesis. In some sense then, it represents a conditional probability, $P(H|E)$. But recall that in a pure Bayesian system, $P(H|E)$ describes the conditional probability of H given that the only relevant evidence is E. If there is other evidence, joint probabilities need to be considered. This is where MYCIN diverges from a pure Bayesian system, with the result that it is easier to write and more efficient to execute, but with the corresponding risk that its behavior will be counterintuitive. In particular, the MYCIN formulas for all three combination scenarios of Figure 8.1 make the assumption that all rules are independent. The burden of guaranteeing independence (at least to the extent that it matters) is on the rule writer. Each of the combination scenarios is vulnerable when this independence assumption is violated.

Let's first consider the scenario in Figure 8.1(a). Our example rule has three antecedents with a single CF rather than three separate rules; this makes the combination rules unnecessary. The rule writer did this because the three antecedents are not independent. To see how much difference MYCIN's independence assumption can make, suppose for a moment that we had instead had three separate rules and that the *CF* of each was 0.6. This could happen and still be consistent with the combined *CF* of 0.7 if the three conditions overlap substantially. If we apply the MYCIN combination formula to the three separate rules, we get

$$MB[h, s_1 \wedge s_2] \qquad = 0.6 + (0.6 \cdot 0.4)$$
$$= 0.84$$

$$MB[h, (s_1 \wedge s_2) \wedge s_3] = 0.84 + (0.6 \cdot 0.16)$$
$$= 0.936$$

This is a substantially different result than the true value, as expressed by the expert, of 0.7.

Now let's consider what happens when independence assumptions are violated in the scenario of Figure 8.1(*c*). Let's consider a concrete example in which:

    S: sprinkler was on last night
    W: grass is wet
    R: it rained last night

We can write MYCIN-style rules that describe predictive relationships among these three events:

```
If: the sprinkler was on last night
then there is suggestive evidence (0.9) that
   the grass will be wet this morning
```

Taken alone, this rule may accurately describe the world. But now consider a second rule:

```
If: the grass is wet this morning
then there is suggestive evidence (0.8) that
   it rained last night
```

Taken alone, this rule makes sense when rain is the most common source of water on the grass. But if the two rules are applied together, using MYCIN's rule for chaining, we get

$$MB[W, S] = 0.8 \qquad\qquad \{\text{sprinkler suggests wet}\}$$
$$MB[R, W] = 0.8 \cdot 0.9 = 0.72 \quad \{\text{wet suggests rains}\}$$

In other words, we believe that it rained because we believe the sprinkler was on. We get this despite the fact that if the sprinkler is known to have been on and to be the cause of the grass being wet, then there is actually almost no evidence for rain (because the wet grass has been explained some other way). One of the major advantages of the modularity of the MYCIN rule system is that it allows us to consider individual antecedent/consequent relationships independently of others. In particular, it lets us talk about the implications of a proposition without going back and considering the evidence that supported it. Unfortunately, this example shows that there is a danger in this approach whenever the justifications of a belief are important to determining its consequences. In this case, we need to know why we believe the grass is wet (e.g., because we observed it to be wet as opposed to because we know the sprinkler was on) in order to determine whether the wet grass is evidence for it having just rained.

It is worth pointing out here that this example illustrates one specific rule structure that almost always causes trouble and should be avoided. Notice that our first rule describes a causal relationship (sprinkler causes wet grass). The second rule, although it looks the same, actually describes an inverse causality relationship (wet grass is caused by rain and thus is evidence for its cause). Although one can derive evidence for a symptom from its cause and for a cause from observing its symptom, it is important that evidence that is derived one way not be used again to go back the other way with no new information. To avoid this problem, many rule-based systems either limit their rules to one structure or clearly partition the two kinds so that they cannot interfere with each other. When we discuss Bayesian networks in the next section, we describe a systematic solution to this problem.

We can summarize this discussion of certainty factors and rule-based systems as follows. The approach makes strong independence assumptions that make it relatively easy to use; at the same time assumptions create dangers if rules are not written carefully so that important dependencies are captured. The approach can serve as the basis of practical application programs. It did so in MYCIN. It has done so in a broad array of other systems that have been built on the EMYCIN platform [van Melle *et al.*, 1981], which is a generalization (often called a *shell*) of MYCIN with all the domain-specific rules stripped out. One reason that this framework is useful, despite its limitations, is that it appears that in an otherwise robust system the exact numbers that are used do not matter very much. The other reason is that the rules were carefully designed to avoid the major pitfalls we have just described. One other interesting thing about this approach is that it appears to mimic quite well [Shultz *et al.*, 1989] the way people manipulate certainties.

8.3 Bayesian Networks

In the last section, we described *CF*'s as a mechanism for reducing the complexity of a Bayesian reasoning system by making some approximations to the formalism. In this section, we describe an alternative approach, *Bayesian networks* [Pearl, 1988], in which we preserve the formalism and rely instead on the modularity of the world we are trying to model. The main idea is that to describe the real world, it is not necessary to use a huge joint probability table in which we list the probabilities of all conceivable combinations of events. Most events are conditionally independent of most other ones, so their interactions need not be considered. Instead, we can use a more local representation in which we will describe clusters of events that interact.

Recall that in Figure 8.1 we used a network notation to describe the various kinds of constraints on likelihoods that propositions can have on each other. The idea of constraint networks turns out to be very powerful. We expand on it in this section as a way to represent interactions among events; we also return to it later in Sections 11.3.1 and 14.3, where we talk about other ways of representing knowledge as sets of constraints.

Let's return to the example of the sprinkler, rain, and grass that we introduced in the last section. Figure 8.2(*a*) shows the flow of constraints we described in MYCIN-style

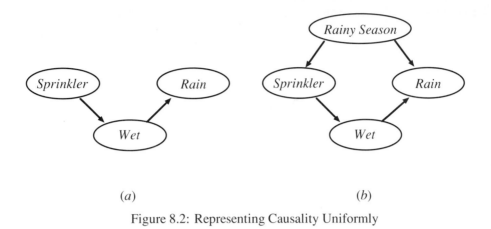

(a)   (b)

Figure 8.2: Representing Causality Uniformly

rules. But recall that the problem that we encountered with that example was that the constraints flowed incorrectly from "sprinkler on" to "rained last night." The problem was that we failed to make a distinction that turned out to be critical. There are two different ways that propositions can influence the likelihood of each other. The first is that causes influence the likelihood of their symptoms; the second is that observing a symptom affects the likelihood of all of its possible causes. The idea behind the Bayesian network structure is to make a clear distinction between these two kinds of influence.

Specifically, we construct a directed acyclic graph (DAG) that represents causality relationships among variables. The idea of a causality graph (or network) has proved to be very useful in several systems, particularly medical diagnosis systems such as CAS-NET [Weiss *et al.*, 1978] and INTERNIST/CADUCEUS [Pople, 1982]. The variables in such a graph may be propositional (in which case they can take on the values TRUE and FALSE) or they may be variables that take on values of some other type (e.g., a specific disease, a body temperature, or a reading taken by some other diagnostic device). In Figure 8.2(*b*), we show a causality graph for the wet grass example. In addition to the three nodes we have been talking about, the graph contains a new node corresponding to the propositional variable that tells us whether it is currently the rainy season.

A DAG, such as the one we have just drawn, illustrates the causality relationships that occur among the nodes it contains. In order to use it as a basis for probabilistic reasoning, however, we need more information. In particular, we need to know, for each value of a parent node, what evidence is provided about the values that the child node can take on. We can state this in a table in which the conditional probabilities are provided. We show such a table for our example in Figure 8.3. For example, from the table we see that the prior probability of the rainy season is 0.5. Then, if it is the rainy season, the probability of rain on a given night is 0.9; if it is not, the probability is only 0.1.

To be useful as a basis for problem solving, we need a mechanism for computing the influence of any arbitrary node on any other. For example, suppose that we have observed that it rained last night. What does that tell us about the probability that it is the

Attribute	Probability
$p(Wet|Sprinkler, Rain)$	0.95
$p(Wet|Sprinkler, \neg Rain)$	0.9
$p(Wet|\neg Sprinkler, Rain)$	0.8
$p(Wet|\neg Sprinkler, \neg Rain)$	0.1
$p(Sprinkler|RainySeason)$	0.0
$p(Sprinkler|\neg RainySeason)$	1.0
$p(Rain|RainySeason)$	0.9
$p(Rain|\neg RainySeason)$	0.1
$p(RainySeason)$	0.5

Figure 8.3: Conditional Probabilities for a Bayesian Network

rainy season? To answer this question requires that the initial DAG be converted to an undirected graph in which the arcs can be used to transmit probabilities in either direction, depending on where the evidence is coming from. We also require a mechanism for using the graph that guarantees that probabilities are transmitted correctly. For example, while it is true that observing wet grass may be evidence for rain, and observing rain is evidence for wet grass, we must guarantee that no cycle is ever traversed in such a way that wet grass is evidence for rain, which is then taken as evidence for wet grass, and so forth.

There are three broad classes of algorithms for doing these computations: a message-passing method [Pearl, 1988], a clique triangulation method [Lauritzen and Spiegelhalter, 1988], and a variety of stochastic algorithms. The idea behind these methods is to take advantage of the fact that nodes have limited domains of influence. Thus, although in principle the task of updating probabilities consistently throughout the network is intractable, in practice it may not be. In the clique triangulation method, for example, explicit arcs are introduced between pairs of nodes that share a common descendent. For the case shown in Figure 8.2(b), a link would be introduced between *Sprinkler* and *Rain*. This explicit link supports assessing the impact of the observation *Sprinkler* on the hypothesis *Rain*. This is important since wet grass could be evidence of either of them, but wet grass plus one of its causes is not evidence for the competing cause since an alternative explanation for the observed phenomenon already exists.

The message-passing approach is based on the observation that to compute the probability of a node A given what is known about other nodes in the network, it is necessary to know three things:

- π - the total support arriving at A from its parent nodes (which represent its causes).

- λ - the total support arriving at A from its children (which represent its symptoms).

- The entry in the fixed conditional probability matrix that relates A to its causes.

Several methods for propagating π and λ messages and updating the probabilities at the nodes have been developed. The structure of the network determines what approach can be used. For example, in singly connected networks (those in which there is only a single path between every pair of nodes), a simpler algorithm can be used than in the case of multiply connected ones. For details, see Pearl [1988].

Finally, there are stochastic, or randomized algorithms for updating belief networks. One such algorithm [Chavez, 1989] transforms an arbitrary network into a Markov chain. The idea is to shield a given node probabilistically from most of the other nodes in the network. Stochastic algorithms run fast in practice, but may not yield absolutely correct results.

8.4   Dempster-Shafer Theory

So far, we have described several techniques, all of which consider individual propositions and assign to each of them a point estimate (i.e., a single number) of the degree of belief that is warranted given the evidence. In this section, we consider an alternative technique, called *Dempster-Shafer theory* [Dempster, 1968; Shafer, 1976]. This new approach considers sets of propositions and assigns to each of them an interval

$$[Belief, Plausibility]$$

in which the degree of belief must lie. Belief (usually denoted *Bel*) measures the strength of the evidence in favor of a set of propositions. It ranges from 0 (indicating no evidence) to 1 (denoting certainty).

Plausibility (*Pl*) is defined to be

$$Pl(s) = 1 - Bel(\neg s)$$

It also ranges from 0 to 1 and measures the extent to which evidence in favor of $\neg s$ leaves room for belief in s. In particular, if we have certain evidence in favor of $\neg s$, then $Bel(\neg s)$ will be 1 and $Pl(s)$ will be 0. This tells us that the only possible value for $Bel(s)$ is also 0.

The belief-plausibility interval we have just defined measures not only our level of belief in some propositions, but also the amount of information we have. Suppose that we are currently considering three competing hypotheses: A, B, and C. If we have no information, we represent that by saying, for each of them, that the true likelihood is in the range $[0, 1]$. As evidence is accumulated, this interval can be expected to shrink, representing increased confidence that we know how likely each hypothesis is. Note that this contrasts with a pure Bayesian approach, in which we would probably begin by distributing the prior probability equally among the hypotheses and thus assert for each that $P(h) = 0.33$. The interval approach makes it clear that we have no information when we start. The Bayesian approach does not, since we could end up with the same probability values if we collected volumes of evidence, which taken together suggest that the three values occur equally often. This difference can matter if one of the decisions that our program needs to make is whether to collect more evidence or to act on the basis of the evidence it already has.

So far, we have talked intuitively about *Bel* as a measure of our belief in some hypothesis given some evidence. Let's now define it more precisely. To do this, we need to start, just as with Bayes' theorem, with an exhaustive universe of mutually exclusive hypotheses. We'll call this the *frame of discernment* and we'll write it as Θ. For example, in a simplified diagnosis problem, Θ might consist of the set $\{All, Flu, Cold, Pneu\}$:

All: allergy
Flu: flu
Cold: cold
Pneu: pneumonia

Our goal is to attach some measure of belief to elements of Θ. However, not all evidence is directly supportive of individual elements. Often it supports sets of elements (i.e., subsets of Θ). For example, in our diagnosis problem, fever might support $\{Flu, Cold, Pneu\}$. In addition, since the elements of Θ are mutually exclusive, evidence in favor of some may have an affect on our belief in the others. In a purely Bayesian system, we can handle both of these phenomena by listing all of the combinations of conditional probabilities. But our goal is not to have to do that. Dempster-Shafer theory lets us handle interactions by manipulating sets of hypotheses directly.

The key function we use is a probability density function, which we denote as m. The function m is defined not just for elements of Θ but for all subsets of it (including singleton subsets, which correspond to individual elements). The quantity $m(p)$ measures the amount of belief that is currently assigned to exactly the set p of hypotheses. If Θ contains n elements, then there are 2^n subsets of Θ. We must assign m so that the sum of all the m values assigned to the subsets of Θ is 1. Although dealing with 2^n values may appear intractable, it usually turns out that many of the subsets will never need to be considered because they have no significance in the problem domain (and so their associated value of m will be 0).

Let's see how m works for our diagnosis problem. Assume that we have no information about how to choose among the four hypotheses when we start the diagnosis task. Then we define m as:

$$\{\Theta\} \quad (1.0)$$

All other values of m are thus 0. Although this means that the actual value must be some one element *All*, *Flu*, *Cold*, or *Pneu*, we do not have any information that allows us to assign belief in any other way than to say that we are sure the answer is somewhere in the whole set. Now suppose we acquire a piece of evidence that suggests (at a level of 0.6) that the correct diagnosis is in the set $\{Flu, Cold, Pneu\}$. Fever might be such a piece of evidence. We update m as follows:

$$\{Flu, Cold, Pneu\} \quad (0.6)$$
$$\{\Theta\} \quad (0.4)$$

At this point, we have assigned to the set $\{Flu, Cold, Pneu\}$ the appropriate belief. The remainder of our belief still resides in the larger set Θ. Notice that we do not make the commitment that the remainder must be assigned to the complement of $\{Flu, Cold, Pneu\}$.

Having defined m, we can now define $Bel(p)$ for a set p as the sum of the values of m for p and for all of its subsets. Thus $Bel(p)$ is our overall belief that the correct answer lies somewhere in the set p.

In order to be able to use m (and thus Bel and Pl) in reasoning programs, we need to define functions that enable us to combine m's that arise from multiple sources of evidence.

Recall that in our discussion of CF's, we considered three combination scenarios, which we illustrated in Figure 8.1. When we use Dempster-Shafer theory, on the other hand, we do not need an explicit combining function for the scenario in Figure 8.1(b) since we have that capability already in our ability to assign a value of m to a set of hypotheses. But we do need a mechanism for performing the combinations of scenarios (a) and (c). Dempster's rule of combination serves both these functions. It allows us to combine any two belief functions (whether they represent multiple sources of evidence for a single hypothesis or multiple sources of evidence for different hypotheses).

Suppose we are given two belief functions m_1 and m_2. Let X be the set of subsets of Θ to which m_1 assigns a nonzero value and let Y be the corresponding set for m_2. We define the combination m_3 of m_1 and m_2 to be

$$m_3(Z) = \frac{\sum_{X \cap Y = Z} m_1(X) \cdot m_2(Y)}{1 - \sum_{X \cap Y = \emptyset} m_1(X) \cdot m_2(Y)}$$

This gives us a new belief function that we can apply to any subset Z of Θ. We can describe what this formula is doing by looking first at the simple case in which all ways of intersecting elements of X and elements of Y generate nonempty sets. For example, suppose m_1 corresponds to our belief after observing fever:

$$\{Flu, Cold, Pneu\} \quad (0.6)$$
$$\Theta \quad\quad\quad\quad\quad (0.4)$$

Suppose m_2 corresponds to our belief after observing a runny nose:

$$\{All, Flu, Cold\} \quad (0.8)$$
$$\Theta \quad\quad\quad\quad\quad (0.2)$$

Then we can compute their combination m_3 using the following table (in which we further abbreviate disease names), which we can derive using the numerator of the combination rule:

		$\{A, F, C\}$	(0.8)	Θ	(0.2)
$\{F, C, P\}$	(0.6)	$\{F, C\}$	(0.48)	$\{F, C, P\}$	(0.12)
Θ	(0.4)	$\{A, F, C\}$	(0.32)	Θ	(0.08)

The four sets that are generated by taking all ways of intersecting an element of X and an element of Y are shown in the body of the table. The value of m_3 that the combination rule associates with each of them is computed by multiplying the values of m_1 and m_2 associated with the elements from which they were derived. Although it did not happen in this simple case, it is possible for the same set to be derived in more than one way during this intersection process. If that does occur, then to compute m_3 for that set, it is necessary to compute the sum of all the individual values that are generated for all the distinct ways in which the set is produced (thus the summation sign in the numerator of the combination formula).

A slightly more complex situation arises when some of the subsets created by the intersection operation are empty. Notice that we are guaranteed by the way we compute m_3 that the sum of all its individual values is 1 (assuming that the sums of all the values of m_1 and m_2 are 1). If some empty subsets are created, though, then some of m_3 will be assigned to them. But from the fact that we assumed that Θ is exhaustive, we know that the true value of the hypothesis must be contained in some nonempty subset of Θ. So we need to redistribute any belief that ends up in the empty subset proportionately across the nonempty ones. We do that with the scaling factor shown in the denominator of the combination formula. If no nonempty subsets are created, the scaling factor is 1, so we were able to ignore it in our first example. But to see how it works, let's add a new piece of evidence to our example. As a result of applying m_1 and m_2, we produced m_3:

$$
\begin{array}{ll}
\{Flu, Cold\} & (0.48) \\
\{All, Flu, Cold\} & (0.32) \\
\{Flu, Cold, Pneu\} & (0.12) \\
\Theta & (0.08)
\end{array}
$$

Now, let m_4 correspond to our belief given just the evidence that the problem goes away when the patient goes on a trip:

$$
\begin{array}{ll}
\{All\} & (0.9) \\
\Theta & (0.1)
\end{array}
$$

We can apply the numerator of the combination rule to produce (where $\emptyset$ denotes the empty set):

		$\{A\}$	(0.9)	Θ	(0.1)
$\{F, C\}$	(0.48)	$\emptyset$	(0.432)	$\{F, C\}$	(0.048)
$\{A, F, C\}$	(0.32)	$\{A, F, C\}$	(0.288)	$\{A, F, C\}$	(0.032)
$\{F, C, P\}$	(0.12)	$\emptyset$	(0.108)	$\{F, C, P\}$	(0.012)
Θ	(0.08)	$\{A\}$	(0.072)	Θ	(0.008)

But there is now a total belief of 0.54 associated with $\emptyset$; only 0.45 is associated with outcomes that are in fact possible. So we need to scale the remaining values by the factor $1 - 0.54 = 0.46$. If we do this, and also combine alternative ways of generating the set $\{All, Flu, Cold\}$, then we get the final combined belief function, m_5:

$$
\begin{array}{ll}
\{Flu, Cold\} & (0.104) \\
\{All, Flu, Cold\} & (0.696) \\
\{Flu, Cold, Pneu\} & (0.026) \\
\{All\} & (0.157) \\
\Theta & (0.017)
\end{array}
$$

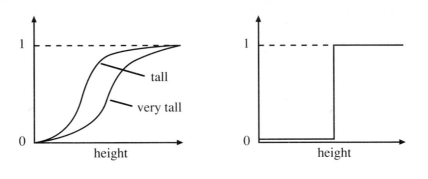

(*a*) Fuzzy Membership   (*b*) Conventional Membership

Figure 8.4: Fuzzy versus Conventional Set Membership

In this example, the percentage of m_5 that was initially assigned to the empty set was large (over half). This happens whenever there is conflicting evidence (as in this case between m_1 and m_4).

8.5   Fuzzy Logic

In the techniques we have discussed so far, we have not modified the mathematical underpinnings provided by set theory and logic. We have instead augmented those ideas with additional constructs provided by probability theory. In this section, we take a different approach and briefly consider what happens if we make fundamental changes to our idea of set membership and corresponding changes to our definitions of logical operations.

The motivation for fuzzy sets is provided by the need to represent such propositions as:

> John is very tall.
> Mary is slightly ill.
> Sue and Linda are close friends.
> Exceptions to the rule are nearly impossible.
> Most Frenchmen are not very tall.

While traditional set theory defines set membership as a boolean predicate, fuzzy set theory allows us to represent set membership as a possibility distribution, such as the ones shown in Figure 8.4(*a*) for the set of tall people and the set of very tall people. Notice how this contrasts with the standard boolean definition for tall people shown in Figure 8.4(*b*). In the latter, one is either tall or not and there must be a specific height that defines the boundary. The same is true for very tall. In the former, one's tallness increases with one's height until the value of 1 is reached.

Once set membership has been redefined in this way, it is possible to define a reasoning system based on techniques for combining distributions [Zadeh, 1979] (or see the papers in the journal *Fuzzy Sets and Systems*). Such reasoners have been applied in control systems for devices as diverse as trains and washing machines.

8.6 Summary

In this chapter we have shown that Bayesian statistics provide a good basis for reasoning under various kinds of uncertainty. We have also, though, talked about its weaknesses in complex real tasks, and so we have talked about ways in which it can be modified to work in practical domains. The thing that all of these modifications have in common is that they substitute, for the huge joint probability matrix that a pure Bayesian approach requires, a more structured representation of the facts that are relevant to a particular problem. They typically do this by combining probabilistic information with knowledge that is represented using one or more other representational mechanisms, such as rules or constraint networks.

Comparing these approaches for use in a particular problem-solving program is not always straightforward, since they differ along several dimensions, for example:

- They provide different mechanisms for describing the ways in which propositions are not independent of each other.

- They provide different techniques for representing ignorance.

- They differ substantially in the ease with which systems that use them can be built and in the computational complexity that the resulting systems exhibit.

We have also presented fuzzy logic as an alternative for representing some kinds of uncertain knowledge. Although there remain many arguments about the relative overall merits of the Bayesian and the fuzzy approaches, there is some evidence that they may both be useful in capturing different kinds of information. As an example, consider the proposition

John was pretty sure that Mary was seriously ill.

Bayesian approaches naturally capture John's degree of certainty, while fuzzy techniques can describe the degree of Mary's illness.

Throughout all of this discussion, it is important to keep in mind the fact that although we have been discussing techniques for representing knowledge, there is another perspective from which what we have really been doing is describing ways of representing *lack* of knowledge. In this sense, the techniques we have described in this chapter are fundamentally different from the ones we talked about earlier. For example, the truth values that we manipulate in a logical system characterize the formulas that we write; certainty measures, on the other hand, describe the exceptions—the facts that do not appear anywhere in the formulas that we have written. The consequences of this distinction show up in the ways that we can interpret and manipulate the formulas that we write. The most important difference is that logical formulas can be treated as though they represent independent propositions. As we have seen throughout this chapter, uncertain assertions cannot. As a result, for example, while implication is transitive in logical systems, we often get into trouble in uncertain systems if we treat it as though it were (as we saw in our first treatment of the sprinkler and grass example). Another difference is that in logical systems it is necessary to find only a single proof to be able to assert the truth value of a proposition. All other proofs, if there are any, can safely be ignored. In uncertain systems, on the other hand, computing belief in a proposition requires that all available reasoning paths be followed and combined.

One final comment is in order before we end this discussion. You may have noticed throughout this chapter that we have not maintained a clear distinction among such concepts as probability, certainty, and belief. This is because although there has been a great deal of philosophical debate over the meaning of these various terms, there is no clear argreement on how best to interpret them if our goal is to create working programs. Although the idea that probability should be viewed as a measure of belief rather than as a summary of past experience is now quite widely held, we have chosen to avoid the debate in this presentation. Instead, we have used all those words with their everyday, undifferentiated meaning, and we have concentrated on providing simple descriptions of how several algorithms actually work. If you are interested in the philosophical issues, see, for example, Shafer [1976] and Pearl [1988].

Unfortunately, although in the last two chapters we have presented several important approaches to the problem of uncertainty management, we have barely scraped the surface of this area. For more information, see Kanal and Lemmer [1986], Kanal and Lemmer [1988], Kanal et al. [1989], Shafer and Pearl [1990], Clark [1990]. In particular, our list of specific techniques is by no means complete. For example, you may wish to look into probabilistic logic [Nilsson, 1986; Halpern, 1989], in which probability theory is combined with logic so that the truth value of a formula is a probability value (between 0 and 1) rather than a boolean value (TRUE or FALSE). Or you may wish to ask not what statistics can do for AI but rather what AI can do for statistics. In that case, see Gale [1986].

8.7   Exercises

1. Consider the following puzzle:

   A pea is placed under one of three shells, and the shells are then manipulated in such a fashion that all three appear to be equally likely to contain the pea. Nevertheless, you win a prize if you guess the correct shell, so you make a guess. The person running the game does know the correct shell, however, and uncovers one of the shells that you did not choose and that is empty. Thus, what remains are two shells: one you chose and one you did not choose. Furthermore, since the uncovered shell did not contain the pea, one of the two remaining shells does contain it. You are offered the opportunity to change your selection to the other shell. Should you?

   Work through the conditional probabilities mentioned in this problem using Bayes' theorem. What do the results tell about what you should do?

2. Using MYCIN's rules for inexact reasoning, compute CF, MB, and MD of h_1 given three observations where

$$
\begin{aligned}
CF(h_1, o_1) &= 0.5 \\
CF(h_1, o_2) &= 0.3 \\
CF(h_1, o_3) &= -0.2
\end{aligned}
$$

3. Show that MYCIN's combining rules satisfy the three properties we gave for them.

4. Consider the following set of propositions:

> patient has spots
> patient has measles
> patient has high fever
> patient has Rocky Mountain Spotted Fever
> patient has previously been innoculated against measles
> patient was recently bitten by a tick
> patient has an allergy

   (a) Create a network that defines the causal connections among these nodes.

   (b) Make it a Bayesian network by constructing the necessary conditional probability matrix.

5. Consider the same propositions again, and assume our task is to identify the patient's disease using Dempster-Shafer theory.

   (a) What is Θ?

   (b) Define a set of m functions that describe the dependencies among sources of evidence and elements of Θ.

   (c) Suppose we have observed spots, fever, and a tick bite. In that case, what is our $Bel(\{RockyMountainSpottedFever\})$?

6. Define fuzzy sets that can be used to represent the list of propositions that we gave at the beginning of Section 8.5.

7. Consider again the ABC Murder story from Chapter 7. In our discussion of it there, we focused on the use of symbolic techniques for representing and using uncertain knowledge. Let's now explore the use of numeric techniques to solve the same problem. For each part below, show how knowledge could be represented. Whenever possible, show how it can be combined to produce a prediction of who committed the murder given at least one possible configuration of the evidence.

   (a) Use MYCIN-style rules and CF's. Example rules might include:

```
If (1) relative (x,y), and
   (2) on speaking terms (x,y),
then there is suggestive evidence (0.7) that
   will-lie-for (x,y)
```

(b) Use Bayesian networks. Represent as nodes such propositions as brother-in-law-lied, Cabot-at-ski-meet, and so forth.

(c) Use Dempster-Shafer theory. Examples of m's might be:

$$m_1 = \begin{array}{lll} \{Abbott, Babbitt\} & (0.8) & \{beneficiaries\ in\ will\} \\ \Theta & (0.2) \end{array}$$

$$m_2 = \begin{array}{lll} \{Abbott, Cabot\} & (0.7) & \{in\ line\ for\ his\ job\} \\ \Theta & (0.3) \end{array}$$

(d) Use fuzzy logic. For example, you might want to define such fuzzy sets as honest people or greedy people and describe Abbott, Babbitt, and Cabot's memberships in those sets.

(e) What kinds of information are easiest (and hardest) to represent in each of these frameworks?

Chapter 9

Weak Slot-and-Filler Structures

In this chapter, we continue the discussion we began in Chapter 4 of slot-and-filler structures. Recall that we originally introduced them as a device to support property inheritance along *isa* and *instance* links. This is an important aspect of these structures. Monotonic inheritance can be performed substantially more efficiently with such structures than with pure logic, and nonmonotonic inheritance is easily supported. The reason that inheritance is easy is that the knowledge in slot-and-filler systems is structured as a set of entities and their attributes. This structure turns out to be a useful one for other reasons besides the support of inheritance, though, including:

- It indexes assertions by the entities they describe. More formally, it indexes binary predicates [such as *team(Three-Finger-Brown, Chicago-Cubs)*] by their first argument. As a result, retrieving the value for an attribute of an entity is fast.

- It makes it easy to describe properties of relations. To do this in a purely logical system requires some higher-order mechanisms.

- It is a form of object-oriented programming and has the advantages that such systems normally have, including modularity and ease of viewing by people.

We describe two views of this kind of structure: semantic nets and frames. We talk about the representations themselves and about techniques for reasoning with them. We do not say much, though, about the specific knowledge that the structures should contain. We call these "knowledge-poor" structures "weak," by analogy with the weak methods for problem solving that we discussed in Chapter 3. In the next chapter, we expand this discussion to include "strong" slot-and-filler structures, in which specific commitments to the content of the representation are made.

9.1 Semantic Nets

The main idea behind semantic nets is that the meaning of a concept comes from the ways in which it is connected to other concepts. In a semantic net, information is represented as a set of nodes connected to each other by a set of labeled arcs, which

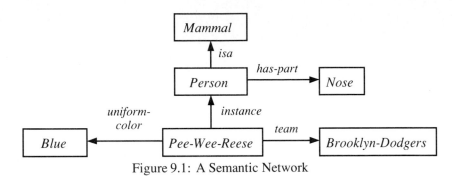

Figure 9.1: A Semantic Network

represent relationships among the nodes. A fragment of a typical semantic net is shown in Figure 9.1.

This network contains examples of both the *isa* and *instance* relations, as well as some other, more domain-specific relations like *team* and *uniform-color*. In this network, we could use inheritance to derive the additional relation

   has-part(Pee-Wee-Reese, Nose)

9.1.1   Intersection Search

One of the early ways that semantic nets were used was to find relationships among objects by spreading activation out from each of two nodes and seeing where the activation met. This process is called *intersection search* [Quillian, 1968]. Using this process, it is possible to use the network of Figure 9.1 to answer questions such as "What is the connection between the Brooklyn Dodgers and blue?"[1] This kind of reasoning exploits one of the important advantages that slot-and-filler structures have over purely logical representations because it takes advantage of the entity-based organization of knowledge that slot-and-filler representations provide.

To answer more structured questions, however, requires networks that are themselves more highly structured. In the next few sections we expand and refine our notion of a network in order to support more sophisticated reasoning.

9.1.2   Representing Nonbinary Predicates

Semantic nets are a natural way to represent relationships that would appear as ground instances of binary predicates in predicate logic. For example, some of the arcs from Figure 9.1 could be represented in logic as

---

[1] Actually, to do this we need to assume that the inverses of the links we have shown also exist.

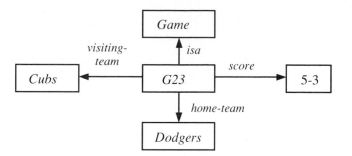

Figure 9.2: A Semantic Net for an *n*-Place Predicate

> *isa(Person, Mammal)*
> *instance(Pee-Wee-Reese, Person)*
> *team(Pee-Wee-Reese, Brooklyn-Dodgers)*
> *uniform-color(Pee-Wee-Reese, Blue)*

But the knowledge expressed by predicates of other arities can also be expressed in semantic nets. We have already seen that many unary predicates in logic can be thought of as binary predicates using some very general-purpose predicates, such as *isa* and *instance*. So, for example,

> *man(Marcus)*

could be rewritten as

> *instance(Marcus, Man)*

thereby making it easy to represent in a semantic net.

Three or more place predicates can also be converted to a binary form by creating one new object representing the entire predicate statement and then introducing binary predicates to describe the relationship to this new object of each of the original arguments. For example, suppose we know that

> *score(Cubs, Dodgers, 5-3)*

This can be represented in a semantic net by creating a node to represent the specific game and then relating each of the three pieces of information to it. Doing this produces the network shown in Figure 9.2.

This technique is particularly useful for representing the contents of a typical declarative sentence that describes several aspects of a particular event. The sentence

> John gave the book to Mary.

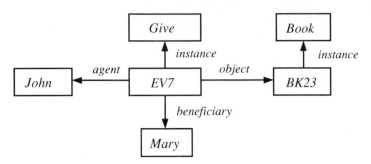

Figure 9.3: A Semantic Net Representing a Sentence

could be represented by the network shown in Figure 9.3.[2] In fact, several of the earliest uses of semantic nets were in English-understanding programs.

9.1.3   Making Some Important Distinctions

In the networks we have described so far, we have glossed over some distinctions that are important in reasoning. For example, there should be a difference between a link that defines a new entity and one that relates two existing entities. Consider the net

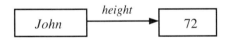

Both nodes represent objects that exist independently of their relationship to each other. But now suppose we want to represent the fact that John is taller than Bill, using the net

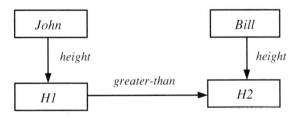

The nodes *H*1 and *H*2 are new concepts representing John's height and Bill's height, respectively. They are defined by their relationships to the nodes *John* and *Bill*. Using these defined concepts, it is possible to represent such facts as that John's height increased, which we could not do before. (The number 72 increased?)

Sometimes it is useful to introduce the arc *value* to make this distinction clear. Thus we might use the following net to represent the fact that John is 6 feet tall and that he is

---

[2]The node labeled *BK23* represents the particular book that was referred to by the phrase "the book." Discovering which particular book was meant by that phrase is similar to the problem of deciding on the correct referent for a pronoun, and it can be a very hard problem. These issues are discussed in Section 15.4.

taller than Bill:

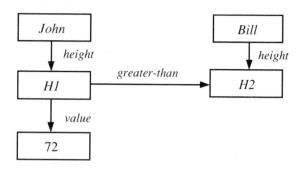

The procedures that operate on nets such as this can exploit the fact that some arcs, such as *height*, define new entities, while others, such as *greater-than* and *value*, merely describe relationships among existing entities.

Another example of an important distinction we have missed is the difference between the properties of a node itself and the properties that a node simply holds and passes on to its instances. For example, it is a property of the node *Person* that it is a subclass of the node *Mammal*. But the node *Person* does not have as one of its parts a nose. Instances of the node *Person* do, and we want them to inherit it.

It is difficult to capture these distinctions without assigning more structure to our notions of node, link, and value. In the next section, when we talk about frame systems, we do that. But first, we discuss a network-oriented solution to a simpler problem; this solution illustrates what can be done in the network model but at what price in complexity.

9.1.4   Partitioned Semantic Nets

Suppose we want to represent simple quantified expressions in semantic nets. One way to do this is to *partition* the semantic net into a hierarchical set of *spaces*, each of which corresponds to the scope of one or more variables [Hendrix, 1977]. To see how this works, consider first the simple net shown in Figure 9.4(*a*). This net corresponds to the statement

The dog bit the mail carrier.

The nodes *Dogs*, *Bite*, and *Mail-Carrier* represent the classes of dogs, bitings, and mail carriers, respectively, while the nodes *d*, *b*, and *m* represent a particular dog, a particular biting, and a particular mail carrier. This fact can easily be represented by a single net with no partitioning.

But now suppose that we want to represent the fact

Every dog has bitten a mail carrier.

or, in logic:

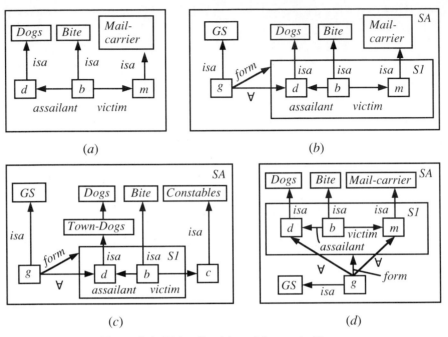

Figure 9.4: Using Partitioned Semantic Nets

$$\forall x : Dog(x) \to \exists y : Mail\text{-}Carrier(y) \land Bite(x, y)$$

To represent this fact, it is necessary to encode the scope of the universally quantified variable x. This can be done using partitioning as shown in Figure 9.4(*b*). The node g stands for the assertion given above. Node g is an instance of the special class GS of general statements about the world (i.e., those with universal quantifiers). Every element of GS has at least two attributes: a *form*, which states the relation that is being asserted, and one or more $\forall$ connections, one for each of the universally quantified variables. In this example, there is only one such variable d, which can stand for any element of the class *Dogs*. The other two variables in the form, b and m, are understood to be existentially quantified. In other words, for every dog d, there exists a biting event b, and a mail carrier m, such that d is the assailant of b and m is the victim.

To see how partitioning makes variable quantification explicit, consider next the similar sentence:

Every dog in town has bitten the constable.

The representation of this sentence is shown in Figure 9.4(*c*). In this net, the node c representing the victim lies outside the form of the general statement. Thus it is not viewed as an existentially quantified variable whose value may depend on the value of d. Instead it is interpreted as standing for a specific entity (in this case, a particular constable), just as do other nodes in a standard, nonpartitioned net.

Figure 9.4(*d*) shows how yet another similar sentence:

Every dog has bitten every mail carrier.

would be represented. In this case, *g* has two ∀ links, one pointing to *d*, which represents any dog, and one pointing to *m*, representing any mail carrier.

The spaces of a partitioned semantic net are related to each other by an inclusion hierarchy. For example, in Figure 9.4(*d*), space *S1* is included in space *SA*. Whenever a search process operates in a partitioned semantic net, it can explore nodes and arcs in the space from which it starts and in other spaces that contain the starting point, but it cannot go downward, except in special circumstances, such as when a *form* arc is being traversed. So, returning to Figure 9.4(*d*), from node *d* it can be determined that *d* must be a dog. But if we were to start at the node *Dogs* and search for all known instances of dogs by traversing *isa* links, we would not find *d* since it and the link to it are in the space *S1*, which is at a lower level than space *SA*, which contains *Dogs*. This is important, since *d* does not stand for a particular dog; it is merely a variable that can be instantiated with a value that represents a dog.

9.1.5   The Evolution into Frames

The idea of a semantic net started out simply as a way to represent labeled connections among entities. But, as we have just seen, as we expand the range of problem-solving tasks that the representation must support, the representation itself necessarily begins to become more complex. In particular, it becomes useful to assign more structure to nodes as well as to links. Although there is no clear distinction between a semantic net and a frame system, the more structure the system has, the more likely it is to be termed a frame system. In the next section we continue our discussion of structured slot-and-filler representations by describing some of the most important capabilities that frame systems offer.

9.2   Frames

A frame is a collection of attributes (usually called slots) and associated values (and possibly constraints on values) that describe some entity in the world. Sometimes a frame describes an entity in some absolute sense; sometimes it represents the entity from a particular point of view (as it did in the vision system proposal [Minsky, 1975] in which the term *frame* was first introduced). A single frame taken alone is rarely useful. Instead, we build frame systems out of collections of frames that are connected to each other by virtue of the fact that the value of an attribute of one frame may be another frame. In the rest of this section, we expand on this simple definition and explore ways that frame systems can be used to encode knowledge and support reasoning.

9.2.1   Frames as Sets and Instances

Set theory provides a good basis for understanding frame systems. Although not all frame systems are defined this way, we do so here. In this view, each frame represents either a class (a set) or an instance (an element of a class). To see how this works, consider the frame system shown in Figure 9.5, which is a slightly modified form of the network we showed in Figure 4.5. In this example, the frames *Person*, *Adult-Male*, *ML-Baseball-Player* (corresponding to major league baseball players), *Pitcher*, and *ML-Baseball-Team* (for major league baseball team) are all classes. The frames *Pee-Wee-Reese* and *Brooklyn-Dodgers* are instances.

The *isa* relation that we have been using without a precise definition is in fact the *subset* relation. The set of adult males is a subset of the set of people. The set of major league baseball players is a subset of the set of adult males, and so forth. Our *instance* relation corresponds to the relation *element-of*. Pee Wee Reese is an element of the set of fielders. Thus he is also an element of all of the supersets of fielders, including major league baseball players and people. The transitivity of *isa* that we have taken for granted in our description of property inheritance follows directly from the transitivity of the subset relation.

Both the *isa* and *instance* relations have inverse attributes, which we call *subclasses* and *all-instances.* We do not bother to write them explicitly in our examples unless we need to refer to them. We assume that the frame system maintains them automatically, either explicitly or by computing them if necessary.

Because a class represents a set, there are two kinds of attributes that can be associated with it. There are attributes about the set itself, and there are attributes that are to be inherited by each element of the set. We indicate the difference between these two by prefixing the latter with an asterisk (*). For example, consider the class *ML-Baseball-Player.* We have shown only two properties of it as a set: It is a subset of the set of adult males. And it has cardinality 624 (i.e., there are 624 major league baseball players). We have listed five properties that all major league baseball players have (*height*, *bats*, *batting-average*, *team*, and *uniform-color*), and we have specified default values for the first three of them. By providing both kinds of slots, we allow a class both to define a set of objects and to describe a prototypical object of the set.

Sometimes, the distinction between a set and an individual instance may not seem clear. For example, the team *Brooklyn-Dodgers*, which we have described as an instance of the class of major league baseball teams, could be thought of as a set of players. In fact, notice that the value of the slot *players* is a set. Suppose, instead, that we want to represent the Dodgers as a class instead of an instance. Then its instances would be the individual players. It cannot stay where it is in the *isa* hierarchy; it cannot be a subclass of *ML-Baseball-Team*, because if it were, then its elements, namely the players, would also, by the transitivity of subclass, be elements of *ML-Baseball-Team*, which is not what we want to say. We have to put it somewhere else in the *isa* hierarchy. For example, we could make it a subclass of major league baseball players. Then its elements, the players, are also elements of *ML-Baseball-Player*, *Adult-Male*, and *Person*. That is acceptable. But if we do that, we lose the ability to inherit properties of the Dodgers from general information about baseball teams. We can still inherit attributes for the elements of the team, but we cannot inherit properties of the team as a whole, i.e., of the set of players. For example, we might like to know what the default size of the team is,

Person
 isa :   *Mammal*
 cardinality :   6,000,000,000
 * *handed* :   *Right*

Adult-Male
 isa :   *Person*
 cardinality :   2,000,000,000
 * *height* :   5-10

ML-Baseball-Player
 isa :   *Adult-Male*
 cardinality :   624
 * *height* :   6-1
 * *bats* :   equal to handed
 * *batting-average* : .252
 * *team* :
 * *uniform-color* :

Fielder
 isa :   *ML-Baseball-Player*
 cardinality :   376
 * *batting-average* : .262

Pee-Wee-Reese
 instance :   *Fielder*
 height :   5-10
 bats :   *Right*
 batting-average :   .309
 team :   *Brooklyn-Dodgers*
 uniform-color :   *Blue*

ML-Baseball-Team
 isa :   *Team*
 cardinality :   26
 * *team-size* :   24
 * *manager* :

Brooklyn-Dodgers
 instance :   *ML-Baseball-Team*
 team-size :   24
 manager :   *Leo-Durocher*
 players :   {*Pee-Wee-Reese*, ...}

Figure 9.5: A Simplified Frame System

that it has a manager, and so on. The easiest way to allow for this is to go back to the idea of the Dodgers as an instance of *ML-Baseball-Team*, with the set of players given as a slot value.

But what we have encountered here is an example of a more general problem. A class is a set, and we want to be able to talk about properties that its elements possess. We want to use inheritance to infer those properties from general knowledge about the set. But a class is also an entity in itself. It may possess properties that belong not to the individual instances but rather to the class as a whole. In the case of *Brooklyn-Dodgers*, such properties included team size and the existence of a manager. We may even want to inherit some of these properties from a more general kind of set. For example, the Dodgers can inherit a default team size from the set of all major league baseball teams. To support this, we need to view a class as two things simultaneously: a subset (*isa*) of a larger class that also contains its elements and an instance (*instance*) of a class of sets, from which it inherits its set-level properties.

To make this distinction clear, it is useful to distinguish between regular classes, whose elements are individual entities, and *metaclasses*, which are special classes whose elements are themselves classes. A class is now an element of (*instance*) some class (or classes) as well as a subclass (*isa*) of one or more classes. A class inherits properties from the class of which it is an instance, just as any instance does. In addition, a class passes inheritable properties down from its superclasses to its instances.

Let's consider an example. Figure 9.6 shows how we could represent teams as classes using this distinction. Figure 9.7 shows a graphic view of the same classes. The most basic metaclass is the class *Class*. It represents the set of all classes. All classes are instances of it, either directly or through one of its subclasses. In the example, *Team* is a subclass (subset) of *Class* and *ML-Baseball-Team* is a subclass of *Team*. The class *Class* introduces the attribute *cardinality*, which is to be inherited by all instances of *Class* (including itself). This makes sense since all the instances of *Class* are sets and all sets have a cardinality.

Team represents a subset of the set of all sets, namely those whose elements are sets of players on a team. It inherits the property of having a cardinality from *Class*. *Team* introduces the attribute *team-size*, which all its elements possess. Notice that *team-size* is like *cardinality* in that it measures the size of a set. But it applies to something different; *cardinality* applies to sets of sets and is inherited by all elements of *Class*. The slot *team-size* applies to the elements of those sets that happen to be teams. Those elements are sets of individuals.

ML-Baseball-Team is also an instance of *Class*, since it is a set. It inherits the property of having a cardinality from the set of which it is an instance, namely *Class*. But it is a subset of *Team*. All of its instances will have the property of having a *team-size* since they are also instances of the superclass *Team*. We have added at this level the additional fact that the default team size is 24, so all instances of *ML-Baseball-Team* will inherit that as well. In addition, we have added the inheritable slot *manager*.

Brooklyn-Dodgers is an instance of a *ML-Baseball-Team*. It is not an instance of *Class* because its elements are individuals, not sets. *Brooklyn-Dodgers* is a subclass of *ML-Baseball-Player* since all of its elements are also elements of that set. Since it is an instance of a *ML-Baseball-Team*, it inherits the properties *team-size* and *manager*, as well as their default values. It specifies a new attribute *uniform-color*, which is to be inherited by all of its instances (who will be individual players).

Class
    instance :   *Class*
    isa :   *Class*
    * *cardinality* :

Team
    instance :   *Class*
    isa :   *Class*
    cardinality :   {the number of teams that exist}
    * *team-size* :   {each team has a size}

ML-Baseball-Team
    instance :   *Class*
    isa :   *Team*
    cardinality :   26 {the number of baseball teams that exist}
    * *team-size* :   24 {default 24 players on a team}
    * *manager* :

Brooklyn-Dodgers
    instance :   *ML-Baseball-Team*
    isa :   *ML-Baseball-Player*
    team-size :   24
    manager :   *Leo-Durocher*
    * *uniform-color* :   *Blue*

Pee-Wee-Reese
    instance :   *Brooklyn-Dodgers*
    instance :   *Fielder*
    uniform-color :   *Blue*
    batting-average :   .309

Figure 9.6: Representing the Class of All Teams as a Metaclass

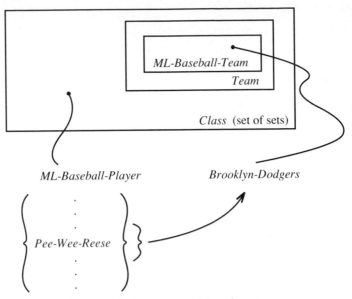

Figure 9.7: Classes and Metaclasses

Finally, *Pee-Wee-Reese* is an instance of *Brooklyn-Dodgers*. That makes him also, by transitivity up *isa* links, an instance of *ML-Baseball-Player*. But recall that in our earlier example we also used the class *Fielder*, to which we attached the fact that fielders have above-average batting averages. To allow that here, we simply make Pee Wee an instance of *Fielder* as well. He will thus inherit properties from both *Brooklyn-Dodgers* and from *Fielder*, as well as from the classes above these. We need to guarantee that when multiple inheritance occurs, as it does here, that it works correctly. Specifically, in this case, we need to assure that *batting-average* gets inherited from *Fielder* and not from *ML-Baseball-Player* through *Brooklyn-Dodgers*. We return to this issue in Section 9.2.5.

In all the frame systems we illustrate, all classes are instances of the metaclass *Class*. As a result, they all have the attribute *cardinality*. We leave the class *Class*, the *isa* links to it, and the attribute *cardinality* out of our descriptions of our examples, though, unless there is some particular reason to include them.

Every class is a set. But not every set should be described as a class. A class describes a set of entities that share significant properties. In particular, the default information associated with a class can be used as a basis for inferring values for the properties of its individual elements. So there is an advantage to representing as a class those sets for which membership serves as a basis for nonmonotonic inheritance. Typically, these are sets in which membership is not highly ephemeral. Instead, membership is based on some fundamental structural or functional properties. To see the difference, consider the following sets:

- People

- People who are major league baseball players

- People who are on my plane to New York

The first two sets can be advantageously represented as classes, with which a substantial number of inheritable attributes can be associated. The last, though, is different. The only properties that all the elements of that set probably share are the definition of the set itself and some other properties that follow from the definition (e.g., they are being transported from one place to another). A simple set, with some associated assertions, is adequate to represent these facts; nonmonotonic inheritance is not necessary.

9.2.2 Other Ways of Relating Classes to Each Other

We have talked up to this point about two ways in which classes (sets) can be related to each other. $Class_1$ can be a subset of $Class_2$. Or, if $Class_2$ is a metaclass, then $Class_1$ can be an instance of $Class_2$. But there are other ways that classes can be related to each other, corresponding to ways that sets of objects in the world can be related.

One such relationship is *mutually-disjoint-with*, which relates a class to one or more other classes that are guaranteed to have no elements in common with it. Another important relationship is *is-covered-by*, which relates a class to a set of subclasses, the union of which is equal to it. If a class *is-covered-by* a set S of mutually disjoint classes, then S is called a *partition* of the class.

For examples of these relationships, consider the classes shown in Figure 9.8, which represent two orthogonal ways of decomposing the class of major league baseball players. Everyone is either a pitcher, a catcher, or a fielder (and no one is more than one of these). In addition, everyone plays in either the National League or the American League, but not both.

9.2.3 Slots as Full-Fledged Objects

So far, we have provided a way to describe sets of objects and individual objects, both in terms of attributes and values. Thus we have made extensive use of attributes, which we have represented as slots attached to frames. But it turns out that there are several reasons why we would like to be able to represent attributes explicitly and describe their properties. Some of the properties we would like to be able to represent and use in reasoning include:

- The classes to which the attribute can be attached, i.e., for what classes does it make sense? For example, weight makes sense for physical objects but not for conceptual ones (except in some metaphorical sense).

- Constraints on either the type or the value of the attribute. For example, the age of a person must be a numeric quantity measured in some time frame, and it must be less than the ages of the person's biological parents.

- A value that all instances of a class must have by the definition of the class.

- A default value for the attribute.

- Rules for inheriting values for the attribute. The usual rule is to inherit down *isa* and *instance* links. But some attributes inherit in other ways. For example, *last-name* inherits down the *child-of* link.

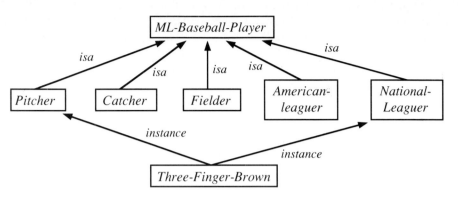

ML-Baseball-Player
    is-covered-by :   {*Pitcher, Catcher, Fielder*},
                                                    {*American-Leaguer, National-Leaguer*}

Pitcher
    isa :   *ML-Baseball-Player*
    mutually-disjoint-with :   {*Catcher, Fielder*}

Catcher
    isa :   *ML-Baseball-Player*
    mutually-disjoint-with :   {*Pitcher, Fielder*}

Fielder
    isa :   *ML-Baseball-Player*
    mutually-disjoint-with :   {*Pitcher, Catcher*}

American-Leaguer
    isa :   *ML-Baseball-Player*
    mutually-disjoint-with :   {*National-Leaguer*}

National-Leaguer
    isa :   *ML-Baseball-Player*
    mutually-disjoint-with :   {*American-Leaguer*}

Three-Finger-Brown
    instance :   *Pitcher*
    instance :   *National-Leaguer*

Figure 9.8: Representing Relationships among Classes

- Rules for computing a value separately from inheritance. One extreme form of such a rule is a procedure written in some procedural programming language such as LISP.

- An inverse attribute.

- Whether the slot is single-valued or multivalued.

In order to be able to represent these attributes of attributes, we need to describe attributes (slots) as frames. These frames will be organized into an *isa* hierarchy, just as any other frames are, and that hierarchy can then be used to support inheritance of values for attributes of slots. Before we can describe such a hierarchy in detail, we need to formalize our notion of a slot.

A slot is a relation. It maps from elements of its domain (the classes for which it makes sense) to elements of its range (its possible values). A relation is a set of ordered pairs. Thus it makes sense to say that one relation (R_1) is a subset of another (R_2). In that case, R_1 is a specialization of R_2, so in our terminology $isa(R_1, R_2)$. Since a slot is a set, the set of all slots, which we will call *Slot*, is a metaclass. Its instances are slots, which may have subslots.

Figures 9.9 and 9.10 illustrate several examples of slots represented as frames. *Slot* is a metaclass. Its instances are slots (each of which is a set of ordered pairs). Associated with the metaclass are attributes that each instance (i.e., each actual slot) will inherit. Each slot, since it is a relation, has a domain and a range. We represent the domain in the slot labeled *domain*. We break up the representation of the range into two parts: *range* gives the class of which elements of the range must be elements; *range-constraint* contains a logical expression that further constrains the range to be elements of *range* that also satisfy the constraint. If *range-constraint* is absent, it is taken to be TRUE. The advantage to breaking the description apart into these two pieces is that type checking is much cheaper than is arbitrary constraint checking, so it is useful to be able to do it separately and early during some reasoning processes.

The other slots do what you would expect from their names. If there is a value for *definition*, it must be propagated to all instances of the slot. If there is a value for *default*, that value is inherited to all instances of the slot unless there is an overriding value. The attribute *transfers-through* lists other slots from which values for this slot can be derived through inheritance. The *to-compute* slot contains a procedure for deriving its value. The *inverse* attribute contains the inverse of the slot. Although in principle all slots have inverses, sometimes they are not useful enough in reasoning to be worth representing. And *single-valued* is used to mark the special cases in which the slot is a function and so can have only one value.

Of course, there is no advantage to representing these properties of slots if there is no reasoning mechanism that exploits them. In the rest of our discussion, we assume that the frame-system interpreter knows how to reason with all of these slots of slots as part of its built-in reasoning capability. In particular, we assume that it is capable of performing the following reasoning actions:

- Consistency checking to verify that when a slot value is added to a frame

  - The slot makes sense for the frame. This relies on the *domain* attribute of the slot.

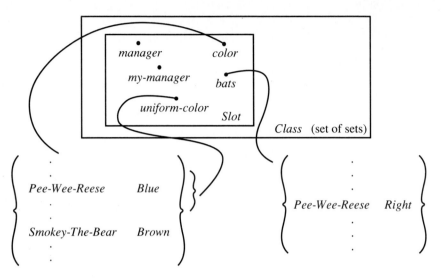

Figure 9.9: Representing Slots as Frames, I

Slot
    isa :   *Class*
    instance :   *Class*
    * *domain* :
    * *range* :
    * *range-constraint* :
    * *definition* :
    * *default* :
    * *transfers-through* :
    * *to-compute* :
    * *inverse* :
    * *single-valued* :

manager
    instance :   *Slot*
    domain :   *ML-Baseball-Team*
    range :   *Person*
    range-constraint :   λx (*baseball-experience* x.*manager*)
    default :
    inverse :   *manager-of*
    single-valued :   TRUE

my-manager
    instance :   *Slot*
    domain :   *ML-Baseball-Player*
    range :   *Person*
    range-constraint : λx (*baseball-experience* x.*my-manager*)
    to-compute : λx (x.*team*).*manager*
    single-valued :   TRUE

color
    instance :   *Slot*
    domain :   *Physical-Object*
    range :   *Color-Set*
    transfers-through :   *top-level-part-of*
    visual-salience :   *High*
    single-valued :   FALSE

uniform-color
    instance :   *Slot*
    isa :   *color*
    domain :   *team-player*
    range :   *Color-Set*
    range-constraint :   not *Pink*
    visual-salience :   *High*
    single-valued :   FALSE

bats
    instance :   *Slot*
    domain :   *ML-Baseball-Player*
    range :   {*Left, Right, Switch*}
    to-compute : λx x.*handed*
    single-valued :   TRUE

Figure 9.10: Representing Slots as Frames, II

   – The value is a legal value for the slot. This relies on the *range* and *range-constraints* attributes.

- Maintenance of consistency between the values for slots and their inverses whenever one is updated.

- Propagation of *definition* values along *isa* and *instance* links.

- Inheritance of *default* values along *isa* and *instance* links.

- Computation of a value of a slot as needed. This relies on the *to-compute* and *transfers-through* attributes.

- Checking that only a single value is asserted for *single-valued* slots. This is usually done by replacing an old value by the new one when it is asserted. An alternative is to force explicit retraction of the old value and to signal a contradiction if a new value is asserted when another is already there.

There is something slightly counterintuitive about this way of defining slots. We have defined the properties *range-constraint* and *default* as parts of a slot. But we often think of them as being properties of a slot associated with a particular class. For example, in Figure 9.5, we listed two defaults for the *batting-average* slot, one associated with major league baseball players and one associated with fielders. Figure 9.11 shows how this can be represented correctly, by creating a specialization of *batting-average* that can be associated with a specialization of *ML-Baseball-Player* to represent the more specific information that is known about the specialized class. This seems cumbersome. It is natural, though, given our definition of a slot as a relation. There are really two relations here, one a specialization of the other. And below we will define inheritance so that it looks for values of either the slot it is given or any of that slot's generalizations.

Unfortunately, although this model of slots is simple and it is internally consistent, it is not easy to use. So we introduce some notational shorthand that allows the four most important properties of a slot (domain, range, definition, and default) to be defined implicitly by how the slot is used in the definitions of the classes in its domain. We describe the domain implicitly to be the class where the slot appears. We describe the range and any range constraints with the clause MUST BE, as the value of an inherited slot. Figure 9.12 shows an example of this notation. And we describe the definition and the default, if they are present, by inserting them as the value of the slot when it appears. The two will be distinguished by prefixing a definitional value with an asterisk (*). We then let the underlying bookkeeping of the frame system create the frames that represent slots as they are needed.

Now let's look at examples of how these slots can be used. The slots *bats* and *my-manager* illustrate the use of the *to-compute* attribute of a slot. The variable x will be bound to the frame to which the slot is attached. We use the dot notation to specify the value of a slot of a frame. Specifically, $x.y$ describes the value(s) of the y slot of frame x. So we know that to compute a frame's value for *my-manager*, it is necessary to find the frame's value for *team*, then find the resulting team's manager. We have simply composed two slots to form a new one.[3] Computing the value of the *bats* slot is even simpler. Just go get the value of the *handed* slot.

---

[3]Notice that since slots are relations rather than functions, their composition may return a set of values.

batting-average
    instance :   *Slot*
    domain :   *ML-Baseball-Player*
    range :   *Number*
    range-constraint : $\lambda x\ (0 \leq x.range\text{-}constraint \leq 1)$
    default :   .252
    single-valued :   TRUE

fielder-batting-average
    instance :   *Slot*
    isa :   *batting-average*
    domain :   *Fielder*
    range :   *Number*
    range-constraint : $\lambda x\ (0 \leq x.range\text{-}constraint \leq 1)$
    default :   .262
    single-valued :   TRUE

Figure 9.11: Associating Defaults with Slots

ML-Baseball-Player
    bats :   MUST BE {*Left*, *Right*, *Switch*}

Figure 9.12: A Shorthand Notation for Slot-Range Specification

The *manager* slot illustrates the use of a range constraint. It is stated in terms of a variable x, which is bound to the frame whose *manager* slot is being described. It requires that any manager be not only a person but someone with baseball experience. It relies on the domain-specific function *baseball-experience*, which must be defined somewhere in the system.

The slots *color* and *uniform-color* illustrate the arrangement of slots in an *isa* hierarchy. The relation *color* is a fairly general one that holds between physical objects and colors. The attribute *uniform-color* is a restricted form of *color* that applies only between team players and the colors that are allowed for team uniforms (anything but pink). Arranging slots in a hierarchy is useful for the same reason that arranging anything else in a hierarchy is: it supports inheritance. In this example, the general slot *color* is known to have high visual salience. The more specific slot *uniform-color* then inherits this property, so it too is known to have high visual salience.

The slot *color* also illustrates the use of the *transfers-through* slot, which defines a way of computing a slot's value by retrieving it from the same slot of a related object. In this example, we used *transfers-through* to capture the fact that if you take an object and chop it up into several top level parts (in other words, parts that are not contained inside each other), then they will all be the same color. For example, the arm of a sofa is the same color as the sofa. Formally, what *transfers-through* means in this example is

John
     height :   72

Bill
     height :

Figure 9.13: Representing Slot-Values

$$color(x, y) \land top\text{-}level\text{-}part\text{-}of(z, x) \rightarrow color(z, y)$$

In addition to these domain-independent slot attributes, slots may have domain-specific properties that support problem solving in a particular domain. Since these slots are not treated explicitly by the frame-system interpreter, they will be useful precisely to the extent that the domain problem solver exploits them.

9.2.4 Slot-Values as Objects

In the last section, we reified the notion of a slot by making it an explicit object that we could make assertions about. In some sense this was not necessary. A finite relation can be completely described by listing its elements. But in practical knowledge-based systems one often does not have that list. So it can be very important to be able to make assertions about the list without knowing all of its elements. Reification gave us a way to do this.

The next step along this path is to do the same thing to a particular attribute-value (an instance of a relation) that we did to the relation itself. We can reify it and make it an object about which assertions can be made. To see why we might want to do this, let us return to the example of John and Bill's height that we discussed in Section 9.1.3. Figure 9.13 shows a frame-based representation of some of the facts. We could easily record Bill's height if we knew it. Suppose, though, that we do not know it. All we know is that John is taller than Bill. We need a way to make an assertion about the value of a slot without knowing what that value is. To do that, we need to view the slot and its value as an object.

We could attempt to do this the same way we made slots themselves into objects, namely by representing them explicitly as frames. There seems little advantage to doing that in this case, though, because the main advantage of frames does not apply to slot values: frames are organized into an *isa* hierarchy and thus support inheritance. There is no basis for such an organization of slot values. So instead, we augment our value representation language to allow the value of a slot to be stated as either or both of:

- A value of the type required by the slot.

- A logical constraint on the value. This constraint may relate the slot's value to the values of other slots or to domain constants.

John
> *height* :   72; λx (x.*height* > *Bill.height*)

Bill
> *height* : λx (x.*height* < *John.height*)

Figure 9.14: Representing Slot-Values with Lambda Notation

If we do this to the frames of Figure 9.13, then we get the frames of Figure 9.14. We again use the lambda notation as a way to pick up the name of the frame that is being described.

9.2.5   Inheritance Revisited

In Chapter 4, we presented a simple algorithm for inheritance. But that algorithm assumed that the *isa* hierarchy was a tree. This is often not the case. To support flexible representations of knowledge about the world, it is necessary to allow the hierarchy to be an arbitrary directed acyclic graph (DAG). We know that acyclic graphs are adequate because *isa* corresponds to the subset relation. Hierarchies that are not trees are called *tangled hierarchies*. Tangled hierarchies require a new inheritance algorithm. In the rest of this section, we discuss an algorithm for inheriting values for single-valued slots in a tangled hierarchy. We leave the problem of inheriting multivalued slots as an exercise.

Consider the two examples shown in Figure 9.15 (in which we return to a network notation to make it easy to visualize the *isa* structure). In Figure 9.15(*a*), we want to decide whether *Fifi* can fly. The correct answer is no. Although birds in general can fly, the subset of birds, ostriches, does not. Although the class *Pet-Bird* provides a path from *Fifi* to *Bird* and thus to the answer that *Fifi* can fly, it provides no information that conflicts with the special case knowledge associated with the the class *Ostrich*, so it should have no affect on the answer. To handle this case correctly, we need an algorithm for traversing the *isa* hierarchy that guarantees that specific knowledge will always dominate more general facts.

In Figure 9.15(*b*), we return to a problem we discussed in Section 7.2.1, namely determining whether Dick is a pacifist. Again, we must traverse multiple *instance* links, and more than one answer can be found along the paths. But in this case, there is no well-founded basis for choosing one answer over the other. The classes that are associated with the candidate answers are incommensurate with each other in the partial ordering that is defined by the DAG formed by the *isa* hierarchy. Just as we found that in Default Logic this theory had two extensions and there was no principled basis for choosing between them, what we need here is an inheritance algorithm that reports the ambiguity; we do not want an algorithm that finds one answer (arbitrarily) and stops without noticing the other.

One possible basis for a new inheritance algorithm is path length. This can be implemented by executing a breadth-first search, starting with the frame for which a slot value is needed. Follow its *instance* links, then follow *isa* links upward. If a path produces a value, it can be terminated, as can all other paths once their length

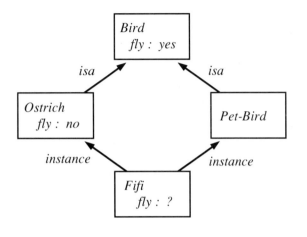

(a)

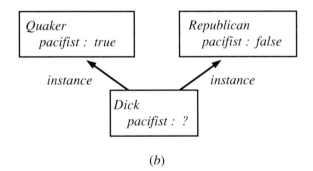

(b)

Figure 9.15: Tangled Hierarchies

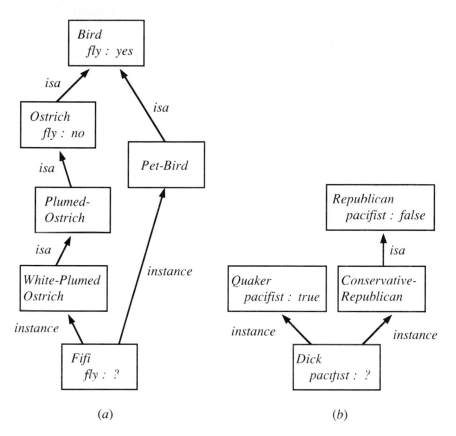

Figure 9.16: More Tangled Hierarchies

exceeds that of the successful path. This algorithm works for both of the examples in Figure 9.15. In (*a*), it finds a value at *Ostrich*. It continues the other path to the same length (*Pet-Bird*), fails to find any other answers, and then halts. In the case of (*b*), it finds two competing answers at the same level, so it can report the contradiction.

But now consider the examples shown in Figure 9.16. In the case of (*a*), our new algorithm reaches *Bird* (via *Pet-Bird*) before it reaches *Ostrich*. So it reports that *Fifi* can fly. In the case of (*b*), the algorithm reaches *Quaker* and stops without noticing a contradiction. The problem is that path length does not always correspond to the level of generality of a class. Sometimes what it really corresponds to is the degree of elaboration of classes in the knowledge base. If some regions of the knowledge base have been elaborated more fully than others, then their paths will tend to be longer. But this should not influence the result of inheritance if no new information about the desired attribute has been added.

The solution to this problem is to base our inheritance algorithm not on path length but on the notion of *inferential distance* [Touretzky, 1986], which can be defined as follows:

$Class_1$ is closer to $Class_2$ than to $Class_3$ if and only if $Class_1$ has an inference path through $Class_2$ to $Class_3$ (in other words, $Class_2$ is between $Class_1$ and $Class_3$).

Notice that inferential distance defines only a partial ordering. Some classes are incommensurate with each other under it.

We can now define the result of inheritance as follows: The set of competing values for a slot S in a frame F contains all those values that

- Can be derived from some frame X that is above F in the *isa* hierarchy

- Are not contradicted by some frame Y that has a shorter inferential distance to F than X does

Notice that under this definition competing values that are derived from incommensurate frames continue to compete.

Using this definition, let us return to our examples. For Figure 9.15(*a*), we had two candidate classes from which to get an answer. But *Ostrich* has a shorter inferential distance to *Fifi* than *Bird* does, so we get the single answer no. For Figure 9.15(*b*), we get two answers, and neither is closer to *Dick* than the other, so we correctly identify a contradiction. For Figure 9.16(*a*), we get two answers, but again *Ostrich* has a shorter inferential distance to *Fifi* than *Bird* does. The significant thing about the way we have defined inferential distance is that as long as *Ostrich* is a subclass of *Bird*, it will be closer to all its instances than *Bird* is, no matter how many other classes are added to the system. For Figure 9.16(*b*), we again get two answers and again neither is closer to *Dick* than the other.

There are several ways that this definition can be implemented as an inheritance algorithm. We present a simple one. It can be made more efficient by caching paths in the hierarchy, but we do not do that here.

Algorithm: Property Inheritance

To retrieve a value V for slot S of an instance F do:

1. Set *CANDIDATES* to empty.

2. Do breadth-first or depth-first search up the *isa* hierarchy from F, following all *instance* and *isa* links. At each step, see if a value for S or one of its generalizations is stored.

   (a) If a value is found, add it to *CANDIDATES* and terminate that branch of the search.

   (b) If no value is found but there are *instance* or *isa* links upward, follow them.

   (c) Otherwise, terminate the branch.

3. For each element C of *CANDIDATES* do:

   (a) See if there is any other element of *CANDIDATES* that was derived from a class closer to F than the class from which C came.

(b) If there is, then, remove *C* from *CANDIDATES*.

4. Check the cardinality of *CANDIDATES*:

   (a) If it is 0, then report that no value was found.

   (b) If it is 1, then return the single element of *CANDIDATES* as *V*.

   (c) If it is greater than 1, report a contradiction.

This algorithm is guaranteed to terminate because the *isa* hierarchy is represented as an acyclic graph.

9.2.6 Frame Languages

The idea of a frame system as a way to represent declarative knowledge has been encapsulated in a series of frame-oriented knowledge representation languages, whose features have evolved and been driven by an increased understanding of the sort of representation issues we have been discussing. Examples of such languages include KRL [Bobrow and Winograd, 1977], FRL [Roberts and Goldstein, 1977], RLL [Greiner and Lenat, 1980], KL-ONE [Brachman, 1979; Brachman and Schmolze, 1985], KRYPTON [Brachman *et al.*, 1985], NIKL [Kaczmarek *et al.*, 1986], CYCL [Lenat and Guha, 1990], conceptual graphs [Sowa, 1984], THEO [Mitchell *et al.*, 1989], and FRAMEKIT [Nyberg, 1988]. Although not all of these systems support all of the capabilities that we have discussed, the more modern of these systems permit elaborate and efficient representation of many kinds of knowledge. Their reasoning methods include most of the ones described here, plus many more, including subsumption checking, automatic classification, and various methods for consistency maintenance.

9.3 Exercises

1. Construct semantic net representations for the following:

   (a) *Pompeian(Marcus)*, *Blacksmith(Marcus)*

   (b) Mary gave the green flowered vase to her favorite cousin.

2. Suppose we want to use a semantic net to discover relationships that could help in disambiguating the word "bank" in the sentence

   John went downtown to deposit his money in the bank.

   The financial institution meaning for bank should be preferred over the river bank meaning.

   (a) Construct a semantic net that contains representations for the relevant concepts.

   (b) Show how intersection search could be used to find the connection between the correct meaning for bank and the rest of the sentence more easily than it can find a connection with the incorrect meaning.

3. Construct partitioned semantic net representations for the following:

   (a) Every batter hit a ball.

   (b) All the batters like the pitcher.

4. Construct one consistent frame representation of all the baseball knowledge that was described in this chapter. You will need to choose between the two representations for team that we considered.

5. Modify the property inheritance algorithm of Section 9.2 to work for multiple-valued attributes, such as the attribute *believes-in-principles*, defined as follows:

   > *believes-in-principles*
   >   *instance* :   *Slot*
   >   *domain* :   *Person*
   >   *range* :   *Philosophical-Principles*
   >   *single-valued* :   FALSE

6. Define the value of a multiple-valued slot S of class C to be the union of the values that are found for S and all its generalizations at C and all its generalizations. Modify your technique to allow a class to exclude specific values that are associated with one or more of its superclasses.

7. Pick a problem area and represent some knowledge about it the way we represented baseball knowledge in this chapter.

Chapter 10

Strong Slot-and-Filler Structures

The slot-and-filler structures described in the previous chapter are very general. Individual semantic networks and frame systems may have specialized links and inference procedures, but there are no hard and fast rules about what kinds of objects and links are good in general for knowledge representation. Such decisions are left up to the builder of the semantic network or frame system.

The three structures discussed in this chapter, *conceptual dependency*, *scripts*, and *CYC*, on the other hand, embody specific notions of what types of objects and relations are permitted. They stand for powerful theories of how AI programs can represent and use knowledge about common situations.

10.1 Conceptual Dependency

Conceptual dependency (often nicknamed CD) is a theory of how to represent the kind of knowledge about events that is usually contained in natural language sentences. The goal is to represent the knowledge in a way that

- Facilitates drawing inferences from the sentences.

- Is independent of the language in which the sentences were originally stated.

Because of the two concerns just mentioned, the CD representation of a sentence is built not out of primitives corresponding to the words used in the sentence, but rather out of conceptual primitives that can be combined to form the meanings of words in any particular language. The theory was first described in Schank [1973] and was further developed in Schank [1975]. It has since been implemented in a variety of programs that read and understand natural language text. Unlike semantic nets, which provide only a structure into which nodes representing information at any level can be placed, conceptual dependency provides both a structure and a specific set of primitives, at a particular level of granularity, out of which representations of particular pieces of information can be constructed.

277

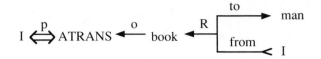

where the symbols have the following meanings:

- Arrows indicate direction of dependency.

- Double arrow indicates two way link between actor and action.

- p indicates past tense.

- ATRANS is one of the primitive acts used by the theory. It indicates transfer of possession.

- o indicates the object case relation.

- R indicates the recipient case relation.

Figure 10.1: A Simple Conceptual Dependency Representation

As a simple example of the way knowledge is represented in CD, the event represented by the sentence

I gave the man a book.

would be represented as shown in Figure 10.1.

In CD, representations of actions are built from a set of primitive acts. Although there are slight differences in the exact set of primitive actions provided in the various sources on CD, a typical set is the following, taken from Schank and Abelson [1977]:

ATRANS	Transfer of an abstract relationship (e.g., give)
PTRANS	Transfer of the physical location of an object (e.g., go)
PROPEL	Application of physical force to an object (e.g., push)
MOVE	Movement of a body part by its owner (e.g., kick)
GRASP	Grasping of an object by an actor (e.g., clutch)
INGEST	Ingestion of an object by an animal (e.g., eat)
EXPEL	Expulsion of something from the body of an animal (e.g., cry)
MTRANS	Transfer of mental information (e.g., tell)
MBUILD	Building new information out of old (e.g., decide)
SPEAK	Production of sounds (e.g., say)
ATTEND	Focusing of a sense organ toward a stimulus (e.g., listen)

A second set of CD building blocks is the set of allowable dependencies among the conceptualizations described in a sentence. There are four primitive conceptual categories from which dependency structures can be built. These are

ACTs	Actions
PPs	Objects (picture producers)
AAs	Modifiers of actions (action aiders)
PAs	Modifiers of PPs (picture aiders)

In addition, dependency structures are themselves conceptualizations and can serve as components of larger dependency structures.

The dependencies among conceptualizations correspond to semantic relations among the underlying concepts. Figure 10.2 lists the most important ones allowed by CD.[1] The first column contains the rules; the second contains examples of their use; and the third contains an English version of each example. The rules shown in the figure can be interpreted as follows:

- Rule 1 describes the relationship between an actor and the event he or she causes. This is a two-way dependency since neither actor nor event can be considered primary. The letter p above the dependency link indicates past tense.

- Rule 2 describes the relationship between a PP and a PA that is being asserted to describe it. Many state descriptions, such as height, are represented in CD as numeric scales

- Rule 3 describes the relationship between two PPs, one of which belongs to the set defined by the other.

- Rule 4 describes the relationship between a PP and an attribute that has already been predicated of it. The direction of the arrow is toward the PP being described.

- Rule 5 describes the relationship between two PPs, one of which provides a particular kind of information about the other. The three most common types of information to be provided in this way are possession (shown as POSS-BY), location (shown as LOC), and physical containment (shown as CONT). The direction of the arrow is again toward the concept being described.

- Rule 6 describes the relationship between an ACT and the PP that is the object of that ACT. The direction of the arrow is toward the ACT since the context of the specific ACT determines the meaning of the object relation.

- Rule 7 describes the relationship between an ACT and the source and the recipient of the ACT.

- Rule 8 describes the relationship between an ACT and the instrument with which it is performed. The instrument must always be a full conceptualization (i.e., it must contain an ACT), not just a single physical object.

---

[1] The table shown in the figure is adapted from several tables in Schank [1973].

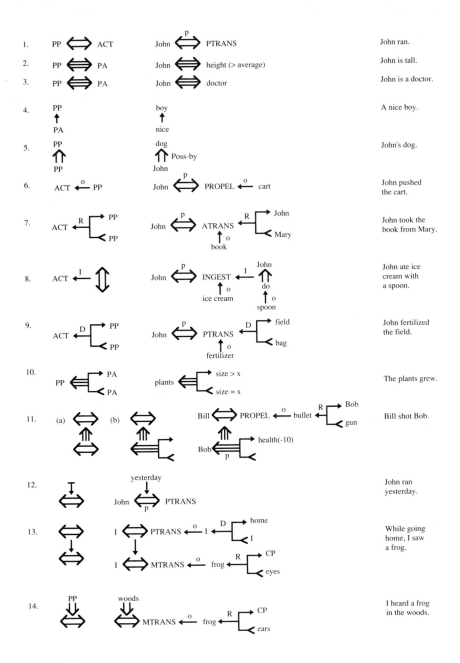

Figure 10.2: The Dependencies of CD

- Rule 9 describes the relationship between an ACT and its physical source and destination.

- Rule 10 represents the relationship between a PP and a state in which it started and another in which it ended.

- Rule 11 describes the relationship between one conceptualization and another that causes it. Notice that the arrows indicate dependency of one conceptualization on another and so point in the opposite direction of the implication arrows. The two forms of the rule describe the cause of an action and the cause of a state change.

- Rule 12 describes the relationship between a conceptualization and the time at which the event it describes occurred.

- Rule 13 describes the relationship between one conceptualization and another that is the time of the first. The example for this rule also shows how CD exploits a model of the human information processing system; *see* is represented as the transfer of information between the eyes and the conscious processor.

- Rule 14 describes the relationship between a conceptualization and the place at which it occurred.

Conceptualizations representing events can be modified in a variety of ways to supply information normally indicated in language by the tense, mood, or aspect of a verb form. The use of the modifier p to indicate past tense has already been shown. The set of conceptual tenses proposed by Schank [1973] includes

p	Past
f	Future
t	Transition
t_s	Start transition
t_f	Finished transition
k	Continuing
?	Interrogative
/	Negative
nil	Present
delta	Timeless
c	Conditional

As an example of the use of these tenses, consider the CD representation shown in Figure 10.3 (taken from Schank [1973]) of the sentence

Since smoking can kill you, I stopped.

The vertical causality link indicates that smoking kills one. Since it is marked c, however, we know only that smoking can kill one, not that it necessarily does. The horizontal causality link indicates that it is that first causality that made me stop smoking. The qualification t_{fp} attached to the dependency between I and INGEST indicates that the smoking (an instance of INGESTING) has stopped and that the stopping happened in the past.

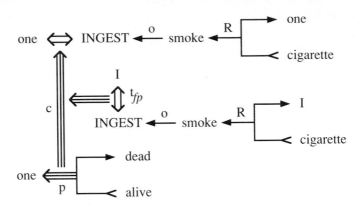

Figure 10.3: Using Conceptual Tenses

There are three important ways in which representing knowledge using the conceptual dependency model facilitates reasoning with the knowledge:

1. Fewer inference rules are needed than would be required if knowledge were not broken down into primitives.

2. Many inferences are already contained in the representation itself.

3. The initial structure that is built to represent the information contained in one sentence will have holes that need to be filled. These holes can serve as an attention focuser for the program that must understand ensuing sentences.

Each of these points merits further discussion.

The first argument in favor of representing knowledge in terms of CD primitives rather than in the higher-level terms in which it is normally described is that using the primitives makes it easier to describe the inference rules by which the knowledge can be manipulated. Rules need only be represented once for each primitive ACT rather than once for every word that describes that ACT. For example, all of the following verbs involve a transfer of ownership of an object:

- Give

- Take

- Steal

- Donate

If any of them occurs, then inferences about who now has the object and who once had the object (and thus who may know something about it) may be important. In a CD representation, those possible inferences can be stated once and associated with the primitive ACT ATRANS.

A second argument in favor of the use of CD representation is that to construct it, we must use not only the information that is stated explicitly in a sentence but also a set

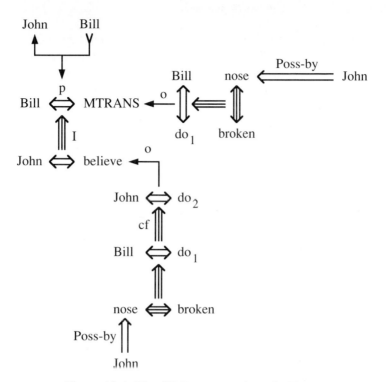

Figure 10.4: The CD Representation of a Threat

of inference rules associated with the specific information. Having applied these rules once, we store these results as part of the representation and they can be used repeatedly without the rules being reapplied. For example, consider the sentence

Bill threatened John with a broken nose.

The CD representation of the information contained in this sentence is shown in Figure 10.4. (For simplicity, *believe* is shown as a single unit. In fact, it must be represented in terms of primitive ACTs and a model of the human information processing system.) It says that Bill informed John that he (Bill) will do something to break John's nose. Bill did this so that John will believe that if he (John) does some other thing (different from what Bill will do to break his nose), then Bill will break John's nose. In this representation, the word "believe" has been used to simplify the example. But the idea behind *believe* can be represented in CD as an MTRANS of a fact into John's memory. The actions do_1 and do_2 are dummy placeholders that refer to some as yet unspecified actions.

A third argument for the use of the CD representation is that unspecified elements of the representation of one piece of information can be used as a focus for the understanding of later events as they are encountered. So, for example, after hearing that

> Bill threatened John with a broken nose.

we might expect to find out what action Bill was trying to prevent John from performing. That action could then be substituted for the dummy action represented in Figure 10.4 as do_2. The presence of such dummy objects provides clues as to what other events or objects are important for the understanding of the known event.

Of course, there are also arguments against the use of CD as a representation formalism. For one thing, it requires that all knowledge be decomposed into fairly low-level primitives. In Section 4.3.3 we discussed how this may be inefficient or perhaps even impossible in some situations. As Schank and Owens [1987] put it,

> CD is a theory of representing fairly simple actions. To express, for example, "John bet Sam fifty dollars that the Mets would win the World Series" takes about two pages of CD forms. This does not seem reasonable.

Thus, although there are several arguments in favor of the use of CD as a model for representing events, it is not always completely appropriate to do so, and it may be worthwhile to seek out higher-level primitives.

Another difficulty with the theory of conceptual dependency as a general model for the representation of knowledge is that it is only a theory of the representation of events. But to represent all the information that a complex program may need, it must be able to represent other things besides events. There have been attempts to define a set of primitives, similar to those of CD for actions, that can be used to describe other kinds of knowledge. For example, physical objects, which in CD are simply represented as atomic units, have been analyzed in Lehnert [1978]. A similar analysis of social actions is provided in Schank and Carbonell [1979]. These theories continue the style of representation pioneered by CD, but they have not yet been subjected to the same amount of empirical investigation (i.e., use in real programs) as CD.

We have discussed the theory of conceptual dependency in some detail in order to illustrate the behavior of a knowledge representation system built around a fairly small set of specific primitive elements. But CD is not the only such theory to have been developed and used in AI programs. For another example of a primitive-based system, see Wilks [1972].

10.2   Scripts

CD is a mechanism for representing and reasoning about events. But rarely do events occur in isolation. In this section, we present a mechanism for representing knowledge about common sequences of events.

A *script* is a structure that describes a stereotyped sequence of events in a particular context. A script consists of a set of slots. Associated with each slot may be some information about what kinds of values it may contain as well as a default value to be used if no other information is available. So far, this definition of a script looks very similar to that of a frame given in Section 9.2, and at this level of detail, the two structures are identical. But now, because of the specialized role to be played by a script, we can make some more precise statements about its structure.

Figure 10.5 shows part of a typical script, the restaurant script (taken from Schank and Abelson [1977]). It illustrates the important components of a script:

Entry conditions   Conditions that must, in general, be satisfied before the events described in the script can occur.

Result   Conditions that will, in general, be true after the events described in the script have occurred.

Props   Slots representing objects that are involved in the events described in the script. The presence of these objects can be inferred even if they are not mentioned explicitly.

Roles   Slots representing people who are involved in the events described in the script. The presence of these people, too, can be inferred even if they are not mentioned explicitly. If specific individuals are mentioned, they can be inserted into the appropriate slots.

Track   The specific variation on a more general pattern that is represented by this particular script. Different tracks of the same script will share many but not all components.

Scenes   The actual sequences of events that occur. The events are represented in conceptual dependency formalism.

Scripts are useful because, in the real world, there are patterns to the occurrence of events. These patterns arise because of causal relationships between events. Agents will perform one action so that they will then be able to perform another. The events described in a script form a giant *causal chain*. The beginning of the chain is the set of entry conditions which enable the first events of the script to occur. The end of the chain is the set of results which may enable later events or event sequences (possibly described by other scripts) to occur. Within the chain, events are connected both to earlier events that make them possible and to later events that they enable.

If a particular script is known to be appropriate in a given situation, then it can be very useful in predicting the occurrence of events that were not explicitly mentioned. Scripts can also be useful by indicating how events that were mentioned relate to each other. For example, what is the connection between someone's ordering steak and someone's eating steak? But before a particular script can be applied, it must be activated (i.e., it must be selected as appropriate to the current situation). There are two ways in which it may be useful to activate a script, depending on how important the script is likely to be:

- For fleeting scripts (ones that are mentioned briefly and may be referred to again but are not central to the situation), it may be sufficient merely to store a pointer to the script so that it can be accessed later if necessary. This would be an appropriate strategy to take with respect to the restaurant script when confronted with a story such as

     Susan passed her favorite restaurant on her way to the museum. She really enjoyed the new Picasso exhibit.

- For nonfleeting scripts it is appropriate to activate the script fully and to attempt to fill in its slots with particular objects and people involved in the current situation.

Script:　RESTAURANT Track:　Coffee Shop Props:　Tables 　　　　Menu 　　　　F = Food 　　　　Check 　　　　Money Roles:　S = Customer 　　　　W = Waiter 　　　　C = Cook 　　　　M = Cashier 　　　　O = Owner	**Scene 1:　Entering** S PTRANS S into restaurant S ATTEND eyes to tables S MBUILD where to sit S PTRANS S to table S MOVE S to sitting position

Scene 2:　Ordering

(Menu on table)　(W brings menu)　　(S asks for menu)
S PTRANS menu to S　　　　　　　S MTRANS signal to W
　　　　　　　　　　　　　　　　W PTRANS W to table
　　　　　　　　　　　　　　　　S MTRANS 'need menu' to W
　　　　　　　　　　　　　　　　W PTRANS W to menu
　　　　　　W PTRANS W to table
　　　　　　W ATRANS menu to S

　　　　S MTRANS W to table
　　　* S MBUILD choice of F
　　　　S MTRANS signal to W
　　　　W PTRANS W to table
　　　　S MTRANS 'I want F' to W

　　　　　　　W PTRANS W to C
　　　　　　　W MTRANS (ATRANS F) to C
　　C MTRANS 'no F' to W
　　W PTRANS W to S　　　　　　　C DO (prepare F script)
　　W MTRANS 'no F' to S　　　　　　to Scene 3
　　(go back to *) or
　　(go to Scene 4 at no pay path)

Scene 3:　Eating
C ATRANS F to W
W ATRANS F to S
S INGEST F
(Option:　Return to Scene 2 to order more;
　otherwise, go to Scene 4)

Scene 4:　Exiting
　　　　　　　　　　S MTRANS to W
　　　　　　　　　　　　　　(W ATRANS check to S)
　　　　W MOVE (write check)
　　　　W PTRANS W to S
　　　　W ATRANS check to S
　　　　S ATRANS tip to W
　　　　S PTRANS S to M
　　　　S ATRANS money to M
(No pay path)　S PTRANS S to out of restaurant

Entry conditions:

S is hungry.
S has money.

Results:

S has less money.
O has more money.
S is not hungry.
S is pleased (optional).

Figure 10.5: The Restaurant Script

The headers of a script (its preconditions, its preferred locations, its props, its roles, and its events) can all serve as indicators that the script should be activated. In order to cut down on the number of times a spurious script is activated, it has proved useful to require that a situation contain at least two of a script's headers before the script will be activated.

Once a script has been activated, there are, as we have already suggested, a variety of ways in which it can be useful in interpreting a particular situation. The most important of these is the ability to predict events that have not explicitly been observed. Suppose, for example, that you are told the following story:

> John went out to a restaurant last night. He ordered steak. When he paid for it, he noticed that he was running out of money. He hurried home since it had started to rain.

If you were then asked the question

> Did John eat dinner last night?

you would almost certainly respond that he did, even though you were not told so explicitly. By using the restaurant script, a computer question-answerer would also be able to infer that John ate dinner, since the restaurant script could have been activated. Since all of the events in the story correspond to the sequence of events predicted by the script, the program could infer that the entire sequence predicted by the script occurred normally. Thus it could conclude, in particular, that John ate. In their ability to predict unobserved events, scripts are similar to frames and to other knowledge structures that represent stereotyped situations. Once one of these structures is activated in a particular situation, many predictions can be made.

A second important use of scripts is to provide a way of building a single coherent interpretation from a collection of observations. Recall that a script can be viewed as a giant causal chain. Thus it provides information about how events are related to each other. Consider, for example, the following story:

> Susan went out to lunch. She sat down at a table and called the waitress. The waitress brought her a menu and she ordered a hamburger.

Now consider the question

> Why did the waitress bring Susan a menu?

The script provides two possible answers to that question:

- Because Susan asked her to. (This answer is gotten by going backward in the causal chain to find out what caused her to do it.)

- So that Susan could decide what she wanted to eat. (This answer is gotten by going forward in the causal chain to find out what event her action enables.)

A third way in which a script is useful is that it focuses attention on unusual events. Consider the following story:

John went to a restaurant. He was shown to his table. He ordered a large
steak. He sat there and waited for a long time. He got mad and left.

The important part of this story is the place in which it departs from the expected
sequence of events in a restaurant. John did not get mad because he was shown to his
table. He did get mad because he had to wait to be served. Once the typical sequence
of events is interrupted, the script can no longer be used to predict other events. So, for
example, in this story, we should not infer that John paid his bill. But we can infer that
he saw a menu, since reading the menu would have occurred before the interruption.
For a discussion of SAM, a program that uses scripts to perform this kind of reasoning,
see Cullingford [1981].

From these examples, we can see how information about typical sequences of events,
as represented in scripts, can be useful in interpreting a particular, observed sequence of
events. The usefulness of a script in some of these examples, such as the one in which
unobserved events were predicted, is similar to the usefulness of other knowledge
structures, such as frames. In other examples, we have relied on specific properties of
the information stored in a script, such as the causal chain represented by the events
it contains. Thus although scripts are less general structures than are frames, and so
are not suitable for representing all kinds of knowledge, they can be very effective for
representing the specific kinds of knowledge for which they were designed.

10.3   CYC

CYC [Lenat and Guha, 1990] is a very large knowledge base project aimed at capturing
human commonsense knowledge. Recall that in Section 5.1, our first attempt to prove
that Marcus was not loyal to Caesar failed because we were missing the simple fact that
all men are people. The goal of CYC is to encode the large body of knowledge that is so
obvious that it is easy to forget to state it explicitly. Such a knowledge base could then
be combined with specialized knowledge bases to produce systems that are less brittle
than most of the ones available today.

Like CD, CYC represents a specific theory of how to describe the world, and like CD,
it can be used for AI tasks such as natural language understanding. CYC, however, is
more comprehensive; while CD provided a specific theory of representation for events,
CYC contains representations of events, objects, attitudes, and so forth. In addition,
CYC is particularly concerned with issues of scale, that is, what happens when we build
knowledge bases that contain millions of objects.

10.3.1   Motivations

Why should we want to build large knowledge bases at all? There are many reasons,
among them:

- Brittleness—Specialized knowledge-based systems are brittle. They cannot cope
  with novel situations, and their performance degradation is not graceful. Programs
  built on top of deep, commonsense knowledge about the world should rest on
  firmer foundations.

- Form and Content—The techniques we have seen so far for representing and using knowledge may or may not be sufficient for the purposes of AI. One good way to find out is to start coding large amounts of commonsense knowledge and see where the difficulties crop up. In other words, one strategy is to focus temporarily on the content of knowledge bases rather than on their form.

- Shared Knowledge—Small knowledge-based systems must make simplifying assumptions about how to represent things like space, time, motion, and structure. If these things can be represented once at a very high level, then domain-specific systems can gain leverage cheaply. Also, systems that share the same primitives can communicate easily with one another.

Building an immense knowledge base is a staggering task, however. We should ask whether there are any methods for acquiring this knowledge automatically. Here are two possibilities:

1. Machine Learning—In Chapter 17, we discuss some techniques for automated learning. However, current techniques permit only modest extensions of a program's knowledge. In order for a system to learn a great deal, it must already know a great deal. In particular, systems with a lot of knowledge will be able to employ powerful analogical reasoning.

2. Natural Language Understanding—Humans extend their own knowledge by reading books and talking with other humans. Since we now have on-line versions of encyclopedias and dictionaries, why not feed these texts into an AI program and have it assimilate all the information automatically? Although there are many techniques for building language understanding systems (see Chapter 15), these methods are themselves very knowledge-intensive. For example, when we hear the sentence

   John went to the bank and withdrew $50.

   we easily decide that "bank" means a financial institution, and not a river bank. To do this, we apply fairly deep knowledge about what a financial institution is, what it means to withdraw money, etc. Unfortunately, for a program to assimilate the knowledge contained in an encyclopedia, that program must already know quite a bit about the world.

The approach taken by CYC is to hand-code (what its designers consider to be) the ten million or so facts that make up commonsense knowledge. It may then be possible to bootstrap into more automatic methods.

10.3.2   CYCL

CYC's knowledge is encoded in a representation language called CYCL. CYCL is a frame-based system that incorporates most of the techniques described in Chapter 9 (multiple inheritance, slots as full-fledged objects, *transfers-through, mutually-disjoint-with*, etc). CYCL generalizes the notion of inheritance so that properties can be inherited along any link, not just *isa* and *instance*. Consider the two statements:

```
Mary
   likes:              ???
   constraints:        (LispConstraint)

LispConstraint
   slotConstrained:    (likes)
   slotValueSubsumes:
       (TheSetOf X (Person allInstances)
          (And (programsIn X LispLanguage)
               (Not (ThereExists Y (Languages allInstances)
                        (And (Not (Equal Y LispLanguage))
                             (programsIn X Y))))))
       propagationDirection:    forward

Bob
   programsIn:     (LispLanguage)

Jane
   programsIn:     (LispLanguage CLanguage)
```

Figure 10.6: Frames and Constraint Expressions in CYC

1. All birds have two legs.

2. All of Mary's friends speak Spanish.

We can easily encode the first fact using standard inheritance—any frame with *Bird* on its *instance* slot inherits the value 2 on its *legs* slot. The second fact can be encoded in a similar fashion if we allow inheritance to proceed along the *friend* relation—any frame with *Mary* on its *friend* slot inherits the value *Spanish* on its *languagesSpoken* slot. CYC further generalizes inheritance to apply to a chain of relations, allowing us to express facts like, "All the parents of Mary's friends are rich," where the value *Rich* is inherited through a composition of the *friend* and *parentOf* links.

In addition to frames, CYCL contains a *constraint language* that allows the expression of arbitrary first-order logical expressions. For example, Figure 10.6 shows how we can express the fact "Mary likes people who program solely in Lisp." *Mary* has a constraint called *lispConstraint*, which restricts the values of her *likes* slot. The *slotValueSubsumes* attribute of *lispConstraint* ensures that Mary's *likes* slot will be filled with at least those individuals that satisfy the logical condition, namely that they program in *LispLanguage* and no others.

The time at which the default reasoning is actually performed is determined by the direction of the *slotValueSubsumes* rule. If the direction is *backward*, the rule is an if-needed rule, and it is invoked whenever someone inquires as to the value of Mary's *likes* slot. (In this case, the rule infers that Mary likes Bob but not Jane.) If the direction is *forward*, the rule is an if-added rule, and additions are automatically propagated to Mary's *likes* slot. For example, after we place LISP on Bob's *programsIn* slot, then the system quickly places Bob on Mary's *likes* slot for us. A truth maintenance system (see Chapter 7) ensures that if Bob ceases to be a Lisp programmer (or if he starts using Pascal), then he will also cease to appear on Mary's *likes* slot.

While forward rules can be very useful, they can also require substantial time and space to propagate their values. If a rule is entered as backward, then the system defers reasoning until the information is specifically requested. CYC maintains a separate background process for accomplishing forward propagations. A knowledge engineer can continue entering knowledge while its effects are propagated during idle keyboard time.[2]

Now let us return to the constraint language itself. Recall that it allows for the expression of facts as arbitrary logical expressions. Since first-order logic is much more powerful than CYC's frame language, why does CYC maintain both? The reason is that frame-based inference is very efficient, while general logical reasoning is computationally hard. CYC actually supports about twenty types of efficient inference mechanisms (including inheritance and transfers-through), each with its own truth maintenance facility. The constraint language allows for the expression of facts that are too complex for any of these mechanisms to handle.

The constraint language also provides an elegant, abstract layer of representation. In reality, CYC maintains two levels of representation: the *epistemological level* (EL) and the *heuristic level* (HL). The EL contains facts stated in the logical constraint language, while the HL contains the same facts stored using efficient inference templates. There is a translation program for automatically converting an EL statement into an efficient HL representation. The EL provides a clean, simple functional interface to CYC so that users and computer programs can easily insert and retrieve information from the knowledge base. The EL/HL distinction represents one way of combining the formal neatness of logic with the computational efficiency of frames.

In addition to frames, inference mechanisms, and the constraint language, CYCL performs consistency checking (e.g., detecting when an illegal value is placed on a slot) and conflict resolution (e.g., handling cases where multiple inference procedures assign incompatible values to a slot).

10.3.3   Control and Meta-Knowledge

Recall our discussion of control knowledge in Chapter 6, where we saw how to take information about control out of a production system interpreter and represent it declaratively using rules. CYCL strives to accomplish the same thing with frames. We have already seen how to specify whether a fact is propagated in the forward or backward direction—this is a type of control information. Associated with each slot is a set of inference mechanisms that can be used to compute values for it. For any given problem, CYC's reasoning is constrained to a small range of relevant, efficient procedures. A query in CYCL can be tagged with a level of effort. At the lowest level of effort, CYC merely checks whether the fact is stored in the knowledge base. At higher levels, CYC will invoke backward reasoning and even entertain metaphorical chains of inference. As the knowledge base grows, it will become necessary to use control knowledge to restrict reasoning to the most relevant portions of the knowledge base. This control knowledge can, of course, be stored in frames.

---

[2] Another idea is to have the system do forward propagation of knowledge during periods of infrequent use, such as at night.

In the tradition of its predecessor RLL (Representation Language Language) [Greiner and Lenat, 1980], many of the inference mechanisms used by CYC are stored explicitly as EL templates in the knowledge base. These templates can be modified like any other frames, and a user can create a new inference template by copying and editing an old one. CYC generates LISP code to handle the various aspects of an inference template. These aspects include recognizing when an EL statement can be transformed into an instance of the template, storing justifications of facts that are deduced (and retracting those facts when the justifications disappear), and applying the inference mechanism efficiently. As with production systems, we can build a more flexible, reflective system by moving inference procedures into a declarative representation.

It should be clear that many of the same control issues exist for frames and rules. Unlike numerical heuristic evaluation functions, control knowledge often has a commonsense, "knowledge about the world" flavor to it. It therefore begins to bridge the gap between two usually disparate types of knowledge: knowledge that is typically used for search control and knowledge that is typically used for natural language disambiguation.

10.3.4   Global Ontology

Ontology is the philosophical study of what exists. In the AI context, ontology is concerned with which categories we can usefully quantify over and how those categories relate to each other. All knowledge-based systems refer to entities in the world, but in order to capture the breadth of human knowledge, we need a well-designed *global ontology* that specifies at a very high level what kinds of things exist and what their general properties are. As mentioned above, such a global ontology should provide a more solid foundation for domain-specific AI programs and should also allow them to communicate with each other.

The highest level concept in CYC is called *Thing*. Everything is an instance of *Thing*. Below this top-level concept, CYC makes several distinctions, including:

- *IndividualObject* versus *Collection*—The CYCL concept *Collection* corresponds to the class CLASS described in Chapter 9. Here are some examples of frames that are instances of *Collection*: *Person, Nation, Nose*. Some instances of *IndividualObject* are *Fred, Greece, Fred'sNose*. These two sets share no common instances, and any instance of *Thing* must be an instance of one of the two sets. Anything that is an instance of *Collection* is a subset of *Thing*. Only *Collections* may have supersets and subsets; only *IndividualObjects* may have parts.

- *Intangible, Tangible,* and *Composite*—Instances of *Intangible* are things without mass, e.g., sets, numbers, laws, and events. Instances of *TangibleObject* are things with mass that have no intangible aspect, e.g., a person's body, an orange, and dirt. Every instance of *TangibleObject* is also an instance of *IndividualObject* since sets have no mass. Instances of *CompositeObject* have two key slots, *physicalExtent* and *intangibleExtent*. For example, a person is a *CompositeObject* whose *physicalExtent* is his body and whose *intangibleExtent* is his mind.

- *Substance*—*Substance* is a subclass of *IndividualObject*. Any subclass of *Substance* is something that retains its properties when it is cut up into smaller pieces.

For example, *Wood* is a *Substance*.[3] A concept like *Table34* can be an instance of both *Wood* (a *Substance*) and *Table* (an *IndividualObject*).

- *Intrinsic* versus *Extrinsic* properties—A property is intrinsic if when an object has that property all parts of the object also have that property. For example, *color* is an intrinsic property. Objects tend to inherit their intrinsic properties from *Substances*. Extrinsic properties include things like *number-of-legs*. Objects tend to inherit their extrinsic properties from *IndividualObjects*.

- *Event* and *Process*—An *Event* is anything with temporal extent, e.g., *Walking*. *Process* is a subclass of *Event*. If every temporal slice of an *Event* is essentially the same as the entire *Event*, then that *Event* is also a *Process*. For example, *Walking* is a *Process*, but *WalkingTwoMiles* is not. This relationship is analogous to *Substance* and *IndividualObject*.

- Slots—*Slot* is a subclass of *Intangible*. There are many types of *Slot*. *BookkeepingSlots* record such information as when a frame was created and by whom. *DefiningSlots* refer not to properties of the frame but to properties of the object represented by the frame. *DefiningSlots* are further divided into intensional, taxonomic, and extensional categories. *QuantitativeSlots* are those which take on a scalar range of values, e.g., *height*, as opposed to *gender*.

- Time—*Events* can have temporal properties, such as *duration* and *startsBefore*. CYC deals with two basic types of temporal measures: intervals, and sets of intervals. A number of basic interval properties, such as *endsDuring*, are defined from the property *before*, which applies to starting and ending times for events. Sets of intervals are built up from basic intervals through operations like union and intersection. Thus, it is possible to state facts like "John goes to the movies at three o'clock every Sunday."

- *Agent*—An important subset of *CompositeObject* is *Agent*, the collection of intelligent beings. *Agents* can be collective (e.g., corporations) or individual (e.g., people). *Agents* have a number of properties, one of which is *beliefs*. Agents often ascribe their own beliefs to other agents in order to facilitate communication. An agent's beliefs may be incorrect, so CYC must be able to distinguish between facts in its own knowledge base (CYC's beliefs) and "facts" that are possibly inconsistent with the knowledge base.

These are but a few of the ontological decisions that the builders of a large knowledge base must make. Other problems arise in the representation of space, causality, structures, and the persistence of objects through time. We return to some of these issues in Chapter 19.

10.3.5 Tools

CYC is a multi-user system that provides each knowledge enterer with a textual and graphical interface to the knowledge base. Users' modifications to the knowledge base

---

[3]Of course, if we cut a substance up *too* finely, it ceases to be the same substance. For each substance type, CYC stores its *granule* size, e.g., *Wood.granule* = *PlantCell*, *Crowd.granule* = *Person*, etc.

are transmitted to a central server, where they are checked and then propagated to other users.

We do not yet have much experience with the engineering problems of building and maintaining very large knowledge bases. In the future, it will be necessary to have tools that check consistency in the knowledge base, point out areas of incompleteness, and ensure that users do not step on each others' toes.

10.4   Exercises

1. Show a conceptual dependency representation of the sentence

    John begged Mary for a pencil.

    How does this representation make it possible to answer the question

    Did John talk to Mary?

2. One difficulty with representations that rely on a small set of semantic primitives, such as conceptual dependency, is that it is often difficult to represent distinctions between fine shades of meaning. Write CD representations for each of the following sentences. Try to capture the differences in meaning between the two sentences of each pair.

    John slapped Bill.
    John punched Bill.

    Bill drank his Coke.
    Bill slurped his Coke.

    Sue likes Dickens.
    Sue adores Dickens.

3. Construct a script for going to a movie from the viewpoint of the movie goer.

4. Consider the following paragraph:

    > Jane was extremely hungry. She thought about going to her favorite restaurant for dinner, but it was the day before payday. So instead she decided to go home and pop a frozen pizza in the oven. On the way, though, she ran into her friend, Judy. Judy invited Jane to go out to dinner with her and Jane instantly agreed. When they got to their favorite place, they found a good table and relaxed over their meal.

    How could the restaurant script be invoked by the contents of this story? Trace the process throughout the story. Might any other scripts also be invoked? For example, how would you answer the question, "Did Jane pay for her dinner?"

5. Would conceptual dependency be a good way to represent the contents of a typical issue of *National Geographic*?

6. State where in the CYC ontology following concepts should fall:

- cat
- court case
- New York Times
- France
- glass of water

Chapter 11

Knowledge Representation Summary

In this chapter, we review the representational schemes that have been discussed so far and we mention briefly some additional representational techniques that are sometimes useful. You may find it useful at this point to reread Chapter 4 for a review of the knowledge representation issues that we outlined there.

11.1 Syntactic-Semantic Spectrum of Representation

One way to review the representational schemes we have just described is to consider an important dimension along which they can be characterized. At one extreme are purely *syntactic* systems, in which no concern is given to the meaning of the knowledge that is being represented. Such systems have simple, uniform rules for manipulating the representation. They do not care what information the representation contains. At the other extreme are purely *semantic* systems, in which there is no unified form. Every aspect of the representation corresponds to a different piece of information, and the inference rules are correspondingly complicated.

So far, we have discussed eight declarative structures in which knowledge can be represented:

- Predicate logic

- Production rules

- Nonmonotonic systems

- Statistical reasoning systems

- Semantic nets

- Frames

- Conceptual dependency

- Scripts

- CYC

Of these, the logical representations (predicate logic and the nonmonotonic systems) and the statistical ones are the most purely syntactic. Their rules of inference are strictly syntactic procedures that operate on well-formed formulas (wff) regardless of what those formulas represent. Production rule systems are primarily syntactic also. The interpreters for these systems usually use only syntactic information (such as the form of the pattern on the left side, the position of the rule in the knowledge base, or the position of the matched object in short-term memory) to decide which rules to fire. Again here we see the similarity between logic and production rules as ways of representing and using knowledge. But it is possible to build production-rule systems that have more semantics embedded in them. For example, in EMYCIN and other systems that provide explicit support for certainty factors, the semantics of certainty factors are used by the rule interpreter to guide its behavior.

Slot-and-filler structures are typically more semantically oriented, although they span a good distance in this spectrum. Semantic nets, as their name implies, are designed to capture semantic relationships among entities, and they are usually employed with a set of inference rules that have been specially designed to handle correctly the specific types of arcs present in the network. (For example, *isa* links are treated differently from most other kinds of links.) Frame systems are typically more highly structured than are semantic nets, and they contain an even larger set of specialized inference rules, including those that implement a whole array of default inheritance rules, as well as other procedures such as consistency checking.

Conceptual dependency moves even further toward being a semantic rather than a syntactic representation. It provides not only the abstract structure of a representation but also a specific indication of what components the representation should contain (such as the primitive ACTs and the dependency relationships). Thus, although CD representations can be thought of as instances of semantic nets, they can be used by more powerful inference mechanisms that exploit specific knowledge about what they contain. And although scripts appear very similar to frames, they are frames in which the slots have been carefully chosen to represent the information that is useful when reasoning about situations. This makes it possible for script manipulation procedures to exploit knowledge about what they are working with in order to solve problems more efficiently. CYC uses both frames and logic (depending on the level at which we view the knowledge) to encode specific types of knowledge and inference aimed at commonsense reasoning. CYC is the most semantic of the systems we have described, since it provides the most built-in knowledge of how to manipulate specific kinds of knowledge structures. It also contains a comprehensive ontology into which new knowledge can be put.

In general, syntactic representations are to knowledge representation what the weak methods of Chapter 3 are to problem-solving. They are, in principle, adequate for any problem. But for hard problems, their generality often means that answers cannot be found quickly. Stronger, more semantically oriented approaches make it possible to use knowledge more effectively to guide search. This does not mean that there is no place for weak or syntactic methods. Sometimes they are adequate, and their simplicity makes a formal analysis of programs that use them much more straightforward than a comparable analysis of a program based on semantic methods. But powerful programs depend on powerful knowledge, some of which is typically embedded in their problem-solving procedures and some of which is embedded in their knowledge representation mechanisms. In fact, as we have seen throughout Part II of this book, it is not usually possible to separate the two facets cleanly.

However, as we have seen in the last few chapters, knowledge representation systems can play the role of support systems that underly specific problem-solving programs. The knowledge representation system is typically expected not just to hold knowledge but also to provide a set of basic inference procedures, such as property inheritance or truth maintenance, that are defined on the knowledge. Specific problem-solving procedures can then be implemented as a level on top of that.

When knowledge representation systems are viewed as modules that are going to be incorporated as black boxes into larger programs, a good argument can be made [Brachman and Levesque, 1984] that their functionality should be restricted to purely syntactic operations about which very precise statements can be made. Essentially, this argument follows standard software engineering principles. To use a module effectively, one must have access to precise functional specifications of that module. If a knowledge representation system performs operations that are highly semantic in nature, it is difficult or impossible to write such a set of specifications. Among the kinds of operations that pose difficulties in this regard are the following:

- Operations whose result is defined to be the first or the best object satisfying some set of specifications. One example of such an operation is the resolution of a contradiction in a default-reasoning system. These operations require heuristics to define first or best and thus cannot usually be described in a straightforward way without appealing to the heuristics.

- Operations that are given resource limitations and whose output depends on how effectively those resources can be used. One common example of such an operation is default reasoning, when it is stated in a form such as, "Assume x unless $\neg x$ can be shown within z inference steps." The semantics of these operations then depend on how the resources happen to be exploited.

Of course, we are not saying that operations with these properties should not be done in reasoning programs. They are necessary. We are only saying that they should be within the control of some domain-specific problem solver rather than hidden within a general-purpose black box.

11.2 Logic and Slot-and-Filler Structures

Slot-and-filler structures have proven very valuable in the efficient storing and retrieving of knowledge for AI programs. They are usually poor, however, when it comes to representing rule-like assertions of the form "If x, y, and z, then conclude w." Predicate logic, on the other hand, does a reasonable job of representing such assertions, although general reasoning using these assertions is inefficient. Slot-and-filler representations are usually more semantic, meaning that their reasoning procedures are more varied, more efficient, and tied more closely to specific types of knowledge.

Hayes [1973] and Nilsson [1980] have shown how slot-and-filler structures can be translated into predicate logic. Concepts become one-place predicates, e.g., *dog*(*x*), and slots become two-place predicates, e.g., *color*(*canary*, *yellow*). Inference mechanisms like property inheritance can be expressed in logical notation, as a series of logical implications, which can then be manipulated with resolution. Working through a translation of a slot-and-filler structure to logic helps clear up what are often imprecisely specified reasoning methods in these structures. In practical terms, however, moving to logic means losing efficiency. For example, a typical slot-and-filler system has procedures for doing property inheritance that are much faster than doing property inheritance via resolution-based theorem proving. Part of the inefficiency of general reasoning methods like resolution can be overcome by intelligent indexing schemes, but the more heavily cross-indexed predicate logic clauses are, the more they come to resemble slot-and-filler structures.

On the other hand, it is difficult to express assertions more complex than inheritance in slot-and-filler structures. Is it possible to create a *hybrid* representational structure that combines the advantages of slot-and-filler structures with the advantages of predicate logic? We have already seen one system (CYC) that maintains both a logical (epistemological level) and frame-based (heuristic level) version of each fact. Another system, called KRYPTON [Brachman *et al.*, 1985], divides its knowledge into two distinct repositories, called the TBox and the ABox. The TBox is a slot-and-filler structure that contains *terminological* information. In it are concepts like "person," "car," and "person with three children." The ABox contains logical assertions, such as "Every person with three children owns a car." The atomic predicates used in ABox assertions refer to concepts defined in the TBox.

In logic-based systems, predicates such as *triangle* and *polygon* are primitive notions. These primitives are tied to one another via assertions, e.g., *isa*(*triangle*, *polygon*) and *isa*(*rectangle*, *polygon*). KRYPTON relates concepts like *triangle* and *polygon* terminologically, in the TBox, rather than assertionally. Thus we can do efficient terminological reasoning in the TBox and more general reasoning in the ABox. Terminological reasoning involves answering questions about subsumption and inheritance, such as "Can something be both a triangle and a rectangle?"

Consider a resolution theorem prover running with assertions in the ABox. A standard operation in resolution is determining when pairs of literals such as $f(x)$ and $\neg f(x)$ are inconsistent. Standard resolution requires that the literals be textually unifiable (except for the negation sign). KRYPTON extends the idea of textual inconsistency to *terminological* inconsistency in order to make the theorem prover more efficient. The TBox can tell that the two assertions *triangle*(*x*) and *rectangle*(*x*) are inconsistent and can thus be resolved against each other. The TBox can also determine the inconsistency of *triangle*(*x*) and $\neg$*polygon*(*x*); moreover, the two assertions $\neg$*rectangle*(*x*) and *polygon*(*x*) can be resolved against each other as long as we add to the resolvent the fact that *x* must have an angle which is not 90 degrees. If TBox computations are very efficient, then ABox proofs will be generated much faster than they would be in a pure logic framework.

11.3 Other Representational Techniques

In the last several chapters, we have described various techniques that can be used to represent knowledge. But our survey is by no means complete. There are other ways of representing knowledge; some of them are quite similar to the ones we have discussed and some are quite different. In this section we briefly discuss three additional methods: constraints, simulation models, and subsymbolic systems. Keep in mind throughout this discussion that it is not always the case that these various representational systems are mutually inconsistent. They often overlap, either in the way they use component representational mechanisms, the reasoning algorithms they support, or the problem-solving tasks for which they are appropriate.

11.3.1 Representing Knowledge as Constraints

Much of what we know about the world can be represented as sets of constraints. We talked in Section 3.5 about a very simple problem, cryptarithmetic, that can be described this way. But constraint-based representations are also useful in more complex problems. For example, we can describe an electronic circuit as a set of constraints that the states of various components of the circuit impose on the states of other components by virtue of being connected together. If the state of one of these components changes, we can propagate the effect of the change throughout the circuit by using the constraints. As a second example, consider the problem of interpreting visual scenes. We can write down a set of constraints that characterize the set of interpretations that can make sense in our physical world. For example, a single edge must be interpreted consistently, at both of its ends, as either a convex or a concave boundary. Finally, as we saw in Section 8.3, there are several kinds of relationships that can be represented as sets of constraints on the likelihoods that we can assign to collections of interdependent events.

In some sense, everything we write in any representational system is a constraint on the world models or problem solutions that we want our program to accept. For example, a wff [e.g., $\forall x : man(x) \rightarrow mortal(x)$] constrains the set of consistent models to those that do not include any man who is not mortal. But there is a very specific sense in which it is useful to talk about a specific class of techniques as constraint-based. Recall that in Section 3.5 we presented an algorithm for constraint satisfaction that was based on the notion of propagating constraints throughout a system until a final state was reached. This algorithm is particularly effective precisely when knowledge is represented in a way that makes it efficient to propagate constraints. This will be true whenever it is easy to locate the objects that a given object influences. This occurs when the objects in the system are represented as a network whose links correspond to constraints among the objects. We considered one example of this when we talked about Bayesian networks in Section 8.3. We consider other examples later in this book. For example, we return to the problem of simulating physical processes, such as electronic circuits, in Section 19.1. We present in Section 14.3 a constraint-propagation solution (known as the Waltz algorithm) to a simple vision problem. And in Section 15.5 we outline a view of natural language understanding as a constraint satisfaction task.

11.3.2   Models and Model-Based Reasoning

For many kinds of problem-solving tasks, it is necessary to model the behavior of some object or system. To diagnose faults in physical devices, such as electronic circuits or electric motors, it is necessary to model the behavior of both the correctly functioning device and some number of ill-functioning variants of it. To evaluate potential designs of such devices requires the same capability. Of course, as soon as we begin to think about modeling such complex entities, it becomes clear that the best we will be able to do is create an approximate model. There are various techniques that we can use to do that.

When we think about constructing a model of some entity in the world, the issue of what we mean by a model soon arises. To what extent should the structure of the model mirror the structure of the object being modeled? Some representational techniques tend to support models whose structure is very different from the structure of the objects being modeled. For example, in predicate logic we write wff's such as $\forall x : raven(x) \rightarrow black(x)$. In the real world, though, this single fact has no single realization; it is distributed across all known ravens. At the other extreme are representations, such as causal networks, in which the physical structure of the world is closely modeled in the structure of the representation.

There are arguments in favor of both ends of this spectrum (and many points in the middle). For example, if the knowledge structure closely matches the problem structure, then the frame problem may be easier to solve. Suppose, for example, that we have a robot-planning program and we want to know if we move a table into another room, what other objects also change location. A model that closely matches the structure of the world (as shown in Figure 11.1(a)) will make answering this question easy, while alternative representations (such as the one shown in Figure 11.1(b)) will not. For more on this issue, see Johnson-Laird [1983]. There are, however, arguments for representations whose structures do not closely model the world. For example, such representations typically do a better job of capturing generalizations and thus of making predictions about some kinds of novel situations.

11.3.3   Subsymbolic Systems

So far, all of the representations that we have discussed are symbolic, in the sense we defined in Section 1.2. There are alternative representations, many of them based on a neural model patterned after the human brain. These systems are often called neural nets or connectionist systems. We discuss such systems in Chapter 18.

11.4   Summary of the Role of Knowledge

In the last several chapters we have focused on the kinds of knowledge that may be useful to programs and on ways of representing and using that knowledge within programs. To sum up, for now, our treatment of knowledge within AI programs, let us return to a brief discussion of the two roles that knowledge can play in those programs.

- It may define the search space and the criteria for determining a solution to a problem. We call this knowledge *essential knowledge*.

(*Livingroom1*:
    contains:
        (*Table1*:
            made-of: *Wood*
            has-on: (*Vase1*:
                        made-of: *Glass*)
                  (*Lamp1*: ...))
      (*Table2*:
          has-on: (*Vase2*: ...)))

(*a*)

in(*Table1*, *Livingroom*)
made-of(*Table1*, *Wood*)
on(*Vase1*, *Table1*)
made-of(*Vase1*, *Glass*)
on(*Vase2*, *Table2*)
on(*Lamp1*, *Table1*)

(*b*)

Figure 11.1: Capturing Structure in Models

- It may improve the efficiency of a reasoning procedure by informing that procedure of the best places to look for a solution. We call that knowledge *heuristic knowledge*.

In formal tasks, such as theorem proving and game playing, there is only a small amount of essential knowledge and the need for a large amount of heuristic knowledge may be challenged by several brute force programs that perform quite successfully (e.g., the chess programs HITECH [Berliner and Ebeling, 1989] and DEEP THOUGHT [Anantharaman *et al.*, 1990]). The real knowledge challenge arises when we tackle naturally occurring problems, such as medical diagnosis, natural language processing, or engineering design. In those domains, substantial bodies of both essential and heuristic knowledge are absolutely necessary.

11.5 Exercises

1. Artificial intelligence systems employ a variety of formalisms for representing knowledge and reasoning with it. For each of the following sets of sentences, indicate the formalism that best facilitates the representation of the knowledge given in the statements in order to answer the question that is posed. Explain your choice briefly. Show how the statements would be encoded in the formalism you have selected. Then show how the question could be answered.

John likes fruit.
Kumquats are fruit.
People eat what they like.
Does John eat kumquats?

Assume that candy contains sugar unless you know
    specifically that it is dietetic.
M&M's are candy.
Diabetics should not eat sugar.
Bill is a diabetic.
Should Bill eat M&M's?

Most people like candy.
Most people who give parties like to serve food that
    their guests like.
Tom is giving a party.
What might Tom like to serve?

When you go to a movie theatre, you usually buy a ticket,
    hand the ticket to the ticket taker, and then go and
    find a seat.
Sometimes you buy popcorn before going to your seat.
When the movie is over, you leave the theatre.
John went to the movies.
Did John buy a ticket?

2. Give five examples of facts that are difficult to represent and manipulate in predicate logic.

3. Suppose you had a predicate logic-based system in which you had represented the information in Figure 4.5. What additional knowledge would you have to include in order to cause properties to be inherited downward in the hierarchy? For example, how could you answer the question of how tall a pitcher is?

4. Property inheritance is a very common form of default reasoning. Consider the semantic net

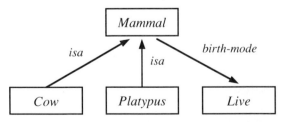

(a) How could the information in this network be represented in a JTMS?

(b) What will happen when the additional fact that the platypus lays eggs is inserted into this system?

Part III

Advanced Topics

Chapter 12

Game Playing

12.1 Overview

Games hold an inexplicable fascination for many people, and the notion that computers might play games has existed at least as long as computers. Charles Babbage, the nineteenth-century computer architect, thought about programming his Analytical Engine to play chess and later of building a machine to play tic tac-toe [Bowden, 1953]. Two of the pioneers of the science of information and computing contributed to the fledgling computer game-playing literature. Claude Shannon [1950] wrote a paper in which he described mechanisms that could be used in a program to play chess. A few years later, Alan Turing described a chess-playing program, although he never built it. (For a description, see Bowden [1953].) By the early 1960s, Arthur Samuel had succeeded in building the first significant, operational game-playing program. His program played checkers and, in addition to simply playing the game, could learn from its mistakes and improve its performance [Samuel, 1963].

There were two reasons that games appeared to be a good domain in which to explore machine intelligence:

- They provide a structured task in which it is very easy to measure success or failure.

- They did not obviously require large amounts of knowledge. They were thought to be solvable by straightforward search from the starting state to a winning position.

The first of these reasons remains valid and accounts for continued interest in the area of game playing by machine. Unfortunately, the second is not true for any but the simplest games. For example, consider chess.

- The average branching factor is around 35.

- In an average game, each player might make 50 moves.

- So in order to examine the complete game tree, we would have to examine 35^{100} positions.

Thus it is clear that a program that simply does a straightforward search of the game tree will not be able to select even its first move during the lifetime of its opponent. Some kind of heuristic search procedure is necessary.

One way of looking at all the search procedures we have discussed is that they are essentially generate-and-test procedures in which the testing is done after varying amounts of work by the generator. At one extreme, the generator generates entire proposed solutions, which the tester then evaluates. At the other extreme, the generator generates individual moves in the search space, each of which is then evaluated by the tester and the most promising one is chosen. Looked at this way, it is clear that to improve the effectiveness of a search-based problem-solving program two things can be done:

- Improve the generate procedure so that only good moves (or paths) are generated.

- Improve the test procedure so that the best moves (or paths) will be recognized and explored first.

In game-playing programs, it is particularly important that both these things be done. Consider again the problem of playing chess. On the average, there are about 35 legal moves available at each turn. If we use a simple legal-move generator, then the test procedure (which probably uses some combination of search and a heuristic evaluation function) will have to look at each of them. Because the test procedure must look at so many possibilities, it must be fast. So it probably cannot do a very accurate job. Suppose, on the other hand, that instead of a legal-move generator, we use a *plausible-move generator* in which only some small number of promising moves are generated. As the number of legal moves available increases, it becomes increasingly important to apply heuristics to select only those that have some kind of promise. (So, for example, it is extremely important in programs that play the game of go [Benson *et al.*, 1979].) With a more selective move generator, the test procedure can afford to spend more time evaluating each of the moves it is given so it can produce a more reliable result. Thus by incorporating heuristic knowledge into both the generator and the tester, the performance of the overall system can be improved.

Of course, in game playing, as in other problem domains, search is not the only available technique. In some games, there are at least some times when more direct techniques are appropriate. For example, in chess, both openings and endgames are often highly stylized, so they are best played by table lookup into a database of stored patterns. To play an entire game then, we need to combine search-oriented and nonsearch-oriented techniques.

The ideal way to use a search procedure to find a solution to a problem is to generate moves through the problem space until a goal state is reached. In the context of game-playing programs, a goal state is one in which we win. Unfortunately, for interesting games such as chess, it is not usually possible, even with a good plausible-move generator, to search until a goal state is found. The depth of the resulting tree (or graph) and its branching factor are too great. In the amount of time available, it is usually possible to search a tree only ten or twenty moves (called *ply* in the game-playing literature) deep. Then, in order to choose the best move, the resulting board positions must be compared to discover which is most advantageous. This is done using a *static evaluation function*, which uses whatever information it has to evaluate individual board positions by estimating how likely they are to lead eventually to a win. Its function is similar to that of the heuristic function h' in the A* algorithm: in the absence of complete information, choose the most promising position. Of course, the static evaluation function could simply be applied directly to the positions generated by the proposed moves. But since it is hard to produce a function like this that is very accurate, it is better to apply it as many levels down in the game tree as time permits.

A lot of work in game-playing programs has gone into the development of good static evaluation functions.[1] A very simple static evaluation function for chess based on piece advantage was proposed by Turing—simply add the values of black's pieces (B), the values of white's pieces (W), and then compute the quotient W/B. A more sophisticated approach was that taken in Samuel's checkers program, in which the static evaluation function was a linear combination of several simple functions, each of which appeared as though it might be significant. Samuel's functions included, in addition to the obvious one, piece advantage, such things as capability for advancement, control of the center, threat of a fork, and mobility. These factors were then combined by attaching to each an appropriate weight and then adding the terms together. Thus the complete evaluation function had the form:

$$c_1 \times pieceadvantage + c_2 \times advancement + c_3 \times centercontrol \dots$$

There were also some nonlinear terms reflecting combinations of these factors. But Samuel did not know the correct weights to assign to each of the components. So he employed a simple learning mechanism in which components that had suggested moves that turned out to lead to wins were given an increased weight, while the weights of those that had led to losses were decreased.

Unfortunately, deciding which moves have contributed to wins and which to losses is not always easy. Suppose we make a very bad move, but then, because the opponent makes a mistake, we ultimately win the game. We would not like to give credit for winning to our mistake. The problem of deciding which of a series of actions is actually responsible for a particular outcome is called the *credit assignment problem* [Minsky, 1963]. It plagues many learning mechanisms, not just those involving games. Despite this and other problems, though, Samuel's checkers program was eventually able to beat its creator. The techniques it used to acquire this performance are discussed in more detail in Chapter 17.

We have now discussed the two important knowledge-based components of a good game-playing program: a good plausible-move generator and a good static evaluation function. They must both incorporate a great deal of knowledge about the particular game being played. But unless these functions are perfect, we also need a search procedure that makes it possible to look ahead as many moves as possible to see what may occur. Of course, as in other problem-solving domains, the role of search can be altered considerably by altering the amount of knowledge that is available to it. But, so far at least, programs that play nontrivial games rely heavily on search.

What search strategy should we use then? For a simple one-person game or puzzle, the A* algorithm described in Chapter 3 can be used. It can be applied to reason forward from the current state as far as possible in the time allowed. The heuristic function h' can be applied at terminal nodes and used to propagate values back up the search graph

---

[1] See Berliner [1979b] for a discussion of some theoretical issues in the design of static evaluation functions.

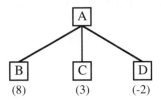

Figure 12.1: One-Ply Search

so that the best next move can be chosen. But because of their adversarial nature, this procedure is inadequate for two-person games such as chess. As values are passed back up, different assumptions must be made at levels where the program chooses the move and at the alternating levels where the opponent chooses. There are several ways that this can be done. The most commonly used method is the *minimax* procedure, which is described in the next section. An alternative approach is the B* algorithm [Berliner, 1979a], which works on both standard problem-solving trees and on game trees.

12.2   The Minimax Search Procedure

The *minimax search procedure* is a depth-first, depth-limited search procedure. It was described briefly in Section 1.3.1. The idea is to start at the current position and use the plausible-move generator to generate the set of possible successor positions. Now we can apply the static evaluation function to those positions and simply choose the best one. After doing so, we can back that value up to the starting position to represent our evaluation of it. The starting position is exactly as good for us as the position generated by the best move we can make next. Here we assume that the static evaluation function returns large values to indicate good situations for us, so our goal is to *maximize* the value of the static evaluation function of the next board position.

  An example of this operation is shown in Figure 12.1. It assumes a static evaluation function that returns values ranging from −10 to 10, with 10 indicating a win for us, −10 a win for the opponent, and 0 an even match. Since our goal is to maximize the value of the heuristic function, we choose to move to B. Backing B's value up to A, we can conclude that A's value is 8, since we know we can move to a position with a value of 8.

  But since we know that the static evaluation function is not completely accurate, we would like to carry the search farther ahead than one ply. This could be very important, for example, in a chess game in which we are in the middle of a piece exchange. After our move, the situation would appear to be very good, but, if we look one move ahead, we will see that one of our pieces also gets captured and so the situation is not as favorable as it seemed. So we would like to look ahead to see what will happen to each of the new game positions at the next move which will be made by the opponent. Instead of applying the static evaluation function to each of the positions that we just generated, we apply the plausible-move generator, generating a set of successor positions for each position. If we wanted to stop here, at two-ply lookahead, we could apply the static evaluation function to each of these positions, as shown in Figure 12.2.

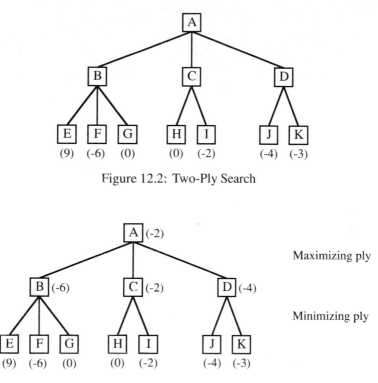

Figure 12.2: Two-Ply Search

Figure 12.3: Backing Up the Values of a Two-Ply Search

But now we must take into account that the opponent gets to choose which successor moves to make and thus which terminal value should be backed up to the next level. Suppose we made move B. Then the opponent must choose among moves E, F, and G. The opponent's goal is to *minimize* the value of the evaluation function, so he or she can be expected to choose move F. This means that if we make move B, the actual position in which we will end up one move later is very bad for us. This is true even though a possible configuration is that represented by node E, which is very good for us. But since at this level we are not the ones to move, we will not get to choose it. Figure 12.3 shows the result of propagating the new values up the tree. At the level representing the opponent's choice, the minimum value was chosen and backed up. At the level representing our choice, the maximum value was chosen.

Once the values from the second ply are backed up, it becomes clear that the correct move for us to make at the first level, given the information we have available, is C, since there is nothing the opponent can do from there to produce a value worse than −2. This process can be repeated for as many ply as time allows, and the more accurate evaluations that are produced can be used to choose the correct move at the top level. The alternation of maximizing and minimizing at alternate ply when evaluations are being pushed back up corresponds to the opposing strategies of the two players and gives this method the name minimax.

Having described informally the operation of the minimax procedure, we now describe it precisely. It is a straightforward recursive procedure that relies on two auxiliary procedures that are specific to the game being played:

1. MOVEGEN(*Position*, *Player*)—The plausible-move generator, which returns a list of nodes representing the moves that can be made by *Player* in *Position*. We call the two players PLAYER-ONE and PLAYER-TWO; in a chess program, we might use the names BLACK and WHITE instead.

2. STATIC(*Position*, *Player*)—The static evaluation function, which returns a number representing the goodness of *Position* from the standpoint of *Player*.[2]

As with any recursive program, a critical issue in the design of the MINIMAX procedure is when to stop the recursion and simply call the static evaluation function. There are a variety of factors that may influence this decision. They include:

- Has one side won?

- How many ply have we already explored?

- How promising is this path?

- How much time is left?

- How stable is the configuration?

For the general MINIMAX procedure discussed here, we appeal to a function, DEEP-ENOUGH, which is assumed to evaluate all of these factors and to return TRUE if the search should be stopped at the current level and FALSE otherwise. Our simple implementation of DEEP-ENOUGH will take two parameters, *Position* and *Depth*. It will ignore its *Position* parameter and simply return TRUE if its *Depth* parameter exceeds a constant cutoff value.

One problem that arises in defining MINIMAX as a recursive procedure is that it needs to return not one but two results:

- The backed-up value of the path it chooses.

- The path itself. We return the entire path even though probably only the first element, representing the best move from the current position, is actually needed.

We assume that MINIMAX returns a structure containing both results and that we have two functions, VALUE and PATH, that extract the separate components.

Since we define the MINIMAX procedure as a recursive function, we must also specify how it is to be called initially. It takes three parameters, a board position, the current depth of the search, and the player to move. So the initial call to compute the best move from the position CURRENT should be

---

[2]This may be a bit confusing, but it need not be. In all the examples in this chapter so far (including Figures 12.2 and 12.3), we have assumed that all values of STATIC are from the point of view of the initial (maximizing) player. It turns out to be easier when defining the algorithm, though, to let STATIC alternate perspectives so that we do not need to write separate procedures for the two levels. It is easy to modify STATIC for this purpose; we merely compute the value of *Position* from PLAYER-ONE's perspective, then invert the value if STATIC's parameter is PLAYER-TWO.

> MINIMAX(CURRENT,0,PLAYER-ONE)

if PLAYER-ONE is to move, or

> MINIMAX(CURRENT,0,PLAYER-TWO)

if PLAYER-TWO is to move.

Algorithm: MINIMAX(Position, Depth, Player)

1. If DEEP-ENOUGH(*Position*, *Depth*), then return the structure

   VALUE = STATIC(*Position*, *Player*);
   PATH = nil

   This indicates that there is no path from this node and that its value is that determined by the static evaluation function.

2. Otherwise, generate one more ply of the tree by calling the function MOVE-GEN(*Position*, *Player*) and setting SUCCESSORS to the list it returns.

3. If SUCCESSORS is empty, then there are no moves to be made, so return the structure that would have been returned if DEEP-ENOUGH had returned true.

4. If SUCCESSORS is not empty, then examine each element in turn and keep track of the best one. This is done as follows.

   Initialize BEST-SCORE to the minimum value that STATIC can return. It will be updated to reflect the best score that can be achieved by an element of SUCCESSORS.

   For each element SUCC of SUCCESSORS, do the following:

   (a) Set RESULT-SUCC to

   MINIMAX(SUCC, *Depth* + 1, OPPOSITE(*Player*))[3]

   This recursive call to MINIMAX will actually carry out the exploration of SUCC.

   (b) Set NEW-VALUE to $-$VALUE(RESULT-SUCC). This will cause it to reflect the merits of the position from the opposite perspective from that of the next lower level.

   (c) If NEW-VALUE > BEST-SCORE, then we have found a successor that is better than any that have been examined so far. Record this by doing the following:

      i. Set BEST-SCORE to NEW-VALUE.

      ii. The best known path is now from CURRENT to SUCC and then on to the appropriate path down from SUCC as determined by the recursive call to MINIMAX. So set BEST-PATH to the result of attaching SUCC to the front of PATH(RESULT-SUCC).

---

[3]OPPOSITE is a function that returns PLAYER-TWO when given PLAYER-ONE, and PLAYER-ONE when given PLAYER-TWO.

5. Now that all the successors have been examined, we know the value of Position as well as which path to take from it. So return the structure

    VALUE = BEST-SCORE
    PATH = BEST-PATH

When the initial call to MINIMAX returns, the best move from CURRENT is the first element on PATH. To see how this procedure works, you should trace its execution for the game tree shown in Figure 12.2.

The MINIMAX procedure just described is very simple. But its performance can be improved significantly with a few refinements. Some of these are described in the next few sections.

12.3   Adding Alpha-Beta Cutoffs

Recall that the minimax procedure is a depth-first process. One path is explored as far as time allows, the static evaluation function is applied to the game positions at the last step of the path, and the value can then be passed up the path one level at a time. One of the good things about depth-first procedures is that their efficiency can often be improved by using branch-and-bound techniques in which partial solutions that are clearly worse than known solutions can be abandoned early. We described a straightforward application of this technique to the traveling salesman problem in Section 2.2.1. For that problem, all that was required was storage of the length of the best path found so far. If a later partial path outgrew that bound, it was abandoned. But just as it was necessary to modify our search procedure slightly to handle both maximizing and minimizing players, it is also necessary to modify the branch-and-bound strategy to include two bounds, one for each of the players. This modified strategy is called *alpha-beta pruning*. It requires the maintenance of two threshold values, one representing a lower bound on the value that a maximizing node may ultimately be assigned (we call this *alpha*) and another representing an upper bound on the value that a minimizing node may be assigned (this we call *beta*).

To see how the alpha-beta procedure works, consider the example shown in Figure 12.4.[4] After examining node F, we know that the opponent is guaranteed a score of −5 or less at C (since the opponent is the minimizing player). But we also know that we are guaranteed a score of 3 or greater at node A, which we can achieve if we move to B. Any other move that produces a score of less than 3 is worse than the move to B, and we can ignore it. After examining only F, we are sure that a move to C is worse (it will be less than or equal to −5) regardless of the score of node G. Thus we need not bother to explore node G at all. Of course, cutting out one node may not appear to justify the expense of keeping track of the limits and checking them, but if we were exploring this tree to six ply, then we would have eliminated not a single node but an entire tree three ply deep.

To see how the two thresholds, alpha and beta, can both be used, consider the example shown in Figure 12.5. In searching this tree, the entire subtree headed by B is searched, and we discover that at A we can expect a score of at least 3. When this

---

[4]In this figure, we return to the use of a single STATIC function from the point of view of the maximizing player.

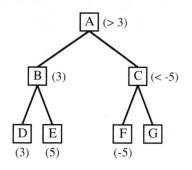

Maximizing ply

Minimizing ply

Figure 12.4: An Alpha Cutoff

alpha value is passed down to F, it will enable us to skip the exploration of L. Let's see why. After K is examined, we see that I is guaranteed a maximum score of 0, which means that F is guaranteed a minimum of 0. But this is less than alpha's value of 3, so no more branches of I need be considered. The maximizing player already knows not to choose to move to C and then to I since, if that move is made, the resulting score will be no better than 0 and a score of 3 can be achieved by moving to B instead. Now let's see how the value of beta can be used. After cutting off further exploration of I, J is examined, yielding a value of 5, which is assigned as the value of F (since it is the maximum of 5 and 0). This value becomes the value of beta at node C. It indicates that C is guaranteed to get a 5 or less. Now we must expand G. First M is examined and it has a value of 7, which is passed back to G as its tentative value. But now 7 is compared to beta (5). It is greater, and the player whose turn it is at node C is trying to minimize. So this player will not choose G, which would lead to a score of at least 7, since there is an alternative move to F, which will lead to a score of 5. Thus it is not necessary to explore any of the other branches of G.

From this example, we see that at maximizing levels, we can rule out a move early if it becomes clear that its value will be less than the current threshold, while at minimizing levels, search will be terminated if values that are greater than the current threshold are discovered. But ruling out a possible move by a maximizing player actually means cutting off the search at a minimizing level. Look again at the example in Figure 12.4. Once we determine that C is a bad move from A, we cannot bother to explore G, or any other paths, at the minimizing level below C. So the way alpha and beta are actually used is that search at a minimizing level can be terminated when a value less than alpha is discovered, while a search at a maximizing level can be terminated when a value greater than beta has been found. Cutting off search at a maximizing level when a high value is found may seem counterintuitive at first, but if you keep in mind that we only get to a particular node at a maximizing level if the minimizing player at the level above chooses it, then it makes sense.

Having illustrated the operation of alpha-beta pruning with examples, we can now explore how the MINIMAX procedure described in Section 12.2 can be modified to exploit this technique. Notice that at maximizing levels, only beta is used to determine whether to cut off the search, and at minimizing levels only alpha is used. But at maximizing levels alpha must also be known since when a recursive call is made

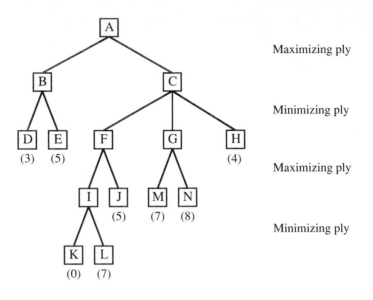

Figure 12.5: Alpha and Beta Cutoffs

to MINIMAX, a minimizing level is created, which needs access to alpha. So at maximizing levels alpha must be known not so that it can be used but so that it can be passed down the tree. The same is true of minimizing levels with respect to beta. Each level must receive both values, one to use and one to pass down for the next level to use.

The MINIMAX procedure as it stands does not need to treat maximizing and minimizing levels differently since it simply negates evaluations each time it changes levels. It would be nice if a comparable technique for handling alpha and beta could be found so that it would still not be necessary to write separate procedures for the two players. This turns out to be easy to do. Instead of referring to alpha and beta, MINIMAX uses two values, USE-THRESH and PASS-THRESH. USE-THRESH is used to compute cutoffs. PASS-THRESH is merely passed to the next level as its USE-THRESH. Of course, USE-THRESH must also be passed to the next level, but it will be passed as PASS-THRESH so that it can be passed to the third level down as USE-THRESH again, and so forth. Just as values had to be negated each time they were passed across levels, so too must these thresholds be negated. This is necessary so that, regardless of the level of the search, a test for greater than will determine whether a threshold has been crossed. Now there need still be no difference between the code required at maximizing levels and that required at minimizing ones.

We have now described how alpha and beta values are passed down the tree. In addition, we must decide how they are to be set. To see how to do this, let's return first to the simple example of Figure 12.4. At a maximizing level, such as that of node A, alpha is set to be the value of the best successor that has yet been found. (Notice that although at maximizing levels it is beta that is used to determine cutoffs, it is alpha whose new value can be computed. Thus at any level, USE-THRESH will be checked for cutoffs and PASS-THRESH will be updated to be used later.) But if the maximizing node is not at the top of the tree, we must also consider the alpha value that was passed down from a higher node. To see how this works, look again at Figure 12.5 and consider what happens at node F. We assign the value 0 to node I on the basis of examining node K. This is so far the best successor of F. But from an earlier exploration of the subtree headed by B, alpha was set to 3 and passed down from A to F. Alpha should not be reset to 0 on the basis of node I. It should stay as 3 to reflect the best move found so far in the entire tree. Thus we see that at a maximizing level, alpha should be set to either the value it had at the next-highest maximizing level or the best value found at this level, whichever is greater. The corresponding statement can be made about beta at minimizing levels. In fact, what we want to say is that at any level, PASS-THRESH should always be the maximum of the value it inherits from above and the best move found at its level. If PASS-THRESH is updated, the new value should be propagated both down to lower levels and back up to higher ones so that it always reflects the best move found anywhere in the tree.

At this point, we notice that we are doing the same thing in computing PASS-THRESH that we did in MINIMAX to compute BEST-SCORE. We might as well eliminate BEST-SCORE and let PASS-THRESH serve in its place.

With these observations, we are in a position to describe the operation of the function MINIMAX-A-B, which requires four arguments, *Position, Depth, Use-Thresh*, and *Pass-Thresh*. The initial call, to choose a move for PLAYER-ONE from the position CURRENT, should be

> MINIMAX-A-B(CURRENT,
> > 0,
> > PLAYER-ONE,
> > maximum value STATIC can compute,
> > minimum value STATIC can compute)

These initial values for *Use-Thresh* and *Pass-Thresh* represent the worst values that each side could achieve.

Algorithm: MINIMAX-A-B(Position, Depth, Player, Use-Thresh, Pass-Thresh)

1. If DEEP-ENOUGH(*Position, Depth*), then return the structure

   VALUE = STATIC(*Position, Player*);
   PATH – nil

2. Otherwise, generate one more ply of the tree by calling the function MOVE-GEN(Position, Player) and setting SUCCESSORS to the list it returns.

3. If SUCCESSORS is empty, there are no moves to be made; return the same structure that would have been returned if DEEP-ENOUGH had returned TRUE.

4. If SUCCESSORS is not empty, then go through it, examining each element and keeping track of the best one. This is done as follows.

   For each element SUCC of SUCCESSORS:

(a) Set RESULT-SUCC to
    MINIMAX-A-B(SUCC, *Depth* + 1, OPPOSITE(*Player*),
       −*Pass-Thresh*, −*Use-Thresh*).

(b) Set NEW-VALUE to −VALUE(RESULT-SUCC).

(c) If NEW-VALUE > *Pass-Thresh*, then we have found a successor that is better than any that have been examined so far. Record this by doing the following.

    i. Set *Pass-Thresh* to NEW-VALUE.

    ii. The best known path is now from CURRENT to SUCC and then on to the appropriate path from SUCC as determined by the recursive call to MINIMAX-A-B. So set BEST-PATH to the result of attaching SUCC to the front of PATH(RESULT-SUCC).

(d) If *Pass-Thresh* (reflecting the current best value) is not better than *Use-Thresh*, then we should stop examining this branch. But both thresholds and values have been inverted. So if *Pass-Thresh* >= *Use-Thresh*, then return immediately with the value
    VALUE = *Pass-Thresh*
    PATH = BEST-PATH

5. Return the structure
   VALUE = *Pass-Thresh*
   PATH = BEST-PATH

The effectiveness of the alpha-beta procedure depends greatly on the order in which paths are examined. If the worst paths are examined first, then no cutoffs at all will occur. But, of course, if the best path were known in advance so that it could be guaranteed to be examined first, we would not need to bother with the search process. If, however, we knew how effective the pruning technique is in the perfect case, we would have an upper bound on its performance in other situations. It is possible to prove that if the nodes are perfectly ordered, then the number of terminal nodes considered by a search to depth d using alpha-beta pruning is approximately equal to twice the number of terminal nodes generated by a search to depth $d/2$ without alpha-beta [Knuth and Moore, 1975]. A doubling of the depth to which the search can be pursued is a significant gain. Even though all of this improvement cannot typically be realized, the alpha-beta technique is a significant improvement to the minimax search procedure. For a more detailed study of the average branching factor of the alpha-beta procedure, see Baudet [1978] and Pearl [1982].

The idea behind the alpha-beta procedure can be extended to cut off additional paths that appear to be at best only slight improvements over paths that have already been explored. In step 4(*d*), we cut off the search if the path we were exploring was not better than other paths already found. But consider the situation shown in Figure 12.6. After examining node G, we see that the best we can hope for if we make move C is a score of 3.2. We know that if we make move B we are guaranteed a score of 3. Since 3.2 is only very slightly better than 3, we should perhaps terminate our exploration of C now. We could then devote more time to exploring other parts of the tree where there may be more to gain. Terminating the exploration of a subtree that offers little possibility for improvement over other known paths is called a *futility cutoff*.

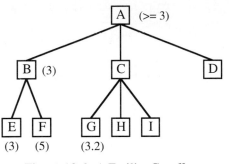

Figure 12.6: A Futility Cutoff

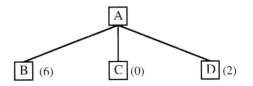

Figure 12.7: The Beginning of a Search

12.4 Additional Refinements

In addition to alpha-beta pruning, there are a variety of other modifications to the minimax procedure that can also improve its performance. Four of them are discussed briefly in this section, and we discuss one other important modification in the next section.

12.4.1 Waiting for Quiescence

As we suggested above, one of the factors that should sometimes be considered in determining when to stop going deeper in the search tree is whether the situation is relatively stable. Consider the tree shown in Figure 12.7. Suppose that when node B is expanded one more level, the result is that shown in Figure 12.8. When we looked one move ahead, our estimate of the worth of B changed drastically. This might happen, for example, in the middle of a piece exchange. The opponent has significantly improved the immediate appearance of his or her position by initiating a piece exchange. If we stop exploring the tree at this level, we assign the value −4 to B and therefore decide that B is not a good move.

   To make sure that such short-term measures do not unduly influence our choice of move, we should continue the search until no such drastic change occurs from one level to the next. This is called waiting for *quiescence*. If we do that, we might get the situation shown in Figure 12.9, in which the move to B again looks like a reasonable move for us to make since the other half of the piece exchange has occurred. A very general algorithm for quiescence can be found in Beal [1990].

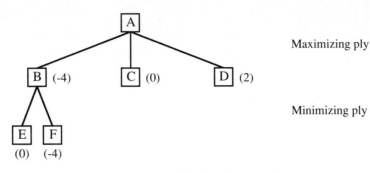

Figure 12.8: The Beginning of an Exchange

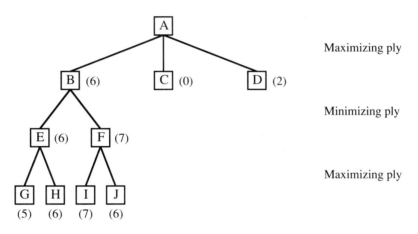

Figure 12.9: The Situation Calms Down

Waiting for quiescence helps in avoiding the *horizon effect*, in which an inevitable bad event can be delayed by various tactics until it does not appear in the portion of the game tree that minimax explores. The horizon effect can also influence a program's perception of good moves. The effect may make a move look good despite the fact that the move might be better if delayed past the horizon. Even with quiescence, all fixed-depth search programs are subject to subtle horizon effects.

12.4.2   Secondary Search

One good way of combating the horizon effect is to double-check a chosen move to make sure that a hidden pitfall does not exist a few moves farther away than the original search explored. Suppose we explore a game tree to an average depth of six ply and, on the basis of that search, choose a particular move. Although it would have been too expensive to have searched the entire tree to a depth of eight, it is not very expensive to search the single chosen branch an additional two levels to make sure that it still looks good. This technique is called *secondary search*.

One particularly successful form of secondary search is called *singular extensions*. The idea behind singular extensions is that if a leaf node is judged to be far superior to its siblings and if the value of the entire search depends critically on the correctness of that node's value, then the node is expanded one extra ply. This technique allows the search program to concentrate on tactical, forcing combinations. It employs a purely syntactic criterion, choosing interesting lines of play without recourse to any additional domain knowledge. The DEEP THOUGHT chess computer [Anantharaman *et al.*, 1990] has used singular extensions to great advantage, finding midgame mating combinations as long as thirty-seven moves, an impossible feat for fixed-depth minimax.

12.4.3 Using Book Moves

For complicated games taken as wholes, it is, of course, not feasible to select a move by simply looking up the current game configuration in a catalogue and extracting the correct move. The catalogue would be immense and no one knows how to construct it. But for some segments of some games, this approach is reasonable. In chess, for example, both opening sequences and endgame sequences are highly stylized. In these situations, the performance of a program can often be considerably enhanced if it is provided with a list of moves (called *book moves*) that should be made. The use of book moves in the opening sequences and endgames, combined with the use of the minimax search procedure for the midgame, provides a good example of the way that knowledge and search can be combined in a single program to produce more effective results than could either technique on its own.

12.4.4 Alternatives to Minimax

Even with the refinements above, minimax still has some problematic aspects. For instance, it relies heavily on the assumption that the opponent will always choose the optimal move. This assumption is acceptable in winning situations where a move that is guaranteed to be good for us can be found. But, as suggested in Berliner [1977], in a losing situation it might be better to take the risk that the opponent will make a mistake. Suppose we must choose between two moves, both of which, if the opponent plays perfectly, lead to situations that are very bad for us, but one is slightly less bad than the other. But further suppose that the less promising move could lead to a very good situation for us if the opponent makes a single mistake. Although the minimax procedure would choose the guaranteed bad move, we ought instead to choose the other one, which is probably slightly worse but possibly a lot better. A similar situation arises when one move appears to be only slightly more advantageous than another, assuming that the opponent plays perfectly. It might be better to choose the less advantageous move if it could lead to a significantly superior situation if the opponent makes a mistake. To make these decisions well, we must have access to a model of the individual opponent's playing style so that the likelihood of various mistakes can be estimated. But this is very hard to provide.

As a mechanism for propagating estimates of position strengths up the game tree, minimax stands on shaky theoretical grounds. Nau [1980] and Pearl [1983] have demonstrated that for certain classes of game trees, e.g., uniform trees with random terminal values, the deeper the search, the *poorer* the result obtained by minimaxing.

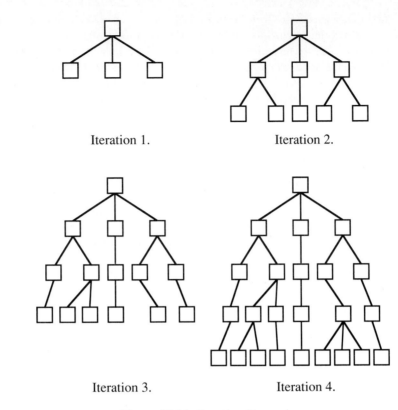

Figure 12.10: Iterative Deepening

This "pathological" behavior of amplifying error-prone heuristic estimates has not been observed in actual game-playing programs, however. It seems that game trees containing won positions and nonrandom distributions of heuristic estimates provide environments that are conducive to minimaxing.

12.5   Iterative Deepening

A number of ideas for searching two-player game trees have led to new algorithms for single-agent heuristic search, of the type described in Chapter 3. One such idea is *iterative deepening*, originally used in a program called CHESS 4.5 [Slate and Atkin, 1977]. Rather than searching to a fixed depth in the game tree, CHESS 4.5 first searched only a single ply, applying its static evaluation function to the result of each of its possible moves. It then initiated a new minimax search, this time to a depth of two ply. This was followed by a three-ply search, then a four-ply search, etc. The name "iterative deepening" derives from the fact that on each iteration, the tree is searched one level deeper. Figure 12.10 depicts this process.

On the face of it, this process seems wasteful. Why should we be interested in any iteration except the final one? There are several reasons. First, game-playing programs are subject to time constraints. For example, a chess program may be required to complete all its moves within two hours. Since it is impossible to know in advance how long a fixed-depth tree search will take (because of variations in pruning efficiency and the need for selective search), a program may find itself running out of time. With iterative deepening, the current search can be aborted at any time and the best move found by the previous iteration can be played. Perhaps more importantly, previous iterations can provide invaluable move-ordering constraints. If one move was judged to be superior to its siblings in a previous iteration, it can be searched first in the next iteration. With effective ordering, the alpha-beta procedure can prune many more branches, and total search time can be decreased drastically. This allows more time for deeper iterations.

Years after CHESS 4.5's success with iterative deepening, it was noticed [Korf, 1985a] that the technique could also be applied effectively to single-agent search to solve problems like the 8-puzzle. In Section 2.2.1, we compared two types of uninformed search, depth-first search and breadth-first search. Depth-first search was efficient in terms of space but required some cutoff depth in order to force backtracking when a solution was not found. Breadth-first search was guaranteed to find the shortest solution path but required inordinate amounts of space because all leaf nodes had to be kept in memory. An algorithm called depth-first iterative deepening (DFID) combines the best aspects of depth-first and breadth-first search.

Algorithm: Depth-First Iterative Deepening

1. Set SEARCH-DEPTH = 1.

2. Conduct a depth first search to a depth of SEARCH-DEPTH. If a solution path is found, then return it.

3. Otherwise, increment SEARCH-DEPTH by 1 and go to step 2.

Clearly, DFID will find the shortest solution path to the goal state. Moreover, the maximum amount of memory used by DFID is proportional to the number of nodes in that solution path. The only disturbing fact is that all iterations but the final one are essentially wasted. However, this is not a serious problem. The reason is that most of the activity during any given iteration occurs at the leaf-node level. Assuming a complete tree, we see that there are as many leaf nodes at level n as there are total nodes in levels 1 through n. Thus, the work expended during the nth iteration is roughly equal to the work expended during all previous iterations. This means that DFID is only slower than depth-first search by a constant factor. The problem with depth-first search is that there is no way to know in advance how deep the solution lies in the search space. DFID avoids the problem of choosing cutoffs without sacrificing efficiency, and, in fact, DFID is the optimal algorithm (in terms of space and time) for uninformed search.

But what about informed, heuristic search? Iterative deepening can also be used to improve the performance of the A* search algorithm [Korf, 1985a]. Since the major practical difficulty with A* is the large amount of memory it requires to maintain the search node lists, iterative deepening can be of considerable service.

Algorithm: Iterative-Deepening-A*

1. Set THRESHOLD = the heuristic evaluation of the start state.

2. Conduct a depth-first search, pruning any branch when its total cost function $(g + h')$ exceeds THRESHOLD.[5] If a solution path is found during the search, return it.

3. Otherwise, increment THRESHOLD by the minimum amount it was exceeded during the previous step, and then go to Step 2.

Like A*, Iterative-Deepening-A* (IDA*) is guaranteed to find an optimal solution, provided that h' is an admissible heuristic. Because of its depth-first search technique, IDA* is very efficient with respect to space. IDA* was the first heuristic search algorithm to find optimal solution paths for the 15-puzzle (a 4x4 version of the 8-puzzle) within reasonable time and space constraints.

12.6   References on Specific Games

In this chapter we have discussed search-based techniques for game playing. We discussed the basic minimax algorithm and then introduced a series of refinements to it. But even with these refinements, it is still difficult to build good programs to play difficult games. Every game, like every AI task, requires a careful combination of search and knowledge.

Chess

Research on computer chess actually predates the field we call artificial intelligence. Shannon [1950] was the first to propose a method for automating the game, and two early chess programs were written by Greenblatt *et al.* [1967] and Newell and Simon [1972].

Chess provides a well-defined laboratory for studying the trade-off between knowledge and search. The more knowledge a program has, the less searching it needs to do. On the other hand, the deeper the search, the less knowledge is required. Human chess players use a great deal of knowledge and very little search—they typically investigate only 100 branches or so in deciding a move. A computer, on the other hand, is capable of evaluating millions of branches. Its chess knowledge is usually limited to a static evaluation function. Deep-searching chess programs have been calibrated on exercise problems in the chess literature and have even discovered errors in the official human analyses of the problems.

A chess player, whether human or machine, carries a numerical rating that tells how well it has performed in competition with other players. This rating lets us evaluate in an absolute sense the relative trade-offs between search and knowledge in this domain. The recent trend in chess-playing programs is clearly away from knowledge and toward faster brute force search. It turns out that deep, full-width search (with pruning) is sufficient for competing at very high levels of chess. Two examples of highly rated chess machines are HITECH [Berliner and Ebeling, 1989] and DEEP THOUGHT [Anantharaman *et al.*, 1990], both of which have beaten human grandmasters and both

---

[5] Recall that g stands for the cost so far in reaching the current node, and h' stands for the heuristic estimate of the distance from the node to the goal.

of which use custom-built parallel hardware to speed up legal move generation and heuristic evaluation.

Checkers

Work on computer checkers began with Samuel [1963]. Samuel's program had an interesting learning component which allowed its performance to improve with experience. Ultimately, the program was able to beat its author. We look more closely at the learning mechanisms used by Samuel in Chapter 17.

Go

Go is a very difficult game to play by machine since the average branching factor of the game tree is very high. Brute force search, therefore, is not as effective as it is in chess. Human go players make up for their inability to search deeply by using a great deal of knowledge about the game. It is probable that go-playing programs must also be knowledge-based, since today's brute-force programs cannot compete with humans. For a discussion of some of the issues involved, see Wilcox [1988].

Backgammon

Unlike chess, checkers, and go, a backgammon program must choose its moves with incomplete information about what may happen. If all the possible dice rolls are considered, the number of alternatives at each level of the search is huge. With current computational power, it is impossible to search more than a few ply ahead. Such a search will not expose the strengths and weaknesses of complex blocking positions, so knowledge-intensive methods must be used. One program that uses such methods is BKG Berliner [1980]. BKG actually does no searching at all but relies instead on positional understanding and understanding of how its goals should change for various phases of play. Like its chess-playing cousins, BKG has reached high levels of play, even beating a human world champion in a short match.

NEUROGAMMON [Tesauro and Sejnowski, 1989] is another interesting backgammon program. It is based on a neural network model that learns from experience. Neurogammon is one of the few competitive game-playing programs that relies heavily on automatic learning.

Othello

Othello is a popular board game that is played on an 8x8 grid with bi-colored pieces. Although computer programs have already achieved world-championship level play [Rosenbloom, 1982; Lee and Mahajan, 1990], humans continue to study the game and international tournaments are held regularly. Computers are not permitted to compete in these tournaments, but it is believed that the best programs are stronger than the best humans. High-performance Othello programs rely on fast brute-force search and table lookup.

The Othello experience may shed some light on the future of computer chess. Will top human players in the future study chess games between World Champion computers in the same way that they study classic human grandmaster matches today? Perhaps it will turn out that the different search versus knowledge trade-offs made by humans and computers will make it impossible for either of them to benefit from the experiences of the other.

Others

Levy [1988] contains a number of classic papers on computer game playing. The papers cover the games listed above as well as bridge, scrabble, dominoes, go-moku, hearts, and poker.

12.7   Exercises

1. Consider the following game tree in which static scores are all from the first player's point of view:

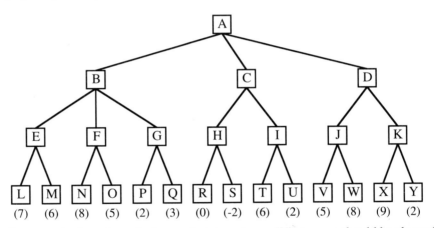

Suppose the first player is the maximizing player. What move should be chosen?

2. In the game tree shown in the previous problem, what nodes would not need to be examined using the alpha-beta pruning procedure?

3. Why does the search in game-playing programs always proceed forward from the current position rather than backward from a goal state?

4. Is the minimax procedure a depth-first or breadth-first search procedure?

5. The minimax algorithm we have described searches a game tree. But for some games, it might be better to search a graph and to check, each time a position is generated, if it has been generated and evaluated before. Under what circumstances would this be a good idea? Modify the minimax procedure to do this.

6. How would the minimax procedure have to be modified to be used by a program playing a three- or four-person game rather than a two-person one?

7. In the context of the search procedure described in Section 12.3, does the ordering of the list of successor positions created by MOVEGEN matter? Why or why not? If it does matter, how much does it matter (i.e., how much effort is reasonable for ordering it)?

8. Implement the alpha-beta search procedure. Use it to play a simple game such as tic-tac-toe.

9. Apply DFID to the water jug problem of Section 2.1.

Chapter 13

Planning

In order to solve most nontrivial problems, it is necessary to combine some of the basic problem-solving strategies discussed in Chapter 3 with one or more of the knowledge representation mechanisms that have just been presented. It is often also useful to divide the problem that must be solved into smaller pieces and to solve those pieces separately, to the extent that that is possible. In this chapter, we describe several techniques for doing this in order to construct plans for solving hard problems.

13.1 Overview

In Chapter 2, we described the process of problem solving as a search through a state space in which each point corresponded to a situation that might arise. The search started with an initial situation and performed a sequence of allowable operations until a situation corresponding to a goal was reached. Then, in Chapter 3, we described a variety of ways of moving through such a search space in an attempt to find a solution to a particular problem. For example, the A* algorithm provides a way of conducting a best-first search through a graph representing a problem space. Each node that is examined in the A* algorithm represents a description of a complete problem state, and each operator describes a way of changing the total state description. For simple problems, such as, say, the 8-puzzle, manipulating the complete state description at one time is easy and reasonable.

However, for more complicated problem domains, it becomes important to be able to work on small pieces of a problem separately and then to combine the partial solutions at the end into a complete problem solution. Unless we can do this, the number of combinations of the states of the components of a problem becomes too large to handle in the amount of time available. There are two ways in which it is important to be able to perform this decomposition.

First of all, we must avoid having to recompute the entire problem state when we move from one state to the next. Instead, we want to consider only that part of the state that may have changed. For example, if we move from one room to another, this does not affect the locations of the doors and the windows in the two rooms. The *frame problem*, which is the problem of how to determine which things change and which do not, becomes increasingly important as the complexity of the problem state increases. It is not difficult to figure out how the state of the 8-puzzle should change after every move, nor is it a lot of work to record explicitly a new copy of the state with the appropriate changes made. Our rules for moving from one state to another can simply describe how one entire board position should be transformed into another.

But if we are considering the problem of guiding a robot around an ordinary house, the situation is much more complex. The description of a single state is very large since it must describe the location of each object in the house as well as that of the robot. A given action on the part of the robot will change only a small part of the total state. If the robot pushes a table across the room, then the locations of the table and all of the objects that were on it will change. But the locations of the other objects in the house will not. Instead of writing rules that describe transformations of one entire state into another, we would like to write rules that describe only the affected parts of the state description. The rest of the description can then be assumed to stay constant.

The second important way in which decomposition can make the solution of hard problems easier is the division of a single difficult problem into several, hopefully easier, subproblems. The AO* algorithm provides a way of doing this when it is possible to decompose the original problem into completely separate subproblems. Although this is sometimes possible, it often is not. Instead, many problems can be viewed as *nearly decomposable* [Simon, 1981], by which we mean that they can be divided into subproblems that have only a small amount of interaction. For example, suppose that we want to move all the furniture out of a room. This problem can be decomposed into a set of smaller problems, each involving moving one piece of furniture out of the room. Within each of these subproblems, considerations such as removing drawers can be addressed separately for each piece of furniture. But if there is a bookcase behind a couch, then we must move the couch before we can move the bookcase. To solve such nearly decomposable problems, we would like a method that enables us to work on each subproblem separately, using techniques such as the ones we have already studied, and then to record potential interactions among subproblems and to handle them appropriately.

Several methods for doing these two kinds of decomposition have been proposed and we investigate them in this chapter. These methods focus on ways of decomposing the original problem into appropriate subparts and on ways of recording and handling interactions among the subparts as they are detected during the problem-solving process. The use of these methods is often called *planning*.

In everyday usage, the word *planning* refers to the process of computing several steps of a problem-solving procedure before executing any of them. When we describe computer problem-solving behavior, the distinction between planning and doing fades a bit since rarely can the computer actually do much of anything besides plan. In solving the 8-puzzle, for example, it cannot actually push any tiles around. So when we discussed the computer solution of the 8-puzzle problem, what we were really doing was outlining the way the computer might generate a plan for solving it. For problems such as the 8-puzzle, the distinction between planning and doing is unimportant.

But in other situations, the distinction may be critical. Recall that in Chapter 2 one of the problem characteristics we discussed was whether solution steps could be ignored or undone if they prove unwise. If they can, then the process of planning a complete solution can proceed just as would an attempt to find a solution by actually trying particular actions. If a dead-end path is detected, then a new one can be explored by backtracking to the last choice point. So, for example, in solving the 8-puzzle, a computer could look for a solution plan in the same way as a person who was actually trying to solve the problem by moving tiles on a board. If solution steps in the real world cannot be ignored or undone, though, planning becomes extremely important. Although real world steps may be irrevocable, computer simulation of those steps is not. So we can circumvent the constraints of the real world by looking for a complete solution in a simulated world in which backtracking is allowed. After we find a solution, we can execute it in the real world.

The success of this approach, however, hinges on another characteristic of a problem's domain: Is its universe predictable? If we look for a solution to a problem by actually carrying out sequences of operations, then at any step of the process we can be sure of the outcome of that step; it is whatever happened. But in an unpredictable universe, we cannot know the outcome of a solution step if we are only simulating it by computer. At best, we can consider the *set* of possible outcomes, possibly in some order according to the likelihood of the outcomes occurring. But then when we produce a plan and attempt to execute it, we must be prepared in case the actual outcome is not what we expected. If the plan included paths for all possible outcomes of each step, then we can simply traverse the paths that turn out to be appropriate. But often there are a great many possible outcomes, most of which are highly unlikely. In such situations, it would be a great waste of effort to formulate plans for all contingencies.

Instead, we have two choices. We can just take things one step at a time and not really try to plan ahead. This is the approach that is taken in *reactive systems*, which we will describe in Section 13.7. Our other choice is to produce a plan that is *likely* to succeed. But then what should we do if it fails? One possibility is simply to throw away the rest of the plan and start the planning process over, using the current situation as the new initial state. Sometimes, this is a reasonable thing to do.

But often the unexpected consequence does not invalidate the entire rest of the plan. Perhaps a small change, such as an additional step, is all that is necessary to make it possible for the rest of the plan to be useful. Suppose, for example, that we have a plan for baking an angel food cake. It involves separating some eggs. While carrying out the plan, we turn out to be slightly clumsy and one of the egg yolks falls into the dish of whites. We do not need to create a completely new plan (unless we decide to settle for some other kind of cake). Instead, we simply redo the egg-separating step until we get it right and then continue with the rest of the plan. This is particularly true for decomposable or nearly decomposable problems. If the final plan is really a composite of many smaller plans for solving a set of subproblems, then if one step of the plan fails, the only part of the remaining plan that can be affected is the rest of the plan for solving that subproblem. The rest of the plan is unrelated to that step. If the problem was only partially decomposable, then any subplans that interact with the affected one may also be affected. So, just as it was important during the planning process to keep track of interactions as they arise, it is important to record information about interactions along with the final plan so that if unexpected events occur at execution time, the interactions can be considered during replanning.

Hardly any aspect of the real world is completely predictable. So we must always be prepared to have plans fail. But, as we have just seen, if we have built our plan by decomposing our problem into as many separate (or nearly separate) subproblems as possible, then the impact on our plan of the failure of one particular step may be quite local. Thus we have an additional argument in favor of the problem-decomposition approach to problem solving. In addition to reducing the combinatorial complexity of the problem-solving process, it also reduces the complexity of the dynamic plan revision process that may be required during the execution of a plan in an unpredictable world (such as the one in which we live).

In order to make it easy to patch up plans if they go awry at execution time, we will find that it is useful during the planning process not only to record the steps that are to be performed but also to associate with each step the reasons why it must be performed. Then, if a step fails, it is easy, using techniques for dependency-directed backtracking, to determine which of the remaining parts of the plan were dependent on it and so may need to be changed. If the plan-generation process proceeds backward from the desired goal state, then it is easy to record this dependency information. If, on the other hand, it proceeded forward from the start state, determining the necessary dependencies may be difficult. For this reason and because, for most problems, the branching factor is smaller going backward, most planning systems work primarily in a *goal-directed* mode in which they search backward from a goal state to an achievable initial state.

In the next several sections, a variety of planning techniques are presented. All of them, except the last, are problem-solving methods that rely heavily on problem decomposition. They deal (to varying degrees of success) with the inevitable interactions among the components that they generate.

13.2   An Example Domain: The Blocks World

The techniques we are about to discuss can be applied in a wide variety of task domains, and they have been. But to make it easy to compare the variety of methods we consider, we should find it useful to look at all of them in a single domain that is complex enough that the need for each of the mechanisms is apparent yet simple enough that easy-to-follow examples can be found. The blocks world is such a domain. There is a flat surface on which blocks can be placed. There are a number of square blocks, all the same size. They can be stacked one upon another. There is a robot arm that can manipulate the blocks. The actions it can perform include:

- UNSTACK(A, B)—Pick up block A from its current position on block B. The arm must be empty and block A must have no blocks on top of it.

- STACK(A, B)—Place block A on block B. The arm must already be holding A and the surface of B must be clear.

- PICKUP(A)—Pick up block A from the table and hold it. The arm must be empty and there must be nothing on top of block A.

- PUTDOWN(A)—Put block A down on the table. The arm must have been holding block A.

Notice that in the world we have described, the robot arm can hold only one block at a time. Also, since all blocks are the same size, each block can have at most one other block directly on top of it.[1]

In order to specify both the conditions under which an operation may be performed and the results of performing it, we need to use the following predicates:

- ON(A, B)—Block A is on block B.

- ONTABLE(A)—Block A is on the table.

- CLEAR(A)—There is nothing on top of block A.

- HOLDING(A)—The arm is holding block A.

- ARMEMPTY—The arm is holding nothing.

Various logical statements are true in this blocks world. For example,

$$[\exists x : \text{HOLDING}(x)] \rightarrow \neg\text{ARMEMPTY}$$
$$\forall x : \text{ONTABLE}(x) \rightarrow \neg\exists y : \text{ON}(x, y)$$
$$\forall x : [\neg\exists y : \text{ON}(y, x)] \rightarrow \text{CLEAR}(x)$$

The first of these statements says simply that if the arm is holding anything, then it is not empty. The second says that if a block is on the table, then it is not also on another block. The third says that any block with no blocks on it is clear.

13.3 Components of a Planning System

In problem-solving systems based on the elementary techniques discussed in Chapter 3, it was necessary to perform each of the following functions:

- Choose the best rule to apply next based on the best available heuristic information.

- Apply the chosen rule to compute the new problem state that arises from its application.

- Detect when a solution has been found.

- Detect dead ends so that they can be abandoned and the system's effort directed in more fruitful directions.

In the more complex systems we are about to explore, techniques for doing each of these tasks are also required. In addition, a fifth operation is often important:

- Detect when an almost correct solution has been found and employ special techniques to make it totally correct.

Before we discuss specific planning methods, we need to look briefly at the ways in which each of these five things can be done.

---

[1] Actually, by careful alignment, two blocks could be placed on top of one, but we ignore that possibility.

ON(A, B, S0) ∧
                       ONTABLE(B, S0) ∧
                       CLEAR(A, S0)

Figure 13.1: A Simple Blocks World Description

Choosing Rules to Apply

The most widely used technique for selecting appropriate rules to apply is first to isolate a set of differences between the desired goal state and the current state and then to identify those rules that are relevant to reducing those differences. If several rules are found, a variety of other heuristic information can be exploited to choose among them. This technique is based on the means-ends analysis method (recall Chapter 3). For example, if our goal is to have a white fence around our yard and we currently have a brown fence, we would select operators whose result involves a change of color of an object. If, on the other hand, we currently have no fence, we must first consider operators that involve constructing wooden objects.

Applying Rules

In the simple systems we have previously discussed, applying rules was easy. Each rule simply specified the problem state that would result from its application. Now, however, we must be able to deal with rules that specify only a small part of the complete problem state. There are many ways of doing this.

One way is to describe, for each action, each of the changes it makes to the state description. In addition, some statement that everything else remains unchanged is also necessary. An example of this approach is described in Green [1969]. In this system, a given state was described by a set of predicates representing the facts that were true in that state. Each distinct state was represented explicitly as part of the predicate. For example, Figure 13.1 shows how a state, called S0, of a simple blocks world problem could be represented.

The manipulation of these state descriptions was done using a resolution theorem prover. So, for example, the effect of the operator UNSTACK(x, y) could be described by the following axiom. (In all the axioms given in this section, all variables are universally quantified unless otherwise indicated.)

$$[\text{CLEAR}(x, s) \wedge \text{ON}(x, y, s)] \rightarrow$$
$$[\text{HOLDING}(x, \text{DO}(\text{UNSTACK}(x, y), s)) \wedge$$
$$\text{CLEAR}(y, \text{DO}(\text{UNSTACK}(x, y), s))]$$

Here, DO is a function that specifies, for a given state and a given action, the new state that results from the execution of the action. The axiom states that if CLEAR(x) and ON(x, y) both hold in state s, then HOLDING(x) and CLEAR(y) will hold in the state that results from DOing an UNSTACK(x, y), starting in state s.

If we execute UNSTACK(A, B) in state S0 as defined above, then we can prove, using our assertions about S0 and our axiom about UNSTACK, that in the state that results from the unstacking operation (we call this state S1),

HOLDING(A, S1) $\wedge$ CLEAR(B, S1)

But what else do we know about the situation in state S1? Intuitively, we know that B is still on the table. But with what we have so far, we cannot derive it. To enable us to do so, we need also to provide a set of rules, called *frame axioms*, that describe components of the state that are not affected by each operator. So, for example, we need to say that

ONTABLE(z, s) $\rightarrow$ ONTABLE(z, DO(UNSTACK(x, y), s))

This axiom says that the ONTABLE relation is never affected by the UNSTACK operator. We also need to say that the ON relation is only affected by the UNSTACK operator if the blocks involved in the ON relation are the same ones involved in the UNSTACK operation. This can be said as

[ON(m, n, s) $\wedge\neg$ EQUAL(m, x)] $\rightarrow$ ON(m, n, DO(UNSTACK(x, y), s))

The advantage of this approach is that a single mechanism, resolution, can perform all the operations that are required on state descriptions. The price we pay for this, however, is that the number of axioms that are required becomes very large if the problem-state descriptions are complex. For example, suppose that we are interested not only in the positions of our blocks but also in their color. Then, for every operation (except possibly PAINT), we would need an axiom such as the following:

COLOR(x, c, s) $\rightarrow$ COLOR(x, c, DO(UNSTACK(y, z), s))

To handle complex problem domains, we need a mechanism that does not require a large number of explicit frame axioms. One such mechanism is that used by the early robot problem-solving system STRIPS [Fikes and Nilsson, 1971] and its descendants. In this approach, each operation is described by a list of new predicates that the operator causes to become true and a list of old predicates that it causes to become false. These two lists are called the ADD and DELETE lists, respectively. A third list must also be specified for each operator. This PRECONDITION list contains those predicates that must be true for the operator to be applied. The frame axioms of Green's system are specified implicitly in STRIPS. Any predicate not included on either the ADD or DELETE list of an operator is assumed to be unaffected by it. This means that, in specifying each operator, we need not consider aspects of the domain that are unrelated to it. Thus we need say nothing about the relationship of UNSTACK to COLOR. Of course, this means that some mechanism other than simple theorem proving must be used to compute complete state descriptions after operations have been performed.

STRIPS-style operators that correspond to the blocks world operations we have been discussing are shown in Figure 13.2. Notice that for simple rules such as these, the PRECONDITION list is often identical to the DELETE list. In order to pick up a block, the robot arm must be empty; as soon as it picks up a block, it is no longer empty. But preconditions are not always deleted. For example, in order for the arm to pick up a block, the block must have no other blocks on top of it. After it is picked up, it still

STACK(x, y)

   P: CLEAR(y) ∧ HOLDING(x)
   D: CLEAR(y) ∧ HOLDING(x)
   A: ARMEMPTY ∧ ON(x, y)

UNSTACK(x, y)

   P: ON(x, y) ∧ CLEAR(x) ∧ ARMEMPTY
   D: ON(x, y) ∧ ARMEMPTY
   A: HOLDING(x) ∧ CLEAR(y)

PICKUP(x)

   P: CLEAR(x) ∧ ONTABLE(x) ∧ ARMEMPTY
   D: ONTABLE(x) ∧ ARMEMPTY
   A: HOLDING(x)

PUTDOWN(x)

   P: HOLDING(x)
   D: HOLDING(x)
   A: ONTABLE(x) ∧ ARMEMPTY

Figure 13.2: STRIPS-Style Operators for the Blocks World

has no blocks on top of it. This is the reason that the PRECONDITION and DELETE lists must be specified separately.

By making the frame axioms implicit, we have greatly reduced the amount of information that must be provided for each operator. This means, among other things, that when a new attribute that objects might possess is introduced into the system, it is not necessary to go back and add a new axiom for each of the existing operators. But how can we actually achieve the effect of the use of the frame axioms in computing complete state descriptions? The first thing we notice is that for complex state descriptions, most of the state remains unchanged after each operation. But if we represent the state as an explicit part of each predicate, as was done in Green's system, then all that information must be deduced all over again for each state. To avoid that, we can drop the explicit state indicator from the individual predicates and instead simply update a single database of predicates so that it always describes the current state of the world. For example, if we start with the situation shown in Figure 13.1, we would describe it as

   ON(A, B) ∧ ONTABLE(B) ∧ CLEAR(A)

After applying the operator UNSTACK(A, B), our description of the world would be

   ONTABLE(B) ∧ CLEAR(A) ∧ CLEAR(B) ∧ HOLDING(A)

This is derived using the ADD and DELETE lists specified as part of the UNSTACK operator.

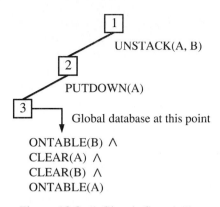

Figure 13.3: A Simple Search Tree

Simply updating a single state description works well as a way of keeping track of the effects of a given sequence of operators. But what happens during the process of searching for the correct operator sequence? If one incorrect sequence is explored, it must be possible to return to the original state so that a different one can be tried. But this is possible even if the global database describes the problem state at the current node of the search graph. All we need to do is record at each node the changes that were made to the global database as we passed through the node. Then, if we backtrack through that node, we can undo the changes. But the changes are described exactly in the ADD and DELETE lists of the operators that have been applied to move from one node to another. So we need only record, along each arc of the search graph, the operator that was applied. Figure 13.3 shows a small example of such a search tree and the corresponding global database. The initial state is the one shown in Figure 13.1 and described in **STRIPS** form above. Notice that we must specify not just the operator (e.g., UNSTACK) but also its arguments in order to be able to undo the changes later.

Now suppose that we want to explore a path different from the one we have just shown. First we backtrack through node 3 by *adding* each of the predicates in PUTDOWN's DELETE list to the global database and *deleting* each of the elements of PUTDOWN's ADD list. After doing that, the database contains

ONTABLE(B) ∧ CLEAR(A) ∧ CLEAR(B) ∧ HOLDING(A)

As we expected, this description is identical to the one we previously computed as the result of applying UNSTACK to the initial situation. If we repeat this process using the ADD and DELETE lists of UNSTACK, we derive a description identical to the one with which we started.

Because an implicit statement of the frame axioms is so important in complex problem domains, all the techniques we look at exploit STRIPS-style descriptions of the available operators.

Detecting a Solution

A planning system has succeeded in finding a solution to a problem when it has found a sequence of operators that transforms the initial problem state into the goal state. How will it know when this has been done? In simple problem-solving systems, this question is easily answered by a straightforward match of the state descriptions. But if entire states are not represented explicitly but rather are described by a set of relevant properties, then this problem becomes more complex. The way it can be solved depends on the way that state descriptions are represented. For any representational scheme that is used, it must be possible to reason with representations to discover whether one matches another. Recall that in Part II we discussed a variety of ways that complex objects could be represented as well as reasoning mechanisms for each representation. Any of those representations (or some combination of them) could be used to describe problem states. Then the corresponding reasoning mechanisms could be used to discover when a solution had been found.

One representational technique has served as the basis for many of the planning systems that have been built. It is predicate logic, which is appealing because of the deductive mechanisms that it provides. Suppose that, as part of our goal, we have the predicate $P(x)$. To see whether $P(x)$ is satisfied in some state, we ask whether we can prove $P(x)$ given the assertions that describe that state and the axioms that define the world model (such as the fact that if the arm is holding something, then it is not empty). If we can construct such a proof, then the problem-solving process terminates. If we cannot, then a sequence of operators that might solve the problem must be proposed. This sequence can then be tested in the same way as the initial state was by asking whether $P(x)$ can be proved from the axioms and the state description that was derived by applying the operators.

Detecting Dead Ends

As a planning system is searching for a sequence of operators to solve a particular problem, it must be able to detect when it is exploring a path that can never lead to a solution (or at least appears unlikely to lead to one). The same reasoning mechanisms that can be used to detect a solution can often be used for detecting a dead end.

If the search process is reasoning forward from the initial state, it can prune any path that leads to a state from which the goal state cannot be reached. For example, suppose we have a fixed supply of paint: some white, some pink, and some red. We want to paint a room so that it has light red walls and a white ceiling. We could produce light red paint by adding some white paint to the red. But then we could not paint the ceiling white. So this approach should be abandoned in favor of mixing the pink and red paints together. We can also prune paths that, although they do not preclude a solution, appear to be leading no closer to a solution than the place from which they started.

If the search process is reasoning backward from the goal state, it can also terminate a path either because it is sure that the initial state cannot be reached or because little progress is being made. In reasoning backward, each goal is decomposed into subgoals. Each of them, in turn, may lead to a set of additional subgoals. Sometimes it is easy to detect that there is no way that all the subgoals in a given set can be satisfied at once. For example, the robot arm cannot be both empty and holding a block. Any path that is attempting to make both of those goals true simultaneously can be pruned immediately. Other paths can be pruned because they lead nowhere. For example, if, in trying to satisfy goal A, the program eventually reduces its problem to the satisfaction of goal A as well as goals B and C, it has made little progress. It has produced a problem even harder than its original one, and the path leading to this problem should be abandoned.

Repairing an Almost Correct Solution

The kinds of techniques we are discussing are often useful in solving *nearly* decomposable problems. One good way of solving such problems is to assume that they are completely decomposable, proceed to solve the subproblems separately, and then check that when the subsolutions are combined, they do in fact yield a solution to the original problem. Of course, if they do, then nothing more need be done. If they do not, however, there are a variety of things that we can do. The simplest is just to throw out the solution, look for another one, and hope that it is better. Although this is simple, it may lead to a great deal of wasted effort.

A slightly better approach is to look at the situation that results when the sequence of operations corresponding to the proposed solution is executed and to compare that situation to the desired goal. In most cases, the difference between the two will be smaller than the difference between the initial state and the goal (assuming that the solution we found did some useful things). Now the problem-solving system can be called again and asked to find a way of eliminating this new difference. The first solution can then be combined with this second one to form a solution to the original problem.

An even better way to patch up an almost correct solution is to appeal to specific knowledge about what went wrong and then to apply a direct patch. For example, suppose that the reason that the proposed solution is inadequate is that one of its operators cannot be applied because at the point it should have been invoked, its preconditions were not satisfied. This might occur if the operator had two preconditions and the sequence of operations that makes the second one true undid the first one. But perhaps, if an attempt were made to satisfy the preconditions in the opposite order, this problem would not arise.

A still better way to patch up incomplete solutions is not really to patch them up at all but rather to leave them incompletely specified until the last possible moment. Then when as much information as possible is available, complete the specification in such a way that no conflicts arise. This approach can be thought of as a *least-commitment* strategy. It can be applied in a variety of ways. One is to defer deciding on the order in which operations will be performed. So, in our previous example, instead of arbitrarily choosing one order in which to satisfy a set of preconditions, we could leave the order unspecified until the very end. Then we would look at the effects of each of the subsolutions to determine the dependencies that exist among them. At that point, an ordering can be chosen.

13.4 Goal Stack Planning

One of the earliest techniques to be developed for solving compound goals that may interact was the use of a goal stack. This was the approach used by STRIPS. In this

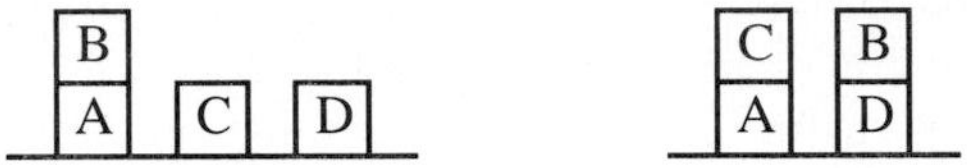

start: ON(B, A) ∧
ONTABLE(A) ∧
ONTABLE(C) ∧
ONTABLE(D) ∧
ARMEMPTY

goal: ON(C, A) ∧
ON(B, D) ∧
ONTABLE(A) ∧
ONTABLE(D)

Figure 13.4: A Very Simple Blocks World Problem

method, the problem solver makes use of a single stack that contains both goals and operators that have been proposed to satisfy those goals. The problem solver also relies on a database that describes the current situation and a set of operators described as PRECONDITION, ADD, and DELETE lists. To see how this method works, let us carry it through for the simple example shown in Figure 13.4.

When we begin solving this problem, the goal stack is simply

ON(C, A) ∧ ON(B, D) ∧ ONTABLE(A) ∧ ONTABLE(D)

But we want to separate this problem into four subproblems, one for each component of the original goal. Two of the subproblems, ONTABLE(A) and ONTABLE(D), are already true in the initial state. So we will work on only the remaining two. Depending on the order in which we want to tackle the subproblems, there are two goal stacks that could be created as our first step, where each line represents one goal on the stack and OTAD is an abbreviation for ONTABLE(A) ∧ ONTABLE(D):

ON(C, A)	ON(B, D)
ON(B, D)	ON(C, A)
ON(C, A) ∧ ON(B, D) ∧ OTAD	ON(C, A) ∧ ON(B, D) ∧ OTAD
[1]	[2]

At each succeeding step of the problem-solving process, the top goal on the stack will be pursued. When a sequence of operators that satisfies it is found, that sequence is applied to the state description, yielding a new description. Next, the goal that is then at the top of the stack is explored and an attempt is made to satisfy it, starting from the situation that was produced as a result of satisfying the first goal. This process continues until the goal stack is empty. Then, as one last check, the original goal is compared to the final state derived from the application of the chosen operators. If any components of the goal are not satisfied in that state (which they might not be if they were achieved at one point and then undone later), then those unsolved parts of the goal are reinserted onto the stack and the process resumed.

To continue with the example we started above, let us assume that we choose first to explore alternative 1. Alternative 2 will also lead to a solution. In fact, it finds one so trivially that it is not very interesting. Exploring alternative 1, we first check to see whether ON(C, A) is true in the current state. Since it is not, we check for operators that could cause it to be true. Of the four operators we are considering, there is only one, STACK, and it would have to be called with C and A. So we place STACK(C, A) on the stack in place of ON(C, A), yielding

> **STACK(C, A)**
> ON(B, D)
> ON(C, A) ∧ ON(B, D) ∧ OTAD

STACK(C, A) replaced ON(C, A) because after performing the STACK we are guaranteed that ON(C, A) will hold. But in order to apply STACK(C, A), its preconditions must hold, so we must establish them as subgoals. Again we must separate a compound goal

> CLEAR(A) ∧ HOLDING(C)

into its components and choose an order in which to work on them. At this point, it is useful to exploit some heuristic knowledge. HOLDING(x) is very easy to achieve. At most, it is necessary to put down something else and then to pick up the desired object. But HOLDING is also very easy to undo. In order to do almost anything else, the robot will need to use the arm. So if we achieve HOLDING first and then try to do something else, we will most likely end up with HOLDING no longer true. So we exploit the heuristic that if HOLDING is one of several goals to be achieved at once, it should be tackled last. This produces the new goal stack

> CLEAR(A)
> HOLDING(C)
> CLEAR(A) ∧ HOLDING(C)
> **STACK(C, A)**
> ON(B, D)
> ON(C, A) ∧ ON(B, D) ∧ OTAD

This kind of heuristic information could be contained in the precondition list itself by stating the predicates in the order in which they should be achieved.

Next we check to see if CLEAR(A) is true. It is not. The only operator that could make it true is UNSTACK(B, A). So we will attempt to apply it. This produces the goal stack

> ON(B, A)
> CLEAR(B)
> ARMEMPTY
> ON(B, A) ∧ CLEAR(B) ∧ ARMEMPTY
> **UNSTACK(B, A)**
> HOLDING(C)
> CLEAR(A) ∧ HOLDING(C)
> **STACK(C, A)**
> ON(B, D)
> ON(C, A) ∧ ON(B, D) ∧ OTAD

This time, when we compare the top element of the goal stack, ON(B, A), to the world model, we see that it is satisfied. So we pop it off and consider the next goal, CLEAR(B). It, too, is already true in the world model, although it was not stated explicitly as one of the initial predicates. But from the initial predicates and the blocks world axiom that says that any block with no blocks on it is clear, a theorem prover could derive CLEAR(B). So that goal, too, can be popped from the stack. The third precondition for UNSTACK(B, A) remains. It is ARMEMPTY, and it is also true in the current world model, so it can be popped off the stack. The next element on the stack is the combined goal representing all of the preconditions for UNSTACK(B, A). We check to make sure it is satisfied in the world model. It will be unless we undid one of its components in attempting to satisfy another. In this case, there is no problem and the combined goal can be popped from the stack.

Now the top element of the stack is the operator UNSTACK(B, A). We are now guaranteed that its preconditions are satisfied, so it can be applied to produce a new world model from which the rest of the problem-solving process can continue. This is done using the ADD and DELETE lists specified for UNSTACK. Meanwhile we record that UNSTACK(B, A) is the first operator of the proposed solution sequence. At this point, the database corresponding to the world model is

> ONTABLE(A) ∧ ONTABLE(C) ∧ ONTABLE(D) ∧
> HOLDING(B) ∧ CLEAR(A)

The goal stack now is

> HOLDING(C)
> CLEAR(A) ∧ HOLDING(C)
> **STACK(C, A)**
> ON(B, D)
> ON(C, A) ∧ ON(B, D) ∧ OTAD

We now attempt to satisfy the goal HOLDING(C). There are two operators that might make HOLDING(C) true: PICKUP(C) and UNSTACK(C, x), where x could be any block from which C could be unstacked. Without looking ahead, we cannot tell which of these operators is appropriate, so we create two branches of the search tree, corresponding to the following goal stacks:

ONTABLE(C)	ON(C, x)
CLEAR(C)	CLEAR(C)
ARMEMPTY	ARMEMPTY
ONTABLE(C) ∧ CLEAR(C) ∧	ON(C, x) ∧ CLEAR(C) ∧
ARMEMPTY	ARMEMPTY
PICKUP(C)	**UNSTACK(C, x)**
CLEAR(A) ∧ HOLDING(C)	CLEAR(A) ∧ HOLDING(C)
STACK(C, A)	**STACK(C, A)**
ON(B, D)	ON(B, D)
ON(C, A) ∧ ON(B, D) ∧ OTAD	ON(C, A) ∧ ON(B, D) ∧ OTAD
[1]	[2]

Notice that for alternative 2, the goal stack now contains a variable *x*, which appears in three places. Although any block could be substituted for *x*, it is important that the same one be matched to each of the *x*'s. Thus it is important that each time a variable is introduced into the goal stack, it be given a name distinct from any other variables already in the stack. And whenever a candidate object is chosen to match a variable, the binding must be recorded so that other occurrences of the same variable will be bound to the same object.

How should our program choose now between alternative 1 and alternative 2? We can tell that picking up C (alternative 1) is better than unstacking it because it is not currently on anything. So to unstack it, we would first have to stack it. Although this could be done, it would be a waste of effort. But how could a program know that? Suppose we decided to pursue alternative 2 first. To satisfy ON(C, *x*), we would have to STACK C onto some block *x*. The goal stack would then be

CLEAR(*x*)
HOLDING(C)
CLEAR(*x*) ∧ HOLDING(C)
STACK(C, *x*)
CLEAR(C)
ARMEMPTY
ON(C, *x*) ∧ CLEAR(C) ∧ ARMEMPTY
UNSTACK(C, *x*)
CLEAR(A) ∧ HOLDING(C)
STACK(C, A)
ON(B, D)
ON(C, A) ∧ ON(B, D) ∧ OTAD

But now notice that one of the preconditions of STACK is HOLDING(C). This is what we were trying to achieve by applying UNSTACK, which required us to apply STACK so that the precondition ON(C, *x*) would be satisfied. So we are back to our original goal. In fact, we now have additional goals as well, since other predicates have also been added to the stack. At this point, this path can be terminated as unproductive. If, however, block C had been on another block in the current state, ON(C, *x*) would have been satisfied immediately with no need to do a STACK and this path would have led to a good solution.

Now we must return to alternative 1, which used PICKUP to get the arm holding C. The top element on the goal stack is ONTABLE(C), which is already satisfied, so we pop it off. The next element is CLEAR(C), which is also satisfied, so we pop it off. The remaining precondition of PICKUP(C) is ARMEMPTY, which is not satisfied since HOLDING(B) is true. There are two operators that could be applied to make ARMEMPTY true: STACK(B, *x*) and PUTDOWN(B). In other words, we can either put B on the table or we can put it on another block. Which should we choose? If we look ahead a bit, we see that we ultimately want to get B onto D. It would be most efficient simply to put it there now. Our program could figure this out by comparing the elements of the ADD lists of the competing operators to the rest of the goal stack. If one of the operators has the fortuitous effect of making any of those goals true, it should be chosen. So we choose to apply STACK(B, D) by binding D to *x* in the STACK operator. This makes the goal stack

    CLEAR(D)
    HOLDING(B)
    CLEAR(D) ∧ HOLDING(B)
    STACK(B, D)
    ONTABLE(C) ∧ CLEAR(C) ∧ ARMEMPTY
    PICKUP(C)
    CLEAR(A) ∧ HOLDING(C)
    STACK(C, A)
    ON(B, D)
    ON(C, A) ∧ ON(B, D) ∧ OTAD

CLEAR(D) and HOLDING(B) are both true. Now the operation STACK(B, D) can be performed, producing the world model

    ONTABLE(A) ∧ ONTABLE(C) ∧ ONTABLE(D) ∧
    ON(B, D) ∧ ARMEMPTY

All of the preconditions for PICKUP(C) are now satisfied so it, too, can be executed. Then all of the preconditions of STACK(C, A) are true, so it can be executed.

Now we can begin work on the second part of our original goal, ON(B, D). But it has already been satisfied by the operations that were used to satisfy the first subgoal. This happened because when we had a choice of ways to get rid of the arm holding B, we scanned back down the goal stack to see if one of the operators would have other useful side effects and we found that one did. So we now pop ON(B, D) off the goal stack. We then do one last check of the combined goal ON(C, A) ∧ ON (B, D) ∧ ONTABLE(A) ∧ ONTABLE(D) to make sure that all four parts still hold, which, of course, they do here. The problem solver can now halt and return as its answer the plan

   1.   UNSTACK(B, A)
   2.   STACK(B, D)
   3.   PICKUP(C)
   4.   STACK(C, A)

In this simple example, we saw a way in which heuristic information can be applied to guide the search process, a way in which an unprofitable path could be detected, and a way in which considering some interaction among goals could help produce a good overall solution. But for problems more difficult than this one, these methods are not adequate.

To see why this method may fail to find a good solution, we attempt to solve the problem shown in Figure 13.5.[2] There are two ways that we could begin solving this problem, corresponding to the goal stacks

ON(A, B)	ON(B, C)
ON(B, C)	ON(A, B)
ON(A, B) ∧ ON(B, C)	ON(A, B) ∧ ON(B, C)
[1]	[2]

---

[2]This problem is often called the *Sussman Anomaly*, because it was carefully studied in Sussman [1975].

start: ON(C, A) ∧
       ONTABLE(A) ∧
       ONTABLE(B) ∧
       ARMEMPTY

goal: ON(A, B) ∧
      ON(B, C)

Figure 13.5: A Slightly Harder Blocks Problem

ON(C, A)
CLEAR(C)
ARMEMPTY
ON(C, A) ∧ CLEAR(C) ∧ ARMEMPTY
UNSTACK(C, A)
ARMEMPTY
CLEAR(A) ∧ ARMEMPTY
PICKUP(A)
CLEAR(B) ∧ HOLDING(A)
STACK(A, B)
ON(B, C)
ON(A, B) ∧ ON(B, C)

Figure 13.6: A Goal Stack

Suppose that we choose alternative 1 and begin trying to get A on B. We will eventually produce the goal stack shown in Figure 13.6.

We can then pop off the stack goals that have already been satisfied, until we reach the ARMEMPTY precondition of PICKUP(A). To satisfy it, we need to PUTDOWN(C). Then we can continue popping until the goal stack is

ON(B, C)
ON(A, B) ∧ ON(B, C)

Then the current state is

ONTABLE(B) ∧
ON(A, B) ∧
ONTABLE(C) ∧
ARMEMPTY

The sequence of operators applied so far is

1. UNSTACK(C, A)
2. PUTDOWN(C)
3. PICKUP(A)
4. STACK(A, B)

Now we can begin to work on satisfying ON(B, C). Without going through all the detail, we can see that our algorithm will attempt to achieve this goal by stacking B on C. But to do that, it has to unstack A from B. By the time we have achieved the goal ON(B, C) and popped it off the stack, we will have executed the following additional sequence of operators:

5. UNSTACK(A, B)
6. PUTDOWN(A)
7. PICKUP(B)
8. STACK(B, C)

The problem state will be

ON(B, C) ∧
ONTABLE(A) ∧
ONTABLE(C) ∧
ARMEMPTY

But now when we check the remaining goal on the stack,

ON(A, B) ∧ ON(B, C)

we discover that it is not satisfied. We have undone ON(A, B) in the process of achieving ON(B, C). The difference between the goal and the current state is ON(A, B), which is now added to the stack so that it can be achieved again. This time, the sequence of operators

9.   PICKUP(A)
10. STACK(A, B)

is found. Now the combined goal is again checked, and this time it is satisfied. The complete plan that has been discovered is

1.	UNSTACK(C, A)	6.	PUTDOWN(A)
2.	PUTDOWN(C)	7.	PICKUP(B)
3.	PICKUP(A)	8.	STACK(B, C)
4.	STACK(A, B)	9.	PICKUP(A)
5.	UNSTACK(A, B)	10.	STACK(A, B)

Although this plan will achieve the desired goal, it does not do so very efficiently. A similar situation would have occurred if we had examined the two major subgoals in the opposite order. The method we are using is not capable of finding an efficient way of solving this problem.

There are two approaches we can take to the question of how a good plan can be found. One is to look at ways to repair the plan we already have to make it more efficient. In this case, that is fairly easy to do. We can look for places in the plan where we perform an operation and then immediately undo it. If we find any such places, we can eliminate both the doing and the undoing steps from the plan. Applying this rule to our plan, we eliminate steps 4 and 5. Once we do that, we can also eliminate steps 3 and 6. The resulting plan

1.	UNSTACK(C, A)		4.	STACK(B, C)
2.	PUTDOWN(C)		5.	PICKUP(A)
3.	PICKUP(B)		6.	STACK(A, B)

contains, in fact, the minimum number of operators needed to solve this problem. But for more complex tasks, the interfering operations may be farther apart in the plan and thus much more difficult to detect. In addition, we wasted a good deal of problem-solving effort producing all the steps that were later eliminated. It would be better if there were a plan-finding procedure that could construct efficient plans directly. In the next section, we present a technique for doing this.

13.5 Nonlinear Planning Using Constraint Posting

The goal-stack planning method attacks problems involving conjoined goals by solving the goals one at a time, in order. A plan generated by this method contains a sequence of operators for attaining the first goal, followed by a complete sequence for the second goal, etc. But as we have seen, difficult problems cause goal interactions. The operators used to solve one subproblem may interfere with the solution to a previous subproblem. Most problems require an intertwined plan in which multiple subproblems are worked on simultaneously. Such a plan is called a *nonlinear plan* because it is not composed of a linear sequence of complete subplans.

As an example of the need for a nonlinear plan, let us return to the Sussman anomaly described in Figure 13.5. A good plan for the solution of this problem is the following:

1. Begin work on the goal ON(A, B) by clearing A, thus putting C on the table.

2. Achieve the goal ON(B, C) by stacking B on C.

3. Complete the goal ON(A, B) by stacking A on B.

This section explores some heuristics and algorithms for tackling nonlinear problems such as this one.

Many ideas about nonlinear planning were present in HACKER [Sussman, 1975], an automatic programming system. The first true nonlinear planner, though, was NOAH [Sacerdoti, 1975]. NOAH was further improved upon by the NONLIN program [Tate, 1977]. The goal stack algorithm of STRIPS was transformed into a goal *set* algorithm by Nilsson [1980]. Subsequent planning systems, such as MOLGEN [Stefik, 1981b] and TWEAK [Chapman, 1987], used *constraint posting* as a central technique.

The idea of constraint posting is to build up a plan by incrementally hypothesizing operators, partial orderings between operators, and bindings of variables within operators. At any given time in the problem-solving process, we may have a set of useful operators but perhaps no clear idea of how those operators should be ordered with respect

State Space Search

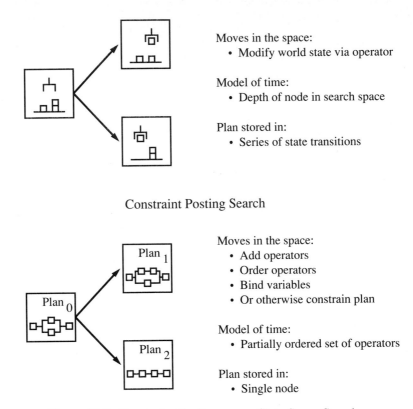

Moves in the space:
- Modify world state via operator

Model of time:
- Depth of node in search space

Plan stored in:
- Series of state transitions

Constraint Posting Search

Moves in the space:
- Add operators
- Order operators
- Bind variables
- Or otherwise constrain plan

Model of time:
- Partially ordered set of operators

Plan stored in:
- Single node

Figure 13.7: Constraint Posting versus State Space Search

to each other. A solution is a partially ordered, partially instantiated set of operators; to generate an actual plan, we convert the partial order into any of a number of total orders. Figure 13.7 shows the difference between the constraint posting method and the planning methods discussed in earlier sections.

We now examine several operations for nonlinear planning in a constraint-posting environment, although many of the operations themselves predate the use of the technique in planning.

Let's incrementally generate a nonlinear plan to solve the Sussman anomaly problem. We begin with the null plan, i.e., a plan with no steps. Next we look at the goal state and posit steps for achieving that goal. Means-ends analysis tells us to choose two steps with respective postconditions ON(A, B) and ON(B, C):

1. Step Addition—Creating new steps for a plan.

2. Promotion—Constraining one step to come before another in a final plan.

3. Declobbering—Placing one (possibly new) step s_2 between two old steps s_1 and s_3, such that s_2 reasserts some precondition of s_3 that was negated (or "clobbered") by s_1.

4. Simple Establishment—Assigning a value to a variable, in order to ensure the preconditions of some step.

5. Separation—Preventing the assignment of certain values to a variable.

Figure 13.8: Heuristics for Planning Using Constraint Posting (TWEAK)

CLEAR(B)	CLEAR(C)
* HOLDING(A)	* HOLDING(B)
STACK(A, B)	STACK(B, C)
ARMEMPTY	ARMEMPTY
ON(A, B)	ON(B, C)
¬CLEAR(B)	¬CLEAR(C)
¬HOLDING(A)	¬HOLDING(B)

Each step is written with its preconditions above it and its postconditions below it. Delete postconditions are marked with a negation symbol ($\neg$). Notice that, at this point, the steps are not ordered with respect to each other. All we know is that we want to execute both of them eventually. Neither can be executed right away because some of their preconditions are not satisfied. An unachieved precondition is marked with a star (*). Both of the *HOLDING preconditions are unachieved because the arm holds nothing in the initial problem state.

Introducing new steps to achieve goals or preconditions is called *step addition*, and it is one of the heuristics we will use in generating nonlinear plans. Step addition is a very basic method dating back to GPS [Newell and Simon, 1963], where means-ends analysis was used to pick operators with postconditions corresponding to desired states. Figure 13.8 lists step addition along with other heuristics we use throughout this example.

To achieve the preconditions of the two steps above, we can use step addition again:

| *CLEAR(A) | *CLEAR(B) |
| ONTABLE(A) | ONTABLE(B) |
*ARMEMPTY	*ARMEMPTY
PICKUP(A)	PICKUP(B)
¬ONTABLE(A)	¬ONTABLE(B)
¬ARMEMPTY	¬ARMEMPTY
HOLDING(A)	HOLDING(B)

Adding these PICKUP steps is not enough to satisfy the *HOLDING preconditions of the STACK steps. This is because there are no ordering constraints present among the steps. If, in the eventual plan, the PICKUP steps were to follow the STACK steps, then the *HOLDING preconditions would need to be satisfied by some other set of steps. We solve this problem by introducing ordering constraints whenever we employ step addition. In this case, we want to say that each PICKUP step should precede its corresponding STACK step[3]:

PICKUP(A) ← STACK(A, B)
PICKUP(B) ← STACK(B, C)

We now have four (partially ordered) steps in our plan and four unachieved preconditions. *CLEAR(A) is unachieved because block A is not clear in the initial state. *CLEAR(B) is unachieved because although B is clear in the initial state, there exists a step STACK(A, B) with postcondition ¬CLEAR(B), and that step might precede the step with *CLEAR(B) as a precondition. To achieve precondition CLEAR(B), we use a second heuristic known as *promotion*. Promotion, first used by Sussman in his HACKER program [Sussman, 1975], amounts to posting a constraint that one step must precede another in the eventual plan. We can achieve CLEAR(B) by stating that the PICKUP(B) step must come before the STACK(A, B) step:

PICKUP(B) ← STACK(A, B)

Let's now turn to the two unachieved *ARMEMPTY preconditions [we deal with *CLEAR(A) a little later]. While the initial state has an empty arm, each of the two pickup operators contain ¬ARMEMPTY postconditions. Either operator could prevent the other from executing. We can use promotion to achieve at least one of the two preconditions:

PICKUP(B) ← PICKUP(A)

Since the initial situation contains an empty arm, and no step preceding PICKUP(B) could make it unempty, the preconditions of PICKUP(B) are all satisfied.

A third heuristic, called *declobbering*, can help achieve the *ARMEMPTY precondition in the PICKUP(A) step. PICKUP(B) asserts ¬ARMEMPTY, but if we can insert

---

[3] $S_1 ← S_2$ means that step S_1 must precede step S_2 in the eventual plan.

another step between PICKUP(B) and PICKUP(A) to reassert ARMEMPTY, then the precondition will be achieved. The STACK(B, C) does the trick, so we post another constraint:

PICKUP(B) ← STACK(B, C) ← PICKUP(A)

The step PICKUP(B) is said to "clobber" PICKUP(A)'s precondition. STACK(B,C) is said to "declobber" it. Declobbering was first used in the NOAH planner [Sacerdoti, 1975], and then in NONLIN. NOAH was the first nonlinear planner to make use of the heuristics we are discussing here. NOAH also used many other heuristics and was able to solve a number of difficult nonlinear planning problems. Still, there were some natural problems that NOAH could not solve. In particular, NOAH's inability to backtrack prevented it from finding many solutions. The NONLIN program included backtracking, but it also failed to solve many hard problems.

Back in our example, the only unachieved precondition left is *CLEAR(A), from the PICKUP(A) step. We can use step addition to achieve it:

$$* ON(x, A)$$
$$* CLEAR(x)$$
$$* ARMEMPTY$$

_____

UNSTACK(x, A)

_____

¬ARMEMPTY
CLEAR(A)
HOLDING(A)
¬ON(x, A)

We introduce the variable x because the only postcondition we are interested in is CLEAR(A). Whatever block is on top of A is irrelevant. Constraint posting allows us to create plans that are incomplete with respect to the order of the steps. Variables allow us to avoid committing to particular instantiations of operators.

Unfortunately, we now have three new unachieved preconditions. We can achieve ON(x, A) easily by constraining the value of x to be block C. This works because block C is on block A in the initial state. This heuristic is called *simple establishment*, and in its most general form, it allows us to state that two different propositions must be ultimately instantiated to the same proposition. In our case:

$x = C$ in step UNSTACK(x, A)

There are still steps that deny the preconditions CLEAR(C) and ARMEMPTY, but we can use promotion to take care of them:

UNSTACK(x, A) ← STACK(B, C)
UNSTACK(x, A) ← PICKUP(A)
UNSTACK(x, A) ← PICKUP(B)

Among the heuristics we have looked at so far, adding a new step is the most problematic because we must always check if the new step clobbers some precondition of a later, already existing step. This has actually happened in our example. The step PICKUP(B) requires ARMEMPTY, but this is denied by the new UNSTACK(x, A) step. One way to solve this problem is to add a new declobbering step to the plan:

HOLDING(C)
——————
PUTDOWN(C)
——————
¬HOLDING(C)
ONTABLE(x)
ARMEMPTY

ordered as:

UNSTACK(x, A) ← PUTDOWN(C) ← PICKUP(B)

Notice that we have seen two types of declobbering, one in which an existing step is used to declobber another, and one in which a new declobbering step is introduced. Fortunately, the precondition of our newest PUTDOWN step is satisfied. In fact, all preconditions of all steps are satisfied, so we are done. All that remains is to use the plan ordering and variable binding constraints to build a concrete plan:

1. UNSTACK(C, A)
2. PUTDOWN(C)
3. PICKUP(B)
4. STACK(B, C)
5. PICKUP(A)
6. STACK(A, B)

This is the same plan we found at the end of Section 13.4. We used four different heuristics to synthesize it: step addition, promotion, declobbering, and simple establishment. (These are sometimes called *plan modification operations*.) Are these four operations, applied in the correct order, enough to solve any nonlinear planning problem? Almost. We require one more, called *separation*. Separation is like simple establishment, in that it concerns variable bindings, but it is used in a declobbering fashion. Suppose step *C1* possibly precedes step *C2* and *C1* possibly denies a precondition of *C2*. We say "possibly" because the propositions may contain variables. Separation allows us to state a constraint that the two propositions must *not* be instantiated in the same way in the eventual plan.

Work on the TWEAK planner presented formal definitions of the five plan modification operations and proved that they were sufficient for solving *any* solvable nonlinear planning problem. In this manner, TWEAK cleaned up the somewhat *ad hoc*, heuristic results in nonlinear planning research. The algorithm to exploit the plan modification operations is quite simple.

Algorithm: Nonlinear Planning (TWEAK)

1. Initialize S to be the set of propositions in the goal state.

2. Remove some unachieved proposition P from S.

3. Achieve P by using step addition, promotion, declobbering, simple establishment, or separation.

4. Review all the steps in the plan, including any new steps introduced by step addition, to see if any of their preconditions are unachieved. Add to S the new set of unachieved preconditions.

5. If S is empty, complete the plan by converting the partial order of steps into a total order, and instantiate any variables as necessary.

6. Otherwise, go to step 2.

Of course, not every sequence of plan modification operations leads to a solution. For instance, we could use step addition *ad infinitum* without ever converging to a useful plan. The nondeterminism of steps 2 and 3 must be implemented as some sort of search procedure. This search can be guided by heuristics; for example, if promotion and step addition will both do the job, it is probably better to try promotion first. TWEAK uses breadth-first dependency-directed backtracking, as well as ordering heuristics.

The example above used most of the plan modification operations, but not in their full generality. We will now be more specific about these operations and how they relate to finding correct plans. The core notion is one of making a proposition *necessarily* true in some state. The *modal truth criterion* tells us exactly when a proposition is true.

> **The Modal Truth Criterion.** A proposition P is necessarily true in a state S if and only if two conditions hold: there is a state T equal or necessarily previous to S in which P is necessarily asserted; and for every step C possibly before S and every proposition Q possibly codesignating[4] with P which C denies, there is a step W necessarily between C and S which asserts R, a proposition such that R and P codesignate whenever P and Q codesignate.

Roughly, this means that P has to be asserted in the initial state or by some previous step and that there can be no clobbering steps without corresponding declobbering steps to save the day. The relationship between the modal truth criterion and the five plan modification operations is shown in Figure 13.9. The figure is simply a logical parse tree of the criterion, from which we can see how the plan modification operations are used to enforce the truth of various parts of the criterion. In the figure, the expression $C_1 \prec C_2$ means step (or state) C_1 necessarily precedes step (or state) C_2. The expression $P \approx Q$ means P and Q codesignate.

The development of a provably correct planner was a noteworthy achievement in the formal (or "neat") style of AI. It cleaned up the complicated, ill-defined planning notions that preceded it and made available a reliable (if not efficient) planner. Now, however, a new round of more informal (or "scruffy") research must follow, concentrating on

---

[4] Two propositions *codesignate* if they can be unified, given the current constraints on variables.

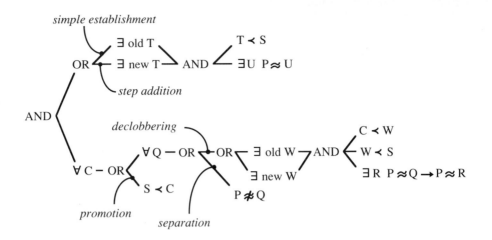

Figure 13.9: The Modal Truth Criterion for Telling whether Proposition *P* Necessarily Holds in State *S*

the weaknesses of such planners. Efficiency is of critical concern in large systems—assured correctness is nice, but a slow planner can be less useful than an incorrect one. Typically, search-based programs can be made faster through the use of heuristic knowledge. Another efficiency issue has to do with the *length* of the plans produced by a planner. Current planners can, unfortunately, generate highly inefficient plans.

Representational issues are just as important as efficiency issues, and the two are closely intertwined. The representation of operators and plans used by TWEAK is at the same time too powerful and too weak. Chapman [1987] proved that even with simple STRIPS-style operators, planning in general is not even decidable, although it is semidecidable: If there is a plan that solves a problem, a planner can find it, but if there is no such plan, the planner may never halt. NP-completeness results suggest that planning is exponentially hard. But it is of no use to look for a simpler representation that might allow for more efficient plan construction—if anything, most domains seem to require operators that are much more complex than the operators used by TWEAK. For example, it is natural to express many preconditions using quantifiers and embedded negation and also to have postconditions with different effects depending on the state of the world. Figure 13.10 depicts a more complex operator structure, of the type used in the PRODIGY planning system [Minton *et al.*, 1989]. As our representation becomes more expressive, the idea of a provably correct, efficient, domain-independent planner becomes more unlikely, and we must again turn to knowledge-intensive heuristic methods.

13.6   Hierarchical Planning

In order to solve hard problems, a problem solver may have to generate long plans. In order to do that efficiently, it is important to be able to eliminate some of the details of

```
(OPERATOR
    (PRECONDITIONS
        (and (...)
                (forall (w ...) ...)
                (not
                        (exists ...)
                        (or ......)))
    (POSTCONDITIONS
        (ADD (...))
        (DELETE (...))
        (if (and (...) (...))
                (ADD (...) (...))
                (DELETE (...) (...))))))
```

Figure 13.10: A Complex Operator

the problem until a solution that addresses the main issues is found. Then an attempt can be made to fill in the appropriate details. Early attempts to do this involved the use of macro-operators, in which larger operators were built from smaller ones [Fikes and Nilsson, 1971]. But in this approach, no details were eliminated from the actual descriptions of the operators. A better approach was developed in the ABSTRIPS system [Sacerdoti, 1974], which actually planned in a hierarchy of *abstraction spaces*, in each of which preconditions at a lower level of abstraction were ignored.

As an example, suppose you want to visit a friend in Europe, but you have a limited amount of cash to spend. It makes sense to check air fares first, since finding an affordable flight will be the most difficult part of the task. You should not worry about getting out of your driveway, planning a route to the airport, or parking your car until you are sure you have a flight.

The ABSTRIPS approach to problem solving is as follows: First solve the problem completely, considering only preconditions whose *criticality value* is the highest possible. These values reflect the expected difficulty of satisfying the precondition. To do this, do exactly what STRIPS did, but simply ignore preconditions of lower than peak criticality. Once this is done, use the constructed plan as the outline of a complete plan and consider preconditions at the next-lowest criticality level. Augment the plan with operators that satisfy those preconditions. Again, in choosing operators, ignore all preconditions whose criticality is less than the level now being considered. Continue this process of considering less and less critical preconditions until all of the preconditions of the original rules have been considered. Because this process explores entire plans at one level of detail before it looks at the lower-level details of any one of them, it has been called *length-first search*.

Clearly, the assignment of appropriate criticality values is crucial to the success of this hierarchical planning method. Those preconditions that no operators can satisfy are clearly the most critical. For example, if we are trying to solve a problem involving a robot moving around in a house and we are considering the operator PUSH-THROUGH-DOOR, the precondition that there exist a door big enough for the robot to get through is of high criticality since there is (in the normal situation) nothing we can do about it if it is not true. But the precondition that the door be open is of lower criticality if we have the operator OPEN-DOOR. In order for a hierarchical planning system to work with STRIPS-like rules, it must be told, in addition to the rules themselves, the appropriate criticality value for each term that may occur in a precondition. Given these values, the basic process can function in very much the same way that nonhierarchical planning does. But effort will not be wasted filling in the details of plans that do not even come close to solving the problem.

13.7 Reactive Systems

So far, we have described a deliberative planning process, in which a plan for completing an entire task is constructed prior to action. There is a very different way, though, that we could approach the problem of deciding what to do. The idea of *reactive systems* [Brooks, 1986; Agre and Chapman, 1987; Kaebling, 1987] is to avoid planning altogether, and instead use the observable situation as a clue to which one can simply react.

A reactive system must have access to a knowledge base of some sort that describes what actions should be taken under what circumstances. A reactive system is very different from the other kinds of planning systems we have discussed because it chooses actions one at a time; it does not anticipate and select an entire action sequence before it does the first thing.

One of the very simplest reactive systems is a thermostat. The job of a thermostat is to keep the temperature constant inside a room. One might imagine a solution to this problem that requires significant amounts of planning, taking into account how the external temperature rises and falls during the day, how heat flows from room to room, and so forth. But a real thermostat uses the simple pair of situation-action rules:

1. If the temperature in the room is k degrees above the desired temperature, then turn the air conditioner on

2. If the temperature in the room is k degrees below the desired temperature, then turn the air conditioner off

It turns out that reactive systems are capable of surprisingly complex behaviors, especially in real world tasks such as robot navigation. We discuss robot tasks in more detail in Chapter 21. The main advantage reactive systems have over traditional planners is that they operate robustly in domains that are difficult to model completely and accurately. Reactive systems dispense with modeling altogether and base their actions directly on their perception of the world. In complex and unpredictable domains, the ability to plan an exact sequence of steps ahead of time is of questionable value. Another advantage of reactive systems is that they are extremely responsive, since they avoid the combinatorial explosion involved in deliberative planning. This makes them attractive for real time tasks like driving and walking.

Of course, many AI tasks do require significant deliberation, which is usually implemented as internal search. Since reactive systems maintain no model of the world and no explicit goal structures, their performance in these tasks is limited. For example, it seems unlikely that a purely reactive system could ever play expert chess. It is possible to provide a reactive system with rudimentary planning capability, but only by explicitly storing whole plans along with the situations that should trigger them. Deliberative planners need not rely on pre-stored plans; they can construct a new plan for each new problem.

Nevertheless, inquiry into reactive systems has served to illustrate many of the shortcomings of traditional planners. For one thing, it is vital to interleave planning and plan execution. Planning is important, but so is action. An intelligent system with limited resources must decide when to start thinking, when to stop thinking, and when to act. Also, goals arise naturally when the system interacts with the environment. Some mechanism for suspending plan execution is needed so that the system can turn its attention to high priority goals. Finally, some situations require immediate attention and rapid action. For this reason, some deliberative planners [Mitchell, 1990] compile out reactive subsystems (i.e., sets of situation-action rules) based on their problem-solving experiences. Such systems learn to be reactive over time.

13.8 Other Planning Techniques

Other planning techniques that we have not discussed include the following.

- Triangle Tables [Fikes *et al.*, 1972; Nilsson, 1980]—Provide a way of recording the goals that each operator is expected to satisfy as well as the goals that must be true for it to execute correctly. If something unexpected happens during the execution of a plan, the table provides the information required to patch the plan.

- Metaplanning [Stefik, 1981a]—A technique for reasoning not just about the problem being solved but also about the planning process itself.

- Macro-operators [Fikes and Nilsson, 1971]—Allow a planner to build new operators that represent commonly used sequences of operators. See Chapter 17 for more details.

- Case-Based Planning [Hammond, 1986]—Re-uses old plans to make new ones. We return to case-based planning in Chapter 19.

13.9 Exercises

1. Consider the following blocks world problem:

start: ON(C, B) ∧
ON(D, A) ∧
ONTABLE(B) ∧
ONTABLE(A) ∧
ARMEMPTY

goal: ON(C, B) ∧
ON(D, A) ∧
ONTABLE(B) ∧
ONTABLE(A)

    (a) Show how STRIPS would solve this problem.

    (b) Show how TWEAK would solve this problem.

    (c) Did these processes produce optimal plans? If not, could they be modified to do so?

2. Consider the problem of devising a plan for cleaning the kitchen.

    (a) Write a set of STRIPS-style operators that might be used. When you describe the operators, take into account such considerations as:

- Cleaning the stove or the refrigerator will get the floor dirty.
- To clean the oven, it is necessary to apply oven cleaner and then to remove the cleaner.
- Before the floor can be washed, it must be swept.
- Before the floor can be swept, the garbage must be taken out.
- Cleaning the refrigerator generates garbage and messes up the counters.
- Washing the counters or the floor gets the sink dirty.

    (b) Write a description of a likely initial state of a kitchen in need of cleaning. Also write a description of a desirable (but perhaps rarely obtained) goal state.

    (c) Show how the technique of planning using a goal stack could be used to solve this problem. (Hint—you may want to modify the definition of an ADD condition so that when a condition is added to the database, its negation is automatically deleted if present.)

3. In Section 13.4, we showed an example of a situation in which a search path could be terminated because it led back to one of its earlier goals. Describe a mechanism by which a program could detect this situation.

4. Consider the problem of swapping the contents of two registers, A and B. Suppose that there is available the single operator $ASSIGN(x, v, lv, ov)$, which assigns the value v, which is stored in location lv, to location x, which previously contained the value ov:

$$ASSIGN(x, v, lv, ov)$$
$$P: CONTAINS(lv, v) \wedge CONTAINS(x, ov)$$
$$D: CONTAINS(x, ov)$$
$$A: CONTAINS(x, v)$$

Assume that there is at least one additional register, C, available.

    (a) What would STRIPS do with this problem?

    (b) What would TWEAK do with this problem?

    (c) How might you design a program to solve this problem?

Chapter 14

Understanding

14.1 What Is Understanding?

To understand something is to transform it from one representation into another, where this second representation has been chosen to correspond to a set of available actions that could be performed and where the mapping has been designed so that for each event, an *appropriate* action will be performed. There is very little absolute in the notion of understanding. If you say to an airline database system "I need to go to New York as soon as possible," the system will have "understood" if it finds the first available plane to New York. If you say the same thing to your best friend, who knows that your family lives in New York, she will have "understood" if she realizes that there may be a problem in your family and you may need some emotional support. As we talk about understanding, it is important to keep in mind that the success or failure of an "understanding" program can rarely be measured in an absolute sense but must instead be measured with respect to a particular task to be performed. This is true both of language-understanding programs and also of understanders in other domains, such as vision.

For people, understanding applies to inputs from all the senses. Computer understanding has so far been applied primarily to images, speech, and typed language. In this chapter we discuss issues that cut across all of these modalities. In Chapter 15, we explore the problem of typed natural language in more detail, and in Chapter 21, we look at speech and vision problems. Although we have defined understanding above as the process of mapping into appropriate *actions*, we are not precluding a view of understanding in which inputs are simply interpreted and stored for later. In such a system, the appropriate action is to store the proper representation. This view of understanding describes what occurs in most image understanding programs and some language understanding programs. Taking direct action describes what happens in systems in which language, either typed or spoken, is used in the interface between user and computer.

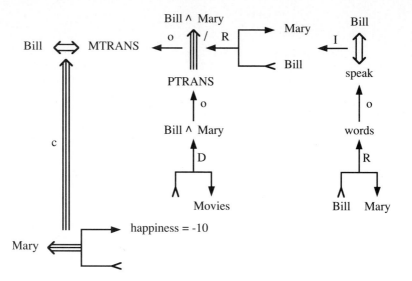

Figure 14.1: The Conceptual Dependency Representation of a Paragraph

14.2 What Makes Understanding Hard?

There are four major factors that contribute to the difficulty of an understanding problem:

1. The complexity of the target representation into which the matching is being done

2. The type of the mapping: one-one, many-one, one-many, or many-many

3. The level of interaction of the components of the source representation

4. The presence of noise in the input to the understander

A few examples will illustrate the importance of each of these factors.

Complexity of the Target Representation

Suppose English sentences are being used for communication with a keyword-based data retrieval system. Then the sentence

I want to read all about the last Presidential election.

would need to be translated into a representation such as

(SEARCH KEYWORDS = ELECTION & PRESIDENT)

But now suppose that English sentences are being used to provide input to a program that records events so that it can answer a variety of questions about those events and their relationships. For example, consider the following story:

> Bill told Mary he would not go to the movies with her.
> Her feelings were hurt.

The result of understanding this story could be represented, using the conceptual dependency model that we discussed in Chapter 10, as shown in Figure 14.1. This representation is considerably more complex than that for the simple query. All other things being equal, constructing such a complex representation is more difficult than constructing a simple one since more information must be extracted from the input sentences. Extracting that information often requires the use of additional knowledge about the world described by the sentences.

Type of Mapping

Recall that understanding is the process of mapping an input from its original form to a more useful one. The simplest kind of mapping to deal with is one-to-one (i.e., each different statement maps to a single target representation that is different from that arising from any other statement). Very few input systems are totally one-to-one. But as an example of an almost one-to-one mapping, consider the language of arithmetic expressions in many programming languages. In such a language, a mapping such as the following might occur:

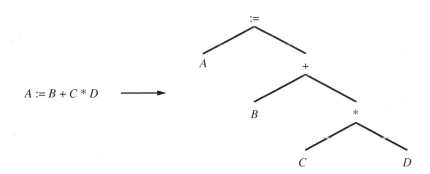

$$A := B + C * D$$

Although one-to-one mappings are, in general, the simplest to perform, they are rare in interesting input systems for several reasons. One important reason is that in many domains, inputs must be interpreted not absolutely, but relatively, with respect to some reference point. For example, when images are being interpreted, size and perspective will change as a function of the viewing position. Thus a single object will look different in different images. To see this, look at Figure 14.2, which shows two line drawings representing the same scene, one of which corresponds to a picture taken close to the scene and one of which represents a picture taken from farther away. A similar phenomenon occurs in English. The word "tall" specifies one height range in the phrase "a tall giraffe" and a different one in the phrase "a tall poodle."

A second reason that many-to-one mappings are frequent is that free variation is often allowed, either because of the physical limitations of the system that produces the inputs or because such variation simply makes the task of generating the inputs manageable. Both of these factors help to explain why natural languages, both in their spoken and their written forms, require many-to-one mappings. Examples from speech abound. No two people speak identically. In fact, one person does not always say a given word the

Figure 14.2: Relative Differences in Pictures of the Same Scene

same way. Figure 14.3 illustrates this problem. It shows a spectrogram produced by
the beginning of the utterance "Alpha gets alpha minus beta." A spectrogram shows
how the sound energy is distributed over the auditory frequency range as a function of
time. In this example, you can see two different patterns, each produced by the word
"alpha." Even when we ignore the variability of the speech signal, natural languages
admit variability because of their richness. This is particularly noticeable when mapping
from a natural language (with its richness of structure and vocabulary) to a small, simple
target representation. So, for example, we might find many-to-one mappings, such as
the following one, occurring in the English front end to a keyword data retrieval system:

<table>
<tr><td>Tell me all about the
    last presidential
    election.</td><td>→</td><td></td></tr>
<tr><td></td><td></td><td>(SEARCH</td></tr>
<tr><td>I'd like to see all the
    stories on the last
    presidential election.</td><td>→</td><td>KEYWORDS =
ELECTION
&
PRESIDENT)</td></tr>
<tr><td>I am interested in the
    last presidential
    election.</td><td>→</td><td></td></tr>
</table>

Many-to-one mappings require that the understanding system know about all the
ways that a target representation can be expressed in the source language. As a result,
they typically require a structured analysis of the input rather than a simple, exact pattern
match. But they often do not require much other knowledge.

One-to-many mappings, on the other hand, often require a great deal of domain
knowledge (in addition to the input itself) in order to make the correct choice among the
available target representations. An example of such a mapping (in which the input can
be said to be *ambiguous*) is the following sentence:

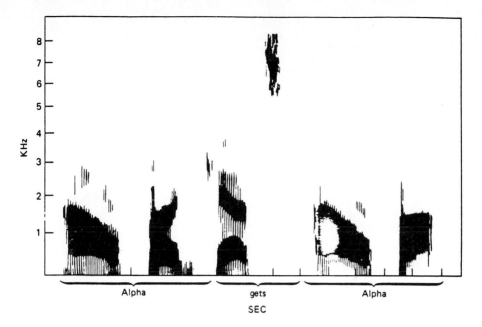

Figure 14.3: Differences in Speech Signals

$\rightarrow$ (They are
       (flying airplanes))

$\rightarrow$ (They (are flying)
       airplanes)

They are flying planes.

$\rightarrow$ (They are
       (flying planing-tools))

$\rightarrow$ (They (are flying)
       planing-tools)

Notice that although this sentence, taken in isolation, is ambiguous, it would usually not be interpreted as being ambiguous by a human listener in a specific context. Clues, both from previous sentences and from the physical context in which the sentence occurs, usually make one of these interpretations appear to be correct. The problem, though, from a processing standpoint, is how to encode this contextual information and how to exploit it while processing each new sentence.

Notice that English, in all its glory, has the properties of both of these last two examples; it involves a *many-to-many* mapping, in which there are many ways to say the same thing and a given statement may have many meanings.

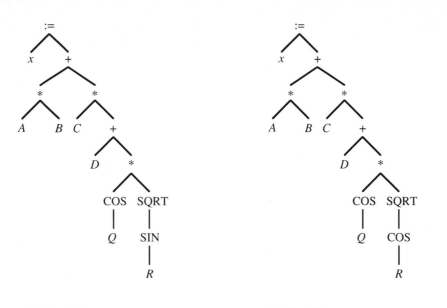

$$x := A * B + C *$$
$$(D + COS(Q) * SQRT(SIN(R)))$$

$$x := A * B + C *$$
$$(D + COS(Q) * SQRT(COS(R)))$$

Figure 14.4: Little Interaction among Components

Level of Interaction among Components

In most interesting understanding contexts, each input is composed of several components (lines, words, symbols, or whatever). The mapping process is the simplest
if each component can be mapped without concern for the other components of the
statement. Otherwise, as the number of interactions increases, so does the complexity
of the mapping.

Programming languages provide good examples of languages in which there is very
little interaction among the components of an input. For example, Figure 14.4 shows
how changing one word of a statement requires only a single change to one node of the
corresponding parse tree.

In many natural language sentences, on the other hand, changing a single word can
alter not just a single node of the interpretation, but rather its entire structure. An example
of this is shown in Figure 14.5. (The triangles in the figure indicate substructures whose
further decomposition is not important.) As these examples show, the components of an
English sentence typically interact more heavily with each other than do the components
of artificial languages, such as programming languages, that have been designed, among
other things, to facilitate processing by computer.

Nonlocality can be a problem at all levels of an understanding process. In the
boy in the park example, the problem is in how to group phrases together. But in
perceptual understanding tasks, this same problem may make it difficult even to decide

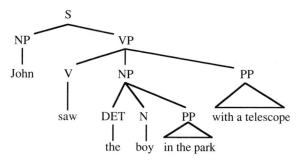

John saw the boy in the park with a telescope.

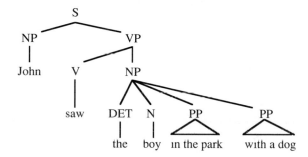

John saw the boy in the park with a dog.

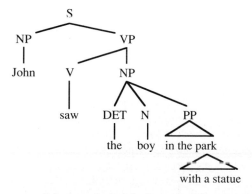

John saw the boy in the park with a statue.

Figure 14.5: More Interaction among Components

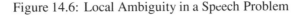

Figure 14.6: Local Ambiguity in a Speech Problem

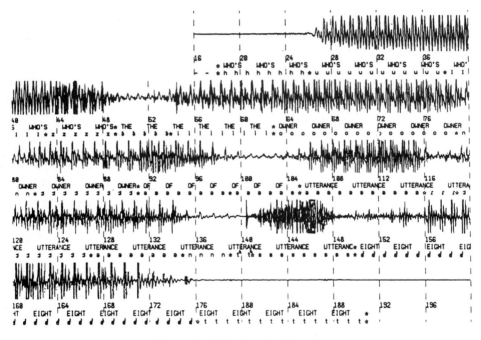

Figure 14.7: A Speech Waveform

on what the basic constituents are. Figure 14.6 shows a simplified example from speech understanding. Assuming that the sounds shown in the figure have been identified, the problem is to group them into words. But the correct grouping cannot be determined without looking at the larger context in which the sounds occurred. Either of the groupings shown is possible, as can be seen from the two sentences in the figure. Figure 14.7 shows an actual speech waveform, in which the lack of local clues, even for segmenting into individual sounds, can be seen.

In image-understanding problems as well, a similar problem involving local indeterminacy arises. Consider the situation shown in Figure 14.8. At this point, lines have been extracted from the original figure and the next task is to separate the figure into objects. But suppose we start at the left and identify the object labeled A. Does it end at the vertical line? It is not possible to tell without looking past the vertical object to see if there is an extension, which, in this case, there is.

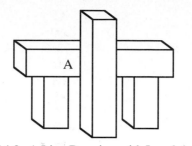

Figure 14.8: A Line Drawing with Local Ambiguity

Noise in the Input

Understanding is the process of interpreting an input and assigning it meaning. Unfortunately, in many understanding situations the input to which meaning should be assigned is not always the input that is presented to the understander. Because of the complex environment in which understanding usually occurs, other things often interfere with the basic input before it reaches the understander. In perceptual tasks, such as speech and image understanding, this problem is common. We rarely have the opportunity to listen to each other against a background of silence. Thus we must take an input signal and separate the speech component from the background noise component in order to understand the speech. The same problem occurs in image understanding. If you look out of your car window in search of a particular store sign, the image you will see of the sign may be interfered with by many things, such as your windshield wipers or the trees alongside the road. Although typed language is less susceptible to noise than is spoken language, noise is still a problem. For example, typing errors are common, particularly if language is being used interactively to communicate with a computer system.

Conclusion

The point of this section has been twofold. On the one hand, it has attempted to describe the sources of complexity in understanding tasks, in order to help you analyze new understanding tasks for tractability. On the other, it has tried to point out specific understanding tasks that turn out, unfortunately, to be hard (such as natural language understanding) but that are nevertheless important in the sense that it would be useful if we could perform them. It is to these understanding tasks that we will need to devote substantial research effort.

14.3   Understanding as Constraint Satisfaction

On the basis of a superficial analysis (such as the one in the last section), many understanding tasks appear impossibly complex. The number of interpretations that can be assigned to individual components of an input is large, and the number of combinations of those components is enormous. But a closer analysis often reveals that many of the combinations cannot actually occur. These natural constraints can be exploited in the understanding process to reduce the complexity from unmanageable to tractable. There are two important steps in the use of constraints in problem solving:

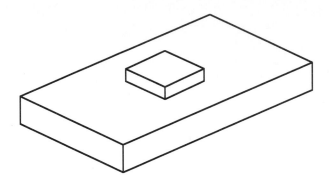

Figure 14.9: A Line Drawing

1. Analyze the problem domain to determine what the constraints are.

2. Solve the problem by applying a constraint satisfaction algorithm that effectively uses the constraints from step 1 to control the search. Recall that we presented such an algorithm in Section 3.5.

In the rest of this section, we look at one example of the use of this approach, the Waltz algorithm for labeling line drawings. In Chapter 15 we then look in depth at the problem of natural language understanding and see how it too can be viewed as a constraint satisfaction process.

Consider the drawing shown in Figure 14.9. Assume either that you have been given this drawing as the input or that lower-level routines have already operated to extract these lines from an input photograph. The next step in the analysis process is to determine the objects described by the lines. To do this, we need first to identify each of the lines in the figure as representing either:

- An Obscuring Edge—A boundary between objects, or between objects and the background

- A Concave Edge—An edge between two faces that form an acute angle when viewed from outside the object

- A Convex Edge—An edge between two faces that form an obtuse angle when viewed from outside the object

For more complex figures, other edge types, such as cracks between coplanar faces and shadow edges between shadows and the background, would also be required. The approach we describe here has, in fact, been extended to handle these other edge types. But to make the explanation straightforward, we consider only these three. In fact, we consider only figures composed exclusively of *trihedral* vertices, which are vertices at which exactly three planes come together. Figure 14.10 shows examples of trihedral figures. Figure 14.11 shows examples of nontrihedral figures.

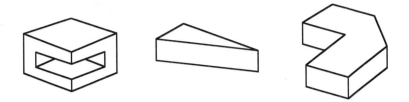

Figure 14.10: Some Trihedral Figures

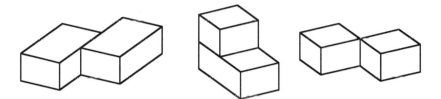

Figure 14.11: Some Nontrihedral Figures

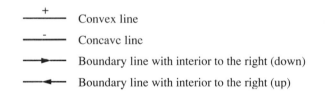

Figure 14.12: Line-Labeling Conventions

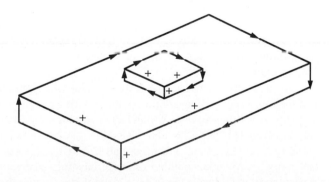

Figure 14.13: An Example of Line Labeling

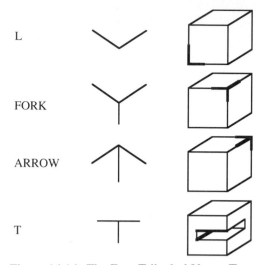

Figure 14.14: The Four Trihedral Vertex Types

Determining the Constraints

The problem we are trying to solve is how to recognize individual objects in a figure. To do that, we intend first to label all the lines in the figure so that we know which ones correspond to boundaries between objects. We use the three line types given above. For boundary lines, we also need to indicate a direction, telling which side of the line corresponds to the object and which to the background. This produces a set of four labels that can be attached to a given line. We use the conventions shown in Figure 14.12 to show line labelings. To illustrate these labelings, Figure 14.13 shows the drawing of Figure 14.9 with each of its lines correctly labeled.

Assuming these four line types, we can calculate that the number of ways of labeling a figure composed of N lines is 4^N. How can we find the correct one? The critical observation here is that every line must meet other lines at a vertex at each of its ends. For the trihedral figures we are considering, there are only four configurations that describe all the possible vertices. These four configurations are shown in Figure 14.14. The rotational position of the vertex is not significant, nor are the sizes of the angles it contains, except that the distinction between acute angles (< 90 degrees) and obtuse angles (> 90 degrees) is important to distinguish between a FORK and an ARROW. If there turn out to be constraints on the kinds of vertices that can occur, then there would be corresponding constraints on the lines entering the vertices and thus the number of possible line labelings would be reduced.

To begin looking for such vertex constraints, we first consider the maximum number of ways that each of the four types of lines might combine with other lines at a vertex. Since an L vertex involves two lines, each of which can have four labels, there must be sixteen ways it could be formed. FORKs, Ts, and ARROWs involve three lines, so they could be formed in sixty-four ways each. Thus there are 208 ways to form a trihedral vertex. But, in fact, only a very small number of these labelings can actually occur in line drawings representing real physical objects. To see this, consider the planes on which the faces that form a vertex of a trihedral figure lie. These three planes must

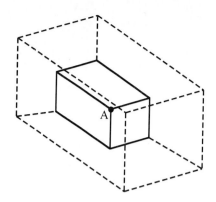

Figure 14.15: A Figure Occupying One Octant

divide 3-space into eight parts (called octants) since each individual face divides the space in half and none of the faces can be coplanar. Trihedral figures may differ in the number of octants that they fill and in the position (which must be one of the unfilled octants) from which they are viewed. Any vertex that can occur in a trihedral figure must correspond to such a division of space with some number (between one and eight) of octants filled, which is viewed from one of the unfilled octants. So to find all the vertex labelings that can occur, we need only consider all the ways of filling the octants and each of the ways of viewing those fillings, and then record the types of the vertices that we find.

To illustrate this process, consider the drawing shown in Figure 14.15, which occupies one of the eight octants formed by the intersection of the planes corresponding to the faces of vertex A. Imagine viewing this figure from each of the remaining seven octants and recording the configuration and the labeling of vertex A. Figure 14.16(u) shows the results of this. When we take those seven descriptions and eliminate rotational and angular variations, we see that only three distinct ones remain, as shown in Figure 14.16(b). If we continue this process for objects filling up to seven octants (there can be no vertices if all eight octants are filled), we get a complete list of the possible trihedral vertices and their labelings (equivalent to that developed by Clowes [1971]). This list is shown in Figure 14.17. Notice that of the 208 labelings that we said were theoretically possible, only eighteen are physically possible. Thus we have found a severe constraint on the way that lines in drawings corresponding to real figures can be labeled.

Of course, at this point we have only found a constraint on the ways in which simple trihedral vertices can be labeled. Many figures, such as those shown in Figure 14.11, contain nontrihedral vertices. In addition, many figures contain shadow areas, which can be of great use in analyzing the scene that is being portrayed. When these variations are considered, there do become more than eighteen allowable vertex labelings. But when these variations are allowed, the number of theoretically possible labelings becomes much larger than 208, and, in fact, the ratio of physically allowable vertices to theoretically possible ones becomes even smaller than 18/208. Thus not only can this approach be extended to larger domains, it must be.

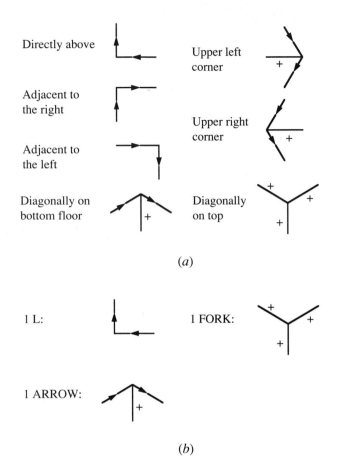

Figure 14.16: The Vertices of a Figure Occupying One Octant

As a result of this analysis, we have been able to articulate one class of constraints that will be needed by a line-labeling procedure. These constraints are static (since the physical rules they are based on never change), and so they do not need to be represented explicitly as part of a problem state. They can be encoded directly into the line-labeling algorithm. The other class of constraints we will need contains the dynamic ones that describe the current options for the labeling of each vertex. These constraints will be represented and manipulated explicitly by the line-labeling algorithm.

Applying Constraints in Analysis Problems

Having analyzed the domain in which we are working and extracted a set of constraints that objects in the domain must satisfy, we need next to apply those constraints to the problem of analyzing inputs in the domain. To do this, we use a form of the constraint satisfaction procedure described in Section 3.5. It turns out that for this problem it is

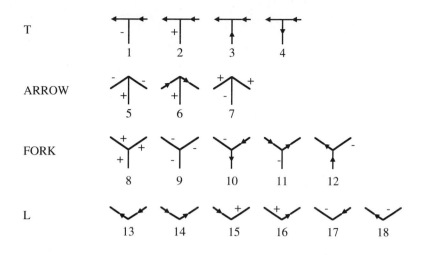

Figure 14.17: The Eighteen Physically Possible Trihedral Vertices

not necessary to use the second part of our constraint satisfaction procedure (the one that makes guesses and results in search). The domain provides sufficiently powerful constraints that it is not necessary to resort to search. Thus the *Waltz algorithm* [Waltz, 1975], which we present here, omits that step entirely.

To label line drawings of the sort we are considering, we first pick one vertex and find all the labelings that are possible for it. Then we move to an adjacent vertex and find all of its possible labelings. The line that we followed to get from the first vertex to the second must end up with only one label, and that label must be consistent with the two vertices it enters. So any labelings for either of the two vertices that require the line to be labeled in a way that is inconsistent with the other vertex can be eliminated. Now another vertex, adjacent to one of the first two, can be labeled. New constraints will arise from this labeling and these constraints can be propagated back to vertices that have already been labeled, so the set of possible labelings for them is further reduced. This process proceeds until all the vertices in the figure have been labeled.

As an example, consider the simple drawing shown in Figure 14.18(*a*). We can begin by labeling all the boundary edges, as shown in Figure 14.18(*b*). Suppose we then begin labeling vertices at vertex 1. The only vertex label that is consistent with the known line labels is 13. At vertex 2, the only consistent label is 6. At each of the remaining boundary vertices, there is also only one labeling choice. These labelings are shown in parentheses in Figure 14.18(*c*). Now consider vertex 7. Just looking at vertex 7 itself, it would appear that any of the five FORK labelings is possible. But from the only labeling we found for vertex 2, we know that the line between vertices 2 and 7 must be labeled +. This makes sense since it obviously represents a convex edge. Using this fact, we can eliminate four of the possible FORK labels. Only label 8 is now possible. The complete labeling just computed is shown in Figure 14.18(*d*). Thus we see that by exploiting constraints on vertex labelings, we have correctly identified vertex 7 as being formed by three convex edges.

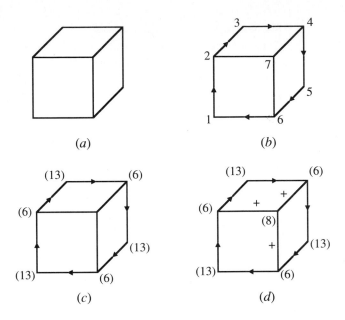

Figure 14.18: A Simple Example of the Labeling Process

We can now specify in more detail this particular version of constraint propagation.

Algorithm: Waltz

1. Find the lines at the border of the scene boundary and label them. These lines can be found by finding an outline such that no vertices are outside it. We do this first because this labeling will impose additional constraints on the other labelings in the figure.

2. Number the vertices of the figure to be analyzed. These numbers will correspond to the order in which the vertices will be visited during the labeling process. To decide on a numbering, do the following:

   (a) Start at any vertex on the boundary of the figure. Since boundary lines are known, the vertices involving them are more highly constrained than are interior ones.

   (b) Move from the vertex along the boundary to an adjacent unnumbered vertex and continue until all boundary vertices have been numbered.

   (c) Number interior vertices by moving from a numbered vertex to some adjacent unnumbered one. By always labeling a vertex next to one that has already been labeled, maximum use can be made of the constraints.

3. Visit each vertex V in order and attempt to label it by doing the following:

(a) Using the set of possible vertex labelings given in Figure 14.17, attach to *V* a list of its possible labelings.

(b) See whether some of these labelings can be eliminated on the basis of local constraints. To do this, examine each vertex *A* that is adjacent to *V* and that has already been visited. Check to see that for each proposed labeling for *V*, there is a way to label the line between *V* and *A* in such a way that at least one of the labelings listed for *A* is still possible. Eliminate from *V*'s list any labeling for which this is not the case.

(c) Use the set of labelings just attached to *V* to constrain the labelings at vertices adjacent to *V*. For each vertex *A* that was visited in the last step, do the following:

    i. Eliminate all labelings of *A* that are not consistent with at least one labeling of *V*.

    ii. If any labelings were eliminated, continue constraint propagation by examining the vertices adjacent to *A* and checking for consistency with the restricted set of labelings now attached to *A*.

    iii. Continue to propagate until there are no adjacent labeled vertices or until there is no change made to the existing set of labelings.

This algorithm will always find the unique, correct figure labeling if one exists. If a figure is ambiguous, however, the algorithm will terminate with at least one vertex still having more than one labeling attached to it.

Actually, this algorithm, as described by Waltz, was applied to a larger class of figures in which cracks and shadows might occur. But the operation of the algorithm is the same regardless of the size of the table of allowable vertex labelings that it uses. In fact, as suggested in the last section, the usefulness of the algorithm increases as the size of the domain increases and thus the ratio of physically possible to theoretically possible vertices decreases. Waltz's program, for example, used shadow information, which appears in the figure locally as shadow lines, as a way of exploiting a global constraint, namely that a single source of light produces consistent shadows.

14.4 Summary

In this chapter we outlined the major difficulties that confront programs designed to perform perceptual tasks. We also described the use of the constraint satisfaction procedure as one way of surmounting some of those difficulties.

Sometimes the problems of speech and image understanding are important in the construction of stand-alone programs to solve one particular task. But they also play an important role in the larger field of *robotics*, which has as its goal the construction of intelligent robots capable of functioning with some degree of autonomy. For such robots, perceptual abilities are essential. We will return to these issues in Chapter 21.

14.5   Exercises

1. One of the reasons that understanding complex perceptual patterns is difficult is that if the pattern is composed of more than one object, a variety of difficult-to-predict phenomena may occur at the junctions between objects. For example, when the phrase "Could you go?" is spoken, a *j* sound appears between the words, "could" and "you." Give another example of boundary interference in speech. Also give one example of it in vision.

2. Which of the following figures are trihedral?

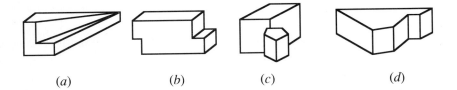

(a)   (b)   (c)   (d)

3. In Section 14.3, we analyzed all the ways that a vertex of a trihedral object that occupies one octant of the space formed by the intersection of its planes could be labeled. Complete this analysis for vertices of objects that occupy two through seven octants.

4. For each of the drawings in Figure 14.10, show how the Waltz algorithm would produce a labeling.

5. In our description of the Waltz algorithm, we first assigned to each vertex V all the labelings that might be attached to it. Then we looked at all adjacent vertices in an attempt to constrain the set of labelings associated with V. And then we went back to each adjacent vertex A to see if the knowledge about V could be used to further constrain the labelings for A. Why could we not simply visit each adjacent vertex once and perform both these steps then?

6. Give an example of an ambiguous figure for which the Waltz algorithm would not find a unique labeling.

Chapter 15

Natural Language Processing

Language is meant for communicating about the world. By studying language, we can come to understand more about the world. We can test our theories about the world by how well they support our attempt to understand language. And, if we can succeed at building a computational model of language, we will have a powerful tool for communicating about the world. In this chapter, we look at how we can exploit knowledge about the world, in combination with linguistic facts, to build computational natural language systems.

Throughout this discussion, it is going to be important to keep in mind that the difficulties we will encounter do not exist out of perversity on the part of some diabolical designer. Instead, what we see as difficulties when we try to analyze language are just the flip sides of the very properties that make language so powerful. Figure 15.1 shows some examples of this. As we pursue our discussion of language processing, it is important to keep the good sides in mind since it is because of them that language is significant enough a phenomenon to be worth all the trouble.

By far the largest part of human linguistic communication occurs as speech. Written language is a fairly recent invention and still plays a less central role than speech in most activities. But processing written language (assuming it is written in unambiguous characters) is easier, in some ways, than processing speech. For example, to build a program that understands spoken language, we need all the facilities of a written language understander as well as enough additional knowledge to handle all the noise and ambiguities of the audio signal.[1] Thus it is useful to divide the entire language-processing problem into two tasks:

- Processing written text, using lexical, syntactic, and semantic knowledge of the language as well as the required real world information

- Processing spoken language, using all the information needed above plus additional knowledge about phonology as well as enough added information to handle the further ambiguities that arise in speech

---

[1] Actually, in understanding spoken language, we take advantage of clues, such as intonation and the presence of pauses, to which we do not have access when we read. We can make the task of a speech-understanding program easier by allowing it, too, to use these cues, but to do so, we must know enough about them to incorporate into the program knowledge of how to use them.

The Problem: English sentences are incomplete descriptions of the information that they are intended to convey:

Some dogs are outside.   I called Lynda to ask her
                                               to the movies.
                                          She said she'd love to go.

         ↓   ↓

Some dogs are on the lawn.   She was home when I called.
Three dogs are on the lawn.   She answered the phone.
Rover, Tripp, and Spot are on the lawn.   I actually asked her.

The Good Side: Language allows speakers to be as vague or as precise as they like. It also allows speakers to leave out things they believe their hearers already know.

The Problem: The same expression means different things in different contexts:

Where's the water? (in a chemistry lab, it must be pure)
Where's the water? (when you are thirsty, it must be potable)
Where's the water? (dealing with a leaky roof, it can be filthy)

The Good Side: Language lets us communicate about an infinite world using a finite (and thus learnable) number of symbols.

The Problem: No natural language program can be complete because new words, expressions, and meanings can be generated quite freely:

I'll fax it to you.

The Good Side: Language can evolve as the experiences that we want to communicate about evolve.

The Problem: There are lots of ways to say the same thing:

Mary was born on October 11.
Mary's birthday is October 11.

The Good Side: When you know a lot, facts imply each other. Language is intended to be used by agents who know a lot.

Figure 15.1: Features of Language That Make It Both Difficult and Useful

In Chapter 14 we described some of the issues that arise in speech understanding, and in Section 21.2.2 we return to them in more detail. In this chapter, though, we concentrate on written language processing (usually called simply *natural language processing*).

Throughout this discussion of natural language processing, the focus is on English. This happens to be convenient and turns out to be where much of the work in the field has occurred. But the major issues we address are common to all natural languages. In fact, the techniques we discuss are particularly important in the task of translating from one natural language to another.

Natural language processing includes both understanding and generation, as well as other tasks such as multilingual translation. In this chapter we focus on understanding, although in Section 15.5 we will provide some references to work in these other areas.

15.1 Introduction

Recall that in the last chapter we defined understanding as the process of mapping from an input form into a more immediately useful form. It is this view of understanding that we pursue throughout this chapter. But it is useful to point out here that there is a formal sense in which a language can be defined simply as a set of strings without reference to any world being described or task to be performed. Although some of the ideas that have come out of this formal study of languages can be exploited in parts of the understanding process, they are only the beginning. To get the overall picture, we need to think of language as a pair (source language, target representation), together with a mapping between elements of each to the other. The target representation will have been chosen to be appropriate for the task at hand. Often, if the task has clearly been agreed on and the details of the target representation are not important in a particular discussion, we talk just about the language itself, but the other half of the pair is really always present.

One of the great philosophical debates throughout the centuries has centered around the question of what a sentence means. We do not claim to have found the definitive answer to that question. But once we realize that understanding a piece of language involves mapping it into some representation appropriate to a particular situation, it becomes easy to see why the questions "What is language understanding?" and "What does a sentence mean?" have proved to be so difficult to answer. We use language in such a wide variety of situations that no single definition of understanding is able to account for them all. As we set about the task of building computer programs that understand natural language, one of the first things we have to do is define precisely what the underlying task is and what the target representation should look like. In the rest of this chapter, we assume that our goal is to be able to reason with the knowledge contained in the linguistic expressions, and we exploit a frame language as our target representation.

15.1.1 Steps in the Process

Before we go into detail on the several components of the natural language understanding process, it is useful to survey all of them and see how they fit together. Roughly, we can break the process down into the following pieces:

- Morphological Analysis—Individual words are analyzed into their components, and nonword tokens, such as punctuation, are separated from the words.

- Syntactic Analysis—Linear sequences of words are transformed into structures that show how the words relate to each other. Some word sequences may be rejected if they violate the language's rules for how words may be combined. For example, an English syntactic analyzer would reject the sentence "Boy the go the to store."

- Semantic Analysis—The structures created by the syntactic analyzer are assigned meanings. In other words, a mapping is made between the syntactic structures and objects in the task domain. Structures for which no such mapping is possible may be rejected. For example, in most universes, the sentence "Colorless green ideas sleep furiously" [Chomsky, 1957] would be rejected as *semantically anomolous*.

- Discourse Integration—The meaning of an individual sentence may depend on the sentences that precede it and may influence the meanings of the sentences that follow it. For example, the word "it" in the sentence, "John wanted it," depends on the prior discourse context, while the word "John" may influence the meaning of later sentences (such as, "He always had.")

- Pragmatic Analysis—The structure representing what was said is reinterpreted to determine what was actually meant. For example, the sentence "Do you know what time it is?" should be interpreted as a request to be told the time.

The boundaries between these five phases are often very fuzzy. The phases are sometimes performed in sequence, and they are sometimes performed all at once. If they are performed in sequence, one may need to appeal for assistance to another. For example, part of the process of performing the syntactic analysis of the sentence "Is the glass jar peanut butter?" is deciding how to form two noun phrases out of the four nouns at the end of the sentence (giving a sentence of the form "Is the x y?"). All of the following constituents are syntactically possible: glass, glass jar, glass jar peanut, jar peanut butter, peanut butter, butter. A syntactic processor on its own has no way to choose among these, and so any decision must be made by appealing to some model of the world in which some of these phrases make sense and others do not. If we do this, then we get a syntactic structure in which the constituents "glass jar" and "peanut butter" appear. Thus although it is often useful to separate these five processing phases to some extent, they can all interact in a variety of ways, making a complete separation impossible.

Specifically, to make the overall language understanding problem tractable, it will help if we distinguish between the following two ways of decomposing a program:

- The processes and the knowledge required to perform the task

- The global control structure that is imposed on those processes

In this chapter, we focus primarily on the first of these issues. It is the one that has received the most attention from people working on this problem. We do not completely ignore the second issue, although considerably less of substance is known about it. For an example of this kind of discussion that talks about interleaving syntactic and semantic processing, see Lytinen [1986].

With that caveat, let's consider an example to see how the individual processes work. In this example, we assume that the processes happen sequentially. Suppose we have an English interface to an operating system and the following sentence is typed:

I want to print Bill's .init file.

Morphological Analysis

Morphological analysis must do the following things:

- Pull apart the word "Bill's" into the proper noun "Bill" and the possessive suffix "'s"

- Recognize the sequence ".init" as a file extension that is functioning as an adjective in the sentence

In addition, this process will usually assign syntactic categories to all the words in the sentence. This is usually done now because interpretations for affixes (prefixes and suffixes) may depend on the syntactic category of the complete word. For example, consider the word "prints." This word is either a plural noun (with the "-s" marking plural) or a third person singular verb (as in "he prints"), in which case the "-s" indicates both singular and third person. If this step is done now, then in our example, there will be ambiguity since "want," "print," and "file" can all function as more than one syntactic category.

Syntactic Analysis

Syntactic analysis must exploit the results of morphological analysis to build a structural description of the sentence. The goal of this process, called *parsing*, is to convert the flat list of words that forms the sentence into a structure that defines the units that are represented by that flat list. For our example sentence, the result of parsing is shown in Figure 15.2. The details of this representation are not particularly significant; we describe alternative versions of them in Section 15.2. What is important here is that a flat sentence has been converted into a hierarchical structure and that that structure has been designed to correspond to sentence units (such as noun phrases) that will correspond to meaning units when semantic analysis is performed. One useful thing we have done here, although not all syntactic systems do, is create a set of entities we call *reference markers*. They are shown in parentheses in the parse tree. Each one corresponds to some entity that has been mentioned in the sentence. These reference markers are useful later since they provide a place in which to accumulate information about the entities as we get it. Thus although we have not tried to do semantic analysis (i.e., assign meaning) at this point, we have designed our syntactic analysis process so that it will find constituents to which meaning can be assigned.

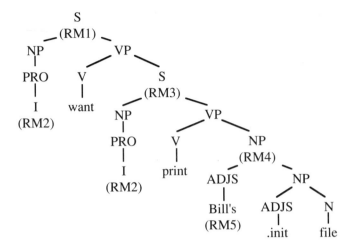

Figure 15.2: The Result of Syntactic Analysis of "I want to print Bill's .init file."

Semantic Analysis

Semantic analysis must do two important things:

- It must map individual words into appropriate objects in the knowledge base or database.

- It must create the correct structures to correspond to the way the meanings of the individual words combine with each other.

For this example, suppose that we have a frame-based knowledge base that contains the units shown in Figure 15.3. Then we can generate a partial meaning, with respect to that knowledge base, as shown in Figure 15.4. Reference marker *RM1* corresponds to the top-level event of the sentence. It is a wanting event in which the speaker (denoted by "I") wants a printing event to occur in which the same speaker prints a file whose extension is ".init" and whose owner is Bill.

Discourse Integration

At this point, we have figured out what kinds of things this sentence is about. But we do not yet know which specific individuals are being referred to. Specifically, we do not know to whom the pronoun "I" or the proper noun "Bill" refers. To pin down these references requires an appeal to a model of the current discourse context, from which we can learn that the current user (who typed the word "I") is *User068* and that the only

User
    isa :   *Person*
    * *login-name* :   must be <string>

User068
    instance :   *User*
    login-name :   *Susan-Black*

User073
    instance :   *User*
    login-name :   *Bill-Smith*

F1
    instance :   *File-Struct*
    name :   stuff
    extension :   .init
    owner :   *User073*
    in-directory :   /wsmith/

File-Struct
    isa :   *Information-Object*

Printing
    isa :   *Physical-Event*
    * *agent* :   must be <animate or program>
    * *object* :   must be <information-object>

Wanting
    isa :   *Mental-Event*
    * *agent* :   must be <animate>
    * *object* :   must be <state or event>

Commanding
    isa :   *Mental-Event*
    * *agent* :   must be <animate>
    * *performer* :   must be <animate or program>
    * *object* :   must be <event>

This-System
    instance :   *Program*

Figure 15.3: A Knowledge Base Fragment

RM1		{the whole sentence}
instance :	*Wanting*	
agent :	*RM2*	{I}
object :	*RM3*	{a printing event}
RM2		{I}
RM3		{a printing event}
instance :	*Printing*	
agent :	*RM2*	{I}
object :	*RM4*	{Bill's .init file}
RM4		{Bill's .init file}
instance :	*File-Struct*	
extension :	.init	
owner :	*RM5*	{Bill}
RM5		{Bill}
instance :	*Person*	
first-name :	Bill	

Figure 15.4: A Partial Meaning for a Sentence

person named "Bill" about whom we could be talking is *User073*. Once the correct referent for Bill is known, we can also determine exactly which file is being referred to: *F1* is the only file with the extension ".init" that is owned by Bill.

Pragmatic Analysis

We now have a complete description, in the terms provided by our knowledge base, of what was said. The final step toward effective understanding is to decide what to do as a result. One possible thing to do is to record what was said as a fact and be done with it. For some sentences, whose intended effect is clearly declarative, that is precisely the correct thing to do. But for other sentences, including this one, the intended effect is different. We can discover this intended effect by applying a set of rules that characterize cooperative dialogues. In this example, we use the fact that when the user claims to want something that the system is capable of performing, then the system should go ahead and do it. This produces the final meaning shown in Figure 15.5.

The final step in pragmatic processing is to translate, when necessary, from the knowledge-based representation to a command to be executed by the system. In this case, this step is necessary, and we see that the final result of the understanding process is

    lpr /wsmith/stuff.init

Meaning
    instance :   *Commanding*
    agent :   *User068*
    performer :   *This-System*
    object :   *P27*
P27
    instance :   *Printing*
    agent :   *This-System*
    object :   *F1*

Figure 15.5: Representing the Intended Meaning

where "lpr" is the operating system's file print command.

Summary

At this point, we have seen the results of each of the main processes that combine to form a natural language system. In a complete system, all of these processes are necessary in some form. For example, it may have seemed that we could have skipped the knowledge-based representation of the meaning of the sentence since the final output of the understanding system bore no relationship to it. But it is that intermediate knowledge-based representation to which we usually attach the knowledge that supports the creation of the final answer.

All of the processes we have described are important in a complete natural language understanding system. But not all programs are written with exactly these components. Sometimes two or more of them are collapsed, as we will see in several sections later in this chapter. Doing that usually results in a system that is easier to build for restricted subsets of English but one that is harder to extend to wider coverage. In the rest of this chapter we describe the major processes in more detail and talk about some of the ways in which they can be put together to form a complete system.

15.2 Syntactic Processing

Syntactic processing is the step in which a flat input sentence is converted into a hierarchical structure that corresponds to the units of meaning in the sentence. This process is called *parsing*. Although there are natural language understanding systems that skip this step (for example, see Section 15.3.3), it plays an important role in many natural language understanding systems for two reasons:

- Semantic processing must operate on sentence constituents. If there is no syntactic parsing step, then the semantics system must decide on its own constituents. If parsing is done, on the other hand, it constrains the number of constituents that semantics can consider. Syntactic parsing is computationally less expensive than is semantic processing (which may require substantial inference). Thus it can play a significant role in reducing overall system complexity.

- Although it is often possible to extract the meaning of a sentence without using grammatical facts, it is not always possible to do so. Consider, for example, the sentences

  - The satellite orbited Mars.

  - Mars orbited the satellite.

  In the second sentence, syntactic facts demand an interpretation in which a planet (Mars) revolves around a satellite, despite the apparent improbability of such a scenario.

Although there are many ways to produce a parse, almost all the systems that are actually used have two main components:

- A declarative representation, called a *grammar*, of the syntactic facts about the language

- A procedure, called a *parser*, that compares the grammar against input sentences to produce parsed structures

15.2.1   Grammars and Parsers

The most common way to represent grammars is as a set of production rules. Although details of the forms that are allowed in the rules vary, the basic idea remains the same and is illustrated in Figure 15.6, which shows a simple context-free, phrase structure grammar for English. Read the first rule as, "A sentence is composed of a noun phrase followed by a verb phrase." In this grammar, the vertical bar should be read as "or." The ε denotes the empty string. Symbols that are further expanded by rules are called *nonterminal symbols*. Symbols that correspond directly to strings that must be found in an input sentence are called *terminal symbols*.

Grammar formalisms such as this one underlie many linguistic theories, which in turn provide the basis for many natural language understanding systems. Modern linguistic theories include: the government binding theory of Chomsky [1981; 1986], GPSG [Gazdar *et al.*, 1985], LFG [Bresnan, 1982], and categorial grammar [Ades and Steedman, 1982; Oehrle *et al.*, 1987]. The first three of these are also discussed in Sells [1986]. We should point out here that there is general agreement that pure, context-free grammars are not effective for describing natural languages.[2] As a result, natural language processing systems have less in common with computer language processing systems (such as compilers) than you might expect.

Regardless of the theoretical basis of the grammar, the parsing process takes the rules of the grammar and compares them against the input sentence. Each rule that matches adds something to the complete structure that is being built for the sentence.

---

[2]There is, however, still some debate on whether context-free grammars are formally adequate for describing natural languages (e.g., Gazdar [1982].)

$$S \rightarrow NP\ VP$$
$$NP \rightarrow the\ NP1$$
$$NP \rightarrow PRO$$
$$NP \rightarrow PN$$
$$NP \rightarrow NP1$$
$$NP1 \rightarrow ADJS\ N$$
$$ADJS \rightarrow \varepsilon\ |\ ADJ\ ADJS$$
$$VP \rightarrow V$$
$$VP \rightarrow V\ NP$$
$$N \rightarrow file\ |\ printer$$
$$PN \rightarrow Bill$$
$$PRO \rightarrow I$$
$$ADJ \rightarrow short\ |\ long\ |\ fast$$
$$V \rightarrow printed\ |\ created\ |\ want$$

Figure 15.6: A Simple Grammar for a Fragment of English

The simplest structure to build is a *parse tree*, which simply records the rules and how they are matched. Figure 15.7 shows the parse tree that would be produced for the sentence "Bill printed the file" using this grammar. Figure 15.2 contained another example of a parse tree, although some additions to this grammar would be required to produce it.

Notice that every node of the parse tree corresponds either to an input word or to a nonterminal in our grammar. Each level in the parse tree corresponds to the application of one grammar rule. As a result, it should be clear that a grammar specifies two things about a language:

- Its weak generative capacity, by which we mean the set of sentences that are contained within the language. This set (called the set of *grammatical sentences*) is made up of precisely those sentences that can be completely matched by a series of rules in the grammar.

- Its strong generative capacity, by which we mean the structure (or possibly structures) to be assigned to each grammatical sentence of the language.

So far, we have shown the result of parsing to be exactly a trace of the rules that were applied during it. This is not always the case, though. Some grammars contain additional information that describes the structure that should be built. We present an example of such a grammar in Section 15.2.2.

But first we need to look at two important issues that define the space of possible parsers that can exploit the grammars we write.

Top-Down versus Bottom-Up Parsing

To parse a sentence, it is necessary to find a way in which that sentence could have been generated from the start symbol. There are two ways that this can be done:

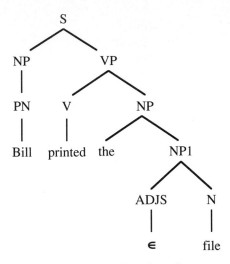

Figure 15.7: A Parse Tree for a Sentence

- *Top-Down Parsing*—Begin with the start symbol and apply the grammar rules forward until the symbols at the terminals of the tree correspond to the components of the sentence being parsed.

- *Bottom-Up Parsing*—Begin with the sentence to be parsed and apply the grammar rules backward until a single tree whose terminals are the words of the sentence and whose top node is the start symbol has been produced.

The choice between these two approaches is similar to the choice between forward and backward reasoning in other problem-solving tasks. The most important consideration is the branching factor. Is it greater going backward or forward? Another important issue is the availability of good heuristics for evaluating progress. Can partial information be used to rule out paths early? Sometimes these two approaches are combined into a single method called *bottom-up parsing with top-down filtering*. In this method, parsing proceeds essentially bottom-up (i.e., the grammar rules are applied backward). But using tables that have been precomputed for a particular grammar, the parser can immediately eliminate constituents that can never be combined into useful higher-level structures.

Finding One Interpretation or Finding Many

As several of the examples above have shown, the process of understanding a sentence is a search process in which a large universe of possible interpretations must be explored to find one that meets all the constraints imposed by a particular sentence. As for any search process, we must decide whether to explore all possible paths or, instead, to explore only a single most likely one and to produce only the result of that one path as the answer.

Suppose, for example, that a sentence processor looks at the words of an input sentence one at a time, from left to right, and suppose that so far, it has seen:

"Have the students who missed the exam—"

There are two paths that the processor could be following at this point:

- "Have" is the main verb of an imperative sentence, such as

    "Have the students who missed the exam take it today."

- "Have" is an auxiliary verb of an interrogative sentence, such as

    "Have the students who missed the exam taken it today?"

There are four ways of handling sentences such as these:

- *All Paths*—Follow all possible paths and build all the possible intermediate components. Many of the components will later be ignored because the other inputs required to use them will not appear. For example, if the auxiliary verb interpretation of "have" in the previous example is built, it will be discarded if no participle, such as "taken," ever appears. The major disadvantage of this approach is that, because it results in many spurious constituents being built and many deadend paths being followed, it can be very inefficient.

- *Best Path with Backtracking*—Follow only one path at a time, but record, at every choice point, the information that is necessary to make another choice if the chosen path fails to lead to a complete interpretation of the sentence. In this example, if the auxiliary verb interpretation of "have" were chosen first and the end of the sentence appeared with no main verb having been seen, the understander would detect failure and backtrack to try some other path. There are two important drawbacks to this approach. The first is that a good deal of time may be wasted saving state descriptions at each choice point, even though backtracking will occur to only a few of those points. The second is that often the same constituent may be analyzed many times. In our example, if the wrong interpretation is selected for the word "have," it will not be detected until after the phrase "the students who missed the exam" has been recognized. Once the error is detected, a simple backtracking mechanism will undo everything that was done after the incorrect interpretation of "have" was chosen, and the noun phrase will be reinterpreted (identically) after the second interpretation of "have" has been selected. This problem can be avoided using some form of dependency-directed backtracking, but then the implementation of the parser is more complex.

- *Best Path with Patchup*—Follow only one path at a time, but when an error is detected, explicitly shuffle around the components that have already been formed. Again, using the same example, if the auxiliary verb interpretation of "have" were chosen first, then the noun phrase "the students who missed the exam" would be interpreted and recorded as the subject of the sentence. If the word "taken" appears next, this path can simply be continued. But if "take" occurs next, the understander can simply shift components into different slots. "Have" becomes the main verb. The noun phrase that was marked as the subject of the sentence becomes the subject of the embedded sentence "The students who missed the exam take it today." And the subject of the main sentence can be filled in as "you," the default subject for imperative sentences. This approach is usually more efficient than the previous two techniques. Its major disadvantage is that it requires interactions among the rules of the grammar to be made explicit in the rules for moving components from one place to another. The interpreter often becomes *ad hoc*, rather than being simple and driven exclusively from the grammar.

- *Wait and See*—Follow only one path, but rather than making decisions about the function of each component as it is encountered, procrastinate the decision until enough information is available to make the decision correctly. Using this approach, when the word "have" of our example is encountered, it would be recorded as some kind of verb whose function is, as yet, unknown. The following noun phrase would then be interpreted and recorded simply as a noun phrase. Then, when the next word is encountered, a decision can be made about how all the constituents encountered so far should be combined. Although several parsers have used some form of wait-and-see strategy, one, PARSIFAL [Marcus, 1980], relies on it exclusively. It uses a small, fixed-size buffer in which constituents can be stored until their purpose can be decided upon. This approach is very efficient, but it does have the drawback that if the amount of lookahead that is necessary is greater than the size of the buffer, then the interpreter will fail. But the sentences on which it fails are exactly those on which people have trouble, apparently because they choose one interpretation, which proves to be wrong. A classic example of this phenomenon, called the *garden path sentence*, is

    The horse raced past the barn fell down.

Although the problems of deciding which paths to follow and how to handle backtracking are common to all search processes, they are complicated in the case of language understanding by the existence of genuinely ambiguous sentences, such as our earlier example "They are flying planes." If it is important that not just one interpretation but rather all possible ones be found, then either all possible paths must be followed (which is very expensive since most of them will die out before the end of the sentence) or backtracking must be forced (which is also expensive because of duplicated computations). Many practical systems are content to find a single plausible interpretation. If that interpretation is later rejected, possibly for semantic or pragmatic reasons, then a new attempt to find a different interpretation can be made.

Parser Summary

As this discussion suggests, there are many different kinds of parsing systems. There are three that have been used fairly extensively in natural language systems:

- Chart parsers [Winograd, 1983], which provide a way of avoiding backup by storing intermediate constituents so that they can be reused along alternative parsing paths.

- Definite clause grammars [Pereira and Warren, 1980], in which grammar rules are written as PROLOG clauses and the PROLOG interpreter is used to perform top-down, depth-first parsing.

- Augmented transition networks (or ATNs) [Woods, 1970], in which the parsing process is described as the transition from a start state to a final state in a transition network that corresponds to a grammar of English.

We do not have space here to go into all these methods. In the next section, we illustrate the main ideas involved in parsing by working through an example with an ATN. After this, we look at one way of parsing with a more declarative representation.

15.2.2 Augmented Transition Networks

An augmented transition network (ATN) is a top-down parsing procedure that allows various kinds of knowledge to be incorporated into the parsing system so it can operate efficiently. Since the early use of the ATN in the LUNAR system [Woods, 1973], which provided access to a large database of information on lunar geology, the mechanism has been exploited in many language-understanding systems. The ATN is similar to a finite state machine in which the class of labels that can be attached to the arcs that define transitions between states has been augmented. Arcs may be labeled with an arbitrary combination of the following:

- Specific words, such as "in."

- Word categories, such as "noun."

- Pushes to other networks that recognize significant components of a sentence. For example, a network designed to recognize a prepositional phrase (PP) may include an arc that asks for ("pushes for") a noun phrase (NP).

- Procedures that perform arbitrary tests on both the current input and on sentence components that have already been identified.

- Procedures that build structures that will form part of the final parse.

Figure 15.8 shows an example of an ATN in graphical notation. Figure 15.9 shows the top-level ATN of that example in a notation that a program could read. To see how an ATN works, let us trace the execution of this ATN as it parses the following sentence:

The long file has printed.

This execution proceeds as follows:

1. Begin in state S.

2. Push to NP.

3. Do a category test to see if "the" is a determiner.

4. This test succeeds, so set the DETERMINER register to DEFINITE and go to state Q6.

5. Do a category test to see if "long" is an adjective.

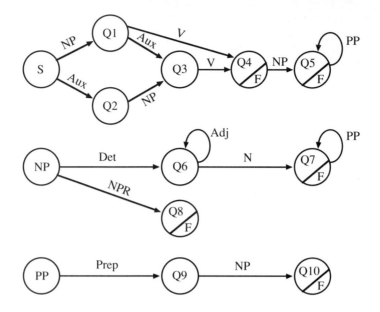

Figure 15.8: An ATN Network for a Fragment of English

6. This test succeeds, so append "long" to the list contained in the ADJS register. (This list was previously empty.) Stay in state Q6.

7. Do a category test to see if "file" is an adjective. This test fails.

8. Do a category test to see if "file" is a noun. This test succeeds, so set the NOUN register to "file" and go to state Q7.

9. Push to PP.

10. Do a category test to see if "has" is a preposition. This test fails, so pop and signal failure.

11. There is nothing else that can be done from state Q7, so pop and return the structure

    (NP (FILE (LONG) DEFINITE))

    The return causes the machine to be in state Q1, with the SUBJ register set to the structure just returned and the TYPE register set to DCL.

12. Do a category test to see if "has" is a verb. This test succeeds, so set the AUX register to NIL and set the V register to "has." Go to state Q4.

13. Push to state NP. Since the next word, "printed," is not a determiner or a proper noun, NP will pop and return failure.

14. The only other thing to do in state Q4 is to halt. But more input remains, so a complete parse has not been found. Backtracking is now required.

```
(S/    (PUSH NP/ T
          (SETR SUBJ *)
          (SETR TYPE (QUOTE DCL))
          (TO Q1))
       (CAT AUX T
          (SETR AUX *)
          (SETR TYPE (QUOTE Q))
          (TO Q2)))
(Q1    (CAT V T
          (SETR AUX NIL)
          (SETR V *)
          (TO Q4))
       (CAT AUX T
          (SETR AUX *)
          (TO Q3)))
(Q2    (PUSH NP/ T
          (SETR SUBJ *)
          (TO Q3)))
(Q3    (CAT V T
          (SETR V *)
          (TO Q4)))
(Q4    (POP (BUILDQ (S + + + (VP +))
                  TYPE SUBJ AUX V) T)
       (PUSH NP/ T
          (SETR VP (BUILDQ (VP (V +) *) V))
          (TO Q5)))
(Q5    (POP (BUILDQ (S + + + +)
                  TYPE SUBJ AUX VP) T)
       (PUSH PP/ T
          (SETR VP (APPEND (GETR VP) (LIST *)))
          (TO Q5)))
```

Figure 15.9: An ATN Grammar in List Form

15. The last choice point was at state Q1, so return there. The registers AUX and V must be unset.

16. Do a category test to see if "has" is an auxiliary. This test succeeds, so set the AUX register to "has" and go to state Q3.

17. Do a category test to see if "printed" is a verb. This test succeeds, so set the V register to "printed." Go to state Q4.

18. Now, since the input is exhausted, Q4 is an acceptable final state. Pop and return the structure

    (S   DCL   (NP (FILE (LONG) DEFINITE))
                 HAS
                 (VP PRINTED))

This structure is the output of the parse.

This example grammar illustrates several interesting points about the use of ATNs. A single subnetwork need only occur once even though it is used in more than one place. A network can be called recursively. Any number of internal registers may be used to contain the result of the parse. The result of a network can be built, using the function BUILDQ, out of values contained in the various system registers. A single state may be both a final state, in which a complete sentence has been found, and an intermediate state, in which only a part of a sentence has been recognized. And, finally, the contents of a register can be modified at any time.

In addition, there are a variety of ways in which ATNs can be used which are not shown in this example:

- The contents of registers can be swapped. For example, if the network were expanded to recognize passive sentences, then at the point that the passive was detected, the current contents of the SUBJ register would be transferred to an OBJ register and the object of the preposition "by" would be placed in the SUBJ register. Thus the final interpretation of the following two sentences would be the same.

    - Bill printed the file.
    - The file was printed by Bill.

- Arbitrary tests can be placed on the arcs. In each of the arcs in this example, the test is specified simply as T (always true). But this need not be the case. Suppose that when the first NP is found, its number is determined and recorded in a register called NUMBER. Then the arcs labeled V could have an additional test placed on them that checked that the number of the particular verb that was found is equal to the value stored in NUMBER. More sophisticated tests, involving semantic markers or other semantic features, can also be performed.

15.2.3   Unification Grammars

ATN grammars have substantial procedural components. The grammar describes the order in which constituents must be built. Variables are explicitly given values, and they must already have been assigned a value before they can be referenced. This procedurality limits the effectiveness of ATN grammars in some cases, for example: in speech processing where some later parts of the sentence may have been recognized clearly while earlier parts are still unknown (for example, suppose we had heard, "The long * * * file printed."), or in systems that want to use the same grammar to support both understanding and generation (e.g., Appelt [1987], Shieber [1988], and Barnett *et al.* [1990]). Although there is no clear distinction between declarative and procedural representations (as we saw in Section 6.1), there is a spectrum and it often turns out that more declarative representations are more flexible than more procedural ones are. So in this section we describe a declarative approach to representing grammars.

When a parser applies grammar rules to a sentence, it performs two major kinds of operations:

- Matching (of sentence constituents to grammar rules)

- Building structure (corresponding to the result of combining constituents)

Now think back to the unification operation that we described in Section 5.4.4 as part of our theorem-proving discussion. Matching and structure building are operations that unification performs naturally. So an obvious candidate for representing grammars is some structure on which we can define a unification operator. Directed acyclic graphs (DAGs) can do exactly that.

Each DAG represents a set of attribute-value pairs. For example, the graphs corresponding to the words "the" and "file" are:

[CAT: DET   [CAT: N
  LEX: the]   LEX: file
                               NUMBER: SING]

Both words have a lexical category (CAT) and a lexical entry. In addition, the word "file" has a value (SING) for the NUMBER attribute. The result of combining these two words to form a simple NP can also be described as a graph:

[NP: [DET: the
      HEAD: file
      NUMBER: SING]]

The rule that forms this new constituent can also be represented as a graph, but to do so we need to introduce a new notation. Until now, all our graphs have actually been trees. To describe graphs that are not trees, we need a way to label a piece of a graph and then point to that piece elsewhere in the graph. So let $\{n\}$ for any value of n be a label, which is to be interpreted as a label for the next constituent following it in the graph. Sometimes, the constituent is empty (i.e., there is not yet any structure that is known to fill that piece of the graph). In that case, the label functions very much like a variable and will be treated like one by the unification operation. It is this degenerate kind of a label that we need in order to describe the NP rule:

NP $\rightarrow$ DET N

We can write this rule as the following graph:

```
[CONSTITUENT1: [CAT: DET
                LEX: {1}]
 CONSTITUENT2: [CAT: N
                LEX: {2}
                NUMBER: {3}]
 BUILD: [NP: [DET: {1}
             HEAD: {2}
             NUMBER: {3}]]]]
```

This rule should be read as follows: Two constituents, described in the subgraphs labeled CONSTITUENT1 and CONSTITUENT2, are to be combined. The first must be of CAT DET. We do not care what its lexical entry is, but whatever it is will be bound to the label {1}. The second constituent must be of CAT N. Its lexical entry will be bound to the label {2}, and its number will be bound to the label {3}. The result of combining these two constituents is described in the subgraph labeled BUILD. This result will be a graph corresponding to an NP with three attributes: DET, HEAD, and NUMBER. The values for all these attributes are to be taken from the appropriate pieces of the graphs that are being combined by the rule.

Now we need to define a unification operator that can be applied to the graphs we have just described. It will be very similar to logical unification. Two graphs unify if, recursively, all their subgraphs unify. The result of a successful unification is a graph that is composed of the union of the subgraphs of the two inputs, with all bindings made as indicated. This process bottoms out when a subgraph is not an attribute-value pair but is just a value for an attribute. At that point, we must define what it means for two values to unify. Identical values unify. Anything unifies with a variable (a label with no attached structure) and produces a binding for the label. The simplest thing to do is then to say that any other situation results in failure. But it may be useful to be more flexible. So some systems allow a value to match with a more general one (e.g., PROPER-NOUN matches NOUN). Others allow values that are disjunctions [e.g., (MASCULINE ∨ FEMININE)], in which case unification succeeds whenever the intersection of the two values is not empty.

There is one other important difference between logical unification and graph unification. The inputs to logical unification are treated as logical formulas. Order matters, since, for example, $f(g(a), h(b))$ is a different formula than $f(h(b), g(a))$. The inputs to graph unification, on the other hand, must be treated as sets, since the order in which attribute-value pairs are stated does not matter. For example, if a rule describes a constituent as

```
[CAT: DET
 LEX: {1}]
```

we want to be able to match a constituent such as

```
[LEX: the
 CAT: DET]
```

Algorithm: Graph-Unify

1. If either $G1$ or $G2$ is an attribute that is not itself an attribute-value pair then:

(a) If the attributes conflict (as defined above), then fail.

(b) If either is a variable, then bind it to the value of the other and return that value.

(c) Otherwise, return the most general value that is consistent with both the original values. Specifically, if disjunction is allowed, then return the intersection of the values.

2. Otherwise, do:

(a) Set variable *NEW* to empty.

(b) For each attribute A that is present (at the top level) in either $G1$ or $G2$ do

i. If A is not present at the top level in the other input, then add A and its value to *NEW*.

ii. If it is, then call Graph-Unify with the two values for A. If that fails, then fail. Otherwise, take the new value of A to be the result of that unification and add A with its value to *NEW*.

(c) If there are any labels attached to $G1$ or $G2$, then bind them to *NEW* and return *NEW*.

A simple parser can use this algorithm to apply a grammar rule by unifying CONSTITUENT1 with a proposed first constituent. If that succeeds, then CONSTITUENT2 is unified with a proposed second constituent. If that also succeeds, then a new constituent corresponding to the value of BUILD is produced. If there are variables in the value of BUILD that were bound during the matching of the constituents, then those bindings will be used to build the new constituent.

There are many possible variations on the notation we have described here. There are also a variety of ways of using it to represent dictionary entries and grammar rules. See Shieber [1986] and Knight [1989] for discussions of some of them.

Although we have presented unification here as a technique for doing syntactic analysis, it has also been used as a basis for semantic interpretation. In fact, there are arguments for using it as a uniform representation for all phases of natural language understanding. There are also arguments against doing so, primarily involving system modularity, the noncompositionality of language in some respects (see Section 15.3.4), and the need to invoke substantial domain reasoning. We will not say any more about this here, but to see how this idea could work, see Allen [1989].

15.3   Semantic Analysis

Producing a syntactic parse of a sentence is only the first step toward understanding it. We must still produce a representation of the *meaning* of the sentence. Because understanding is a mapping process, we must first define the language into which we are trying to map. There is no single, definitive language in which all sentence meanings can be described. All of the knowledge representation systems that were described in Part II are candidates, and having selected one or more of them, we still need to define the vocabulary (i.e., the predicates, frames, or whatever) that will be used on top of the structure. In the rest of this chapter, we call the final meaning representation language, including both the representational framework and the specific meaning vocabulary, the *target language*. The choice of a target language for any particular natural language understanding program must depend on what is to be done with the meanings once they are constructed. There are two broad families of target languages that are used in NL systems, depending on the role that the natural language system is playing in a larger system (if any).

When natural language is being considered as a phenomenon on its own, as, for example, when one builds a program whose goal is to read text and then answer questions about it, a target language can be designed specifically to support language processing. In this case, one typically looks for primitives that correspond to distinctions that are usually made in language. Of course, selecting the right set of primitives is not easy. We discussed this issue briefly in Section 4.3.3, and in Chapter 10 we looked at two proposals for a set of primitives, conceptual dependency and CYC.

When natural language is being used as an interface language to another program (such as a database query system or an expert system), then the target language must be a legal input to that other program. Thus the design of the target language is driven by the backend program. This was the case in the simple example we discussed in Section 15.1.1. But even in this case, it is useful, as we showed in that example, to use an intermediate knowledge-based representation to guide the overall process. So, in the rest of this section, we assume that the target language we are building is a knowledge-based one.

Although the main purpose of semantic processing is the creation of a target language representation of a sentence's meaning, there is another important role that it plays. It imposes constraints on the representations that can be constructed, and, because of the structural connections that must exist between the syntactic structure and the semantic one, it also provides a way of selecting among competing syntactic analyses. Semantic processing can impose constraints because it has access to knowledge about what makes sense in the world. We already mentioned one example of this, the sentence, "Is the glass jar peanut butter?" There are other examples in the rest of this section.

Lexical Processing

The first step in any semantic processing system is to look up the individual words in a dictionary (or *lexicon*) and extract their meanings. Unfortunately, many words have several meanings, and it may not be possible to choose the correct one just by looking at the word itself. For example, the word "diamond" might have the following set of meanings:

- A geometrical shape with four equal sides

- A baseball field

- An extremely hard and valuable gemstone

To select the correct meaning for the word "diamond" in the sentence,

Joan saw Susan's diamond shimmering from across the room.

it is necessary to know that neither geometrical shapes nor baseball fields shimmer, whereas gemstones do.

Unfortunately, if we view English understanding as mapping from English words into objects in a specific knowledge base, lexical ambiguity is often greater than it seems in everyday English. For, example, consider the word "mean." This word is ambiguous in at least three ways: it can be a verb meaning "to signify"; it can be an adjective meaning "unpleasant" or "cheap"; and it can be a noun meaning "statistical average." But now imagine that we have a knowledge base that describes a statistics program and its operation. There might be at least two distinct objects in that knowledge base, both of which correspond to the "statistical average" meaning of "mean." One object is the statistical concept of a mean; the other is the particular function that computes the mean in this program. To understand the word "mean" we need to map it into some concept in our knowledge base. But to do that, we must decide which of these concepts is meant. Because of cases like this, lexical ambiguity is a serious problem, even when the domain of discourse is severely constrained.

The process of determining the correct meaning of an individual word is called *word sense disambiguation* or *lexical disambiguation*. It is done by associating, with each word in the lexicon, information about the contexts in which each of the word's senses may appear. Each of the words in a sentence can serve as part of the context in which the meanings of the other words must be determined.

Sometimes only very straightforward information about each word sense is necessary. For example, the baseball field interpretation of "diamond" could be marked as a LOCATION. Then the correct meaning of "diamond" in the sentence "I'll meet you at the diamond" could easily be determined if the fact that *at* requires a TIME or a LOCATION as its object were recorded as part of the lexical entry for *at*. Such simple properties of word senses are called *semantic markers*. Other useful semantic markers are

- PHYSICAL-OBJECT

- ANIMATE-OBJECT

- ABSTRACT-OBJECT

Using these markers, the correct meaning of "diamond" in the sentence "I dropped my diamond" can be computed. As part of its lexical entry, the verb "drop" will specify that its object must be a PHYSICAL-OBJECT. The gemstone meaning of "diamond" will be marked as a PHYSICAL-OBJECT. So it will be selected as the appropriate meaning in this context.

This technique has been extended by Wilks [1972; 1975a; 1975b] in his *preference semantics*, which relies on the notion that requirements, such as the one described above for an object that is a LOCATION, are rarely hard-and-fast demands. Rather, they can best be described as preferences. For example, we might say that verbs such as "hate" prefer a subject that is animate. Thus we have no difficulty in understanding the sentence

Pop hates the cold.

as describing the feelings of a man and not those of soft drinks. But now consider the sentence

My lawn hates the cold.

Now there is no animate subject available, and so the metaphorical use of lawn acting as an animate object should be accepted.

Unfortunately, to solve the lexical disambiguation problem completely, it becomes necessary to introduce more and more finely grained semantic markers. For example, to interpret the sentence about Susan's diamond correctly, we must mark one sense of diamond as SHIMMERABLE, while the other two are marked NONSHIMMERABLE. As the number of such markers grows, the size of the lexicon becomes unmanageable. In addition, each new entry into the lexicon may require that a new marker be added to each of the existing entries. The breakdown of the semantic marker approach when the number of words and word senses becomes large has led to the development of other ways in which correct senses can be chosen. We return to this issue in Section 15.3.4.

Sentence-Level Processing

Several approaches to the problem of creating a semantic representation of a sentence have been developed, including the following:

- Semantic grammars, which combine syntactic, semantic, and pragmatic knowledge into a single set of rules in the form of a grammar. The result of parsing with such a grammar is a semantic, rather than just a syntactic, description of a sentence.

- Case grammars, in which the structure that is built by the parser contains some semantic information, although further interpretation may also be necessary.

- Conceptual parsing, in which syntactic and semantic knowledge are combined into a single interpretation system that is driven by the semantic knowledge. In this approach, syntactic parsing is subordinated to semantic interpretation, which is usually used to set up strong expectations for particular sentence structures.

- Approximately compositional semantic interpretation, in which semantic processing is applied to the result of performing a syntactic parse. This can be done either incrementally, as constituents are built, or all at once, when a structure corresponding to a complete sentence has been built.

In the following sections, we discuss each of these approaches.

15.3.1   Semantic Grammars

A *semantic grammar* [Burton, 1976; Hendrix *et al.*, 1978; Hendrix and Lewis, 1981] is a context-free grammar in which the choice of nonterminals and production rules is governed by semantic as well as syntactic function. In addition, there is usually a semantic action associated with each grammar rule. The result of parsing and applying all the associated semantic actions is the meaning of the sentence. This close coupling of semantic actions to grammar rules works because the grammar rules themselves are designed around key semantic concepts.

S → what is FILE-PROPERTY of FILE?
    {query FILE.FILE-PROPERTY}
S → I want to ACTION
    {command ACTION}
FILE-PROPERTY → the FILE-PROP
    {FILE-PROP}
FILE-PROP → extension | protection | creation date | owner
    {value}
FILE → FILE-NAME | FILE1
    {value}
FILE1 → USER's FILE2
    {FILE2.owner: USER}
FILE1 → FILE2
    {FILE2}
FILE2 → EXT file
    {instance: file-struct
     extension: EXT}
EXT → .init | .txt | .lsp | .for | .ps | .mss
    value
ACTION → print FILE
    {instance: printing
     object: FILE}
ACTION → print FILE on PRINTER
    {instance: printing
     object: FILE
     printer: PRINTER}
USER → Bill | Susan
    {value}

Figure 15.10: A Semantic Grammar

An example of a fragment of a semantic grammar is shown in Figure 15.10. This grammar defines part of a simple interface to an operating system. Shown in braces under each rule is the semantic action that is taken when the rule is applied. The term "value" is used to refer to the value that is matched by the right-hand side of the rule. The dotted notation $x.y$ should be read as the y attribute of the unit x. The result of a successful parse using this grammar will be either a command or a query.

A semantic grammar can be used by a parsing system in exactly the same ways in which a strictly syntactic grammar could be used. Several existing systems that have used semantic grammars have been built around an ATN parsing system, since it offers a great deal of flexibility.

Figure 15.11 shows the result of applying this semantic grammar to the sentence

I want to print Bill's .init file.

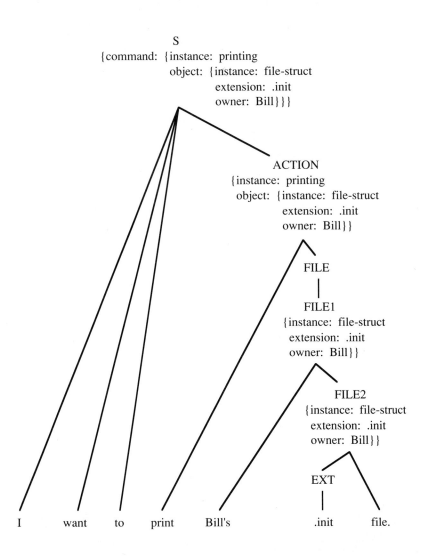

Figure 15.11: The Result of Parsing with a Semantic Grammar

Notice that in this approach, we have combined into a single process all five steps of Section 15.1.1 with the exception of the final part of pragmatic processing in which the conversion to the system's command syntax is done.

The principal advantages of semantic grammars are the following:

- When the parse is complete, the result can be used immediately without the additional stage of processing that would be required if a semantic interpretation had not already been performed during the parse.

- Many ambiguities that would arise during a strictly syntactic parse can be avoided since some of the interpretations do not make sense semantically and thus cannot be generated by a semantic grammar. Consider, for example, the sentence "I want to print stuff.txt on printer3." During a strictly syntactic parse, it would not be possible to decide whether the prepositional phrase, "on printer3" modified "want" or "print." But using our semantic grammar, there is no general notion of a prepositional phrase and there is no attachment ambiguity.

- Syntactic issues that do not affect the semantics can be ignored. For example, using the grammar shown above, the sentence, "What is the extension of .lisp file?" would be parsed and accepted as correct.

There are, however, some drawbacks to the use of semantic grammars:

- The number of rules required can become very large since many syntactic generalizations are missed.

- Because the number of grammar rules may be very large, the parsing process may be expensive.

After many experiments with the use of semantic grammars in a variety of domains, the conclusion appears to be that for producing restricted natural language interfaces quickly, they can be very useful. But as an overall solution to the problem of language understanding, they are doomed by their failure to capture important linguistic generalizations.

15.3.2 Case Grammars

Case grammars [Fillmore, 1968; Bruce, 1975] provide a different approach to the problem of how syntactic and semantic interpretation can be combined. Grammar rules are written to describe syntactic rather than semantic regularities. But the structures the rules produce correspond to semantic relations rather than to strictly syntactic ones. As an example, consider the two sentences and the simplified forms of their conventional parse trees shown in Figure 15.12.

Although the semantic roles of "Susan" and "the file" are identical in these two sentences, their syntactic roles are reversed. Each is the subject in one sentence and the object in another.

Using a case grammar, the interpretations of the two sentences would both be

(printed (agent Susan)
     (object File))

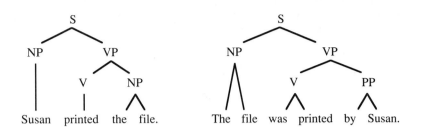

Figure 15.12: Syntactic Parses of an Active and a Passive Sentence

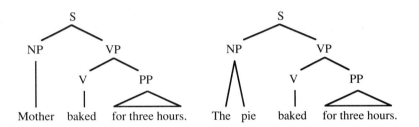

Figure 15.13: Syntactic Parses of Two Similar Sentences

Now consider the two sentences shown in Figure 15.13.

The syntactic structures of these two sentences are almost identical. In one case, "Mother" is the subject of "baked," while in the other "the pie" is the subject. But the relationship between Mother and baking is very different from that between the pie and baking. A case grammar analysis of these two sentences reflects this difference. The first sentence would be interpreted as

    (baked (agent Mother)
        (timeperiod 3-hours))

The second would be interpreted as

    (baked (object Pie)
        (timeperiod 3-hours))

In these representations, the semantic roles of "mother" and "the pie" are made explicit. It is interesting to note that this semantic information actually does intrude into the syntax of the language. While it is allowed to conjoin two parallel sentences (e.g., "the pie baked" and "the cake baked" become "the pie and the cake baked"), this is only possible if the conjoined noun phrases are in the same case relation to the verb. This accounts for the fact that we do not say, "Mother and the pie baked."

Notice that the cases used by a case grammar describe relationships between verbs and their arguments. This contrasts with the grammatical notion of surface case, as exhibited, for example, in English, by the distinction between "I" (nominative case) and "me" (objective case). A given grammatical, or surface, case can indicate a variety of semantic, or deep, cases.

There is no clear agreement on exactly what the correct set of deep cases ought to be, but some obvious ones are the following:

- (A) Agent—Instigator of the action (typically animate)

- (I) Instrument—Cause of the event or object used in causing the event (typically inanimate)

- (D) Dative—Entity affected by the action (typically animate)

- (F) Factitive—Object or being resulting from the event

- (L) Locative—Place of the event

- (S) Source—Place from which something moves

- (G) Goal—Place to which something moves

- (B) Beneficiary—Being on whose behalf the event occurred (typically animate)

- (T) Time—Time at which the event occurred

- (O) Object—Entity that is acted upon or that changes, the most general case

The process of parsing into a case representation is heavily directed by the lexical entries associated with each verb. Figure 15.14 shows examples of a few such entries. Optional cases are indicated in parentheses.

Languages have rules for mapping from underlying case structures to surface syntactic forms. For example, in English, the "unmarked subject"[3] is generally chosen by the following rule:

> If A is present, it is the subject. Otherwise, if I is present, it is the subject.
> Else the subject is O.

These rules can be applied in reverse by a parser to determine the underlying case structure from the superficial syntax.

Parsing using a case grammar is usually *expectation-driven*. Once the verb of the sentence has been located, it can be used to predict the noun phrases that will occur and to determine the relationship of those phrases to the rest of the sentence.

ATNs provide a good structure for case grammar parsing. Unlike traditional parsing algorithms in which the output structure always mirrors the structure of the grammar rules that created it, ATNs allow output structures of arbitrary form. For an example of their use, see Simmons [1973], which describes a system that uses an ATN parser to translate English sentences into a semantic net representing the case structures of sentences. These semantic nets can then be used to answer questions about the sentences.

---

[3] The unmarked subject is the one that is used by default; it signals no special focus or emphasis in the sentence.

open   [_ _ O (I) (A)]
        The door opened.
        John opened the door.
        The wind opened the door.
        John opened the door with a chisel.

die   [_ _ D]
        John died.

kill   [_ _ D (I) A]
        Bill killed John.
        Bill killed John with a knife.

run   [_ _ A]
        John ran.

want   [_ _ A O]
        John wanted some ice cream.
        John wanted Mary to go to the store.

Figure 15.14: Some Verb Case Frames

The result of parsing in a case representation is usually not a complete semantic description of a sentence. For example, the constituents that fill the case slots may still be English words rather than true semantic descriptions stated in the target representation. To go the rest of the way toward building a meaning representation, we still require many of the steps that are described in Section 15.3.4.

15.3.3   Conceptual Parsing

Conceptual parsing, like semantic grammars, is a strategy for finding both the structure and the meaning of a sentence in one step. Conceptual parsing is driven by a dictionary that describes the meanings of words as conceptual dependency (CD) structures.

Parsing a sentence into a conceptual dependency representation is similar to the process of parsing using a case grammar. In both systems, the parsing process is heavily driven by a set of expectations that are set up on the basis of the sentence's main verb. But because the representation of a verb in CD is at a lower level than that of a verb in a case grammar (in which the representation is often identical to the English word that is used), CD usually provides a greater degree of predictive power. The first step in mapping a sentence into its CD representation involves a syntactic processor that extracts the main noun and verb. It also determines the syntactic category and aspectual class of the verb (i.e., stative, transitive, or intransitive). The conceptual processor then takes over. It makes use of a verb-ACT dictionary, which contains an entry for each environment in which a verb can appear. Figure 15.15 (taken from Schank [1973]) shows the dictionary entries associated with the verb "want." These three entries correspond to the three

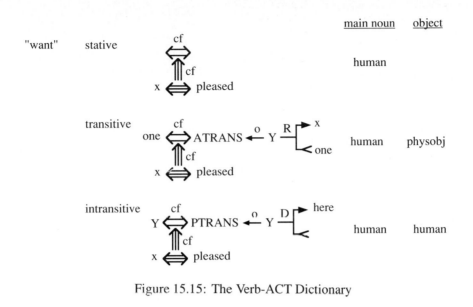

	main noun	object
"want" stative	human	
transitive	human	physobj
intransitive	human	human

Figure 15.15: The Verb-ACT Dictionary

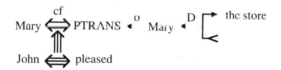

Figure 15.16: A CD Structure

kinds of wanting:

- Wanting something to happen

- Wanting an object

- Wanting a person

Once the correct dictionary entry is chosen, the conceptual processor analyzes the rest of the sentence looking for components that will fit into the empty slots of the verb structure. For example, if the stative form of "want" has been found, then the conceptual processor will look for a conceptualization that can be inserted into the structure. So, if the sentence being processed were

John wanted Mary to go to the store.

the structure shown in Figure 15.16 would be built.

The conceptual processor examines possible interpretations in a well-defined order. For example, if a phrase of the form "with PP" (recall that a PP is a picture producer) occurs, it could indicate any of the following relationships between the PP and the conceptualization of which it is a part:

1. Object of the instrumental case

2. Additional actor of the main ACT

3. Attribute of the PP just preceding it

4. Attribute of the actor of the conceptualization

Suppose that the conceptual processor were attempting to interpret the prepositional phrase in the sentence

>   John went to the park with the girl.

First, the system's immediate memory would be checked to see if a park with a girl has been mentioned. If so, a reference to that particular object is generated and the process terminates. Otherwise, the four possibilities outlined above are investigated in the order in which they are presented. Can "the girl" be an instrument of the main ACT (PTRANS) of this sentence? The answer is no, because only MOVE and PROPEL can be instruments of a PTRANS and their objects must be either body parts or vehicles. "Girl" is neither of these. So we move on to consider the second possibility. In order for "girl" to be an additional actor of the main ACT, it must be animate. It is. So this interpretation is chosen and the process terminates. If, however, the sentence had been

>   John went to the park with the fountain.

the process would not have stopped since a fountain is inanimate and cannot move. Then the third possibility would have been considered. Since parks can have fountains, it would be accepted and the process would terminate there. For a more detailed description of the way a conceptual processor based on CD works, see Schank [1973], Rieger [1975], and Riesbeck [1975].

This example illustrates both the strengths and the weaknesses of this approach to sentence understanding. Because a great deal of semantic information is exploited in the understanding process, sentences that would be ambiguous to a purely syntactic parser can be assigned a unique interpretation. Unfortunately, the amount of semantic information that is required to do this job perfectly is immense. All simple rules have exceptions. For example, suppose the conceptual processor described above were given the sentence

>   John went to the park with the peacocks.

Since peacocks are animate, they would be acceptable as additional actors of the main verb, "went." Thus, the interpretation that would be produced would be that shown in Figure 15.17(a), while the more likely interpretation, in which John went to a park containing peacocks, is shown in Figure 15.17(b). But if the possible roles for a prepositional phrase introduced by "with" were considered in the order necessary for

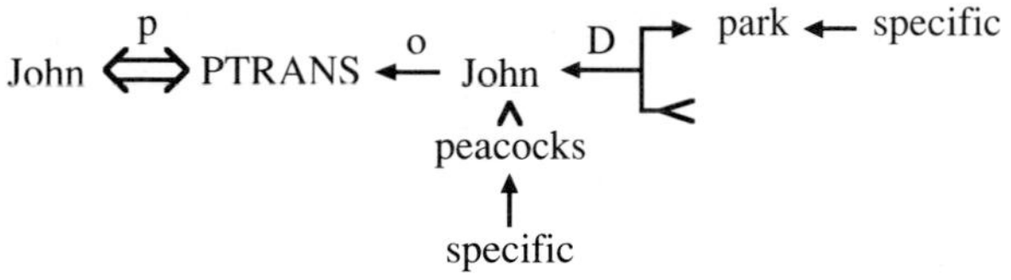

John went to the park with the peacocks.

(*a*)

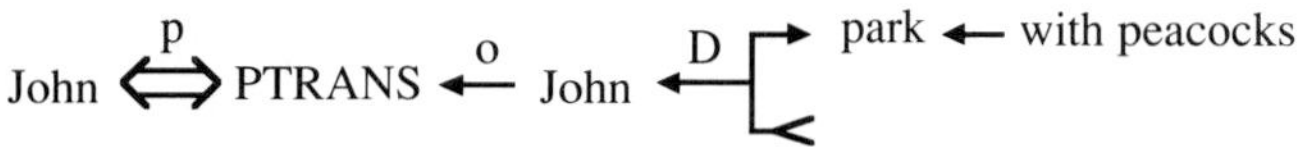

John went to the park with the peacocks.

(*b*)

Figure 15.17: Two CD Interpretations of a Sentence

this sentence to be interpreted correctly, then the previous example involving the phrase, "with Mary," would have been misunderstood.

The problem is that the simple check for the property ANIMATE is not sufficient to determine acceptability as an additional actor of a PTRANS. Additional knowledge is necessary. Some more knowledge can be inserted within the framework we have described for a conceptual processor. But to do a very good job of producing correct semantic interpretations of sentences requires knowledge of the larger context in which the sentence appears. Techniques for exploiting such knowledge are discussed in the next section.

15.3.4 Approximately Compositional Semantic Interpretation

The final approach to semantics that we consider here is one in which syntactic parsing and semantic interpretation are treated as separate steps, although they must mirror each other in well-defined ways. This is the approach to semantics that we looked at briefly in Section 15.1.1 when we worked through the example sentence "I want to print Bill's .init file."

If a strictly syntactic parse of a sentence has been produced, then a straightforward way to generate a semantic interpretation is the following:

1. Look up each word in a lexicon that contains one or more definitions for the word, each stated in terms of the chosen target representation. These definitions must describe how the idea that corresponds to the word is to be represented, and they may also describe how the idea represented by this word may combine with the ideas represented by other words in the sentence.

2. Use the structure information contained in the output of the parser to provide additional constraints, beyond those extracted from the lexicon, on the way individual

words may combine to form larger meaning units.

We have already discussed the first of these steps (in Section 15.3). In the rest of this section, we discuss the second.

Montague Semantics

Recall that we argued in Section 15.1.1 that the reason syntactic parsing was a good idea was that it produces structures that correspond to the structures that should result from semantic processing. If we investigate this idea more closely, we arrive at a notion called *compositional semantics*. The main idea behind compositional semantics is that, for every step in the syntactic parsing process, there is a corresponding step in semantic interpretation. Each time syntactic constituents are combined to form a larger syntactic unit, their corresponding semantic interpretations can be combined to form a larger semantic unit. The necessary rules for combining semantic structures are associated with the corresponding rules for combining syntactic structures. We use the word "compositional" to describe this approach because it defines the meaning of each sentence constituent to be a composition of the meanings of its constituents with the meaning of the rule that was used to create it. The main theoretical basis for this approach is modern (i.e., post-Fregean) logic; the clearest linguistic application is the work of Montague [Dowty *et al.*, 1981; Thomason, 1974].

As an example of this approach to semantic interpretation, let's return to the example that we began in Section 15.1.1. The sentence is

I want to print Bill's .init file.

The output of the syntactic parsing process was shown in Figure 15.2, and a fragment of the knowledge base that is being used to define the target representation was shown in Figure 15.3. The result of semantic interpretation was also shown there in Figure 15.4. Although the exact form of semantic mapping rules in this approach depends on the way that the syntactic grammar is defined, we illustrate the idea of compositional semantic rules in Figure 15.18.

The first two rules are examples of verb-mapping rules. Read these rules as saying that they map from a partial syntactic structure containing a verb, its subject, and its object, to some unit with the attributes instance, agent, and object. These rules do two things. They describe the meaning of the verbs ("want" or "print") themselves in terms of events in the knowledge base. They also state how the syntactic arguments of the verbs (their subjects and objects) map into attributes of those events. By the way, do not get confused by the use of the term "object" in two different senses here. The syntactic object of a sentence and its semantic object are two different things. For historical reasons (including the standard usage in case grammars as described in Section 15.3.2), they are often called the same thing, although this problem is sometimes avoided by using some other name, such as *affected-entity*, for the semantic object. Alternatively, in some knowledge bases, much more specialized names, such as *printed-thing*, are sometimes used as attribute names.

The third and fourth rules are examples of modifier rules. Like the verb rules, they too must specify both their own constituent's contribution to meaning as well as how it combines with the meaning of the noun phrase or phrases to which it is attached.

"want"	$\rightarrow$	*Unit*
subject : RM_i		*instance* : *Wanting*
object : RM_j		*agent* : RM_i
		object : RM_j

"print"	$\rightarrow$	*Unit*
subject : RM_i		*instance* : *Printing*
object : RM_j		*agent* : RM_i
		object : RM_j

".init"	$\rightarrow$	*Unit* for NP_1 plus
modifying NP_1		*extension* : .init

possessive marker	$\rightarrow$	*Unit* for NP_2 plus
NP_1's NP_2		*owner* : NP_1

"file"	$\rightarrow$	*Unit*
		instance : *File-Struct*

"Bill"	$\rightarrow$	*Unit*
		instance : *Person*
		first-name : Bill

Figure 15.18: Some Semantic Interpretation Rules

The last two rules are simpler. They define the meanings of nouns. Since nouns do not usually take arguments, these rules specify only single-word meanings; they do not need to describe how the meanings of larger constituents are derived from their components.

One important thing to remember about these rules is that since they define mappings from words into a knowledge base, they implicitly make available to the semantic processing system all the information contained in the knowledge base itself. For example, Figure 15.19 contains a description of the semantic information that is associated with the word "want" after applying the semantic rule associated with the verb and retrieving semantic constraints associated with wanting events in the knowledge base. Notice that we now know where to pick up the agent for the wanting ($RM1$) and we know some property that the agent must have. The semantic interpretation routine will reject any interpretation that does not satisfy all these constraints.

This compositional approach to defining semantic interpretation has proved to be a very powerful idea. (See, for example, the Absity system described in Hirst [1987].) Unfortunately, there are some linguistic constructions that cannot be accounted for naturally in a strictly compositional system. Quantified expressions have this property. Consider, for example, the sentence

Every student who hadn't declared a major took an English class.

Unit
    instance :   *Wanting*
    agent : RM_i
                 must be <animate>
    object : RM_j
                 must be <state or event>

Figure 15.19: Combining Mapping Knowledge with the Knowledge Base

There are several ways in which the relative scopes of the quantifiers in this sentence can be assigned. In the most likely, both existential quantifiers are within the scope of the universal quantifier. But, in other readings, they are not. These include readings corresponding to, "There is a major such that every student who had not declared it took an English class," and "There is an English class such that every student who had not declared some major took it." In order to generate these meanings compositionally from the parse, it is necessary to produce a separate parse for each scope assignment. But there is no syntactic reason to do that, and it requires substantial additional effort. An alternative is to generate a single parse and then to use a noncompositional algorithm to generate as many alternative scopes as desired.

As a second example, consider the sentence, "John only eats meat on Friday and Mary does too." The syntactic analysis of this sentence must include the verb phrase constituent, "only eats meat on Friday," since that is the constituent that is picked up by the elliptical expression "does too." But the meaning of the first clause has a structure more like

$$only(meat, \{x \mid John\ eats\ x\ on\ Friday\})$$

which can be read as, "Meat is the only thing that John eats on Friday."

Extended Reasoning with a Knowledge Base

A significant amount of world knowledge may be necessary in order to do semantic interpretation (and thus, sometimes, to get the correct syntactic parse). Sometimes the knowledge is needed to enable the system to choose among competing interpretations. Consider, for example, the sentences

1. John made a huge wedding cake with chocolate icing.

2. John made a huge wedding cake with Bill's mixer.

3. John made a huge wedding cake with a giant tower covered with roses.

4. John made a cherry pie with a giant tower covered with roses.

Let's concentrate on the problem of deciding to which constituent the prepositional phrase should be attached and of assigning a meaning to the preposition "with." We have two main choices: either the phrase attaches to the action of making the cake and "with" indicates the instrument relation, or the prepositional phrase attaches to the noun phrase describing the dessert that was made, in which case "with" describes an additional component of the dessert. The first two sentences are relatively straightforward if we imagine that our knowledge base contains the following facts:

- Foods can be components of other foods.

- Mixers are used to make many kinds of desserts.

But now consider the third sentence. A giant tower is neither a food nor a mixer. So it is not a likely candidate for either role. What is required here is the much more specific (and culturally dependent) fact that

- Wedding cakes often have towers and statues and bridges and flowers on them.

The highly specific nature of this knowledge is illustrated by the fact that the last of these sentences does not make much sense to us since we can find no appropriate role for the tower, either as part of a pie or as an instrument used during pie making.

Another use for knowledge is to enable the system to accept meanings that it has not been explicitly told about. Consider the following sentences as examples:

1. Sue likes to read Joyce.

2. Washington backed out of the summit talks.

3. The stranded explorer ate squirrels.

Suppose our system has only the following meanings for the words "Joyce," "Washington," and "squirrel" (actually we give only the relevant parts of the meanings):

1. Joyce—*instance*: *Author*; *last-name*: Joyce

2. Washington—*instance*: *City*; *name*: Washington

3. squirrel—*isa*: *Rodent*; ...

But suppose that we also have only the following meanings for the verbs in these sentences:

1. read—*isa*: *Mental-Event*; *object*: must be <printed-material>

2. back out—*isa*: *Mental-Event*; *agent*: must be <animate-entity>

3. eat—*isa*: *Ingestion-Event*; *object*: must be <food>

The problem is that it is not possible to construct coherent interpretations for any of these sentences with these definitions. An author is not a <printed-material>. A city is not an <animate-entity>. A rodent is not a <food>. One solution is to create additional dictionary entries for the nouns: Joyce as a set of literary works, Washington as the people who run the U.S. government, and a squirrel as a food. But a better solution is to use general knowledge to derive these meanings when they are needed. By better, here we mean that since less knowledge must be entered by hand, the resulting system will be less brittle. The general knowledge that is necessary to handle these examples is:

- The name of a person can be used to refer to things the person creates. Authoring is a kind of creating.

- The name of a place can be used to stand for an organization headquartered in that place if the association between the organization and the place is salient in the context. An organization can in turn stand for the people who run it. The headquarters of the U.S. government is in Washington.

- Food (meat) can be made out of almost any animal. Usually the word for the animal can be used to refer to the meat made from the animal.

Of course, this problem can become arbitrarily complex. For example, metaphors are a rich source for linguistic expressions [Lakoff and Johnson, 1980]. And the problem becomes even more complex when we move beyond single sentences and attempt to extract meaning from texts and dialogues. We delve briefly into those issues in Section 15.4.

The Interaction between Syntax and Semantics

If we take a compositional approach to semantics, then we apply semantic interpretation rules to each syntactic constituent, eventually producing an interpretation for an entire sentence. But making a commitment about what to do implies no specific commitment about when to do it. To implement a system, however, we must make some decision on how control will be passed back and forth between the syntactic and the semantic processors. Two extreme positions are:

- Every time a syntactic constituent is formed, apply semantic interpretation to it immediately.

- Wait until the entire sentence has been parsed, and then interpret the whole thing.

There are arguments in favor of each approach. The theme of most of the arguments is search control and the opportunity to prune dead-end paths. Applying semantic processing to each constituent as soon as it is produced allows semantics to rule out right away those constituents that are syntactically valid but that make no sense. Syntactic processing can then be informed that it should not go any further with those constituents. This approach would pay off, for example, for the sentence, "Is the glass jar peanut butter?" But this approach can be costly when syntactic processing builds constituents that it will eventually reject as being syntactically unacceptable, regardless of their semantic acceptability. The sentence, "The horse raced past the barn fell down," is an example of this. There is no point in doing a semantic analysis of the sentence "The horse raced past the barn," since that constituent will not end up being part of any complete syntactic parse. There are also additional arguments for waiting until a complete sentence has been parsed to do at least some parts of semantic interpretation. These arguments involve the need for large constituents to serve as the basis of those semantic actions, such as the ones we discussed in Section 15.3.4, that are hard to define completely compositionally. There is no magic solution to this problem. Most systems use one of these two extremes or a heuristically driven compromise position.

15.4   Discourse and Pragmatic Processing

To understand even a single sentence, it is necessary to consider the discourse and pragmatic context in which the sentence was uttered (as we saw in Section 15.1.1). These issues become even more important when we want to understand texts and dialogues, so in this section we broaden our concern to these larger linguistic units. There are a number of important relationships that may hold between phrases and parts of their discourse contexts, including:

- Identical entities. Consider the text

    - Bill had a red balloon.
    - John wanted it.

  The word "it" should be identified as referring to the red balloon. References such as this are called *anaphoric references* or *anaphora*.

- Parts of entities. Consider the text

    - Sue opened the book she just bought.
    - The title page was torn.

  The phrase "the title page" should be recognized as being part of the book that was just bought.

- Parts of actions. Consider the text

    - John went on a business trip to New York.
    - He left on an early morning flight.

  Taking a flight should be recognized as part of going on a trip.

- Entities involved in actions. Consider the text

    - My house was broken into last week.
    - They took the TV and the stereo.

  The pronoun "they" should be recognized as referring to the burglars who broke into the house.

- Elements of sets. Consider the text

    - The decals we have in stock are stars, the moon, item and a flag.
    - I'll take two moons.

  The moons in the second sentence should be understood to be some of the moons mentioned in the first sentence. Notice that to understand the second sentence at all requires that we use the context of the first sentence to establish that the word "moons" means moon decals.

- Names of individuals. Consider the text

  - Dave went to the movies.

  Dave should be understood to be some person named Dave. Although there are many, the speaker had one particular one in mind and the discourse context should tell us which.

- Causal chains. Consider the text

  - There was a big snow storm yesterday.
  - The schools were closed today.

  The snow should be recognized as the reason that the schools were closed.

- Planning sequences. Consider the text

  - Sally wanted a new car.
  - She decided to get a job.

  Sally's sudden interest in a job should be recognized as arising out of her desire for a new car and thus for the money to buy one.

- Illocutionary force. Consider the sentence

  - It sure is cold in here.

  In many circumstances, this sentence should be recognized as having, as its intended effect, that the hearer should do something like close the window or turn up the thermostat.

- Implicit presuppositions. Consider the query

  - Did Joe fail CS101?

  The speaker's presuppositions, including the fact that CS101 is a valid course, that Joe is a student, and that Joe took CS101, should be recognized so that if any of them is not satisfied, the speaker can be informed.

In order to be able to recognize these kinds of relationships among sentences, a great deal of knowledge about the world being discussed is required. Programs that can do multiple-sentence understanding rely either on large knowledge bases or on strong constraints on the domain of discourse so that only a more limited knowledge base is necessary. The way this knowledge is organized is critical to the success of the understanding program. In the rest of this section, we discuss briefly how some of the knowledge representations described in Chapters 9 and 10 can be exploited by a language-understanding program. In particular, we focus on the use of the following kinds of knowledge:

- The current focus of the dialogue

- A model of each participant's current beliefs

- The goal-driven character of dialogue

- The rules of conversation shared by all participants

Although these issues are complex, we discuss them only briefly here. Most of the hard problems are not peculiar to natural language processing. They involve reasoning about objects, events, goals, plans, intentions, beliefs, and likelihoods, and we have discussed all these issues in some detail elsewhere. Our goal in this section is to tie those reasoning mechanisms into the process of natural language understanding.

15.4.1 Using Focus in Understanding

There are two important parts of the process of using knowledge to facilitate understanding:

- Focus on the relevant part(s) of the available knowledge base.

- Use that knowledge to resolve ambiguities and to make connections among things that were said.

The first of these is critical if the amount of knowledge available is large. Some techniques for handling this were outlined in Section 4.3.5, since the problem arises whenever knowledge structures are to be used.

The linguistic properties of coherent discourse, however, provide some additional mechanisms for focusing. For example, the structure of task-oriented discourses typically mirrors the structure of the task. Consider the following sequence of (highly simplified) instructions:

> To make the torte, first make the cake, then, while the cake is baking, make the filling. To make the cake, combine all ingredients. Pour them into the pans, and bake for 30 minutes. To make the filling, combine the ingredients. Mix until light and fluffy. When the cake is done, alternate layers of cake and filling.

This task decomposes into three subtasks: making the cake, making the filling, and combining the two components. The structure of the paragraph of instructions is: overall sketch of the task, instructions for step 1, instructions for step 2, and then instructions for step 3.

A second property of coherent discourse is that dramatic changes of focus are usually signaled explicitly with phrases such as "on the other hand," "to return to an earlier topic," or "a second issue is."

Assuming that all this knowledge has been used successfully to focus on the relevant part(s) of the knowledge base, the second issue is how to use the focused knowledge to help in understanding. There are as many ways of doing this as there are discourse phenomena that require it. In the last section, we presented a sample list of those phenomena. To give one example, consider the problem of finding the meaning of definite noun phrases. Definite noun phrases are ones that refer to specific individual objects, for example, the first noun phrase in the sentence, "The title page was torn." The title page in question is assumed to be one that is related to an object that is currently in focus. So the procedure for finding a meaning for it involves searching for ways in which a title page could be related to a focused object. Of course, in some sense, almost any object in a knowledge base relates somehow to almost any other. But some relations are far more salient than others, and they should be considered first. Highly salient relations include *physical-part-of*, *temporal-part-of*, and *element-of*. In this example, *physical-part-of* relates the title page to the book that is in focus as a result of its mention in the previous sentence.

Other ways of using focused information also exist. We examine some of them in the remaining parts of this section.

15.4.2 Modeling Beliefs

In order for a program to be able to participate intelligently in a dialogue, it must be able to represent not only its own beliefs about the world, but also its knowledge of the other dialogue participant's beliefs about the world, that person's beliefs about the computer's beliefs, and so forth. The remark "She knew I knew she knew I knew she knew"[4] may be a bit extreme, but we do that kind of thinking all the time. To make computational models of belief, it is useful to divide the issue into two parts: those beliefs that can be assumed to be shared among all the participants in a linguistic event and those that cannot.

Modeling Shared Beliefs

Shared beliefs can be modeled without any explicit notion of belief in the knowledge base. All we need to do is represent the shared beliefs as facts, and they will be accessed whenever knowledge about anyone's beliefs is needed. We have already discussed techniques for doing this. For example, much of the knowledge described in Chapter 10 is exactly the sort that people presume is shared by other people they are communicating with. Scripts, in particular, have been used extensively to aid in natural language understanding. Recall that scripts record commonly occurring sequences of events. There are two steps in the process of using a script to aid in language understanding:

- Select the appropriate script(s) from memory.

- Use the script(s) to fill in unspecified parts of the text to be understood.

Both of these aspects of reasoning with scripts have already been discussed in Section 10.2. The story-understanding program SAM [Cullingford, 1981] demonstrated the usefulness of such reasoning with scripts in natural language understanding. To understand a story, SAM first employed a parser that translated the English sentences into their conceptual dependency representation. Then it built a representation of the entire text using the relationships indicated by the relevant scripts.

---

[4]From Kingsley Amis' *Jake's Thing*.

Modeling Individual Beliefs

As soon as we decide to represent individual beliefs, we need to introduce some explicit predicate(s) to indicate that a fact is believed. Up until now, belief has been indicated only by the presence or absence of assertions in the knowledge base. To model belief, we need to move to a logic that supports reasoning about belief propositions. The standard approach is to use a *modal logic* such as that defined in Hintikka [1962]. Logic, or "classical" logic, deals with the truth or falsehood of different statements as they are. Modal logic, on the other hand, concerns itself with the different "modes" in which a statement may be true. Modal logics allow us to talk about the truth of a set of propositions not only in the current state of the real world, but also about their truth or falsehood in the past or the future (these are called *temporal logics*), and about their truth or falsehood under circumstances that might have been, but were not (these are sometimes called *conditional logics*). We have already used one idea from modal logic, namely the notion *necessarily true*. We used it in Section 13.5, when we talked about nonlinear planning in TWEAK.

Modal logics also allow us to talk of the truth or falsehood of statements concerning the beliefs, knowledge, desires, intentions, and obligations of people and robots, which may, in fact be, respectively, false, unjustified, unsatisfiable, irrational, or mutually contradictory. Modal logics thus provide a set of powerful tools for understanding natural language utterances, which often involve reference to other times and circumstances, and to the mental states of people.

In particular, to model individual belief we define a modal operator BELIEVE, that enables us to make assertions of the form BELIEVE(A, P), which is true whenever A believes P to be true. Notice that this can occur even if P is believed by someone else to be false or even if P is false.

Another useful modal operator is KNOW:

$$\text{BELIEVE}(A, P) \land P \rightarrow \text{KNOW}(A, P)$$

A third useful modal operator is KNOW-WHAT(A, P), which is true if A knows the value of the function P. For example, we might say that A knows the value of his age.

An alternative way to represent individual beliefs is to use the idea of knowledge base partitioning that we discussed in Section 9.1. Partitioning enables us to do two things:

1. Represent efficiently the large set of beliefs shared by the participants. We discussed one way of doing this above.

2. Represent accurately the smaller set of beliefs that are not shared.

Requirement 1 makes it imperative that shared beliefs not be duplicated in the representation. This suggests that a single knowledge base must be used to represent the beliefs of all the participants. But requirement 2 demands that it be possible to separate the beliefs of one person from those of another. One way to do this is to use partitioned semantic nets. Figure 15.20 shows an example of a partitioned belief space.

Three different belief spaces are shown:

- S1 believes that Mary hit Bill.

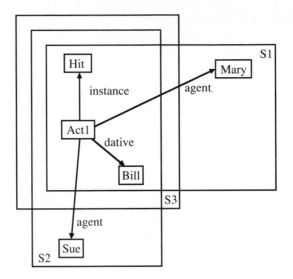

Figure 15.20: A Partitioned Semantic Net Showing Three Belief Spaces

- S2 believes that Sue hit Bill.

- S3 believes that someone hit Bill. It is important to be able to handle incomplete beliefs of this kind, since they frequently serve as the basis for questions, such as, in this case, "Who hit Bill?"

15.4.3   Using Goals and Plans for Understanding

Consider the text

> John was anxious to get his daughter's new bike put together before Christmas Eve. He looked high and low for a screwdriver.

To understand this story, we need to recognize that John had

1. A goal, getting the bike put together.

2. A plan, which involves putting together the various subparts until the bike is complete. At least one of the resulting subplans involves using a screwdriver to screw two parts together.

Some of the common goals that can be identified in stories of all sorts (including children's stories, newspaper reports, and history books) are

- Satisfaction goals, such as sleep, food, and water.

- Enjoyment goals, such as entertainment and competition.

- Achievement goals, such as possession, power, and status.

- Preservation goals, such as health and possessions.

- Pleasing goals, which involve satisfying some other kind of goal for someone else.

- Instrumental goals, which enable preconditions for other, higher-level goals.

To achieve their goals, people exploit plans. In Chapter 13, we talked about several computational representations of plans. These representations can be used to support natural language processing, particularly if they are combined with a knowledge base of operators and stored plans that describe the ways that people often accomplish common goals. These stored operators and plans enable an understanding system to form a coherent representation of a text even when steps have been omitted, since they specify things that must have occurred in the complete story. For example, to understand this simple text about John, we need to make use of the fact that John was exploiting the operator USE (by A of P to perform G), which can be described as:

USE(A, P, G):
      precondition: KNOW-WHAT(A, LOCATION(P))
            NEAR(A, P)
            HAS-CONTROL-OF(A, P)
            READY(P)
      postcondition: DONE(G)

In other words, for A to use P to perform G, A must know the location of P, A must be near P, A must have control of P (for example, I cannot use a screwdriver that you are holding and refuse to give to me), and P must be ready for use (for example, I cannot use a broken screwdriver).

In our story, John's plan for constructing the bike includes using a screwdriver. So he needs to establish the preconditions for that use. In particular, he needs to know the location of the screwdriver. To find that out, he makes use of the operator LOOK-FOR:

LOOK-FOR(A, P):
      precondition: CAN-RECOGNIZE(A, P)
      postcondition: KNOW-WHAT(A, LOCATION(P))

A story understanding program can connect the goal of putting together the bike with the activity of looking for a screwdriver by recognizing that John is looking for a screwdriver so that he can use it as part of putting the bike together.

Often there are alternative operators or plans for achieving the same goal. For example, to find out where the screwdriver was, John could have asked someone. Thus the problem of constructing a coherent interpretation of a text or a discourse may involve considering many partial plans and operators.

Plan recognition has served as the basis for many understanding programs. PAM [Wilensky, 1981] is an early example; it translated stories into a CD representation.

Another such program was BORIS [Dyer, 1983]. BORIS used a memory structure called the Thematic Abstraction Unit to organize knowledge about plans, goals, interpersonal relationships, and emotions. For other examples, see Allen and Perrault [1980] and Sidner [1985].

15.4.4 Speech Acts

Language is a form of behavior. We use it as one way to accomplish our goals. In essence, we make communicative plans in much the same sense that we make plans for anything else [Austin, 1962]. In fact, as we just saw in the example above, John could have achieved his goal of locating a screwdriver by asking someone where it was rather than by looking for it. The elements of communicative plans are called *speech acts* [Searle, 1969]. We can axiomatize speech acts just as we axiomatized other operators in the previous section, except that we need to make use of modal operators that describe states of belief, knowledge, wanting, etc. For example, we can define the basic speech act A INFORM B of P as follows:

$$INFORM(A, B, P)$$
$$precondition: BELIEVE(A, P)$$
$$KNOW\text{-}WHAT(A, LOCATION(B))$$
$$postcondition: BELIEVE(B, BELIEVE(A, P))$$
$$BELIEVE\text{-}IN(B, A) \rightarrow BELIEVE(B, P)$$

To execute this operation, A must believe P and A must know where B is. The result of this operator is that B believes that A believes P, and if B believes in the truth of what A says, then B also believes P.

We can define other speech acts similarly. For example, we can define ASK-WHAT (in which A asks B the value of some predicate P):

$$ASK\text{-}WHAT(A, B, P):$$
$$precondition: KNOW\text{-}WHAT(A, LOCATION(B))$$
$$KNOW\text{-}WHAT(B, P)$$
$$WILLING\text{-}TO\text{-}PERFORM$$
$$(B, INFORM(B, A, P))$$
$$postcondition: KNOW\text{-}WHAT(A, P)$$

This is the action that John could have performed as an alternative way of finding a screwdriver.

We can also define other speech acts, such as A REQUEST B to perform R:

$$REQUEST(A, B, R)$$
$$precondition: KNOW\text{-}WHAT(A, LOCATION(B))$$
$$CAN\ PERFORM(B, R)$$

WILLING-TO-PERFORM(B, R)
postcondition: WILL(PERFORM(B, R))

15.4.5 Conversational Postulates

Unfortunately, this analysis of language is complicated by the fact that we do not always say exactly what we mean. Instead, we often use *indirect speech acts*, such as "Do you know what time it is?" or "It sure is cold in here." Searle [1975] presents a linguistic theory of such indirect speech acts. Computational treatments of this phenomenon usually rely on models of the speaker's goals and of ways that those goals might reasonably be achieved by using language. See, for example, Cohen and Perrault [1979].

Fortunately, there is a certain amount of regularity in people's goals and in the way language can be used to achieve them. This regularity gives rise to a set of *conversational postulates*, which are rules about conversation that are shared by all speakers. Usually these rules are followed. Sometimes they are not, but when this happens, the violation of the rules communicates something in itself. Some of these conversational postulates are:

- Sincerity Conditions—For a request by A of B to do R to be sincere, A must want B to do R, A must assume B can do R, A must assume B is willing to do R, and A must believe that B would not have done R anyway. If A attempts to verify one of these conditions by asking a question of B, that question should normally be interpreted by B as equivalent to the request R. For example,

    A: Can you open the door?

- Reasonableness Conditions—For a request by A of B to do R to be reasonable, A must have a reason for wanting R done, A must have a reason for assuming that B can do R, A must have a reason for assuming that B is willing to do R, and A must have a reason for assuming that B was not already planning to do R. Reasonableness conditions often provide the basis for challenging a request. Together with the sincerity conditions described above, they account for the coherence of the following interchange:

    A: Can you open the door?
    B: Why do you want it open?

- Appropriateness Conditions—For a statement to be appropriate, it must provide the correct amount of information, it must accurately reflect the speaker's beliefs, it must be concise and unambiguous, and it must be polite. These conditions account for A's response in the following interchange:

    A: Who won the race?
    B: Someone with long, dark hair.
    A: I thought you knew all the runners.

    A inferred from B's incomplete response that B did not know who won the race, because if B had known she would have provided a name.

Of course, sometimes people "cop out" of these conventions. In the following dialogue, *B* is explicitly copping out:

A: Who is going to be nominated for the position?
B: I'm sorry, I cannot answer that question.

But in the absence of such a cop out, and assuming a cooperative relationship between the parties to a dialogue, the shared assumption of these postulates greatly facilitates communication. For a more detailed discussion of conversational postulates, see Grice [1975] and Gordon and Lakoff [1975].

We can axiomatize these conversational postulates by augmenting the preconditions for the speech acts that we have already defined. For example, we can describe the sincerity conditions by adding the following clauses to the precondition for REQUEST(*A*, *B*, *R*):

WANT(*A*, PERFORM(*B*, *R*))
BELIEVE(*A*, CAN-PERFORM(*B*, *R*))
BELIEVE(*A*, WILLING-TO-PERFORM(*B*, *R*))
BELIEVE(*A*, ¬WILL(PERFORM(*B*, *R*)))

If we assume that each participant in a dialogue is following these conventions, then it is possible to infer facts about the participants' belief states from what they say. Those facts can then be used as a basis for constructing a coherent interpretation of a discourse as a whole.

To summarize, we have just described several techniques for representing knowledge about how people act and talk. This knowledge plays an important role in text and discourse understanding, since it enables an understander to fill in the gaps left by the original writer or speaker. It turns out that many of these same mechanisms, in particular those that allow us to represent explicitly the goals and beliefs of multiple agents, will also turn out to be useful in constructing distributed reasoning systems, in which several (at least partially independent) agents interact to achieve a single goal. We come back to this topic in Section 16.3.

15.5   Summary

In this chapter, we presented a brief introduction to the surprisingly hard problem of language understanding. Recall that in Chapter 14, we showed that at least one understanding problem, line labeling, could effectively be viewed as a constraint satisfaction problem. One interesting way to summarize the natural language understanding problem that we have described in this chapter is to view it too as a constraint satisfaction problem. Unfortunately, many more kinds of constraints must be considered, and even when they are all exploited, it is usually not possible to avoid the guess and search part of the constraint satisfaction procedure. But constraint satisfaction does provide a reasonable framework in which to view the whole collection of steps that together create a meaning for a sentence. Essentially each of the steps described in this chapter exploits a particular kind of knowledge that contributes a specific set of constraints that must be satisfied by any correct final interpretation of a sentence.

Syntactic processing contributes a set of constraints derived from the grammar of the language. It imposes constraints such as:

- Word order, which rules out, for example, the constituent, "manager the key," in the sentence, "I gave the apartment manager the key."

- Number agreement, which keeps "trial run" from being interpreted as a sentence in "The first trial run was a failure."

- Case agreement, which rules, out, for example, the constituent, "me and Susan gave one to Bob," in the sentence, "Mike gave the program to Alan and me and Susan gave one to Bob."

Semantic processing contributes an additional set of constraints derived from the knowledge it has about entities that can exist in the world. It imposes constraints such as:

- Specific kinds of actions involve specific classes of participants. We thus rule out the baseball field meaning of the word "diamond" in the sentence, "John saw Susan's diamond shimmering from across the room."

- Objects have properties that can take on values from a limited set. We thus rule out Bill's mixer as a component of the cake in the sentence, "John made a huge wedding cake with Bill's mixer."

Discourse processing contributes a further set of constraints that arise from the structure of coherent discourses. These include:

- The entities involved in the sentence must either have been introduced explicitly or they must be related to entities that were. Thus the word "it" in the discourse "John had a cold. Bill caught it," must refer to John's cold. This constraint can propagate through other constraints. For example, in this case, it can be used to determine the meaning of the word "caught" in this discourse, in contrast to its meaning in the discourse, "John threw the ball. Bill caught it."

- The overall discourse must be coherent. Thus, in the discourse, "I needed to deposit some money, so I went down to the bank," we would choose the financial institution reading of bank over the river bank reading. This requirement can even cause a later sentence to impose a constraint on the interpretation of an earlier one, as in the discourse, "I went down to the bank. The river had just flooded, and I wanted to see how bad things were."

And finally, pragmatic processing contributes yet another set of constraints. For example,

- The meaning of the sentence must be consistent with the known goals of the speaker. So, for example, in the sentence, "Mary was anxious to get the bill passed this session, so she moved to table it," we are forced to choose the (normally British) meaning of table (to put it on the table for discussion) over the (normally American) meaning (to set it aside for later).

There are many important issues in natural language processing that we have barely touched on here. To learn more about the overall problem, see Allen [1987], Cullingford [1986], Dowty *et al.* [1985], and Grosz *et al.* [1986]. For more information on syntactic processing, see Winograd [1983] and King [1983]. See Joshi *et al.* [1981] for more discussion of the issues involved in discourse understanding. Also, we have restricted our discussion to natural language understanding. It is often useful to be able to go the other way as well, that is, to begin with a logical description and render it into English. For discussions of natural language generation systems, see McKeown and Swartout [1987] and McDonald and Bolc [1988]. By combining understanding and generation systems, it is possible to attack the problem of *machine translation*, by which we understand text written in one language and then generate it in another language. See Slocum [1988], Nirenburg [1987], Lehrberger and Bourbeau [1988], and Nagao [1989] for discussions of a variety of approaches to this problem.

15.6   Exercises

1. Consider the sentence

   The old man's glasses were filled with sherry.

   What information is necessary to choose the correct meaning for the word "glasses"? What information suggests the incorrect meaning?

2. For each of the following sentences, show a parse tree. For each of them, explain what knowledge, in addition to the grammar of English, is necessary to produce the correct parse. Expand the grammar of Figure 15.6 as necessary to do this.

   - John wanted to go to the movie with Sally.
   - John wanted to go to the movie with Robert Redford.
   - I heard the story listening to the radio.
   - I heard the kids listening to the radio.
   - All books and magazines that deal with controversial topics have been removed from the shelves.
   - All books and magazines that come out quarterly have been removed from the shelves.

3. In the following paragraph, show the antecedents for each of the pronouns. What knowledge is necessary to determine each?

   > John went to the store to buy a shirt. The salesclerk asked him if he could help him. He said he wanted a blue shirt. The salesclerk found one and he tried it on. He paid for it and left.

4. Consider the following sentence:

   Put the red block on the blue block on the table.

   (a) Show all the syntactically valid parses of this sentence. Assume any standard grammatical formalism you like.

(b) How could semantic information and world knowledge be used to select the appropriate meaning of this command in a particular situation?

After you have done this, you might want to look at the discussion of this problem in Church and Patil [1982].

5. Each of the following sentences is ambiguous in at least two ways. Because of the type of knowledge represented by each sentence, different target languages may be useful to characterize the different meanings. For each of the sentences, choose an appropriate target language and show how the different meanings would be represented:

- Everyone doesn't know everything.
- John saw Mary and the boy with a telescope.
- John flew to New York.

6. Write an ATN grammar that recognizes verb phrases involving auxiliary verbs. The grammar should handle such phrases as

- "went"
- "should have gone"
- "had been going"
- "would have been going"
- "would go"

Do not expect to produce an ATN that can handle all possible verb phrases. But do design one with a reasonable structure that handles most common ones, including the ones above. The grammar should create structures that reflect the structures of the input verb phrases.

7. Show how the ATN of Figures 15.8 and 15.9 could be modified to handle passive sentences.

8. Write the rule "S → NP VP" in the graph notation that we defined in Section 15.2.3. Show how unification can be used to enforce number agreement between the subject and the verb.

9. Consider the problem of providing an English interface to a database of employee records.

(a) Write a semantic grammar to define a language for this task.

(b) Show a parse, using your grammar, of each of the two sentences
   What is Smith's salary?
   Tell me who Smith's manager is.

(c) Show parses of the two sentences of part (b) using a standard syntactic grammar of English. Show the fragment of the grammar that you use.

(d) How do the parses of parts (b) and (c) differ? What do these differences say about the differences between syntactic and semantic grammars?

10. How would the following sentences be represented in a case structure:

    (a) The plane flew above the clouds.

    (b) John flew to New York.

    (c) The co-pilot flew the plane.

11. Both case grammar and conceptual dependency produce representations of sentences in which noun phrases are described in terms of their semantic relationships to the verb. In what ways are the two approaches similar? In what ways are they different? Is one a more general version of the other? As an example, compare the representation of the sentence

    John broke the window with a hammer.

    in the two formalisms.

12. Use compositional semantics and a knowledge base to construct a semantic interpretation of each of the following sentences:

    (a) A student deleted my file.

    (b) John asked Mary to print the file.

    To do this, you will need to do all the following things:

    • Define the necessary knowledge base objects.

    • Decide what the output of your parser will be assumed to be.

    • Write the necessary semantic interpretation rules.

    • Show how the process proceeds.

13. Show how conversational postulates can be used to get to the most common, coherent interpretation of each of the following discourses:

    (a)   A: Do you have a comb?

    (b)   A: Would Jones make a good programmer?
           B: He's a great guy. Everyone likes him.

    (c)   A (in a store): Do you have any money?
           B (A's friend): What do you want to buy?

14. Winograd and Flores [1986] present an argument that it is wrong to attempt to make computers understand language. Analyze their arguments in light of what was said in this chapter.

Chapter 16

Parallel and Distributed AI

Recent years have seen significant advances in parallel computation and distributed systems. What are the implications of these advances for AI? There are three main areas in which parallel and distributed architectures can contribute to the study of intelligent systems:

- Psychological modeling

- Improving efficiency

- Helping to organize systems in a modular fashion

These areas are often overlapping and complementary. For example, consider the production system model that we described in Chapter 2. The ideas of short-term and long-term memory, independently operating productions, matching, and so forth first arose in the psychological literature. When researchers began building AI systems based on these principles, they realized that parallel computers might be used to increase significantly the speed at which the systems could run. Even on single processor systems, however, the production system architecture turned out to have many benefits over conventional programming. One benefit is better modularity. When rules operate more or less independently, it is easy to add, delete, or modify them without changing the structure of the entire program. In this chapter, we discuss all these issues. First we briefly discuss psychological modeling. Then, in the following two sections we present some specific techniques that can be exploited in constructing parallel and distributed reasoning systems.

16.1 Psychological Modeling

The production system was originally proposed as a model of human information processing, and it continues to play a role in psychological modeling. Some production system models stress the sequential nature of production systems, i.e., the manner in which short-term memory is modified over time by the rules. Other models stress the parallel aspect, in which all productions match and fire simultaneously, no matter how many there are. Both types of models have been used to explain timing data from experiments on human problem solving.

SOAR [Laird *et al.*, 1987] is the production system architecture that we mentioned in Chapter 6. SOAR has a dual mission. On the one hand, it is intended as an architecture for building integrated AI systems; on the other hand, it is intended as a model of human intelligence [Newell, 1991]. SOAR incorporates both sequential and parallel aspects of production systems by operating in cycles. In the *elaboration phase* of the processing cycle, productions fire in parallel. In the *decision phase*, operators and states are chosen, and working memory is modified, thus setting the stage for another elaboration phase. By tying these phases to particular timings, SOAR accounts for a number of psychological phenomena.

Another approach to psychological modeling draws its inspiration from the physical organization of the human brain itself. While individual neurons are quite slow compared to digital computer circuits, there are vast numbers of these richly interconnected components, and they all operate concurrently. If we wish to model the brain or use it as a source of ideas for AI, we must consider the powers and constraints imposed by the brain's architecture at the neural level. Unfortunately, we do not understand very well how neurons are wired in the brain, so modeling at this level is difficult. But we return to this idea in Chapter 18, where we describe the use of *neural networks* as a way of representing and using knowledge.

16.2   Parallelism in Reasoning Systems

AI programs consume significant time and space resources. It is therefore important that AI algorithms make use of advances in parallel computation. In this section, we describe several ways of doing this without substantially changing the programs that we write. Then, in the next section, we explore ways in which techniques from parallel and distributed computing can be used in the overall design of AI systems.

16.2.1   Parallelizing AI Architectures

As we mentioned above, production systems have both sequential and parallel aspects. The question arises, how much speedup can we expect from parallel processing? There are several sources of parallel speedup in production systems:

- Match-level parallelism, in which multiple processors are used to speed up the handling of individual match-resolve-act cycles

    - Production-level parallelism, in which all of the productions match themselves against working memory in parallel

    - Condition-level parallelism, in which all of the conditions of a single production are matched in parallel

    - Action-level parallelism, in which all of the actions of a single production are executed in parallel

- Task-level parallelism, in which several cycles are executed simultaneously

The amount of task-level parallelism available is completely dependent on the nature of the task. In a medical diagnosis system, for example, each production firing might be dependent on the previous production firing, thus enabling a long, sequential chain of reasoning to occur. However, if the system were diagnosing five patients simultaneously, productions involving different patients would not interact with one another and could be executed in parallel.

Match-level parallelism is more widely applicable. Since production systems spend nearly all of their time in the matching phase, it was expected early on that match-level parallelism would lead to vast speedups. In a system with a thousand productions, for example, one processor could be assigned to every production, possibly speeding up every match cycle by a factor of a thousand. However, as Gupta [1985] showed, having n processors does not lead to an n-fold speedup. Some reasons for this effect are:

1. Only a few productions are affected by each change in working memory. With some bookkeeping to save state information, sequential implementations such as RETE [Forgy, 1982] (Section 6.4.2) can avoid processing large numbers of productions. Parallel implementations must be judged with respect to the speedups they offer over efficient sequential algorithms, not inefficient ones.

2. Some productions are very expensive to match, while others are cheap. This means that many processors may sit idle waiting for others to finish. When processors are idle, the speedup available from parallel processing diminishes.

3. Overhead resulting from communication costs among multiple processors can further reduce the benefits of parallelism.

Other architectures behave differently with respect to parallel implementation. The brain-style architectures mentioned above are naturally parallel; in fact, simulating them on sequential machines is often prohibitive because of the high degree of parallelism they assume. In Section 16.3, we discuss some other parallel AI architectures.

16.2.2 Parallelizing AI Programming Languages

In the last section, we discussed the benefits of parallelizing a particular kind of program, namely a production system interpreter. Other frequently used interpreters in AI include those for the programming languages LISP and PROLOG.

Writing parallel programs is a difficult task for humans, and there is some hope that parallel implementations of these languages (perhaps augmented with parallel programming constructs) will make effective speedups more practical. Parallel LISP models include Multilisp [Halstead, 1988], QLISP [Gabriel and McCarthy, 1988], and the Paralation Model [Sabot, 1988]. Parallel PROLOG models include Concurrent PROLOG [Shapiro, 1987], PARLOG [Clark and Gregory, 1986], and Guarded Horn Clauses [Ueda, 1985].

Research into parallel logic programming languages was an important focus of the Japanese Fifth Generation project [ICOT, 1984]. Languages like PROLOG immediately suggest two types of parallelism. In *OR-parallelism*, multiple paths to the same goal are taken in parallel. For example, suppose we have the following clauses:

```
uncle(X,Y)  :- mother(Z,Y),  sibling(X,Z).
uncle(X,Y)  :- father(Z,Y),  sibling(X,Z).
```

Then the query

```
?- uncle(John,Bill)
```

could be satisfied in two different ways since John could be the sibling of Bill's mother or of Bill's father. A sequential implementation would try to satisfy the first condition, and then, if that failed, try the second condition. There is no reason, however, why these two paths could not be pursued in parallel.[1]

In *AND-parallelism*, the portions of a conjunctive goal are pursued in parallel. Consider the clause:

```
infieldfly(X)  :- fly(X), infieldcatchable(X),
                   occupiedbase(first),  outs(zero).
```

Here, the four conditions can be checked in parallel, possibly leading to a four-fold speedup in processing `infieldfly` queries. Such AND-parallelism is not so straightforward when variables are shared across goals, as in:

```
uncle(X,Y)  :- mother(Z,Y),  sibling(X,Z).
```

The `mother(Z,Y)` and `sibling(X,Z)` conditions cannot be satisfied independently, since they must instantiate the variable Z in the same manner.

Research on parallel logic programming shares the same goal as that on parallel production systems: to permit the efficient execution of high-level, easily written code for AI systems.

16.2.3   Parallelizing AI Algorithms

Some problems are more amenable to parallel solutions than others. While nine authors may be able to write a book much faster than one author (if they each write separate chapters), nine women cannot bear a child any faster than one can. Likewise, throwing more processors at an AI problem may not bring the desired benefits. One example of an inherently sequential problem in AI is unification (recall Section 5.4.4). While multiple processors can help somewhat [Vitter and Simons, 1986], formal arguments [Dwork *et al.*, 1984] show that vast speedups in the unification of large terms are not possible.

Many problems can be solved efficiently by parallel methods, but it is not always a simple matter to convert a sequential algorithm into an efficient parallel one. Some AI algorithms whose parallel aspects have been studied are best-first search [Kumar *et al.*, 1988], alpha-beta pruning [Hsu, 1989], constraint satisfaction [Kasif, 1986], natural language parsing [Thompson, 1989], resolution theorem proving [Cheng and Juang, 1987], and property inheritance [Fahlman, 1979].

---

[1] In PROLOG, clauses are matched sequentially from top to bottom. If PROLOG programmers write code that depends on this behavior, OR-parallelism may yield undesired results.

16.2.4 Custom Parallel Hardware

Finally, we must ask how these parallel algorithms can be implemented in hardware. One approach is to code an algorithm in a programming language supported by a general-purpose parallel computer. Another approach is to build custom parallel hardware that directly implements a single algorithm. This last approach has led to striking performance increases, as demonstrated in the SPHINX [Lee and Hon, 1988] speech recognition system, where real-time performance was achieved through the use of a beam search accelerator [Bisiani *et al.*, 1989], and in the DEEP THOUGHT chess machine [Hsu, 1989], which uses a parallel tree-search algorithm for searching game trees.

16.3 Distributed Reasoning Systems

In all of our discussions of problem-solving systems until now, we have focused on the design of single systems. In this section, we expand our view, and look at *distributed reasoning systems*. We define a distributed reasoning system to be one that is composed of a set of separate modules (often called *agents* since each module is usually expected to act as a problem-solving entity in its own right) and a set of communication paths between them. This definition is intentionally very vague. It admits systems everywhere along a spectrum that ranges from tightly coupled systems in which there is a completely centralized control mechanism and a shared knowledge base to ones in which both control and knowledge are fully distributed. In fact, of course, most real distributed reasoning systems lie somewhere in the middle. This definition also includes systems that are distributed at varying levels of granularity, although we do not intend it to include systems with very fine granularity (such as connectionist systems in which the individual nodes do not perform reasoning in the same sense that we have been using the term).

For many kinds of applications, distributed reasoning systems have significant advantages over large monolithic systems. These advantages can include:

1. System Modularity—It is easier to build and maintain a collection of quasi-independent modules than one huge one.[2]

2. Efficiency—Not all knowledge is needed for all tasks. By modularizing it, we gain the ability to focus the problem-solving system's efforts in ways that are most likely to pay off.

3. Fast Computer Architectures—As problem solvers get more complex, they need more and more cycles. Although machines continue to get faster, the real speed-ups are beginning to come not from a single processor with a huge associated memory, but from clusters of smaller processors, each with its own memory. Distributed systems are better able to exploit such architectures.

4. Heterogeneous Reasoning—The problem-solving techniques and knowledge representation formalisms that are best for working on one part of a problem may not be the best for working on another part.

---

[2]In this respect, reasoning programs are no different from other large programs [Dijkstra, 1972].

5. Multiple Perspectives—The knowledge required to solve a problem may not reside in the head of a single person. It is very difficult to get many diverse people to build a single, coherent knowledge base, and sometimes it is impossible because their models of the domain are actually inconsistent.

6. Distributed Problems—Some problems are inherently distributed. For example, there may be different data available in each of several distinct physical locations.

7. Reliability—If a problem is distributed across agents on different systems, problem solving can continue even if one system fails.

An architecture for distributed reasoning must provide:

1. A mechanism for ensuring that the activities of the various agents in the system are coordinated so that the overall problem-solving system achieves its goal(s).

2. A communication structure that enables information to be passed back and forth among agents.

3. Distributed versions of the necessary reasoning techniques. These mechanisms are likely to differ from their monolithic counterparts since they will be presumed to operate on a set of local knowledge bases rather than on a global one that can be assumed to possess a set of global properties (such as consistency).

In the rest of this section, we address each of these issues.

16.3.1 Coordination and Cooperation

The biggest issue that needs to be faced in the design of any distributed reasoning system is how the actions of the individual agents can be coordinated so that they work together effectively. There are a variety of approaches that can be taken here, including the following:

- One agent is in charge. That master agent makes a plan and distributes pieces of the plan to other "slave" agents, who then do as they are told and report back their results. They may also communicate with other slave agents if necessary to accomplish their goals.

- One agent is in charge and that agent decomposes the problem into subproblems, but then negotiation occurs to decide what agents will take responsibility for which subtasks.

- No one agent is in charge, although there is a single shared goal among all the agents. They must cooperate both in forming a plan and in executing it.

- No one agent is in charge, and there is no guarantee that a single goal will be shared among all the agents. They may even compete with each other.

Although these approaches differ considerably, there is one modification to a simple, single agent view of reasoning that is necessary to support all of them in anything other than a trivial way. We need a way to represent models of agents, including what they know, what they can do, and what their goals are. Fortunately, what we need is exactly the set of mechanisms that we introduced in Section 15.4. But now, instead of using modal operators and predicates (such as BELIEVE, KNOW, KNOW-WHAT, CAN-PERFORM, and WILLING-TO-PERFORM) to model writers and speakers, we use them to model agents in a distributed system. Using such operators, it is possible for each agent to build a model of both itself and the other agents with which it must interact. The self-descriptive model is necessary to enable the agent to know when it should get help from others and to allow it to represent itself accurately to other agents who may wish to get help from it. The model of other agents is necessary to enable an agent to know how best to get help from them.

Planning for Multi-agent Execution

The least distributed form of distributed reasoning is that in which a single agent:

1. Decomposes the goal into subgoals, and

2. Assigns the subgoals to the various other agents

This kind of reasoning is usually called *multi-agent planning*. The first step, problem decomposition, is essentially the same as it is for single-agent planning systems. Ideally, the decomposition results in a set of subproblems that are mutually independent. This is often not possible, however, so various of the techniques that we described in Chapter 13 must be exploited.

Once a decomposition has been produced, the subproblems must be allocated to the available agents for execution. At this point, distributed planning differs from single agent planning in the following important ways:

- Unless all the slave agents are identical, the master agent must have access to models of the capabilities of the various slaves. These models make it possible to allocate tasks to the agents that are best able to perform them.

- Even if all the slave agents are identical, the master must do load balancing to assure that the overall goal is completed as soon as possible.

- Once the tasks have been distributed, synchronization among the slaves is necessary unless all the tasks are completely independent. In single-agent planning, dependencies are usually handled at plan creation time. In a multiple agent system, it is not usually possible to do that, since any such static scheme will be defeated if the various agents take unpredictable amounts of time to perform their tasks.

Let's consider this last issue in a bit more detail. Suppose the task is to do spelling correction on a document with several chapters, and then to print it. We can distribute this among several spelling correcting agents and one printing agent. But to get the desired result, we need to ensure that the printing agent does not begin printing any chapter until spelling correction on that chapter is complete. Distributed reasoning systems exploit a wide variety of synchronization techniques to guarantee this, ranging from simple ones (e.g., in which the printing process does not begin until all the spelling correctors are done and have so informed the master) to more sophisticated ones in which the slave processes communicate directly with each other (e.g., the spelling correctors each inform the printer when they have finished). These more sophisticated techniques require that each slave agent be told some information about the other slaves at the time that it is given its task.

For relatively simple tasks, such as the one we just described, the various agents can communicate effectively with each other just by announcing when operations have been completed. For other kinds of tasks, though, it is not enough to know when an agent has completed its task. It may also be necessary to know what state the system is in during task execution. For example, suppose that there is a single resource that the various agents share, such as an input or output device. Then one agent may want to know whether any other is currently using the device. To support this kind of interaction, it is useful to introduce a state-based model, such as that described by Georgeff [1983; 1984]. In this kind of a model, each available action is characterized as a sequence of state changes that it effects. The various agents may share a single model, which they all update as necessary, or they may each have their own model, in which case they must also inform all other relevant agents whenever they make a change to their internal state that could be important externally.

Planning and Negotiation: Contract Nets

A slightly more distributed kind of reasoning occurs when a single agent performs the problem decomposition but then negotiates with the other agents to determine who will take on which subtasks. The *contract net* mechanism [Davis and Smith, 1983] supports this kind of interaction. In a contract net, there are two roles that the agents can assume:

1. Manager, who decomposes a problem, looks for contractors to attack pieces of the problem, and monitors the problem's execution.

2. Contractor, who executes a subtask, possibly by actually doing the job and possibly by recursively becoming a manager and subcontracting subparts of the job to other contractors.

Managers and contractors find each other through a process of bidding:

1. A manager announces a task.

2. Contractors evaluate the task with respect to their own abilities and the resource requirements necessary to accomplish it.

3. Contractors make bids to the manager.

4. The manager chooses a single contractor and waits for the result.

Thus managers and contractors select each other by communicating in a completely distributed fashion. A node can be both a manager and a contractor simultaneously; rather than sit idle, waiting for results from its contractors, a manager can take on work in the meantime.

Distributed Control and Communication

So far, we have focused on systems in which there is a single agent who maintains control of the overall problem-solving process. In this section, we look at the problem of *distributed planning*, in which there is no such centralized controller. In the extreme form of such systems, we can make no assumptions about how the various agents will behave. But without any such assumptions, it is impossible to construct problem-solving algorithms. So we start by assuming that each agent is rational. We can define rationality as follows:

> An agent is *rational* if it behaves in a manner that is optimal with respect to its goals.

Unfortunately, in a complex world, an agent may not have enough processing power to behave optimally. This leads to a slightly weaker, but more useful, notion of bounded rationality [Simon, 1957]:

> *Bounded rationality* is a property of an agent that behaves in a manner that is as nearly optimal with respect to its goals as its resources allow.

Bounded rationality is akin to the notion of satisficing that we discussed in Chapter 2.

Using these ideas, we can define techniques that an individual agent can use to attain its goals, taking into account what will probably happen as a result of what the other agents in its environment are likely to do. Sometimes, the other agents are cooperating to achieve the same goal. Sometimes they are working on other goals, which may be competitive or simply orthogonal. We consider two classes of approaches to this problem:

- Planning with communication

- Planning without communication

The first approach is one in which the agents can communicate freely with each other during problem solving. In this case, the agents can each create their own plans, which are composed both of problem-solving actions and of communication actions of the sort we described in Section 15.4. Sometimes the communication actions are addressed to a specific other agent who is believed to be able to satisfy a request (either for information or to perform some other task). In other systems, the agents do not know explicitly about each other. Instead, each agent can broadcast to a shared memory structure, which other agents can be counted on to read. Each agent can then reply to those messages to which it chooses to pay attention. We describe one specific way of implementing such a broadcast structure as a blackboard system in Section 16.3.2.

One specific technique that several communicating agents can use is called the *functionally accurate, cooperative* (FA/C) approach [Lesser and Corkill, 1981] to distributed problem solving. Each agent begins by forming a tentative, incomplete plan. These plans are then shared among the agents, who are able to help refine each other's plans by adding information that they possess. Ideally, the entire system converges on a complete plan.

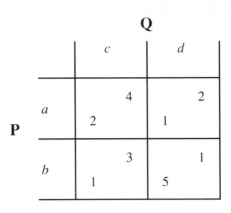

Figure 16.1: A Payoff Matrix for Two Agents and Two Actions

The second approach is one in which we assume that the agents cannot communicate. This may seem to be a very serious restriction, but it is useful to consider it both because it does sometimes arise in the extreme (perhaps because the agents are geographically isolated) and because it often arises at small granularity levels where the cost of constant communication may come to dominate the cost of actual problem solving.

If we assume that the agents cannot communicate and that they are all rational, then we can use many of the standard notions of game theory to describe how each of them should act. The most basic technique is that of a payoff matrix, such as the one shown in Figure 16.1. We assume that there are only two agents, P and Q, and that there are only two actions that each of them can perform (*a* and *b* for P, and *c* and *d* for Q). Then the matrix shows the payoff for each of them for each of the possible joint actions. The number in the lower left of each box is the payoff for P; the number in the upper right is the payoff for Q. Each agent's goal is to maximize its own payoff. For example, P comes out best if it makes move *b* and Q makes move *d*. On the other hand, Q comes out best if P makes move *a* and Q makes move *c*.

Of course, no one of the agents can force such a dual move. Each must make its own decision independently. In this case, for example, P should choose move *a* (rather than *b*, even though the best case for P included move *b*). Why? The answer is that P should assume that Q will behave rationally. In this matrix, the *c* column dominates the *d* column for Q, by which we mean that in every row, the payoff for Q is higher in the *c* column than in the *d* column. Thus Q can be predicted to choose *c*, and P should plan accordingly. Given that Q will choose *c*, P sees that it does better to choose move *a* than move *b*.

We can now view our discussion of game-playing programs (Chapter 12) from a different perspective, that of noncommunicating agents trying to solve their own goals. Both payoff matrices and tree-search algorithms can be generalized to more than two players (e.g., Korf [1989]), but there are some important differences. In board games, players usually take turns making moves, whereas payoff matrices model the kind of simultaneous decision making common in the real world. Also, games are usually zero-sum, meaning that one player's gain is another player's loss. Payoff matrices are sometimes zero-sum, but need not be. See Genesereth *et al.* [1987] and Rosenschein and Breese [1989] for more substantial discussions of operations on payoff matrices.

16.3.2   Communication: Blackboards and Messages

The specific communication architectures that have been proposed to support distributed reasoning fall into two classes with respect to communication structure:

- *Blackboard systems*, in which communication takes place through a shared knowledge structure called a blackboard. Modules can post items on the blackboard, and they can read and act on messages that are posted by other modules.

- *Message-passing systems*, in which one reasoning module sends messages (both requests for services and information as well as replies to such requests) to one or more other modules whose names are explicitly known.

Although on the surface, these two techniques appear quite different, they turn out in practice to offer essentially the same support for distributed reasoning. In fact, they can be used to simulate each other, as we see below. In the rest of this section, we describe examples of each approach.

Blackboard Systems

The blackboard approach to the organization of large AI programs was first developed in the context of the HEARSAY-II speech-understanding project [Erman *et al.*, 1980]. The idea behind the blackboard approach is simple. The entire system consists of:

- A set of independent modules, called knowledge sources (or KSs), that contain the system's domain-specific knowledge

- A blackboard, which is the shared data structure through which the knowledge sources communicate with each other

- A control system, which determines the order in which knowledge sources will operate on the entries on the blackboard

To see how these pieces work together, let's look at the HEARSAY-II system. Here, the KSs correspond to the levels of knowledge about speech, language (syllables, words, phrases, and sentences), and the task being discussed. The blackboard contains hypotheses about interpretations at each of these levels. Control is performed by a specialized knowledge source that reasons about such factors as cost of execution and likelihood of achieving a result.

When a KS is activated (as described below), it examines the current contents of the blackboard and applies its knowledge either to create a new *hypothesis* and write it on the blackboard, or to modify an existing one. Although the execution of the entire HEARSAY-II system consists of the asynchronous execution of a collection of KSs, the execution of an individual KS is a sequential process. Once a KS is activated, it executes without being interrupted until it is finished.

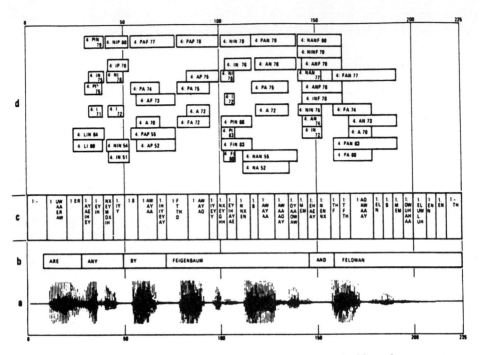

Figure 16.2: A Snapshot of a HEARSAY-II Blackboard

The hypotheses on the blackboard are arranged along two dimensions: level (from small, low-level hypotheses about individual sounds to large, high-level hypotheses about the meaning of an entire sentence) and time (corresponding to periods of the utterance being analyzed). The goal of the system is to create a single hypothesis that represents a solution to a problem. For HEARSAY-II, such a solution would be an acceptable interpretation of an entire utterance. Figures 16.2 and 16.3 show a snapshot of a HEARSAY-II blackboard. Figure 16.2 shows the lowest three levels of the blackboard, and Figure 16.3 shows the top three. The levels are the following:

a. The waveform corresponding to the sentence "Are any by Feigenbaum and Feld-man?"

b. The correct words shown just for reference

c. The sound segments

d. The syllable classes

e. The words as created by one word KS

f. The words as created by a second word KS

g. Word sequences

h. Phrases

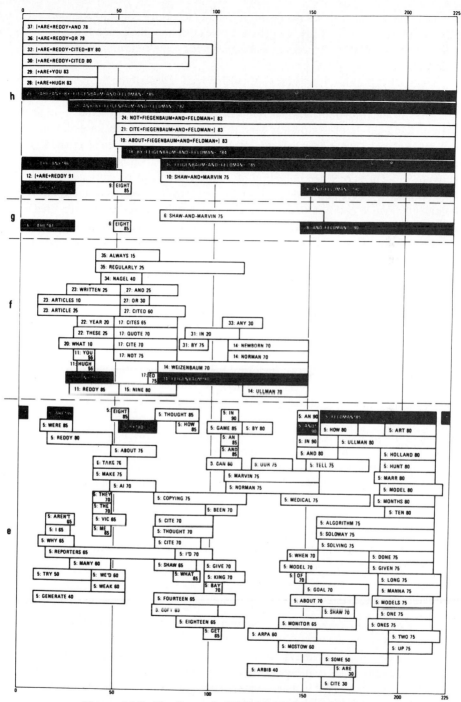

Figure 16.3: The Rest of a HEARSAY-II Blackboard

Associated with each KS is a set of *triggers* that specify conditions under which the KS should be activated. These triggers are an example of the general idea of a *demon*, which is, conceptually, a procedure that watches for some condition to become true and then activates an associated process.[3]

When a trigger fires, it creates an *activation record* describing the KS that should be activated and the specific event that fired the trigger. This latter information can be used to focus the attention of the KS when it is actually activated. Of course, a single event, such as the addition of a particular kind of hypothesis to the blackboard, could cause several triggers to fire at once, causing several activation records to be created. The KS that caused the triggering event to occur need not know about any of these subsequent activations. The actual determination of which KS should be activated next is done by a special KS, called the *scheduler*, on the basis of its knowledge about how best to conduct the search in the particular domain. The scheduler uses ratings supplied to it by each of the independent KSs. If the scheduler ever discovers that there are no activation records pending, then the system's execution terminates. For more information on the HEARSAY-II scheduler, see Hayes-Roth and Lesser [1977].

The techniques developed in HEARSAY-II have since been generalized in several multipurpose blackboard systems, including HEARSAY-III [Balzer *et al.*, 1980; Erman *et al.*, 1981], GBB [Corkill *et al.*, 1987], and BB1 [Hayes-Roth, 1985; Hayes-Roth and Hewett, 1989]. For example, the use of time as an explicit dimension on the blackboard is not appropriate in all domains, so it has been removed from these more general systems.

But these new blackboard systems also provide facilities that HEARSAY-II lacked. In HEARSAY-II, control was data-driven. This worked well for speech understanding. But for other kinds of problem solving, other kinds of control are more appropriate. Examples include control that is driven either by goals or by plans. The newer blackboard systems provide explicit support for these other control mechanisms. One important way in which they do that is to allow the use of multiple blackboards. Although this idea can also be exploited as a way to modularize domain reasoning, one of its important uses is to exploit one blackboard for reasoning in the problem domain and another for controlling that reasoning. In addition, these systems provide a goal-structured agenda mechanism that can be used in the control space to allow problem solving to be driven by an explicit goal structure. See Englemore and Morgan [1989] and Jagannathan *et al.* [1989] for further descriptions of these systems and some applications that have been built on top of them.

Message-Passing Systems

Message-passing systems provide an alternative way for agents in a distributed reasoning system to communicate with each other. In such a framework, the agents tend to know more about each other than they do in a blackboard system. This knowledge enables them to direct their messages to those agents who are most likely to be able to do what needs to be done. As an example of a message-passing distributed system, we describe MACE [Gasser *et al.*, 1987], which provides a general architecture for distributed reasoning

---

[3]Of course, demons usually are not actually implemented as processes that watch for things, but rather the things they are watching for are set up to activate them when appropriate.

systems (in the same sense that systems such as BB1 provide a general architecture for blackboard systems). A MACE system is composed of five kinds of components:

1. Problem-solving agents, which are specialized to a problem domain

2. System agents, which provide such facilities as command interpretation, error handling, tracing

3. Facilities, which are built-in functions that agents can use for such things as pattern matching and simulation

4. A description database, which maintains descriptions of the agents

5. Kernels, of which there is one for each processor, which handle such functions as message routing and I/O transfers

A MACE problem-solving agent maintains models of other agents. A model that an agent *P* has of some other agent *A* contains the following information:

1. Name: *A*'s name

2. Class: *A*'s class

3. Address: *A*'s location

4. Role: *A*'s relationship to *P*. This relationship can be identity, creator, or member of an organization.

5. Skills: *P*'s knowledge about what *A* can do

6. Goals: *P*'s beliefs about *A*'s goals

7. Plans: *P*'s beliefs about *A*'s plans for achieving its goals

This architecture supports many of the kinds of distributed reasoning systems that we have been discussing. Let's consider a few.

First, suppose we want to build a system in which a controlling agent will decompose the problem and then negotiate with other agents to perform subtasks using a contract net mechanism. Then each of the agents can be represented as a problem-solving agent in MACE. The manager decomposes the problem. It then sends requests for bids to all the other agents, about which it knows nothing except their addresses. As the other agents respond, the manager can build up its model of them. Using that model, it can choose the agents to whom it wishes to award bids. The chosen agents perform their tasks and then send reply messages to the manager.

At another extreme, suppose we want to build a system that is composed of competing agents. We can model such a system in a MACE architecture, again by building a set of problem-solving agents, but this time their models of each other must be more sophisticated. In particular, it will be necessary to model each other's goals and plans.

Although MACE directly supports a message-passing communication protocol, it can be used to simulate a blackboard system. A single problem-solving agent, or a collection of them, can be used to simulate each blackboard knowledge source. Additional agents can simulate the blackboard itself. Agents send messages to the blackboard, which in turn routes the messages to the other agents that should be triggered as a result of the posting.

As this example suggests, there really is no dichotomy between blackboard and message-passing systems so much as there is a continuum. At one extreme, an agent can do nothing but broadcast its message to everyone. At the other, an agent can do nothing except send its message to a specific other agent. There are many in-between positions that can be very useful. For example, an agent may not know exactly which other agent should receive its message, but it may know that it is some agent belonging to a particular class. In a message-passing architecture, this can be implemented by arranging agents into a hierarchy of classes and allowing messages to be sent to a class and thus delivered to all members of the class. In a blackboard system, this same capability can be implemented by creating a type hierarchy for blackboard elements. Then each KS is marked with the types of elements that will be considered as triggering events. When an element is posted, only those KSs that are defined for elements of that type will be given a chance to trigger on it.

16.3.3 Distributed Reasoning Algorithms

So far we have discussed various issues that arise when planning and plan execution are distributed across multiple agents. But we have not considered any modifications to any other reasoning algorithms. We have implicitly assumed that such standard procedures as matching and inheritance would work in a distributed system just as they do in a single-agent system. In many cases they do. But there are some reasoning algorithms, particularly ones that operate globally on a knowledge base, that need to be redesigned to support distributed reasoning. We consider one example of such an algorithm here.

Consider again the justification-based truth maintenance system (JTMS) that we described in Section 7.5.2. The JTMS works by considering an entire knowledge base and labeling the nodes in the knowledge base so that the labeling is consistent and well-founded. Both of these are global properties. But consider a distributed reasoning system in which there are several agents, each of which has its own knowledge base. Although we expect that each of these knowledge bases will be locally consistent, we do not want to insist that, taken together, they be globally consistent. This is important, since one of the benefits of a distributed system is that agents that represent different points of view and positions can interact. So what does it mean to label the nodes in such an inconsistent knowledge base?

A second question arises when we extend the notion of a JTMS to a distributed system. In a single-agent system, a justification is created as part of the reasoning process. It stays with the resulting node and can be used to update the belief status of the node if any of the assumptions on which the reasoning depended ever change. But what if one agent does the reasoning and then communicates its result to another? It may not make sense to communicate the justification, since it may involve knowledge-base objects that the receiver of the result knows nothing about. This will often happen if one agent asks another to solve a problem about which it knows very little.

Both of these problems can be solved by introducing the idea of a distributed truth maintenance system. In this system, interagent justifications work as follows. Assume $A1$ solves a problem and reports the result to $A2$. Then $A1$ also reports to

*A*2 a justification that says "Because *A*1 says so." This justification is treated by *A*2 essentially like a premise justification. But *A*1 must also remember the justification, and it must remember that it sent this justification to *A*2. If the justification ever becomes invalid in *A*1, then *A*1 must send a message to *A*2 saying that *A*1 no longer says so. At that point, the conclusion must go OUT in *A*2 unless there exists some other justification that is still valid.

Node labeling in the distributed truth maintenance system works similarly to node labeling in a single-agent system except that we need to redefine consistency. Rather than insisting on global consistency, we instead insist on extended local consistency, by which we mean that the labels within the knowledge base of a single agent must be consistent and the labels that are attached to nodes that have been explicitly shared among agents must be consistent across agents. But we do not insist that the labels attached to nodes that have not been explicitly shared be consistent across agents. For more information on how to do this, see Bridgeland and Huhns [1990]. For a similar discussion of ways to create a distributed assumption-based truth maintenance system, see Mason and Johnson [1989].

16.4 Summary

In this chapter, we discussed parallel and distributed aspects of AI. We examined psychological factors as well as efficiency concerns. The last section described the issues that arise when we attempt to extend the problem-solving mechanisms of earlier chapters to distributed reasoning systems. We have by no means covered all of them. For more information in this area, see the the following collections: Huhns [1987], Bond and Gasser [1988], and Gasser and Huhns [1989].

Before we end this chapter, we should point out that as distributed systems become more complex, it becomes harder to see how best to organize them. One thing that has proved promising is to look for analogies in the organization of other complex systems. One of the most promising sources of such analogies is the structure of human organizations, such as societies and corporations. A team or a corporation or a government is, after all, a distributed goal-oriented system. We have already seen one example of this idea, namely the bidding that is exploited in the contract net framework. See Fox [1981], Malone [1987], and Kornfeld and Hewitt [1981] for further discussion of this idea.

Another source of ideas is the way a single human brain functions. The book, *The Society of Mind* [Minsky, 1985] explores the notion that single minds are also distributed systems, composed of collections of heterogeneous agents that simultaneously cooperate and compete.

16.5 Exercises

1. Consider a situation in which one agent *A*1 requests help from a second agent *A*2 to help find a movie it would like. *A*1 knows what it likes and *A*2 knows about movies.

    (a) Using the belief and communication operators that we have defined (plus any others that you find it useful to define), write a plan that could be used by $A1$.

    (b) Write a similar plan for $A2$.

2. Consider the following payoff matrix:

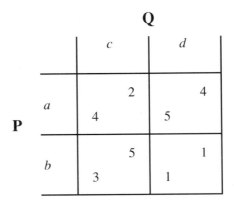

    If Q assumes P is rational, what move should Q make?

3. Show how the HEARSAY-II blackboard system could be extended to support the whole natural language understanding process that we described in Chapter 15.

4. Show how a speech understanding system could be built using a MACE-style architecture.

Chapter 17

Learning

17.1 What Is Learning?

One of the most often heard criticisms of AI is that machines cannot be called intelligent until they are able to learn to do new things and to adapt to new situations, rather than simply doing as they are told to do. There can be little question that the ability to adapt to new surroundings and to solve new problems is an important characteristic of intelligent entities. Can we expect to see such abilities in programs? Ada Augusta, one of the earliest philosophers of computing, wrote that

> The Analytical Engine has no pretensions whatever to *originate* anything.
> It can do whatever we *know how to order it* to perform. [Lovelace, 1961]

This remark has been interpreted by several AI critics as saying that computers cannot learn. In fact, it does not say that at all. Nothing prevents us from telling a computer how to interpret its inputs in such a way that its performance gradually improves.

Rather than asking in advance whether it is possible for computers to "learn," it is much more enlightening to try to describe exactly what activities we mean when we say "learning" and what mechanisms could be used to enable us to perform those activities. Simon [1983] has proposed that learning denotes

> ... changes in the system that are adaptive in the sense that they enable the system to do the same task or tasks drawn from the same population more efficiently and more effectively the next time.

As thus defined, learning covers a wide range of phenomena. At one end of the spectrum is *skill refinement*. People get better at many tasks simply by practicing. The more you ride a bicycle or play tennis, the better you get. At the other end of the spectrum lies *knowledge acquisition*. As we have seen, many AI programs draw heavily on knowledge as their source of power. Knowledge is generally acquired through experience, and such acquisition is the focus of this chapter.

Knowledge acquisition itself includes many different activities. Simple storing of computed information, or *rote learning*, is the most basic learning activity. Many computer programs, e.g., database systems, can be said to "learn" in this sense, although most people would not call such simple storage learning. However, many AI programs are able to improve their performance substantially through rote-learning techniques, and we will look at one example in depth, the checker-playing program of Samuel [1963].

Another way we learn is through taking advice from others. Advice taking is similar to rote learning, but high-level advice may not be in a form simple enough for a program to use directly in problem solving. The advice may need to be first *operationalized*, a process explored in Section 17.3.

People also learn through their own problem-solving experience. After solving a complex problem, we remember the structure of the problem and the methods we used to solve it. The next time we see the problem, we can solve it more efficiently. Moreover, we can generalize from our experience to solve related problems more easily. In contrast to advice taking, learning from problem-solving experience does not usually involve gathering new knowledge that was previously unavailable to the learning program. That is, the program remembers its experiences and generalizes from them, but does not add to the transitive closure[1] of its knowledge, in the sense that an advice-taking program would, i.e., by receiving stimuli from the outside world. In large problem spaces, however, efficiency gains are critical. Practically speaking, learning can mean the difference between solving a problem rapidly and not solving it at all. In addition, programs that learn through problem-solving experience may be able to come up with qualitatively better solutions in the future.

Another form of learning that does involve stimuli from the outside is *learning from examples*. We often learn to classify things in the world without being given explicit rules. For example, adults can differentiate between cats and dogs, but small children often cannot. Somewhere along the line, we induce a method for telling cats from dogs based on seeing numerous examples of each. Learning from examples usually involves a teacher who helps us classify things by correcting us when we are wrong. Sometimes, however, a program can discover things without the aid of a teacher.

AI researchers have proposed many mechanisms for doing the kinds of learning described above. In this chapter, we discuss several of them. But keep in mind throughout this discussion that learning is itself a problem-solving process. In fact, it is very difficult to formulate a precise definition of learning that distinguishes it from other problem-solving tasks. Thus it should come as no surprise that, throughout this chapter, we will make extensive use of both the problem-solving mechanisms and the knowledge representation techniques that were presented in Parts I and II.

17.2   Rote Learning

When a computer stores a piece of data, it is performing a rudimentary form of learning. After all, this act of storage presumably allows the program to perform better in the future (otherwise, why bother?). In the case of data caching, we store computed values so that we do not have to recompute them later. When computation is more expensive than recall, this strategy can save a significant amount of time. Caching has been used

---

[1]The transitive closure of a program's knowledge is that knowledge plus whatever the program can logically deduce from it.

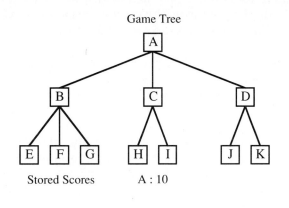

Figure 17.1(a) content:

Game Tree

Stored Scores   A : 10

(*a*)

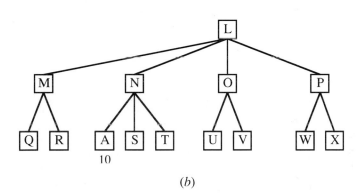

(*b*)

Figure 17.1: Storing Backed-Up Values

in AI programs to produce some surprising performance improvements. Such caching is known as *rote learning*.

In Chapter 12, we mentioned one of the earliest game-playing programs, Samuel's checkers program [Samuel, 1963]. This program learned to play checkers well enough to beat its creator. It exploited two kinds of learning: rote learning, which we look at now, and parameter (or coefficient) adjustment, which is described in Section 17.4.1. Samuel's program used the minimax search procedure to explore checkers game trees. As is the case with all such programs, time constraints permitted it to search only a few levels in the tree. (The exact number varied depending on the situation.) When it could search no deeper, it applied its static evaluation function to the board position and used that score to continue its search of the game tree. When it finished searching the tree and propagating the values backward, it had a score for the position represented by the root of the tree. It could then choose the best move and make it. But it also recorded the board position at the root of the tree and the backed up score that had just been computed for it. This situation is shown in Figure 17.1(*a*).

Now suppose that in a later game, the situation shown in Figure 17.1(*b*) were to arise. Instead of using the static evaluation function to compute a score for position A, the stored value for A can be used. This creates the effect of having searched an additional several ply since the stored value for A was computed by backing up values from exactly such a search.

Rote learning of this sort is very simple. It does not appear to involve any sophisticated problem-solving capabilities. But even it shows the need for some capabilities that will become increasingly important in more complex learning systems. These capabilities include:

- Organized Storage of Information—In order for it to be faster to use a stored value than it would be to recompute it, there must be a way to access the appropriate stored value quickly. In Samuel's program, this was done by indexing board positions by a few important characteristics, such as the number of pieces. But as the complexity of the stored information increases, more sophisticated techniques are necessary.

- Generalization—The number of distinct objects that might potentially be stored can be very large. To keep the number of stored objects down to a manageable level, some kind of generalization is necessary. In Samuel's program, for example, the number of distinct objects that could be stored was equal to the number of different board positions that can arise in a game. Only a few simple forms of generalization were used in Samuel's program to cut down that number. All positions are stored as though White is to move. This cuts the number of stored positions in half. When possible, rotations along the diagonal are also combined. Again, though, as the complexity of the learning process increases, so too does the need for generalization.

At this point, we have begun to see one way in which learning is similar to other kinds of problem solving. Its success depends on a good organizational structure for its knowledge base.

17.3   Learning by Taking Advice

A computer can do very little without a program for it to run. When a programmer writes a series of instructions into a computer, a rudimentary kind of learning is taking place: The programmer is a sort of teacher, and the computer is a sort of student. After being programmed, the computer is now able to do something it previously could not. Executing the program may not be such a simple matter, however. Suppose the program is written in a high-level language like LISP. Some interpreter or compiler must intervene to change the teacher's instructions into code that the machine can execute directly.

People process advice in an analogous way. In chess, the advice "fight for control of the center of the board" is useless unless the player can translate the advice into concrete moves and plans. A computer program might make use of the advice by adjusting its static evaluation function to include a factor based on the number of center squares attacked by its own pieces.

Mostow [1983] describes a program called FOO, which accepts advice for playing hearts, a card game. A human user first translates the advice from English into a representation that FOO can understand. For example, "Avoid taking points" becomes:

(avoid (take-points me) (trick))

FOO must *operationalize* this advice by turning it into an expression that contains concepts and actions FOO can use when playing the game of hearts. One strategy FOO can follow is to UNFOLD an expression by replacing some term by its definition. By UNFOLDing the definition of avoid, FOO comes up with:

(achieve (not (during (trick) (take-points me))))

FOO considers the advice to apply to the player called "me." Next, FOO UNFOLDs the definition of trick:

(achieve (not (during
                (scenario
                  (each p1 (players) (play-card p1))
                  (take-trick (trick-winner)))
                (take-points me))))

In other words, the player should avoid taking points during the scenario consisting of (1) players playing cards and (2) one player taking the trick. FOO then uses *case analysis* to determine which steps could cause one to take points. It rules out step 1 on the basis that it knows of no intersection of the concepts take-points and play-card. But step 2 could affect taking points, so FOO UNFOLDs the definition of take-points:

(achieve (not (there-exists c1 (cards-played)
                (there-exists c2 (point-cards)
                  (during (take (trick-winner) c1)
                    (take me c2))))))

This advice says that the player should avoid taking point-cards during the process of the trick-winner taking the trick. The question for FOO now is: Under what conditions does (take me c2) occur during (take (trick-winner) c1)? By using a technique called *partial match*, FOO hypothesizes that points will be taken if me = trick-winner and c2 = c1. It transforms the advice into:

(achieve (not (and (have-points (cards-played))
                  (= (trick-winner) me))))

This means "Do not win a trick that has points." We have not traveled very far conceptually from "avoid taking points," but it is important to note that the current vocabulary is one that FOO can understand in terms of actually playing the game of hearts. Through a number of other transformations, FOO eventually settles on:

(achieve (>= (and (in-suit-led (card-of me))
                  (possible (trick-has-points)))
              (low (card-of me))))

In other words, when playing a card that is the same suit as the card that was played first, if the trick possibly contains points, then play a low card. At last, FOO has translated the rather vague advice "avoid taking points" into a specific, usable heuristic. FOO is able to play a better game of hearts after receiving this advice. A human can watch FOO play, detect new mistakes, and correct them through yet more advice, such as "play high cards when it is safe to do so." The ability to operationalize knowledge is critical for systems that learn from a teacher's advice. It is also an important component of explanation-based learning, another form of learning discussed in Section 17.6.

17.4   Learning in Problem Solving

In the last section, we saw how a problem solver could improve its performance by taking advice from a teacher. Can a program get better *without* the aid of a teacher? It can, by generalizing from its own experiences.

17.4.1   Learning by Parameter Adjustment

Many programs rely on an evaluation procedure that combines information from several sources into a single summary statistic. Game-playing programs do this in their static evaluation functions, in which a variety of factors, such as piece advantage and mobility, are combined into a single score reflecting the desirability of a particular board position. Pattern classification programs often combine several features to determine the correct category into which a given stimulus should be placed. In designing such programs, it is often difficult to know *a priori* how much weight should be attached to each feature being used. One way of finding the correct weights is to begin with some estimate of the correct settings and then to let the program modify the settings on the basis of its experience. Features that appear to be good predictors of overall success will have their weights increased, while those that do not will have their weights decreased, perhaps even to the point of being dropped entirely.

Samuel's checkers program [Samuel, 1963] exploited this kind of learning in addition to the rote learning described above, and it provides a good example of its use. As its static evaluation function, the program used a polynomial of the form

$$c_1t_1 + c_2t_2 + \cdots + c_{16}t_{16}$$

The t terms are the values of the sixteen features that contribute to the evaluation. The c terms are the coefficients (weights) that are attached to each of these values. As learning progresses, the c values will change.

The most important question in the design of a learning program based on parameter adjustment is "When should the value of a coefficient be increased and when should it be decreased?" The second question to be answered is then "By how much should the value be changed?" The simple answer to the first question is that the coefficients of terms that predicted the final outcome accurately should be increased, while the coefficients of poor predictors should be decreased. In some domains, this is easy to do. If a pattern classification program uses its evaluation function to classify an input and it gets the right answer, then all the terms that predicted that answer should have their weights increased. But in game-playing programs, the problem is more difficult. The program does not get any concrete feedback from individual moves. It does not find out for sure until the end of the game whether it has won. But many moves have contributed to that final outcome. Even if the program wins, it may have made some bad moves along the way. The problem of appropriately assigning responsibility to each of the steps that led to a single outcome is known as the *credit assignment problem.*

Samuel's program exploits one technique, albeit imperfect, for solving this problem. Assume that the initial values chosen for the coefficients are good enough that the total evaluation function produces values that are fairly reasonable measures of the correct score even if they are not as accurate as we hope to get them. Then this evaluation function can be used to provide feedback to itself. Move sequences that lead to positions with higher values can be considered good (and the terms in the evaluation function that suggested them can be reinforced).

Because of the limitations of this approach, however, Samuel's program did two other things, one of which provided an additional test that progress was being made and the other of which generated additional nudges to keep the process out of a rut:

- When the program was in learning mode, it played against another copy of itself. Only one of the copies altered its scoring function during the game; the other remained fixed. At the end of the game, if the copy with the modified function won, then the modified function was accepted. Otherwise, the old one was retained. If, however, this happened very many times, then some drastic change was made to the function in an attempt to get the process going in a more profitable direction.

- Periodically, one term in the scoring function was eliminated and replaced by another. This was possible because, although the program used only sixteen features at any one time, it actually knew about thirty-eight. This replacement differed from the rest of the learning procedure since it created a sudden change in the scoring function rather than a gradual shift in its weights.

This process of learning by successive modifications to the weights of terms in a scoring function has many limitations, mostly arising out of its lack of exploitation of any knowledge about the structure of the problem with which it is dealing and the logical relationships among the problem's components. In addition, because the learning procedure is a variety of hill climbing, it suffers from the same difficulties as do other hill-climbing programs. Parameter adjustment is certainly not a solution to the overall learning problem. But it is often a useful technique, either in situations where very little additional knowledge is available or in programs in which it is combined with more knowledge-intensive methods. We have more to say about this type of learning in Chapter 18.

17.4.2 Learning with Macro-Operators

We saw in Section 17.2 how rote learning was used in the context of a checker-playing program. Similar techniques can be used in more general problem-solving programs. The idea is the same: to avoid expensive recomputation. For example, suppose you are faced with the problem of getting to the downtown post office. Your solution may involve getting in your car, starting it, and driving along a certain route. Substantial planning may go into choosing the appropriate route, but you need not plan about how to go about starting your car. You are free to treat START-CAR as an atomic action, even though it really consists of several actions: sitting down, adjusting the mirror, inserting the key, and turning the key. Sequences of actions that can be treated as a whole are called *macro-operators*.

Macro-operators were used in the early problem-solving system STRIPS [Fikes and Nilsson, 1971; Fikes *et al.*, 1972]. We discussed the operator and goal structures of STRIPS in Section 13.2, but STRIPS also has a learning component. After each problem-solving episode, the learning component takes the computed plan and stores it away as a macro-operator, or MACROP. A MACROP is just like a regular operator except that it consists of a sequence of actions, not just a single one. A MACROP's preconditions are the initial conditions of the problem just solved, and its postconditions correspond to the goal just achieved. In its simplest form, the caching of previously computed plans is similar to rote learning.

Suppose we are given an initial blocks world situation in which ON(C, B) and ON(A, Table) are both true. STRIPS can achieve the goal ON(A, B) by devising a plan with the four steps UNSTACK(C, B), PUTDOWN(C), PICKUP(A), STACK(A, B). STRIPS now builds a MACROP with preconditions ON(C, B), ON(A, Table) and postconditions ON(C, Table), ON(A, B). The body of the MACROP consists of the four steps just mentioned. In future planning, STRIPS is free to use this complex macro-operator just as it would use any other operator.

But rarely will STRIPS see the exact same problem twice. New problems will differ from previous problems. We would still like the problem solver to make efficient use of the knowledge it gained from its previous experiences. By *generalizing* MACROPs before storing them, STRIPS is able to accomplish this. The simplest idea for generalization is to replace all of the constants in the macro-operator by variables. Instead of storing the MACROP described in the previous paragraph, STRIPS can generalize the plan to consist of the steps UNSTACK(x_1, x_2), PUTDOWN(x_1), PICKUP(x_3), STACK(x_3, x_2), where x_1, x_2, and x_3 are variables. This plan can then be stored with preconditions ON(x_1, x_2), ON(x_3, Table) and postconditions ON(x_1, Table), ON(x_2, x_3). Such a MACROP can now apply in a variety of situations.

Generalization is not so easy, however. Sometimes constants must retain their specific values. Suppose our domain included an operator called STACK-ON-B(x), with preconditions that both x and B be clear, and with postcondition ON(x, B). Consider the same problem as above:

start: ON(C, B)   goal: ON(A, B)

STRIPS might come up with the plan UNSTACK(C, B), PUTDOWN(C), STACK-ON-B(A). Let's generalize this plan and store it as a MACROP. The precondition becomes ON(x_3, x_2), the postcondition becomes ON(x_1, x_2), and the plan itself becomes

UNSTACK(x_3, x_2), PUTDOWN(x_3), STACK-ON-B(x_1). Now, suppose we encounter a slightly different problem:

start: ON(E, C)   goal: ON(A, C)
ON(D, B)

The generalized MACROP we just stored seems well-suited to solving this problem if we let x_1 = A, x_2 = C, and x_3 = E. Its preconditions are satisfied, so we construct the plan UNSTACK(E, C), PUTDOWN(E), STACK-ON-B(A). But this plan does not work. The problem is that the postcondition of the MACROP is overgeneralized. This operation is only useful for stacking blocks onto B, which is not what we need in this new example. In this case, this difficulty will be discovered when the last step is attempted. Although we cleared C, which is where we wanted to put A, we failed to clear B, which is were the MACROP is going to try to put it. Since B is not clear, STACK-ON-B cannot be executed. If B had happened to be clear, the MACROP would have executed to completion, but it would not have accomplished the stated goal.

In reality, STRIPS uses a more complex generalization procedure. First, all constants are replaced by variables. Then, for each operator in the parameterized plan, STRIPS reevaluates its preconditions. In our example, the preconditions of steps 1 and 2 are satisfied, but the only way to ensure that B is clear for step 3 is to assume that block x_2, which was cleared by the UNSTACK operator, is actually block B. Through "re-proving" that the generalized plan works, STRIPS locates constraints of this kind.

More recent work on macro-operators appears in Korf [1985b]. It turns out that the set of problems for which macro-operators are critical are exactly those problems with *nonserializable subgoals*. Nonserializability means that working on one subgoal will necessarily interfere with the previous solution to another subgoal. Recall that we discussed such problems in connection with nonlinear planning (Section 13.5). Macro-operators can be useful in such cases, since one macro-operator can produce a small global change in the world, even though the individual operators that make it up produce many undesirable local changes.

For example, consider the 8-puzzle. Once a program has correctly placed the first four tiles, it is difficult to place the fifth tile without disturbing the first four. Because disturbing previously solved subgoals is detected as a bad thing by heuristic scoring functions, it is strongly resisted. For many problems, including the 8-puzzle and Rubik's cube, weak methods based on heuristic scoring are therefore insufficient. Hence, we either need domain-specific knowledge, or else a new weak method. Fortunately, we can *learn* the domain-specific knowledge we need in the form of macro-operators. Thus, macro-operators can be viewed as a weak method for learning. In the 8-puzzle, for example, we might have a macro—a complex, prestored sequence of operators—for placing the fifth tile without disturbing any of the first four tiles externally (although in fact they are disturbed within the macro itself). Korf [1985b] gives an algorithm for learning a complete set of macro-operators. This approach contrasts with STRIPS, which learned its MACROPs gradually, from experience. Korf's algorithm runs in time proportional to the time it takes to solve a single problem without macro-operators.

17.4.3   Learning by Chunking

Chunking is a process similar in flavor to macro-operators. The idea of chunking comes from the psychological literature on memory and problem solving. Its computational basis is in production systems, of the type studied in Chapter 6. Recall that in that chapter we described the SOAR system and discussed its use of control knowledge. SOAR also exploits chunking [Laird *et al.*, 1986] so that its performance can increase with experience. In fact, the designers of SOAR hypothesize that chunking is a universal learning method, i.e., it can account for all types of learning in intelligent systems.

SOAR solves problems by firing productions, which are stored in long-term memory. Some of those firings turn out to be more useful than others. When SOAR detects a useful sequence of production firings, it creates a chunk, which is essentially a large production that does the work of an entire sequence of smaller ones. As in MACROPs, chunks are generalized before they are stored.

Recall from Section 6.5 that SOAR is a uniform processing architecture. Problems like choosing which subgoals to tackle and which operators to try (i.e., search control problems) are solved with the same mechanisms as problems in the original problem space. Because the problem solving is uniform, chunking can be used to learn general search control knowledge in addition to operator sequences. For example, if SOAR tries several different operators, but only one leads to a useful path in the search space, then SOAR builds productions that help it choose operators more wisely in the future.

SOAR has used chunking to replicate the macro-operator results described in the last section. In solving the 8-puzzle, for example, SOAR learns how to place a given tile without permanently disturbing the previously placed tiles. Given the way that SOAR learns, several chunks may encode a single macro-operator, and one chunk may participate in a number of macro sequences. Chunks are generally applicable toward any goal state. This contrasts with macro tables, which are structured toward reaching a particular goal state from any initial state. Also, chunking emphasizes how learning can occur during problem solving, while macro tables are usually built during a preprocessing stage. As a result, SOAR is able to learn within trials as well as across trials. Chunks learned during the initial stages of solving a problem are applicable in the later stages of the same problem-solving episode. After a solution is found, the chunks remain in memory, ready for use in the next problem.

The price that SOAR pays for this generality and flexibility is speed. At present, chunking is inadequate for duplicating the contents of large, directly-computed macro-operator tables.

17.4.4   The Utility Problem

PRODIGY [Minton *et al.*, 1989], which we described in Section 6.5, also acquires control knowledge automatically. PRODIGY employs several learning mechanisms. One mechanism uses *explanation-based learning* (EBL), a learning method we discuss in Section 17.6. PRODIGY can examine a trace of its own problem-solving behavior and try to explain why certain paths failed. The program uses those explanations to formulate control rules that help the problem solver avoid those paths in the future. So while SOAR learns primarily from examples of successful problem solving, PRODIGY also learns from its failures.

A major contribution of the work on EBL in PRODIGY [Minton, 1988] was the identification of the *utility problem* in learning systems. While new search control knowledge can be of great benefit in solving future problems efficiently, there are also some drawbacks. The learned control rules can take up large amounts of memory and the search program must take the time to consider each rule at each step during problem solving. Considering a control rule amounts to seeing if its postconditions are desirable and seeing if its preconditions are satisfied. This is a time-consuming process. So while learned rules may reduce problem-solving time by directing the search more carefully, they may also increase problem-solving time by forcing the problem solver to consider them. If we only want to minimize the number of node expansions in the search space, then the more control rules we learn, the better. But if we want to minimize the total CPU time required to solve a problem, we must consider this trade-off.

PRODIGY maintains a utility measure for each control rule. This measure takes into account the average savings provided by the rule, the frequency of its application, and the cost of matching it. If a proposed rule has a negative utility, it is discarded (or "forgotten"). If not, it is placed in long-term memory with the other rules. It is then monitored during subsequent problem solving. If its utility falls, the rule is discarded. Empirical experiments have demonstrated the effectiveness of keeping only those control rules with high utility. Utility considerations apply to a wide range of learning systems. For example, for a discussion of how to deal with large, expensive chunks in SOAR, see Tambe and Rosenbloom [1989].

17.5 Learning from Examples: Induction

Classification is the process of assigning, to a particular input, the name of a class to which it belongs. The classes from which the classification procedure can choose can be described in a variety of ways. Their definition will depend on the use to which they will be put.

Classification is an important component of many problem-solving tasks. In its simplest form, it is presented as a straightforward recognition task. An example of this is the question "What letter of the alphabet is this?" But often classification is embedded inside another operation. To see how this can happen, consider a problem-solving system that contains the following production rule:

```
If:   the current goal is to get from place A to place B, and
      there is a WALL separating the two places
then: look for a DOORWAY in the WALL and go through it.
```

To use this rule successfully, the system's matching routine must be able to identify an object as a wall. Without this, the rule can never be invoked. Then, to apply the rule, the system must be able to recognize a doorway.

Before classification can be done, the classes it will use must be defined. This can be done in a variety of ways, including:

- Isolate a set of features that are relevant to the task domain. Define each class by a weighted sum of values of these features. Each class is then defined by a scoring function that looks very similar to the scoring functions often used in other situations, such as game playing. Such a function has the form:

$$c_1 t_1 + c_2 t_2 + c_3 t_3 + \cdots$$

  Each t corresponds to a value of a relevant parameter, and each c represents the weight to be attached to the corresponding t. Negative weights can be used to indicate features whose presence usually constitutes negative evidence for a given class.

  For example, if the task is weather prediction, the parameters can be such measurements as rainfall and location of cold fronts. Different functions can be written to combine these parameters to predict sunny, cloudy, rainy, or snowy weather.

- Isolate a set of features that are relevant to the task domain. Define each class as a structure composed of those features.

  For example, if the task is to identify animals, the body of each type of animal can be stored as a structure, with various features representing such things as color, length of neck, and feathers.

There are advantages and disadvantages to each of these general approaches. The statistical approach taken by the first scheme presented here is often more efficient than the structural approach taken by the second. But the second is more flexible and more extensible.

Regardless of the way that classes are to be described, it is often difficult to construct, by hand, good class definitions. This is particularly true in domains that are not well understood or that change rapidly. Thus the idea of producing a classification program that can evolve its own class definitions is appealing. This task of constructing class definitions is called *concept learning*, or *induction*. The techniques used for this task must, of course, depend on the way that classes (concepts) are described. If classes are described by scoring functions, then concept learning can be done using the technique of coefficient adjustment described in Section 17.4.1. If, however, we want to define classes structurally, some other technique for learning class definitions is necessary. In this section, we present three such techniques.

17.5.1   Winston's Learning Program

Winston [1975] describes an early structural concept learning program. This program operated in a simple blocks world domain. Its goal was to construct representations of the definitions of concepts in the blocks domain. For example, it learned the concepts *House*, *Tent*, and *Arch* shown in Figure 17.2. The figure also shows an example of a near miss for each concept. A *near miss* is an object that is not an instance of the concept in question but that is very similar to such instances.

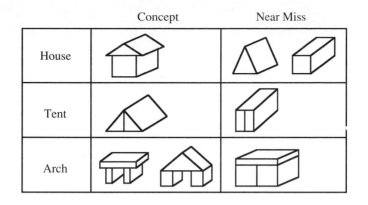

Figure 17.2: Some Blocks World Concepts

The program started with a line drawing of a blocks world structure. It used procedures such as the one described in Section 14.3 to analyze the drawing and construct a semantic net representation of the structural description of the object(s). This structural description was then provided as input to the learning program. An example of such a structural description for the *House* of Figure 17.2 is shown in Figure 17.3(*a*). Node A represents the entire structure, which is composed of two parts: node B, a *Wedge*, and node C, a *Brick*. Figures 17.3(*b*) and 17.3(*c*) show descriptions of the two *Arch* structures of Figure 17.2. These descriptions are identical except for the types of the objects on the top; one is a *Brick* while the other is a *Wedge*. Notice that the two supporting objects are related not only by *left-of* and *right-of* links, but also by a *does-not-marry* link, which says that the two objects do not *marry*. Two objects *marry* if they have faces that touch and they have a common edge. The *marry* relation is critical in the definition of an *Arch*. It is the difference between the first arch structure and the near miss arch structure shown in Figure 17.2.

The basic approach that Winston's program took to the problem of concept formation can be described as follows:

1. Begin with a structural description of one known instance of the concept. Call that description the concept definition.

2. Examine descriptions of other known instances of the concept. Generalize the definition to include them.

3. Examine descriptions of near misses of the concept. Restrict the definition to exclude these.

Steps 2 and 3 of this procedure can be interleaved.

Steps 2 and 3 of this procedure rely heavily on a comparison process by which similarities and differences between structures can be detected. This process must function in much the same way as does any other matching process, such as one to determine whether a given production rule can be applied to a particular problem state. Because differences as well as similarities must be found, the procedure must perform

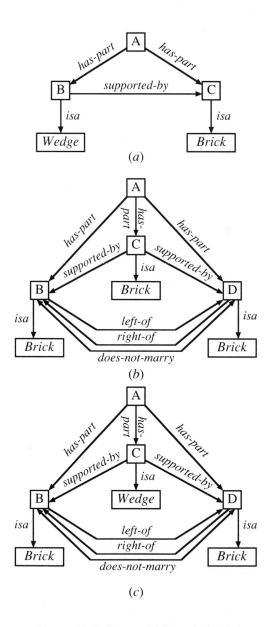

Figure 17.3: Structural Descriptions

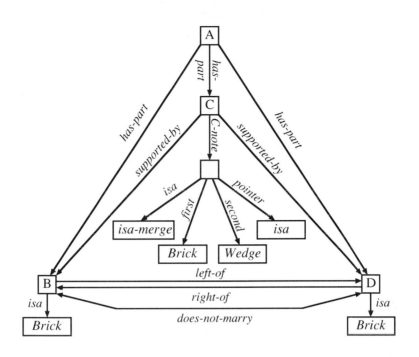

Figure 17.4: The Comparison of Two Arches

not just literal but also approximate matching. The output of the comparison procedure is a skeleton structure describing the commonalities between the two input structures. It is annotated with a set of comparison notes that describe specific similarities and differences between the inputs.

To see how this approach works, we trace it through the process of learning what an arch is. Suppose that the arch description of Figure 17.3(*b*) is presented first. It then becomes the definition of the concept *Arch*. Then suppose that the arch description of Figure 17.3(*c*) is presented. The comparison routine will return a structure similar to the two input structures except that it will note that the objects represented by the nodes labeled C are not identical. This structure is shown as Figure 17.4. The *c-note* link from node C describes the difference found by the comparison routine. It notes that the difference occurred in the *isa* link, and that in the first structure the *isa* link pointed to *Brick*, and in the second it pointed to *Wedge*. It also notes that if we were to follow *isa* links from *Brick* and *Wedge*, these links would eventually merge. At this point, a new description of the concept *Arch* can be generated. This description could say simply that node C must be either a *Brick* or a *Wedge*. But since this particular disjunction has no previously known significance, it is probably better to trace up the *isa* hierarchies of *Brick* and *Wedge* until they merge. Assuming that that happens at the node *Object*, the *Arch* definition shown in Figure 17.5 can be built.

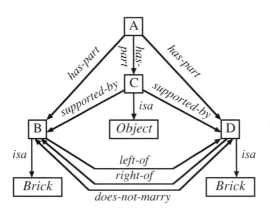

Figure 17.5: The Arch Description after Two Examples

Next, suppose that the near miss arch shown in Figure 17.2 is presented. This time, the comparison routine will note that the only difference between the current definition and the near miss is in the *does-not-marry* link between nodes *B* and *D*. But since this is a near miss, we do not want to broaden the definition to include it. Instead, we want to restrict the definition so that it is specifically excluded. To do this, we modify the link *does-not-marry*, which may simply be recording something that has happened by chance to be true of the small number of examples that have been presented. It must now say *must-not-marry*. The *Arch* description at this point is shown in Figure 17.6. Actually, *must-not-marry* should not be a completely new link. There must be some structure among link types to reflect the relationship between *marry*, *does-not-marry*, and *must-not-marry*.

Notice how the problem-solving and knowledge representation techniques we covered in earlier chapters are brought to bear on the problem of learning. Semantic networks were used to describe block structures, and an *isa* hierarchy was used to describe relationships among already known objects. A matching process was used to detect similarities and differences between structures, and hill climbing allowed the program to evolve a more and more accurate concept definition.

This approach to structural concept learning is not without its problems. One major problem is that a teacher must guide the learning program through a carefully chosen sequence of examples. In the next section, we explore a learning technique that is insensitive to the order in which examples are presented.

17.5.2   Version Spaces

Mitchell [1977; 1978] describes another approach to concept learning called *version spaces*. The goal is the same: to produce a description that is consistent with all positive examples but no negative examples in the training set. But while Winston's system did this by evolving a single concept description, version spaces work by maintaining a

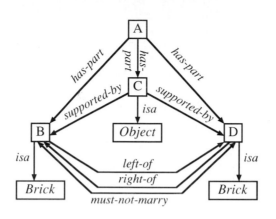

Figure 17.6: The Arch Description after a Near Miss

Car023
origin :	*Japan*
manufacturer :	*Honda*
color :	*Blue*
decade :	*1970*
type :	*Economy*

Figure 17.7: An Example of the Concept *Car*

set of possible descriptions and evolving that set as new examples and near misses are presented. As in the previous section, we need some sort of representation language for examples so that we can describe exactly what the system sees in an example. For now we assume a simple frame-based language, although version spaces can be constructed for more general representation languages. Consider Figure 17.7, a frame representing an individual car.

Now, suppose that each slot may contain only the discrete values shown in Figure 17.8. The choice of features and values is called the *bias* of the learning system. By being embedded in a particular program and by using particular representations, every learning system is biased, because it learns some things more easily than others. In our example, the bias is fairly simple—e.g., we can learn concepts that have to do with car manufacturers, but not car owners. In more complex systems, the bias is less obvious. A clear statement of the bias of a learning system is very important to its evaluation.

Concept descriptions, as well as training examples, can be stated in terms of these slots and values. For example, the concept "Japanese economy car" can be represented as in Figure 17.9. The names x_1, x_2, and x_3 are variables. The presence of x_2, for example, indicates that the color of a car is not relevant to whether the car is a Japanese

origin	$\in$	*{Japan, USA, Britain, Germany, Italy}*
manufacturer	$\in$	*{Honda, Toyota, Ford, Chrysler, Jaguar, BMW, Fiat}*
color	$\in$	*{Blue, Green, Red, White}*
decade	$\in$	*{1950, 1960, 1970, 1980, 1990, 2000}*
type	$\in$	*{Economy, Luxury, Sports}*

Figure 17.8: Representation Language for Cars

origin :	*Japan*
manufacturer :	x_1
color :	x_2
decade :	x_3
type :	*Economy*

Figure 17.9: The Concept "Japanese economy car"

economy car. Now the learning problem is: Given a representation language such as in Figure 17.8, and given positive and negative training examples such as those in Figure 17.7, how can we produce a concept description such as that in Figure 17.9 that is consistent with all the training examples?

Before we proceed to the version space algorithm, we should make some observations about the representation. Some descriptions are more general than others. For example, the description in Figure 17.9 is more general than the one in Figure 17.7. In fact, the representation language defines a partial ordering of descriptions. A portion of that partial ordering is shown in Figure 17.10.

The entire partial ordering is called the *concept space*, and can be depicted as in Figure 17.11. At the top of the concept space is the null description, consisting only of variables, and at the bottom are all the possible training instances, which contain no variables. Before we receive any training examples, we know that the target concept lies somewhere in the concept space. For example, if every possible description is an instance of the intended concept, then the null description is the concept definition since it matches everything. On the other hand, if the target concept includes only a single example, then one of the descriptions at the bottom of the concept space is the desired concept definition. Most target concepts, of course, lie somewhere in between these two extremes.

As we process training examples, we want to refine our notion of where the target concept might lie. Our current hypothesis can be represented as a subset of the concept space called the *version space*. The version space is the largest collection of descriptions that is consistent with all the training examples seen so far.

How can we represent the version space? The version space is simply a set of descriptions, so an initial idea is to keep an explicit list of those descriptions. Unfortunately, the number of descriptions in the concept space is exponential in the number of features and values. So enumerating them is prohibitive. However, it turns out that

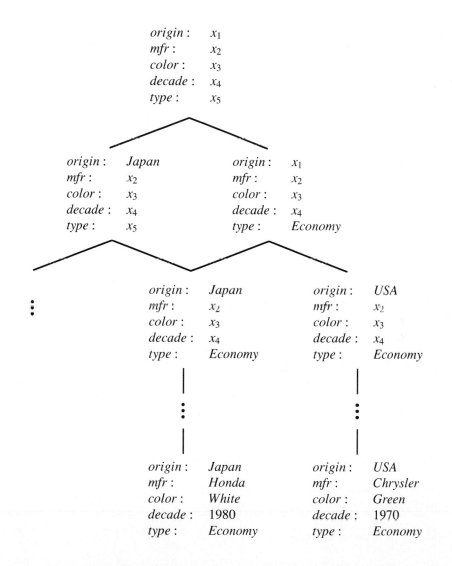

Figure 17.10: Partial Ordering of Concepts Specified by the Representation Language

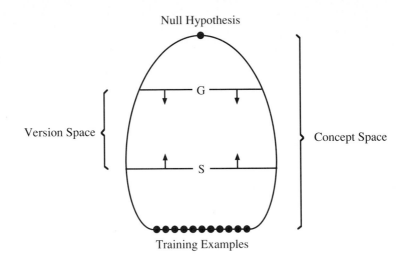

Figure 17.11: Concept and Version Spaces

the version space has a concise representation. It consists of two subsets of the concept space. One subset, called G, contains the most *general* descriptions consistent with the training examples seen so far; the other subset, called S, contains the most *specific* descriptions consistent with the training examples. The version space is the set of all descriptions that lie between some element of G and some element of S in the partial order of the concept space.

This representation of the version space is not only efficient for storage, but also for modification. Intuitively, each time we receive a positive training example, we want to make the S set more general. Negative training examples serve to make the G set more specific. If the S and G sets converge, our range of hypotheses will narrow to a single concept description. The algorithm for narrowing the version space is called the *candidate elimination algorithm*.

Algorithm: Candidate Elimination

Given: A representation language and a set of positive and negative examples expressed in that language.

Compute: A concept description that is consistent with all the positive examples and none of the negative examples.

1. Initialize G to contain one element: the null description (all features are variables).

2. Initialize S to contain one element: the first positive example.

3. Accept a new training example.

   If it is a *positive example*, first remove from G any descriptions that do not cover the example. Then, update the S set to contain the most specific set of descriptions in the version space that cover the example and the current elements of the S set.

origin :	Japan	origin :	Japan	origin :	Japan
mfr :	Honda	mfr :	Toyota	mfr :	Toyota
color :	Blue	color :	Green	color :	Blue
decade :	1980	decade :	1970	decade :	1990
type :	Economy	type :	Sports	type :	Economy

| (+) | (−) | (+) |

origin :	USA	origin :	Japan
mfr :	Chrysler	mfr :	Honda
color :	Red	color :	White
decade :	1980	decade :	1980
type :	Economy	type :	Economy

| (−) | (+) |

Figure 17.12: Positive and Negative Examples of the Concept "Japanese economy car"

That is, generalize the elements of S as little as possible so that they cover the new training example.

If it is a *negative* example, first remove from S any descriptions that cover the example. Then, update the G set to contain the most general set of descriptions in the version space that *do not* cover the example. That is, specialize the elements of G as little as possible so that the negative example is no longer covered by any of the elements of G.

4. If S and G are both singleton sets, then if they are identical, output their value and halt. If they are both singleton sets but they are different, then the training cases were inconsistent. Output this result and halt. Otherwise, go to step 3.

Let us trace the operation of the candidate elimination algorithm. Suppose we want to learn the concept of "Japanese economy car" from the examples in Figure 17.12. G and S both start out as singleton sets. G contains the null description (see Figure 17.11), and S contains the first positive training example. The version space now contains all descriptions that are consistent with this first example:[2]

$G = \{(x_1, x_2, x_3, x_4, x_5)\}$
$S = \{(Japan, Honda, Blue, 1980, Economy)\}$

Now we are ready to process the second example. The G set must be specialized in such a way that the negative example is no longer in the version space. In our representation language, specialization involves replacing variables with constants. (Note: The G set must be specialized only to descriptions that are *within* the current version space, not outside of it.) Here are the available specializations:

---

[2]To make this example concise, we skip slot names in the descriptions. We just list slot values in the order in which the slots have been shown in the preceding figures.

$$G = \{(x_1, Honda, x_3, x_4, x_5), (x_1, x_2, Blue, x_4, x_5),$$
$$(x_1, x_2, x_3, 1980, x_5), (x_1, x_2, x_3, x_4, Economy)\}$$

The S set is unaffected by the negative example. Now we come to the third example, a positive one. The first order of business is to remove from the G set any descriptions that are inconsistent with the positive example. Our new G set is:

$$G = \{(x_1, x_2, Blue, x_4, x_5), (x_1, x_2, x_3, x_4, Economy)\}$$

We must now generalize the S set to include the new example. This involves replacing constants with variables. Here is the new S set:

$$S = \{(Japan, x_2, Blue, x_4, Economy)\}$$

At this point, the S and G sets specify a version space (a space of candidate descriptions) that can be translated roughly into English as: "The target concept may be as specific as 'Japanese, blue economy car,' or as general as either 'blue car' or 'economy car.'"

Next, we get another negative example, a car whose *origin* is *USA*. The S set is unaffected, but the G set must be specialized to avoid covering the new example. The new G set is:

$$G = \{(Japan, x_2, Blue, x_4, x_5), (Japan, x_2, x_3, x_4, Economy)\}$$

We now know that the car must be Japanese, because *all* of the descriptions in the version space contain *Japan* as *origin*.[3] Our final example is a positive one. We first remove from the G set any descriptions that are inconsistent with it, leaving:

$$G = \{(Japan, x_2, x_3, x_4, Economy)\}$$

We then generalize the S set to include the new example:

$$S = \{(Japan, x_2, x_3, x_4, Economy)\}$$

S and G are both singletons, so the algorithm has converged on the target concept. No more examples are needed.

There are several things to note about the candidate elimination algorithm. First, it is a *least-commitment* algorithm. The version space is pruned as little as possible at each step. Thus, even if all the positive training examples are Japanese cars, the algorithm will not reject the possibility that the target concept may include cars of other origin—until it receives a negative example that forces the rejection. This means that if the training data are sparse, the S and G sets may never converge to a single description; the system may learn only partially specified concepts. Second, the algorithm involves exhaustive, breadth-first search through the version space. We can see this in the algorithm for

---

[3] It could be the case that our target concept is "not Chrysler," but we will ignore this possibility because our representation language is not powerful enough to express negation and disjunction.

updating the G set. Contrast this with the depth-first behavior of Winston's learning program. Third, in our simple representation language, the S set always contains exactly one element, because any two positive examples always have exactly one generalization. Other representation languages may not share this property.

The version space approach can be applied to a wide variety of learning tasks and representation languages. The algorithm above can be extended to handle continuously valued features and hierarchical knowledge (see Exercises). However, version spaces have several deficiencies. One is the large space requirements of the exhaustive, breadth-first search mentioned above. Another is that inconsistent data, also called *noise*, can cause the candidate elimination algorithm to prune the target concept from the version space prematurely. In the car example above, if the third training instance had been mislabeled $(-)$ instead of $(+)$, the target concept of "Japanese economy car" would never be reached. Also, given enough erroneous negative examples, the G set can be specialized so far that the version space becomes empty. In that case, the algorithm concludes that *no* concept fits the training examples.

One solution to this problem [Mitchell, 1978] is to maintain several G and S sets. One G set is consistent with all the training instances, another is consistent with all but one, another with all but two, etc. (and the same for the S set). When an inconsistency arises, the algorithm switches to G and S sets that are consistent with most, but not all, of the training examples. Maintaining multiple version spaces can be costly, however, and the S and G sets are typically very large. If we assume *bounded inconsistency*, i.e., that instances close to the target concept boundary are the most likely to be misclassified, then more efficient solutions are possible. Hirsh [1990] presents an algorithm that runs as follows. For each instance, we form a version space consistent with that instance plus other nearby instances (for some suitable definition of nearby). This version space is then intersected with the one created for all previous instances. We keep accepting instances until the version space is reduced to a small set of candidate concept descriptions. (Because of inconsistency, it is unlikely that the version space will converge to a singleton.) We then match each of the concept descriptions against the entire data set, and choose the one that classifies the instances most accurately.

Another problem with the candidate elimination algorithm is the learning of disjunctive concepts. Suppose we wanted to learn the concept of "European car," which, in our representation, means either a German, British, or Italian car. Given positive examples of each, the candidate elimination algorithm will generalize to cars of any *origin*. Given such a generalization, a negative instance (say, a Japanese car) will only cause an inconsistency of the type mentioned above.

Of course, we could simply extend the representation language to include disjunctions. Thus, the concept space would hold descriptions such as "Blue car of German or British origin" and "Italian sports car or German luxury car." This approach has two drawbacks. First, the concept space becomes much larger and specialization becomes intractable. Second, generalization can easily degenerate to the point where the S set contains simply one large disjunction of all positive instances. We must somehow force generalization while allowing for the introduction of disjunctive descriptions. Mitchell [1978] gives an iterative approach that involves several passes through the training data. On each pass, the algorithm builds a concept that covers the largest number of positive training instances without covering any negative training instances. At the end of the pass, the positive training instances covered by the new concept are removed from the

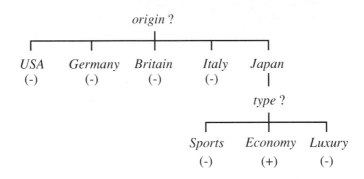

Figure 17.13: A Decision Tree

training set, and the new concept then becomes one disjunct in the eventual disjunctive concept description. When all positive training instances have been removed, we are left with a disjunctive concept that covers all of them without covering any negative instances.

There are a number of other complexities, including the way in which features interact with one another. For example, if the *origin* of a car is *Japan*, then the *manufacturer* cannot be *Chrysler*. The version space algorithm as described above makes no use of such information. Also in our example, it would be more natural to replace the *decade* slot with a continuously valued *year* field. We would have to change our procedures for updating the *S* and *G* sets to account for this kind of numerical data.

17.5.3   Decision Trees

A third approach to concept learning is the induction of *decision trees*, as exemplified by the ID3 program of Quinlan [1986]. ID3 uses a tree representation for concepts, such as the one shown in Figure 17.13. To classify a particular input, we start at the top of the tree and answer questions until we reach a leaf, where the classification is stored. Figure 17.13 represents the familiar concept "Japanese economy car." ID3 is a program that builds decision trees automatically, given positive and negative instances of a concept.[4]

ID3 uses an iterative method to build up decision trees, preferring simple trees over complex ones, on the theory that simple trees are more accurate classifiers of future inputs. It begins by choosing a random subset of the training examples. This subset is called the *window*. The algorithm builds a decision tree that correctly classifies all examples in the window. The tree is then tested on the training examples outside the window. If all the examples are classified correctly, the algorithm halts. Otherwise, it adds a number of training examples to the window and the process repeats. Empirical evidence indicates that the iterative strategy is more efficient than considering the whole training set at once.

---

[4]Actually, the decision tree representation is more general: Leaves can denote any of a number of classes, not just positive and negative.

So how does ID3 actually construct decision trees? Building a node means choosing some attribute to test. At a given point in the tree, some attributes will yield more information than others. For example, testing the attribute *color* is useless if the color of a car does not help us to classify it correctly. Ideally, an attribute will separate training instances into subsets whose members share a common label (e.g., positive or negative). In that case, branching is terminated, and the leaf nodes are labeled.

There are many variations on this basic algorithm. For example, when we add a test that has more than two branches, it is possible that one branch has no corresponding training instances. In that case, we can either leave the node unlabeled, or we can attempt to guess a label based on statistical properties of the set of instances being tested at that point in the tree. Noisy input is another issue. One way of handling noisy input is to avoid building new branches if the information gained is very slight. In other words, we do not want to overcomplicate the tree to account for isolated noisy instances. Another source of uncertainty is that attribute values may be unknown. For example a patient's medical record may be incomplete. One solution is to guess the correct branch to take; another solution is to build special "unknown" branches at each node during learning.

When the concept space is very large, decision tree learning algorithms run more quickly than their version space cousins. Also, disjunction is more straightforward. For example, we can easily modify Figure 17.13 to represent the disjunctive concept "American car or Japanese economy car," simply by changing one of the negative $(-)$ leaf labels to positive $(+)$. One drawback to the ID3 approach is that large, complex decision trees can be difficult for humans to understand, and so a decision tree system may have a hard time explaining the reasons for its classifications.

17.6   Explanation-Based Learning

The previous section illustrated how we can induce concept descriptions from positive and negative examples. Learning complex concepts using these procedures typically requires a substantial number of training instances. But people seem to be able to learn quite a bit from single examples. Consider a chess player who, as Black, has reached the position shown in Figure 17.14. The position is called a "fork" because the white knight attacks both the black king and the black queen. Black must move the king, thereby leaving the queen open to capture. From this single experience, Black is able to learn quite a bit about the fork trap: the idea is that if any piece *x* attacks both the opponent's king and another piece *y*, then piece *y* will be lost. We don't need to see dozens of positive and negative examples of fork positions in order to draw these conclusions. From just one experience, we can learn to avoid this trap in the future and perhaps to use it to our own advantage.

What makes such single-example learning possible? The answer, not surprisingly, is knowledge. The chess player has plenty of domain-specific knowledge that can be brought to bear, including the rules of chess and any previously acquired strategies. That knowledge can be used to identify the critical aspects of the training example. In the case of the fork, we know that the double simultaneous attack is important while the precise position and type of the attacking piece is not.

Much of the recent work in machine learning has moved away from the empirical, data-intensive approach described in the last section toward this more analytical,

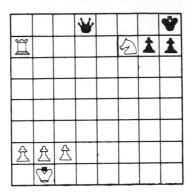

Figure 17.14: A Fork Position in Chess

knowledge-intensive approach. A number of independent studies led to the characterization of this approach as *explanation-based learning*. An EBL system attempts to
learn from a single example x by explaining why x is an example of the target concept.
The explanation is then generalized, and the system's performance is improved through
the availability of this knowledge.

Mitchell *et al.* [1986] and DeJong and Mooney [1986] both describe general frameworks for EBL programs and give general learning algorithms. We can think of EBL
programs as accepting the following as input:

- A Training Example—What the learning program "sees" in the world, e.g., the
  car of Figure 17.7

- A Goal Concept—A high-level description of what the program is supposed to
  learn

- An Operationality Criterion—A description of which concepts are usable

- A Domain Theory—A set of rules that describe relationships between objects and
  actions in a domain

From this, EBL computes a *generalization* of the training example that is sufficient to
describe the goal concept, and also satisfies the operationality criterion.

Let's look more closely at this specification. The training example is a familiar
input—it is the same thing as the example in the version space algorithm. The goal
concept is also familiar, but in previous sections, we have viewed the goal concept as an
output of the program, not an input. The assumption here is that the goal concept is not
operational, just like the high-level card-playing advice described in Section 17.3. An
EBL program seeks to operationalize the goal concept by expressing it in terms that a
problem-solving program can understand. These terms are given by the operationality
criterion. In the chess example, the goal concept might be something like "bad position
for Black," and the operationalized concept would be a generalized description of
situations similar to the training example, given in terms of pieces and their relative
positions. The last input to an EBL program is a domain theory, in our case, the rules of

chess. Without such knowledge, it is impossible to come up with a correct generalization of the training example.

Explanation-based generalization (EBG) is an algorithm for EBL described in Mitchell *et al.* [1986]. It has two steps: (1) explain and (2) generalize. During the first step, the domain theory is used to prune away all the unimportant aspects of the training example with respect to the goal concept. What is left is an *explanation* of why the training example is an instance of the goal concept. This explanation is expressed in terms that satisfy the operationality criterion. The next step is to generalize the explanation as far as possible while still describing the goal concept. Following our chess example, the first EBL step chooses to ignore White's pawns, king, and rook, and constructs an explanation consisting of White's knight, Black's king, and Black's queen, each in their specific positions. Operationality is ensured: all chess-playing programs understand the basic concepts of piece and position. Next, the explanation is generalized. Using domain knowledge, we find that moving the pieces to a different part of the board is still bad for Black. We can also determine that other pieces besides knights and queens can participate in fork attacks.

In reality, current EBL methods run into difficulties in domains as complex as chess, so we will not pursue this example further. Instead, let's look at a simpler case. Consider the problem of learning the concept *Cup* [Mitchell *et al.*, 1986]. Unlike the arch-learning program of Section 17.5.1, we want to be able to generalize from a single example of a cup. Suppose the example is:

- Training Example:

   owner(Object23, Ralph) ∧ *has-part(Object23, Concavity12)* ∧
   is(Object23, Light) ∧ *color(Object23, Brown)* ∧ ···

Clearly, some of the features of *Object23* are more relevant to its being a cup than others. So far in this chapter, we have seen several methods for isolating relevant features. These methods all require many positive and negative examples. In EBL we instead rely on domain knowledge, such as:

- Domain Knowledge:

   is(x, Light) ∧ *has-part(x, y)* ∧ *isa(y, Handle)* → *liftable(x)*
   has-part(x, y) ∧ *isa(y, Bottom)* ∧ *is(y, Flat)* → *stable(x)*
   has-part(x, y) ∧ *isa(y, Concavity)* ∧ *is(y, Upward-Pointing)* → *open-vessel(x)*

We also need a goal concept to operationalize:

- Goal Concept: *Cup*

   x is a Cup iff *x* is *liftable*, *stable*, and *open-vessel*.

- Operationality Criterion: Concept definition must be expressed in purely structural terms (e.g., *Light*, *Flat*, etc.).

Given a training example and a functional description, we want to build a general structural description of a cup. The first step is to explain why *Object23* is a cup. We do this by constructing a proof, as shown in Figure 17.15. Standard theorem-proving

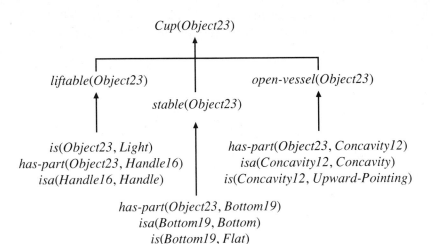

Figure 17.15: An Explanation

techniques can be used to find such a proof. Notice that the proof isolates the relevant features of the training example; nowhere in the proof do the predicates *owner* and *color* appear. The proof also serves as a basis for a valid generalization. If we gather up all the assumptions and replace constants with variables, we get the following description of a cup:

$$has\text{-}part(x, y) \land isa(y, Concavity) \land is(y, Upward\text{-}Pointing) \land$$
$$has\text{-}part(x, z) \land isa(z, Bottom) \land is(z, Flat) \land$$
$$has\text{-}part(x, w) \land isa(w, Handle) \land is(x, Light)$$

This definition satisfies the operationality criterion and could be used by a robot to classify objects.

Simply replacing constants by variables worked in this example, but in some cases it is necessary to retain certain constants. To catch these cases, we must reprove the goal. This process, which we saw earlier in our discussion of learning in STRIPS, is called *goal regression*.

As we have seen, EBL depends strongly on a domain theory. Given such a theory, why are examples needed at all? We could have operationalized the goal concept *Cup* without reference to an example, since the domain theory contains all of the requisite information. The answer is that examples help to focus the learning on relevant operationalizations. Without an example cup, EBL is faced with the task of characterizing the entire range of objects that satisfy the goal concept. Most of these objects will never be encountered in the real world, and so the result will be overly general.

Providing a tractable domain theory is a difficult task. There is evidence that humans do not learn with very primitive relations. Instead, they create incomplete and inconsistent domain theories. For example, returning to chess, such a theory might include concepts like "weak pawn structure." Getting EBL to work in ill-structured domain theories is an active area of research (see, e.g., Tadepalli [1989]).

EBL shares many features of all the learning methods described in earlier sections. Like concept learning, EBL begins with a positive example of some concept. As in learning by advice taking, the goal is to operationalize some piece of knowledge. And EBL techniques, like the techniques of chunking and macro-operators, are often used to improve the performance of problem-solving engines. The major difference between EBL and other learning methods is that EBL programs are built to take advantage of domain knowledge. Since learning is just another kind of problem solving, it should come as no surprise that there is leverage to be found in knowledge.

17.7 Discovery

Learning is the process by which one entity acquires knowledge. Usually that knowledge is already possessed by some number of other entities who may serve as teachers. *Discovery* is a restricted form of learning in which one entity acquires knowledge without the help of a teacher.[5] In this section, we look at three types of automated discovery systems.

17.7.1 AM: Theory-Driven Discovery

Discovery is certainly learning. But it is also, perhaps more clearly than other kinds of learning, problem solving. Suppose that we want to build a program to discover things, for example, in mathematics. We expect that such a program would have to rely heavily on the problem-solving techniques we have discussed. In fact, one such program was written by Lenat [1977; 1982]. It was called AM, and it worked from a few basic concepts of set theory to discover a good deal of standard number theory.

AM exploited a variety of general-purpose AI techniques. It used a frame system to represent mathematical concepts. One of the major activities of AM is to create new concepts and fill in their slots. An example of an AM concept is shown in Figure 17.16. AM also uses heuristic search, guided by a set of 250 heuristic rules representing hints about activities that are likely to lead to "interesting" discoveries. Examples of the kind of heuristics AM used are shown in Figure 17.17. Generate-and-test is used to form hypotheses on the basis of a small number of examples and then to test the hypotheses on a larger set to see if they still appear to hold. Finally, an agenda controls the entire discovery process. When the heuristics suggest a task, it is placed on a central agenda, along with the reason that it was suggested and the strength with which it was suggested. AM operates in cycles, each time choosing the most promising task from the agenda and performing it.

In one run, AM discovered the concept of prime numbers. How did it do that? Having stumbled onto the natural numbers, AM explored operations such as addition, multiplication, and their inverses. It created the concept of divisibility and noticed that some numbers had very few divisors. AM has a built-in heuristic that tells it to explore

---

[5] Sometimes, there is no one in the world who has the knowledge we seek. In that case, the kind of action we must take is called *scientific discovery*.

name : *Prime-Numbers*
definitions :
    origin : *Number-of-divisors-of*$(x) = 2$
    predicate-calculus : *Prime*$(x) \Leftrightarrow (\forall z)(z \mid x \Rightarrow (z = 1 \otimes z = x))$
    iterative : *(for $x > 1$)* : For i from 2 to $\sqrt{x}, i \nmid x$
examples : 2, 3, 5, 7, 11, 13, 17
    boundary : 2, 3
    boundary-failures : 0, 1
    failures : 12
generalizations : *Number, numbers with an even number of divisors*
specializations : *Odd primes, prime pairs, prime uniquely addables*
conjecs : *Unique factorization, Goldbach's conjecture, extrema of number-of-divisors-of*
intus : *A metaphor to the effect that primes are the building blocks of all numbers*
analogies :
    Maximally divisible numbers are converse extremes of number-of-divisors-of
    Factor a nonsimple group into simple groups
interest : *Conjectures tying primes to times, to divisors of, to related operations*
worth : 800

Figure 17.16: An AM Concept: Prime Number

- If f is a function from A to B and B is ordered, then consider the elements of A that are mapped into extremal elements of B. Create a new concept representing this subset of A.

- If some (but not most) examples of some concept X are also examples of another concept Y, create a new concept representing the intersection of X and Y.

- If very few examples of a concept X are found, then add to the agenda the task of finding a generalization of X.

Figure 17.17: Some AM Heuristics

extreme cases. It attempted to list all numbers with zero divisors (finding none), one divisor (finding one: 1), and two divisors. AM was instructed to call the last concept "primes." Before pursuing this concept, AM went on to list numbers with three divisors, such as 49. AM tried to relate this property with other properties of 49, such as its being odd and a perfect square. AM generated other odd numbers and other perfect squares to test its hypotheses. A side effect of determining the equivalence of perfect squares with numbers with three divisors was to boost the "interestingness" rating of the divisor concept. This led AM to investigate ways in which a number could be broken down into factors. AM then noticed that there was only one way to break a number down into prime factors (known as the Unique Factorization Theorem).

Since breaking down numbers into multiplicative components turned out to be interesting, AM decided, by analogy, to pursue additive components as well. It made several uninteresting conjectures, such as that every number could be expressed as a sum of 1's. It also found more interesting phenomena, such as that many numbers were expressible as the sum of two primes. By listing cases, AM determined that all even numbers greater than 2 seemed to have this property. This conjecture, known as Goldbach's Conjecture, is widely believed to be true, but a proof of it has yet to be found in mathematics.

AM contains a great many general-purpose heuristics such as the ones it used in this example. Often different heuristics point in the same place. For example, while AM discovered prime numbers using a heuristic that involved looking at extreme cases, another way to derive prime numbers is to use the following two rules:

- If there is a strong analogy between A and B but there is a conjecture about A that does not hold for all elements of B, define a new concept that includes the elements of B for which it does hold.

- If there is a set whose complement is much rarer than itself, then create a new concept representing the complement.

There is a strong analogy between addition and multiplication of natural numbers. But that analogy breaks down when we observe that all natural numbers greater than 1 can be expressed as the sum of two smaller natural numbers (excluding the identity). This is not true for multiplication. So the first heuristic described above suggests the creation of a new concept representing the set of composite numbers. Then the second heuristic suggests creating a concept representing the complement of that, namely the set of prime numbers.

Two major questions came out of the work on AM. One question was: "Why was AM ever turned off?" That is, why didn't AM simply keep discovering new interesting facts about numbers, possibly facts unknown to human mathematics? Lenat [1983b] contends that AM's performance was limited by the static nature of its heuristics. As the program progressed, the concepts with which it was working evolved away from the initial ones, while the heuristics that were available to work on those concepts stayed the same. To remedy this problem, it was suggested that heuristics be treated as full fledged concepts that could be created and modified by the same sorts of processes (such as generalization, specialization, and analogy) as are concepts in the task domain. In other words, AM would run in discovery mode in the domain of "Heuretics," the study of heuristics themselves, as well as in the domain of number theory. An extension of AM called EURISKO [Lenat, 1983a] was designed with this goal in mind.

The other question was: "Why did AM work as well as it did?" One source of power for AM was its huge collection of heuristics about what constitute interesting things. But AM had another less obvious source of power, namely, the natural relationship between number theoretical concepts and their compact representations in AM [Lenat and Brown, 1983]. AM worked by syntactically mutating old concept definitions— stored essentially as short LISP programs—in the hopes of finding new, interesting concepts. It turns out that a mutation in a small LISP program very likely results in another well-formed, meaningful LISP program. This accounts for AM's ability to generate so many novel concepts. But while humans interpret AM as exploring number theory, it was actually exploring the space of small LISP programs. AM succeeded in large part because of this intimate relationship between number theory and LISP programs. When AM and EURISKO were applied to other domains, including the study of heuristics themselves, problems arose. Concepts in these domains were larger and more complex than number theory concepts, and the syntax of the representation

n	T	p	V	pV	pV/T	pV/nT
1	300	100	24.96			
1	300	200	12.48			
1	300	300	8.32	2496		
1	310			2579.2		
1	320			2662.4	8.32	
2	320				16.64	
3	320				24.96	8.32

Figure 17.18: BACON Discovering the Ideal Gas Law

language no longer closely mirrored the semantics of the domain. As a result, syntactic mutation of a concept definition almost always resulted in an ill-formed or useless concept, severely hampering the discovery procedure.

Perhaps the moral of AM is that learning is a tricky business. We must be careful how we interpret what our AI programs are doing [Ritchie and Hanna, 1984]. AM had an implicit *bias* toward learning concepts in number theory. Only after that bias was explicitly recognized was it possible to understand why AM performed well in one domain and poorly in another.

17.7.2   BACON: Data-Driven Discovery

AM showed how discovery might occur in a theoretical setting. Empirical scientists see things somewhat differently. They are confronted with data from the world and must make sense of it. They make hypotheses, and in order to validate them, they design and execute experiments. Scientific discovery has inspired a number of computer models. Langley *et al.* [1981a] present a model of data-driven scientific discovery that has been implemented as a program called BACON, named after Sir Francis Bacon, an early philosopher of science.

BACON begins with a set of variables for a problem. For example, in the study of the behavior of gases, some variables are p, the pressure on the gas, V, the volume of the gas, n, the amount of gas in moles, and T, the temperature of the gas. Physicists have long known a law, called the *ideal gas law*, that relates these variables. BACON is able to derive this law on its own. First, BACON holds the variables n and T constant, performing experiments at different pressures p_1, p_2, and p_3. BACON notices that as the pressure increases, the volume V decreases. Therefore, it creates a theoretical term pV. This term is constant. BACON systematically moves on to vary the other variables. It tries an experiment with different values of T, and finds that pV changes. The two terms are linearly related with an intercept of 0, so BACON creates a new term pV/T. Finally, BACON varies the term n and finds another linear relation between n and pV/T. For all values of n, p, V, and T, $pV/nT = 8.32$. This is, in fact, the ideal gas law. Figure 17.18 shows BACON's reasoning in a tabular format.

BACON has been used to discover a wide variety of scientific laws, such as Kepler's third law, Ohm's law, the conservation of momentum, and Joule's law. The heuristics BACON uses to discover the ideal gas law include noting constancies, finding linear relations, and defining theoretical terms. Other heuristics allow BACON to postulate intrinsic properties of objects and to reason by analogy. For example, if BACON finds a regularity in one set of parameters, it will attempt to generate the same regularity in a similar set of parameters. Since BACON's discovery procedure is state-space search, these heuristics allow it to reach solutions while visiting only a small portion of the search space. In the gas example, BACON comes up with the ideal gas law using a minimal number of experiments.

A better understanding of the science of scientific discovery may lead one day to programs that display true creativity. Much more work must be done in areas of science that BACON does not model, such as determining what data to gather, choosing (or creating) instruments to measure the data, and using analogies to previously understood phenomena. For a thorough discussion of scientific discovery programs, see Langley *et al.* [1987].

17.7.3   Clustering

A third type of discovery, called *clustering*, is very similar to induction, as we described it in Section 17.5. In inductive learning, a program learns to classify objects based on the labelings provided by a teacher. In clustering, no class labelings are provided. The program must discover for itself the natural classes that exist for the objects, in addition to a method for classifying instances.

AUTOCLASS [Cheeseman *et al.*, 1988] is one program that accepts a number of training cases and hypothesizes a set of classes. For any given case, the program provides a set of probabilities that predict into which class(es) the case is likely to fall. In one application, AUTOCLASS found meaningful new classes of stars from their infrared spectral data. This was an instance of true discovery by computer, since the facts it discovered were previously unknown to astronomy. AUTOCLASS uses statistical Bayesian reasoning of the type discussed in Chapter 8.

17.8   Analogy

Analogy is a powerful inference tool. Our language and reasoning are laden with analogies. Consider the following sentences:

- Last month, the stock market was a roller coaster.

- Bill is like a fire engine.

- Problems in electromagnetism are just like problems in fluid flow.

Underlying each of these examples is a complicated mapping between what appear to be dissimilar concepts. For example, to understand the first sentence above, it is necessary to do two things: (1) pick out one key property of a roller coaster, namely that it travels up and down rapidly and (2) realize that physical travel is itself an analogy for numerical fluctuations (in stock prices). This is no easy trick. The space of possible analogies is very large. We do not want to entertain possibilities such as "the stock market is like a roller coaster because it is made of metal."

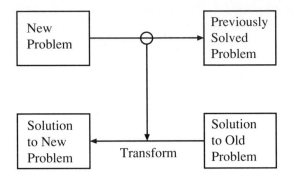

Figure 17.19: Transformational Analogy

Lakoff and Johnson [1980] make the case that everyday language is filled with such analogies and metaphors. An AI program that is unable to grasp analogy will be difficult to talk to and, consequently, difficult to teach. Thus, analogical reasoning is an important factor in learning by advice taking. It is also important to learning in problem solving.

Humans often solve problems by making analogies to things they already understand how to do. This process is more complex than storing macro-operators (as discussed in Section 17.4.2) because the old problem might be quite different from the new problem on the surface. The difficulty comes in determining what things are similar and what things are not. Two methods of analogical problem solving that have been studied in AI are *transformational* and *derivational* analogy.

17.8.1   Transformational Analogy

Suppose you are asked to prove a theorem in plane geometry. You might look for a previous theorem that is very similar and "copy" its proof, making substitutions when necessary. The idea is to transform a solution to a previous problem into a solution for the current problem. Figure 17.19 shows this process.

An example of transformational analogy is shown in Figure 17.20 [Anderson and Kline, 1979]. The program has seen proofs about points and line segments; for example, it knows a proof that the line segment RN is exactly as long as the line segment OY, given that RO is exactly as long as NY. The program is now asked to prove a theorem about angles, namely that the angle BD is equivalent to the angle CE, given that angles BC and DE are equivalent. The proof about line segments is retrieved and transformed into a proof about angles by substituting the notion of line for point, angle for line segment, AB for R, AC for O, AD for N, and AE for Y.

Carbonell [1983] describes one method for transforming old solutions into new solutions. Whole solutions are viewed as states in a problem space called *T-space*. *T-operators* prescribe the methods of transforming solutions (states) into other solutions. Reasoning by analogy becomes search in T-space: starting with an old solution, we use means-ends analysis or some other method to find a solution to the current problem.

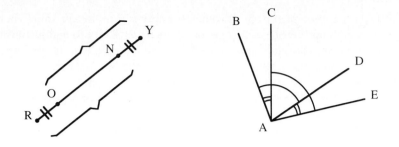

Old Proof: New Proof:

RO = NY   (given)   BAC = DAE
ON = ON   (reflexive)   CAD = CAD
RO + ON = ON + NY   (additive)   BAC + CAD = CAD + DAE
RN = OY   (transitive)   BAD = CAE

Figure 17.20: Solving a Problem by Transformational Analogy

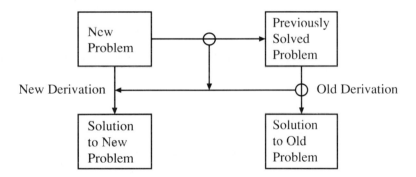

Figure 17.21: Derivational Analogy

17.8.2 Derivational Analogy

Notice that transformational analogy does not look at *how* the old problem was solved: it only looks at the final solution. Often the twists and turns involved in solving an old problem are relevant to solving a new problem. The detailed history of a problem-solving episode is called its *derivation*. Analogical reasoning that takes these histories into account is called derivational analogy (see Figure 17.21).

Carbonell [1986] claims that derivational analogy is a necessary component in the transfer of skills in complex domains. For example, suppose you have coded an efficient sorting routine in Pascal, and then you are asked to recode the routine in LISP. A line-by-line translation is not appropriate, but you will reuse the major structural and control decisions you made when you constructed the Pascal program. One way to model this behavior is to have a problem-solver "replay" the previous derivation and modify it when necessary. If the original reasons and assumptions for a step's existence still hold in the new problem, the step is copied over. If some assumption is no longer valid, another assumption must be found. If one cannot be found, then we can try to find justification for some alternative stored in the derivation of the original problem. Or perhaps we can try some step marked as leading to search failure in the original derivation, if the reasons for failure conditions are not valid in the current derivation.

Analogy in problem solving is a very open area of research. For a survey of recent work, see Hall [1989].

17.9   Formal Learning Theory

Like many other AI problems, learning has attracted the attention of mathematicians and theoretical computer scientists. Inductive learning in particular has received considerable attention. Valiant [1984] describes a "theory of the learnable" which classifies problems by how difficult they are to learn. Formally, a device learns a concept if it can, given positive and negative examples, produce an algorithm that will classify future examples correctly with probability $1/h$. The complexity of learning a concept is a function of three factors: the error tolerance (h), the number of binary features present in the examples (t), and the size of the rule necessary to make the discrimination (f). If the number of training examples required is polynomial in h, t, and f, then the concept is said to be *learnable*.

Some interesting results have been demonstrated for concept learning. Consider the problem of learning conjunctive feature descriptions. For example, from the list of positive and negative examples of elephants shown in Figure 17.22, we want to induce the description "gray, mammal, large." It has been shown that in conjunctive learning the number of randomly chosen training examples is proportional to the logarithm of the total number of features [Haussler, 1988; Littlestone, 1988].[6] Since very few training examples are needed to solve this induction problem, it is called *learnable*. Even if we restrict the learner to *positive* examples only, conjunctive learning can be achieved when the number of examples is linearly proportional to the number of attributes [Ehrenfeucht *et al.*, 1989]. Learning from positive examples only is a phenomenon not modeled by least-commitment inductive techniques such as version spaces. The introduction of the error tolerance h makes this possible: After all, even if all the elephants in our training set are gray, we may later encounter a genuine elephant that happens to be white. Fortunately, we can extend the size of our randomly sampled training set to ensure that the probability of misclassifying an elephant as something else (such as a polar bear) is an arbitrarily small $1/h$.

Formal techniques have been applied to a number of other learning problems. For example, given positive and negative examples of strings in some regular language, can we efficiently induce the finite automaton that produces all and only the strings in that language? The answer is no; an exponential number of computational steps is required [Kearns and Valiant, 1989].[7] However, if we allow the learner to make specific queries (e.g., "Is string x in the language?"), then the problem *is* learnable [Angluin, 1987].

---

[6]However, the number of examples must be *linear* in the number of *relevant* attributes, i.e., the number of attributes that appear in the learned conjunction.

[7]The proof of this result rests on some unproven hypotheses about the complexity of certain number theoretic functions.

gray?	mammal?	large?	vegetarian?	wild?		
+	+	+	+	+	+	(*Elephant*)
+	+	+	−	+	+	(*Elephant*)
+	+	−	+	+	−	(*Mouse*)
−	+	+	+	+	−	(*Giraffe*)
+	−	+	−	+	−	(*Dinosaur*)
+	+	+	+	−	+	(*Elephant*)

Figure 17.22: Six Positive and Negative Examples of the Concept *Elephant*

It is difficult to tell how such mathematical studies of learning will affect the ways in which we solve AI problems in practice. After all, people are able to solve many exponentially hard problems by using knowledge to constrain the space of possible solutions. Perhaps mathematical theory will one day be used to quantify the use of such knowledge, but this prospect seems far off. For a critique of formal learning theory as well as some of the inductive techniques described in Section 17.5, see Amsterdam [1988].

17.10 Neural Net Learning and Genetic Learning

The very first efforts in machine learning tried to mimic animal learning at a neural level. These efforts were quite different from the symbolic manipulation methods we have seen so far in this chapter. Collections of idealized neurons were presented with stimuli and prodded into changing their behavior via forms of reward and punishment. Researchers hoped that by imitating the learning mechanisms of animals, they might build learning machines from very simple parts. Such hopes proved elusive. However, the field of neural network learning has seen a resurgence in recent years, partly as a result of the discovery of powerful new learning algorithms. Chapter 18 describes these algorithms in detail.

While neural network models are based on a computational "brain metaphor," a number of other learning techniques make use of a metaphor based on evolution. In this work, learning occurs through a selection process that begins with a large population of random programs. Learning algorithms inspired by evolution are called *genetic algorithms* [Holland, 1975; de Jong, 1988; Goldberg, 1989].

17.11 Summary

The most important thing to conclude from our study of automated learning is that learning itself is a problem-solving process. We can cast various learning strategies in terms of the methods of Chapters 2 and 3.

- Learning by taking advice

    - Initial state: high-level advice

  – Final state: an operational rule

  – Operators: unfolding definitions, case analysis, matching, etc.

- Learning from examples

  – Initial state: collection of positive and negative examples

  – Final state: concept description

  – Search algorithms: candidate elimination, induction of decision trees

- Learning in problem solving

  – Initial state: solution traces to example problems

  – Final state: new heuristics for solving new problems efficiently

  – Heuristics for search: generalization, explanation-based learning, utility considerations

- Discovery

  – Initial state: some environment

  – Final state: unknown

  – Heuristics for search: interestingness, analogy, etc.

A learning machine is the dream system of AI. As we have seen in previous chapters, the key to intelligent behavior is having a lot of knowledge. Getting all of that knowledge into a computer is a staggering task. One hope of sidestepping the task is to let computers acquire knowledge independently, as people do. We do not yet have programs that can extend themselves indefinitely. But we have discovered some of the reasons for our failure to create such systems. If we look at actual learning programs, we find that the more knowledge a program starts with, the more it can learn. This finding is satisfying, in the sense that it corroborates our other discoveries about the power of knowledge. But it is also unpleasant, because it seems that fully self-extending systems are, for the present, still out of reach.

Research in machine learning has gone through several cycles of popularity. Timing is always an important consideration. A learning program needs to acquire new knowledge and new problem-solving abilities, but knowledge and problem-solving are topics still under intensive study. If we do not understand the nature of the thing we want to learn, learning is difficult. Not surprisingly, the most successful learning programs operate in fairly well-understood areas (like planning), and not in less well-understood areas (like natural language understanding).

17.12   Exercises

1. Would it be reasonable to apply Samuel's rote-learning procedure to chess? Why (not)?

2. Implement the candidate elimination algorithm for version spaces. Choose a concept space with several features (for example, the space of books, computers, animals, etc.) Pick a concept and demonstrate learning by presenting positive and negative examples of the concept.

3. In Section 17.5.2, the concept "Japanese economy car" was learned through the presentation of five positive and negative examples. Give a sequence of *four* examples that accomplishes the same goal. In general, what properties of a positive example make it most useful? What makes a negative example most useful?

4. Recall the problem of learning disjunctive concepts in version spaces. We discussed learning a concept like "European car," where a European car was defined as a car whose *origin* was either *Germany, Italy,* or *Britain.* Suppose we expand the number of discrete values the slot *origin* might take to include the values *Europe* and *Imported.* Suppose further that we have the following *isa* hierarchy at our disposal:

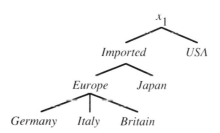

The diagram reflects facts such as "Japanese cars are a subset of imported cars" and "Italian cars are a subset of European cars." How could we modify the candidate elimination algorithm to take advantage of this knowledge? Propose new methods of updating the sets G and S that would allow us to learn the concept "European car" in one pass through a set of adequate training examples.

5. AM exploited a set of 250 heuristics designed to guide AM's behavior toward interesting mathematical concepts. A classic work by Polya [1957] describes a set of heuristics for solving mathematical problems. Unfortunately, Polya's heuristics are not specified in enough detail to make them implementable in a program. In particular, they lack precise descriptions of the situations in which they are appropriate (i.e., the left sides if they are viewed as productions). Examine some of Polya's rules and refine them so that they could be implemented in a problem-solving program with a structure similar to AM's.

6. Consider the problem of building a program to learn a grammar for a language such as English. Assume that such a program would be provided, as input, with a set of pairs, each consisting of a sentence and a representation of the meaning of the sentence. This is analogous to the experience of a child who hears a sentence and sees something at the same time. How could such a program be built using the techniques discussed in this chapter?

Chapter 18

Connectionist Models

In our quest to build intelligent machines, we have but one naturally occurring model: the human brain. One obvious idea for AI, then, is to simulate the functioning of the brain directly on a computer. Indeed, the idea of building an intelligent machine out of artificial neurons has been around for quite some time. Some early results on brainlike mechanisms were achieved by McCulloch and Pitts [1943], and other researchers pursued this notion through the next two decades, e.g., Ashby [1952], Minsky [1954], Minsky and Selfridge [1961], Block [1962], and Rosenblatt [1962]. Research in neural networks came to virtual halt in the 1970s, however, when the networks under study were shown to be very weak computationally. Recently, there has been a resurgence of interest in neural networks. There are several reasons for this, including the appearance of faster digital computers on which to simulate larger networks, the interest in building massively parallel computers, and, most important, the discovery of new neural network architectures and powerful learning algorithms.

The new neural network architectures have been dubbed "connectionist" architectures. For the most part, these architectures are not meant to duplicate the operation of the human brain, but rather to receive inspiration from known facts about how the brain works. They are characterized by having:

- A large number of very simple neuronlike processing elements.

- A large number of weighted connections between the elements. The weights on the connections encode the knowledge of a network.

- Highly parallel, distributed control.

- An emphasis on learning internal representations automatically.

Connectionist researchers conjecture that thinking about computation in terms of the "brain metaphor" rather than the "digital computer metaphor" will lead to insights into the nature of intelligent behavior.

Computers are capable of amazing feats. They can effortlessly store vast quantities of information. Their circuits operate in nanoseconds. They can perform extensive arithmetic calculations without error. Humans cannot approach these capabilities. On the other hand, humans routinely perform "simple" tasks such as walking, talking, and commonsense reasoning. Current AI systems cannot do any of these things better than humans can. Why not? Perhaps the structure of the brain is somehow suited to these tasks and not suited to tasks such as high-speed arithmetic calculation. Working under constraints similar to those of the brain may make traditional computation more difficult, but it may lead to solutions to AI problems that would otherwise be overlooked.

What constraints, then, does the brain offer us? First of all, individual neurons are extremely slow devices when compared to their counterparts in digital computers. Neurons operate in the millisecond range, an eternity to a VLSI designer. Yet, humans can perform extremely complex tasks, such as interpreting a visual scene or understanding a sentence, in just a tenth of a second. In other words, we do in about a hundred steps what current computers cannot do in 10 million steps. How can this be possible? Unlike a conventional computer, the brain contains a huge number of processing elements that act in parallel. This suggests that in our search for solutions, we should look for massively parallel algorithms that require no more than 100 time steps [Feldman and Ballard, 1985].

Also, neurons are failure-prone devices. They are constantly dying (you have certainly lost a few since you began reading this chapter), and their firing patterns are irregular. Components in digital computers, on the other hand, must operate perfectly. Why? Such components store bits of information that are available nowhere else in the computer: the failure of one component means a loss of information. Suppose that we built AI programs that were not sensitive to the failure of a few components, perhaps by using redundancy and distributing information across a wide range of components? This would open up the possibility of very large-scale implementations. With current technology, it is far easier to build a *billion-component* integrated circuit in which 95 percent of the components work correctly than it is to build a *million-component* machine that functions perfectly [Fahlman and Hinton, 1987].

Another thing people seem to be able to do better than computers is handle fuzzy situations. We have very large memories of visual, auditory, and problem-solving episodes, and one key operation in solving new problems is finding closest matches to old situations. Approximate matching is something brain-style models seem to be good at, because of the diffuse and fluid way in which knowledge is represented.

The idea behind connectionism, then, is that we may see significant advances in AI if we approach problems from the point of view of brain-style computation. Connectionist AI is quite different from the symbolic approach covered in the other chapters of this book. At the end of this chapter, we discuss the relationship between the two approaches.

18.1 Introduction: Hopfield Networks

The history of AI is curious. The first problems attacked by AI researchers were problems such as chess and theorem proving, because they were thought to require the essence of intelligence. Vision and language understanding—processes easily mastered by five-year olds—were not thought to be difficult. These days, we have expert chess programs and expert medical diagnosis programs, but no programs that can match the basic perceptual skills of a child. Neural network researchers contend that there is a basic mismatch between standard computer information processing technology and the technology used by the brain.

In addition to these perceptual tasks, AI is just starting to grapple with the fundamental problems of memory and commonsense reasoning. Computers are notorious
for their lack of common sense. Many people believe that common sense derives from
our massive store of knowledge and, more important, our ability to access relevant
knowledge quickly, effortlessly, and at the right time.

When we read the description "gray, large, mammal," we automatically think of
elephants and their associated features. We access our memories *by content*. In traditional implementations, access by content involves expensive searching and matching
procedures. Massively parallel networks suggest a more efficient method.

Hopfield [1982] introduced a neural network that he proposed as a theory of memory.
A Hopfield network has the following interesting features:

- Distributed Representation—A memory is stored as a pattern of activation across
  a set of processing elements. Furthermore, memories can be superimposed on one
  another; different memories are represented by different patterns over the *same*
  set of processing elements.

- Distributed, Asynchronous Control—Each processing element makes decisions
  based only on its own local situation. All these local actions add up to a global
  solution.

- Content-Addressable Memory—A number of patterns can be stored in a network. To retrieve a pattern, we need only specify a portion of it. The network
  automatically finds the closest match.

- Fault Tolerance—If a few processing elements misbehave or fail completely, the
  network will still function properly.

How are these features achieved? A simple Hopfield net is shown in Figure 18.1.
Processing elements, or *units*, are always in one of two states, active or inactive. In
the figure, units colored black are active and units colored white are inactive. Units are
connected to each other with weighted, symmetric connections. A positively weighted
connection indicates that the two units tend to activate each other. A negative connection
allows an active unit to deactivate a neighboring unit.

The network operates as follows. A random unit is chosen. If any of its neighbors
are active, the unit computes the sum of the weights on the connections to those active
neighbors. If the sum is positive, the unit becomes active, otherwise it becomes inactive.
Another random unit is chosen, and the process repeats until the network reaches a stable
state, i.e., until no more units can change state. This process is called *parallel relaxation*.
If the network starts in the state shown in Figure 18.1, the unit in the lower left corner
will tend to activate the unit above it. This unit, in turn, will attempt to activate the unit
above *it*, but the inhibitory connection from the upper-right unit will foil this attempt,
and so on.

This network has only four distinct stable states, which are shown in Figure 18.2.
Given any initial state, the network will necessarily settle into one of these four
configurations.[1] The network can be thought of as "storing" the patterns in Figure 18.2.
Hopfield's major contribution was to show that given any set of weights and any initial

---

[1] The stable state in which all units are inactive can only be reached if it is also the initial state.

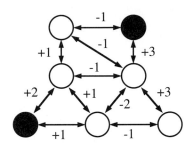

Figure 18.1: A Simple Hopfield Network

state, his parallel relaxation algorithm would eventually steer the network into a stable state. There can be no divergence or oscillation.

The network can be used as a content-addressable memory by setting the activities of the units to correspond to a partial pattern. To retrieve a pattern, we need only supply a portion of it. The network will then settle into the stable state that best matches the partial pattern. An example is shown in Figure 18.3.

Parallel relaxation is nothing more than search, albeit of a different style than the search described in the early chapters of this book. It is useful to think of the various states of a network as forming a search space, as in Figure 18.4. A randomly chosen state will transform itself ultimately into one of the *local minima*, namely the nearest stable state. This is how we get the content-addressable behavior.[2] We also get error-correcting behavior. Suppose we read the description, "gray, large, fish, eats plankton." We imagine a whale, even though we know that a whale is a mammal, not a fish. Even if the initial state contains inconsistencies, a Hopfield network will settle into the solution that violates the fewest constraints offered by the inputs. Traditional match-and-retrieve procedures are less forgiving.

Now, suppose a unit occasionally fails, say, by becoming active or inactive when it should not. This causes no major problem: surrounding units will quickly set it straight again. It would take the unlikely concerted effort of many errant units to push the network into the wrong stable state. In networks of thousands of more highly interconnected units, such fault tolerance is even more apparent—units and connections can disappear completely without adversely affecting the overall behavior of the network.

So parallel networks of simple elements can compute interesting things. The next important question is: What is the relationship between the weights on the network's connections and the local minima it settles into? In other words, if the weights encode the knowledge of a particular network, then how is that knowledge acquired? In Chapter 17 we saw several ways to acquire symbolic structures and descriptions. Such acquisition was quite difficult. One feature of connectionist architectures is that their method of representation (namely, real-valued connection weights) lends itself very nicely to

---

[2]In Figure 18.4, state B is depicted as being lower than state A because fewer constraints are violated. A constraint is violated, for example, when two active units are connected by a negatively weighted connection.

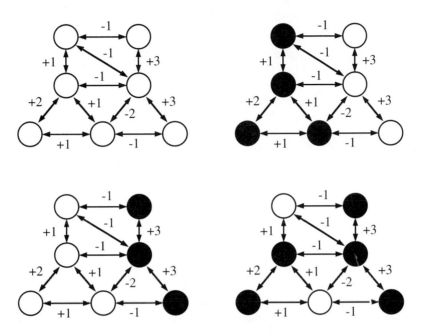

Figure 18.2: The Four Stable States of a Particular Hopfield Net

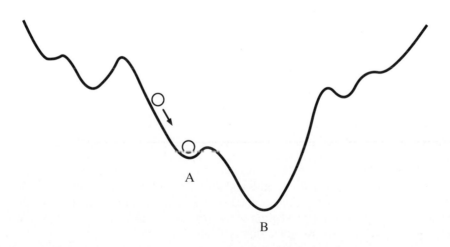

Figure 18.3: A Hopfield Net as a Model of Content-Addressable Memory

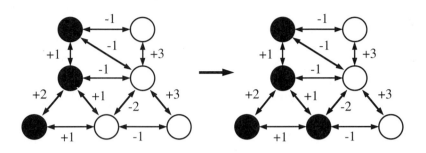

Figure 18.4: A Simplified View of What a Hopfield Net Computes

automatic learning.

In the next section, we look closely at learning in several neural network models, including perceptrons, backpropagation networks, and Boltzmann machines, a variation of Hopfield networks. After this, we investigate some applications of connectionism. Then we see how networks with feedback can deal with temporal processes and how distributed representations can be made efficient.

18.2   Learning in Neural Networks

18.2.1   Perceptrons

The *perceptron*, an invention of Rosenblatt [1962], was one of the earliest neural network models. A perceptron models a neuron by taking a weighted sum of its inputs and sending the output 1 if the sum is greater than some adjustable threshold value (otherwise it sends 0). Figure 18.5 shows the device. Notice that in a perceptron, unlike a Hopfield network, connections are unidirectional.

The inputs $(x_1, x_2, \ldots, x_n)$ and connection weights $(w_1, w_2, \ldots, w_n)$ in the figure are typically real values, both positive and negative. If the presence of some feature x_i tends to cause the perceptron to fire, the weight w_i will be positive; if the feature x_i inhibits the perceptron, the weight w_i will be negative. The perceptron itself consists of the weights, the summation processor, and the adjustable threshold processor. Learning is a process of modifying the values of the weights and the threshold. It is convenient to implement the threshold as just another weight w_0, as in Figure 18.6. This weight can be thought of as the propensity of the perceptron to fire irrespective of its inputs. The perceptron of Figure 18.6 fires if the weighted sum is greater than zero.

A perceptron computes a binary function of its input. Several perceptrons can be combined to compute more complex functions, as shown in Figure 18.7.

Such a group of perceptrons can be trained on sample input-output pairs until it learns to compute the correct function. The amazing property of perceptron learning

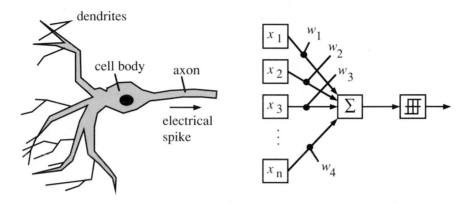

Figure 18.5: A Neuron and a Perceptron

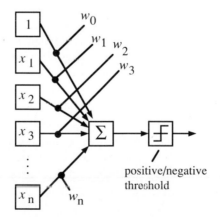

Figure 18.6: Perceptron with Adjustable Threshold Implemented as Additional Weight

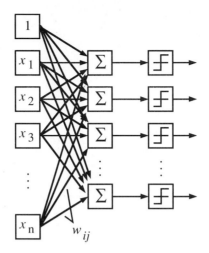

Figure 18.7: A Perceptron with Many Inputs and Many Outputs

is this: Whatever a perceptron can compute, it can *learn* to compute! We demonstrate this in a moment. At the time perceptrons were invented, many people speculated that intelligent systems could be constructed out of perceptrons (see Figure 18.8).

Since the perceptrons of Figure 18.7 are independent of one another, they can be separately trained. So let us concentrate on what a single perceptron can learn to do. Consider the pattern classification problem shown in Figure 18.9. This problem is *linearly separable*, because we can draw a line that separates one class from another. Given values for x_1 and x_2, we want to train a perceptron to output 1 if it thinks the input belongs to the class of white dots and 0 if it thinks the input belongs to the class of black dots. Pattern classification is very similar to *concept learning*, which was discussed in Chapter 17. We have no explicit rule to guide us; we must induce a rule from a set of training instances. We now see how perceptrons can learn to solve such problems.

First, it is necessary to take a close look at what the perceptron computes. Let $\vec{x}$ be an input vector $(x_1, x_2, \ldots, x_n)$. Notice that the weighted summation function $g(x)$ and the output function $o(x)$ can be defined as:

$$g(x) = \sum_{i=0}^{n} w_i x_i$$

$$o(x) = \begin{cases} 1 & \text{if } g(x) > 0 \\ 0 & \text{if } g(x) < 0 \end{cases}$$

Consider the case where we have only two inputs (as in Figure 18.9). Then:

$$g(x) = w_0 + w_1 x_1 + w_2 x_2$$

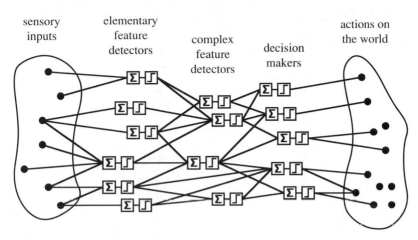

Figure 18.8: An Early Notion of an Intelligent System Built from Trainable Perceptrons

If $g(x)$ is exactly zero, the perceptron cannot decide whether to fire. A slight change in inputs could cause the device to go either way. If we solve the equation $g(x) = 0$, we get the equation for a line:

$$x_2 = \frac{w_1}{w_2}x_1 \quad \frac{w_0}{w_2}$$

The location of the line is completely determined by the weights w_0, w_1, and w_2. If an input vector lies on one side of the line, the perceptron will output 1; if it lies on the other side, the perceptron will output 0. A line that correctly separates the training instances corresponds to a perfectly functioning perceptron. Such a line is called a *decision surface*. In perceptrons with many inputs, the decision surface will be a hyperplane through the multidimensional space of possible input vectors. The problem of *learning* is one of locating an appropriate decision surface.

We present a formal learning algorithm later. For now, consider the informal rule:

> If the perceptron fires when it should not fire, make each w_i smaller by an amount proportional to x_i. If the perceptron fails to fire when it should fire, make each w_i larger by a similar amount.

Suppose we want to train a three-input perceptron to fire only when its first input is on. If the perceptron fails to fire in the presence of an active x_1, we will increase w_1 (and we may increase other weights). If the perceptron fires incorrectly, we will end up decreasing weights that are not w_1. (We will never decrease w_1 because undesired firings only occur when x_1 is 0, which forces the proportional change in w_1 also to be 0.) In addition, w_0 will find a value based on the total number of incorrect firings versus incorrect misfirings. Soon, w_1 will become large enough to overpower w_0, while w_2 and w_3 will not be powerful enough to fire the perceptron, even in the presence of both x_2 and x_3.

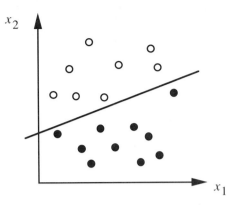

Figure 18.9: A Linearly Separable Pattern Classification Problem

Now let us return to the functions $g(x)$ and $o(x)$. While the sign of $g(x)$ is critical to determining whether the perceptron will fire, the magnitude is also important. The absolute value of $g(x)$ tells how *far* a given input vector $\vec{x}$ lies from the decision surface. This gives us a way of characterizing how good a set of weights is. Let $\vec{w}$ be the weight vector $(w_0, w_1, \ldots, w_n)$, and let X be the subset of training instances *misclassified* by the current set of weights. Then define the *perceptron criterion function*, $J(\vec{w})$, to be the sum of the distances of the misclassified input vectors from the decision surface:

$$J(\vec{w}) = \sum_{\vec{x} \in X} \left| \sum_{i=0}^{n} w_i x_i \right| = \sum_{\vec{x} \in X} |\vec{w}\vec{x}|$$

To create a better set of weights than the current set, we would like to reduce $J(\vec{w})$. Ultimately, if all inputs are classified correctly, $J(\vec{w}) = 0$.

How do we go about minimizing $J(\vec{w})$? We can use a form of local-search hill climbing known as *gradient descent*. We have already seen in Chapter 3 how we can use hill-climbing strategies in symbolic AI systems. For our current purposes, think of $J(\vec{w})$ as defining a surface in the space of all possible weights. Such a surface might look like the one in Figure 18.10.

In the figure, weight w_0 should be part of the weight space but is omitted here because it is easier to visualize J in only three dimensions. Now, some of the weight vectors constitute solutions, in that a perceptron with such a weight vector will classify all its inputs correctly. Note that there are an infinite number of solution vectors. For any solution vector $\vec{w}_s$, we know that $J(\vec{w}_s) = 0$. Suppose we begin with a random weight vector $\vec{w}$ that is not a solution vector. We want to slide down the J surface. There is a mathematical method for doing this—we compute the gradient of the function $J(\vec{w})$. Before we derive the gradient function, we reformulate the perceptron criterion function to remove the absolute value sign:

$$J(\vec{w}) = \sum_{\vec{x} \in X} \vec{w} \begin{cases} \vec{x} \text{ if } \vec{x} \text{ is misclassified as a negative example} \\ -\vec{x} \text{ if } \vec{x} \text{ is misclassified as a positive example} \end{cases}$$

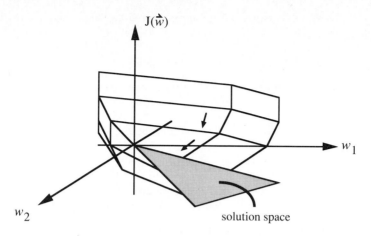

Figure 18.10: Adjusting the Weights by Gradient Descent, Minimizing $J(\vec{w})$

Recall that X is the set of misclassified input vectors.

Now, here is ∇J, the gradient of $J(\vec{w})$ with respect to the weight space:

$$\nabla J(\vec{w}) = \sum_{\vec{x} \in X} \begin{cases} \vec{x} \text{ if } \vec{x} \text{ is misclassified as a negative example} \\ -\vec{x} \text{ if } \vec{x} \text{ is misclassified as a positive example} \end{cases}$$

The gradient is a vector that tells us the direction to move in the weight space in order to reduce $J(\vec{w})$. In order to find a solution weight vector, we simply change the weights in the direction of the gradient, recompute $J(\vec{w})$, recompute the new gradient, and iterate until $J(\vec{w}) = 0$. The rule for updating the weights at time $t + 1$ is:

$$\vec{w}_{t+1} = \vec{w}_t + \eta \nabla J$$

Or in expanded form:

$$\vec{w}_{t+1} = \vec{w}_t + \eta \sum_{\vec{x} \in X} \begin{cases} \vec{x} \text{ if } \vec{x} \text{ is misclassified as a negative example} \\ -\vec{x} \text{ if } \vec{x} \text{ is misclassified as a positive example} \end{cases}$$

η is a scale factor that tells us how far to move in the direction of the gradient. A small η will lead to slower learning, but a large η may cause a move through weight space that "overshoots" the solution vector. Taking η to be a constant gives us what is usually called the "fixed-increment perceptron learning algorithm":

Algorithm: Fixed-Increment Perceptron Learning

Given: A classification problem with n input features $(x_1, x_2, \ldots, x_n)$ and two output classes.

Compute: A set of weights $(w_0, w_1, w_2, \ldots, w_n)$ that will cause a perceptron to fire whenever the input falls into the first output class.

1. Create a perceptron with $n+1$ inputs and $n+1$ weights, where the extra input x_0 is always set to 1.

2. Initialize the weights $(w_0, w_1, \ldots, w_n)$ to random real values.

3. Iterate through the training set, collecting all examples *misclassified* by the current set of weights.

4. If all examples are classified correctly, output the weights and quit.

5. Otherwise, compute the vector sum S of the misclassified input vectors, where each vector has the form $(x_0, x_1, \ldots, x_n)$. In creating the sum, add to S a vector $\vec{x}$ if $\vec{x}$ is an input for which the perceptron incorrectly *fails to fire*, but add vector $-\vec{x}$ if $\vec{x}$ is an input for which the perceptron incorrectly *fires*. Multiply the sum by a scale factor η.

6. Modify the weights $(w_0, w_1, \ldots, w_n)$ by adding the elements of the vector S to them. Go to step 3.

The perceptron learning algorithm is a search algorithm. It begins in a random initial state and finds a solution state. The search space is simply all possible assignments of real values to the weights of the perceptron, and the search strategy is gradient descent. Gradient descent is identical to the hill-climbing strategy described in Chapter 3, except that we view good as "down" rather than "up."

So far, we have seen two search methods employed by neural networks, *gradient descent* in perceptrons and *parallel relaxation* in Hopfield networks. It is important to understand the relation between the two. Parallel relaxation is a problem-solving strategy, analogous to state space search in symbolic AI. Gradient descent is a learning strategy, analogous to techniques such as version spaces. In both symbolic and connectionist AI, learning is viewed as a type of problem solving, and this is why search is useful in learning. But the ultimate goal of learning is to get a system into a position where it can solve problems better. Do not confuse learning algorithms with others.

The *perceptron convergence theorem*, due to Rosenblatt [1962], guarantees that the perceptron will find a solution state, i.e., it will learn to classify any linearly separable set of inputs. In other words, the theorem shows that in the weight space, there are no local minima that do not correspond to the global minimum. Figure 18.11 shows a perceptron learning to classify the instances of Figure 18.9. Remember that every set of weights specifies some decision surface, in this case some two-dimensional line. In the figure, k is the number of passes through the training data, i.e., the number of iterations of steps 3 through 6 of the fixed-increment perceptron learning algorithm.

The introduction of perceptrons in the late 1950s created a great deal of excitement. Here was a device that strongly resembled a neuron and for which well-defined learning algorithms were available. There was much speculation about how intelligent systems could be constructed from perceptron building blocks. In their book *Perceptrons*, Minsky and Papert [1969] put an end to such speculation by analyzing the computational capabilities of the devices. They noticed that while the convergence theorem guaranteed correct classification of linearly separable data, most problems do not supply such nice data. Indeed, the perceptron is incapable of learning to solve some very simple problems. One example given by Minsky and Papert is the exclusive-or (XOR) problem: Given

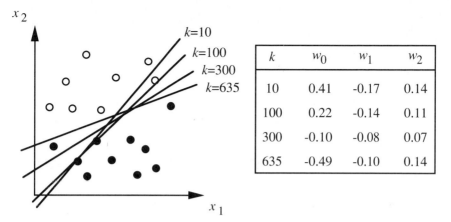

k	w_0	w_1	w_2
10	0.41	-0.17	0.14
100	0.22	-0.14	0.11
300	-0.10	-0.08	0.07
635	-0.49	-0.10	0.14

Figure 18.11: A Perceptron Learning to Solve a Classification Problem

two binary inputs, output 1 if *exactly* one of the inputs is on and output 0 otherwise. We can view XOR as a pattern classification problem in which there are four patterns and two possible outputs (see Figure 18.12).

The perceptron cannot learn a linear decision surface to separate these different outputs, *because no such decision surface exists.* No single line can separate the 1 outputs from the 0 outputs. Minsky and Papert gave a number of problems with this property including telling whether a line drawing is connected, and separating figure from ground in a picture. Notice that the deficiency here is not in the perceptron learning algorithm, but in the way the perceptron represents knowledge.

If we could draw an elliptical decision surface, we could encircle the two "1" outputs in the XOR space. However, perceptrons are incapable of modeling such surfaces. Another idea is to employ two separate line-drawing stages. We could draw one line to isolate the point ($x_1 = 1, x_2 = 1$) and then another line to divide the remaining three points into two categories. Using this idea, we can construct a "multilayer" perceptron (a series of perceptrons) to solve the problem. Such a device is shown in Figure 18.13.

Note how the output of the first perceptron serves as one of the inputs to the second perceptron, with a large, negatively weighted connection. If the first perceptron sees the input ($x_1 = 1, x_2 = 1$), it will send a massive inhibitory pulse to the second perceptron, causing that unit to output 0 regardless of its other inputs. If either of the inputs is 0, the second perceptron gets no inhibition from the first perceptron, and it outputs 1 if either of the inputs is 1.

The use of multilayer perceptrons, then, solves our knowledge representation problem. However, it introduces a serious learning problem: The convergence theorem does not extend to multilayer perceptrons. The perceptron learning algorithm can correctly adjust weights between inputs and outputs, but it cannot adjust weights between perceptrons. In Figure 18.13, the inhibitory weight "−9.0" was hand-coded, not learned. At the time *Perceptrons* was published, no one knew how multilayer perceptrons could be made to learn. In fact, Minsky and Papert speculated:

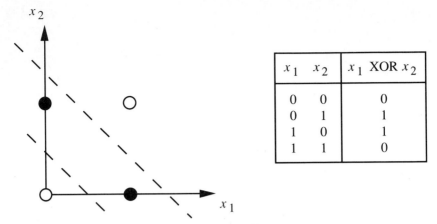

Figure 18.12: A Classification Problem, XOR, That Is Not Linearly Separable

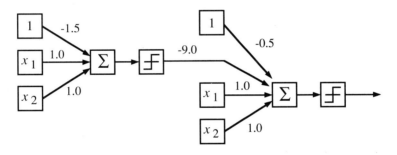

Figure 18.13: A Multilayer Perceptron That Solves the XOR Problem

> The perceptron ... has many features that attract attention: its linearity, its intriguing learning theorem ... there is no reason to suppose that any of these virtues carry over to the many-layered version. Nevertheless, we consider it to be an important research problem to elucidate (or reject) our intuitive judgement that the extension is sterile.

Despite the identification of this "important research problem," actual research in perceptron learning came to a halt in the 1970s. The field saw little interest until the 1980s, when several learning procedures for multilayer perceptrons—also called multilayer networks—were proposed. The next few sections are devoted to such learning procedures.

18.2.2   Backpropagation Networks

As suggested by Figure 18.8 and the *Perceptrons* critique, the ability to train multilayer networks is an important step in the direction of building intelligent machines from neuronlike components. Let's reflect for a moment on why this is so. Our goal is to take a relatively amorphous mass of neuronlike elements and teach it to perform useful tasks. We would like it to be fast and resistant to damage. We would like it to generalize from the inputs it sees. We would like to build these neural masses on a very large scale, and we would like them to be able to learn efficiently. Perceptrons got us part of the way there, but we saw that they were too weak computationally. So we turn to more complex, multilayer networks.

What can a multilayer network compute? The simple answer is: *anything*! Given a set of inputs, we can use summation-threshold units as simple AND, OR, and NOT gates by appropriately setting the threshold and connection weights. We know that we can build any arbitrary combinational circuit out of those basic logical units. In fact, if we are allowed to use feedback loops, we can build a general-purpose computer with them.

The major problem is learning. The knowledge representation system employed by neural nets is quite opaque: the nets *must* learn their own representations because programming them by hand is impossible. Perceptrons had the nice property that whatever they could compute, they could learn to compute. Does this property extend to multilayer networks? The answer is yes, sort of. Backpropagation is a step in that direction.

It will be useful to deal first with a subclass of multilayer networks, namely *fully connected, layered, feedforward* networks. A sample of such a network is shown in Figure 18.14. In this figure, x_i, h_i, and o_i represent unit activation levels of input, *hidden*, and output units. Weights on connections between the input and hidden layers are denoted here by $w1_{ij}$, while weights on connections between the hidden and output layers are denoted by $w2_{ij}$. This network has three layers, although it is possible and sometimes useful to have more. Each unit in one layer is connected in the forward direction to every unit in the next layer. Activations flow from the input layer through the hidden layer, then on to the output layer. As usual, the knowledge of the network is encoded in the weights on connections between units. In contrast to the parallel relaxation method used by Hopfield nets, backpropagation networks perform a simpler computation. Because activations flow in only one direction, there is no need for an iterative relaxation process. The activation levels of the units in the output layer determine the output of the network.

The existence of hidden units allows the network to develop complex feature detectors, or internal representations. Figure 18.15 shows the application of a three layer network to the problem of recognizing digits. The two-dimensional grid containing the numeral "7" forms the input layer. A single hidden unit might be strongly activated by a horizontal line in the input, or perhaps a diagonal. The important thing to note is that the behavior of these hidden units is automatically learned, not preprogrammed. In Figure 18.15, the input grid appears to be laid out in two dimensions, but the fully connected network is unaware of this 2-D structure. Because this structure can be important, many networks permit their hidden units to maintain only local connections to the input layer (e.g., a different 4 by 4 subgrid for each hidden unit).

The hope in attacking problems like handwritten character recognition is that the neural network will not only learn to classify the inputs it is trained on but that it will *generalize* and be able to classify inputs that it has not yet seen. We return to generalization in the next section.

A reasonable question at this point is: "All neural nets seem to be able to do

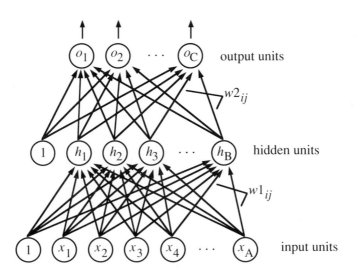

Figure 18.14: A Multilayer Network

is classification. Hard AI problems such as planning, natural language parsing, and theorem proving are not simply classification tasks, so how do connectionist models address these problems?" Most of the problems we see in this chapter are indeed classification problems, because these are the problems that neural networks are best suited to handle at present. A major limitation of current network formalisms is how they deal with phenomena that involve time. This limitation is lifted to some degree in work on recurrent networks (see Section 18.4), but the problems are still severe. Hence, we concentrate on classification problems for now.

Let's now return to backpropagation networks. The unit in a backpropagation network requires a slightly different activation function from the perceptron. Both functions are shown in Figure 18.16. A backpropagation unit still sums up its weighted inputs, but unlike the perceptron, it produces a real value between 0 and 1 as output, based on a sigmoid (or S-shaped) function, which is continuous and differentiable, as required by the backpropagation algorithm. Let *sum* be the weighted sum of the inputs to a unit. The equation for the unit's output is given by:

$$output = \frac{1}{1 + e^{-sum}}$$

Notice that if the sum is 0, the output is 0.5 (in contrast to the perceptron, where it must be either 0 or 1). As the sum gets larger, the output approaches 1. As the sum gets smaller, on the other hand, the output approaches 0.

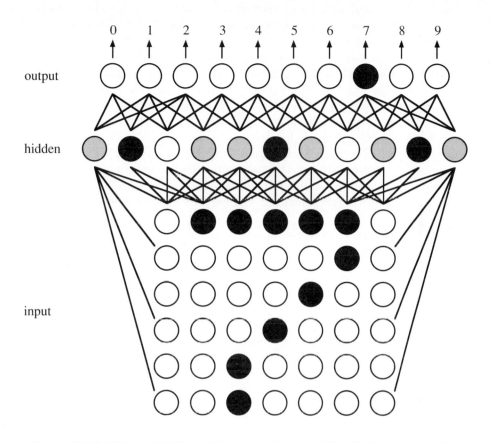

Figure 18.15: Using a Multilayer Network to Learn to Classify Handwritten Digits

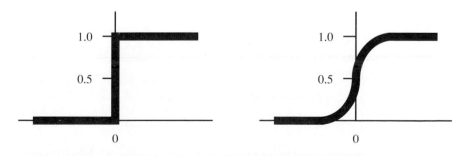

Figure 18.16: The Stepwise Activation Function of the Perceptron (*left*), and the Sigmoid Activation Function of the Backpropagation Unit (*right*)

Like a perceptron, a backpropagation network typically starts out with a random set of weights. The network adjusts its weights each time it sees an input-output pair. Each pair requires two stages: a forward pass and a backward pass. The forward pass involves presenting a sample input to the network and letting activations flow until they reach the output layer. During the backward pass, the network's actual output (from the forward pass) is compared with the target output and error estimates are computed for the output units. The weights connected to the output units can be adjusted in order to reduce those errors. We can then use the error estimates of the output units to derive error estimates for the units in the hidden layers. Finally, errors are propagated back to the connections stemming from the input units.

Unlike the perceptron learning algorithm of the last section, the backpropagation algorithm usually updates its weights incrementally, after seeing each input-output pair. After it has seen all the input-output pairs (and adjusted its weights that many times), we say that one *epoch* has been completed. Training a backpropagation network usually requires many epochs.

Refer back to Figure 18.14 for the basic structure on which the following algorithm is based.

Algorithm: Backpropagation

Given: A set of input-output vector pairs.

Compute: A set of weights for a three-layer network that maps inputs onto corresponding outputs.

1. Let A be the number of units in the input layer, as determined by the length of the training input vectors. Let C be the number of units in the output layer. Now choose B, the number of units in the hidden layer.[3] As shown in Figure 18.14, the input and hidden layers each have an extra unit used for thresholding; therefore, the units in these layers will sometimes be indexed by the ranges $(0, \ldots, A)$ and $(0, \ldots, B)$. We denote the activation levels of the units in the input layer by x_j, in the hidden layer by h_j, and in the output layer by o_j. Weights connecting the input layer to the hidden layer are denoted by $w1_{ij}$, where the subscript i indexes the input units and j indexes the hidden units. Likewise, weights connecting the hidden layer to the output layer are denoted by $w2_{ij}$, with i indexing to hidden units and j indexing output units.

2. Initialize the weights in the network. Each weight should be set randomly to a number between -0.1 and 0.1.

$$w1_{ij} = random(-0.1, 0.1) \quad \text{for all} \quad i = 0, \ldots, A, \ j = 1, \ldots, B$$

$$w2_{ij} = random(-0.1, 0.1) \quad \text{for all} \quad i = 0, \ldots, B, \ j = 1, \ldots, C$$

3. Initialize the activations of the thresholding units. The values of these thresholding units should never change.

---

[3] Successful large-scale networks have used topologies like 203-80-26 [Sejnowski and Rosenberg, 1987], 960-9-45 [Pomerleau, 1989], and 459-24-24-1 [Tesauro and Sejnowski, 1989]. A larger hidden layer results in a more powerful network, but too much power may be undesirable (see Section 18.2.3).

$$x_0 = 1.0$$

$$h_0 = 1.0$$

4. Choose an input-output pair. Suppose the input vector is x_i and the target output vector is y_i. Assign activation levels to the input units.

5. Propagate the activations from the units in the input layer to the units in the hidden layer using the activation function of Figure 18.16:

$$h_j = \frac{1}{1 + e^{-\sum_{i=0}^{A} w1_{ij}x_i}} \quad \text{for all} \quad j = 1, \ldots, B$$

Note that i ranges from 0 to A. $w1_{0j}$ is the thresholding weight for hidden unit j (its propensity to fire irrespective of its inputs). x_0 is always 1.0.

6. Propagate the activations from the units in the hidden layer to the units in the output layer.

$$o_j = \frac{1}{1 + e^{-\sum_{i=0}^{B} w2_{ij}h_i}} \quad \text{for all} \quad j = 1, \ldots, C$$

Again, the thresholding weight $w2_{0j}$ for output unit j plays a role in the weighted summation. h_0 is always 1.0.

7. Compute the errors[4] of the units in the output layer, denoted $\delta 2_j$. Errors are based on the network's actual output (o_j) and the target output (y_j).

$$\delta 2_j = o_j(1 - o_j)(y_j - o_j) \quad \text{for all} \quad j = 1, \ldots, C$$

8. Compute the errors of the units in the hidden layer, denoted $\delta 1_j$.

$$\delta 1_j = h_j(1 - h_j) \sum_{i=1}^{C} \delta 2_i \cdot w2_{ji} \quad \text{for all} \quad j = 1, \ldots, B$$

9. Adjust the weights between the hidden layer and output layer.[5] The learning rate is denoted η; its function is the same as in perceptron learning. A reasonable value of η is 0.35.

---

[4]The error formula is related to the derivative of the activation function. The mathematical derivation behind the backpropagation learning algorithm is beyond the scope of this book.

[5]Again, we omit the details of the derivation. The basic idea is that each hidden unit tries to minimize the errors of output units to which it connects.

$$\Delta w2_{ij} = \eta \cdot \delta 2_j \cdot h_i \quad \text{for all} \quad i = 0, \ldots, B, \; j = 1, \ldots, C$$

10. Adjust the weights between the input layer and the hidden layer.

$$\Delta w1_{ij} = \eta \cdot \delta 1_j \cdot x_i \quad \text{for all} \quad i = 0, \ldots, A, \; j = 1, \ldots, B$$

11. Go to step 4 and repeat. When all the input-output pairs have been presented to the network, one epoch has been completed. Repeat steps 4 to 10 for as many epochs as desired.

The algorithm generalizes straightforwardly to networks of more than three layers.[6] For each extra hidden layer, insert a forward propagation step between steps 6 and 7, an error computation step between steps 8 and 9, and a weight adjustment step between steps 10 and 11. Error computation for hidden units should use the equation in step 8, but with i ranging over the units in the next layer, not necessarily the output layer.

The speed of learning can be increased by modifying the weight modification steps 9 and 10 to include a momentum term α. The weight update formulas become:

$$\Delta w2_{ij}(t+1) = \eta \cdot \delta 2_j \cdot h_i + \alpha \Delta w2_{ij}(t)$$

$$\Delta w1_{ij}(t+1) = \eta \cdot \delta 1_j \cdot x_i + \alpha \Delta w1_{ij}(t)$$

where h_i, x_i, $\delta 1_j$ and $\delta 2_j$ are measured at time $t+1$. $\Delta w_{ij}(t)$ is the change the weight experienced during the previous forward-backward pass. If α is set to 0.9 or so, learning speed is improved.[7]

Recall that the activation function has a sigmoid shape. Since infinite weights would be required for the actual outputs of the network to reach 0.0 and 1.0, binary target outputs (the y_j's of steps 4 and 7 above) are usually given as 0.1 and 0.9 instead. The sigmoid is required by backpropagation because the derivation of the weight update rule requires that the activation function be continuous and differentiable.

The derivation of the weight update rule is more complex than the derivation of the fixed-increment update rule for perceptrons, but the idea is much the same. There is an error function that defines a surface over weight space, and the weights are modified in the direction of the gradient of the surface. See Rumelhart et al. [1986] for details. Interestingly, the error surface for multilayer nets is more complex than the error surface for perceptrons. One notable difference is the existence of local minima. Recall the bowl-shaped space we used to explain perceptron learning (Figure 18.10). As we

---

[6] A network with one hidden layer can compute any function that a network with many hidden layers can compute: with an exponential number of hidden units, one unit could be assigned to every possible input pattern. However, learning is sometimes faster with multiple hidden layers, especially if the input is highly nonlinear, i.e., hard to separate with a series of straight lines.

[7] Empirically, best results have come from letting α be zero for the first few training passes, then increasing it to 0.9 for the rest of training. This process first gives the algorithm some time to find a good general direction, and then moves it in that direction with some extra speed.

modified weights, we moved in the direction of the bottom of the bowl; eventually, we reached it. A backpropagation network, however, may slide down the error surface into a set of weights that does not solve the problem it is being trained on. If that set of weights is at a local minimum, the network will never reach the optimal set of weights. Thus, we have no analogue of the perceptron convergence theorem for backpropagation networks.

There are several methods of overcoming the problem of local minima. The momentum factor α, which tends to keep the weight changes moving in the same direction, allows the algorithm to skip over small minima. *Simulated annealing*, discussed later in Section 18.2.4, is also useful. Finally, adjusting the shape of a unit's activation function can have an effect on the network's susceptibility to local minima.

Fortunately, backpropagation networks rarely slip into local minima. It turns out that, especially in larger networks, the high-dimensional weight space provides plenty of degrees of freedom for the algorithm. The lack of a convergence theorem is not a problem in practice. However, this pleasant feature of backpropagation was not discovered until recently, when digital computers became fast enough to support large-scale simulations of neural networks. The backpropagation algorithm was actually derived independently by a number of researchers in the past, but it was discarded as many times because of the potential problems with local minima. In the days before fast digital computers, researchers could only judge their ideas by proving theorems about them, and they had no idea that local minima would turn out to be rare in practice. The modern form of backpropagation is often credited to Werbos [1974], LeCun [1985], Parker [1985], and Rumelhart *et al.* [1986].

Backpropagation networks are not without real problems, however, with the most serious being the slow speed of learning. Even simple tasks require extensive training periods. The XOR problem, for example, involves only five units and nine weights, but it can require many, many passes through the four training cases before the weights converge, especially if the learning parameters are not carefully tuned. Also, simple backpropagation does not scale up very well. The number of training examples required is superlinear in the size of the network.

Since backpropagation is inherently a parallel, distributed algorithm, the idea of improving speed by building special-purpose backpropagation hardware is attractive. However, fast new variations of backpropagation and other learning algorithms appear frequently in the literature, e.g., Fahlman [1988]. By the time an algorithm is transformed into hardware and embedded in a computer system, the algorithm is likely to be obsolete.

18.2.3 Generalization

If all possible inputs and outputs are shown to a backpropagation network, the network will (probably, eventually) find a set of weights that maps the inputs onto the outputs. For many AI problems, however, it is impossible to give all possible inputs. Consider face recognition and character recognition. There are an infinite number of orientations and expressions to a face, and an infinite number of fonts and sizes for a character, yet humans learn to classify these objects easily from only a few examples. We would hope that our networks would do the same. And, in fact, backpropagation shows promise as a generalization mechanism. If we work in a domain (such as the classification domains just discussed) where similar inputs get mapped onto similar outputs, backpropagation

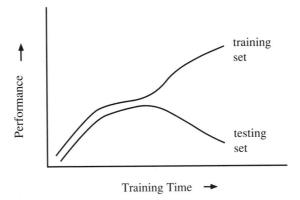

Figure 18.17: A Common Generalization Effect in Neural Network Learning

will interpolate when given inputs it has never seen before. For example, after learning to distinguish a few different sized As from a few different sized Bs, a network will usually be able to distinguish *any* sized A from *any* sized B. Also, generalization will help overcome any undesirable noise in the inputs.

There are some pitfalls, however. Figure 18.17 shows the common generalization effect during a long training period. During the first part of the training, performance on the training set improves as the network adjusts its weights through backpropagation. Performance on the test set (examples that the network is *not* allowed to learn on) also improves, although it is never quite as good as the training set. After a while, network performance reaches a plateau as the weights shift around, looking for a path to further improvement. Ultimately, such a path is found, and performance on the training set improves again. But performance on the test set gets worse. Why? The network has begun to memorize the individual input-output pairs rather than settling for weights that generally describe the mapping for all cases. With thousands of real-valued weights at its disposal, backpropagation is theoretically capable of storing entire training sets; with enough hidden units, the algorithm could learn to assign a hidden unit to every distinct input pattern in the training set. It is a testament to the power of backpropagation that this actually happens in practice.

Of course, that much power is undesirable. There are several ways to prevent backpropagation from resorting to a table-lookup scheme. One way is to stop training when a plateau has been reached, on the assumption that any other improvement will come through "cheating." Another way is to add deliberately small amounts of noise to the training inputs. The noise should be enough to prevent memorization, but it should not be so much that it confuses the classifier. A third way to help generalization is to reduce the number of hidden units in the network, creating a bottleneck between the input and output layers. Confronted with a bottleneck, the network will be forced to come up with compact internal representations of its inputs.

Finally, there is the issue of exceptions. In many domains, there are general rules, but there are also exceptions to the rules. For example, we can generally make the past tense of an English verb by adding "-ed" to it, but this is not true of verbs like "sing," "think," and "eat." When we show many present and past tense pairs to a network, we would like it to generalize in spite of the exceptions—but not to generalize so far that the exceptions are lost. Backpropagation performs fairly well in this regard, as do simple perceptrons, as reported in Rumelhart and McClelland [1986a].

18.2.4 Boltzmann Machines

A Boltzmann machine is a variation on the idea of a Hopfield network. Recall that pairs of units in a Hopfield net are connected by symmetric weights. Units update their states asynchronously by looking at their local connections to other units.

In addition to serving as content-addressable memories, Hopfield networks can solve a wide variety of constraint satisfaction problems. The idea is to view each unit as a "hypothesis," and to place positive weights on connections between units representing compatible or mutually supporting hypotheses, and negative weights on connections between units representing incompatible hypotheses. As the Hopfield net settles into a stable state, it attempts to assign truth and falsity to the various hypotheses while violating as few constraints as possible. We see examples of how neural networks attack real-world constraint satisfaction problems in Section 18.3.

The main problem with Hopfield networks is that they settle into local minima. Having many local minima is good for building content-addressable memories, but for constraint satisfaction tasks, we need to find the *globally* optimal state of the network. This state corresponds to an interpretation that satisfies as many interacting constraints as possible. Unfortunately, Hopfield networks cannot find global solutions because they settle into stable states via a completely distributed algorithm. If a network reaches a stable state like state A in Figure 18.4, then no single unit is willing to change its state in order to move uphill, so the network will never reach globally optimal state B. If several units decided to change state simultaneously, the network might be able to scale the hill and slip into state B. We need a way to push networks into globally optimal states while maintaining our distributed approach.

At about the same time that Hopfield networks were developed, a new search technique, called *simulated annealing*, appeared in the literature. Simulated annealing, described in Chapter 3, is a technique for finding globally optimal solutions to combinatorial problems. Hinton and Sejnowski [1986] combined Hopfield networks and simulated annealing to produce networks called *Boltzmann machines*.

To understand how annealing applies, go back to Figure 18.4 and imagine it as a black box. Imagine further a ball rolling around in the box. If we could not see into the black box, how could we coax the ball into the deepest valley? By shaking the box, of course. Now, if we shake too violently, the ball will bounce from valley to valley at random. That is, if the ball were in valley A, it might jump to valley B; but if the ball were in valley B, it might jump to valley A. If we shake too *softly*, however, the ball might find itself in valley A, unable to jump out. The answer suggested by annealing is to shake the box violently at first, then gradually slow down. At some point, the probability of the ball jumping from A to B will be larger than the probability of jumping from B to A. The ball will very likely find its way to valley B, and as the shaking becomes softer, it will be unable to escape. This is what we want.

How is this idea implemented in a neural network? Units in Boltzmann machines update their individual binary states by a *stochastic* rather than deterministic rule. The probability that any given unit will be active is given by p:

$$p = \frac{1}{1 + e^{\Delta E/T}}$$

where ΔE is the sum of the unit's active input lines and T is the "temperature" of the network. Stochastic updating of units is very similar to updating in Hopfield nets, except for the temperature factor. At high temperatures, units display random behavior, while at very low temperatures, units behave as in Hopfield nets. Annealing is the process of gradually moving from a high temperature down to a low temperature. The randomness added by the temperature helps the network escape from local minima.

There is a learning procedure for Boltzmann machines, i.e., a procedure that assigns weights to connections between units given a training set of initial states and final states. We do not go into the algorithm here; interested readers should see Hinton and Sejnowski [1986]. Boltzmann learning is more time-consuming than backpropagation,[8] because of the complex annealing process, but it has some advantages. For one thing, it is easier to use Boltzmann machines to solve constraint satisfaction problems. Unlike backpropagation networks, Boltzmann machines do not make a clear division between "input" and "output." For example, a Boltzmann machine might have three important sets of units, any two of which could have their values "clamped," or fixed, like the input layer of a backpropagation net—activations in the third set of units would be determined by parallel relaxation.

If the annealing is carried out properly, Boltzmann machines can avoid local minima and learn to compute any computable function of fixed-sized inputs and outputs.

18.2.5   Reinforcement Learning

What if we train our networks not with sample outputs but with punishment and reward instead? This process is certainly sufficient to train animals to perform relatively interesting tasks. Barto [1985] describes a network which learns as follows: (1) the network is presented with a sample input from the training set, (2) the network computes what it thinks should be the sample output, (3) the network is supplied with a real-valued judgment by the teacher, (4) the network adjusts its weights, and the process repeats. A positive value in step 3 indicates good performance, while a negative value indicates bad performance. The network seeks a set of weights that will prevent negative reinforcement in the future, much as an experimental rat seeks behaviors that will prevent electric shocks.

18.2.6   Unsupervised Learning

What if a neural network is given *no* feedback for its outputs, not even a real-valued reinforcement? Can the network learn anything useful? The unintuitive answer is yes.

---

[8]One deterministic variation of Boltzmann learning [Peterson and Anderson, 1987] promises to be more efficient.

	has-hair?	has-scales?	has-feathers?	flies?	lives in water?	lays eggs?
Dog	1	0	0	0	0	0
Cat	1	0	0	0	0	0
Bat	1	0	0	1	0	0
Whale	1	0	0	0	1	0
Canary	0	0	1	1	0	1
Robin	0	0	1	1	0	1
Ostrich	0	0	1	1	0	1
Snake	0	1	0	0	0	1
Lizard	0	1	0	0	0	1
Alligator	0	1	0	0	1	1

Figure 18.18: Data for Unsupervised Learning

This form of learning is called *unsupervised learning* because no teacher is required.[9] Given a set of input data, the network is allowed to play with it to try to discover regularities and relationships between the different parts of the input.

Learning is often made possible through some notion of which features in the input set are important. But often we do not know in advance which features are important, and asking a learning system to deal with raw input data can be computationally expensive. Unsupervised learning can be used as a "feature discovery" module that precedes supervised learning.

Consider the data in Figure 18.18. The group of ten animals, each described by its own set of features, breaks down naturally into three groups: mammals, reptiles, and birds. We would like to build a network that can learn which group a particular animal belongs to, and to generalize so that it can identify animals it has not yet seen. We can easily accomplish this with a six-input, three-output backpropagation network. We simply present the network with an input, observe its output, and update its weights based on the errors it makes. Without a teacher, however, the error cannot be computed, so we must seek other methods.

Our first problem is to ensure that only one of the three output units becomes active for any given input. One solution to this problem is to let the network settle, find the output unit with the highest level of activation, and set that unit to 1 and all other output units to 0. In other words, the output unit with the highest activation is the only one we consider to be active. A more neural-like solution is to have the output units fight among themselves for control of an input vector. The scheme is shown in Figure 18.19. The input units are directly connected to the output units, as in the perceptron, but the output units are also connected to each other via prewired negative, or inhibitory, connections. The output unit with the most activation along its input lines initially will most strongly

---

[9]One analogue of unsupervised learning in symbolic AI is *discovery* (Section 17.7).

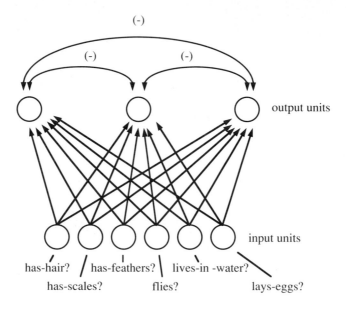

Figure 18.19: A Competitive Learning Network

dampen its competitors. As a result, the competitors will become weaker, losing their power of inhibition over the stronger output unit. The stronger unit then becomes even stronger, and its inhibiting effect on the other output units becomes overwhelming. Soon, the other output units are all completely inactive. This type of mutual inhibition is called *winner-take-all* behavior. One popular unsupervised learning scheme based on this behavior is known as *competitive learning*.

In competitive learning, output units fight for control over portions of the input space. A simple competitive learning algorithm is the following:

1. Present an input vector.

2. Calculate the initial activation for each output unit.

3. Let the output units fight until only one is active.

4. Increase the weights on connections between the active output unit and active input units. This makes it more likely that the output unit will be active next time the pattern is repeated.

One problem with this algorithm is that one output unit may learn to be active all the time—it may claim all the space of inputs for itself. For example, if all the weights on a unit's input lines are large, it will tend to bully the other output units into submission. Learning will only further increase those weights.

The solution, originally due to Rosenblatt (and described in Rumelhart and Zipser [1986]), is to ration the weights. The sum of the weights on a unit's input lines is limited to 1. Increasing the weight of one connection requires that we decrease the weight of some other connection. Here is the learning algorithm.

Algorithm: Competitive Learning

Given: A network consisting of n binary-valued input units directly connected to any number of output units.

Produce: A set of weights such that the output units become active according to some natural division of the inputs.

1. Present an input vector, denoted $(x_1, x_2, \ldots, x_n)$.

2. Calculate the initial activation for each output unit by computing a weighted sum of its inputs.[10]

3. Let the output units fight until only one is active.[11]

4. Adjust the weights on the input lines that lead to the single active output unit:

$$\Delta w_j = \eta \; \frac{x_j}{m} - \eta \; w_j \quad \text{for all} \quad j = 1, \ldots, n$$

where w_j is the weight on the connection from input unit j to the active output unit, x_j is the value of the jth input bit, m is the number of input units that are active in the input vector that was chosen in step 1, and η is the learning rate (some small constant). It is easy to show that if the weights on the connections feeding into an output unit sum to 1 before the weight change, then they will still sum to 1 afterward

5. Repeat steps 1 to 4 for all input patterns for many epochs.

The weight update rule in step 4 makes the output unit more prone to fire when it sees the same input again. If the same input is presented over and over, the output unit will eventually adjust its weights for maximum activation on that input. Because input vectors arrive in a mixed fashion, however, output units never settle on a perfect set of weights. The hope is that each will find a natural group of input vectors and gravitate toward it, that is, toward high activations when presented with those inputs. The algorithm halts when the weight changes become very small.

The competitive learning algorithm works well in many cases, but it has some problems. Sometimes, one output unit will always win, despite the existence of more than one cluster of input vectors. If two clusters are close together, one output unit may learn weights that give it a high level of activation when presented with an input from either cluster. In other words, it may oscillate between the two clusters. Normally, another output unit will win occasionally and move to claim one of the two clusters. However, if the other output units are completely unexcitable by the input vectors, they may never win the competition. One solution, called "leaky learning," is to change

---

[10]There is no reason to pass the weighted sum through a sigmoid function, as we did with backpropagation, because we only calculate activation levels for the purpose of singling out the most highly activated output unit.

[11]As mentioned earlier, any method for determining the most highly activated output unit is sufficient. Simulators written in a serial programming language may dispense with the neural circuitry and simply compare activations levels to find the maximum.

the weights belonging to relatively inactive output units as well as the most active one. The weight update rule for losing output units is the same as in the algorithm above, except that they move their weights with a much smaller η (learning rate). An alternative solution is to adjust the sensitivity of an output unit through the use of a bias, or adjustable threshold. Recall that this bias mechanism was used in perceptrons and corresponded to the propensity of a unit to fire irrespective of its inputs. Output units that seldom win in the competitive learning process can be given larger biases. In effect, they are given control over a larger portion of the input space. In this way, units that consistently lose are eventually given a chance to win and adjust their weights in the direction of a particular cluster.

18.3   Applications of Neural Networks

Connectionist models can be divided [Touretzky, 1989b] into the following categories based on the complexity of the problem and the network's behavior:

- Pattern recognizers and associative memories

- Pattern transformers

- Dynamic inferencers

Most of the examples we have seen so far fall into the first category. In this section, we also see networks that fall into the second category. General inferencing in connectionist networks is still at a primitive stage.

18.3.1   Connectionist Speech

Speech recognition is a difficult perceptual task (as we see in Chapter 21). Connectionist networks have been applied to a number of problems in speech recognition; for a survey, see Lippmann [1989]. Figure 18.20 shows how a three-layer backpropagation network can be trained to discriminate between different vowel sounds. The network is trained to output one of ten vowels, given a pair of frequencies taken from the speech waveform. Note the nonlinear decision surfaces created by backpropagation learning.

Speech production—the problem of translating text into speech rather than vice versa—has also been attacked with neural networks. Speech production is easier than speech recognition, and high performance programs are available. NETtalk [Sejnowski and Rosenberg, 1987], a network that learns to pronounce English text, was one of the first systems to demonstrate that connectionist methods could be applied to real-world tasks.

Linguists have long studied the rules governing the translation of text into speech units called *phonemes*. For example, the letter "x" is usually pronounced with a "ks" sound, as in "box" and "axe." A traditional approach to the problem would be to write all these rules down and use a production system to apply them. Unfortunately, most of the rules have exceptions—consider "xylophone"—and these exceptions must also be programmed in. Also, the rules may interact with one another in unpleasant, unforeseen ways. A connectionist approach is simply to present a network with words and their

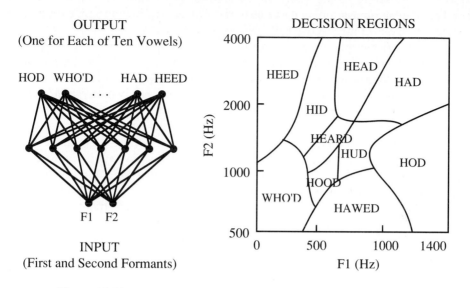

Figure 18.20: A Network That Learns to Distinguish Vowel Sounds

pronunciations, and hope that the network will discover the regularities and remember the exceptions. NETtalk succeeds fairly well at this task with a backpropagation network of the type described in Section 18.2.2.

We can think of NETtalk as an exercise in "extensional programming" [Cottrell *et al.*, 1987]. There exists some complex relationship between text and speech, and we program that relationship into the computer by showing it examples from the real world. Contrast this with traditional, "intensional programming," in which we write rules or specialized algorithms without reference to any particular examples. In the former case, we hope that the network generalizes to translate new words correctly; in the latter case, we hope that the algorithm is general enough to handle whatever words it receives. Extensional programming is a powerful technique because it drastically cuts down on knowledge acquisition time, a major bottleneck in the construction of AI systems. However, current learning methods are not adequate for the extensional programming of very complex tasks, such as the translation of English sentences into Japanese.

18.3.2   Connectionist Vision

Humans achieve significant visual prowess with limited visual hardware. Only the center of the retina maintains good spatial resolution; as a result, we must constantly shift our attention among various points of interest. Each snapshot lasts only about two hundred milliseconds. Since individual neural firing rates usually lie in the millisecond range, each scene must be interpreted in about a hundred computational steps. To compound the problem, each interpretation must be rapidly integrated with previous interpretations to enable the construction of a stable three-dimensional model of the world. These severe timing constraints strongly suggest that human vision is highly parallel. Connectionism offers many methods for studying both the engineering and biological aspects of massively parallel vision.

Parallel relaxation plays an important role in connectionist vision systems [Ballard *et al.*, 1983; Ballard, 1984]. Recall our discussion of parallel relaxation search in Hopfield networks and Boltzmann machines. In a typical system, some neural units receive their initial activation levels from a video camera and then these activations are iteratively modified based on the influences of nearby units. One use for relaxation is detecting edges. If many units think they are located on an edge border, they can override any dissenters. The relaxation process settles on the most likely set of edges in the scene. While traditional vision programs running on serial computing engines must reason about which regions of a scene require edge detection processing, the connectionist approach simply assumes massively parallel machinery [Fahlman and Hinton, 1987].

Visual interpretation also requires the integration of many constraint sources. For example, if two adjacent areas in the scene have the same color and texture, then they are probably part of the same object. If these constraints can be encoded in a network structure, then parallel relaxation is an attractive technique for combining them. Because relaxation treats constraints as "soft"—i.e., it will violate one constraint if necessary to satisfy the others—it achieves a global best-fit interpretation even in the presence of local ambiguity or noise.

18.3.3 Combinatorial Problems

Parallel relaxation can also be used to solve many other constraint satisfaction problems. Hopfield and Tank [1985] show how a Hopfield network can be programmed to come up with approximate solutions to the traveling salesman problem. The system employs n^2 neural units, where n is the number of cities to be toured. Figure 18.21 shows how tours themselves are represented. Each row stands for one city. The tour proceeds horizontally across the columns. The starting city is marked by the active unit in column 1, the next city by column 2, etc. The tour shown in Figure 18.21 goes through cities D, B, E, H, G, F, C, A, and back to D.

Like all Hopfield networks, this n by n array contains a number of weighted connections. The connection weights are initialized to reflect exactly the constraints of a particular problem instance.[12] First of all, every unit is connected with a negative weight to every other unit in its *column*, because only one city at a time can be visited. Second, every unit inhibits every other unit in its *row*, because each city can only be visited once. Third, units in adjacent columns inhibit each other in proportion to the distances between cities represented by their rows. For example, if city D is far from city G, then the fourth unit in column 3 will strongly inhibit the seventh units in columns 2 and 4. There is some global excitation, so in the absence of strong inhibition, individual units will prefer to be active.

Notice that each unit represents some hypothesis about the position of a particular city in a short tour. To find that tour, we start out by giving our units random activation values. Once all the weights are set, the units update themselves asynchronously

---

[12] Note that these connection weights are hand-coded, not learned.

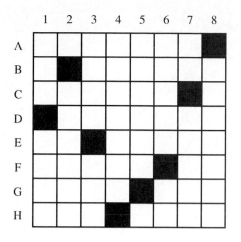

Figure 18.21: The Representation of a Traveling Salesman Tour in a Hopfield Network

according to the rule described in Section 18.1.[13] This updating continues until a stable state is reached. Stable states of the network correspond to short tours because conflicts between constraints are minimal. Hopfield and Tank [1985] have used these networks to come up with quick, approximate solutions to traveling salesman problems (but see Wilson and Pawley [1988] for a critique of their results). Many other combinatorial problems, such as graph-coloring, can be cast as constraint satisfaction problems and solved with parallel relaxation networks.

18.3.4 Other Applications

Other tasks successfully tackled by neural networks include learning to play backgammon [Tesauro and Sejnowski, 1989], to classify sonar signals [Gorman and Sejnowski, 1988], to compress images [Cottrell *et al.*, 1987], and to drive a vehicle along a road [Pomerleau, 1989]. While there are other techniques for attacking all these problems, learning-based connectionist systems can often be built more quickly and with less expertise than their traditional counterparts.

18.4 Recurrent Networks

One clear deficiency of neural network models compared to symbolic models is the difficulty in getting neural network models to deal with temporal AI tasks such as planning and natural language parsing. Recurrent networks, or networks with loops, are an attempt to remedy this situation.

Consider trying to teach a network how to shoot a basketball through a hoop. We can present the network with an input situation (distance and height of hoop, initial position

---

[13] Actually, the units used by Hopfield and Tank [1985] take on real activation values (determined by a sigmoid curve) not binary values. By changing the shape of the sigmoid during processing, the network achieves some of the same results as does simulated annealing.

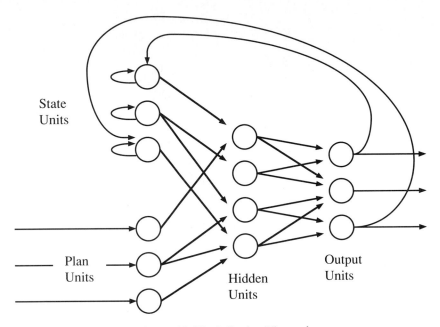

State
Units

Plan
Units

Hidden
Units

Output
Units

Figure 18.22: A Jordan Network

of muscles), but we need more than a single output vector. We need a series of output
vectors: first move the muscles this way, then this way, then this way, etc. Jordan [1986]
has invented a network that can do something like this. It is shown in Figure 18.22.
The network's *plan units* stay constant. They correspond to an instruction like "shoot
a basket." The *state units* encode the current state of the network. The *output units*
simultaneously give commands (e.g., move arm x to position y) and update the state
units. The network never settles into a stable state; instead it changes at each time step.

Recurrent networks can be trained with the backpropagation algorithm. At each step,
we compare the activations of the output units with the desired activations and propagate
errors backward through the network. When training is completed, the network will
be capable of performing a sequence of actions. Features of backpropagation, such as
automatic generalization, also hold for recurrent networks. A few modifications are
useful, however. First of all, we would like the state units to change smoothly. For
example, we would not like to move from a crouched position to a jumping position
instantaneously. Smoothness can be implemented as a change in the weight update
rule; essentially, the "error" of an output becomes a combination of real error and the
magnitude of the change in the state units. Enforcing the smoothness constraint turns
out to be very important in fast learning, as it removes many of the weight-manipulation
options available to backpropagation.

A major problem in supervised learning systems lies in correcting the network's
behavior. If enough training data can be amassed, then target outputs can be provided
for many input vectors. Recurrent networks have special training problems, however,
because it is difficult to specify completely a series of target outputs. In shooting
basketballs, for example, the feedback comes from the external world (i.e., where the

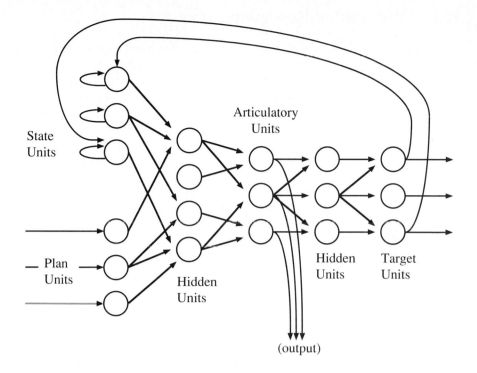

State
Units

Articulatory
Units

Plan
Units

Hidden
Units

Hidden
Units

Target
Units

(output)

Figure 18.23: A Recurrent Network with a Mental Model

basketball lands), not from a teacher showing how to move each muscle. To get around this difficulty, we can learn a *mental model*, a mapping that relates the network's outputs to events in the world. Once such a model is known, the system can learn sequential tasks by backpropagating the errors it sees in the real world. So it is necessary to learn two different things: the relationship between the plan and the network's output, and the relationship between the network's output and the real world.

Networks of this type are described by Jordan [1988]. Figure 18.23 shows such a network, which is essentially the same as a Jordan net except for the addition of two more layers: another hidden layer and a layer representing results as seen in the world. First, the latter portion of the network is trained (using backpropagation) on various pairs of outputs and targets until the network gets a good feel for how its outputs affect the real world. After these rough weights are established, the whole network is trained using real-world feedback until it is able to perform accurately.

Another type of recurrent network is described in Elman [1990]. In this model, activation levels are explicitly copied from hidden units to state units. Networks of this kind have been used in a number of applications, including natural language parsing.

18.5 Distributed Representations

As we have seen, the long-term knowledge of a connectionist network is stored as a set of weights on connections between units. This general scheme admits many kinds of representations, just as the basic slot-and-filler structure left room for all the representations discussed in Chapters 9 and 10. Connectionist networks can be divided roughly into two classes: those that use *localist* representations and those that use *distributed* representations.

NETL [Fahlman, 1979] is a highly parallel system that employs a localist representation. Each node in a NETL network stands for one concept in a semantic network. For example, there is a node for "elephant," a node for "gray," etc. When the network is considering an elephant, the elephant unit becomes active. This unit then activates neighboring units, such as units for gray, large, and mammal. The reverse process works nicely as a content-addressable memory.

Distributed representations [Hinton *et al.*, 1986], on the other hand, do not use individual units to represent concepts; they use patterns of activations over many units. We have already seen one example of how this works: A Hopfield network provides a distributed representation for a content-addressable memory, in which each structure is stored as a collection of active units. One might be tempted to say that digital computers also use distributed representations. After all, a small integer is stored in a distributed fashion, as a pattern of activation over eight storage locations, each of which represents one bit of data. An extreme localist approach, on the other hand, would be to use 256 bits per integer, only one of which could be active at any given time. However, besides storing objects as patterns across many units, distributed representations have another important property, namely that stored objects may be superimposed on one another. One set of units can thus store many different objects. It is clearly impossible to store two 8-bit integers in one 8-bit place-holder, so we do not view such an encoding as a truly distributed representation.

Distributed representations have several advantages over localist ones. For one thing, they are more resistant to damage. If NETL loses its "elephant" unit somehow, then it immediately loses all ability to reason or remember about elephants. This fragility is undesirable if our goal is to build very large systems from unreliable parts. Also, it does not conform to what we know about human and animal memory. Lashley [1929] performed a number of classic experiments concerning memories in rats. Lashley wanted to find out in which part of its brain a rat stores its knowledge of how to run a particular maze. In the experiments, rats' brains were lesioned in many different places. Performance degraded in all rats in proportion to the size of the lesion, but the location of the lesion had no special effect on performance. Lashley concluded that the memory of how to run the maze was somehow stored in a distributed fashion across the entire rat cortex. Such a memory organization has been described using a hologram metaphor, in reference to the holographic storage medium, which allows the reconstruction of the entire image from just a portion of the recording (although the reconstructed image may be of poorer quality than the original). Work on distributed representations brings this metaphor down to an implementational level.

In addition to being more robust than localist representations, distributed representations can also be more efficient. Consider the problem of describing the locations of objects on a two-dimensional 8 by 8 grid [Hinton *et al.*, 1986]. In a symbolic implemen-

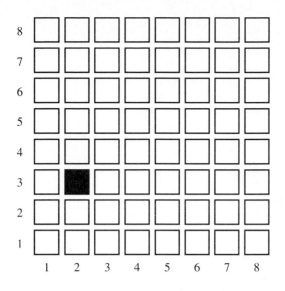

Figure 18.24: A Localist Representation of Location (2 3) on an 8 by 8 Grid

tation, this task is easy: A location can be stored simply as a list of two numbers, e.g., (2 3). Multiple object locations can be stored easily in this notation, as a list of lists: ((2 3) (6 5) (7 1)). How can we accomplish the same task with neuronlike units? The localist approach is to maintain an array of sixty-four units, one unit for every possible location (see Figure 18.24). A more efficient approach would be to use a group of eight units for the x-axis and another group of eight units for the y-axis, as in Figure 18.25. To represent the location (2 3), we activate two units: the second unit of the x-axis group and the third unit of the y-axis group. The other 14 units remain inactive. This method is not very damage resistant, however, and it will not support the representation of multiple object locations. To represent both (2 3) and (6 5) would require turning on two x-axis units and two y-axis units. But then we get the following *binding problem*: it is impossible to tell which of the four x-y pairs (2 3), (2 5), (6 3), and (6 5) correspond to actual object locations.

There is a distributed representation for solving this problem—it is called *coarse coding*. In coarse coding, we divide the space of possible object locations into a number of large, overlapping, circular zones. See, for example, Figure 18.26, in which units are depicted as small dots and their receptive fields as large circles. A unit becomes active if any object is located within its receptive field. There is a unit associated with each zone—the zone is called the unit's *receptive field*.[14] Whenever an object is located in a unit's receptive field, the unit becomes active. By looking at a single active unit, we cannot tell with any accuracy where an object is located, but by looking at the pattern of activity across all the units, we can actually be quite precise. Consider that the intersection of several circular zones associated with a group of units may be a

---

[14]The term *receptive field* comes from the study of vision. A receptive field of a retinal cell is an area of the retina that the cell is responsible for. The cell is triggered by light in that area.

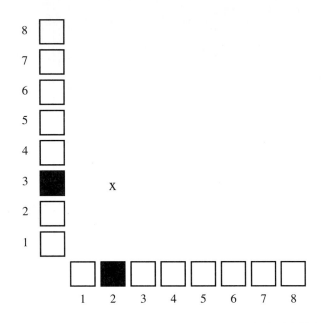

Figure 18.25: A More Efficient Representation, Requiring Only 16 Units, but Unable to Store Multiple Locations

very small area—if only those units are active, we can be fairly precise about where the object is located. In fact, as the receptive fields become larger, i.e., as the individual units become *less* discriminating about object locations, the whole representation becomes *more* accurate, because the regions of intersection become smaller. In the end, we can represent multiple objects with some precision without paying the price of the localist representation scheme.

One drawback to distributed representations is that they cannot store many densely packed objects. A localist or symbolic system could easily represent the three distinct objects at (4 4), (4 5), and (5 4), but a distributed scheme would be confounded by the loss of information caused by the effect of many objects on a single unit's receptive field. On the other hand, psychological experiments have shown that a similar *interference effect* is very likely a cause of forgetting in human memory [Gleitman, 1981]. A more serious deficiency concerning distributed representations lies in the difficulty of interpreting, acquiring, and modifying them by hand. Thus, they are usually used in conjunction with automatic learning mechanisms of the type discussed in Section 18.2.

18.6   Connectionist AI and Symbolic AI

The connectionist approach to AI is quite different from the traditional symbolic approach. Both approaches are certainly joined at the problem; both try to address difficult issues in search, knowledge representation, and learning. Let's list some of the methods used by both:

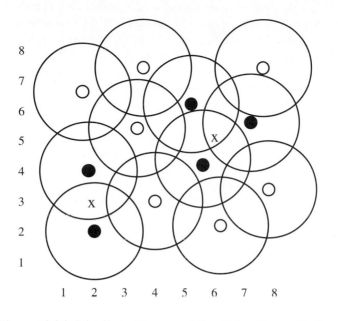

Figure 18.26: Distributed Representation Using Coarse Coding

1. Connectionist

   - Search—Parallel relaxation.
   - Knowledge Representation—Very large number of real-valued connection strengths. Structures often stored as distributed patterns of activation.
   - Learning—Backpropagation, Boltzmann machines, reinforcement learning, unsupervised learning.

2. Symbolic

   - Search—State space traversal.
   - Knowledge Representation—Predicate logic, semantic networks, frames, scripts.
   - Learning—Macro-operators, version spaces, explanation-based learning, discovery.

The approaches have different strengths and weaknesses. One major allure of connectionist systems is that they employ knowledge representations that seem to be more learnable than their symbolic counterparts. Nearly all connectionist systems have a strong learning component. However, neural network learning algorithms usually involve a large number of training examples and long training periods compared to their symbolic cousins. Also, after a network has learned to perform a difficult task, its knowledge is usually quite opaque, an impenetrable mass of connection weights. Getting the network to explain its reasoning, then, is difficult. Of course, this may not be a bad thing. Humans, for example, appear to have little access to the procedures they use for many tasks such as speech recognition and vision. It is no accident that the most promising uses for neural networks are in these areas of low-level perception.

Connectionist knowledge representation offers other advantages besides learnability. Touretzky and Geva [1987] discuss the fluidity and richness of connectionist representations. In connectionist models, concepts are represented as feature vectors, sets of activation values over groups of units. Similar concepts are given similar feature vector representations. In symbolic models, on the other hand, concepts are usually given atomic labels that bear no surface relation to each other, such as *Car* and *Porsche*. Links (like *isa*) are used to describe relationships between concepts. When the relationships become more fuzzy than *isa*, however, symbolic systems have difficulty doing matching. For example, consider the phrases "mouth of a bird" and "nose of a bird." People have no trouble mapping these phrases onto the concept *Beak*. A connectionist system could perform this fuzzy match by considering that *Nose*, *Mouth*, and *Beak* have similar feature value representations. Moreover, symbolic systems do not handle multiple, related shades of meaning very well. Consider the sentence, "The newspaper changed its format." Usually, the word "newspaper" is interpreted either as (1) something made of black and white paper or (2) a group of people in charge of producing a daily periodical. In the sentence above, however, it is impossible to choose between the two readings. In symbolic systems, different word senses are represented as independent atomic objects. Connectionist models offer several ways of maintaining multiple meanings: the simultaneous activations of different units (localist), the superposition of activity patterns (distributed), and the choice of intermediate feature vectors. The third method involves choosing a representation that shares some features of one meaning and some feature of another, but the intermediate representation itself has no single, corresponding symbolic concept.

A major part of this book has been devoted to the study of search in symbolic systems. It is difficult to see how connectionist systems will tackle difficult problems that state-space search addresses (e.g., chess, theorem-proving, and planning). Parallel relaxation search, however, does have some advantages over symbolic search. First of all, it maps naturally onto highly parallel hardware. When such hardware becomes widely available, parallel relaxation methods will be extremely efficient. More importantly, parallel relaxation search may prove even more efficient because it makes use of states that have no analogues in symbolic search. We saw this phenomenon briefly in Section 18.3.3 when we considered a Hopfield network that comes up with short traveling salesman tours. In the process of settling into a solution state, the network enters and exits many "impossible" states, such as ones in which a city is visited twice, or ones in which the traveler is in two places at the same time. Eventually, a valid solution state falls out of the relaxation process. In contrast, a symbolic system can only expand new search nodes that correspond to valid, possible states of the world.

A good deal of connectionist research concerns itself with modeling human mental processes. Neural networks seem to display many psychologically and biologically plausible features such as content-addressable memory, fault tolerance, distributed representations, and automatic generalization. Can we integrate these desirable properties into symbolic AI systems? Certainly, high-level theories of cognition can incorporate such features as new psychological primitives. Practically speaking, we may want to use connectionist architectures for low-level tasks such as vision, speech recognition, and memory, feeding results from these modules into symbolic AI programs. Another idea is to take a symbolic notion and implement it in a connectionist framework. Touretzky and Hinton [1988] describe a connectionist production system, and Derthick [1988] describes a connectionist semantic network.

A third idea is to program a symbolic system with the basic principles that are necessary to perform a task and then use the symbolic system to guide the performance of a neural network, which refines its behavior as it acquires experience. An example of this approach is described by Handelman *et al.* [1989], who describe a robot arm that can throw a ball at a target. Initially, a symbolic system guides the behavior of the arm. Each throw produces a training case, which is fed to a neural network. The symbolic system monitors the progress of the network, which is acquiring the fine motor control that the symbolic system lacks. When the network's behavior exceeds a set criterion, control of the arm is turned over to it.

Ultimately, connectionists would like to see symbolic structures "emerge" naturally from complex interactions among simple units, in the same way that "wetness" emerges from the combination of hydrogen and oxygen, although it is an intrinsic property of neither.

Most of the promising advantages of connectionist systems described in this section are just that: promising. A great deal of work remains to be done to turn these promises into results. Only time will tell how influential connectionist models will be in the evolution of AI research. In any case, connectionists can at least point to the brain as an existence proof that neural networks, in some form, are capable of exhibiting intelligent behavior.

18.7   Exercises

1. Consider a Hopfield net with the symmetric, weighted connections of Figure 18.1. If all the units are initially active, which of the four states in Figure 18.2 will the network settle into?

2. Implement the fixed-increment perceptron learning algorithm. Invent a three-feature linearly separable classification problem on which to test your program.

3. Implement the backpropagation learning algorithm for a fully connected three-layer network. Be sure to include parameters for layer sizes, learning rate (η), and number of training epochs. Test your implementation first on the OR problem:

Input Vector	Target Output Vector
(0.0, 0.0)	(0.1)
(0.0, 1.0)	(0.9)
(1.0, 0.0)	(0.9)
(1.0, 1.0)	(0.9)

Then on the XOR problem:

Input Vector	Target Output Vector
(0.0, 0.0)	(0.1)
(0.0, 1.0)	(0.9)
(1.0, 0.0)	(0.9)
(1.0, 1.0)	(0.1)

Initially, use two hidden units, set $\eta = 0.35$, and run for 6000 training epochs. (Each epoch consists of forward and backward propagation of each of the four training examples.) Modify your program to use the momentum factor $\alpha = 0.9$. Did adding momentum significantly decrease the number of training epochs required for learning?

4. Here is a toy problem for testing generalization in networks. Suppose that there are eight political issues on which every political party must decide, and suppose further that those decisions are binary (for example, to legalize gambling or not, to increase military spending or not, etc.). We can then represent the platform of a political party as a vector of eight ones and zeros. Individuals who belong to political parties may have beliefs that differ slightly from their party's platform. Your job is to train a backpropagation network to compute the political platform of the party that most closely matches a given individual's beliefs.

Generate four random 8-bit vectors to represent the platforms of four political parties. For each party, generate nine individuals who belong to that party. The beliefs of an individual, like those of a party, are represented as an 8-bit vector. One of the nine individuals should agree entirely with the party platform, and the other eight should differ on exactly one issue (1 bit). Now generate 36 input-output pairs, by juxtaposing individuals with the platforms of their respective political parties. Each input is 8 bits, and each output is 8 bits.

Input Vector	Target Output Vector
$individual_1$	$party_1$
$individual_2$	$party_1$
. . .	. . .
$individual_9$	$party_1$
$individual_{10}$	$party_2$
$individual_{11}$	$party_2$
. . .	. . .
$individual_{18}$	$party_2$
. . .	. . .
. . .	. . .
$individual_{36}$	$party_4$

Next, remove five of the input-output pairs. These five will make up the "testing set"; the other 31 will make up the "training set." Create a backpropagation network with eight input units, eight hidden units, and eight output units. Train the network on the 31 vectors in the training set until performance is very high. Now test the network on the five input-output pairs it has never seen before. How well does it perform? Experiment with the different sizes of testing and training sets, as well as hidden layers of different sizes. Finally, how does the network perform when given individuals whose beliefs are not so close to one of the four parties?

5. Many people consider connectionism to be irrelevant to AI, because it studies intelligence at such a low level. They argue that intelligence should be modeled at a higher, more abstract level. They often relate connectionism to symbolic AI with a software metaphor that runs: "If you want to study the behavior of a complex LISP program, then you should inspect its input and outputs, its functions, its data, its general flow of control, but you should not be concerned about the particular hardware the program happens to be running on. The same goes for the study of intelligence." Read both Broadbent [1985] and Rumelhart and McClelland [1986b], and comment on this line of reasoning.

6. In contrast to those who view connectionism merely as an implementational theory, others believe that connectionist models are too abstract and that we should look more closely at the organization of the brain for clues about how to organize artificial networks. Consider the following facts about the brain [Crick and Asanuma, 1986; Rosenzweig and Leiman, 1982], and comment on how they might affect current connectionist models of memory, learning, and problem solving:

   - Neurons excite and inhibit one another, but an individual neuron is either purely excitatory or purely inhibitory. Neuron A cannot excite neuron B while inhibiting neuron C.

   - Neurons communicate through their firing rates, which range from a few spikes per second to perhaps 500 spikes per second. Neuron firing is asynchronous; there appears to be no global clock. There are two types of neural summation: (1) spatial summation, in which the effects of various connecting neurons are added together and (2) temporal summation, in which asynchronously arriving impulses are likely to cause a neuron to fire when they all arrive closely together in time. As a corollary of (2), one neuron can have a very great effect on another by firing very rapidly.

   - Some behavioral functions, such as vision and language, appear to be localized in the brain. Destruction of small portions of the brain can result in the complete inability to perform certain cognitive tasks.

   - The human brain has at least 150 billion neurons and probably 1000 to 10,000 connections per neuron. The brain of a rat is 700 times smaller. The proportion of the brain taken up by the cortex is much larger in humans than in rats.

   - Neurons are not connected symmetrically: if the axon of neuron A leads to neuron B, then the axon of neuron B probably does not lead back to neuron A.

   - There are many different types of neurons. Some types do not project out of their local area of the brain, while the axons of other types travel long distances.

7. *Life* is a one-player game invented by John Conway. The game is played on an infinite two-dimensional grid of square cells. At any given time, a cell is either living or dead. Patterns of cells transform themselves according to a simple set of rules:

   - If a cell is living, it continues to live if surrounded by exactly two or three living cells. If it is surrounded by more than three living cells, it dies of overcrowding; if less than two of its neighbors is alive, it dies of loneliness.

   - If a cell is dead, it becomes living only if it is surrounded by exactly three living cells. Otherwise, it remains dead.

   For example:

   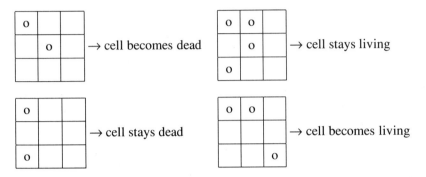

   (a) Create input-output pairs for every possible configuration of a cell and its eight neighbors. There will be 512 (2^9) different input vectors. Associated with each input vector will be one output bit: 0 if the next state of the cell is dead, 1 if living. Use the rules above to compute the proper output for each input vector.

   (b) Train a three-layer backpropagation network to learn the behavior of a Life cell. Use two hidden units.

   (c) Print out the set of weights and biases learned by the network. Now derive a set of (symbolic) rules that concisely describes how the network is actually computing its output. Focus on the behaviors of the two hidden units—how do they respond to their inputs, and what effects do they have on the eventual output?

   (d) Compare the rules you derived in part (c) with the rules you used to create the data in part (a).

Chapter 19

Common Sense

Computers have an entirely deserved reputation for lacking common sense. Anyone who has ever received a bill for $0.00 from an accounting program can attest to this fact. An AI program may possess more knowledge than an accounting program, but it still computes using primitives that it knows nothing about. For example, consider the following interaction between a medical diagnosis system and a human (adapted from Lenat and Guha [1990]):

> *System*: How old is the patient?
> *Human (looking at his 1957 Chevrolet)*: 33.
> *System*: Are there any spots on the patient's body?
> *Human (noticing rust spots)*: Yes.
> *System*: What color are the spots?
> *Human*: Reddish-brown.
> *System*. The patient has measles (probability 0.9).

Obviously, the system does not really know what measles are, what spots are, or what the difference between cars and people is. Even within its specialty, the system is unaware of fundamental facts, for example, that humans have two arms. Clearly, what the system lacks is knowledge. So far in this book, we have seen a number of techniques that can be used to enable an AI program to represent and reason with commonsense knowledge. For example, in predicate logic, one can state facts such as "if you die, you are dead at all later times." Frames can describe everyday objects, and scripts can describe the typical sequences of events. Nonmonotonic logics can support default reasoning, an important aspect of common sense.

As of yet, however, no program can match the commonsense reasoning powers of a five-year-old child. This is due, in part, to the large amount of knowledge required for common sense. In Section 10.3, we discussed the CYC program, one attempt to codify this information in a large knowledge base. In this chapter, we look more closely at the kinds of knowledge such a system must possess. In particular, we investigate how to understand and predict physical processes, how to model the behavior of materials, and how to reason about time and space. Memory is another key aspect to common sense. We look at how a memory can organize experiences, generalize them, and use them to solve new problems.

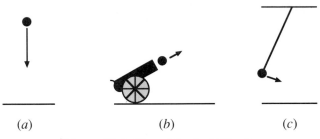

(a) (b) (c)

Figure 19.1: Three Physical Situations

19.1   Qualitative Physics

People know a great deal about the how the physical world works. Consider the three situations shown in Figure 19.1.

Anyone can predict what will happen in these scenarios. In situation (a), the ball will probably bounce on the ground several times, then come to rest. In situation (b), the ball will travel upward and to the right, then downward. In situation (c), the ball will swing repeatedly from left to right, finally coming to rest in the middle. Now, how can we build a computer program to do this kind of reasoning?

The obvious answer is to program in the equations governing the physical motion of objects. These equations date back to classical physics and appear in every introductory physics textbook. For example, if the initial velocity of the ball in Figure 19.1(b) is v_0, and the angle of its departure from the ground is θ, then the ball's position t seconds after being launched is given by:

$$
\begin{aligned}
\textit{height} &= v_0 \cdot t \cdot \sin(\theta) - \tfrac{1}{2}gt^2 \\
\textit{distance} &= v_0 \cdot t \cdot \cos(\theta)
\end{aligned}
$$

We can do the same thing for Figures 19.1(a) and (c). For Figure 19.1(a), we need to know the coefficient of elasticity, and for Figure 19.1(c), we need to know the length of the string, the initial velocity of the ball, and its original horizontal displacement.

There are two problems with this approach. First, most people do not know these equations, yet they are perfectly capable of predicting what will happen in physical situations. Also, unlike equations, people do not need exact, numerical measures. They need only *qualitative* descriptions, such as the ones given at the beginning of this section. People seem to reason more abstractly than the equations would indicate. The goal of qualitative physics is to understand how to build and reason with abstract, numberless representations.

One might object to qualitative physics on the grounds that computers are actually well-suited to model physical processes with numerical equations. After all, a computer's ability to solve simultaneous equations far outstrips that of a human. However, we cannot escape common sense so easily. Equations themselves say nothing about when they should be used; this is usually left up to a human physicist. The common-sense knowledge employed by the physicist is part of what we must model. While some sort of qualitative physics seems necessary for automating the solution of physics problems, it is not sufficient by itself. The goal of qualitative physics is not to replace traditional physics but rather to provide a foundation for programs that can reason about the physical world. One such program might be a physics expert system.

As a further illustration of the need for qualitative models, consider a scene in which a glass of water leans precariously against a book on top of a cluttered desk. When the book is moved, the glass begins to tip over. At present, no set of differential equations can accurately model exactly how the spilling water will flow across the desk. Even if such a model existed, it would be impossible to measure the initial conditions accurately enough to make an accurate prediction. Yet anyone in this situation can immediately visualize what is likely to happen and take rapid action to prevent it.

19.1.1 Representing Qualitative Information

Qualitative physics seeks to understand physical processes by building models of them. A model is an abstract representation that eliminates irrelevant details. For example, if we want to predict the motion of a ball, we may want to consider its mass and velocity, but probably not its color. Traditional physical models are built up from real-valued variables, rates of change, expressions, equations, and states. Qualitative physics provides similar building blocks, ones which are more abstract and nonnumeric.

- Variables—In traditional physics, real-valued variables are used to represent features of objects, such as position, velocity, angle, and temperature. Qualitative physics retains this notion, but restricts each variable to a small finite set of possible values. For example, the amount of water in a pot might be represented as one of {*empty, between, full*}, and its temperature as {*frozen, between, boiling*}.

- Quantity Spaces—A small set of discrete values for a variable is called a *quantity space*. The elements of a quantity space are usually ordered with respect to each other so that one value can be said to be smaller than another.[1]

- Rates of Change—Variables take on different values at different times. A real-valued rate of change (dx/dt) can be modeled qualitatively with the quantity space {*decreasing, steady, increasing*}.

- Expressions—Variables can be combined to form expressions. Consider representing the volume of water in a glass as {*empty, between, full*}. If we pour the contents of one glass into another, how much water will the second glass contain? We can add two qualitative values with the following chart:

  empty + empty = empty
  empty + between = between
  empty + full = full
  between + between = {between, full}
  between + full = full + overflow
  full + full = full + overflow

  Notice that qualitative addition differs from its quantitative counterpart, in part because the result of qualitative addition may be ambiguous. For example, if both

---

[1] In some variations [Raiman, 1986], it is possible to state that one value is *much* larger than another, or that two values are unequal but very close to one another.

glasses are between empty and full, it is impossible to know whether combining them will result in a full glass or not.

- Equations—Expressions and variables can be linked to one another via equations. The simplest equation states that variable x increases as variable y increases. This gives us an abstract representation of the actual function relating x and y (it may be linear, quadratic, or logarithmic, for example).

- States—Traditional physics models a process as a set of variables whose values evolve over time. A state is a single snapshot in which each variable possesses one value. Within qualitative physics, there are several different ways of formulating state information. One idea [de Kleer, 1979] is to combine qualitative state variables with symbolic descriptions. For example, the state of Figure 19.1(a) might be represented as (BALL-1, IN-AIR, DOWN). In order to predict the behavior of devices, de Kleer and Brown [1984] represent a state as a network of connected components. Forbus [1984] presents a state organization centered on processes and their influences.

19.1.2   Reasoning with Qualitative Information

No matter how states are represented, we need some way to reason about the information contained in them. A common reasoning method in qualitative physics is called *qualitative simulation* [Kuipers, 1986]. The idea is to construct a sequence of discrete "episodes" that occur as qualitative variables change values. States are linked to other states by qualitative rules. Some rules are very general. For example, one simulation rule states that variables reach closer values before reaching further ones, and another rule states that changing from one value to another consumes some finite amount of time. Other rules, such as the rules governing the motion of objects through the air, are more specific.

In systems that contain more than one object, rules must apply to all objects simultaneously. For example, consider an electrical device with many components. Because the components are connected, they influence one another. The constraint satisfaction technique (Chapters 3 and 14) is one efficient way of propagating a change in one component to other nearby components.

Since combining qualitative values can lead to ambiguity, a qualitative simulation must sometimes split into two or more possible paths. A network of all possible states and transitions for a qualitative system is called an *envisionment*. Figure 19.2 shows an envisionment of the bouncing ball system of Figure 19.1(a). This network allows a computer to reason about the behavior of the ball without recourse to numerical simulation. There are often many paths through an envisionment. Each path is called a *history*.

Envisionments are useful in a number of applications. Most importantly, envisionments provide explanations for physical systems, and those explanations can be used to predict future behavior. In addition, if a system is an artificial one, such as a mechanical device, envisionments can be used to diagnose problems that occur when components fail to behave correctly. Envisionments can also be used to represent and/or repair inaccurate mental models that people may have. For more information about envisionments and qualitative simulation, see Weld and de Kleer [1988].

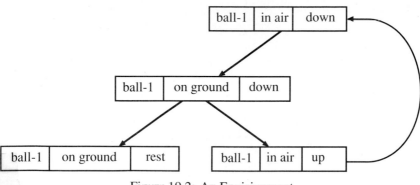

Figure 19.2: An Envisionment

In order to write programs that automatically construct envisionments, we must represent qualitative knowledge about the behavior of particular kinds of processes, substances, spaces, devices, and so on. In the next section, we look at how to codify some of this knowledge.

19.2 Commonsense Ontologies

A computer program that interacts with the real world must be able to reason about things like time, space, and materials. As fundamental and commonsensical as these concepts may be, modeling them turns out to present some thorny problems.

19.2.1 Time

While physicists and philosophers still debate the true nature of time, we all manage to get by on a few basic commonsense notions. These notions help us to decide when to initiate actions, how to reason about others' actions, and how to determine relationships between events. For instance, if we know that the Franco-Prussian War preceded World War I and that the Battle of Verdun occurred during World War I, then we can easily infer that the Battle of Verdun must have occurred sometime after the Franco-Prussian War. A commonsense theory of time must account for reasoning of this kind.

The most basic notion of time is that it is occupied by events. These events occur during intervals, continuous spaces of time. What kinds of things might we want to say about an interval? An interval has a starting point and an ending point, and a duration defined by these points. Intervals can be related to other intervals, as we saw in the last paragraph. It turns out that there are exactly thirteen ways in which two non-empty time intervals can relate to one another. Figure 19.3 shows these relationships. As is clear from the figure, there are actually only seven distinct relationships: the relationship of equality plus six other relationships that have their own inverses.

Now we can state rules for drawing inferences about time intervals. For example, common sense tells us that the IS-BEFORE relation is transitive. That is, if event a occurred before event b and if event b occurred before event c, then event a must have

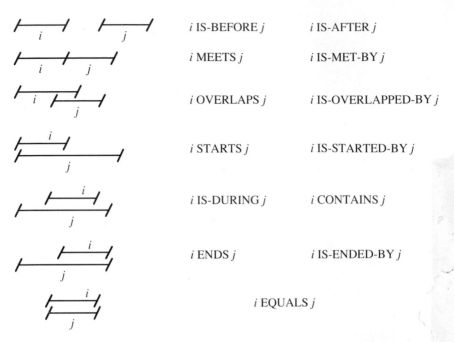

Figure 19.3: Thirteen Possible Relationships between Two Time Intervals

occurred before event c. How many such axioms will we need before we capture all of our basic commonsense notions of time? We can greatly simplify matters if we define some interval relationships in terms of other more basic ones. In fact, we can reduce all the relations in Figure 19.3 to the single relation MEETS. Here is the definition of the relation IS-BEFORE:

$$i \text{ IS-BEFORE } j \equiv \exists k : (i \text{ MEETS } k) \wedge (k \text{ MEETS } j)$$

In other words, if i IS-BEFORE j, then there must be some k in between that MEETS both i and j. When the rest of the relations are defined similarly, MEETS becomes the only primitive relation, and we can write all our commonsense axioms in terms of it. Our first axiom states that points where intervals MEET are unique:

$$\forall i, j : \quad (\exists k : (i \text{ MEETS } k) \wedge (j \text{ MEETS } k)) \rightarrow$$
$$(\forall l : (i \text{ MEETS } l) \leftrightarrow (j \text{ MEETS } l))$$

In other words, i and j cannot MEET k at different points in time, so every event has a unique starting time. We can write a similar axiom to state that every event has a unique ending time. Next, we state that given two places where intervals meet, exactly one of the following three conditions must hold: the places are the same, the first place precedes the second, or the second precedes the first.[2]

---

[2] In this formula $\oplus$ should be read as "exclusive-or." $p \oplus q \oplus r$ is logical shorthand for $(p \wedge \neg q \wedge \neg r) \vee (\neg p \wedge q \wedge \neg r) \vee (\neg p \wedge \neg q \wedge r)$.

$$\forall i, j, k, l: \quad (i \text{ MEETS } j) \wedge (k \text{ MEETS } l) \rightarrow$$
$$(i \text{ MEETS } l) \oplus$$
$$\exists m : (i \text{ MEETS } m) \wedge (m \text{ MEETS } l) \oplus$$
$$\exists m : (k \text{ MEETS } m) \wedge (m \text{ MEETS } j)$$

There are two more axioms. One states that there are always intervals surrounding any given interval. This axiom turns out to be useful, although it prohibits any reasoning about infinite time intervals.

$$\forall i : \exists j, k : (j \text{ MEETS } i) \wedge (i \text{ MEETS } k)$$

Finally, we can state that for any two intervals that MEET, there exists a continuous interval that is the union of the two:

$$\forall i, j: \quad (i \text{ MEETS } j) \rightarrow$$
$$\exists a, b, (i+j) :$$
$$(a \text{ MEETS } i) \wedge (j \text{ MEETS } b) \wedge$$
$$(a \text{ MEETS } (i+j)) \wedge ((i+j) \text{ MEETS } b)$$

These axioms encode a rich commonsense theory of time. They allow us to derive many facts, such as the transitivity of the IS-BEFORE relation. Suppose we know that a IS-BEFORE b and that b IS-BEFORE c. By the definition of IS-BEFORE, there must be some interval d that lies between a and b, i.e., a MEETS d and d MEETS b. By the union axiom, we can deduce the existence of an interval $(d + b)$ such that there is an x that MEETS $(d + b)$ and a y that IS-MET-BY $(d + b)$. By the uniqueness of starting points, we can conclude that a also meets $(d + b)$. Since b IS-BEFORE c, there must be an e between them. We can now construct another union interval $(d + b + e)$, which we can prove MEETS c and IS-MET-BY a. Therefore a IS-BEFORE c.

This may seem like a roundabout way of doing things, and it is. There is nothing in the axioms themselves that dictates how they should be used in real programs. In fact, efficient implementations represent all thirteen temporal relations explicitly, making use of precompiled tables that record how the relations can interact. Constraint satisfaction is a useful technique for making inferences about these relations [Kautz, 1986]. The logical statements above are just a concise way of writing down one particular commonsense theory of time.

19.2.2 Space

In this book, we have often used examples from the blocks world. Primitives in this world include block names, actions like PICKUP and STACK, and predicates like $ON(x, y)$. These primitives constitute a useful abstraction, but eventually we must break them down. If we want a real robot to achieve $ON(x, y)$, then that robot had better know what ON really means, where x and y are located, how big they are, how they are shaped, how to align x on top of y so that x won't fall off, and so forth. These requirements become more apparent if we want to issue commands like "place block x near block y" or "lean block x up against block y." Commonsense notions of space are critical for living in the real world.

Objects have spatial extent, while events have temporal extent. We might therefore try to expand our commonsense theory of time into a commonsense theory of space. Because space is three-dimensional, there are far more than thirteen possible spatial relationships between two objects. For instance, consider one block perfectly aligned on top of another. The objects are EQUAL in the length and width dimensions, while they MEET in the height dimension. If the top block is smaller than the bottom one but still centered on top of it, then they still MEET in the height dimension, but we must use the spatial equivalent of IS-DURING to describe the length and width relationships. The main problem with this approach is that it generates a vast number of relations (namely $13^3 = 2197$), many of which are not very commonsensical. Moreover, a number of interesting spatial relations, such as "x curves around y," are not included. So we must consider another approach.

In our discussion of qualitative physics, we saw how to build abstract models by transforming real-valued variables into discrete quantity spaces. We can also view objects and spaces at various levels of abstraction. For instance, we can view a three-dimensional piece of paper as a two-dimensional sheet; similarly, we can view a three-dimensional highway as a one-dimensional curve. Hobbs [1985] proposed one very general mechanism for creating and manipulating abstract models. With this mechanism, we start out with a full-blown theory of the world, and then we construct a simpler, more abstract model by extracting a set of *relevant properties*. We then group objects into classes whose members are indistinguishable from each other as far as their relevant properties go. For example, as we drive along a highway, our major relevant property might be DISTANCE-TO-GOAL. This property effectively reduces the bits of concrete in the three-dimensional highway into a one-dimensional curve, where each point on the curve has a unique DISTANCE-TO-GOAL value. In a similar fashion, we can map real time intervals onto discrete time steps, spatial coordinates onto a two-dimensional grid, and so on. Choosing a set of relevant properties amounts to viewing the world at a particular level of *granularity*. Since different granularities are systematically related to each other, we can reason in a simplified model with relative assurance that our actions will be implementable in the real world.

The idea of granularity can be used to build a commonsense model of space [Kautz, 1985]. The basic idea is to define relations over spaces. The first relation is INSIDE(x, y, g), where x and y are spaces occupied by particular objects and g is the level of granularity at which those objects are viewed. For example, water is INSIDE a glass if the three-dimensional space taken up by the water is completely contained within the three-dimensional space taken up by the glass. If we view a highway as a three-dimensional slab of concrete, then a car driving along the highway would be considered ADJACENT to the highway, but not INSIDE of it. However, if some granularity g views the highway as a one-dimensional curve, then the relation INSIDE(*Car, Highway, g*) holds for as long as the car stays on the road. This is because the car and its position on the road are indistinguishable at that level of granularity.

We can now define a number of useful properties for curves, lines, surfaces, planes, and volumes. For example, here is the definition of a terminal point p of a curve c:

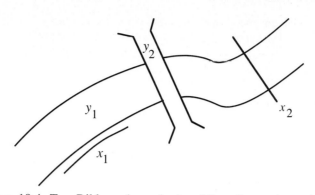

Figure 19.4: Two Ribbons (y_1 and y_2) and Two Curves (x_1 and x_2)

$$\text{TERMINAL}(p, c) \equiv$$
$$\text{INSIDE}(p, c) \wedge$$
$$\forall c_1, c_2 : \text{INSIDE}(c_1, c) \wedge \text{INSIDE}(c_2, c)$$
$$\wedge \text{INSIDE}(p, c_1) \wedge \text{INSIDE}(p, c_2)$$
$$\rightarrow \text{INSIDE}(c_1, c_2) \vee \text{INSIDE}(c_2, c_1)$$

In other words, p is a TERMINAL of c if, whenever two subcurves of c both include p, one must be a subcurve of the other. We can similarly define curve segments, adjoining curves, loops, and forks. Another useful class to define is that of a RIBBON:

$$\text{RIBBON}(object, side_1, side_2)$$

A ribbon is essentially a curve viewed at a coarser level of granularity, resulting in a two dimensional ribbonlike shape. Our world contains many objects that are usefully viewed as ribbons, e.g., rivers and bridges (Figure 19.4). We can define several properties of curves as they relate to ribbons. For example,

$$\text{ALONG}(x, y) \quad \equiv \quad \text{CURVE}(x) \wedge \text{RIBBON}(y, s_1, s_2) \wedge$$
$$\forall z : \text{INSIDE}(z, x) \rightarrow \text{ADJACENT}(z, y)$$

$$\text{ACROSS}(x, y) \quad \equiv \quad \text{CURVE}(x) \wedge \text{RIBBON}(y, s_1, s_2) \wedge$$
$$\text{PERPENDICULAR}(x, \text{AXIS}(y, s_1, s_2)) \wedge$$
$$\text{ADJACENT}(x, y) \wedge \text{ADJACENT}(x, s_1) \wedge$$
$$\text{ADJACENT}(x, s_2)$$

These definitions assume that we have defined the terms PERPENDICULAR, AXIS, and ADJACENT, and that we have supplied the commonsense axiom that an object x is ADJACENT to an object y if any part of x is ADJACENT to y.

A robot could use the ALONG relation to plot a course down the river's edge. It could similarly use the ACROSS relation to navigate to the other side of the river. Unfortunately, the ACROSS relation is not enough, as the robot might try to cross the river without using the bridge. The robot is still missing one fact: you can't walk on water. That's common sense.

19.2.3   Materials

Why can't you walk on water? What happens if you turn a glass of water upside down? What happens when you pour water into the soil of a potted plant?

Liquids present a particularly interesting and challenging domain to formalize. Hayes [1985] presented one attempt to describe them. Before we can write down any properties of liquids, we must decide what kinds of objects those properties will describe. In the last section, we defined spatial relations in terms of the spaces occupied by objects, not in terms of the objects themselves. It is particularly useful to take this point of view with liquids, since liquid "objects" can be split and merged so easily. For example, if we consider a river to be a piece of liquid, then what happens to the river when the liquid flows out into the ocean? Instead of continually changing our characterization of the river, it is more convenient to view the river as a fixed space occupied by water.

Containers play an important role in the world of liquids. Since we do not want to refer to liquid objects, we must have another way of stating how much liquid is in a container. We can define a CAPACITY function to bound the amount of liquid l that a space s can hold. The space is FULL when the AMOUNT equals the CAPACITY.

$$\text{CAPACITY}(s) \geq \text{AMOUNT}(l, s) > \text{none}$$
$$\text{FULL}(s) \equiv \text{AMOUNT}(l, s) = \text{CAPACITY}(s)$$

We can also define an AMOUNT function:

$$\text{AMOUNT}(Water, Glass) > \text{none}$$

This statement means, "There is water in the glass." Here, *Water* refers to the generic concept of water and *Glass* refers to the space enclosed by a particular glass.

Spaces have a number of other properties besides CAPACITY and FULL. Recall that spaces can be linked to one another by the INSIDE relation. In addition, a space can be *free* or not. A space is free if it is not wholly contained inside a solid object. In addition, every space is bounded on all sides by a set of two-dimensional regions, called *faces*. If a free face (one not part of a solid object) separates two free spaces, it is called a *portal*. Liquids can flow from one free space to another via a portal. Two objects are said to be *joined* if they share a common face. To summarize:

$$\text{FREE}(s) \equiv \neg \exists o : \text{SOLID}(o) \wedge \text{INSIDE}(s, o)$$
$$\text{FACE}(f, s) \equiv f \text{ is some 2-D bounding region of } s$$
$$\text{PORTAL}(f) \equiv \exists s_1, s_2 : \text{FACE}(f, s_1) \wedge \text{FACE}(f, s_2) \wedge$$
$$\text{FREE}(s_1) \wedge \text{FREE}(s_2) \wedge \text{FREE}(f)$$
$$\text{JOINED}(o_1, o_2, f) \equiv \text{FACE}(f, o_1) \wedge \text{FACE}(f, o_2)$$

We can now define a closed container as a hollow object with no portals:

$$\text{CLOSED-CONTAINER}(c) \equiv$$
$$(\exists s : \text{INSIDE}(s, c) \wedge \text{FREE}(s)) \wedge$$
$$(\neg \exists s, f : \text{INSIDE}(s, c) \wedge \text{JOINED}(s, c, f) \wedge \neg \text{PORTAL}(f))$$

An open container has (at least) one portal at the top:

OPEN-CONTAINER$(c) \equiv$
  $(\exists s : \text{INSIDE}(s, c) \wedge \text{FREE}(s)) \wedge$
  $(\forall s, f : \text{INSIDE}(s, c) \wedge \text{JOINED}(s, c, f) \rightarrow$
    $f = \text{TOP}(c) \wedge \neg \text{PORTAL}(f))$

Liquids make things wet. To model wetness, we will find it useful to imagine a solid object as being surrounded by a very thin free space. This space is broken up into a set of thin *outer* spaces corresponding to the various faces of the object. Objects that touch share these outer spaces.

SURROUND$(o) \equiv$ thin space surrounding object o
$\forall o : \text{FREE}(\text{SURROUND}(o))$
OUTER$(d, o) \equiv \exists f : \text{FACE}(f, o)$ and d is the thin free space just outside f
TOUCHING$(o_1, o_2) \equiv \exists d : \text{OUTER}(d, o_1) \wedge \text{OUTER}(d, o_2)$
$\forall d, o : \text{OUTER}(d, o) \rightarrow \text{INSIDE}(d, \text{SURROUND}(o))$
$\forall s, o : \text{FREE}(s) \wedge \text{INSIDE}(o, s) \rightarrow \text{INSIDE}(\text{SURROUND}(o), s)$

The last two facts state that SURROUND(o) contains all its outer spaces, and that any larger, free space containing object o also contains SURROUND(o). Now we can define wetness as a relation between an outer space d and some generic liquid l:

WET-BY$(d, l) \equiv \text{CAPACITY}(d) \geq \text{AMOUNT}(l, d) > none$
IS-WET$(o) \equiv \exists d, l : \text{OUTER}(d, o) \wedge \text{WET-BY}(d, l)$
IS-WET-ALL-OVER$(o) \equiv \forall d : \text{OUTER}(d, o) \rightarrow \exists l : \text{WET-BY}(d, l)$

Suppose our robot encounters a room with six inches of water on the floor. What will happen if the robot touches the floor? By the definition of TOUCHING, we have:

$\exists d_1 : \text{OUTER}(d_1, Robot) \wedge \text{OUTER}(d_1, Floor)$

Since the floor only has one face, d, we can conclude:

OUTER$(d, Robot) \wedge \text{OUTER}(d, Floor)$

Combining the first clause with the fact WET-BY$(d, Water)$ gives us IS-WET$(Robot)$. In other words, the robot will get wet. Recall that at the end of the last section, our robot was about to try crossing a river without using a bridge. It might find this fact useful:

INSIDE$(s_1, s_2) \wedge \text{FREE}(s_1) \wedge \text{FULL}(s_2, l) \rightarrow \text{FULL}(s_1, l)$

It is straightforward to show that if the robot is submerged, it will be wet all over. Predicting that the robot will become submerged in the first place requires some envisionment. We need a rule that says one dense solid object must be supported by another solid object, or else it will tend to move downward. One property of liquids is that they do not support dense solid objects.

We also need general rules describing how liquids themselves behave over time. Consider all the possible forms that a liquid may take at a given instant. Hayes [1985] distinguishes between "lazy, still" liquids, "lazy, moving" liquids and "energetic, moving" liquids. Energetic, moving liquids are liquids being propelled by some active force, for example, oil being pumped through a pipeline. Lazy liquids are liquids in their natural state. Sometimes they are moving, as in river water and rain, and sometimes they are still. Liquids in any of these forms can also be either bulk or divided. Most of the time we deal with bulk liquid, but sometimes we encounter mist, dew, or rain. Finally, liquids can be either unsupported, on a surface, or in a container.

What happens to these types of liquids? Figure 19.5 shows five envisionments for lazy, bulk liquids. A containment event can become a falling event if the container tips. The falling event becomes a wetting event and then a spreading one. Depending on where the spreading takes place, further falling or flowing events may ensue. When all the liquid has left the container, the spreading will stop, and sometime afterward, a drying event will begin.

Other materials behave differently. Solids can be rigid or flexible. A string can be used to pull an object but not to push it. Solids can also be particulate (like sand), in which case they share many of the same behaviors as liquids. Gases are also similar to liquids. Also, some solids soak up liquid (sponges, dirt), while others are watertight.

We can see that commonsense knowledge representation has a strongly taxonomic flavor. A lot of work has been done in these and other areas, but much more also remains to be worked out.

19.3 Memory Organization

Memory is central to commonsense behavior. Human memory contains an immense amount of knowledge about the world. So far, we have only discussed a tiny fraction of that knowledge. Memory is also the basis for learning. A system that cannot learn cannot, in practice, possess common sense.

A complete theory of human memory has not yet been discovered, but we do have a number of facts at our disposal. Some of these facts come from neurobiology (e.g., [Kandel and Schwartz, 1985]), while others are psychological in nature. Computer models of neural memory (such as the Hopfield network of Chapter 18) are interesting, but they do not serve as theories about how memory is used in everyday, commonsense reasoning. Psychology and AI seek to address these issues.

Psychological studies suggest several distinctions in human memory. One distinction is between short-term memory (STM) and long-term memory (LTM). We know that a person can only hold a few items at a time in STM, but the capacity of LTM is very large. LTM storage is also fairly permanent. The production system is one computer model of the STM-LTM structure. Perceptual information is stored directly in STM, also called working memory. Production rules, stored in LTM, match themselves against items in STM. Productions fire, modify STM, and repeat.

LTM is often divided into *episodic memory* and *semantic memory*. Episodic memory contains information about past personal experiences, usually stored from an autobiographical point of view. For example, a college graduation, a wedding, or a concert may all form episodic memories. Semantic memory, on the other hand, contains facts like "Birds fly." These facts are no longer connected with personal experiences.

Work on modeling semantic memory began with Quillian [1969]. This model soon

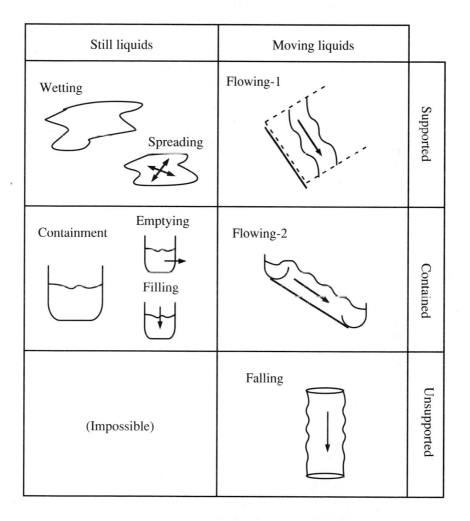

Figure 19.5: Five Envisionments for Lazy, Bulk Liquids

developed into the idea of semantic networks and from there into the other slot-and-filler structures we saw in Chapters 9 and 10. Semantic memory is especially useful in programs that understand natural language.

Models for episodic memory grew out of research on scripts. Recall that a script is a stereotyped sequence of events, such as those involved in going to the dentist. One obvious question to ask is: How are scripts acquired? Surely they are acquired through personal experience. But a particular experience often includes details that we do not want to include in a script. For example, just because we once saw *The New Yorker* magazine in a dentist's waiting room, that doesn't mean that *The New Yorker* should be part of the dentist script. The problem is that if a script contains too many details, it will not be matched and retrieved correctly when new, similar situations arise.

In general, it is difficult to know which script to retrieve (as we discussed in Section 4.3.5). One reason for this is that scripts are too monolithic. It is hard to do any kind of partial matching. It is also hard to modify a script. More recent work reduces scripts to individual *scenes*, which can be shared across multiple structures. Stereotypical sequences of scenes are strung together into memory organization packets (MOPs) [Schank, 1977]. Usually, three distinct MOPs encode knowledge about an event sequence. One MOP represents the physical sequence of events, such as entering a dentist's office, sitting in the waiting room, reading a magazine, sitting in the dentist's chair, etc. Another MOP represents the set of social events that take place. These are events that involve personal interactions. A third MOP revolves around the goals of the person in the particular episode. Any of these MOPs may be important for understanding new situations.

MOPs organize scenes, and they themselves are further organized into higher-level MOPs. For example, the MOP for visiting the office of a professional may contain a sequence of abstract general scenes, such as talking to an assistant, waiting, and meeting. High-level MOPs contain no actual memories, so where do they come from?

New MOPs are created upon the failure of expectations. When we use scripts for story understanding, we are able to locate interesting parts of the story by noticing places where events do not conform to the script's expectations. In a MOP-based system, if an expectation is repeatedly violated, then the MOP is generalized or split. Eventually, episodic memories can fade away, leaving only a set of generalized MOPs. These MOPs look something like scripts, except that they share scenes with one another.

Let's look at an example. The first time you go to the dentist, you must determine how things work from scratch since you have no prior experience. In doing so, you store detailed accounts of each scene and string them together into a MOP. The next time you visit the dentist, that MOP provides certain expectations, which are mostly met. You are able to deal with the situation easily and make inferences that you could not make the first time. If any expectation fails, this provides grounds for modifying the MOP. Now, suppose you later visit a doctor's office. As you begin to store episodic scenes, you notice similarities between these scenes and scenes from the dentist MOP. Such similarities provide a basis for using the dentist MOP to generate expectations. Multiple trips to the doctor will result in a doctor MOP that is slightly different from the dentist MOP. Later experiences with visiting lawyers and government officials will result in other MOPs. Ultimately, the structures shared by all of these MOPs will cause a generalized MOP to appear. Whenever you visit a professional's office in the future, you can use the generalized MOP to provide expectations.

With MOPs, memory is both a constructive and reconstructive process. It is constructive because new experiences create new memory structures. It is reconstructive because even if the details of a particular episode are lost, the MOP provides information about what was likely to have happened. The ability to do this kind of reconstruction is an important feature of human memory.

There are several MOP-based computer programs. CYRUS [Kolodner, 1984] is a program that contains episodes taken from the life of a particular individual. CYRUS can answer questions that require significant amounts of memory reconstruction. The IPP program [Lebowitz, 1983] accepts stories about terrorist attacks and stores them in an episodic memory. As it notices similarities in the stories, it creates general memory structures. These structures improve its ability to understand. MOPTRANS [Lytinen, 1984] uses a MOP-based memory to understand sentences in one language and translate them into another.

19.4 Case-Based Reasoning

We now turn to the role of memory in general problem solving. Most AI programs solve problems by reasoning from first principles. They can explain their reasoning by reporting the string of deductions that led from the input data to the conclusion. With human experts, however, we often observe a different type of explanation. An expert encountering a new problem is usually reminded of similar cases seen in the past, remembering the results of those cases and perhaps the reasoning behind those results. New problems are solved by analogy with old ones and the explanations are often couched in terms of prior experiences. Medical expertise, for example, seems to follow this pattern, and legal education is also case-oriented.

Computer systems that solve new problems by analogy with old ones are often called *case-based reasoning* (CBR) systems. A CBR system draws its power from a large case library, rather than from a set of first principles. In order to be successful, CBR systems must answer the following questions:

1. How are cases organized in memory?

2. How are relevant cases retrieved from memory?

3. How can previous cases be adapted to new problems?

4. How are cases originally acquired?

The memory structures we discussed in the previous section are clearly relevant to CBR. Those structures were used primarily in text understanding applications, however. Now we look at general memory-based problem solving.

To use a memory effectively, we must have a rich indexing mechanism. When we are presented with a problem, we should be reminded of relevant past experiences, but not be inundated with a lot of useless memories. The obvious idea is to index past episodes by the features present in them. For example, any experience having to do with a car would be filed under *Car*, as well as under other indices. But we must have some scheme for distinguishing important indices from unimportant ones. Otherwise, everything will remind us of everything else, and we will be unable to focus on memories that will best help us to solve our current problem. But important features are not always the most obvious ones. Here is an example from Schank [1977], called the "steak and haircut" story:

> X described how his wife would never cook his steak as rare as he liked it. When X told this to Y, Y was reminded of a time, 30 years earlier, when he tried to get his hair cut in England and the barber just wouldn't cut it as short as he wanted it.

Clearly, the indices *Steak*, *Wife*, and *Rare* are insufficient to remind Y of the barbershop episode. We need more general indices, such as *Provide-Service*, *Refusal*, and *Extreme*. Dyer [1983] also takes up this theme, embodied in a program that deduces adages and morals from narratives.

Some features are only important in certain contexts. For example, suppose it is cloudy. If your problem is to plan a picnic, you might want to retrieve other episodes involving cloudy days. But if your problem is to write a computer program, then the fact that it is cloudy is probably incidental. Because important features vary from domain to domain, a general CBR system must be able to learn a proper set of indices from experience. Both the inductive and explanation-based learning techniques described in Chapter 17 have been used for this task.

Recall that in our discussion of production systems, we talked about how rules and states could be organized into a RETE network for efficient matching. We also discussed matching frames and scripts in Section 4.3.5. Something similar is required for CBR, since the number of cases can be very large. The data structure for the case itself is also important. A case is usually stored as a monolithic structure, although in some variations, cases can be stored piecemeal. The former strategy is efficient when it is possible to obtain almost-perfect matches; the latter strategy is better in complex problem-solving domains.

The result of the retrieval process is usually a set of cases. The next step is to take the best case and adapt it to the current situation. One method for choosing the best case is the use of *preference heuristics* [Kolodner, 1989]. Here are some examples:

- Goal-Directed Preference—Prefer cases that involve the same goal as the current situation.

- Salient-Feature Preference—Prefer cases that match the most important features, or those that match the largest number of important features.

- Specificity Preference—Prefer cases that match features exactly over those that match features generally.

- Frequence Preference—Prefer frequently matched cases.

- Recency Preference—Prefer recently matched cases.

- Ease-of-Adaptation Preference—Prefer cases with features that are easily adapted to new situations.

Since even the best case will not match the current situation exactly, it will have to be adapted. At the simplest level, this involves mapping new objects onto old ones (e.g., *Steak* onto *Hair*, and *Rare* onto *Short*). When old cases represent entire problem-solving episodes, adaptation can be quite complex. CHEF [Hammond, 1986] is an example of a case-based planner, a program whose cases are actually complete plans for solving problems in the domain of cooking. CHEF's case library is augmented with a plan-modification library indexed by plan types and change types. CHEF first looks at the retrieved plan and sees if it satisfies the current goals. If any goal is unsatisfied, then the plan-modification library is consulted. The library may suggest a list of steps to be added to the plan, deleted from the plan, or substituted for existing steps. This modification process is not guaranteed to succeed, however, and so CHEF includes a plan repair module that uses domain knowledge to explain why the new plan fails, if it does. Once a complete, working plan is created, it is executed and then stored in the case library for future reference.

We have said nothing yet about how cases are acquired originally. In fact, most CBR systems draw on a small library of cases that are entered by hand. Of course, we will eventually be able to transform large bodies of on-line texts, such as legal cases, into large case libraries. Another approach is to bootstrap gradually from rule-based search into CBR. The idea is to start solving problems with a heuristic search engine. Each time a problem is solved, it is automatically stored in a case library. As the library grows, it becomes possible to solve some new problems by analogy with old ones. This idea is very similar to some of the learning techniques we saw in Section 17.4—the acquisition of search control rules, for example. This brings up the issue of whether it is better to store whole cases in memory or to store smaller bits of control knowledge instead. There are a number of trade-offs involved. First is the ease of modification. Central to case-based reasoning is the idea that stored cases can be adapted and modified. Search control rules are more procedural. Once learned, they are hard to modify. If a search control rule starts to perform badly, it is usually deleted in toto. Another trade-off involves indexing. Search control rules are fully indexed: they apply in exactly the situations to which they are relevant. Cases, on the other hand, are usually indexed heuristically, as we saw above. Finally, search control rules are explicitly generalized at storage time. In CBR, generalization occurs over time as a by-product of the retrieval and adaptation process. Aggressive generalization makes it easy to solve new problems quickly, but in less complete domains, where proper generalizations are unknown, an aggressive strategy can be inefficient and even incorrect.

19.5 Exercises

1. Consider a toy balloon hooked up to a bottle of compressed air. As the air is released, the balloon expands. Using qualitative measures, list the quantity spaces of variables and rates of change in this system. Construct an envisionment for the system, and write down one possible history.

2. Express all the temporal relations in Figure 19.3 in terms of the single relation MEETS.

3. Suppose you know the following facts:

- The Franco-Prussian War took place before World War I.
- The Battle of Verdun took place during World War I.

Convert these facts into logical statements in terms of the MEETS relation. Use the commonsense axioms of time given in Section 19.2.1 to show that the Franco-Prussian War must have occurred before the Battle of Verdun.

4. Using the axioms in Section 19.2.2, show that a robot submerged under water will be wet all over.

5. Case-based reasoning shares many of the same ideas of learning by analogy (Section 17.8). Briefly discuss how transformational and derivational analogy could apply in case-based reasoning systems.

6. Forgetting is one aspect of human memory that is not usually modeled in computer systems. Under what circumstances might a case-based reasoning system benefit from the ability to forget?

Chapter 20

Expert Systems

Expert systems solve problems (such as the ones in Figure 1.1) that are normally solved by human "experts." To solve expert-level problems, expert systems need access to a substantial domain knowledge base, which must be built as efficiently as possible. They also need to exploit one or more reasoning mechanisms to apply their knowledge to the problems they are given. Then they need a mechanism for explaining what they have done to the users who rely on them. One way to look at expert systems is that they represent applied AI in a very broad sense. They tend to lag several years behind research advances, but because they are tackling harder and harder problems, they will eventually be able to make use of all of the kinds of results that we have described throughout this book. So this chapter is in some ways a review of much of what we have already discussed.

The problems that expert systems deal with are highly diverse. There are some general issues that arise across these varying domains. But it also turns out that there are powerful techniques that can be defined for specific classes of problems. Recall that in Section 2.3.8 we introduced the notion of problem classification and we described some classes into which problems can be organized. Throughout this chapter we have occasion to return to this idea, and we see how some key problem characteristics play an important role in guiding the design of problem-solving systems. For example, it is now clear that tools that are developed to support one classification or diagnosis task are often useful for another, while different tools are useful for solving various kinds of design tasks.

20.1 Representing and Using Domain Knowledge

Expert systems are complex AI programs. Almost all the techniques that we described in Parts I and II have been exploited in at least one expert system. However, the most widely used way of representing domain knowledge in expert systems is as a set of production rules, which are often coupled with a frame system that defines the objects that occur in the rules. In Section 8.2, we saw one example of an expert system rule, which was taken from the MYCIN system. Let's look at a few additional examples drawn from some other representative expert systems. All the rules we show are English versions of the actual rules that the systems use. Differences among these rules illustrate some of the important differences in the ways that expert systems operate.

R1 [McDermott, 1982; McDermott, 1984] (sometimes also called XCON) is a program that configures DEC VAX systems. Its rules look like this:

```
If: the most current active context is distributing
        massbus devices, and
      there is a single-port disk drive that has not been
        assigned to a massbus, and
      there are no unassigned dual-port disk drives, and
        the number of devices that each massbus should
        support is known, and
      there is a massbus that has been assigned at least
        one disk drive and that should support additional
        disk drives,
      and the type of cable needed to connect the disk drive
        to the previous device on the massbus is known
then: assign the disk drive to the massbus.
```

Notice that R1's rules, unlike MYCIN's, contain no numeric measures of certainty. In the task domain with which R1 deals, it is possible to state exactly the correct thing to be done in each particular set of circumstances (although it may require a relatively complex set of antecedents to do so). One reason for this is that there exists a good deal of human expertise in this area. Another is that since R1 is doing a design task (in contrast to the diagnosis task performed by MYCIN), it is not necessary to consider all possible alternatives; one good one is enough. As a result, probabilistic information is not necessary in R1.

PROSPECTOR [Duda *et al.*, 1979; Hart *et al.*, 1978] is a program that provides advice on mineral exploration. Its rules look like this:

```
If: magnetite or pyrite in disseminated or veinlet form is
        present
then: (2, -4) there is favorable mineralization and texture
        for the propylitic stage.
```

In PROSPECTOR, each rule contains two confidence estimates. The first indicates the extent to which the presence of the evidence described in the condition part of the rule suggests the validity of the rule's conclusion. In the PROSPECTOR rule shown above, the number 2 indicates that the presence of the evidence is mildly encouraging. The second confidence estimate measures the extent to which the evidence is necessary to the validity of the conclusion, or stated another way, the extent to which the lack of the evidence indicates that the conclusion is not valid. In the example rule shown above, the number -4 indicates that the absence of the evidence is strongly discouraging for the conclusion.

DESIGN ADVISOR [Steele *et al.*, 1989] is a system that critiques chip designs. Its rules look like:

```
If: the sequential level count of ELEMENT is greater than 2,
      UNLESS the signal of ELEMENT is resetable
then: critique for poor resetability
```

```
DEFEAT: poor resetability of ELEMENT
due to: sequential level count of ELEMENT greater than 2
by: ELEMENT is directly resetable
```

The DESIGN ADVISOR gives advice to a chip designer, who can accept or reject the advice. If the advice is rejected, the system can exploit a justification-based truth maintenance system to revise its model of the circuit. The first rule shown here says that an element should be criticized for poor resetability if its sequential level count is greater than two, unless its signal is currently believed to be resetable. Resetability is a fairly common condition, so it is mentioned explicitly in this first rule. But there is also a much less common condition, called direct resetability. The DESIGN ADVISOR does not even bother to consider that condition unless it gets in trouble with its advice. At that point, it can exploit the second of the rules shown above. Specifically, if the chip designer rejects a critique about resetability and if that critique was based on a high level count, then the system will attempt to discover (possibly by asking the designer) whether the element is directly resetable. If it is, then the original rule is defeated and the conclusion withdrawn.

Reasoning with the Knowledge

As these example rules have shown, expert systems exploit many of the representation and reasoning mechanisms that we have discussed. Because these programs are usually written primarily as rule-based systems, forward chaining, backward chaining, or some combination of the two, is usually used. For example, MYCIN used backward chaining to discover what organisms were present; then it used forward chaining to reason from the organisms to a treatment regime. R1, on the other hand, used forward chaining. As the field of expert systems matures, more systems that exploit other kinds of reasoning mechanisms are being developed. The DESIGN ADVISOR is an example of such a system; in addition to exploiting rules, it makes extensive use of a justification-based truth maintenance system.

20.2 Expert System Shells

Initially, each expert system that was built was created from scratch, usually in LISP. But, after several systems had been built this way, it became clear that these systems often had a lot in common. In particular, since the systems were constructed as a set of declarative representations (mostly rules) combined with an interpreter for those representations, it was possible to separate the interpreter from the domain-specific knowledge and thus to create a system that could be used to construct new expert systems by adding new knowledge corresponding to the new problem domain. The resulting interpreters are called *shells*. One influential example of such a shell is EMYCIN (for Empty MYCIN) [Buchanan and Shortliffe, 1984], which was derived from MYCIN.

There are now several commercially available shells that serve as the basis for many of the expert systems currently being built. These shells provide much greater flexibility in representing knowledge and in reasoning with it than MYCIN did. They typically support rules, frames, truth maintenance systems, and a variety of other reasoning mechanisms.

Early expert system shells provided mechanisms for knowledge representation, reasoning, and explanation. Later, tools for knowledge acquisition were added, as we see in Section 20.4. But as experience with using these systems to solve real world problems grew, it became clear that expert system shells needed to do something else as well. They needed to make it easy to integrate expert systems with other kinds of programs. Expert systems cannot operate in a vacuum, any more than their human counterparts can. They need access to corporate databases, and access to them needs to be controlled just as it does for other systems. They are often embedded within larger application programs that use primarily conventional programming techniques. So one of the important features that a shell must provide is an easy-to-use interface between an expert system that is written with the shell and a larger, probably more conventional, programming environment.

20.3   Explanation

In order for an expert system to be an effective tool, people must be able to interact with it easily. To facilitate this interaction, the expert system must have the following two capabilities in addition to the ability to perform its underlying task:

- Explain its reasoning. In many of the domains in which expert systems operate, people will not accept results unless they have been convinced of the accuracy of the reasoning process that produced those results. This is particularly true, for example, in medicine, where a doctor must accept ultimate responsibility for a diagnosis, even if that diagnosis was arrived at with considerable help from a program. Thus it is important that the reasoning process used in such programs proceed in understandable steps and that enough meta-knowledge (knowledge about the reasoning process) be available so the explanations of those steps can be generated.

- Acquire new knowledge and modifications of old knowledge. Since expert systems derive their power from the richness of the knowledge bases they exploit, it is extremely important that those knowledge bases be as complete and as accurate as possible. But often there exists no standard codification of that knowledge; rather it exists only inside the heads of human experts. One way to get this knowledge into a program is through interaction with the human expert. Another way is to have the program learn expert behavior from raw data.

TEIRESIAS [Davis, 1982; Davis, 1977] was the first program to support explanation and knowledge acquisition. TEIRESIAS served as a front-end for the MYCIN expert system. A fragment of a TEIRESIAS-MYCIN conversation with a user (a doctor) is shown in Figure 20.1. The program has asked for a piece of information that it needs in order to continue its reasoning. The doctor wants to know why the program wants the information, and later asks how the program arrived at a conclusion that it claimed it had reached.

Is the patient's illness with ORGANISM-1 a hospital-acquired
infection?
** WHY
[i.e., WHY is it important to determine whether or not the
infection with ORGANISM-1 was acquired while the patient
was hospitalized?]
[2.0] This will aid in determining the category of
        ORGANISM-1. It has already been established that
 [2.1] the gram stain of ORGANISM-1 is gramneg, and
 [2.2] the morphology of ORGANISM-1 is rod, and
 [2.3] the aerobicity of ORGANISM-1 is facultative
       Therefore, if
 [2.4] the infection with ORGANISM-1 was not acquired
       while the patient was hospitalized, then
there is strongly suggestive evidence (.8) that the
category of ORGANISM-1 is enterobacteriaceae
[ALSO: there is weakly suggestive evidence (.1) that
the identity of ORGANISM-1 is pseudomonas-aeruginosa]
[RULE037]
** HOW [2.3]
[i.e., HOW was it established that the aerobicity of
ORGANISM-1 is facultative?]
The following were used:
 [3.1] RULE027 indicated there is strongly suggestive
       evidence (.8) that the aerobicity of ORGANISM-1
       is facultative.
 [3.2] RULE033 indicated there is weakly suggestive
       evidence (.2) that the aerobicity of ORGANISM-1
       is not facultative.
Since this gave a cumulative CF of (.6) for facultative,
the evidence indicates that the aerobicity of ORGANISM-1
is facultative.

Figure 20.1: A Portion of a Dialogue with TEIRESIAS

An important premise underlying TEIRESIAS's approach to explanation is that the behavior of a program can be explained simply by referring to a trace of the program's execution. There are ways in which this assumption limits the kinds of explanations that can be produced, but it does minimize the overhead involved in generating each explanation. To understand how TEIRESIAS generates explanations of MYCIN's behavior, we need to know how that behavior is structured.

MYCIN attempts to solve its goal of recommending a therapy for a particular patient by first finding the cause of the patient's illness. It uses its production rules to reason backward from goals to clinical observations. To solve the top-level diagnostic goal, it looks for rules whose right sides suggest diseases. It then uses the left sides of those rules (the preconditions) to set up subgoals whose success would enable the rules to be invoked. These subgoals are again matched against rules, and their preconditions are used to set up additional subgoals. Whenever a precondition describes a specific piece of clinical evidence, MYCIN uses that evidence if it already has access to it. Otherwise, it asks the user to provide the information. In order that MYCIN's requests for information will appear coherent to the user, the actual goals that MYCIN sets up are often more general than they need be to satisfy the preconditions of an individual rule. For example, if a precondition specifies that the identity of an organism is X, MYCIN will set up the goal "infer identity." This approach also means that if another rule mentions the organism's identity, no further work will be required, since the identity will be known.

We can now return to the trace of TEIRESIAS-MYCIN's behavior shown in Figure 20.1. The first question that the user asks is a "WHY" question, which is assumed to mean "Why do you need to know that?" Particularly for clinical tests that are either expensive or dangerous, it is important for the doctor to be convinced that the information is really needed before ordering the test. (Requests for sensitive or confidential information present similar difficulties.) Because MYCIN is reasoning backward, the question can easily be answered by examining the goal tree. Doing so provides two kinds of information:

- What higher-level question might the system be able to answer if it had the requested piece of information? (In this case, it could help determine the category of ORGANISM-1.)

- What other information does the system already have that makes it think that the requested piece of knowledge would help? (In this case, facts [2.1] to [2.4].)

When TEIRESIAS provides the answer to the first of these questions, the user may be satisfied or may want to follow the reasoning process back even further. The user can do that by asking additional "WHY" questions.

When TEIRESIAS provides the answer to the second of these questions and tells the user what it already believes, the user may want to know the basis for those beliefs. The user can ask this with a "HOW" question, which TEIRESIAS will interpret as "How did you know that?" This question also can be answered by looking at the goal tree and chaining backward from the stated fact to the evidence that allowed a rule that determined the fact to fire. Thus we see that by reasoning backward from its top-level goal and by keeping track of the entire tree that it traverses in the process, TEIRESIAS-MYCIN can do a fairly good job of justifying its reasoning to a human user. For more details of this process, as well as a discussion of some of its limitations, see Davis [1982].

The production system model is very general, and without some restrictions, it is hard to support all the kinds of explanations that a human might want. If we focus on a particular type of problem solving, we can ask more probing questions. For example, SALT [Marcus and McDermott, 1989] is a knowledge acquisition program used to build expert systems that design artifacts through a *propose-and-revise* strategy. SALT is capable of answering questions like WHY-NOT ("why didn't you assign value x to this parameter?") and WHAT-IF ("what would happen if you did?"). A human might ask these questions in order to locate incorrect or missing knowledge in the system as a precursor to correcting it. We now turn to ways in which a program such as SALT can support the process of building and refining knowledge.

20.4 Knowledge Acquisition

How are expert systems built? Typically, a knowledge engineer interviews a domain expert to elicit expert knowledge, which is then translated into rules. After the initial system is built, it must be iteratively refined until it approximates expert-level performance. This process is expensive and time-consuming, so it is worthwhile to look for more automatic ways of constructing expert knowledge bases. While no totally automatic knowledge acquisition systems yet exist, there are many programs that interact with domain experts to extract expert knowledge efficiently. These programs provide support for the following activities:

- Entering knowledge

- Maintaining knowledge base consistency

- Ensuring knowledge base completeness

The most useful knowledge acquisition programs are those that are restricted to a particular problem-solving paradigm, e.g., diagnosis or design. It is important to be able to enumerate the roles that knowledge can play in the problem-solving process. For example, if the paradigm is diagnosis, then the program can structure its knowledge base around symptoms, hypotheses, and causes. It can identify symptoms for which the expert has not yet provided causes. Since one symptom may have multiple causes, the program can ask for knowledge about how to decide when one hypothesis is better than another. If we move to another type of problem solving, say designing artifacts, then these acquisition strategies no longer apply, and we must look for other ways of profitably interacting with an expert. We now examine two knowledge acquisition systems in detail.

MOLE [Eshelman, 1988] is a knowledge acquisition system for heuristic classification problems, such as diagnosing diseases. In particular, it is used in conjunction with the *cover-and-differentiate* problem-solving method. An expert system produced by MOLE accepts input data, comes up with a set of candidate explanations or classifications that cover (or explain) the data, then uses differentiating knowledge to determine which one is best. The process is iterative, since explanations must themselves be justified, until ultimate causes are ascertained.

MOLE interacts with a domain expert to produce a knowledge base that a system called MOLE-p (for MOLE-performance) uses to solve problems. The acquisition proceeds through several steps:

1. Initial knowledge base construction. MOLE asks the expert to list common symptoms or complaints that might require diagnosis. For each symptom, MOLE prompts for a list of possible explanations. MOLE then iteratively seeks out higher-level explanations until it comes up with a set of ultimate causes. During this process, MOLE builds an influence network similar to the belief networks we saw in Chapter 8.

   Whenever an event has multiple explanations, MOLE tries to determine the conditions under which one explanation is correct. The expert provides *covering* knowledge, that is, the knowledge that a hypothesized event might be the cause of a certain symptom. MOLE then tries to infer *anticipatory* knowledge, which says that if the hypothesized event does occur, then the symptom will definitely appear. This knowledge allows the system to rule out certain hypotheses on the basis that specific symptoms are absent.

2. Refinement of the knowledge base. MOLE now tries to identify the weaknesses of the knowledge base. One approach is to find holes and prompt the expert to fill them. It is difficult, in general, to know whether a knowledge base is complete, so instead MOLE lets the expert watch MOLE-p solving sample problems. Whenever MOLE-p makes an incorrect diagnosis, the expert adds new knowledge. There are several ways in which MOLE-p can reach the wrong conclusion. It may incorrectly reject a hypothesis because it does not feel that the hypothesis is needed to explain any symptom. It may advance a hypothesis because it is needed to explain some otherwise inexplicable hypothesis. Or it may lack differentiating knowledge for choosing between alternative hypotheses.

   For example, suppose we have a patient with symptoms A and B. Further suppose that symptom A could be caused by events X and Y, and that symptom B can be caused by Y and Z. MOLE-p might conclude Y, since it explains both A and B. If the expert indicates that this decision was incorrect, then MOLE will ask what evidence should be used to prefer X and/or Z over Y.

MOLE has been used to build systems that diagnose problems with car engines, problems in steel-rolling mills, and inefficiencies in coal-burning power plants. For MOLE to be applicable, however, it must be possible to preenumerate solutions or classifications. It must also be practical to encode the knowledge in terms of covering and differentiating.

But suppose our task is to design an artifact, for example, an elevator system. It is no longer possible to preenumerate all solutions. Instead, we must assign values to a large number of parameters, such as the width of the platform, the type of door, the cable weight, and the cable strength. These parameters must be consistent with each other, and they must result in a design that satisfies external constraints imposed by cost factors, the type of building involved, and expected payloads.

One problem-solving method useful for design tasks is called *propose-and-revise*. Propose-and-revise systems build up solutions incrementally. First, the system proposes an extension to the current design. Then it checks whether the extension violates any global or local constraints. Constraint violations are then fixed, and the process repeats. It turns out that domain experts are good at listing overall design constraints and at providing local constraints on individual parameters, but not so good at explaining how to arrive at global solutions. The SALT program [Marcus and McDermott, 1989] provides mechanisms for elucidating this knowledge from the expert.

Like MOLE, SALT builds a dependency network as it converses with the expert. Each node stands for a value of a parameter that must be acquired or generated. There are three kinds of links: *contributes-to, constrains,* and *suggests-revision-of.* Associated with the first type of link are procedures that allow SALT to generate a value for one parameter based on the value of another. The second type of link, *constrains,* rules out certain parameter values. The third link, *suggests-revision-of,* points to ways in which a constraint violation can be fixed. SALT uses the following heuristics to guide the acquisition process:

1. Every noninput node in the network needs at least one *contributes-to* link coming into it. If links are missing, the expert is prompted to fill them in.

2. No *contributes-to* loops are allowed in the network. Without a value for at least one parameter in the loop, it is impossible to compute values for any parameter in that loop. If a loop exists, SALT tries to transform one of the *contributes-to* links into a *constrains* link.

3. Constraining links should have *suggests-revision-of* links associated with them. These include *constrains* links that are created when dependency loops are broken.

Control knowledge is also important. It is critical that the system propose extensions and revisions that lead toward a design solution. SALT allows the expert to rate revisions in terms of how much trouble they tend to produce.

SALT compiles its dependency network into a set of production rules. As with MOLE, an expert can watch the production system solve problems and can override the system's decision. At that point, the knowledge base can be changed or the override can be logged for future inspection.

The process of interviewing a human expert to extract expertise presents a number of difficulties, regardless of whether the interview is conducted by a human or by a machine. Experts are surprisingly inarticulate when it comes to how they solve problems. They do not seem to have access to the low-level details of what they do and are especially inadequate suppliers of any type of statistical information. There is, therefore, a great deal of interest in building systems that automatically induce their own rules by looking at sample problems and solutions. With inductive techniques, an expert needs only to provide the conceptual framework for a problem and a set of useful examples.

For example, consider a bank's problem in deciding whether to approve a loan. One approach to automating this task is to interview loan officers in an attempt to extract their domain knowledge. Another approach is to inspect the record of loans the bank has made in the past and then try to generate automatically rules that will maximize the number of good loans and minimize the number of bad ones in the future.

META-DENDRAL [Mitchell, 1978] was the first program to use learning techniques to construct rules for an expert system automatically. It built rules to be used by DEN-DRAL, whose job was to determine the structure of complex chemical compounds. META-DENDRAL was able to induce its rules based on a set of mass spectrometry data; it was then able to identify molecular structures with very high accuracy. META-DENDRAL used the version space learning algorithm, which we discussed in Chapter 17. Another popular method for automatically constructing expert systems is the induction of decision trees, data structures we described in Section 17.5.3. Decision tree expert systems have been built for assessing consumer credit applications, analyzing hypothyroid conditions, and diagnosing soybean diseases, among many other applications.

Statistical techniques, such as multivariate analysis, provide an alternative approach to building expert-level systems. Unfortunately, statistical methods do not produce concise rules that humans can understand. Therefore it is difficult for them to explain their decisions.

For highly structured problems that require deep causal chains of reasoning, learning techniques are presently inadequate. There is, however, a great deal of research activity in this area, as we saw in Chapter 17.

20.5   Summary

Since the mid-1960s, when work began on the earliest of what are now called expert
systems, much progress has been made in the construction of such programs. Experience
gained in these efforts suggests the following conclusions:

- These systems derive their power from a great deal of domain-specific knowledge,
  rather than from a single powerful technique.

- In successful systems, the required knowledge is about a particular area and is
  well defined. This contrasts with the kind of broad, hard-to-define knowledge
  that we call common sense. It is easier to build expert systems than ones with
  common sense.

- An expert system is usually built with the aid of one or more experts, who must
  be willing to spend a great deal of effort transferring their expertise to the system.

- Transfer of knowledge takes place gradually through many interactions between
  the expert and the system. The expert will never get the knowledge right or
  complete the first time.

- The amount of knowledge that is required depends on the task. It may range from
  forty rules to thousands.

- The choice of control structure for a particular system depends on specific characteristics of the system.

- It is possible to extract the nondomain-specific parts from existing expert systems
  and use them as tools for building new systems in new domains.

Four major problems facing current expert systems are:

- Brittleness—Because expert systems only have access to highly specific domain
  knowledge, they cannot fall back on more general knowledge when the need
  arises. For example, suppose that we make a mistake in entering data for a
  medical expert system, and we describe a patient who is 130 years old and weighs
  40 pounds. Most systems would not be able to guess that we may have reversed
  the two fields since the values aren't very plausible. The CYC system, which
  we discussed in Section 10.3, represents one attempt to remedy this problem
  by providing a substrate of commonsense knowledge on which specific expert
  systems can be built.

- Lack of Meta-Knowledge—Expert systems do not have very sophisticated knowledge about their own operation. They typically cannot reason about their own
  scope and limitations, making it even more difficult to deal with the brittleness
  problem.

- Knowledge Acquisition—Despite the development of the tools that we described in Section 20.4, acquisition still remains a major bottleneck in applying expert systems technology to new domains.

- Validation—Measuring the performance of an expert system is difficult because we do not know how to quantify the use of knowledge. Certainly it is impossible to present formal proofs of correctness for expert systems. One thing we can do is pit these systems against human experts on real-world problems. For example, MYCIN participated in a panel of experts in evaluating ten selected meningitis cases, scoring higher than any of its human competitors [Buchanan, 1982].

There are many issues in the design and implementation of expert systems that we have not covered. For example, there has been a substantial amount of work done in the area of real-time expert systems [Laffey *et al.*, 1988]. For more information on the whole area of expert systems and to get a better feel for the kinds of applications that exist, look at Weiss and Kulikowski [1984], Harmon and King [1985], Rauch-Hindin [1986], Waterman [1986], and Prerau [1990].

20.6 Exercises

1. Rule-based systems often contain rules with several conditions in their left sides.

    (a) Why is this true in MYCIN?
    (b) Why is this true in R1?

2. Contrast expert systems and neural networks (Chapter 18) in terms of knowledge representation, knowledge acquisition, and explanation. Give one domain in which the expert system approach would be more promising and one domain in which the neural network approach would be more promising.

Chapter 21

Perception and Action

In the first chapter of this book, we proposed a definition of AI based on the nature of the problems it tackles, namely those for which humans currently outperform computers. So far, we have discussed primarily cognitive tasks, but there are many other tasks that also fall within this realm. In basic perceptual and motor skills, even lower animals possess phenomenal capabilities compared to computers.

Perception involves interpreting sights, sounds, smells, and touch. Action includes the ability to navigate through the world and manipulate objects. In order to build robots that live in the world, we must come to understand these processes. Figure 21.1 shows a design for a complete autonomous robot. Most of AI is concerned only with cognition, the idea being that when intelligent programs are developed, we will simply add sensors and effectors to them. But problems in perception and action are substantial in their own right and are being tackled by researchers in the field of robotics.

In the past, robotics and AI have been largely independent endeavors, and they have developed different techniques to solve different problems. We attempt to characterize the field of robotics at the end of this chapter, but for now, we should note one key difference between AI programs and robots: While AI programs usually operate in computer-simulated worlds, robots must operate in the physical world. As an example, consider making a move in chess. An AI program can search millions of nodes in a game tree without ever having to sense or touch anything in the real world. A complete chess-playing robot, on the other hand, must be capable of grasping pieces, visually interpreting board positions, and carrying on a host of other actions.

The distinction between real and simulated worlds has several implications:

- The input to an AI program is symbolic in form, e.g., an 8-puzzle configuration or a typed English sentence. The input to a robot is typically an analog signal, such as a two-dimensional video image or a speech waveform.

- Robots require special hardware for perceiving and affecting the world, while AI programs require only general-purpose computers.

- Robot sensors are inaccurate, and their effectors are limited in precision. There is always some degree of uncertainty about exactly where the robot is located,

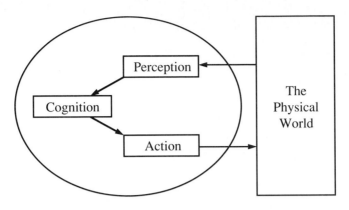

Figure 21.1: A Design for an Autonomous Robot

and where objects and obstacles stand in relation to it. Robot effectors are also limited in precision.

- Many robots must react in real time. A robot fighter plane, for example, cannot afford to search optimally or to stop monitoring the world during a LISP garbage collection.

- The real world is unpredictable, dynamic, and uncertain. A robot cannot hope to maintain a correct and complete description of the world. This means that a robot must consider the trade-off between devising and executing plans. This trade-off has several aspects. For one thing, a robot may not possess enough information about the world for it to do any useful planning. In that case, it must first engage in information-gathering activity. Furthermore, once it begins executing a plan, the robot must continually monitor the results of its actions. If the results are unexpected, then re-planning may be necessary.

  Consider the problem of traveling across town. We might decide to take a bus, but without a bus schedule, it is impossible to complete the plan. So we make a plan for acquiring a schedule and execute it in the world. Now we can plan our route. The bus we want to take may be scheduled to arrive at 5:22 p.m., but the probability of it coming at exactly 5:22 p.m. is actually very small. We should stick to our plan and wait, even if the bus is late. After a while, if the bus still has not come, we must make a new plan.

- Because robots must operate in the real world, searching and backtracking can be costly. Consider the problem of moving furniture into a room. Operating in a simulated world with full information, an AI program can come up with an optimal plan by best-first search. Preconditions of operators can be checked quickly, and if an operator fails to apply, another can be tried. Checking preconditions in the real world, however, can be time-consuming if the robot does not have full information. For example, one operator may require that an object weigh less than fifty pounds. Navigating to the object and applying a force to it may take the robot several minutes. At that rate, it is impossible to traverse and backtrack over a large search space. Worse still, it may be impossible to evaluate a projected arrangement of furniture without actually moving the pieces first.

Recent years have seen efforts to integrate research in robotics and AI. The old idea of simply attaching sensors and effectors to existing AI programs has given way to a serious rethinking of basic AI algorithms in light of the problems involved in dealing with the physical world. Research in robotics is likewise affected by AI techniques, since reasoning about goals and plans is essential for mapping perceptions onto appropriate actions. In this chapter, we explore the interface between robotics and AI. We do not delve too deeply into purely robotic issues, but instead focus on how the AI techniques we have seen in this book can be used and/or modified to handle problems that arise in dealing with the physical world.

At this point, one might ask whether physical robots are necessary for research purposes. Since current AI programs already operate in simulated worlds, why not build more realistic simulations, which better model the real world? Such simulators do exist, for example, Carbonell and Hood [1986] and Langley *et al.* [1981b]. There are several advantages to using a simulated world: Experiments can be conducted very rapidly, conditions can easily be replicated, programs can return to previous states at no cost, and sensory input can be treated in a high-level fashion. Furthermore, simulators require no fragile, expensive mechanical parts. The major drawback to simulators is figuring out exactly which factors to build in. Experience with real robots continues to expose tough problems that do not arise even in the most sophisticated simulators. The world turns out—not surprisingly—to be an excellent model of itself, and a readily available one.

21.1 Real-Time Search

We now turn to heuristic search, as exemplified in AI by the A* algorithm. While A* is guaranteed to find an optimal path from the initial state to the goal state, the algorithm has a number of limitations in the real world. For one, the exponential complexity of A* limits the size of problems it can realistically solve, and forces us to consider a limited search horizon. Also, having incomplete information about the world can further limit that search horizon. For example, consider the task of navigating from one room to another in an unfamiliar building. The search horizon is limited to how far one can (literally) see at any given time. It is necessary to take steps in the physical world in order to see beyond the horizon, despite the fact that the steps may be nonoptimal ones. Finally, real-time tasks like driving require continuous monitoring and reacting. Because heuristic search is time-consuming, we cannot afford to work out optimal solutions ahead of time.

There is a variation of A* that addresses these issues. It is called Real-Time-A* (RTA*) [Korf, 1988]. This algorithm commits to a real-world action every k seconds, where k is some constant that depends on the depth of the search horizon. Each time RTA* carries out an action, it restarts the search from that point. Thus, RTA* is able to make progress toward a goal state without having to plan a complete sequence of solution steps in advance. RTA* was inspired to a degree by work on computer games.

As we mentioned in Chapter 12, game-playing programs must commit to irrevocable moves because of time constraints.

Algorithm: Real-Time-A*

1. Set NODE to be the start state.

2. Generate the successors of NODE. If any of the successors is a goal state, then quit.

3. Estimate the value of each successor by performing a fixed-depth search starting at that successor. Use depth-first search. Evaluate all leaf nodes using the A* heuristic function $f = g + h'$, where g is the distance to the leaf node and h' is the predicted distance to the goal. Pass heuristic estimates up the search tree in such a way that the f value of each internal node is set to the minimum of the values of its children.[1]

4. Set NODE to the successor with the lowest score, and take the corresponding action in the world. Store the old NODE in a table along with the heuristic score of the second-best successor. (With this strategy, we can never enter into a fixed loop, because we never make the same decision at the same node twice.) If this node is ever generated again in step 2, simply look up the heuristic estimate in the table instead of redoing the fixed-depth search of step 3.

5. Go to step 2.

We can adjust the depth to which we search in step 3, depending on how much time we want to spend planning versus executing actions in the world. Provided that every part of the search space is accessible from every other part, RTA* is guaranteed to find a path to a solution state if one exists. The path may not be an optimal one, however. The deeper we search in step 3, the shorter our average solution paths will be. Of course, the task itself may impose limits on how deep we can search, as a result of incomplete information.

RTA* is just one example of a limited-horizon search algorithm. Another algorithm, due to Hansson and Mayer [1989], uses Bayesian inference. Dean and Boddy [1988] define a related notion, the *anytime* algorithm. An anytime algorithm is one that can be interrupted and queried at any point during its computation. The longer the algorithm runs, the more accurate its answer is.

Now we turn to more specific techniques aimed at various perceptual and motor problems. Later, we investigate architectures for integrating perception, action, and cognition. It should be noted that this is only a brief survey of a very large and active field of research. Those interested in investigating these issues more deeply should consult robotics texts such as Brady [1982] and Craig [1985].

---

[1] It is possible to prune the search tree using a technique called *alpha pruning*, a single-agent analogue of alpha-beta pruning. Alpha pruning is a branch-and-bound technique of the type we encountered in Chapter 2.

21.2 Perception

We perceive our environment through many channels: sight, sound, touch, smell, taste. Many animals possess these same perceptual capabilities, and others are able to monitor entirely different channels. Robots, too, can process visual and auditory information, and they can also be equipped with more exotic sensors, such as laser rangefinders, speedometers, and radar.

Two extremely important sensory channels for humans are vision and spoken language. It is through these two faculties that we gather almost all of the knowledge that drives our problem-solving behaviors.

21.2.1 Vision

Accurate machine vision opens up a new realm of computer applications. These applications include mobile robot navigation, complex manufacturing tasks, analysis of satellite images, and medical image processing. In this section, we investigate how we can transform raw camera images into useful information about the world.

A video camera provides a computer with an image represented as a two-dimensional grid of intensity levels. Each grid element, or *pixel*, may store a single bit of information (that is, black/white) or many bits (perhaps a real-valued intensity measure and color information). A visual image is composed of thousands of pixels. What kinds of things might we want to do with such an image? Here are four operations, in order of increasing complexity:

1. Signal Processing—Enhancing the image, either for human consumption or as input to another program.

2. Measurement Analysis—For images containing a single object, determining the two-dimensional extent of the object depicted.

3. Pattern Recognition—For single-object images, classifying the object into a category drawn from a finite set of possibilities.

4. Image Understanding—For images containing many objects, locating the objects in the image, classifying them, and building a three-dimensional model of the scene.

See Niblack [1986] for algorithms that perform the first two operations. The third operation, pattern recognition, varies in its difficulty. It is possible to classify two-dimensional (2-D) objects, such as machine parts coming down a conveyor belt, but classifying 3-D objects is harder because of the large number of possible orientations for each object. Image understanding is the most difficult visual task, and it has been the subject of the most study in AI. While some aspects of image understanding reduce to measurement analysis and pattern recognition, the entire problem remains unsolved, because of difficulties that include the following:

- An image is two-dimensional, while the world is three-dimensional. Some information is necessarily lost when an image is created.

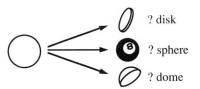

Figure 21.2: An Ambiguous Image

- One image may contain several objects, and some objects may partially occlude others, as we saw earlier in Figure 14.8.

- The value of a single pixel is affected by many different phenomena, including the color of the object, the source of the light, the angle and distance of the camera, the pollution in the air, etc. It is hard to disentangle these effects.

As a result, 2-D images are highly ambiguous. Given a single image, we could construct any number of 3-D worlds that would give rise to the image. For example, consider the ambiguous image of Figure 21.2. It is impossible to decide what 3-D solid it portrays. In order to determine the most likely interpretation of a scene, we have to apply several types of knowledge.

For example, we may invoke knowledge about low-level image features, such as shadows and textures. Figure 21.3 shows how such knowledge can help to disambiguate the image. Having multiple images of the same object can also be useful for recovering 3-D structure. The use of two or more cameras to acquire multiple simultaneous views of an object is called stereo vision. Moving objects (or moving cameras) also supply multiple views. Of course, we must also possess knowledge about how motion affects images that get produced. Still more information can be gathered with a laser rangefinder, a device that returns an array of distance measures much like sonar does. While rangefinders are still somewhat expensive, integration of visual and range data will soon become commonplace. Integrating different sense modalities is called *sensor fusion*. Other image factors we might want to consider include shading, color, and reflectance.

High-level knowledge is also important for interpreting visual data. For example, consider the ambiguous object at the center of Figure 21.4(*a*). While no low-level image features can tell us what the object is, the object's surroundings provide us with top-down expectations. Expectations are critical for interpreting visual scenes, but resolving expectations can be tricky. Consider the scene shown in Figure 21.4(*b*). All objects in this scene are ambiguous; the same shapes might be interpreted elsewhere as an amoeba, logs in a fireplace, and a basketball. As a result, there are no clear-cut top-down expectations. But the preferred interpretations of egg, bacon, and plate reinforce each other mutually, providing the necessary expectations.

So how can we bring all of this knowledge to bear in an organized fashion? One possible architecture for vision is shown in Figure 21.5. The very first step is to convert the analog video signal into a digital image. The next step is to extract image features like edges and regions. Edges can be detected by algorithms that look for sets of adjacent pixels with differing values. Since pixel values are affected by many factors, small edges

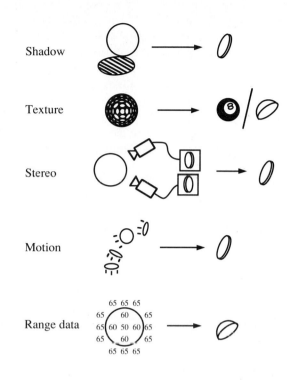

Figure 21.3: Using Low-Level Knowledge to Interpret an Image

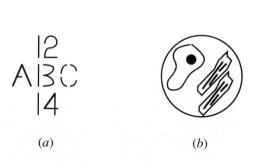

(a)　　　　　　　　　(b)

Figure 21.4: Using High-Level Knowledge to Interpret an Image

with similar orientations must be grouped into larger ones [Ballard and Brown, 1982]. Regions, on the other hand, are found by grouping similar pixels together. Edge and region detection are computationally intensive processes, but ones that can be readily mapped onto parallel hardware. The next step is to infer 3-D orientations for the various regions. Texture, illumination, and range data are all useful for this task. Assumptions about the kinds of objects that are portrayed can also be valuable, as we saw in the Waltz labeling algorithm (Section 14.3). Next, surfaces are collected into 3-D solids. Small solids are combined into larger, composite objects. At this point, the scene is segmented into discrete entities. The final step involves matching these entities against a knowledge base in order to pick the most likely interpretations for them. Organizing such a knowledge base of objects is difficult, though the knowledge-structuring techniques we studied in Part II are useful. As we demonstrated above, it may be impossible to interpret objects in isolation. Therefore, higher-level modules can pass hypotheses back down to lower-level modules, which check for predictions made by the hypotheses.

This is only one way of structuring an image understanding program. It highlights the spectrum of low- to high-level knowledge required for 3-D vision. As with other AI tasks, the success of a vision program depends critically on the way it represents and applies knowledge. For more information on computer vision, see Marr [1982], Ballard and Brown [1982], and Horn [1986].

21.2.2   Speech Recognition

Natural language understanding systems usually accept typed input, but for a number of applications this is not acceptable. Spoken language is a more natural form of communication in many human-computer interfaces. Speech recognition systems have been available for some time, but their limitations have prevented widespread use. Below are five major design issues in speech systems. These issues also provide dimensions along which systems can be compared with one another.

- Speaker Dependence versus Speaker Independence—A speaker-independent system can listen to any speaker and translate the sounds into written text. Speaker independence is hard to achieve because of the wide variations in pitch and accent. It is easier to build a speaker-dependent system, which can be trained on the voice patterns of a single speaker. The system will only work for that one speaker. It can be retrained on another voice, but then it will no longer work for the original speaker.

- Continuous versus Isolated-Word Speech—Interpreting isolated-word speech, in which the speaker pauses between each word, is easier than interpreting continuous speech. This is because boundary effects cause words to be pronounced differently in different contexts. For example, the spoken phrase "could you" contains a j sound, and despite the fact it contains two words, there is no empty space between them in the speech wave. The ability to recognize continuous speech is very important, however, since humans have difficulty speaking in isolated words.

- Real Time versus Offline Processing—Highly interactive applications require that a sentence be translated into text as it is being spoken, while in other situations,

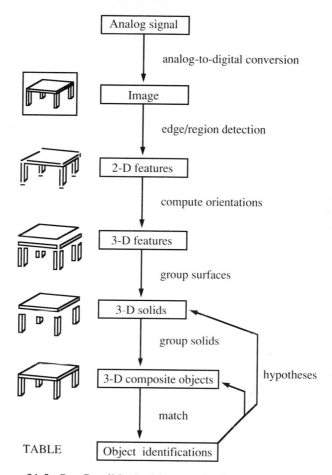

Figure 21.5: One Possible Architecture for Image Understanding

it is permissible to spend minutes in computation. Real-time speeds are hard to achieve, especially when higher-level knowledge is involved.

- Large versus Small Vocabulary—Recognizing utterances that are confined to small vocabularies (e.g., 20 words) is easier than working with large vocabularies (e.g., 20,000 words). A small vocabulary helps to limit the number of word candidates for a given speech segment.

- Broad versus Narrow Grammar—An example of a narrow grammar is the one for phone numbers: S → XXX-XXXX, where X is any number between zero and nine. Syntactic and semantic constraints for unrestricted English are much harder to represent, as we saw in Chapter 15. The narrower the grammar is, the smaller the search space for recognition will be.

Existing speech systems make various compromises. Early systems, like DRAGON [Baker, 1975], HEARSAY [Lesser *et al.*, 1975], and HARPY [Lowerre, 1976] dealt with single-user, continuous speech, and vocabularies up to a thousand words. They achieved word accuracy rates of 84 to 97 percent. TANGORA [IBM speech recognition group, 1985] moved to speaker independence and a large, 20,000-word vocabulary, but sacrificed continuous speech. TANGORA is 97 percent accurate. One system built at Bell Labs for recognizing continuous, speaker-independent digit recognition (for phone numbers) has also produced 97 percent accuracy [Rabiner *et al.*, 1988]. SPHINX [Lee and Hon, 1988] is the first system to achieve high accuracy (96 percent) on real-time, speaker independent, continuous speech with a vocabulary of 1000 words.

What techniques do these systems use? HEARSAY used a blackboard architecture, of the kind we discussed in Chapter 16. Using this method, various knowledge sources enter positive and negative evidence for different hypotheses, and the blackboard integrates all the evidence. Low-level phonemic knowledge sources provide information that high-level knowledge sources can use to make hypotheses about what words appear in the input. The high-level knowledge sources can then generate expectations that can be checked by the low-level ones.

The HARPY system also used knowledge to direct its reasoning, but it precompiled all that knowledge into a very large network of phonemes. In the network model, an interpreter tries to find the path through the network that best matches the spoken input. This path can be found with any number of heuristic search techniques, for example, beam search. HARPY was much faster than HEARSAY, but the blackboard architecture that HEARSAY used was more general and easily extensible.

Most modern speech systems are learning systems. In other words, they accept sample inputs and interpretations, and modify themselves appropriately until they are able to transform speech waveforms into written words. So far, statistical learning methods have proven most useful for learning this type of transformation. The statistical method used in the SPHINX system is called *hidden Markov modeling*. A hidden Markov model (HMM) is a collection of states and transitions. Each transition leaving a state is marked with (1) the probability with which that transition is taken, (2) an output symbol, and (3) the probability that the output symbol is emitted when the transition is taken. The problem of decoding a speech waveform turns into the problem of finding the most likely path (set of transitions) through an appropriate HMM. It is possible to tune the probabilities of an HMM automatically so that these paths correspond to correct interpretations of the waveform. The technique for doing this is called the *forward-backward algorithm*.

Connectionist systems also show promise as a learning mechanism for speech recognition. One problem with connectionist models is that they do not deal very well with time-varying data. New types of networks, such as recurrent and time-delay networks [Waibel *et al.*, 1989], are being employed to overcome these difficulties.

In our discussion of vision in Section 21.2.1, we saw that higher-level sources of knowledge can be used to manage uncertainty at lower levels. Speech recognition also has sources of higher-level knowledge. We have already studied some of these in Chapter 15. Syntactic knowledge can be used to identify constituent phrases, semantic knowledge to disambiguate word senses, discourse knowledge to dereference pronouns, and so forth. Early speech recognition systems sought to make use of this higher-level knowledge in order to constrain the interpretation at the lower levels. As we saw in

Chapter 14, a speech system that cannot decide between "the cat's cares are few" and "the cat scares are few" can invoke high-level knowledge to choose one alternative over the other.

However, modern speech systems perform fairly well without any sophisticated syntactic or semantic models of language. Instead, simple statistical models are used. For example, SPHINX uses a *word-pair grammar*, which tells it which words can legally appear adjacent to one another in the input. TANGORA uses a *trigram grammar*, which, given the previous two words in the input, yields the probability that a given word will occur next.

Still, no speech system is 100 percent accurate. There has recently been renewed interest in integrating speech recognition and natural language processing in order to overcome the final hurdle. For example, ATNs and unification-based grammars can be used to constrain the hypotheses made by a speech system. Thus far, integration has proved difficult, because natural language grammars do not offer much in the way of constraints.

In the speech recognition literature, there is a quantitative measure of grammar, called *perplexity*. Perplexity measures the number of words that can legally appear next in the input (on average). The telephone number recognition task has a perplexity of 10, because at any decision point, there are ten alternatives. On a sample 1000-word English task, a word-pair grammar may reduce the perplexity from 1000 down to 60. A bigram grammar may reduce it further, perhaps to 20 [Lee and Hon, 1988].

While natural language grammars accurately predict word categories (such as noun and verb), they say nothing about which words within a category are likely to show up in the input. For example, given the word "the," a grammar might hypothesize that the next word is either an adjective or a noun. But this knowledge does us little good when there are thousands of possible adjectives and nouns to choose from. Thus, it is natural to turn to statistical, or collocational, facts about language. For example, if the word "doctor" is recognized, then one might expect to hear the word "nurse" later in the input, but not "Norse." Collocational data, unlike more complex syntactic and semantic structures, can be extracted automatically from large on-line bodies of text. Ultimately, we want to substitute semantic and discourse information for statistical data. If we know the conversation is about doctors, and if we know that doctors and nurses typically work together, then we should be able to generate the proper expectations. Such a strategy will require large knowledge bases and a deeper understanding of semantics and discourse.

21.3 Action

Mobility and intelligence seem to have evolved together. Immobile creatures have little use for intelligence, while it is intelligence that puts mobility to effective use. In this section, we investigate the nature of mobility in terms of how robots navigate through the world and manipulate objects.

21.3.1 Navigation

Navigation means moving around the world: planning routes, reaching desired destinations without bumping into things, and so forth. Like vision and speech recognition,

Figure 21.6: A Path Planning Problem

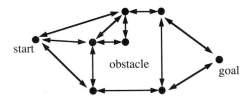

Figure 21.7: Constructing a Visibility Graph

this is something humans do fairly easily.

Many classic AI planning problems involve navigation. The STRIPS system, for example, gave high-level instructions to a robot moving through a set of rooms, carrying objects from one to another. Plans to solve goals like "move box A into room X" contained operators like MOVE(Y, X), meaning "move from room Y to room X." The planner did not concern itself with how this movement was to be realized in the world; from its perspective, the manner of movement was something akin to teleportation. A real robot, however, must consider the low-level details involved in getting from here to there.

Navigational problems are surprisingly complex. For example, suppose that there are obstacles in the robot's path, as in Figure 21.6. The problem of *path planning* is to plot a continuous set of points connecting the initial position of the robot to its desired position.

If the robot is so small as to be considered a point, the problem can be solved straightforwardly by constructing a *visibility graph*. Let S be the set consisting of the initial and final positions as well as the vertices of all obstacles. To form the visibility graph, we connect every pair of points in S that are visible from one another, as shown in Figure 21.7. We can then search the graph (perhaps using the A* algorithm) to find an optimal path for the robot.

Most robots have bulky extent, however, and we must take this into account when we plan paths. Consider the problem shown in Figure 21.8, where the robot has a pentagonal

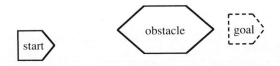

Figure 21.8: Another Path Planning Problem

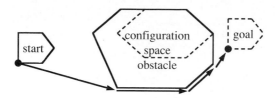

Figure 21.9: Constructing Configuration Space Obstacles

shape. Fortunately, we can reduce this problem to the previous path-planning problem. The algorithm is as follows: First choose a point P on the surface of the robot, then increase the size of the obstacles so that they cover all points that P cannot enter, because of the physical size and shape of the robot. Now, simply construct and search a visibility graph based on P and the vertices of the new obstacles, as in Figure 21.9. The basic idea is to reduce the robot to a point P and do path planning in an artificially constructed space, known as *configuration space*, or *c-space* [Lozano-Perez et al., 1984].

If we want to allow rotations, we can represent the robot as a combination of point P and some angle of rotation θ. The robot can now be considered as a point moving through three-dimensional space (x, y, θ). Obstacles can be transformed into three-dimensional c-space objects, and a visibility graph can again be created and searched.

An alternative approach to obstacle avoidance is the use of *potential fields* [Khatib, 1986]. With this technique, the direction of a moving robot is continually recomputed as a function of its current position relative to obstacles and its destination. The robot is essentially repelled by obstacles and attracted to the destination point. This approach is especially useful for correcting positioning errors that accumulate during a robot's journey and for dealing with unexpected obstacles. It can be combined with configuration space path planning to enable robust navigation [Krogh and Thorpe, 1986].

Road following is another navigational task that has received a great deal of attention. The object of road following is to steer a moving vehicle so that it stays centered on a road and avoids obstacles. Much of the problem comes in locating the edges of the road despite varying light, weather, and ground conditions. At present, this control task is feasible only for fairly slow-moving vehicles [Shafer and Whittaker, 1989]. Increases in speed demand more reactivity and thus more real-time computation.

21.3.2 Manipulation

Robots have found numerous applications in industrial settings. Robot manipulators are able to perform simple repetitive tasks, such as bolting and fitting automobile parts, but these robots are highly task-specific. It is a long-standing goal in robotics to build robots that can be programmed to carry out a wide variety of tasks.

A manipulator is composed of a series of links and joints, usually terminating in an *end-effector*, which can take the form of a two-pronged gripper, a humanlike hand, or any of a variety of tools. One general manipulation problem is called *pick-and-place*, in which a robot must grasp an object and move it to a specific location. For example, consider Figure 21.10, where the goal is to place a peg in a hole.

There are two main subtasks here. The first is to design a robot motion that ends

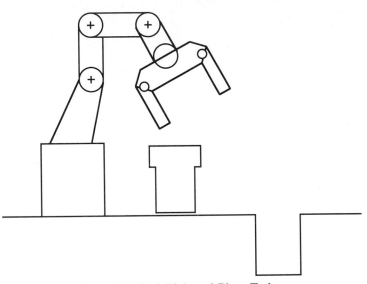

Figure 21.10: A Pick-and-Place Task

with the object stably grasped between the two fingers of the robot. Clearly some form of path planning, as discussed above, can be used to move the arm toward the object, but we need to modify the technique when it comes to the fine motion involved in the grasp itself. Here, uncertainty is a critical problem. Even with the vision techniques of Section 21.2.1, a robot can never be sure of the precise location of the peg or the arm. Therefore it would be a mistake to plan a grasp motion in which the gripper is spread only wide enough to permit the peg to pass, as in Figure 21.11(a). A better strategy is to open the gripper wide, then close gradually as the gripper gets near the peg, as in Figure 21.11(b). That way, if the peg turns out to be located some small distance away from where we thought it was, the grasp will still succeed. Although this strategy depends less on precise vision, it requires some tactile sensitivity in order to terminate the grasp. Unless we take special care in designing grasping motions, uncertainty can lead to disasters. For example, should the left side of the gripper touch the peg one second before the right side does, the peg may fall, thus foiling the grasp. Brost [1988] and Mason et al. [1988] give robust algorithms for grasping a wide variety of objects.

After the peg is stably grasped, the robot must place it in the hole. This subtask resembles the path-planning problem, although it is complicated by the fact that moving the peg through 3-D space requires careful orchestration of the arm's joints. Also, we must seriously consider the problems introduced by uncertainty. Figure 21.12(a) shows a naive strategy for placing the peg. Failure will result from even a slight positioning error, because the peg will jam flatly on the outer surface. A better strategy is shown in Figure 21.12(b). We slide the peg along the surface, applying downward pressure so that the peg enters the hole at an angle. After this happens, we straighten the peg gradually and push it down into the hole.

This type of motion, which reacts to forces generated by the world, is called *compli-*

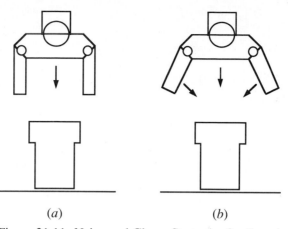

(a) (b)

Figure 21.11: Naive and Clever Strategies for Grasping

ant motion. Compliant motion is very robust in the face of uncertainty. Humans employ compliant motion in a wide variety of activities, such as writing on chalkboards.

So given a pick-and-place problem, how can we automatically generate a sequence of compliant motions? One approach [Lozano-Perez *et al.*, 1984] is to use the familiar problem-solving process of backward chaining. Our initial and goal states for the peg-in-hole problem are represented as points in configuration space, as shown in Figure 21.13. First, we compute the set of points in c-space from which we are guaranteed to reach the goal state in a single compliant motion, assuming a certain degree of uncertainty in initial position and direction of movement and certain facts about relative friction. This set of points is called the goal state's *strong pre-image*.[2] In Figure 21.13, the strong pre-image of the goal state is shown in gray. Now we use backward chaining to design a set of motions that is guaranteed to get us from the initial state to some point in the goal state's strong pre-image. Recursively applying this procedure will eventually yield a set of motions that, while individually uncertain, combine to form a guaranteed plan.

21.4 Robot Architectures

Now let us turn to what happens when we put it all together—perception, cognition, and action. There are many decisions involved in designing an architecture that integrates all these capabilities, among them:

- What range of tasks is supported by the architecture?

- What type of environment (e.g., indoor, outdoor, space) is supported?

- How are complex behaviors turned into sequences of low-level actions?

- Is control centralized or distributed?

---

[2]The set of points from which it is *possible* to reach the state in a single motion is called the state's *weak pre-image*.

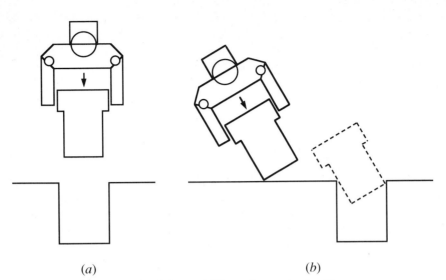

(a)   (b)

Figure 21.12: Naive and Clever Strategies for Placement

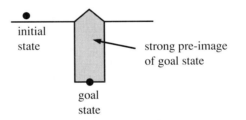

Figure 21.13: Planning with Uncertainty in Configuration Space

- How are numeric and symbolic representations merged?

- How does the architecture represent the state of the world?

- How quickly can the architecture react to changes in the environment?

- How does the architecture decide when to plan and when to act?

With these issues in mind, let's look briefly at a few existing robot architectures.

CODGER [Shafer *et al.*, 1986] is an architecture for controlling vehicles in outdoor road-following tasks. CODGER uses a blackboard structure to organize incoming perceptual data. The system's control is centralized and hierarchical—all numerical data from sensors are fused in order to build up a consistent model of the world. This model is represented symbolically. CODGER has been used to build a system for driving the experimental NAVLAB [Shafer and Whittaker, 1989] vehicle, a commercial van that has been altered for computer control via electric and hydraulic servos. The

NAVLAB is completely self-contained, with room for several on-board computers and researchers.

Brooks [1986] describes the *subsumption* architecture for building autonomous robots for indoor navigation and manipulation. Behaviors are built up from layers of simple, numeric finite-state machines. Bottom layers consist of reactive, instinctual behaviors such as obstacle avoidance and wandering. Upper layers consist of behaviors like object identification and reasoning about object motions. The various behaviors operate in a decentralized fashion, computing independently, and suppressing or informing one another. Such an organization encourages reactivity—for example, high-level navigation behavior is suppressed abruptly when an obstacle moves to block a robot's path. In fact, the subsumption architecture takes reactivity to the extreme. Separate modules monitor only the sensors that affect their behavior, and there are no explicit goals, plans, or world models in these systems. They simply react to the situation at hand. For example, the task of one such robot is to wander the halls, picking up soda cans and depositing them in a bin. When the robot locates a can, several modules steer the robot toward it. Modules governing the robot arm continuously monitor the physical wheels of the robot. When the wheels stop, the arm extends to grasp the can. Notice that all these motions are decentralized and reactive; nowhere in the robot is there any explicit plan for how to pick up the soda can, or how to pick up soda cans in general.

This kind of organization presents a perspective on problem solving similar to the one we described in Section 13.7. Advantages of the subsumption architecture include simplicity and speed, since programs for controlling such robots are simple enough that they can be rendered easily into hardware. Also, modeling the real world is a very difficult task, one that the subsumption architecture avoids. On the other hand, it is not clear that the subsumption architecture will scale up to complex planning problems. Subsumption robots tend to lack the flexibility that traditional problem solvers display in being able to reason about a wide variety of tasks. Also, they lack the ability to reflect on their own actions. For example, if the wheels of the soda can robot should stop turning because of a loose connection, the robot arm will mindlessly extend forward in search of a nonexistent can. While the CODGER architecture emphasizes data fusion, subsumption robots emphasize data fission. A series of subsumption robots have been built, and they demonstrate how reactive systems are capable of much more interesting and varied behavior than was previously thought. It is unknown whether these architectures are capable of achieving tasks that seem to require significant amounts of planning.

TCA [Simmons and Mitchell, 1989] is an architecture that combines the idea of reactive systems with traditional AI planning. TCA is a distributed system with centralized control, designed to control autonomous robots for long periods in unstructured environments, such as the surface of Mars. TCA particularly addresses issues that arise in the context of multiple goals and limited resources. The architecture provides mechanisms for hierarchical task management and allows action based on incomplete plans. Because robots gather new information by moving through the world, TCA permits plans to be terminated early should higher-priority goals arise. Some situations require highly reactive behavior. TCA achieves high-speed response by parallelizing planning and execution whenever possible. For example, in designing walking motions over rough terrain, TCA plans one step, initiates it, and then begins to plan the next step before the leg motion has been completed.

Another program for combining heuristic problem solving with reactivity is called THEO-Agent [Mitchell, 1990]. THEO-Agent contains two subsystems, a reactive engine and a general problem solver (called THEO [Mitchell *et al.*, 1989]). When the reactive subsystem fails to suggest a course of action, the problem solver creates a plan for the robot. As it executes the plan, the robot uses explanation-based learning to create new reactive modules. Thus, the robot becomes increasingly reactive with experience. Robo-SOAR [Laird *et al.*, 1989], an extension of the SOAR problem-solving system, is another learning robot architecture.

PRS [Georgeff and Lansky, 1987] is a symbolic robot planning system that interleaves planning and execution. In PRS, goals represent robot behaviors, not world states. PRS contains procedures for turning goals into subgoals or iterations thereof. A procedure can be invoked by either the presence of a goal or the presence of some sensory input. Thus, the robot is capable of goal-directed behavior but can also react when the world changes or when plans fail. Goals and procedures are represented symbolically, and a central reasoner uses a stack to oversee the invocation of procedures.

21.5 Summary

The field of robotics is often described as the subfield of AI that is concerned with perceptual and motor tasks. As Figure 21.1 suggests, the tables can easily be turned, and AI could well be the subfield of robotics that deals with cognition. Indeed, Brady [1985] has proposed a definition of robotics with this flavor:

> Robotics is the intelligent connection of perception to action.

Another definition, suggested by Grossman,[3] reads as follows:

> A robot is anything that is surprisingly animate.

The word "surprisingly" suggests a moving-target definition. It should be noted that the first automatic dishwashing machines were called robots by their designers. But after a while, it became less surprising that a machine could wash dishes, and the term "robot" fell away. This characterization of robotics is similar to the one we proposed for AI in Chapter 1. There, we characterized AI as the study of problems in which humans currently perform better than computers. As a result, programs that solve calculus problems are no longer considered artificial intelligence.[4]

These moving-target definitions accurately differentiate actual AI work and robotics work. AI tends to focus on uniquely human capabilities, while robotics aims to produce physical, animate behaviors. As we have seen in this chapter, however, many interesting problems lie at the intersection of AI and robotics, and only by combining techniques from both fields will we be able to design intelligent robots that live in the world.

---

[3]David Grossman, after-dinner speech delivered at the 7th NSF Grantees Conference, Ithaca, NY, 1979.

[4]We must be careful here. When movable-type printing was first introduced, it was called *artificial writing*, because it seemed to be automating what scribes had been doing for previous centuries. Of course, printing only automates a small portion of the writing process. It is often more enlightening to view AI programs and robots as tools for enhancing human capabilities, rather than as independent, autonomous agents [Hill, 1989].

21.6 Exercises

1. Describe scenarios in which the following features are critical:

   (a) Reactivity—The robot must react quickly to a changing environment.

   (b) Robustness—The robot must act appropriately, in spite of incomplete or inexact sensory data.

   (c) Recoverability—When a plan fails to bring about expected results, the robot must find another way to achieve its goal.

   Why aren't the planning techniques described in Chapter 13 sufficient to ensure these characteristics?

2. Describe three different ways of combining speech recognition with a natural language understanding system. Compare and contrast them in terms of expected performance and ease of implementation.

3. Say each of the following phrases very slowly, and write down the sounds you use. Then gradually speed up, and continue to write down the sounds. Finally, say them the way you would in ordinary speech. How do the sounds change as you move through each series? What are the implications of these changes for continuous speech recognition?

   (a) could you

   (b) boy's school

   (c) the store, the elevator

   (d) sharp point

   (e) stop it

   (f) want to go

4. Create a search graph, labeled with heuristic estimates, that shows the RTA* algorithm entering the same node twice. Explain what would happen if RTA* did not keep track of previously visited states.

5. In Section 21.1, we said that the RTA* algorithm is guaranteed to find a path to a solution state if such a path exists and if every part of the search space is accessible from every other part. Why is this second qualification necessary? Give an example in which, without it, a solution will not be found.

6. Consider the following variation on the peg-in-hole problem:

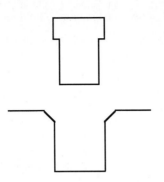

Explain, using the concept of a strong pre-image, why this problem is easier than the standard peg-in-hole problem of Figure 21.10.

Chapter 22

Conclusion

22.1 Components of an AI Program

We have now surveyed the major techniques of artificial intelligence. From our discussion of them, it should be clear that there are two important classes of AI techniques:

- Methods for representing and using knowledge

- Methods for conducting heuristic search

These two aspects interact heavily with each other. The choice of a knowledge representation framework determines the kind of problem-solving methods that can be applied. For example, if knowledge is represented as formulas in predicate logic, then resolution can be used to derive new inferences. If, on the other hand, knowledge is represented in semantic nets, then network search routines must be used. Or, if knowledge is represented as a set of weights in a neural network, then some form of network search (e.g., relaxation or forward propagation) must be exploited.

If there is one single message that this book has tried to convey, it is the crucial part that knowledge plays in AI programs. Although much of the book has been devoted to other topics, particularly to search techniques, it is important to keep in mind that the power of those techniques lies in their ability to use knowledge effectively to solve particular problems. Because of the importance of the role of knowledge in problem-solving programs, it is worth reviewing here what that role is.

Knowledge serves two important functions in AI programs. The first is to define what can be done to solve a problem and to specify what it means to have solved the problem. We can call knowledge that does this *essential knowledge*. The second is to provide advice on how best to go about solving a problem efficiently. We can call such knowledge *heuristic knowledge*.

The goal of this book has been to say enough about the use of knowledge in problem-solving programs to enable you to build one. Go do it. And have fun.

22.2 Exercises

1. What do you think is the main result to come out of AI research in the last 20 years? Give a brief justification of your answer.

2. Why are table-driven programs so important in AI?

3. What is the role of matching in AI programs? Give several examples of its use.

4. How do the topics of knowledge representation and problem-solving techniques interact with each other? Give examples.

5. Dreyfus [1972] presents a criticism of AI in which it is argued that AI is not possible. Read through it, and using the material presented in this book, refute the arguments.

6. Using what you have learned in this book, comment briefly on each line below. Feel free to augment your answer with diagrams or illustrations.

   Question. How many AI people does it take to change a lightbulb?

   Answer. At least 67.

   The Problem Space Group (5)

   One to define the goal state
   One to define the operators
   One to describe the universal problem solver
   One to hack the production system
   One to indicate about how it is a model of human lightbulb-changing behavior

   The Logical Formalism Group (12)

   One to figure out how to describe lightbulb changing in predicate logic
   One to show the adequacy of predicate logic
   One to show the inadequacy of predicate logic
   One to show that lightbulb logic is nonmonotonic
   One to show that it isn't nonmonotonic
   One to incorporate nonmonotonicity into predicate logic
   One to determine the bindings for the variables
   One to show the completeness of the solution
   One to show the consistency of the solution
   One to hack a theorem prover for lightbulb resolution
   One to indicate how it is a description of human lightbulb-changing behavior
   One to call the electrician

   The Statistical Group (1)

   One to point out that, in the real world, a lightbulb is never "on" or
       "off," but usually somewhere in between

The Planning Group (4)

One to define STRIPS-style operators for lightbulb changing
One to show that linear planning is not adequate
One to show that nonlinear planning is adequate
One to show that people don't plan; they simply react to lightbulbs

The Robotics Group (7)

One to build a vision system to recognize the dead bulb
One to build a vision system to locate a new bulb
One to figure out how to grasp the lightbulb without breaking it
One to figure out the arm solutions that will get the arm to the socket
One to organize the construction teams
One to hack the planning system
One to indicate how the robot mimics human motor behavior in lightbulb changing

The Knowledge Engineering Group (6)

One to study electricians changing lightbulbs
One to arrange for the purchase of the Lisp machines
One to assure the customer that this is a hard problem and that great
    accomplishments in theory will come from support of this effort
The same one can negotiate the project budget
One to study related research
One to indicate how it is a description of human lightbulb-changing behavior
One to call the Lisp hackers

The Lisp Hackers (7)

One to bring up the network
One to order the Chinese food
Four to hack on the Lisp debugger, compiler, window system, and microcode
One to write the lightbulb-changing program

The Connectionist Group (6)

One to claim that lightbulb changing can only be achieved through
    massive parallelism
One to build a backpropagation network to direct the robot arm
One to assign initial random weights to the connections in the network
One to train the network by showing it how to change a lightbulb
    (training shall consist of 500,000 repeated epochs)
One to tell the media that the network learns "just like a human does"
One to compare the performance of the resulting system with that of
    traditional symbolic approaches (optional)

The Natural Language Group (5)

One to collect sample utterances from the lightbulb domain
One to build an English understanding program for the lightbulb-changing robot
One to build a speech recognition system
One to tell lightbulb jokes to the robot in between bulb-changing tasks
One to build a language generation component so that the robot
    can make up its own lightbulb jokes

The Learning Group (4)

One to collect twenty lightbulbs
One to collect twenty "near misses"
One to write a concept learning program that learns to identify lightbulbs
One to show that the program found a local maximum in the space of
    lightbulb descriptions

The Game-Playing Group (5)

One to design a two-player game tree with the robot as one player and the
    lightbulb as the other
One to write a minimax search algorithm that assumes optimal play
    on the part of the lightbulb
One to build special-purpose hardware to enable 24-ply search
One to enter the robot in a human lightbulb-changing tournament
One to state categorically that lightbulb changing is "no longer considered AI"

The Psychological Group (5)

One to build an apparatus which will time lightbulb-changing performance
One to gather and run subjects
One to mathematically model the behavior
One to call the expert systems group
One to adjust the resulting system, so that it drops the right number of bulbs

References

Ades, A. and M. Steedman. 1982. On the order of words. *Linguistics and Philosophy* 4:517–558.

Agre, P. E. and D. Chapman. 1987. Pengi: An implementation of a theory of activity. In *Proceedings AAAI-87*, 268–272.

Aho, A., J. Hopcroft, and J. Ullman. 1983. *Data Structures and Algorithms*. Reading, MA: Addison-Wesley.

Allen, J. 1987. *Natural Language Understanding*. Menlo Park, CA: Benjamin/Cummings.

Allen, J. 1989. Natural language understanding. In *The Handbook of Artificial Intelligence Volume IV*, ed. A. Barr, P. R. Cohen, and E. A. Feigenbaum. Reading, MA: Addison-Wesley.

Allen, J. and C. R. Perrault. 1980. Analyzing intention in utterances. *Artificial Intelligence* 15(3):143–178. (Reprinted in *Readings in Natural Language Processing* (1986), ed. B. Grosz, published by Morgan Kaufmann, Los Altos, CA, pp. 441 458).

Amsterdam, J. 1988. Some philosophical problems with formal learning theory. In *Proceedings AAAI-88*.

Anantharaman, T., M. Campbell, and F. Hsu. 1990. Singular extensions: Adding selectivity to brute force searching. *Artificial Intelligence* 43(1).

Anderson, J. R. 1983. *The Architecture of Cognition*. Cambridge, MA: Harvard University Press.

Anderson, J. R. 1985. *Cognitive Psychology and Its Implications, 2d ed*. San Francisco: Freeman.

Anderson, J. R. and P. J. Kline. 1979. A learning system and its psychological implications. In *Proceedings IJCAI-79*.

Angluin, D. 1987. Learning regular sets from queries and counterexamples. *Information and Computation* 75(2):87–106.

Appelt, D. E. 1987. Bidirectional grammars and the design of natural language generation systems. In *Theoretical Issues in Natural Language Processing (TINLAP 3)*.

Ashby, W. R. 1952. *Design for a Brain*. New York: Wiley.

Austin, J. L. 1962. *How to Do Things with Words*. Cambridge, MA: Harvard University Press.

Baker, J. 1975. The DRAGON system—an overview. *IEEE Transactions on Acoustics, Speech, and Signal Processing* 23(1).

Ballard, D. H. 1984. Parameter nets. *Artificial Intelligence* 22(3):235–267.

Ballard, D. H. and C. Brown. 1982. *Computer Vision*. Englewood Cliffs, NJ: Prentice-Hall.

Ballard, D. H., G. E. Hinton, and T. J. Sejnowski. 1983. Parallel visual computation. *Nature* 306(5938):21–26.

Balzer, R., L. D. Erman, P. E. London, and C. Williams. 1980. Hearsay-III: A domain-independent framework for expert systems. In *Proceedings AAAI-80*.

Barnett, J., K. Knight, I. Mani, and E. A. Rich. 1990. Knowledge and natural language processing. *Communications of the ACM* 33(8).

Barr, A., E. A. Feigenbaum, and P. R. Cohen. 1981. *The Handbook of Artificial Intelligence*. Los Altos, CA: Morgan Kaufman.

Barto, A. G. 1985. Learning by statistical cooperation of self-interested neuron-like computing elements. *Human Neurobiology* 4(4).

Baudet, G. M. 1978. On the branching factor of the alpha-beta pruning algorithm. *Artificial Intelligence* 10(2):173–199.

Beal, D. F. 1990. A generalised quiescence search algorithm. *Artificial Intelligence* 43(1).

Benson, D. B., B. R. Hilditch, and J. D. Starkey. 1979. Tree analysis techniques in Tsumego. In *Proceedings IJCAI-79*.

Berliner, H. J. 1977. Search and knowledge. In *Proceedings IJCAI-77*.

Berliner, H. J. 1979a. The B* tree search algorithm: A best-first proof procedure. *Artificial Intelligence* 12(1).

Berliner, H. J. 1979b. On the construction of evaluation functions for large domains. In *Proceedings IJCAI-79*.

Berliner, H. J. 1980. Backgammon computer program beats world champion. *Artificial Intelligence* 14(1).

Berliner, H. J. and C. Ebeling. 1989. Pattern knowledge and search: The SUPREM architecture. *Artificial Intelligence* 38(2).

Bisiani, R., T. Anantharaman, and L. Butcher. 1989. BEAM: An accelerator for speech recognition. In *IEEE International Conference on Acoustics, Speech, and Signal Processing*.

Bledsoe, W. W. 1977. Non-resolution theorem proving. *Artificial Intelligence* 9(1).

Block, H. D. 1962. The perceptron: A model for brain functioning. *Reviews of Modern Physics* 34(1):123–135.

Bobrow, D. G. 1975. Dimensions of representation. In *Representation and Understanding*, ed. D. G. Bobrow and A. Collins. New York: Academic Press.

Bobrow, D. G. and A. Collins. 1975. *Representation and Understanding*. New York: Academic Press.

Bobrow, D. G. and T. Winograd. 1977. An overview of KRL, a knowledge representation language. *Cognitive Science* 1(1).

Bond, A. H. and L. Gasser, eds. 1988. *Readings in Distributed Artificial Intelligence*. San Mateo, CA: Morgan Kaufmann.

Bowden, B. V. 1953. *Faster Than Thought*. London: Pitman.

Boyer, R. S. and J. S. Moore. 1988. *A Computational Logic Handbook*. Boston: Academic Press.

Brachman, R. J. 1979. On the epistemological status of semantic networks. In *Associative Networks*, ed. N. V. Findler. New York: Academic Press.

Brachman, R. J. 1985. I lied about the trees. *The AI Magazine* 6(3):80–93.

Brachman, R. J., V. P. Gilbert, and H. J. Levesque. 1985. An essential hybrid reasoning system: Knowledge and symbol level accounts of KRYPTON. In *Proceedings IJCAI-85*.

Brachman, R. J. and H. J. Levesque. 1984. The tractability of subsumption in frame-based description languages. In *Proceedings AAAI-84*.

Brachman, R. J. and H. J. Levesque, eds. 1985. *Readings in Knowledge Representation*. Los Altos, CA: Morgan Kaufmann.

Brachman, R. J. and J. Schmolze. 1985. An overview of the KL-ONE knowledge representation system. *Cognitive Science* 9(2).

Brady, M., ed. 1982. *Robot Motion: Planning and Control*. Cambridge, MA: MIT Press.

Brady, M. 1985. Artificial intelligence and robotics. *Artificial Intelligence* 26(1).

Bratko, I. 1986. *Prolog Programming for Artificial Intelligence*. Reading, MA: Addison-Wesley.

Bresnan, J., ed. 1982. *The Mental Representation of Grammatical Relations*. Cambridge, MA: MIT Press.

Bridgeland, D. M. and M. N. Huhns. 1990. Distributed truth maintenance. In *Proceedings AAAI-90*.

Broadbent, D. 1985. A question of levels: Comment on McClelland and Rumelhart. *Journal of Experimental Psychology: General* 114:189–192.

Brooks, R. A. 1986. A robust layered control system for a mobile robot. *IEEE Journal of Robotics and Automation* RA-2(1).

Brost, R. C. 1988. Automatic grasp planning in the presence of uncertainty. *International Journal of Robotics Research* 7(1).

Brownston, L., R. Farrell, E. Kant, and N. Martin. 1985. *Programming Expert Systems in OPS5: An Introduction to Rule-Based Programming*. Reading, MA: Addison-Wesley.

Bruce, B. 1975. Case systems for natural language. *Artificial Intelligence* 6(4):327–360.

Buchanan, B. G. 1982. New research on expert systems. In *Machine Intelligence*, vol. 10, ed. J. E. Hayes, D. Michie, and Y. H. Pao, 269–299. Edinburgh: Edinburgh University Press.

Buchanan, B. G. and E. H. Shortliffe. 1984. *Rule-Based Expert Systems: The MYCIN Experiments of the Stanford Heuristic Programming Project*. Reading, MA: Addison-Wesley.

Burton, R. R. 1976. *Semantic Grammar: An Engineering Technique for Constructing Natural Language Understanding Systems*. Tech. Rep. 3453, Bolt Beranek and Newman, Boston, MA.

Carbonell, J. G. 1980. POLITICS: An experiment in subjective understanding and integrated reasoning. In *Inside Computer Understanding: Five Programs Plus Miniatures*, ed. R. C. Schank and C. K. Riesbeck. Hillsdale, NJ: Erlbaum.

Carbonell, J. G. 1983. Learning by analogy. In *Machine Learning, An Artificial Intelligence Approach*, ed. R. S. Michalski, J. G. Carbonell, and T. M. Mitchell. Palo Alto, CA: Tioga Press.

Carbonell, J. G. 1986. Derivational analogy: A theory of reconstructive problem solving and expertise acquisition. In *Machine Learning, Volume II*, ed. R. S. Michalski, J. G. Carbonell, and T. M. Mitchell. Los Altos, CA: Morgan Kaufman.

Carbonell, J. G. and G. Hood. 1986. The World Modelers Project: Learning in a reactive environment. In *Machine Learning: A Guide to Current Research*, ed. T. Mitchell, J. G. Carbonell, and R. S. Michalski. Boston: Kluwer.

Chandrasekaran, B. 1986. Generic tasks in knowledge-based reasoning: High-level building blocks for expert system design. *IEEE Expert* 1(3):23–30.

Chandy, K. and J. Misra. 1989. *Parallel Program Design: A Foundation*. Reading, MA: Addison-Wesley.

Chang, C. L. and R. C. Lee. 1973. *Symbolic Logic and Mechanical Theorem Proving*. New York: Academic Press.

Chapman, D. 1987. Planning for conjunctive goals. *Artificial Intelligence* 32(3).

Charniak, E. 1978. With spoon in hand this must be the eating frame. In *Proceedings of the Second Workshop on Theoretical Issues in Natural Language Processing (TINLAP 2)*.

Charniak, E. and D. McDermott. 1985. *Introduction to Artificial Intelligence*. Reading, MA: Addison-Wesley.

Chavez, R. M. 1989. *An Empirical Evaluation of a Randomized Algorithm for Probabilistic Inference*. Tech. Rep. KSL-89-31, Knowledge Systems Laboratory, Department of Computer Science, Stanford University, Stanford, CA.

Cheeseman, P. 1985. In defense of probability. In *Proceedings IJCAI-85*.

Cheeseman, P., M. Self, J. Kelly, W. Taylor, D. Freeman, and J. Stutz. 1988. Bayesian classification. In *Proceedings AAAI-88*.

Cheng, P. and J. Juang. 1987. A parallel resolution procedure based on connection graph. In *Proceedings AAAI-87*.

Chomsky, N. 1957. *Syntactic Structures*. The Hague: Mouton.

Chomsky, N. 1981. *Lectures on Government and Binding*. Dordrecht, Holland: Foris.

Chomsky, N. 1986. *Knowledge of Language, Its Nature, Origin and Use*. New York: Praeger.

Church, K. and R. Patil. 1982. Coping with syntactic ambiguity or how to put the block in the box on the table. *Journal of Computational Linguistics* 8:139–149.

Clark, D. A. 1990. Numerical and symbolic approaches to uncertainty management in AI. *Artificial Intelligence Review* 4:109–146.

Clark, K. L. 1978. Negation as failure. In *Logic and Databases*, ed. H. Gallaire and J. Minker, 293–322. New York: Plenum Press. (Reprinted in *Readings in Nonmonotonic Reasoning* (1987), ed. M. Ginsberg, published by Morgan Kaufmann, Los Altos, CA, pp. 311-325).

Clark, K. L. and S. Gregory. 1986. Parlog: Parallel programming in logic. *ACM Transactions on Programming Languages and Systems* 8(1).

Clocksin, W. F. and C. S. Mellish. 1984. *Programming in Prolog, 2d ed*. New York: Springer-Verlag.

Clowes, M. B. 1971. On seeing things. *Artificial Intelligence* 2(1).

Cohen, P. R. and C. R. Perrault. 1979. Elements of a plan-based theory of speech acts. *Cognitive Science* 3(3):177–212.

Colby, K. 1975. *Artificial Paranoia*. New York: Pergamon Press.

Corkill, D. D., K. Q. Gallagher, and P. M. Johnson. 1987. Achieving flexibility, efficiency, and generality in blackboard architectures. In *Proceedings AAAI-87*.

Cottrell, G. W., P. Munro, and D. Zipser. 1987. Learning internal representations from grayscale images: An example of extensional programming. In *Proceedings of the Ninth Annual Conference of the Cognitive Science Society*.

Craig, J. J. 1985. *Introduction to Robotics*. Reading, MA: Addison-Wesley.

Crick, F. H. C. and C. Asanuma. 1986. Certain aspects of the anatomy and physiology of the cerebral cortex. In *Parallel Distributed Processing*, ed. D. E. Rumelhart, J. L. McClelland, and the PDP Research Group. Cambridge, MA: MIT Press.

Cullingford, R. E. 1981. SAM. In *Inside Computer Understanding*, ed. R. C. Schank and C. K. Riesbeck. Hillsdale, NJ: Erlbaum.

Cullingford, R. E. 1986. *Natural Language Processing: A Knowledge Engineering Approach*. Totowa, NJ: Rowman and Allanheld.

Davis, M. and H. Putnam. 1960. A computing procedure for quantification theory. *Journal of the ACM* 7:201–215.

Davis, R. 1977. Interactive transfer of expertise: Acquisition of new inference rules. In *Proceedings IJCAI-77*.

Davis, R. 1980. Meta-rules: Reasoning about control. *Artificial Intelligence* 15(3).

Davis, R. 1982. Applications of meta level knowledge to the construction, maintenance and use of large knowledge bases. In *Knowledge-Based Systems in Artificial Intelligence*, ed. R. Davis and D. B. Lenat. New York: McGraw-Hill.

Davis, R. and R. G. Smith. 1983. Negotiation as a metaphor for distributed problem solving. *Artificial Intelligence* 20(1).

de Champeaux, D. and L. Sint. 1977. An improved bi-directional heuristic search algorithm. *Journal of the ACM* 24(2):177–191.

de Jong, K. 1988. Learning with genetic algorithms: An overview. *Machine Learning* 3:121–138.

de Kleer, J. 1979. The origin and resolution of ambiguities in causal arguments. In *Proceedings IJCAI-79*.

de Kleer, J. 1986. An Assumption-Based TMS. *Artificial Intelligence* 28(2):127–162. (Reprinted in *Readings in Nonmonotonic Reasoning* (1987), ed. M. Ginsberg, published by Morgan Kaufmann, Los Altos, CA, pp. 280-297).

de Kleer, J. and J. S. Brown. 1984. A qualitative physics based on confluences. *Artificial Intelligence* 24:7–83.

de Kleer, J. and B. C. Williams. 1987. Diagnosing multiple faults. *Artificial Intelligence* 32(1):97–130. (Reprinted in *Readings in Nonmonotonic Reasoning* (1987), ed. M. Ginsberg, published by Morgan Kaufmann, Los Altos, CA, pp. 372-388).

Dean, T. and M. Boddy. 1988. An analysis of time-dependent planning. In *Proceedings AAAI-88*.

DeJong, G. and R. Mooney. 1986. Explanation-based learning: An alternative view. *Machine Learning* 1(2).

Dempster, A. P. 1968. A generalization of Bayesian inference. *Journal of the Royal Statistical Society, Series B* 30:205–247.

Derthick, M. 1988. *Mundane Reasoning by Parallel Constraint Satisfaction*. PhD thesis, Carnegie Mellon University, Pittsburgh, PA, Pittsburgh, PA.

Dijkstra, E. 1972. Notes on structured programming. In *Structured Programming*, ed. O.-J. Dahl, E. W. Dijkstra, and C. A. R. Hoare. New York: Academic Press.

Dijkstra, E. 1976. *A Discipline of Programming*. Englewood Cliffs, N. J.: Prentice-Hall.

Dowty, D. R., L. Karttunen, and A. M. Zwicky. 1985. *Natural Language Parsing: Psychological, Computational and Theoretical Perspectives*. New York: Cambridge University Press.

Dowty, D. R., R. Wall, and S. Peters. 1981. *Introduction to Montague Semantics*. Dordrecht: Reidel.

Doyle, J. 1979. A truth maintenance system. *Artificial Intelligence* 12(3).

Dreyfus, H. 1972. *What Computers Can't Do: A Critique of Artificial Reason*. New York: Harper and Row.

Duda, R. O., P. E. Hart, K. Konolige, and R. Reboh. 1979. *A Computer-Based Consultant for Mineral Exploration*. Tech. rep., SRI International.

Dwork, C., P. C. Kanellakis, and J. C. Mitchell. 1984. On the sequential nature of unification. *Journal of Logic Programming* 1.

Dyer, M. 1983. *In-Depth Understanding*. Cambridge, MA: MIT Press.

Ehrenfeucht, A., D. Haussler, M. Kearns, and L. G. Valiant. 1989. A general lower bound on the number of examples needed for learning. *Information and Computation* 82(3).

Elman, J. L. 1990. Finding structure in time. *Cognitive Science* 14(2).

Englemore, R. and T. Morgan, eds. 1989. *Blackboard Systems*. Reading, MA: Addison-Wesley.

Erman, L. D., F. Hayes-Roth, V. R. Lesser, and R. D. Reddy. 1980. The Hearsay-II speech-understanding system: Integrating knowledge to resolve uncertainty. *ACM Computing Surveys* 12(2).

Erman, L. D., P. E. London, and S. F. Fickas. 1981. The design and an example use of Hearsay III. In *Proceedings IJCAI-81*.

Ernst, G. W. and A. Newell. 1969. *GPS: A Case Study in Generality and Problem Solving*. New York: Academic Press.

Eshelman, L. 1988. Mole: A knowledge-acquisition tool for cover-and-differentiate systems. In *Automating Knowledge Acquisition for Expert Systems*, ed. S. Marcus. Boston: Kluwer.

Etherington, D. W. 1988. *Reasoning with Incomplete Information*. Los Altos, CA: Morgan Kaufmann.

Etzioni, O. 1989. *Tractable Decision-Analytic Control*. Tech. Rep. CMU-CS-89-119, Computer Science Department, Carnegie Mellon University, Pittsburgh, PA.

Fahlman, S. E. 1979. *NETL: A System for Representing and Using Real-World Knowledge*. Cambridge, MA: MIT Press.

Fahlman, S. E. 1988. Faster-learning variations on back-propagation: An empirical study. In *Proceedings of the 1988 Connectionist Models Summer School*, 38–51. San Mateo, CA: Morgan Kaufmann.

Fahlman, S. E. and G. E. Hinton. 1987. Connectionist architectures for artificial intelligence. *IEEE Computer* 20(1):100–109.

Feigenbaum, E. A. 1963. The simulation of verbal learning behavior. In *Computers and Thought*, ed. E. A. Feigenbaum and J. Feldman. New York: McGraw-Hill.

Feigenbaum, E. A. and J. A. Feldman, eds. 1963. *Computers and Thought*. New York: McGraw-Hill.

Feldman, J. A. and D. H. Ballard. 1985. Connectionist models and their properties. *Cognitive Science* 6(3):205–254.

Fikes, R. E., P. E. Hart, and N. J. Nilsson. 1972. Learning and executing generalized robot plans. *Artificial Intelligence* 3(4):251–288.

Fikes, R. E. and N. J. Nilsson. 1971. STRIPS: A new approach to the application of theorem proving to problem solving. *Artificial Intelligence* 2(3–4):189–208.

Fillmore, C. 1968. The case for case. In *Universals in Linguistic Theory*, ed. E. Bach and R.T. Harms. New York: Holt.

Findler, N. V., ed. 1979. *Associative Networks: Representation and Use of Knowledge by Computer*. New York: Academic Press.

Forbus, K. 1984. Qualitative process theory. *Artificial Intelligence* 24(1).

Forgy, C. L. 1982. Rete: A fast algorithm for the many pattern/many object pattern match problem. *Artificial Intelligence* 19(1):17–37.

Fox, M. S. 1981. An organizational view of distributed systems. *IEEE Transactions on Systems, Man and Cybernetics* 11:70–80. (Reprinted in *Readings in Distributed Artificial Intelligence* (1988), ed. A. H. Bond and L. Gasser, published by Morgan Kaufmann, San Mateo, CA).

Gabriel, R. and J. McCarthy. 1988. Qlisp. In *Parallel Computation and Computers for Artificial Intelligence*, ed. J. Kowalik. Boston: Kluwer.

Gale, W. A., ed. 1986. *Artificial Intelligence and Statistics*. Reading, MA: Addison-Wesley.

Gardner, H. 1985. *The Mind's New Science*. New York: Basic Books.

Gasser, L., C. Braganza, and N. Herman. 1987. Implementing distributed artificial intelligence systems using MACE. In *Proceedings of the Third IEEE Conference on Artificial Intelligence Applications*, 315–320. (Reprinted in *Readings in Distributed Artificial Intelligence* (1988), ed. A. H. Bond and L. Gasser, published by Morgan Kaufmann, San Mateo, CA).

Gasser, L. and M. N. Huhns, eds. 1989. *Distributed Artificial Intelligence, Volume II*. London: Pitman. (Available from Morgan Kaufmann, San Mateo, CA).

Gazdar, G. 1982. Phrase structure grammar. In *The Nature of Syntactic Representation*, ed. P. Jacobson and G. K. Pullum, 131–186. Dordrecht, Holland: D. Reidel.

Gazdar, G., E. Klein, G. K. Pullum, and I. Sag. 1985. *Generalized Phrase Structure Grammar*. Cambridge, MA: Harvard University Press.

Gelernter, H., J. R. Hansen, and D. W. Loveland. 1963. Empirical explorations of the geometry theorem proving machine. In *Computers and Thought*, ed. E. A. Feigenbaum and J. Feldman. New York: McGraw-Hill.

Gelperin, D. 1977. On the optimality of A*. *Artificial Intelligence* 8(1).

Genesereth, M., M. L. Ginsberg, and J. S. Rosenschein. 1987. Cooperation without communication. In *Proceedings AAAI-87*. (Reprinted in *Readings in Distributed Artificial Intelligence* (1988), ed. A. H. Bond and L. Gasser, published by Morgan Kaufmann, San Mateo, CA).

Genesereth, M. and N. Nilsson. 1987. *Logical Foundations of Artificial Intelligence*. Los Altos, CA: Morgan Kaufmann.

Georgeff, M. 1983. Communication and interaction in multi-agent planning. In *Proceedings AAAI-83*. (Reprinted in *Readings in Distributed Artificial Intelligence* (1988), ed. A. H. Bond and L. Gasser, published by Morgan Kaufmann, San Mateo, CA).

Georgeff, M. 1984. A theory of action for multi-agent planning. In *Proceedings AAAI-84*. (Reprinted in *Readings in Distributed Artificial Intelligence* (1988), ed. A. H. Bond and L. Gasser, published by Morgan Kaufmann, San Mateo, CA).

Georgeff, M. and A. Lansky. 1987. Reactive reasoning and planning. In *Proceedings AAAI-87*.

Ginsberg, M. L., ed. 1987. *Readings in Nonmonotonic Reasoning*. Los Altos, CA: Morgan Kaufmann.

Gleitman, H. 1981. *Psychology*. New York: W. W. Norton.

Goldberg, D. 1989. *Genetic Algorithms in Search, Optimization, and Machine Learning*. Reading, MA: Addison-Wesley.

Gordon, D. and G. Lakoff. 1975. Conversational postulates. In *Studies in Syntax, Vol. III*, ed. P. Cole and J. L. Morgan. New York: Seminar Press.

Gorman, R. and T. J. Sejnowski. 1988. Analysis of hidden units in a layered network to classify sonar targets. *Neural Networks* 1(1):75–89.

Green, C. 1969. Application of theorem proving to problem solving. In *Proceedings IJCAI-69*.

Greenblatt, R. B., D. E. Eastlake, and S. D. Crocker. 1967. The Greenblatt chess program. In *Proceedings of the 1967 Joint Computer Conference*, 801–810.

Greiner, R. and D. B. Lenat. 1980. A representation language language. In *Proceedings AAAI-80*.

Grice, H. P. 1975. Logic and conversation. In *Studies in Syntax, Vol. III*, ed. P. Cole and J. L. Morgan. New York: Seminar Press.

Grosz, B. J., K. Spark Jones, and B. L. Webber. 1986. *Readings in Natural Language Processing*. Los Altos, CA: Morgan Kaufmann.

Gupta, A. 1985. *Parallelism in Production Systems*. PhD thesis, Carnegie Mellon University, Pittsburgh, PA.

Hall, R. 1989. Computational approaches to analogical reasoning. *Artificial Intelligence* 39(1).

Halpern, J. Y. 1986. *Theoretical Aspects of Reasoning About Knowledge*. Los Altos, CA: Morgan Kaufmann.

Halpern, J. Y. 1989. An analysis of first-order logics of probability. In *Proceedings IJCAI-89*.

Halstead, Jr., R. 1988. Parallel computing using Multilisp. In *Parallel Computation and Computers for Artificial Intelligence*, ed. J. Kowalik. Boston: Kluwer.

Hammond, K. 1986. Chef: a model of case-based planning. In *Proceedings AAAI-86*.

Handelman, D. A., S. H. Lane, and J. J. Gelfand. 1989. Integrating knowledge-based system and neural network techniques for robotic skill acquisition. In *Proceedings IJCAI-89*.

Hanks, S. and D. McDermott. 1986. Default reasoning, nonmonotonic logics, and the frame problem. In *Proceedings AAAI-86*. (Reprinted in *Readings in Nonmonotonic Reasoning* (1987), ed. M. Ginsberg, published by Morgan Kaufmann, Los Altos, CA, pp. 390-395).

Hansson, O. and A. Mayer. 1989. Heuristic search as evidential reasoning. In *Proceedings of the Fifth Workshop on Uncertainty in AI*.

Harmon, P. and D. King. 1985. *Artificial Intelligence in Business*. New York: Wiley.

Hart, P. E., R. O. Duda, and M. T. Einaudi. 1978. *A Computer-Based Consultation System for Mineral Exploration*. Tech. rep., SRI International.

Hart, P. E., N. J. Nilsson, and B. Raphael. 1968. A formal basis for the heuristic determination of minimum cost paths. *IEEE Transactions on SSC* 4:100–107.

Hart, P. E., N. J. Nilsson, and B. Raphael. 1972. Correction to 'A formal basis of the heuristic determination of minimum cost paths'. *SIGART Newsletter* 37:28–29.

Haussler, D. 1988. Quantifying inductive bias: AI learning algorithms and Valiant's learning framework. *Artificial Intelligence* 36(2).

Hayes, Patrick J. 1973. The frame problem and related problems in artificial intelligence. In *Artificial and Human Thinking*, ed. A. Elithorn and D. Jones. San Francisco: Jossey-Bass.

Hayes, Patrick J. 1985. Naive physics I: Ontology for liquids. In *Formal Theories of the Common Sense World*, ed. J. Hobbs and R. C. Moore, 71–107. Norwood, NJ: Ablex.

Hayes-Roth, B. 1985. A blackboard architecture for control. *Artificial Intelligence* 26(3):251–321.

Hayes-Roth, B. and M. Hewett. 1989. BB1: An implementation of the blackboard control architecture. In *Blackboard Systems*, ed. R. Englemore and T. Morgan, 297–314. Reading, MA: Addison-Wesley.

Hayes-Roth, F. and V. R. Lesser. 1977. Focus of attention in the Hearsay-II system. In *Proceedings IJCAI-77*.

Heckerman, D. 1986. Probabilistic interpretations for MYCIN's certainty factors. In *Uncertainty in Artificial Intelligence*, ed. L. N. Kanal and J. F. Lemmer, 167–196. New York: North Holland.

Hendrix, G. G. 1977. Expanding the utility of semantic networks through partitioning. In *Proceedings IJCAI-77*.

Hendrix, G. G. and W. H. Lewis. 1981. Transportable natural-language interfaces to databases. In *Proceedings of the 19th Annual Meeting of the Association for Computational Linguistics*.

Hendrix, G. G., E. D. Sacerdoti, D. Sagalowicz, and J. Slocum. 1978. Developing a natural language interface to complex data. *ACM Transactions on Database Systems* 3:105–147.

Henle, P. 1965. *Language, Thought, and Culture*. Ann Arbor: University of Michigan Press.

Hennessey, W. 1989. *Common Lisp*. New York: McGraw-Hill.

Hill, W. 1989. The mind at AI: Horseless carriage to clock. *AI Magazine* 10(2).

Hintikka, J. 1962. *Knowledge and Belief*. Ithaca, NY: Cornell University Press.

Hinton, G. E., J. L. McClelland, and D. E. Rumelhart. 1986. Distributed representations. In *Parallel Distributed Processing*, ed. D. E. Rumelhart, J. L. McClelland, and the PDP Research Group, 77–109. Cambridge, MA: MIT Press.

Hinton, G. E. and T. J. Sejnowski. 1986. Learning and relearning in Boltzmann Machines. In *Parallel Distributed Processing*, ed. D. E. Rumelhart, J. L. McClelland, and the PDP Research Group, 282–317. Cambridge, MA: MIT Press.

Hirsh, H. 1990. Learning from data with bounded inconsistency. In *Proceedings of the Seventh International Conference on Machine Learning*, 32–39.

Hirst, G. 1987. *Semantic Interpretation against Ambiguity*. New York: Cambridge University Press.

Hoare, C. A. R. 1985. *Communicating Sequential Processes*. Englewood Cliffs, NJ: Prentice-Hall.

Hobbs, J. 1985. Granularity. In *Proceedings IJCAI-85*.

Holland, J. H. 1975. *Adaptation in Natural and Artificial Systems*. Ann Arbor, MI: University of Michigan Press.

Hopfield, J. J. 1982. Neural networks and physical systems with emergent collective computational abilities. *Proceedings of the National Academy of Sciences USA* 79(8):2554–2558.

Hopfield, J. J. and D. W. Tank. 1985. 'Neural' computation of decisions in optimization problems. *Biological Cybernetics* 52(3):141–152.

Horn, B. 1986. *Robot Vision*. Cambridge, MA: MIT Press.

Hsu, F. 1989. *Large Scale Parallelization of Alpha-Beta Search: An Algorithmic and Architectural Study with Computer Chess*. PhD thesis, Carnegie Mellon University, Pittsburgh, PA.

Huhns, M. N., ed. 1987. *Distributed Artificial Intelligence*. London: Pitman. (Available from Morgan Kaufmann, San Mateo, CA).

IBM speech recognition group. 1985. A real-time, isolated-word, speech recognition system for dictation transcription. In *IEEE International Conference on Acoustics, Speech, and Signal Processing*.

ICOT. 1984. *International Conference on Fifth Generation Computer Systems*. Amsterdam: North-Holland.

Jagannathan, V., R. Dodhiawala, and L. S. Baum, eds. 1989. *Blackboard Architectures and Applications*. Boston: Academic Press.

Johnson-Laird, P. 1983. *Towards a Cognitive Science of Language, Inference, and Consciousness*. Cambridge, MA: Harvard University Press.

Jordan, M. I. 1986. Attractor dynamics and parallelism in a connectionist sequential machine. In *Proceedings of the Eighth Annual Conference of the Cognitive Science Society*. Hillsdale, NJ: Erlbaum.

Jordan, M. I. 1988. Supervised learning and systems with excess degrees of freedom. In *Proceedings of the 1988 Connectionist Models Summer School*, 62–75. San Mateo, CA: Morgan Kaufmann.

Joshi, A. K., B. L. Webber, and I. A. Sag, eds. 1981. *Elements of Discourse Understanding*. Cambridge: Cambridge University Press.

Kaczmarek, T., R. Bates, and G. Robbins. 1986. Recent developments in NIKL. In *Proceedings AAAI-86*.

Kaebling, L. P. 1987. An architecture for intelligent reactive systems. In *Reasoning About Actions and Plans*, ed. M. Georgeff and A. L. Lansky, 395–410. Palo Alto, CA: Morgan Kaufmann.

Kahneman, D., P. Slovic, and A. Tversky, eds. 1982. *Judgement under Uncertainty: Heuristics and Biases*. New York: Cambridge University Press.

Kanal, L. N. and J. F. Lemmer, eds. 1986. *Uncertainty in Artificial Intelligence*. New York: North-Holland.

Kanal, L. N. and J. F. Lemmer, eds. 1988. *Uncertainty in Artificial Intelligence 2*. New York: North-Holland.

Kanal, L. N., T. E. Levitt, and J. F. Lemmer, eds. 1989. *Uncertainty in Artificial Intelligence 3*. New York: North-Holland.

Kandel, E. R. and J. H. Schwartz. 1985. *Principles of Neural Science, 2d ed*. New York: Elsevier.

Kasif, S. 1986. On the parallel complexity of some constraint satisfaction problems. In *Proceedings AAAI-86*.

Kautz, H. 1985. Formalizing spatial concepts and spatial language. In *Commonsense Summer: Final Report*. Stanford, CA: Center for the Study of Language and Information (CSLI). (Tech. Rep. CSLI-85-35).

Kautz, H. 1986. Constraint propagation algorithms for temporal reasoning. In *Proceedings AAAI-86*, 377–382.

Kearns, M. and L. G. Valiant. 1989. Cryptographic limitations on learning boolean formulae and finite automata. In *Proceedings of the ACM Symposium on the Theory of Computing*.

Khatib, O. 1986. Real-time obstacle avoidance for manipulators and mobile robots. *International Journal of Robotics Research* 5(1).

King, M. 1983. *Parsing Natural Language*. New York: Academic Press.

Kirkpatrick, S., Gelatt, Jr., C. D., and M. P. Vecchi. 1983. Optimization by simulated annealing. *Science* 220(4598).

Knight, K. 1989. Unification: A multidisciplinary survey. *ACM Computing Surveys* 21(1).

Knuth, D. E. and R. W. Moore. 1975. An analysis of alpha-beta pruning. *Artificial Intelligence* 6(4).

Kolodner, J. 1984. *Retrieval and Organizational Strategies in Conceptual Memory: A Computer Model*. Hillsdale, NJ: Erlbaum.

Kolodner, J. 1989. Judging which is the "best" case for a case-based reasoner. In *Proceedings of the Case-Based Reasoning Workshop*.

Konolige, K. 1987. On the relations between default theories and autoepistemic logic. In *Proceedings IJCAI-87*.

Korf, R. 1985a. Depth-first iterative-deepening: An optimal admissible tree search. *Artificial Intelligence* 27(1).

Korf, R. 1985b. Macro-operators: A weak method for learning. *Artificial Intelligence* 26(1).

Korf, R. 1988. Real-time heuristic search: New results. In *Proceedings AAAI-88*.

Korf, R. 1989. Generalized game trees. In *Proceedings IJCAI-89*.

Kornfeld, W. A. and C. E. Hewitt. 1981. The scientific community metaphor. *IEEE Transactions on Systems, Man and Cybernetics* 11(1):24–33. (Reprinted in *Readings in Distributed Artificial Intelligence* (1988), ed. A. H. Bond and L. Gasser, published by Morgan Kaufmann, San Mateo, CA).

Krogh, B. H. and C. Thorpe. 1986. Integrated path planning and dynamic steering control for autonomous vehicles. In *Proceedings of the IEEE Conference on Robotics and Automation*.

Kuipers, B. 1986. Qualitative simulation. *Artificial Intelligence* 29:289–338.

Kumar, V., K. Ramesh, and V. Rao. 1988. Parallel best-first search of state-space graphs: A summary of results. In *Proceedings AAAI-88*.

Laffey, T. J., P. A. Cox, J. L. Schmidt, S. M. Kao, and J. Y. Read. 1988. Real-time knowledge-based systems. *AI Magazine* 9(1):27–45.

Laird, J. E., A. Newell, and P. S. Rosenbloom. 1987. Soar: An architecture for general intelligence. *Artificial Intelligence* 33(1).

Laird, J. E., P. S. Rosenbloom, and A. Newell. 1986. Chunking in Soar: The anatomy of a general learning mechanism. *Machine Learning* 1(1).

Laird, J. E., E. S. Yager, C. M. Tuck, and M. Hucka. 1989. Learning in tele-autonomous systems using Soar. In *Proceedings of the 1989 NASA Conference on Space Telerobotics*.

Lakoff, G. and M. Johnson. 1980. *Metaphors We Live By*. Chicago: University of Chicago Press.

Langley, P., G. L. Bradshaw, and H. A. Simon. 1981a. BACON.5: The discovery of conservation laws. In *Proceedings IJCAI-81*.

Langley, P., D. Nicholas, D. Klahr, and G. Hood. 1981b. A simulated world for modeling learning and development. In *Proceedings of the Third Annual Conference of the Cognitive Science Society*.

Langley, P., H. A. Simon, G. L. Bradshaw, and J. M. Zytkow. 1987. *Scientific Discovery*. Cambridge, MA: The MIT Press.

Lashley, K. S. 1929. *Brain Mechanisms and Intelligence: A Quantitative Study of Injuries to the Brain*. Chicago: Chicago University Press.

Lauritzen, S. L. and D. J. Spiegelhalter. 1988. Local computations with probabilities on graphical structures and their applications to expert systems. *Journal of the Royal Statistical Society, Series B* 50(19):157–224.

Lebowitz, M. 1983. Generalization from natural language text. *Cognitive Science* 7(1):1–40.

LeCun, Y. 1985. Une procedure d'apprentissage pour réseau à seauil asymétrique (A learning procedure for asymmetric threshold networks). In *Proceedings of Cognitiva 85*, 599–604. (Paris).

Lee, K.-F. and H. W. Hon. 1988. Large-vocabulary speaker-independent continuous speech recognition. In *IEEE International Conference on Acoustics, Speech, and Signal Processing*.

Lee, K.-F. and S. Mahajan. 1990. The development of a world class othello program. *Artificial Intelligence* 43(1).

Lehnert, W. C. 1978. *The Process of Question Answering: A Computer Simulation of Cognition*. Hillsdale, NJ: Erlbaum.

Lehrberger, J. and L. Bourbeau. 1988. *Machine Translation: Linguistic Characteristics of MT Systems and General Methodology of Evaluation*. Philadelphia: Benjamins.

Lenat, D. B. 1977. Automated theory formation in mathematics. In *Proceedings IJCAI-77*.

Lenat, D. B. 1982. AM: An artificial intelligence approach to discovery in mathematics as heuristic search. In *Knowledge-Based Systems in Artificial Intelligence*, ed. R. Davis and D. B. Lenat. New York: McGraw-Hill.

Lenat, D. B. 1983a. EURISKO: A program that learns new heuristics and domain concepts. The nature of heuristics III: Program design and results. *Artificial Intelligence* 21(1–2).

Lenat, D. B. 1983b. Theory formation by heuristic search—The nature of heuristics II: Background and examples. *Artificial Intelligence* 21(1–2).

Lenat, D. B. and J. S. Brown. 1983. Why AM and Eurisko appear to work. In *Proceedings AAAI-83*.

Lenat, D. B. and R. V. Guha. 1990. *Building Large Knowledge-Based Systems*. Reading, MA: Addison-Wesley.

Lesser, V. R. and D. D. Corkill. 1981. Functionally accurate, cooperative distributed systems. *IEEE Transactions on Systems, Man, and Cybernetics* 11(1):81–96. (Reprinted in *Readings in Distributed Artificial Intelligence* (1988), ed. A. H. Bond and L. Gasser, published by Morgan Kaufmann, San Mateo, CA).

Lesser, V. R., R. Fennell, L. Erman, and R. Reddy. 1975. The Hearsay II speech understanding system. *IEEE Transactions on Acoustics, Speech, and Signal Processing* 23(1).

Levy, D. N. L. 1988. *Computer Games*. New York: Springer-Verlag.

Lifschitz, V. 1985. Closed-world databases and circumscription. *Artificial Intelligence* 27(2):229–235. (Reprinted in *Readings in Nonmonotonic Reasoning* (1987), ed. M. Ginsberg, published by Morgan Kaufmann, Los Altos, CA, pp. 334-336).

Lindsay, R. K. 1963. Inferential memory as the basis of machines which understand natural language. In *Computers and Thought*, ed. E. A. Feigenbaum and J. Feldman. New York: McGraw-Hill.

Lindsay, R. K., B. G. Buchanan, E. A. Feigenbaum, and J. Lederberg. 1980. *Applications of Artificial Intelligence for Organic Chemistry: The Dendral Project*. New York: McGraw-Hill.

Lippmann, R. P. 1989. Review of research on neural nets for speech. *Neural Computation* 1(1).

Littlestone, N. 1988. Learning quickly when irrelevant attributes abound: A new linear threshold algorithm. *Machine Learning* 2(4).

Lovelace, A. 1961. Notes upon L. F. Menabrea's sketch of the Analytical Engine invented by Charles Babbage. In *Charles Babbage and His Calculating Engines*, ed. P. Morrison and E. Morrison. New York: Dover.

Lowerre, B. 1976. *The HARPY Speech Recognition System*. PhD thesis, Carnegie Mellon University, Pittsburgh, PA.

Lozano-Perez, T., M. Mason, and R. Taylor. 1984. Automatic synthesis of fine-motion strategies for robots. *International Journal of Robotics Research* 3(1).

Lytinen, S. 1984. Frame selection in parsing. In *Proceedings AAAI-84*.

Lytinen, S. 1986. Dynamically combining syntax and semantics in natural language processing. In *Proceedings AAAI-86*.

Malone, T. W. 1987. Modeling coordination in organizations and markets. *Management Science* 33(10):1317–1332. (Reprinted in *Readings in Distributed Artificial Intelligence* (1988), ed. A. H. Bond and L. Gasser, published by Morgan Kaufmann, San Mateo, CA).

Marcus, M. P. 1980. *A Theory of Syntactic Recognition for Natural Language*. Cambridge, MA: MIT Press.

Marcus, S. and J. McDermott. 1989. SALT: A knowledge acquisition language for propose-and-revise systems. *Artificial Intelligence* 39(1).

Marr, D. 1982. *Vision: A computational investigation into the human representation and processing of visual information*. San Francisco: W. H. Freeman.

Martelli, A. 1977. On the complexity of admissible search algorithms. *Artificial Intelligence* 8(1):1–13.

Martelli, A. and U. Montanari. 1973. Additive and/or graphs. In *Proceedings IJCAI-73*.

Martelli, A. and U. Montanari. 1978. Optimization decision trees through heuristically guided search. *Communications of the ACM* 21(12).

Mason, C. L. and R. R. Johnson. 1989. DATMS: A framework for distributed assumption based reasoning. In *Distributed Artificial Intelligence Volume II*, ed. L. Gasser and M. N. Huhns, 293–317. San Mateo, CA: Morgan Kaufmann.

Mason, M., K. Goldberg, and R. Taylor. 1988. *Planning Sequences of Squeeze-grasps to Orient and Grasp Polygonal Objects*. Tech. Rep. CMU CS 88 127, Computer Science Department, Carnegie Mellon University, Pittsburgh, PA.

McAllester, D. A. 1980. *An Outlook on Truth Maintenance*. Tech. Rep. AI Memo 551, MIT Artificial Intelligence Lab, Cambridge, MA.

McCarthy, J. 1980. Circumscription—a form of non-monotonic reasoning. *Artificial Intelligence* 13(1–2).

McCarthy, J. 1986. Applications of circumscription to formalizing commonsense knowledge. *Artificial Intelligence* 28(1):89–116. (Reprinted in *Readings in Nonmonotonic Reasoning* (1987), ed. M. Ginsberg, published by Morgan Kaufmann, Los Altos, CA, pp. 153-166).

McCarthy, J. and Patrick J. Hayes. 1969. Some philosophical problems from the standpoint of artificial intelligence. In *Machine Intelligence 4*, ed. B. Meltzer and D. Michie. Edinburgh: Edinburgh University Press.

McCorduck, P. 1979. *Machines Who Think*. San Francisco: Freeman.

McCulloch, W. S. and W. Pitts. 1943. A logical calculus of the ideas immanent in neural nets. *Bulletin of Mathematical Biophysics* 5:115–137.

McDermott, D. and J. Doyle. 1980. Non-monotonic logic I. *Artificial Intelligence* 13(1–2).

McDermott, J. 1982. R1: A rule-based configurer of computer systems. *Artificial Intelligence* 19(1):39–88.

McDermott, J. 1984. R1 revisited: Four years in the trenches. *AI Magazine* 5(3).

McDermott, J. 1988. Preliminary steps toward a taxonomy of problem-solving methods in automating knowledge acquisition for expert systems. In *Automating Knowledge Acquisition for Expert Systems*, ed. S. Marcus, 225–266. Boston: Kluwer.

McDonald, D. D. and L. Bolc. 1988. *Natural Language Generation Systems*. New York: Springer-Verlag.

McKeown, K. R. and W. R. Swartout. 1987. Language generation and explanation. In *Annual Review of Computer Science, Volume 2*. Palo Alto: Annual Reviews.

Minsky, M. 1954. *Neural Nets and the Brain-Model Problem*. PhD thesis, Princeton University, Princeton, NJ.

Minsky, M. 1963. Steps toward artificial intelligence. In *Computers and Thought*, ed. E. A. Feigenbaum and J. Feldman. New York: McGraw-Hill.

Minsky, M. 1975. A framework for representing knowledge. In *The Psychology of Computer Vision*, ed. P. Winston. New York: McGraw-Hill.

Minsky, M. 1985. *The Society of Mind*. New York: Simon & Schuster, Inc.

Minsky, M. and S. Papert. 1969. *Perceptrons*. Cambridge, MA: MIT Press. (Expanded edition (1988) also published by MIT Press).

Minsky, M. and O. G. Selfridge. 1961. Learning in neural nets. In *Proceedings of the Fourth London Symposium on Information Theory*. New York: Academic Press.

Minton, S. 1988. *Learning Search Control Knowledge: An Explanation-Based Approach*. Boston, MA: Kluwer.

Minton, S., J. G. Carbonell, C. A. Knoblock, D. R. Kuokka, O. Etzioni, and Y. Gil. 1989. Explanation-based learning: A problem solving perspective. *Artificial Intelligence* 40(1–3):63–118.

Miranker, D. P. 1987. Treat: A better match algorithm for AI production systems. In *Proceedings AAAI-87*, 42–47.

Mitchell, T. M. 1977. Version spaces: A candidate elimination approach to rule learning. In *Proceedings IJCAI-77*.

Mitchell, T. M. 1978. *Version Spaces: An Approach to Concept Learning*. PhD thesis, Stanford University, Stanford, CA.

Mitchell, T. M. 1990. Becoming increasingly reactive. In *Proceedings AAAI-90*.

Mitchell, T. M., J. Allen, P. Chalasani, J. Cheng, O. Etzioni, M. Ringuette, and J. Schlimmer. 1989. Theo: A framework for self-improving systems. In *Architectures for Intelligence*, ed. K. VanLehn. Hillsdale, NJ.: Erlbaum.

Mitchell, T. M., R. M. Keller, and S. T. Kedar-Cabelli. 1986. Explanation-based generalization: A unifying view. *Machine Learning* 1(1).

Moore, R. C. 1985. Semantical considerations on nonmonotonic logic. *Artificial Intelligence* 25(1):75–94. (Reprinted in *Readings in Nonmonotonic Reasoning* (1987), ed. M. Ginsberg, published by Morgan Kaufmann, Los Altos, CA, pp. 127-136).

Mostow, D. J. 1983. Machine transformation of advice into a heuristic search procedure. In *Machine Learning, An Artificial Intelligence Approach*, ed. R. S. Michalski, J. G. Carbonell, and T. M. Mitchell. Palo Alto, CA: Tioga Press.

Nagao, M. 1989. *Machine Translation Summit*. Tokyo: Ohmsha.

Nau, D. S. 1980. Pathology on game trees: A summary of results. In *Proceedings AAAI-80*.

Newell, A. 1973. Production systems: Models of control structures. In *Visual Information Processing*, ed. W.G. Chase. New York: Academic Press.

Newell, A. 1982. The knowledge level. *Artificial Intelligence* 18(1).

Newell, A. 1991. *Unified Theories of Cognition*. Cambridge, MA: Harvard University Press. In press.

Newell, A., J. C. Shaw, and H. A. Simon. 1963. Empirical explorations with the logic theory machine: A case study in heuristics. In *Computers and Thought*, ed. E. A. Feigenbaum and J. Feldman. New York: McGraw-Hill.

Newell, A. and H. A. Simon. 1963. GPS, a program that simulates human thought. In *Computers and Thought*, ed. E. A. Feigenbaum and J. Feldman. New York: McGraw-Hill.

Newell, A. and H. A. Simon. 1972. *Human Problem Solving*. Englewood Cliffs, NJ: Prentice-Hall.

Newell, A. and H. A. Simon. 1976. Computer science as empirical inquiry: Symbols and search. *Communications of the ACM* 19(3):113–126.

Niblack, W. 1986. *An Introduction to Digital Image Processing*. Englewood Cliffs, NJ: Prentice/Hall.

Nilsson, N. J. 1980. *Principles of Artificial Intelligence*. Palo Alto, CA: Morgan Kaufmann.

Nilsson, N. J. 1986. Probabilistic logic. *Artificial Intelligence* 28(1):71–87.

Nirenburg, S. 1987. *Machine Translation: Theoretical and Methodological Issues*. Cambridge, England: Cambridge University Press.

Norman, D. A. 1981. *Perspectives on Cognitive Science*. Norwood, NJ: Ablex.

Nyberg, E. 1988. *The FrameKit User's Guide*. Tech. Rep. CMU-CMT-88-MEMO, Center for Machine Translation, Carnegie Mellon University, Pittsburgh, PA.

Oehrle, R., E. Bach, and D. Wheeler, eds. 1987. *Categorial Grammars and Natural Language Structures*. Dordrecht, Holland: Reidel.

Oflazer, K. 1987. *Partitioning in Parallel Processing of Production Systems*. PhD thesis, Computer Science Department, Carnegie Mellon University, Pittsburgh, PA.

Parker, D. B. 1985. *Learning-Logic*. Tech. Rep. TR-47, MIT Center for Computational Research in Economics and Management Science, Cambridge, MA.

Paulos, J. A. 1980. *Mathematics and Humor*. Chicago: University of Chicago Press.

Pearl, J. 1982. The solution for the branching factor of the alpha-beta pruning algorithm and its optimality. *Communications of the ACM* 25(8):559–564.

Pearl, J. 1983. On the nature of pathology in game searching. *Artificial Intelligence* 20(4):427–453.

Pearl, J. 1988. *Probabilistic Reasoning in Intelligent Systems*. Palo Alto: Morgan Kaufmann.

Pereira, F. C. N and D. H. D. Warren. 1980. Definite clause grammars for language analysis—a survey of the formalism and a comparison with augmented transition networks. *Artificial Intelligence* 13(3):231–278.

Peterson, C. and J. R. Anderson. 1987. A mean field theory learning algorithm for neural nets. *Complex Systems* 1(5):995–1015.

Pohl, I. 1971. Bi-directional search. In *Machine Intelligence 6*, ed. B. Meltzer and D. Michie. New York: American Elsevier.

Polya, G. 1957. *How to Solve It*. Princeton, NJ: Princeton University Press.

Pomerleau, D. 1989. ALVINN: An autonomous land vehicle in a neural network. In *Advances in Neural Information Processing Systems I*, ed. D. Touretzky, 305–313. San Mateo, CA: Morgan Kaufmann.

Pople, H. E. 1982. Heuristic methods for imposing structure on ill structured problems: The structuring of medical diagnosis. In *Artifical Intelligence in Medicine*, ed. P. Szolovits, 119–185. Colorado: Westview Press.

Prerau, D. S. 1990. *Developing and Managing Expert Systems: Proven Techniques for Business and Industry*. Reading, MA: Addison-Wesley.

Quillian, R. 1968. Semantic memory. In *Semantic Information Processing*, ed. M. Minsky. Cambridge, MA: MIT Press.

Quillian, R. 1969. The teachable language comprehender. *Communications of the ACM* 12:459–475.

Quine, W. V. 1961. *From a Logical Point of View, 2nd ed.* New York: Harper.

Quine, W. V. and J. S. Ullian. 1978. *The Web of Belief.* New York: Random House.

Quinlan, J. R. 1986. Induction of decision trees. *Machine Learning* 1(1).

Rabiner, L., J. Wilpon, and F. K. Soong. 1988. High performance connected digit recognition using hidden Markov models. In *IEEE International Conference on Acoustics, Speech, and Signal Processing.*

Raiman, O. 1986. Order of magnitude reasoning. In *Proceedings AAAI-86.*

Rauch-Hindin, W. B. 1986. *Artificial Intelligence in Business, Science, and Industry: Volume I—Fundamentals, Volume II—Applications.* Englewoods Cliffs, NJ: Prentice-Hall.

Reichenbach, H. 1947. *Elements of Symbolic Logic.* New York: Free Press.

Reiter, R. 1978. On closed world data bases. In *Logic and Data Bases*, ed. H. Gallaire and J. Minker, 55–76. New York: Plenum Press. (Reprinted in *Readings in Nonmonotonic Reasoning* (1987), ed. M. Ginsberg, published by Morgan Kaufmann, Los Altos, CA, pp. 300-310).

Reiter, R. 1980. A logic for default reasoning. *Artificial Intelligence* 13(1–2).

Reiter, R. 1987a. Nonmonotonic reasoning. *Annual Review of Computer Science* 147–186.

Reiter, R. 1987b. A theory of diagnosis from first principles. *Artificial Intelligence* 32(1):57–95. (Reprinted in *Readings in Nonmonotonic Reasoning* (1987), ed. M. Ginsberg, published by Morgan Kaufmann, Los Altos, CA, pp. 352-371).

Reiter, R. and G. Criscuolo. 1981. On interacting defaults. In *Proceedings IJCAI-81.* (Reprinted in *Readings in Nonmonotonic Reasoning* (1987), ed. M. Ginsberg, published by Morgan Kaufmann, Los Altos, CA, pp. 94-100).

Rich, E. A. 1983. Default reasoning as likelihood reasoning. In *Proceedings AAAI-83.*

Rieger, C. 1975. Conceptual memory. In *Conceptual Information Processing*, ed. R. C. Schank. Amsterdam: North-Holland.

Riesbeck, C. K. 1975. Conceptual analysis. In *Conceptual Information Processing*, ed. R. C. Schank. Amsterdam: North-Holland.

Ritchie, G. D. and F. K. Hanna. 1984. AM: A case study in AI methodology. *Artificial Intelligence* 23(3):249–268.

Roberts, R. B. and I. P. Goldstein. 1977. *The FRL Manual.* Tech. rep., MIT Artificial Intelligence Laboratory.

Robinson, J. A. 1965. A machine-oriented logic based on the resolution principle. *Journal of the ACM* 12(1):23–41.

Rosenblatt, F. 1962. *Principles of Neurodynamics: Perceptrons and the Theory of Brain Mechanisms.* Washington, D.C.: Spartan Books.

Rosenbloom, P. S. 1982. A world-championship level Othello program. *Artificial Intelligence* 19(3).

Rosenschein, J. S. and J. S. Breese. 1989. Communication-free interactions among rational agents: A probabilistic approach. In *Distributed Artificial Intelligence Volume II*, ed. L. Gasser and M. N. Huhns, 99–118. San Mateo, CA: Morgan Kaufmann.

Rosenzweig, M. R. and A. L. Leiman. 1982. *Physiological Psychology.* Lexington, MA: D. C. Heath and Company.

Rumelhart, D. E., G. E. Hinton, and R. J. Williams. 1986. Learning internal representations by error propagation. In *Parallel Distributed Processing*, ed. D. E. Rumelhart, J. L. McClelland, and the PDP Research Group, 318–362. Cambridge, MA: MIT Press.

Rumelhart, D. E. and J. L. McClelland. 1986a. On learning the past tenses of English verbs. In *Parallel Distributed Processing*, ed. D. E. Rumelhart, J. L. McClelland, and the PDP Research Group, 216–271. Cambridge, MA: MIT Press.

Rumelhart, D. E. and J. L. McClelland. 1986b. PDP models and general issues in cognitive science. In *Parallel Distributed Processing*, ed. D. E. Rumelhart, J. L. McClelland, and the PDP Research Group. Cambridge, MA: MIT Press.

Rumelhart, D. E. and D. Zipser. 1986. Feature discovery by competitive learning. In *Parallel Distributed Processing*, ed. D. E. Rumelhart, J. L. McClelland, and the PDP Research Group, 151–193. Cambridge, MA: MIT Press.

Sabot, G. 1988. *The Paralation Model: Architecture-Independent Parallel Programming*. Cambridge, MA: MIT Press.

Sacerdoti, E. D. 1974. Planning in a hierarchy of abstraction spaces. *Artificial Intelligence* 5(2):115–135.

Sacerdoti, E. D. 1975. The nonlinear nature of plans. In *Proceedings IJCAI-75*.

Samuel, A. L. 1963. Some studies in machine learning using the game of checkers. In *Computers and Thought*, ed. E. A. Feigenbaum and J. Feldman. New York: McGraw-Hill.

Schank, R. C. 1973. Identification of conceptualizations underlying natural language. In *Computer Models of Thought and Language*, ed. R. C. Schank and K. M. Colby. San Francisco: Freeman.

Schank, R. C. 1975. *Conceptual Information Processing*. Amsterdam: North-Holland.

Schank, R. C. 1977. *Dynamic Memory: A Theory of Reminding and Learning in Computers and People*. New York: Cambridge University Press.

Schank, R. C. and R. P. Abelson. 1977. *Scripts, Plans, Goals, and Understanding*. Hillsdale, NJ: Erlbaum.

Schank, R. C. and J. G. Carbonell. 1979. Re: The Gettysburg Address: Representing social and political acts. In *Associative Networks: Representation and Use of Knowledge by Computers*, ed. N. Findler. New York: Academic Press.

Schank, R. C. and K. Colby. 1973. *Computer Models of Thought and Language*. San Francisco: Freeman.

Schank, R. C. and C. Owens. 1987. *Ten Problems in Artificial Intelligence*. Tech. Rep. 514, Computer Science Department, Yale University, New Haven, CT.

Searle, J. R. 1969. *Speech Acts*. Cambridge: Cambridge University Press.

Searle, J. R. 1975. Indirect speech acts. In *Syntax and Semantics 3: Speech Acts*, ed. P. Cole and J. Morgan. New York: Academic Press.

Sejnowski, T. J. and C. R. Rosenberg. 1987. Parallel networks that learn to pronounce English text. *Complex Systems* 1(1):145–168.

Sells, P. 1986. *Lectures on Contemporary Syntactic Theories*. CSLI Lecture Notes, distributed by University of Chicago Press.

Shafer, G. 1976. *A Mathematical Theory of Evidence*. Princeton, NJ: Princeton University Press.

Shafer, G. and J. Pearl, eds. 1990. *Readings in Uncertain Reasoning*. Los Altos, CA: Morgan Kaufmann.

Shafer, S., A. Stentz, and C. Thorpe. 1986. An architecture for sensor fusion in a mobile robot. In *IEEE International Conference on Robotics and Automation*, 2002–2010.

Shafer, S. and W. Whittaker. 1989. *Development of an Integrated Mobile Robot System at Carnegie Mellon University*. Tech. Rep. CMU-RI-TR-89-22, Robotics Institute, Carnegie Mellon University, Pittsburgh, PA.

Shannon, C. E. 1950. Programming a computer for playing chess. *Philosophical Magazine [Series 7]* 41:256–275.

Shapiro, E. Y., ed. 1987. *Concurrent Prolog: Collected Papers*. Cambridge, MA: MIT Press.

Shapiro, S. and D. Eckroth, eds. 1987. *Encyclopedia of Artificial Intelligence*. New York: Wiley.

Shieber, S. M. 1986. *An Introduction to Unification-Based Approaches to Grammar*. CSLI Lecture Notes, distributed by University of Chicago Press.

Shieber, S. M. 1988. A uniform architecture for parsing and generation. In *Proceedings of the 12th International Conference on Computational Linguistics*, 614–619.

Shoham, Y. 1987. Nonmonotonic logics: Meaning and utility. In *Proceedings IJCAI-87*.

Shortliffe, E. H. 1976. *Computer-Based Medical Consultations: MYCIN*. New York: Elsevier.

Shortliffe, E. H. and B. G. Buchanan. 1975. A model of inexact reasoning in medicine. *Mathematical Biosciences* 23:351–379.

Shrobe, H., ed. 1988. *Exploring Artificial Intelligence*. San Mateo, CA: Morgan Kaufman.

Shultz, T. R., P. D. Zelago, and D. J. Engleberg. 1989. Managing uncertainty in rule-based reasoning. In *Proceedings of the Eleventh Annual Conference of the Cognitive Science Society*.

Sidner, C. 1985. Plan parsing for intended response recognition in discourse. *Computational Intelligence* 1(1):1–10.

Simmons, Reid and T. M. Mitchell. 1989. A task control architecture for mobile robots. In *AAAI Spring Symposium on Robot Navigation*.

Simmons, Robert F. 1973. Semantic networks: Their computation and use for understanding English sentences. In *Computer Models of Thought and Language*, ed. R. C. Schank and K. M. Colby. San Francisco: Freeman.

Simon, H. A. 1957. *Models of Man*. New York: Wiley.

Simon, H. A. 1981. *The Sciences of the Artificial, 2d ed*. Cambridge, MA: MIT Press.

Simon, H. A. 1983. Why should machines learn? In *Machine Learning, An Artificial Intelligence Approach*, ed. R. S. Michalski, J. G. Carbonell, and T. M. Mitchell. Palo Alto, CA: Tioga Press.

Simon, H. A. and L. Siklossy. 1972. *Representation and Meaning*. Englewood Cliffs, NJ: Prentice-Hall.

Slate, D. and L. Atkin. 1977. Chess 4.5—the Northwestern University chess program. In *Chess Skill in Man and Machine*, ed. P. W. Frey. New York: Springer-Verlag.

Slocum, J. 1988. *Machine Translation Systems*. Cambridge: Cambridge University Press.

Smolensky, P. 1988. On the proper treatment of connectionism. *Behavioral and Brain Sciences* 2(1).

Sowa, J. F. 1984. *Conceptual Structures*. Reading, MA: Addison-Wesley.

Stallman, R. M. and G. J. Sussman. 1977. Forward reasoning and dependency-directed backtracking in a system for computer-aided circuit analysis. *Artificial Intelligence* 9(2).

Steele, G. L. 1990. *Common LISP: The Language, Second Edition*. Bedford, MA: Digital Press.

Steele, R., S. S. Richardson, and M. A. Winchell. 1989. Design advisor: A knowledge-based integrated circuit design critic. In *Innovative Applications of Artificial Intelligence*, ed. H. Schorr and A. Rappaport, 213–224. Menlo Park: AAAI Press.

Stefik, M. 1981a. Planning and meta-planning (MOLGEN: Part 2). *Artificial Intelligence* 16(2):141–169.

Stefik, M. 1981b. Planning with constraints (MOLGEN: Part 1). *Artificial Intelligence* 16(2):111–139.

Stickel, M. E. 1988. Resolution theorem proving. In *Annual Review of Computer Science, Volume 3*. Palo Alto: Annual Reviews.

Sussman, G. J. 1975. *A Computer Model of Skill Acquisition*. Cambridge, MA: MIT Press.

Tadepalli, P. 1989. Lazy explanation-based learning: A solution to the intractable theory problem. In *Proceedings IJCAI-89*, 694–700.

Tambe, M. and P. S. Rosenbloom. 1989. Eliminating expensive chunks by restricting expressiveness. In *Proceedings IJCAI-89*, 731–737.

Tanimoto, S. L. 1987. *The Elements of Artificial Intelligence*. Rockville, MD: Computer Science Press.

Tate, A. 1977. Generating project networks. In *Proceedings IJCAI-77*.

Tesauro, G. and T. J. Sejnowski. 1989. A parallel network that learns to play backgammon. *Artificial Intelligence* 39(3).

Thomason, R., ed. 1974. *Formal Philosophy: Selected Papers of Richard Montague*. New Haven, CT: Yale University Press.

Thompson, H. 1989. Chart parsing for loosely coupled parallel systems. In *International Workshop on Parsing Technologies*, 320–328.

Touretzky, D. 1986. *The Mathematics of Inheritance Systems*. Palo Alto, CA: Morgan Kaufmann.

Touretzky, D. 1989a. *Common Lisp: A Gentle Introduction to Symbolic Computation*. Menlo Park, CA: Benjamin/Cummings.

Touretzky, D. 1989b. Connectionism and compositional semantics. In *Advances in Connectionist and Neural Computational Theory*, ed. J. A. Barnden and J. B. Pollack. Norwood, NJ: Ablex.

Touretzky, D. and S. Geva. 1987. A distributed connectionist representation for concept structures. In *Proceedings of the Ninth Annual Conference of the Cognitive Science Society*.

Touretzky, D. and G. E. Hinton. 1988. A distributed connectionist production system. *Cognitive Science* 12(3):423–466.

Turing, A. 1963. Computing machinery and intelligence. In *Computers and Thought*, ed. E. A. Feigenbaum and J. Feldman. New York: McGraw-Hill.

Tversky, A. and D. Kahneman. 1974. Judgement under uncertainty: Heuristics and biases. *Science* 185:1124–1131.

Ueda, K. 1985. Guarded horn clauses. In *Proceedings of Logic Programming '85*, ed. E. Wada. New York: Springer-Verlag.

Valiant, L. G. 1984. A theory of the learnable. *Communications of the ACM* 27(11).

van Melle, W., A. C. Scott, J. S. Bennett, and M. A. Peairs. 1981. *The EMYCIN Manual*. Tech. rep., Heuristic Programming Project, Stanford University, CA.

Vitter, J. S. and R. A. Simons. 1986. New classes for parallel complexity: A study of unification and other complete problems for P. *IEEE Transactions on Computers* C-35(5).

Waibel, A., H. Sawai, and K. Shikano. 1989. Consonant and phoneme recognition by modular construction of large phonemic time-delay neural networks. In *IEEE International Conference on Acoustics, Speech, and Signal Processing*.

Waltz, D. L. 1975. Understanding line drawings of scenes with shadows. In *The Psychology of Computer Vision*, ed. P. Winston. New York: McGraw-Hill.

Waterman, D. A. 1986. *A Guide to Expert Systems*. Reading, MA: Addison-Wesley.

Waterman, D. A. and F. Hayes-Roth. 1978. *Pattern-Directed Inference Systems*. New York: Academic Press.

Webber, B. L. and N. J. Nilsson. 1981. *Readings in Artificial Intelligence*. Palo Alto, CA: Morgan Kaufmann.

Weiss, S. M. and C. A. Kulikowski. 1984. *A Practical Guide to Designing Expert Systems*. Totowa, NJ: Rowman & Allanheld.

Weiss, S. M., C. A. Kulikowski, S. Amarel, and A. Safir. 1978. A model-based method for computer-aided medical decision-making. *Artificial Intelligence* 11(1–2):145–172.

Weizenbaum, J. 1966. ELIZA—a computer program for the study of natural language communication between man and machine. *Communications of the ACM* 9(1):36–44.

Weld, D. S. and J. de Kleer, eds. 1988. *Readings in Qualitative Reasoning about Physical Systems*. Palo Alto, CA: Morgan Kaufmann.

Werbos, P. J. 1974. *Beyond Regression: New Tools for Prediction and Analysis in the Behavioral Sciences*. PhD thesis, Harvard University, Cambridge, MA.

Whitehead, A. N. and B. Russell. 1950. *Principia Mathematica, 2nd ed*. Cambridge: Cambridge University Press.

Wilcox, B. 1988. Computer Go. In *Computer Games*, ed. D. N. L. Levy. New York: Springer-Verlag.

Wilensky, R. 1981. PAM. In *Inside Computer Understanding*, ed. R. C. Schank and C. K. Riesbeck. Hillsdale, NJ: Erlbaum.

Wilensky, R. 1986. *Common LISPcraft*. New York: W. W. Norton.

Wilks, Y. A. 1972. *Grammar, Meaning and the Machine Analysis of Language*. London: Routledge and Kegan Paul.

Wilks, Y. A. 1975a. Preference semantics. In *Formal Semantics of Natural Language*, ed. E. L. Keenan. Cambridge: Cambridge University Press.

Wilks, Y. A. 1975b. A preferential, pattern-seeking semantics for natural language. *Artificial Intelligence* 6(1).

Wilson, G. V. and G. S. Pawley. 1988. On the stability of the travelling salesman problem algorithm of Hopfield and Tank. *Biological Cybernetics* 58(1):63–70.

Winograd, T. 1978. On primitives, prototypes, and other semantic anomalies. In *Proceedings of the Second Workshop on Theoretical Issues in Natural Language Processing (TINLAP 2)*.

Winograd, T. 1983. *Language as a Cognitive Process: Syntax*. Reading, MA: Addison-Wesley.

Winograd, T. and F. Flores. 1986. *Understanding Computers and Cognition: A New Foundation for Design*. Norwood, NJ: Ablex.

Winston, P. H. 1975. Learning structural descriptions from examples. In *The Psychology of Computer Vision*, ed. P. H. Winston. New York: McGraw-Hill.

Winston, P. H. 1984. *Artificial Intelligence*. Reading, MA: Addison-Wesley.

Winston, P. H. and B. Horn. 1989. *LISP*. Reading, MA: Addison-Wesley.

Woods, W. A. 1970. Transition network grammars for natural language analysis. *Communications of the ACM* 13(10):591–606.

Woods, W. A. 1973. Progress in natural language understanding: An application to Lunar geology. In *Proceedings of the AFIPS Conference 42*. AFIPS Press.

Woods, W. A. 1975. What's in a link: Foundations for semantic networks. In *Representation and Understanding*, ed. D. G. Bobrow and A. Collins. New York: Academic Press.

Wos, L., R. Overbeek, W. Lusk, and J. Boyle. 1984. *Automated Reasoning: Introduction and Applications*. Englewood Cliffs, NJ: Prentice-Hall.

Zadeh, L. A. 1979. A theory of approximate reasoning. In *Machine Intelligence 9*, ed. J. Hayes, D. Michie, and L. I. Mikulich, 149–194. New York: Halstead Press.

Acknowledgments

The following copyrighted material was reprinted here with the permission of the publisher:

Newell, A. and H. A. Simon, "Computer Science as Empirical Inquiry: Symbols and Search," *Communications of the ACM*, Vol. 19, No. 3, Mar. 1976, p. 116. Copyright © 1976, Association for Computing Machinery. (Quotations appear in Chapter 1).

Morrison, P. and E. Morrison, *Charles Babbage and His Calculating Engines*, Dover Publications, Copyright © 1961, pp. 248, 284. (Quotations appear in Chapters 1 and 17).

Carbonell, J. G., "Politics," p. 275. In *Inside Computer Understanding*, Schank, R. C., ed. Copyright ©1981, Lawrence Erlbaum Associates. (Quotation appears in Chapter 1).

Polya, G., *How to Solve It: A New Aspect of Mathematical Method*, p. *vii*. Copyright 1945, © renewed 1973 by Princeton University Press; second edition copyright © 1957 by G. Polya. (Quotation appears in Chapter 2).

Weizenbaum, J., "ELIZA—A Computer Program for the Study of Natural Language Communication between Man and Machine," *Communications of the ACM*, Vol. 9, No. 1, Jan. 1966, pp. 36. Copyright © 1966, Association for Computing Machinery. (Appears as Figure 6.6).

Woods, W. A., "Transition Network Grammars for Natural Language Analysis," *Communications of the ACM*, Vol. 13, 1970, pp. 592, 594. Copyright © 1970, Association for Computing Machinery. (Appears as Figures 15.8 and 15.9).

Quine, W. V. and J. S. Ullian, *The Web of Belief, Second Edition*, pp. 17–19. Copyright © 1970, 1978 by Random House, Inc. (Quotation appears in Chapter 7).

Erman, L., F. Hayes-Roth, V. Lesser and R. Reddy, "Hearsay-II Speech Understanding System," *Computing Surveys*, Vol. 12, No. 2, 1980, pp. 224–225, Copyright © 1980, Association for Computing Machinery. (Appears as Figures 14.3 and 14.7).

Carbonell, J. G., "Derivational Analogy: A Theory of Reconstructive Problem Solving and Expertise Acquisition," pp. 376, 277. In *Machine Learning: An Artificial Intelligence Approach, Volume II*, Michalski, R. S., J. G. Carbonell, and T. Mitchell, eds. Copyright © 1986, Morgan Kaufmann Publications, Inc. (Appears as Figures 17.19 and 17.21).

Schank, R. C. and R. Abelson, *Scripts, Plans, Goals, and Understanding*, Copyright © 1977, Lawrence Erlbaum Associates, Inc., pp. 12–14, 43–44. (Appears as list of ACTs in Chapter 10, and as Figure 10.5).

Schank, R. C., "Identification of Conceptualizations Underlying Natural Language," pp. 195, 206, 213, 229. In *Computer Models of Thought and Language*, R. C. Schank and K. Colby, eds. Copyright © 1973, W. H. Freeman. (Appears as Figure 10.2, list of conceptual tenses in Chapter 10, and Figures 10.3, 10.4, and 15.15).

Waltz, D., "Understanding Line Drawings of Scenes with Shadows," pp. 20, 31. In *The Psychology of Computer Vision*, P. Winston, ed. Copyright © 1975, McGraw-Hill. (Appears as Figures 14.8 and 14.15).

Minsky, M. and S. Papert, *Perceptrons*, pp. 231–232. Copyright © 1969, MIT Press. (Quotation appears in Chapter 18).

Hendrix, G., "Expanding the Utility of Semantic Networks through Partitioning," *Proc. IJCAI 4*, pp. 119–120. Copyright © 1975, Morgan Kaufmann Publications, Inc. (Appears as Figure 9.4).

Davis, R. and D. Lenat, *Knowledge Based Systems in Artificial Intelligence*, pp. 16, 21–25, 270, 284. Copyright © 1982, McGraw-Hill. (Appears as Figure 17.16, and the trace of AM in Chapter 17).

Simon, H. A., "Why Should Machines Learn?" p. 28. In *Machine Learning: An Artificial Intelligence Approach*, Michalski, R. S., J. G. Carbonell, and T. Mitchell, eds. Copyright © 1983, Tioga Press. (Quotation appears in Chapter 17).

Turing, A. M., "Computing Machinery and Intelligence," p. 23. In *Computers and Thought*, Feigenbaum, E. A. and J. Feldman, eds. Copyright © 1963, McGraw Hill. (Quotation appears in Chapter 1).

Quine, W. V. O., *From a Logical Point of View*, Copyright © 1953, 1961, 1980 by the President and Fellows of Harvard College, p. 9. (Quotation appears in Chapter 4).

Minsky, M., "A Framework for Representing Knowledge," p. 252. In *The Psychology of Computer Vision*, Winston, P., ed. Copyright © 1975, McGraw-Hill. (Appears as Figure 4.11).

Chapman, D., "Planning for Conjunctive Goals," *Artificial Intelligence*, vol. 32, p. 342. Copyright © 1987 by Elsevier Science Publishers B.V. (North Holland). (Appears as Figure 13.9).

Lippmann, R. P., "Review of Research on Neural Nets for Speech," *Neural Computation*, Vol. 1, No. 1, 1989, p. 10. Copyright © 1989, MIT Press. (Appears as Figure 18.20).

Mitchell, T. M., R. M. Keller and S. T. Kedar-Cabelli, "Explanation-Based Generalization: A Unifying View," *Machine Learning*, Vol. 1, No. 1, 1986, p. 59. Copyright © 1986, Kluwer Academic Publishers. (Appears as Figure 17.15).

Schank, R. C., *Dynamic Memory: A Theory of Reminding and Learning in Computers and People*, p. 47. Copyright © 1977 by Cambridge University Press. (Quotation appears in Chapter 19).

Author Index

Subject Index